Contract Law

New Features in Contract Law

Reiner Schulze (Ed.)

Sellier. European Law Publishers

ISBN 978-3-86653-036-2

Die Deutsche Nationalbibliothek verzeichnet diese Publikation in der Deutschen Nationalbibliografie; detaillierte bibliografische Daten sind im Internet über http://dnb.d-nb.de abrufbar.

© 2007 by Sellier. European Law Publishers.

Dieses Werk einschließlich aller seiner Teile ist urheberrechtlich geschützt. Jede Verwertung außerhalb der engen Grenzen des Urheberrechtsgesetzes ist ohne Zustimmung des Verlages unzulässig und strafbar. Das gilt insbesondere für Vervielfältigungen, Übersetzungen, Mikroverfilmungen und die Einspeicherung und Verarbeitung in elektronischen Systemen.

Gestaltung: Sandra Sellier, München. Herstellung: Karina Hack, München. Druck und Bindung: AZ Druck und Datentechnik, Kempten. Gedruckt auf säurefreiem, alterungsbeständigem Papier. Printed in Germany.

Foreword

"New features of Contract Law" was the theme of a series of lectures held at the Centre for European Private Law at the Westfälische Wilhelms-Universität Münster in 2006. The lectures of this series are published in this volume. It further contains lectures on the same theme delivered at the concluding symposium of the research network "Uniform Terminology for European Private Law", which ran from 2002 to 2006 with funding from the European Commission. Participating in this research network were the universities of Turin (co-ordinating institution), Barcelona, Lyon, Nijmegen, Münster, Oxford and Warsaw.

The preparation and publication of this compendium occurs at a time of intense scholarly work towards a "Common Frame of Reference" for European contract law. Several authors of this volume participate in these works; and some contributions refer to this project. If this volume can make a contribution to the debate on some of the issues concerning the future development of European contract law through the "Common Frame of Reference" then it has fulfilled the purpose intended by the series of lectures upon which it was based.

For the efficient preparation and printing of the contributions I thank the authors and the publishers. I am particularly grateful to the research assistants Christian Rodorff and David Kraft for the responsible and dependable execution of the editorial and linguistic work.

Münster, April 2007   *Reiner Schulze*

Contributors

John N. Adams
Professor Emeritus of Law, University of Sheffield, UK; Adjunct Professor, University of Notre Dame London Law Centre, UK

Hugh Beale
Professor of Law, University of Warwick, UK; Law Commissioner for England and Wales (Commercial and Common Law)

Giuditta Cordero Moss
Professor of Law, University of Oslo, Norway

Barbara Dauner-Lieb
Professor for Civil, Commercial and Corporate Law, Labour Law and European Private Law, Director of the Institute for Labour Law and Commercial Law, University of Cologne, Germany and Judge at the Constitutional Court of North Rhine-Westphalia, Germany

Michele Graziadei
Professor for Comparative Private Law, University of Eastern Piemont, Alessandria, Italy

Thomas Gutmann
Professor for Civil Law and Legal Philosophy, University of Münster, Germany

Geraint Howells
Professor of Law, Lancaster University, UK; Barrister, Gough Square Chambers

Simon James
Partner, Clifford Chance LLP, London, UK

Paul Lagarde
Professor Emeritus of Law, University Paris I Panthéon-Sorbonne, France

Matthias Lehmann
Lecturer for Civil Law, Private International Law and Comparative Law, University of Bayreuth, Germany

Peter Møgelvang-Hansen
Professor of Law, Copenhagen Business School, Denmark

Salvatore Patti
Professor of Law, University of Rome La Sapienza, Italy

Thomas Pfeiffer
Professor of Law, University of Heidelberg, Germany

John C. Reitz
Professor of Law, Associate Dean for International and Comparative Law Programmes, University of Iowa College of Law, USA

Judith Rochfeld
Professor of Law, University Paris XI Paris-Sud, France

Martin Schmidt-Kessel
Professor of Law and Dean of Law Faculty, University of Osnabrück, Germany

Reiner Schulze
Professor of Law and Dean of Law Faculty, University of Münster, Germany

Alessandro Somma
Professor of Law, University of Ferrara, Italy

Stefano Troiano
Professor of Law, University of Verona, Italy

Christian Twigg-Flesner
Senior Lecturer in Private Law, University of Hull, UK

Antoni Vaquer
Professor for Civil Law, University of Lleida, Spain

Fryderyk Zoll
Professor of Law, Jagiellonen University, Krakow, Poland

Contents

Contributors   V

Introduction

The New Challenges in Contract Law   3
Reiner Schulze (Münster)

Part I
Freedom of Contract and Protection of Weaker Parties

Der Schutz der schwächeren Vertragspartei –
rechtshistorische und rechtspolitische Aspekte   25
Alessandro Somma (Ferrara)

Zwang und Ausbeutung beim Vertragsschluss   49
Thomas Gutmann (Münster)

Diskriminierungsschutz und Vertragsrecht –
Entwicklungstendenzen im Rechtsvergleich   67
Matthias Lehmann (Bayreuth)

Das Antidiskriminierungsrecht in der Acquis-Gruppe und
die fehlende Umsetzung von Antidiskriminierungsrichtlinien in das polnische Zivilrecht   85
Fryderyk Zoll (Krakau)

A Special Private Law for B2C? Silver Bullet or Blind Alley?   107
Barbara Dauner-Lieb (Cologne)

Consumer Concepts for a European Code?   119
Geraint Howells (Lancaster)

Part II
Preparation and Formation of the Contract

The Function of Letters of Intent and their
Recognition in Modern Legal Systems 139
Giuditta Cordero Moss (Oslo)

New Mechanisms for Concluding Contracts 161
Thomas Pfeiffer (Heidelberg)

The Binding Effects of Advertising 169
Peter Møgelvang-Hansen (Copenhagen)

Part III
Performance and Remedies

Remedies for Breach of Contract in European Private Law –
Principles of European Contract Law, Acquis Communautaire
and Common und Frame of Reference 183
Martin Schmidt-Kessel (Osnabrück)

La proposition de réforme des sanctions de l'inexécution du
contrat dans l'Avant-projet de réforme du
Code civil français et l'influence européenne 197
Judith Rochfeld (Paris)

Third Party Questions: The Privity Problem 213
John N. Adams (Sheffield)

Part IV
Legal Pluralism and International Challenges

Political Economy and Contract Law 247
John C. Reitz (Iowa)

Remarques sur la proposition de règlement de la
Commission européenne sur la loi applicable aux
obligations contractuelles (Rome I) 277
Paul Lagarde (Paris)

Time to Slice and Dice in the Contractual Kitchen? 299
Simon James (London)

Variations on the Concept of Contract in a European Perspective:
Some Unresolved Issues 311
Michele Graziadei (Alessandria)

Standard terms in International Commercial Law –
the example of documentary credits 325
Christian Twigg-Flesner (Hull)

Part V
National Experience and Supranational Law

The Common Frame of Reference in general –
a resumé of the current status 343
Hugh Beale (Warwick)

Die Terminologie des italienischen Zivilgesetzbuches
auf dem Gebiet der allgemeinen Vertragsbedingungen:
Probleme der Übersetzung 363
Salvatore Patti (Rom)

Das Konzept der „Reasonableness" als Mittel zur
Harmonisierung des Europäischen Vertragsrechts:
Probleme und Perspektiven aus der Sicht des
italienischen Rechtssystems 375
Stefano Troiano (Verona)

Traces of Paulian Action in Community Law 421
Antoni Vaquer (Lleida)

Introduction

The New Challenges in Contract Law

Reiner Schulze (Münster)

I. Facets of the global challenge

Contract law is facing new challenges. They predominantly arise from the deep-seated change currently underway in business, politics and law and which is usually summarised under the term globalisation.[1] It not only affects cross border contractual relationships, rather it increasingly also impacts on contractual practice in the national context. Certain facets of this change must be mentioned (I.), before we take a closer look at specific challenges for European contract law (II.) and focus on some illustrative research themes concerning the new developments of contract law (III.)

1. The globalisation of contract law

Before the middle of the 20th century important legal points of origin for the development which later extended into "globalisation" were already emerging. In addition to the founding of the United Nations (UN) in 1944 they include in particular the ratification of the General Agreement on Tariffs and Trade (GATT) in 1947, which opened the way for the establishment of the World Trade Organization (WTO) in 1994.[2] Against this background, in the second half of the 20th century the political and economic importance of efforts to reach uniform rules for contracts for international transactions grew. Central hereto since the 1920s were the works on a harmonisation of contract law for cross border deliveries of

---

[1] See e.g. W. *Twining*, Globalization and Legal Theory, Evanston 2001; M. *Barr/ R. Avi-Yonah*, Globalization, Law and Development: Introduction and Overview, Michigan Journal of International Law, 2004, pp. 1 et seq.; H. *Van Loon*, Globalisation and the Hague Conference on Private International Law, International Law FORUM du droit international, 2000, pp. 230 et seq.

[2] See e.g. M. *Matsushita/T. J. Schoenbaum/P. C. Mavroidis*, The World Trade Organization: law, practice, and policy, 2nd edition Oxford 2006; A. F. *Lowenfeld*, International Economic Law, Oxford 2003; C. *Herrmann/W. Weiß/C. Ohler*, Welthandelsrecht, 2nd edition, Munich 2007.

goods. The success of these efforts with the conclusion of the Hague Convention of 1964[3] constitute the beginning of a new era for the area of contract law, in which the needs of world trade became a material factor in its development.

The Hague Sales law however was essentially created by states of the western world. An important precursor of globalisation over the next decade were the negotiations for the Vienna Convention on Contracts for the International Sale of Goods (CISG) of 1980, which displaced the Hague sales law. The need for change arose from the last wave of decolonisation until 1960 when numerous new states entered the international legal community. From their perspective the Hague sales law was in no way the representative of the whole world. Together with other states of the so-called third world they therefore demanded a part in the creation of this law.[4]

In the 1990s there followed a further great change in the topography of contract law: With the transition of the former socialist countries of central and eastern Europe to market economies contract law acquired fundamental economic importance and a central position in the legal orders. In China a corresponding gradual change had already begun to take root, in the course of which a uniform contract law for the People's Republic of China emerged in 1999 and a civil code is currently being prepared. For a large part of mankind it is only these most recent developments which gave contract law the prominent importance (or at least opened the way), that it already enjoyed in the western world.

2. Technological change

Alongside the aforementioned political changes, above all technological change created new conditions and challenges for contract law in the course of globalisation. Improved production technologies and in particular cost effective transportation technologies promoted the emergence of world wide production channels and distribution systems. In contract law this is expressed for example in new, complex combinations of numerous bilateral contracts and in many kinds of multilateral "network contracts". The reduction of transportation costs as a consequence of new technolo-

---

[3] Convention relating to a Uniform Law on the International Sale of Goods, The Hague, 1.7.1964.

[4] P. Schlechtriem/I. Schwenzer (eds.), Commentary on the Convention for the International Sale of Goods (CISG), 2nd (English) edition, Munich 2005, Introduction, p. 2, with further references; P. Schlechtriem/I. Schwenzer (eds.), Kommentar zum einheitlichen UN-Kaufrecht (CISG), 4th (German) edition, Munich 2004, Einleitung, p. 29.

gies also calls into question the traditional assumption that, in the context of non-performance of obligations from international contracts, supplementary performance is regularly too burdensome. It is therefore for instance worthwhile reconsidering whether UN sales law is still up to date, insofar as a fundamental breach of contract does not entitle the debtor to effect supplementary performance, but entitles the creditor to simultaneously terminate the contract (cf. Art. 49 (1) lit. a CISG).[5]

One particular technological challenge for contract law, which is perhaps comparable with that of industrialisation in the 19th century, are the changes in communication and market behaviour through the "electronic revolution". New communications technologies have made physical proximity and personal contact unnecessary in numerous transactions and enabled contracting on a global scale, not only for high value transactions but also for the provision of everyday goods of services. A lively international discussion attends the consequences for numerous legal issues of preparation, conclusion and performance of such contracts in e-commerce.[6] A number of issues must be considered in this context, which arise for substantive law and private international law in the area of contract law. They arise from the peculiarities of electronic communication in relation to the classification of statements in personal, territorial and temporal terms and the actions of the contractual parties. For example, this communication before, during and after conclusion of contract can occur more or less irrespective of location and without the contractual parties' mutual knowledge of one another's personal identity or domicile. Furthermore a very far reaching automisation of the processes for different phases and eventualities of preparation and performance of contract can make it difficult to apply the traditional criteria for the determination of the relevant contractual party's conduct in personal and temporal terms.

3. Change in contractual language and style

The political and technological changes of recent decades, with the immense increase in cross border delivery of goods and services, of international capital movement and mobility for professional and personal reasons, have not only led to a corresponding increase in the number of

---

[5] R. *Schulze*, Gemeinsamer Referenzrahmen und acquis communautaire, Zeitschrift für Euopäisches Privatrecht (ZEuP) 2007, pp. 130 et seq (140).
[6] See for example J. *Dickie*, Producers and Consumers in EU E-commerce Law, Oxford 2005; G. *Spindler/F. Börner*, E-Commerce-Recht in Europa und den USA, Berlin 2003; D. W. *Dorn/C. Krämer* (eds.), E-Commerce – Produkte und Dienstleistungen im Internet – die rechtlichen Grundlagen, Berlin 2003.

international contracts. They have also considerably increased the importance of international contract law in business practice and law firms and also attracted increasing attention from the academic community. A further consequence was the emergence and the rapid expansion of new contractual designs and types. "Franchising", "Factoring", "Merger and Acquisition" or "Swap" entered common international usage and not only for international contracts. Moreover, they have also found entry into national laws and also denote internal contractual relationships in the framework of the relevant legal order.

The spread of such notions also indicates the increasing use of the English language in contract law. At least for international transactions English has clearly established itself as the dominant contractual language for business. Furthermore, English appears to be more commonly used in certain branches of the economy, also outside of the common law states, as the contractual language for purely internal transactions. This tendency of business follows academia, insofar as the multilateral exchange of experience on national contract laws for example at international congresses is frequently conducted in English. Despite the bond between legal language and the relevant legal tradition, recourse to a global lingua franca clearly proves to be indispensable, to enable communication between considerably more than one hundred legal orders each with its own contract law.

Associated with contractual language, international practice has in part increasingly adapted contractual style to the model of the English speaking countries and their common law tradition. This is particularly evident in the widespread adoption of detailed provisions in contractual documents to cover all future developments and conceivable disputes. Such extensive contractual texts are less used in the continental European civil tradition because the great codifications can complement the contractual text with their precise provisions, with the general clauses on "good faith" and "good morals" providing a corrective in the individual case. Nevertheless, the common law tradition in this respect appears to influence not only international contractual practice, but – spread disseminated in particular by the internationally established law firms – in part also the design of contracts for internal transactions in civil law countries.

4. Freedom of contract and needs of protection

a) The aforementioned changes, which predominantly occurred in business practice and without state regulation, indicate that freedom of contract and private autonomy are immensely significant for the new developments in contract law (b). This is admittedly only one side of the coin which characterises contract law and private law as a whole in view of the challenges of globalisation. To look at this *alone* would correspond to the somewhat (neo-) liberal political objective rather than the considerably complex reality of current legal developments. Indeed, on the other side of the coin the regulatory functions of private law and the corresponding regulation by states and supranational institutions have increased, to ensure framework conditions for private action and to reduce structural disparities: (c).

b) The developments of international contract law occur largely outside of the areas which individual states, with their traditional regulatory mechanisms, namely their legislation, can or want to regulate. A decisive driving force is the freedom and power of individual persons, businesses and self-regulating associations. The independent construction of legal relationships on this basis replaces to a certain extent lacking state regulation and in part even state law enforcement.

Material actors in this further development of contract law in the context of private autonomy include – together with the internationally orientated law firms – the numerous large and small businesses with cross border business activity as well as the international business associations, chambers of commerce and institutions (such as "UNIDROIT" in Rome)[7]. They have designed and disseminated many kinds of standard terms, model contracts and codes of conduct. International contractual practice – and frequently also internal contractual practice – thus flows from sets of terms and bodies of rules which emerged without legislative action by the state.[8] In this way – alongside private international law and international uniform law (such as UN sales law) – a third area of contract law for cross border transactions has strongly developed: the self made "transnational" law of business, which is frequently (in whole or in part) termed "lex mercatoria".[9]

Consequently, wide areas of international business contract law are not based on state legislation, but on the independent design of the parties and the self regulation of business, i.e. on individual and collectively ap-

---

[7] International Institute for the Unification of Private Law (UNIDROIT), see M. J. *Bonell*, An International Restatement of Contract Law: The UNIDROIT Principles Of International Commercial Contracts, 3rd edition, Ardsley, New York 2005.

[8] See for example in this volume Part II, G. *Cordero Moss*, The Function of Letters of Intent and their Recognition in Modern Legal Systems; Part IV, C. *Twigg-Flesner*, Standard terms in International Commercial Law – the example of documentary credits.

[9] See e.g. U. *Blaurock*, Übernationales Recht des Internationalen Handels, ZEuP 1993, pp. 247 et seq.; K. P. *Berger* in A. S. *Hartkamp*/M. *Hesselink* (eds.), Towards a European Civil Code, 3rd edition, Dordrecht 2004, pp. 43 et seq.

plied private autonomy. This fundament of substantive contract law is also reflected in the procedures for the settlement of disputes. The main role here for international contracts – and to a considerable extent also for domestic contracts between businesses – is not played by the state courts, but the self-organised jurisdiction of business: the arbitration courts and their arbitration procedures. Thus, on an international level something is happening to a great extent which Friedrich Carl von Savigny described for national law (and what he in the national legal understanding of his time saw as connected to the "Volksgeist" [spirit of the nation]): the emergence of a law "durch innere, stillwirkende Kräfte, nicht durch die Willkür eines Gesetzgebers" ("through organic, silently working forces, not through the arbitrariness of a legislator").[10]

c) The prominent role of private autonomy has as its counterpart the protective function of the state to ensure the conditions for the exercise of this freedom including the avoidance of gross distortions of parity between the contractual parties. This fundament of modern contract law has not lost meaning through globalisation. It is however less bound to specific national traditions than previously; rather, it is part of the exchange of experience and transfer of legal concepts between the individual legal orders and the international tendencies of legal development.

Not least the concept of human rights and a series of international treaties have thus at least contributed to many states improving traditional, or introducing new instruments of private law to protect bodily integrity, property (including foreign investments) and privacy – for example in respect of injunctions; on the scope of damages, in part including strict liability, non-pecuniary damages and punitive damages; in unjust enrichment etc. In no way less significant in the course of globalisation have become other state mandates in respect of regulating competition (in antitrust law and in fair trading law) and protection of industrial property (particularly protection of copyright, patents and other forms of "intellectual property"). It is the development of worldwide regulatory instruments and state-enforced protective standards in precisely these areas which provide the necessary correlative of the worldwide abolition of state barriers to trade.

In contract law itself one can ascertain tendencies to strengthen protective functions above all insofar as they seek to reduce or compensate for structural disparities between the contractual parties[11] and protect

---

[10] F.C. *von Savigny*, Vom Beruf unsrer Zeit für Gesetzgebung und Rechtswissenschaft, Heidelberg 1814, p. 14 (translation by the author).

[11] On this issue see in this volume Part I, A. *Somma*, Der Schutz der schwächeren Vertragspartei – rechtshistorische und rechtspolitische Aspekte; *T. Gutmann*, Zwang und Ausbeutung beim Vertragsschluss.

against discrimination.[12] Alongside contracts of employment[13] – which in many countries only became a specific area of protective legislative activity in recent decades – this concerns certain types of contracts and problems in the relations between businesses (for example franchise contracts[14]) and in particular consumer contracts.[15] Since the programmatic speech of John F. Kennedy[16], considerable legislative activity has concerned consumer law and above all consumer contract law in many states in recent decades. Irrespective of the different national regulatory models for consumer protection (specific statutes for different areas, uniform consumer code, integration into the civil code etc.) the notional separation of consumer contracts (B2C contracts) as opposed to contracts between businesses (B2B contracts) counts as one of the conventional, fundamental divisions in contract law in an international context.

5. International and supranational law

a) Although the states thus retain important regulatory functions in the area of contract law including international contractual relationships, the individual state often cannot fulfil these tasks alone. It has therefore become a fundamental characteristic of modern contract law that the regulatory and protective function of the legislator in this area is increasingly tackled with the help of international co-operation and international institutions.

This internationalisation of contract law is not limited to individual concrete projects (such as the preparation of a specific international Convention as the basis for a uniform law in several states). Moreover, it

---

[12] On this issue see in this volume Part I, M. *Lehmann*, Diskriminierungsschutz und Vertragsrecht – Entwicklungstendenzen im Rechtsvergleich; F. *Zoll*, Das Antidiskriminierungsrecht in der Acquis-Gruppe und die fehlenden Umsetzung von Antidiskriminierungsrichtlinien in das polnische Zivilrecht.

[13] See in this volume Part IV, J. C. *Reitz*, Political Economy and Contract Law.

[14] With various solution approaches such as disclosure provisions in civil codes or specific statutes, supplementary international Codes of Ethics etc.; C. *Joerges*, (ed.), Franchising and the Law: Theoretical and Comparative Approaches in Europe and the United States, Baden-Baden 1991; R. *Schulze* (ed.), Franchising im Europäischen Privatrecht, Baden-Baden 2001.

[15] See thereto in this volume Part I, B. *Dauner-Lieb*, A Special Private Law for B to C? Silver Bullet or Blind Alley?; G. *Howells*, Consumer Concepts for a European Code.

[16] Harvard Business School, 23.1.1954, available at: http://www.jfklibrary.org/Historical+Resources/Archives/Reference+Desk/Speeches/JFK/JFK+Pre-Pres/002PREPRES12SPEECHES_54JAN23A.htm.

has acquired a durable, institutional character through the activity for example of UNIDROIT in Rome. Insofar as these institutions draft model laws and proposals for new international agreements (such as in respect of Factoring and Leasing) or promote the uniform application of existing international contract law,[17] they make a considerable contribution to the further internationalisation of contract law. In this way international uniform law can take over part of the regulatory function for which purely national, isolated legislation is only insufficiently suitable in view of globalisation. In addition to transnational law, which is primarily based on private autonomy, international unitary law which arose as a result of internationally co-ordinated state legislation, thus proves an indispensable answer to the challenges of globalisation.

b) A further answer to these challenges consists of the emergence of supranational contract law. It goes beyond harmonisation of laws via international uniform law insofar as supranational law does not come into force by way of domestic legislation of individual states. Rather, states transfer part of their sovereignty to a supranational Community and entitle it to enact its own legislation.

To a considerable degree such supranational law in the area of contract law is currently arising in the European Community.[18] It takes its place alongside the national contract law of the member states. In this way a new kind of legal pluralism develops in place of the all encompassing, closed system of national law, which corresponds with the monistic tradition of national legal thinking. In Europe, which contract law applies in each state of the Community and which is to be applied in its courts is no longer decided by the national legislator alone, but in part also by the supranational Community. Accordingly, it is not only the national courts which decide on the interpretation of this law, but in part also the court of the Community. In applying contract law lawyers must therefore, as "servants of two masters", overcome the difficulty of bridging the differences and possible contradictions between the different sources of law.

---

[17] For example the United Nations Commission on International Trade Law (UNCITRAL) provides a database (CLOUT) containing court decisions and arbitral awards relating to the Conventions and Model Laws that have emanated from the work of the Commission.

[18] In further detail *post* II. The European challenge.

II. The European Challenge

1. The dualism of national and supranational law

New conditions for contract law in Europe were created with the emergence and expansion of European Community law in the second half of the 20th century. Contract law was previously almost exclusively a component of the national laws of the European states. These national laws had over the preceding centuries displaced both the older Ius commune – the one time common law of lawyers on the European continent – as well as the various local laws (apart from exceptions for individual regions and areas). As a result of this development, contract law in Europe in the middle of the 20th century essentially consisted, on the one hand, of a multitude of different national laws on the European continent, which comparative law tried to order into different areas of law, and, on the other hand, of the Common Law in England, Wales and Ireland (as well as some mixed jurisdictions).

Since the 1950s this situation changed as the supranational law of the European Communities emerged alongside the national laws of the European states. The dualism of national and supranational law initially encompassed above all areas of public law. Since the 1980s however the number of European legislative acts which affect areas of private law has continually grown. European Community law has extended to core areas of contract law such as late payment or – for consumer contracts – standard contract terms and contractual conformity of goods.[19]

This legislative activity of the Community has set in chain a series of innovative accents in the area of contract law. In particular, it further developed information duties in the precontractual area, established the legal institution of withdrawal for various areas, strengthened protection against discrimination beyond the level existing in most member states and gave a new basis for the binding effects of advertising.[20] These innovations through Community law influenced the law of the member states not only to the extent that they transposed directives of the European Community in line with their Treaty obligations. Moreover, member states frequently voluntarily extended the directives beyond their scope of application as prescribed by Community law – so called extended transposition (e.g. by extending the right of withdrawal prescribed by the

---

[19] Late Payments Directive 2000/35/EC of 29.6.2000, OJ L 200, 8.8.2000, pp. 35 et seq; Unfair Contract Terms Directive 93/13/EEC of 5.4.1993, OJ L 95, 21.4.1993, pp. 29 et seq; Consumer Sales Directive 1999/44/EC of 25.5.1999, OJ L 171, 7.7.1999, pp. 12 et seq.

[20] See thereto in this volume Part II, P. Møgelvang-Hansen, The Binding Effects of Advertising.

"doorstep selling directive"[21] to contracts concluded in public areas, or by extending the directive provisions on consumer contracts to apply to all contracts; cf. in German law § 312 BGB and § 434 BGB). The great extent to which the legislative activity of the Community has thus influenced contract law in the member states is evident both in the reforms in the new eastern member states as well as in the old member states,[22] in particular the modernisation of the law of obligations in Germany in 2002.

2. The concept of European Contract Law

The multitude of European provisions, which affect contract law, did not however initially develop on the basis of a common concept of European contract law. Rather, the aims of the directives regularly related to specific policy aims of the European Community and the recitals of the directives were restricted to the corresponding considerations (above all consumer protection und promotion of the internal market, but also protection of small and medium sized businesses etc.). A co-ordination of notions and content between the directives, which related to different policy areas, and often also between the directives within a policy area or "sector", was to a large extent missing. Although these directives related to general issues of contract law – from precontractual duties to conclusion and performance of contract and remedies – in contrast to member state law, an overarching terminological and systematic framework was lacking.

Since the end of the 1990s however this began to change. Of course the scholarly inquiry into European private law and in particular with European contract law at the time had already begun in the 1980s. In the centre of it all was the project of a group of legal scholars around Ole Lando, to draft "Principles of European Contract Law" (PECL).[23] At the time however this group was to a certain extent intellectually ahead of

---

[21] Doorstep Selling Directive 85/577/EEC of 20.12.1985, OJ L 372, 31.12.1985, pp. 31 et seq.

[22] On the current state of development see the recent work S. *Vogenauer/S. Weatherill* (eds.), The Harmonisation of European Contract Law: Implications for European Private Laws, Business and Legal Practice, Oxford 2006; on the German modernisation of the law of obligations R. *Schulze/H. Schulte-Nölke* (eds.), Die Schuldrechtsreform vor dem Hintergrund des Gemeinschaftsrechts, Tübingen 2001.

[23] O. *Lando/H. Beale* (eds.), Principles of European Contract Law, Parts I & II, The Hague 2000; O. *Lando/E. Clive/A. Prüm/R. Zimmerman* (eds.), Principles of European Contract Law, Part III, The Hague 2003.

how European law was actually developing. Indeed, the European Community had at the time only enacted relatively little legislation in the area of contract law. Accordingly, the "Lando Commission" had to delve into national laws to extract principles for the European contract law it was pursuing. Through comparative analysis of the national laws it sought general principles – and later, increasingly also "best solutions" – for its academic proposal of a European contract law.

With the increasing number of European directives affecting contract law and corresponding decisions of the European Court of Justice, a cleft began to emerge between this actually existing law of the European Community in the area of contract law on the one hand and, on the other hand, the scholarly drafts such as the PECL, which, far removed from this legislative activity were based on comparative analysis of the member state traditions. To bridge this gap became the object of scholarly works since the end of the 1990s.[24] For this it was necessary to incorporate existing Community law – the acquis communautaire in the area of contract law – as its own subject into the research alongside the comparative law inquiry into the laws of the member states. This "acquis"-related research concerns itself above all with the issue of the extent to which the multifarious individual provisions of Community law in the various legislative acts that affect contract law reveal overarching principles and structures (without this always being intended by the European legislator when enacting the relevant legislation). In this way, in recent years the "Principles of the Existing EC Contract Law" ("Acquis Principles") were compiled.[25]

3. The action plan for a more coherent European contract law

The European Commission initiated a public discussion on the extension and lacking coherence of Community law provisions, which concern con-

---

[24] In closer detail see R. *Schulze*, European Private Law and Existing EC Law, European Review of Private Law (ERPL) 2005, pp. 3 et seq; *idem*, Gemeinsamer Referenzrahmen und acquis communautaire, ZEuP 2007, pp. 130 et seq. (132).

[25] Principles of the Existing EC Contract Law (Acquis Principles), with comments, Part 1, Munich 2007; the second part of the proposed draft (Chapter 8: "Remedies") is foreseen for publication in ERPL 2007; see also the German translation of the Acquis Principles (without comments) ZEuP 2007, pp. 896 et seq.

tract law, initially through the Communication of July 2001.[26] On the basis of this discussion, a new phase in the development of European contract law begun with the action plan for a more coherent European contract law of February 2003.[27] The Commission did not limit itself with this action plan to the previously predominant isolated consideration of individual areas and regulatory aims within the policy areas of the EC Treaty. Moreover, it expressly adopted the concept of a European contract law, which overarches the individual policy areas and sectors. This action plan recognises, that general principles, definitions and rules for a series of areas must be worked out, to give European contract law the necessary consistence.

The action plan foresees as an important step in this direction the compilation of a "Common Frame of Reference" (CFR).[28] Its "basis sources" constitute – according to the aforementioned developments and the associated research tasks – above all common principles of the national laws, and also analysis of the acquis communautaire and the principles of existing Community law[29]. In accordance with these "basic sources" two research approaches are thereby combined: on the one hand the comparative law works, which extend and develop the "Principles of European Contract Law" of the "Lando Commission"; on the other hand the works on the basis of the existing community law. The former is the subject of the "study group",[30] the latter predominantly the "Acquis group".[31] The first draft of the "Common Frame of Reference" shall be compiled by the end of 2007 by an international network of scholars (in dialogue with representatives of interested parties from business, professional and consumer associations, so called "stakeholders").

---

[26] Communication from the Commission to the Council and the European Parliament on European Contract Law, Brussels, 11.07.2001 COM(2001) 398 final.
[27] Communication from the Commission to the Council and the European parliament, A More Coherent European Contract Law, An Action Plan, Brussels, 12.02.2003, COM(2003) 68 final ("Action Plan").
[28] See in this volume Part V, H. Beale, The Common Frame of Reference in general – a resumé of the current status.
[29] Action Plan (note 27), No. 63.
[30] On the Study Group on European Civil Code see http://www.sgecc.net .
[31] On the European Research Group on Existing EC Private Law (Acquis Group) see http://www.acquis-group.org.

4. The next steps towards a European contract law

Two essential bases for the "Common Frame of Reference" are already present: the "Principles of European Contract Law" and the "Acquis-Principles". For the rest of 2007 there thus remains the challenge of fusing these two main components together into a unified whole. This should not be particularly difficult where these parts complement each other. For example the "Acquis Principles" exhaustively address areas such as withdrawal rights and protection against discrimination, not however the PECL. By contrast the PECL contain comprehensive provisions for example on rescission for mistake and the details of conclusion of contract, whereas less on this is to be found in the "Acquis Principles", lacking basis in Community law. Likewise it should not be too difficult to combine both sets of rules where they overlap each other, providing the principles of existing EC law accord with the comparative law solutions. However, in particular those areas in which principles of existing Community law and the comparative law solutions diverge from each other will have to be discussed in detail.[32]

For instance in respect of the requirements for termination of contract it will have to be reconsidered whether the relevant principles of Community law on the basis of the consumer sales directive are more appropriate for the needs of the internal market than the provisions of the PECL, which essentially follow the CISG. Whereas Art. 9:301, 8:103 PECL (following Art. 49 (1) (a) CISG) requires a fundamental breach, in Community law (and, following it, the new German law of obligations) it is sufficient that the breach is *not minor*, for which admittedly it generally only provides for supplementary performance within a reasonable period of time (Art. 3 (2), (5) and (6) consumer sales directive). For European contract law this appears preferable at least because both supplementary performance and return are easier – in view of reduced transportation costs,[33] removed barriers to trade in the internal market and the European judicial co-operation – than when the CISG came into being.

Following publication of the first proposal of the "Common Frame of Reference", in 2008 the important task and the great chance will exist, to examine and improve the proposal of the academic network in as wide and intensive a public discussion as possible. Only if the Frame of Reference corresponds to the needs of business practice in the European internal market for both businesses and consumers will it be accepted by the institutions of the European Community and the citizens of the Union.

---

[32] For example the requirements of the English remedy of termination of contract; see *post* III. Illustrative areas.

[33] See R. *Schulze*, Gemeinsamer Referenzrahmen und acquis communautaire, ZEuP 2007, pp. 130 et seq.

This discussion on the quality of the proposal will at the same time prepare the political discussion of the coming years, of how the European institutions will use the "Common Frame of Reference" for the future development of European contract law. Probably the function of the frame of reference will at least be to serve as an orientation aid for the European legislator when enacting new measures or reviewing existing ones. Beyond that, according to the action plan it shall be discussed whether the frame of reference should constitute the basis for an "optional instrument".[34] This eventual "optional instrument" would contain rules, which businesses and citizens in particular could choose for cross border contracts. It would be a common European contract law, which could be available alongside national contract law. For the European internal market it could fulfil part of the role which for the world market must be played for the most part by the transnational law of business, but in comparison to a codified contract law perhaps with a lack of completeness, certainty and balance.[35]

III. Illustrative areas

From the wide spectrum of research tasks in respect of the changes in contract law in the international and European context, only certain limited subjects can be named here by means of illustration. Likewise a comprehensive inventory of the current state of older and more modern research in these fields is beyond the scope of this volume, even though a rich basis for the current discussion can be found in this research, as the seminal works by Schlesinger et al[36] and Kötz[37] show.

I. Notion of contract

Precisely the fundamental issues of the notion of contract and the associated concepts of freedom of contract and the binding nature of the contract must be reconsidered in view of the internationalisation and Europeanisation of contract law. The rate at which international business and

---

[34] Action plan (note 27) No. 56.
[35] See in this volume Part IV, S. *James*, Time to Slice and Dice in the Contractual Kitchen?
[36] R. B. *Schlesinger et al*, Formation of Contract, A Study of the Common Core of Legal Systems (2 Volumes), New York 1968.
[37] H. *Kötz/A. Flessner*, Europäisches Vertragsrecht, Volume 1, Tübingen 1996; english edition H. *Kötz/A. Flessner*, European Contract Law, Volume 1, Oxford 1998.

contractual relations increase and spread will confront lawyers of every country not only with numerous individual issues. They will also have to deal with fundamental perceptions and general principles concerning contracts and formation of contract in other legal orders and legal traditions. This confrontation is precipitated not only through the traditional "loophole" of private international law, by which the rules on conflicts of laws can lead to application of foreign law. Rather, increasingly also uniform law on the basis of international Conventions – from UN sales law to the European Convention on Human Rights – are proving to be a challenge beyond the scope of the "own" national tradition incorporating "foreign" case law and legal experience into the own legal practice (proceeding in particular from the "autonomous" interpretation of uniform law). The spread of transnational law and the practice of international arbitration courts are having similar effects.

Against this background two contributions in this volume address some of the issues which arise from the notion of contract and freedom of contract.[38] In addition, new challenges clearly arise on the issue of the material basis for the binding nature of the contract. For lawyers in most countries of the European continent for more than a century it was more or less self evident in this respect that the *agreement* of the parties was central. The encounter with some other legal orders – namely in Scandinavian countries – can however divert attention to the reciprocal *promises* as the starting point for the binding effect[39] (and thereby, under a new dimension, bring current attention to a hot topic of discussion of the 18th and 19th centuries in Europe).[40]

Against the background of these different lines of tradition, current thinking in European contract law even seems to be considering a far reaching relativisation of the hitherto predominant concept of contract: The "Principles of European Contract Law" and probably also the planned draft "Common Frame of Reference" (if it follows them) attaches more or less the same significance to a unilateral promise as to bilateral binding through contract: "*A promise which is intended to be legally binding without acceptance is binding*" (Art. 2:107 PECL). The advantages and disadvantages of such a general rule, which is not restricted to certain forms of unilateral promise (such as reward in German law; § 657 BGB) may be

---

[38] Part IV, M. *Graziadei*, Variations on the Concept of Contract in a European Perspective: Some Unresolved Issues; Part I, T. *Gutmann*, Zwang und Ausbeutung beim Vertragsschluss.

[39] See P. *Møgelvang-Hansen* in B. *Dahl/T. Melchior/D. Tamm* (eds.), Danish Law in a European Perspective, Copenhagen 2002, p. 237.

[40] B. *Schmidlin*, Die beiden Vertragsmodelle des europäischen Zivilrechts, in: R. *Zimmermann* et al (eds.), Rechtsgeschichte und Rechtsdogmatik, Heidelberg 1999.

one of the points to be reconsidered in the discussion on the "Common Frame of Reference". At least a clarification is desireable that (and how) such a unilateral promise to one person or to the public must be expressed.

2. Mechanisms of conclusion of contract

Related to such fundamental issues of the concept of contract and the relationship between contract and unilateral promise, traditional models of conclusion of contract must be reconsidered. In view of international and European developments, in particular the idea that the contract is generally concluded by acceptance of an offer seems questionable. This scheme which traditionally underlies German law has proven to be too narrow for the requirements of practice. For international sales of goods the CISG has retained the division into offer and acceptance; this does not however support any strict scheme, but also recognises for example the corresponding declarations on conclusion of contract.[41] For European contract law the "Principles of European Contract Law" provide in a separate section rules on "offer and acceptance". They contain however at the end of this section a kind of enabling clause for other forms of conclusion of contract: "*The rules in this section apply with appropriate adaptations even though the process of conclusion of a contract cannot be analysed into offer and acceptance*" (Art. 2:211 PECL).[42]

Both bodies of rules thus recognise that that the strict orientation on the offer – acceptance scheme has proven to be too narrow for business practice. Moreover, one must have regard to numerous different forms of gradually occurring conclusions of contract. In these the precontractual or contractual duties and the determination of the content of the contract can solidify over many stages of the process.[43] These new mechanisms of conclusion of contract need close examination both in respect of

---

[41] P. *Schlechtriem/I. Schwenzer* (eds.), Commentary on the Convention for the International Sale of Goods (CISG), 2nd (English) edition, Munich 2005, Introduction to Art. 14-24, para 2; P. *Schlechtriem/I. Schwenzer* (eds.), Kommentar zum einheitlichen UN-Kaufrecht (CISG), 4th (German) edition, Munich 2004, Vor Art. 14-24, para 2.

[42] See my recent paper R. *Schulze*, Precontractual Duties and Conlcusion of Contract in European Law, ERPL 2005, pp. 841et seq.

[43] See the fundamental work of S. *Van Erp*, Contract als Rechtsbetrekking, Tilburg 1990; M. *Fontaine*, Mélange offerts à Pierre Van Ommerslanghe, Brussels, 2000, pp. 115 et seq.; J. M. *Mousseron*, Études offerts à Alfred Jauffret, Aix-Marseille 1974, pp. 509 et seq.; cf. M. *Demoulin/T. Motero* in M. *Fontaine* (ed.), Le Processus du Formation du Contrat, Brussels, Paris 2002.

their individual instruments (such as letters of intent[44]) as well as in respect of their effects in specific legal contexts (such as in European consumer law or in electronic commerce[45]), in order to cogently assess the implications of modern contractual practice for the doctrine of conclusion of contract (in particular in respect of the "magical point in time" at which contractual obligations arise[46]).

3. Precontractual public statements

Closely related to the scheme of gradual conclusion of contract is the issue of the binding effect of public precontractual statements. In view of the immense role, which advertising has acquired worldwide in the marketing of goods and services, it belongs to the greatest challenges for scholarly discussion and legislation. Advertising measures of the future seller (or provider of services) or of a third party (in particular of the manufacturer or of an earlier link in the business chain) often significantly influence the buyer's perception of the subject matter of the contract long before initiation of contractual negotiations. They can have a decisive impact on the decision to conclude the contract, without them having to be mentioned by the parties themselves during contractual negotiations (and without for example the seller being aware in concrete terms of exactly which advertising statements of the manufacturer are decisive for the decision to buy). One innovative accent, which European Community law has set in the area of contract law, is that such precontractual statements acquire a binding effect through Art. 2 (2) consumer sales directive[47] and Art. 3 (2) package travel directive.[48] The latter named directive incorporates alongside B2C contracts also B2B contracts. For contracts of sale some member states (such as Germany and Austria) in transposing the consumer sales directive have extended the binding effect of pre-contractual public statements beyond consumer contracts to all contracts of sale. Following this tendency the Acquis Princi-

---

[44] See in this volume Part II, G. *Cordero Moss*, The Function of Letters of Intent and their Recognition in Modern Legal Systems.
[45] On this and further areas in this volume see Part II, T. *Pfeiffer*, New Mechanisms for Concluding Contracts.
[46] T. *Pfeiffer* in R. *Schulze*/M. *Ebers*/H. C. *Grigoleit* (eds.), Informationspflichten und Vertragsschluss im Acquis communautaire, Tübingen 2003, pp. 103 et seq. (110).
[47] Consumer Sales Directive 1999/44/EC of 25.5.1999, OJ L 171, 7.7.1999, pp. 12 et seq.
[48] Package Travel Directive 90/314/EEC of 13.6.1990, OJ L 158, 23.6.1990, pp. 59 et seq.

ples for future contract law propose corresponding general rules (Art. 4:105, 4:106 ACQP).[49]

4. Further areas

What the aforementioned examples for the fundaments and the mechanisms of conclusion of contract as well as precontractual statements have shown applies no less for other areas. Some contributions in this volume explore in closer detail performance of the contract and remedies.[50]

It is also evident for example for the right of withdrawal, as in the course of an international development it was adopted in numerous countries (partly in connection with already existing legal institutions, partly as an innovation) in a relatively short space of time. Against the background of the worldwide spread of the concept of instruments of consumer protection[51] European Community law also in this area has given impulse for the national laws of most member states. Whereas 20 years ago this legal institution was unknown in most of the legal orders in Europe, it is now one of the everyday instruments in contract law practice.[52] For European contract law the Acquis Principles propose a unification of the provisions on the exercise and effect of this instrument as well as a more coherent formulation of the right of withdrawal for contracts concluded outside of business premises (Art. 5:101 to Art. 5:202 Acquis Principles).[53] The continuing development will show to what extent for this area of contract law European Community law can serve as a model not only for national laws in Europe, but also in the framework of international discussion.

---

[49] In closer detail see in this volume Part II, P. Møgelvang-Hansen, The Binding Effects of Advertising.
[50] Part III, M. Schmidt-Kessel, Remedies for Breach of Contract in European Private Law – PECL, Aquis and CFR; J. Rochfeld, La proposition de réforme des sanctions l'inexécution du contrat dans l'Avant-projet de réforme du Code civil français et l'influence européenne; J. N. Adams, Third Party Questions: The Privity Problem.
[51] See ante I. 4.
[52] M. B. M. Loos, A uniform and efficient right of withdrawal from consumer contracts, ZEuP 2007, pp. 5 et seq. with further references.
[53] On this approach see R. Schulze, Precontractual Duties and Conlcusion of Contract in European Law, ERPL 2005, pp. 841 et seq. (857).

IV. Summary

Only some examples for these changes in contract law could be briefly introduced: the new issues on the notion of contract as one legal system encounters different legal traditions and bodies of rules; the new mechanisms of conclusion of contract; the legal answers to the growing importance of advertising and other precontractual statements; the spread of the right of withdrawal as an instrument of consumer protection. All these examples – and further ones which are addressed in this compendium – concern developments and problems which are not limited to any one country. Rather, they show that the changes and the challenges in modern contract law are part of a world-wide change in economic relationships, which are given legal form with the help of contracts. Just as in this change cross border trade relationships and transactions, international free trade and common markets have increased in significance as oppose to national transactions and markets, so too different kinds of law of international contractual relationships have acquired more meaning for legal practice and academia. Transnational law, which developed above all on the basis of private autonomy, private international law, international uniform law and supranational law thus complement one another. They transfer the complementary elements of contract law to the international level: freedom of contract on the one hand and, on the other hand, regulation to protect the rights and parity of the contractual parties.

At the same time these different kinds of international contract law increase the transfer of legal ideas and solutions from one legal order to another and lead to the adoption of concepts of international law at the national level. Businesses which operate across borders; increasingly also consumers who, with the aid of e-commerce, want to use newly opened markets; the international law firms, who want to transfer their international practice to the national level; representatives from politics and business who want to make their country a forum for concluding contracts and an attractive location for investors – they all strengthen the tendency, in a continuing process, to adapt their national laws to the international mainstream in one point or another. The modernisation of the law of obligations in Germany in 2002 with its recourse to the international sales law of the CISG and the supranational law of the European Community is a significant example. This in no way however removes all deep-rooted systematic and terminological differences between the individual legal orders. But it appears to lead to more and more crucial issues and new challenges of contract law being discussed in an international framework.

Part I
Freedom of Contract and
Protection of Weaker Parties

Der Schutz der schwächeren Vertragspartei – rechtshistorische und rechtspolitische Aspekte

Alessandro Somma (Ferrara)

I. Schwäche und Recht: Individuelle Schwäche und soziale Schwäche

Schwäche ist ein allgemeiner sprachlicher Ausdruck, den man in rechtlichen Überlegungen häufig wiederfindet. Unter anderem wird er in Bezug auf den Güter- und Dienstleistungsverkehr gebraucht, um Situationen zu veranschaulichen, in denen das Vertragsrecht – nachdem es die Bedingungen festgelegt hat, unter denen der Verkehr zu erfolgen hat – Ausnahmen zulässt, um Situationen der Unterlegenheit eines Vertragspartners anzugehen. Allerdings ist es offensichtlich, dass der genannte Ausdruck keine endgültigen Szenarien heraufbeschwören kann: zu zahlreich sind die Begriffe von Schwäche und die jeweils von den Juristen diskutierten und auf verschiedenartige rechtspolitische Modelle zurückzuführenden Eingriffsmöglichkeiten. Man könnte auch sagen: Schwäche ist ein technischer Ausdruck, der je nach dem Zusammenhang, in dem er gebraucht wird, unterschiedliche Werte zum Ausdruck bringt.[1]

In diesen Anmerkungen möchte ich mich drei Eingriffsmodellen zur Schwäche widmen. Zu diesem Zweck werde ich auf einige historische Ereignisse Bezug nehmen, die notwendig, aber auch ausreichend sind, um die Eckdaten dieser drei Modelle in ihrer Verbindung mit der Art von Staat zu umreißen, auf die die jeweils angewandte Regelung des Güter- und Dienstleistungsverkehrs Bezug nimmt. Des Weiteren werde ich eine Unterscheidung treffen, die von Anfang an klargestellt werden sollte: die Unterscheidung zwischen individueller und sozialer Schwäche. Mit der letzteren meine ich Situationen, in denen der Zustand der Unterlegenheit als strukturell im Verhältnis zu den Bedingungen, die aus dem typischen Kontext des Vertragsschlusses entstehen und von einer ursprünglichen Unfähigkeit zur Selbstbestimmung abhängen, angesehen wird. Erstere ist hingegen in den Fällen anerkannt, in denen man von individueller Schwäche spricht: Fälle, die eine vielleicht vom Zusammenhang abhän-

---

[1] Zur Trennung von Techniken und Werten s. A. *Somma*, Tecniche e valori nella ricerca comparatistica, Turin, 2005, insbes. S. 64 ff.

gige Unterlegenheit betreffen, die aber nicht deswegen als strukturell im Verhältnis zu typischen Szenarien angesehen wird.

Eingriffe in Bezug auf individuelle Schwäche sind typisch für den modernen Staat: der Staat, in dem sich die formale Trennung von Politik und Wirtschaft vollzieht. Ein solcher Eingriff stimmt mit dem Gedanken überein, dass das Recht das Ergebnis eines sozialen Konflikts grundsätzlich in sich aufnehmen muss, ohne durch andere als die zur Wiederherstellung der Fähigkeit zur Selbstbestimmung auf dem Markt notwendigen Voraussetzungen bedingt zu werden.

Ein solches Modell kommt in Schwierigkeiten, sobald sich ein politisches Eingreifen zur Ordnung des Wirtschaftssystems und zum Schutz vor seinem Scheitern als notwendig erweist. Eine erste Antwort auf diese Notwendigkeit ist der Übergang vom modernen Staates zum totalitären Staat: ein Staat, der dazu berufen ist, den Wirtschaftsliberalismus zu reformieren, aber gleichzeitig den politischen Liberalismus auszuhöhlen. In diesem Zusammenhang erfolgt ein Eingreifen in soziale Schwäche seitens des Vertragsrechts durch Hervorhebung des sie bestimmenden Zusammenhangs; dies erfolgt jedoch zum Zwecke der Wiederherstellung des Gleichgewichts des Wirtschaftssystems und nicht auch deshalb, um direkt solidarisch in den Mechanismus der Umverteilung von Reichtum einzugreifen.

Dieses letztgenannte Ziel charakterisiert hingegen das für den Sozialstaat typische Eingreifen in soziale Schwäche: ein Staat, der dazu berufen ist, mit privaten und nicht nur mit öffentlichen Instrumenten[2] auf das Ergebnis des sozialen Konflikts einzuwirken und zwar zu Zwecken, die die Teilnahme an demokratischer Konfrontation und nicht auch – bzw. nicht vorwiegend – die Aufrechterhaltung des Wirtschaftssystems betreffen.

Die drei hier genannten Eingriffsmodelle folgen zeitlich aufeinander: das für den modernen Staat typische Modell charakterisiert das gesamte 19. Jahrhundert, befindet sich aber Anfang des 20. Jahrhunderts in der Krise. Die Antwort auf diese Krise – nämlich das vom totalitären Staat verwirklichte Modell – charakterisiert sodann die Epoche zwischen den zwei Weltkriegen, während sich in dem darauf folgenden Zeitraum das im Sozialstaat entwickelte Modell verwirklicht.

Es muss nicht weiter darauf hingewiesen werden, dass mit der Betonung des Aufeinanderfolgens verschiedener Formen des Eingreifens in Schwäche nicht beabsichtigt wird, eine Evolutionstheorie über das Wesen des Vertragsrechts aufzustellen. Andere haben von einem Übergang eines „*autonomous*" Rechts zu einem „*responsive*" Recht gesprochen – ersteres bezeichnend für eine politische Macht, die dem Markt die Bestimmung der Zwecke überlässt, derentwegen soziale Konflikte beizulegen

---

[2] Z.B. *P. Barcellona*, I controlli della libertà contrattuale (1965), in: *S. Rodotà* (Hrsg.), Il diritto privato nella società moderna, Bologna, 1971, S. 285.

sind, letzteres hingegen Produkt des Sozialstaats. Andere haben auch vor der Gefahr einer Rückkehr zu einem Recht „repressiven" Charakters der totalitären Systeme gewarnt.[3] Und wenn die jüngsten Entwicklungen im Gemeinschaftsvertragsrecht eine solche Hypothese zwar nicht bestätigen, so veranlassen sie doch sicherlich dazu, Tendenzen im genannten Sinne festzustellen – vor allem in Bezug auf die Reformtendenzen der Institutionen des Wirtschaftsliberalismus.[4]

II. Schwäche im modernen Staat: Unsichtbare Hand und freie Bildung vertraglicher Einigung

Nach einem zwischen dem 18. und 19. Jahrhundert vertretenen Grundsatz ist dem modernen Staat die Aufgabe anvertraut, die Konzentration der Herrschaft in den Händen des Fürsten und die des Eigentums in den Händen des Individuums zu verwirklichen.[5] Damit soll der Sinn der Überwindung der Modelle im weitesten Sinne feudaler Natur betont werden, die auf einer Verwicklung von Politik und Wirtschaft beruhten[6] und damit die Verabsolutierung des freien Marktes als Mechanismus der Umverteilung von Reichtum behinderten.

So ist die Feudalgesellschaft eine nach Schichten strukturierte politische Gesellschaft, die als solche die auf familiären und sozialen Bindungen beruhenden zwischenmenschlichen Beziehungen betont und die Allokation von Ressourcen mit Hilfe von Mechanismen wie redistributiven Transaktionen und der gesellschaftlich verpflichtenden Schenkung verwirklicht.[7] Der moderne Staat ist hingegen eine nach Klassen strukturierte Wirtschaftsgesellschaft, in der die Pflicht des Einzelnen zum Motor der zwischenmenschlichen Beziehungen wird, die sich in kalte, monetäre

---

[3] Ph. *Nonet* und Ph. *Selzenick*, Law and society in transition, New York, 1978, S. 14 und 117.

[4] Zitate in: A. *Somma*, Social justice and the market in European Contract Law, in: Eur. Rev. Contract Law, 2006, S. 181 ff. und ders., Exporting Economic Democracy. Social Justice and Private Law from the Point of View of Non-European Countries, in T. Wilhelmsson (ed.), Private Law and the Many Cultures of Europe, The Hague etc., 2007.

[5] Der von Seneca stammende Grundsatz findet sich z.B. in Exposé des motifs de la loi relative à la propriété par le conseiller d'état Portalis, in: Code civil des français, 4. Bd, Paris, 1804, S. 31.

[6] S. nur O. *Brunner*, Storia sociale dell'Europa nel Medioevo (1978), Bologna, 1988, S. 39 ff.

[7] Vor allem K. *Polanyi*, Economie primitive, arcaiche e moderne (1968), Turin, 1980, S. 5 ff.

Verhältnisse verwandeln.⁸ Eine Gesellschaft, die den Übergang von Formen des durch Ständeverhältnisse charakterisierten Zusammenlebens in von der freien Einigung der Individuen geprägte Formen verwirklicht: die berühmte Bewegung vom Status zum Vertrag.⁹

Mit anderen Worten ist der freie Markt bzw. der Tausch von Gütern und Dienstleistungen durch das freie Aufeinandertreffen von Angebot und Nachfrage die Institution, innerhalb der sich die Handelnden unter Betonung ihrer Autonomie bzw. jedenfalls unabhängig von der sozialen Dimension ihrer Handlungen gegenüberstehen. Er ist die Institution, die sich in dem Moment behauptet, in dem sich die Entsozialisierung der Wirtschaft verwirklicht: eine Situation, in der der Markt „aus den gesamten gesellschaftlichen Beziehungen ausgegliedert" erscheint und die Preise nicht „vor dem Austausch bestehen" bzw. „nicht einfach vom Umfang von Angebot und Nachfrage beeinflusst werden".¹⁰

Die Hervorhebung der Dimension des Individuums ist somit ein fester Bestandteil der Diskussionen über den freien Markt: Diskussionen, in denen er als Maßstab für die „Autonomie der am Tausch beteiligten Einzelnen in ihrem Kampf um Preis und Konkurrenz" hervorgehoben wird.¹¹ Die Epoche, in der sich die Entsozialisierung der Wirtschaft verwirklicht, ist im Übrigen die Zeit, in der ein menschliches Modell triumphiert, das sich in den folgenden Jahrhunderten behaupten wird. Das Individuum wird als homo oeconomicus angesehen: die Fähigkeit zur rationalen Selbstbestimmung auf dem Markt macht ihm eine kühle Kosten-Nutzen-Analyse möglicher Verhaltensalternativen möglich.¹² Das ist die Bedeutung der Arbeiten, die der schottischen Aufklärung zu verdanken sind und die aus der Erweiterung auf das Studium menschlichen Verhaltens der in der Naturphilosophie verwendeten Methode und der Notwendigkeit der Individualisierung einheitlicher Modelle stammen.¹³

Der Mythos des homo oeconomicus steht mit einer weiteren in jener Zeit ausgearbeiteten Konstruktion in Zusammenhang, nach der „die Betrachtung des eigenen Vorteils" den Einzelnen „natürlicherweise oder vielmehr notwendigerweise" darauf hinführt, „den für die Gesellschaft vorteilhaftesten Einsatz zu bevorzugen". Der Einzelne werde von „einer

---

⁸ Z.B. G. *Simmel*, Filosofia del denaro (1900), Turin, 1984, S. 436.
⁹ H. *Summer Maine*, Diritto antico (1861), Mailand, 1998, S. 129 f.
¹⁰ A. *Caillé*, L'origine del mercato e i suoi rapporti con la democrazia (1998), in: A. Salsano (Hrsg.), Karl Polanyi, Mailand, 2003, S. 210.
¹¹ M. *Weber*, Economia e società (1922), 1. Bd., Mailand, 1999, S. 77.
¹² E. *Soranger*, Lebensformen, Halle, 1921, insbes. S. 148.
¹³ So schon G. *Solari*, Socialismo e diritto privato (1906), Mailand, 1980, S. 37.

unsichtbaren Hand geleitet, um ein Ziel zu erreichen, das nicht in seinen Absichten stand":[14] die „privaten Laster" führen zu „öffentlichen Vorteilen".[15]

Die Ordnung, die diese Voraussetzungen umzusetzen beabsichtigt – die also die Fähigkeit der Mitglieder zur Selbstbestimmung auf dem Markt anerkennen und fördern will – begreift den Vertrag als eine Art vorübergehenden Stillstand im Konflikt zwischen den auf dem Markt Handelnden und weist dem Vertragsrecht die Aufgabe zu, den Inhalt getreu in sich aufzunehmen und für seine Beachtung zu sorgen. Eine solche Ordnung legt ein Vertragsrecht fest, das auf dem Grundsatz der Herrschaft des Wollens basiert und begreift die Schwäche der Parteien als eine Situation, in der dem Prozess der freien Bildung des Willens Hindernisse entgegenstehen. Nur in diesen Fällen sind heteronome und korrigierende Eingriffe erlaubt, die jedoch als Umsetzung eines nicht zum Ausdruck gebrachten Willens des Interessierten und nicht als Fremdbestimmung seines vertraglichen Verhaltens gedacht sind.

Die Wiedergabe eines ähnlichen Schemas finden wir im französischen Code Civil wieder, dessen Vertragsrecht der Partei beisteht, deren Konsens sich aufgrund eines Irrtums gebildet hat oder durch Drohung oder arglistige Täuschung hervorgerufen worden ist (Art. 1109) und heteronome Eingriffe nur dann zulässt, wenn diese von Gründen getragen werden, die die Moral oder Erlaubtheit des Geschäfts betreffen. Das wird bestätigt, wenn man an die causa des Vertrags denkt – eine essenzielle, aber schon durch das bloße „gegenseitige Interesse der Parteien oder der Wohltätigkeit einer von ihnen"[16] erfüllte Voraussetzung – die erlaubt (art. 1108) und nicht „vom Gesetz verboten sein oder gegen die guten Sitten oder die öffentliche Ordnung verstoßen" (Art. 1133) darf. Nur unter diesen Bedingungen sind die Verträge „legal zustande gekommene Vereinbarungen", die „in Vertretung eines Gesetz zwischen denjenigen, die sie begründet haben, stehen" (Art. 1134 Abs. 1).

Und das alles, während die Bezugnahme auf Treu und Glauben als für die Ausführung des Vertrags verbindlicher Maßstab (Art. 1134 Abs. 3) eine Aufgabe erfüllt, die lediglich formell auf die Absicht, privates Handeln zu kontrollieren, zurückzuführen ist. Die Bezugnahme betrifft die Ausweitung der für die „sog. Handlungen nach Treu und Glauben" vorgesehenen Regelungen auf alle Verträge und spielt damit auf den Umstand an, dass die Gerichte bei den „sog. streng rechtlichen Handlungen ... sämtliche Rechtsfolgen", die auf die „Gleichheit" zurückzuführen sind,

---

[14] A. Smith, La ricchezza delle nazioni (1776), Rom, 1995, S. 389 f.
[15] B. Mandeville, La favola delle api (1714), Rom und Bari, 2002.
[16] A.R. Bousquet, Explication du code civil, 3. Bd., Avignon, 1805, S. 212.

beachten müssen (Art. 1135).[17] In Wirklichkeit reduziert sich alles auf eine Hervorhebung dessen, was im römischen Recht (das oft neben das Naturrecht gestellt wird) als Funktion von Treu und Glauben angesehen wurde: die Verstärkung der Bindung an das gegebene Wort durch die Aufforderung der Vertragspartner zu einem von „Treue" und „Loyalität"[18] geprägten kollaborativen Verhalten.

Dieser Darstellung folgt auch die Regelung des vertraglichen Ungleichgewichts, die das französische Zivilgesetzbuchs vom Modell Justinians ableitet (Art. 1674). Die Norm geht von einem lediglich arithmetischen Ungleichgewicht aus und behält den Schutz nur demjenigen Vertragspartner vor, den man für schutzbedürftig hielt: den Verkäufer von unbeweglichen Sachen – und insbesondere von Grundstücken – der nach traditioneller Auffassung dem Druck eines von „Gier erfüllten" Käufers ausgesetzt ist, der „den Kauf eines Gutes oft in betrügerischer Absicht annimmt".[19] Trotzdem beeilen sich die Kommentatoren des Code Civil mit der Klarstellung, dass die Norm in Wirklichkeit die Reaktion auf einen Einigungsmangel darstellt, der „der arglistigen Täuschung nahe kommt"[20] und relativieren somit die Bezugnahme auf den wirtschaftlichen und sozialen Zusammenhang, auf dem das römische Konzept von Schwäche aufbaut.

Bei genauerem Hinsehen ist die Epoche, über die wir hier sprechen, noch nicht von einer Überbetonung der Herrschaft des Wollens charakterisiert. Dies geht unter anderem aus Überlegungen zu Treu und Glauben im Vertragsrecht – Ausdruck für die Aufforderung zur Bindung an das gegebene Wort – hervor, die dem von ethischen Vorstellungen beeinflussten römischen Recht entlehnt sind. Letztere werden in der Literatur, auf der die Abfassung des Code Civil aufbaut, in einer Form hervorgehoben, die dazu führt, im Naturrecht (auch demjenigen, das in den Normen romanistischer Natur nicht aufgenommen ist) eine Ordnung zu sehen, auf der die bindende Kraft der Vereinbarungen zu gründen ist.[21] Und das Ganze ist auf einer Linie mit der in der Erklärung der Menschen- und Bürgerrechte von 1789 enthaltenen Klarstellung, wonach „der Zweck einer jeden politischen Vereinigung die Bewahrung der natürlichen und unabdingbaren Rechte des Menschen ist" (Art. 2).

---

[17] Z.B. A.M. *Demante* und E. *Colmet de Santerre*, Cours analytique de code civil, 2. Aufl., 5. Bd., Paris, 1883, S. 64.
[18] F. *Gorphe*, Le principe de la bonne foi, Paris, 1928, S. 11.
[19] J. *Cujacii* Observatorium et emendationum libri XXVIII, in: Opera, 1. Bd., Fratr. Giochetti, Prati, 1836, Sp. 732 (XVI. Buch, XVIII. Kap).
[20] Rapport fait au Tribunat par Favard, in: Code civil des français (wie Fn. 5), 5. Bd., S. 107.
[21] A.-J. *Arnaud*, Les origines doctrinales du code civil français, Paris, 1969, S. 209 ff.

Diese Situation verändert sich insbesondere auf deutschem Gebiet zur Zeit der umfassenden Aufnahme der Philosophie Kants. Ihr ist die endgütige Aufgabe der Ansicht zu verdanken, wonach das Naturrecht jeder historischen Grundlage entbehrt und ihm deshalb die Anerkennung als Quelle zu beachtender Pflichten versagt wird. Letztere können einzig und allein vom positiven Recht aufgestellt werden und lediglich zu dem – gerade angesprochenen – Zweck, die Initiativen des Einzelnen innerhalb eines die Selbstbestimmung der Handelnden betonenden Systems zu koordinieren.

Das sind die Voraussetzungen, unter denen der Begründer der historischen Rechtsschule die Unterscheidung zwischen „Sittlichkeit" und „Recht" betont – insofern als es „kein Widerspruch" ist, „wenn im einzelnen Fall die Möglichkeit unsittlicher Ausübung eines wirklich vorhandenen Rechts behauptet wird" – und letzterem die Aufgabe anvertraut, die „unsichtbare Grenze, innerhalb welcher das Daseyn und die Wirksamkeit jedes Einzelnen einen sichern, freyen Raum gewinne" auszumachen, ohne gleichzeitig in der „Entwicklung" anderer „hemmend" zu sein.[22]

Bei solchen Überlegungen spielt der Grundsatz von Treu und Glauben im Vertragsrecht keinerlei Rolle. Genauso wie in der französischen Literatur behauptet man, dass er die „bey rechtlichen Menschen geltenden Sitten" betrifft und zu einem „Schutz" führt, der mit Sicherheit „stärker als man in blos juristischer Betrachtung anzunehmen geneigt seyn mag", ist. Im Übrigen sind die in Frage stehenden Sitten nicht auf die Rechtssphäre zurückführbar und haben deshalb – anders als auf französischem Gebiet – keinerlei formale Relevanz. Vor allem aber werden sie nicht als Ausdruck „edler Gesinnung, Grosmuth, Aufopferung, auf welche durchschnittlich zu rechnen nie geraten seyn möchte" angesehen. Ein ehrliches Verhalten kann auch aus „Selbstsucht" herrühren und nur deshalb beachtet werden, da aus ihm „das schwer zu entbehrende Zutrauen Anderer"[23] herrührt.

Ganz offensichtlich werden diese Bemerkungen in der Formulierung des BGB bestätigt, unter anderem durch den Verweis auf die Lehre hinsichtlich der Definition zahlreicher der verwendeten Konzepte. Man steht der Partei bei, die im Prozess der freien Bildung der Einigung durch einen Irrtum über den Inhalt der Erklärung (§ 119), durch arglistige Täuschung oder widerrechtliche Drohung (§ 123) behindert wird. Die Kontrolle des Vertrags ist auf die Fälle beschränkt, in denen es um die Erlaubtheit (§ 134) oder Moral (§ 138 Abs. 1) geht und eventuell um den Umstand, dass die Leistungen „in einem auffälligen Missverhältnis stehen" (§ 138 Abs. 2). Im letztgenannten Fall ist jedoch die Bezugnahme auf das subjek-

---

[22] F.C. von Savigny, System des heutigen Römischen Rechts, 1. Bd., Berlin, 1840, S. 331 f.
[23] F.C. von Savigny (wie Fn. 22), Bd. 5, Berlin, 1841, S. 108.

tive Element und damit die Ablehnung der vom gemeinen Recht geerbten Tradition, ausdrücklich:[24] das Missverhältnis stellt nur dann ein Indiz für Schwäche dar, wenn es aus der Ausnutzung eines Zustands von Unterlegenheit herrührt.

Dieser Rahmen verändert sich nicht durch Bezugnahmen auf Treu und Glauben „mit Rücksicht auf die Verkehrssitte" als Maßstab für die Auslegung von Verträgen (§ 157) und das Verhalten des Schuldners (§ 242). Die Literatur romanistischer Bildung hält die Berufung auf Treu und Glauben für eine vom gemeinen Recht – genauer gesagt von der erwähnten Verallgemeinerung der „so genannten Handlungen nach Treu und Glauben" [25] – geerbte Angelegenheit. Das behaupten auch die Autoren germanistischer Bildung,[26] die noch dazu betonen, dass das Bürgerliche Gesetzbuch in der Sache die im französischen Code civil in den Art. 1134 und 1135 enthaltene Lösung aufgenommen hat.[27]

Und das alles während die Weigerung, die Regelung des Ratenkaufs in das Gesetzbuch aufzunehmen – und im folgenden die des Mietvertrags – die Absicht betont, all die Fälle als bloße Ausnahme anzusehen, in denen die Schwäche der Vertragspartner insoweit, als sie sozialer Natur ist, Bedeutung gewinnt.[28] Soziale Schwäche kann einer Rechtsordnung mit Sicherheit Sorgen bereiten; nach den Theorien dieser Zeit zur Funktion des Sozialstaats sollte eine Reaktion hierauf jedoch vorzugsweise mit öffentlichen Instrumenten erfolgen, die die konzeptuelle Reinheit des Privatrechtssystems nicht anzugreifen vermögen.

III. Krise des modernen Staates und Entwicklung sozialer Kooperationsmodelle

Bis zu diesem Punkt wurden also Überlegungen zur Schwäche gemessen an einem Marktmodell, das auf dem Mythos der Selbstbestimmung der Vertragspartner sowie dem Glauben beruht, dass das Gemeinwohl einzig und allein aus bedingungslosen wirtschaftlichen Handlungen herrührt.

---

[24] B. *Mugdan* (Hrsg.), Die gesammelte Materialien zum Bürgerlichen Gesetzbuch für das Deutsche Reich, 2. Bd., Berlin, 1899, S. 178.

[25] B. *Windscheid*, Lehrbuch des Pandektenrechts, 8. Aufl., 2, Frankfurt M., 1900, S. 19.

[26] Z.B. G. *Beseler*, System des gemeinen deutschen Privatrechts, 1. Bd., Leipzig, 1847, S. 270.

[27] So auch die Motive zu dem Entwurfe eines bürgerlichen Gesetzbuches für das Deutsche Reich, 2. Bd., Leipzig und Berlin, 1888, S. 198.

[28] In der Sache hat Gierke wirksam von einem „duale(n) Schuldrecht" gesprochen: vgl. O. *Gierke*, Die soziale Aufgabe des Privatrechts, Berlin, 1889.

Eine genauere Analyse dieser Überzeugung bringt jedoch die Tatsache ans Licht, dass der Mythos der Selbstbestimmung Freiheiten betrifft, die von Anfang an nur relativ und somit nicht absolut verstanden werden. Der durch die Wirtschaft genährte Individualismus ist – anders als der, auf den sich die Politik normalerweise bezieht – tatsächlich utilitaristischer und nicht universalistischer Natur. Die Theoretiker der „unsichtbaren Hand" betonen das persönliche Interesse insofern als es die Produktion ankurbelt und damit den „Reichtum der Nationen" vergrößert, der als Maßstab für den „Vorteil der Gesellschaft" und den „Fortschritt" gilt.[29] Und die Politik wiederum nährt solche Vorhaben insoweit, als sie ihrerseits im Fortschritt die Voraussetzung für das Wachstum der Bevölkerung sieht und damit – neben Erhöhung von Produktion und Export – auch für die Vergrößerung der staatlichen Militärmacht.[30]

Mit anderen Worten sind die Freiheiten, derer sich die Wirtschaft bedient, funktionalisierbar; von der Politik werden sie in dem Moment funktionalisiert, in dem sich eine Koordination der Marktkräfte, die über die von der „unsichtbaren Hand" versicherten hinausgeht, als notwendig erweist: der freie Markt stellt das Ergebnis eines Entsozialisierungsprozesses der Wirtschaft dar, der umgekehrt werden muss, um dem Recht die Aufgabe zuzuweisen, eine Art von Ordnung zu schaffen.[31] Und das geschieht spätestens am Anfang des 20. Jahrhunderts, als die Veränderungen des Wirtschaftssystems endgültig den „Individualismus begraben" haben, genauso wie die Französische Revolution „den Feudalismus umgestürzt hat".[32]

Das wirkt sich auf das Modell von Vertragsverhältnissen aus, auf das die Juristen direkt oder indirekt Bezug nehmen. Wie wir gesehen haben, ist das Modell, das den homo oeconomicus – und die unsichtbare Hand – als Maßstab nimmt, ein Konfliktmodell: der Vertrag stellt einen momentanen und freien Stillstand zwischen den wirtschaftlich Handelnden dar, und das Recht hat dabei die Aufgabe, für seine Beachtung zu sorgen. Nunmehr hat sich die Perspektive geändert: die Politik – und damit das Recht – zielt auf eine mehr oder weniger einschneidende Koordination der Produktionskräfte ab und erkennt zu diesem Zweck die Absicht der Vertragsparteien nur insoweit an, als sie zu einem Ergebnis führt, das sich auf einer Linie mit den von der angesprochenen Koordination verfolgten Zwecken befindet.

---

[29] A. *Smith* (wie Fn. 14), S. 119.

[30] M. *Foucault*, Sicurezza, territorio popolazione (1977–78), in: ders, I corsi al Collège de France (1994), Mailand, 1999, S. 78.

[31] K. *Polanyi*, La grande trasformazione (1944), Turin, 1974, insbes. S. 297 ff.

[32] N. *Stolfi*, La rivoluzione francese e la guerra mondiale, in: Riv. dir. pubbl., 1922, I, S. 388 und 404 ff.

Eine ähnliche Darstellung findet sich offensichtlich auch – zumindest potentiell – in Überlegungen zu den Kodifikationen des 19. Jahrhunderts wieder. Das geht insbesondere aus der deutschen Literatur hervor, die letzten Endes anerkennt, dass – durch die Behauptung der Bindung an das gegebene Wort – die Bezugnahme auf Treu und Glauben nicht zur Betonung des Inhalts der wirtschaftlichen Handlung führt, so wie er von den Vertragspartnern gewollt war. Die genannte Bezugnahme verweist auf das, „was bei dem Schuldverhältnis nach den Zwecken des Geschäfts und der Sitte anständig und gerecht denkender Menschen von dem anderen Teile erwartet werden dürfte"[33] – womit ein endlich nicht nur von den „Gesetzes- oder Vertragsbuchstaben", sondern auch und vor allem vom „subjektives Meinen und Belieben"[34] losgelöster „objektiver Maßstab" vorgeschrieben wird.

Bezeichnender sind Überlegungen hinsichtlich der Notwendigkeit, dass der Vertrag – neben dem Verweis auf objektive Verhaltensmodelle – nicht mehr länger Konfliktmodell ist, sondern zu einem Kooperationsmodell wird; d.h., mit anderen Worten, dass er eine Situation betrifft, in der die gegenseitige Zusammenarbeit der Parteien erwartet wird.

Dabei wird nicht auf die bloße Zusammenarbeit zur Erreichung eines gemeinsamen Zwecks angespielt: dies würde zwar eine Vermehrung der Eingriffsmöglichkeiten auch außerhalb der individuellen Schwäche der Vertragsparteien zur Folge haben, jedoch würde der Eingriff weiterhin die konkreten, den Parteien jeweils zugewiesenen Interessen in den Mittelpunkt stellen. Vielmehr wird auf eine Zusammenarbeit im Hinblick auf Ergebnisse angespielt, die der Einigung selbst nicht eigen sind bzw. von der Rechtsordnung jedenfalls in dem Maße anerkannt werden, in dem sie mit den jeweils geschützten superindividuellen Interessen vereinbar sind. Ich werde noch die Gelegenheit haben, zu zeigen, dass hierdurch nicht nur die Einbeziehung der sozialen Schwäche neben der individuellen Schwäche erfolgt, sondern dass es sich gleichzeitig, um dem entgegenzuwirken, um einen Eingriff anderer Natur handelt: er wird nämlich zu einem Instrument der Wirtschaftspolitik, nicht aber zu einem Ziel der Sozialpolitik.

Die Aufforderung zur Zusammenarbeit der Vertragsparteien – eventuell ohne Bestimmung der Zwecke, an denen sie sich orientieren soll – rührt von Anschauungen bzgl. des Zusammenlebens her, die in Anbetracht der unterschiedlichen politisch-normativen Ansichten und der jeweiligen Ursprungsordnung ihrer Anhänger transversaler Natur sind. Nur bei-

---

[33] H. *Dernburg*, Die Schuldverhältnisse nach dem Rechte des Deutschen Reichs und Preussens, 4. Aufl., 1. Bd., Halle, 1909, S. 29.

[34] O. *Gierke*, Deutsches Privatrecht, 3. Bd., Leipzig, 1917, S. 64., s. auch *Staudinger-Kuhlenbeck*, in: Kommentar zum BGB, 7./8. Aufl., Berlin, 1912, § 242, S. 23.

spielhaft kann hier an die Literatur neokantianischer Tendenz erinnert werden, in der eine Vision des Vertrags als eine der „Idee einer Menschengemeinschaft, in der ein Jeder die Zwecke des Anderen zu den seinigen macht"[35] angepasste Angelegenheit gefördert wird. Weiterhin kann auf den Gedanken der Katholiken verwiesen werden, nach dem „der Vertrag nicht ein Herrschaftsakt eines Willens ist, der Recht schafft, sondern ein Angleichungsprozess des privaten Willens an die Verwendung der gemeinsamen Mühen, die auf die Zufriedenstellung der gegenseitigen individuellen Interessen gerichtet sind".[36]

Von den Lehren, in denen die Kritik des Individualismus utilitaritischer Art und das diesbezügliche Auffinden eines alternativen Weges im Mittelpunkt stehen, wird insbesondere das Thema der Kooperation zwischen den Vertragspartnern entwickelt. Es verbindet sich genau in diesem Bereich mit Konstruktionen, die sich auf den Zweck, angesichts dessen der soziale Konflikt beizulegen ist, konzentrieren; insbesondere betont man die Notwendigkeit, ihn mit Hilfe des Rechts zu überwachen. Und tatsächlich werden private Handlungen in Anbetracht „eher des Zwecks als des Willens, der sie bestimmt" von der Ordnung anerkannt und geschützt: oder mit anderen Worten in Bezugnahme auf ihre „Funktion", die „sozial" sein muss. Und noch etwas: „damit eine Willenshandlung rechtliche Wirkungen erzeugen kann", muss sie „zulässig" sein, und vor allem ist es unverzichtbar, dass sie „von einem gewissen Zweck bestimmt wird und dass dieser Zweck ein Zweck sozialer Solidarität ist".[37]

In der Überzeugung der Angemessenheit des Prinzips der Privatautonomie und ihrer Zusätze, gibt es offensichtlich noch Autoren, die den traditionalen Theorien treu geblieben sind. Und trotzdem zeigt die Rechtsprechung, wie wir wissen, klare Zeichen von Unzufriedenheit in Anbetracht der von der Vergangenheit geerbten Konstruktionen der Lehre und fördert ihre Neuinterpretation im Lichte der neuen Überzeugung. Verlangen dieser Art kommen im übrigen direkt aus dem Wirtschaftssystem, das eingreifende Maßnahmen, die einerseits auf die Herstellung eines Klimas sozialen Friedens und andererseits auf die Verwirklichung von Formen der Sozialisierung von Unternehmensrisiken gerichtet sind, nunmehr für unabdingbar hält. Maßnahmen, die mit anderen Worten den Wirtschaftsliberalismus reformieren, ihn aber nicht einmal radikal umgestalten, geschweige denn begraben.

Beteuerungen in diesem Sinne stammen auf italienischem Gebiet von vielen Vertretern der Schulen sozialen Privatrechts. Sie stellen ausführlich die Ziele dar, in deren Namen dem Recht die Aufgabe der Beilegung

---

[35] R. *Stammler*, Das Recht der Schuldverhältnisse, Berlin, 1897, S. 41.
[36] R. *Saleilles*, De la déclaration de volonté, Paris, 1901, S. 229.
[37] L. *Duguit*, Les transformation générales du droit privé, 2. Aufl., Paris, 1920, S. 73 und 96.

sozialer Konflikte anvertraut werden soll: „niemand hat zu befürchten, dass ich hier einen Klassenkampf predige, ich meine dagegen, dass alle Gliedmaßen desselben Körpers sind und dass der Schaden des einen der Schaden des anderen ist".[38] Allerdings fördert das soziale Privatrecht – wie von seinen Gegnern hervorgehoben wird – die Verwechslung von Produktionsinteressen und allgemeinen Interessen, und behindert doch die Gleichsetzung von allgemeinen und nationalen Interessen.[39]

IV. Schwäche im totalitären Staat: Kooperation und Produktivismus im Vertragsrecht

Dieser weitere Schritt charakterisiert die Literatur nationalistischer Natur, die mit neuartigem Nachdruck den Staat zum Schlichter des Konflikts erhebt und dadurch ein zum klassischen Liberalismus und zum Sozialismus alternatives Wirtschaftsmodell kooperativer Natur fördert. Ein Modell, das in der Lage ist, „ein Bewusstsein" zu erzeugen, „das die Klasseninteressen überwinden wird und zu einem globalen Produktionsinteresse und damit zu nationalen, mit den Produktionsinteressen untrennbar verbundenen Interessen, führen wird".[40] Das führt mit Sicherheit nicht zu einem Untergang des Konkurrenzmechanismus: es bestimmt lediglich seine Reglementierung, die ihm durch die Feststellung auferlegt wird, dass ansonsten „die Produktion kostspieliger würde".[41] Und das Hauptziel ist die Förderung einer „Politik des Produktivismus": ein „hässliches Wort, das jedoch in äußerst wirksamer Art und Weise die komplexe, aus politischen Maßnahmen und wirtschaftlichen Vorkehrungen bestehende Handlung zum Ausdruck bringt", die „das Problem des Reichtums in das bedeutendere Problem der Größe der Nation einordnet".[42]

Es ist bekannt, dass die nationalistische Idee nicht nur wegen der Aushöhlung des politischen Liberalismus, sondern auch aufgrund der Reform des Wirtschaftsliberalismus zu den Hauptbezugspunkten der Entwicklung

---

[38] E. *Gianturco*, L'individualismo e il socialismo nel diritto contrattuale (1891), in: Opere giuridiche, 2. Bd., Rom, 1947, S. 266. S. auch G. *Salvioli*, I difetti sociali delle leggi vigenti, 2. Aufl., Palermo, 1906, S. 25.

[39] Z.B. E. *Betti*, Sul codice delle obbligazioni, in: Mon. trib., 1939, S. 421.

[40] A. *Rocco*, Il congresso nazionalista di Roma (1919), in Scritti e discorsi politici, 2. Bd, Mailand, 1938, S. 478 f.

[41] A. *Rocco*, Che cosa è il nazionalismo e che cosa vogliono i nazionalisti (wie Fn. 40), 1. Bd, S. 84.

[42] G. *Olivetti*, L'industria e il fascismo, in: G.L. *Pomba* (Hrsg.), La civiltà fascista, Turin, 1928, S. 331.

der faschistischen Lehre hinzuzurechnen ist.[43] Unter diesen Gesichtspunkten wird die Reform eines Vertragsrechts gefördert, mit der eine „Reduzierung der Wirksamkeit des Willensdogmas" erreicht und somit „das Prinzip von Solidarität oder Sozialität"[44] aufgestellt werden kann: „die rechtliche Ordnung gewährt nicht der bloßen individuellen Laune Schutz, sondern den nützlichen Funktionen, die sozial relevant sind und als solche rechtlichen Schutz verdienen".[45] In der Überzeugung, dass der Gedanke, nach dem „der Grund des Nutzens der Mittelpunkt jeder Handlung bleiben muss"[46] weiterhin Geltung hat, betont man darauf zu achten, dass dies nicht zu einer Art von „Ablehnung klassischer Wirtschaft" führt.

Das italienische Zivilgesetzbuch von 1942 setzt ein ähnliches Schema um, indem es unter anderem den kooperativen Charakter des aufgenommenen Vertragsmodells betont: seine Tendenz zur Überwindung der Gegenüberstellung der Vertragsparteien und sein Ziel, die von der Ordnung verfolgte wirtschaftliche Entwicklung zu fördern. Unter diesem Gesichtspunkt wird die Überwindung der Unterscheidung von Handels- und Zivilrecht gefördert. Ersteres wird, insoweit als sich an einem objektiven System inspiriert, als Klassenrecht betrachtet, das dem Kaufmann eine Machtposition verleiht und gleichzeitig die Schwäche seines Vertragspartners bestimmt.[47]

So verstanden stellt die Vereinheitlichung des Vertragsrechts das Ergebnis von Überlegungen dar, die den typischen Handlungszusammenhang und damit die soziale Schwäche hervorheben. Es handelt sich jedoch um Überlegungen, die mit Kooperationsmodellen in Verbindung stehen und daher das Ungleichgewicht zwischen den Vertragspartnern insoweit angehen, als es ein Element darstellt, das das vorhandene Wirtschaftssystem und sein Wachstum destabilisiert. Beispielhaft in diesem Sinne ist die Bezugnahme auf die sog. Pflicht zum Handeln nach Treu und Glauben, die als ein Instrument betrachtet wird, durch das „Interes-

---

[43] Zitate in A. *Somma*, Liberali in camicia nera, in: A. *Mazzacane*, A. *Somma* und M. *Stolleis* (Hrsg.), Der Korporativismus in den südeuropäischen Diktaturen, Frankfurt a.M., 2005, S. 63 ff.

[44] Rede von Minister Guardasigilli Dino Grandi vor der Commissione delle Assemblee legislative per la riforma dei codici, in: Foro it., 1940, IV, Sp. 23.

[45] Relazione al Re n. 8 zit. v. G. *Scarpello*, M. *Stella Richter* und G. *Dallari*, Codice civile – Libro delle obbligazioni, Milano, 1942, S. 156 f.

[46] A. *De Stefani* und L. *Moroso*, La logica del sistema corporativo, in: Riv. int. sc. soc., 1933, S. 409.

[47] Relazione al Re nn. 1 ff. zit. v. G. *Scarpello*, M. *Stella Richter* und G. *Dallari*, Codice civile – Libro del Lavoro (wie Fn. 45), p. 2.

senkonflikte beigelegt" und „Egoismus und Betrug gebremst"⁴⁸ werden können: unverzichtbare Bedingungen, damit eine „Harmonie der gegenseitigen Interessen und der höherwertigen Interessen des Wirtschaftslebens der Nation, mit denen sie organisch verbunden sind" ⁴⁹ geschaffen wird.

Das ist ein in der mit der Neuordnung der kapitalistischen Ordnung befassten Literatur und Rechtsprechung stetig vorhandenes Modell: der „vertragliche Dirigismus bestätigt sich in allen Ländern, ohne Unterscheidung zwischen liberalen Regierungsformen und totalitären Organisationen".⁵⁰ Natürlich bewährt sich der neue Kurs in den letztgenannten mit geringeren Schwierigkeiten hinsichtlich des Abbaus des demokratischen Mechanismus. Und trotzdem ergeben sich – bei einer Bewertung der Reformbedingungen des Wirtschaftsliberalismus – keinerlei grundlegende Unterschiede zwischen den Erfahrungen, bei denen es den Institutionen des politischen Liberalismus gelingt, noch erhalten zu bleiben und denjenigen, bei denen sie ausgehöhlt sind.

Unter erstere fällt sicherlich Frankreich – wo die faschistische Diktatur nur die erste Hälfte der vierziger Jahre des 20. Jahrhunderts eingenommen hat – das seit den dreißiger Jahren Ansichten in der Lehre kennt, die den italienischen aus den zwanziger Jahren sehr ähneln. In diesem Sinn wird die Vertragsfreiheit vor heteronomer Kontrolle leidenschaftlich verteidigt und damit begründet, dass die Ordnung nunmehr Ausdruck der „Linksrichtung" sei, die durch die „politische Tyrannei derjenigen, die die Macht der Masse vertreten" verursacht werde. Diese Verteidigung mündet durch die Wiederentdeckung der „Macht, zu dirigieren"⁵¹ in das Verlangen, das Allgemeinwohl zu schützen, und hat die imminente Verurteilung des „freien Spiels des privaten Willens" in all den Fällen zur Folge, in denen es den „Schutz der höherwertigen Interessen der sozialen Ordnung" ⁵² nicht fördert.

Zu den Erfahrungen, bei denen die Reform des Wirtschaftsliberalismus von einem Untergang des politischen Liberalismus begleitet wird, ist dagegen die nationalsozialistische Ordnung mit ihrem Versuch der Überarbeitung der individuellen Initiative und des Konkurrenzprinzips zu zäh-

---

[48] M. *Ghiron*, Art. 1366, in: Codice civile – Libro delle obbligazioni – Commentario, hrsg. von M. D'Amelio und E. Finzi, 1. Bd, Florenz, 1948, S. 495.
[49] W. *d'Avanzo*, Art. 1175, in: Codice civile (wie Fn. 48), S. 15.
[50] L. *Josserand*, Cours de droit civil positif français, 2. Bd, Paris, 1939, S. 223 f.
[51] G. *Ripert*, Le régime démocratique et le droit civil moderne, Paris, 1936, S. 44 und 450 f.
[52] P. *Durand*, La contrainte légale dans la formation du rapport contractuel, in: Rev. trim. dr. civ., 1944, S. 97.

len.⁵³ Ein Versuch, der zur Ausarbeitung eines Vertragsrechts geführt hat, das nicht weit von demjenigen des faschistischen Italiens entfernt liegt. Auch die Nationalsozialisten betonen die Kooperation der Parteien: „es interessiert die Gemeinschaft mit Sicherheit, dass das Schuldverhältnis nicht mehr ein Verhältnis des Kampfes zwischen Schuldner und Gläubiger ist und dass der eine Teil nicht die Freiheit besitzt, sich jeglichen Mittels im Kampf mit der anderen zu bedienen".⁵⁴ Und auch die Nationalsozialisten verwenden die Kooperation zu Zwecken, die über die Erwartungen der Vertragsparteien hinausgehen und mit „dem nationalen Interesse an der sozialen Funktion des Vertrags" ⁵⁵ übereinstimmen: eine Funktion, die eine „sinnvolle Güterverteilung" und eine „Erreichung immer höherer Leistungen"⁵⁶ bezweckt.

Diese und andere Konstruktionen kooperativer Natur können auf einen Gedanken zurückgeführt werden, der gerade in der nationalsozialistischen Epoche herangereift ist: der ordoliberale Gedanke. Seine Vertreter entwickeln Überlegungen zum Thema der individuellen Freiheit, die das Wesen des Wirtschaftsliberalismus betreffen und denen die Schicksale, die dem politischen Liberalismus vorbehalten sind, letztendlich gleichgültig sind. Ordoliberal ist tatsächlich der Gedanke, wonach der klassische Liberalismus und seine utilitaristischen Spuren bekämpft werden müssen: der Liberalismus, durch den „die materialistischen Werte über die menschlichen Werte gestellt werden" und in dem sich die „wirtschaftliche Macht" in ein bloßes „egoistische(s) Interesse"⁵⁷ verwandelt. An seiner Statt ist ein System zu errichten, in dem ein starker Staat, der dazu fähig ist, „vernünftig und planend" das Produktionssystem zu „lenken" und „den Bedeutungsgehalt der Gemeinschaft im den wirtschaftlichen Handlungen gewidmeten Volk"⁵⁸ anzukurbeln. Alles jedoch, ohne den Mechanismus der Konkurrenz anzugreifen, der als eine wirksame „Art der Auslese in der Form des Kampfes"⁵⁹ angesehen wird.

---

⁵³ S. statt vieler *H.-U. Wehler*, Deutsche Gesellschaftsgeschichte, 4. Bd., München, 2003, S. 96 ff.

⁵⁴ *G. Vassalli*, Per un diritto unico delle obbligazioni, in: Lo Stato, 1939, S. 104, der auf diese Weise eine in der nationalsozialistischen Litratur zum Vertrag aufgestellte Behauptung zusammenfasst.

⁵⁵ *W. Siebert*, Contrato y libertad de contratación en el nuevo sistema del derecho alemán, in: Rev. der. priv., 1942, S. 454.

⁵⁶ *H. Stoll*, Vertrag und Unrecht, 1. HalbBd., Tübingen, 1943, S. 43.

⁵⁷ *H. Peter*, Sozialpolitik und freier Wettbewerb, in: *G. Schmölders* (Hrsg.), Der Wettbewerb als Mittel volkswirtschaftlicher Leistungssteigerung und Leistungsauslese, Berlin, 1942, S. 199.

⁵⁸ *F. Böhm*, Die Ordnung der Wirtschaft, Berlin, 1937, S. 8 f.

⁵⁹ *J. Jessen*, Wettbewerb als grundsätzliche historisch-politische Frage, in: *G. Schmölders* (wie Fn. 57), S. 9.

Es wurde bereits gesagt, dass Anschauungen dieser Art auch dort verbreitet sind, wo sich der Untergang des politischen Liberalismus nicht verwirklicht hat. Dort, wo er sich verwirklicht hat, folgt die Literatur auch dann ordoliberalen Thematiken, wenn sie der Diktatur – wie so viele Vertreter der Bewegung, der ihre Ausarbeitung zu verdanken ist – nicht nahe steht.

Dies zeigt sich beispielhaft an einem bekannten deutschen Beitrag, der dem Thema der Standardverträge gewidmet und in den dreißiger Jahren erschienen ist. Dort liest man, dass die Vertragsfreiheit von der Rechtsordnung begrenzt werden muss, um zu vermeiden, dass „im Zeichen jener Freiheit der Starke den Schwachen ausbeutet". Allerdings geht es nicht darum, Elemente – den typischen Zusammenhang, in dem der Vertragsschluss stattfindet – zur Geltung zu bringen, durch die zur Hervorhebung einer Schwäche der Vertragspartner neben der bloß individuellen Schwäche beigetragen werden soll. Die Bezugnahme auf objektive Umstände verbindet sich in der Tat mit einer eindringlichen Aufforderung zur Kooperation der Parteien, die darauf ausgerichtet ist, nicht nur die Position des schwächeren Vertragsteils, sondern vor allem die „Gesamtheit, deren wirtschaftliches Wohl gefährdet und deren Rechtsbewusstsein gekränkt wird durch den Egoismus eines Einzelnen oder einer Sondergruppe" zu schützen: die Vertragsfreiheit „ist dem Einzelnen nur im Dienste nicht gegen die Gemeinschaft verliehen".[60]

Derselbe Beitrag fordert den Rückgriff auf eine präventive verwaltungsrechtliche Kontrolle zumindest derjenigen Allgemeinen Geschäftsbedingungen, die als „wirtschaftlich und sozial wichtig"[61] betrachtet werden. Das liegt auf einer Linie mit dem Gedanken, dass der Schwächere in Funktion des Wirtschaftswachstums geschützt wird – und stellt damit keinen Anspruch dar, der einem Recht entspricht – woraus sich die Zuständigkeit der Exekutive ergibt. In den Vorarbeiten zum nationalsozialistischen Volksgesetzbuch wird eine solche Lösung erwogen, aber gleichzeitig werden Formen des Schutzes des schwächeren Vertragsteils am Maßstab des homo oeconomicus vorgesehen. Besonderer Nachdruck wird nämlich dem vertraglichen Transparenzgebot und ganz allgemein der Notwendigkeit verliehen, dass der schwächere Vertragsteil in der Lage sein muss, rationale Erwägungen hinsichtlich des Geschäfts anzustellen.[62]

Ganz ähnlich ist der vom faschistischen Recht eingeschlagene Weg. Die gesetzliche Regelung der allgemeinen Geschäftsbedingungen (Art.

---

[60] L. *Raiser*, Das Recht der Allgemeinen Geschäftsbedingungen, Hamburg, 1935, S. 277.

[61] L. *Raiser*, (wie Fn. 60), S. 103 f.

[62] Dazu – auch bzgl. einer Quellenauswahl – C. *Harth*, Der „richtige Vertrag" im Nationalsozialismus, in: D. *Gosewinkel* (Hrsg.), Wirtschaftskontrolle und Recht in der nationalsozialistischen Diktatur, Frankfurt M., 2005, S. 124 ff.

1341) und der mittels Formularen und Vordrucken geschlossenen Verträge (Art. 1342) wird wegen der Umstände, unter denen typischerweise der Abschluss des Geschäfts erfolgt, vereinzelt als Instrument des Schutzes der schwächeren Vertragspartei dargestellt.[63] Allerdings handelt es sich dabei um einen mittels Informationsmechanismen verwirklichten Schutz – nämlich die Notwendigkeit der zweifachen Unterschrift – der sich auf einer Linie mit der Überlegung befindet, dass die Schwäche eines Vertragspartners individuell ist und von der fehlenden Information hinsichtlich der Bedingungen des Geschäfts bzw. von der zu geringen Sorgfalt bei ihrer Bewertung abhängt.

Die italienische Literatur, die Überlegungen zum Massengeschäft anstellt und dieses durch den Rückgriff auf „typische Verträge" – „Form einer kategorischen Regelung, die sich vom arbeitsrechtlichen Kollektivvertrag nur dadurch unterscheidet, dass der Beitritt der anderen vertragsschließenden Kategorie fehlt"[64] – charakterisiert sieht, behauptet außerdem die Notwendigkeit ihrer Festlegung im Bereich kooperativer Strukturen.[65] Im Übrigen bezweckt der Faschismus – neben der Verbindung von Arbeitnehmern und Arbeitgebern – die Realisierung eines Bündnisses zwischen letzteren und den Verbrauchern. In die gleiche Richtung geht auch die Bestimmung, die den Körperschaften die Aufgabe erteilt, die Preise „für die wirtschaftlichen Leistungen und Dienste" und für „die der Öffentlichkeit angebotenen Verbrauchsgüter nach privilegierenden Bedingungen"[66] zu bestimmen: und all das unter Mitwirkung der Vertreter der faschistischen Partei in „Vertretung der großen anonymen Masse der Verbraucher".[67]

V. Die Entdeckung sozialer Schwäche und das Vertragsrecht als Instrument der Umverteilung von Reichtum

Im totalitären Staat wohnt man somit einem Resozialisierungsprozess der Wirtschaft bei, wie er von den Befürwortern des ordoliberalen Denkens erwünscht wird. Das Gleiche geschieht auch dort, wo die Krise des modernen Staates keine faschistische Diktatur zur Folge hat. Wie ich bereits

---

[63] Relazione al Re, n. 78, zit. v. G. *Pandolfelli*, G. *Scarpello*, M. *Stella Richter* und G. *Dallari*, Codice civile (wie Fn. 45), S. 170.
[64] D. *Guidi*, Regime corporativo e diritto commerciale, in: Dir. e prat. comm., 1928, S. 12 f.
[65] Vgl. C. *Vivante*, L'autonomia del diritto commerciale e il sistema corporativo, in Dir. e prat. comm., 1929, S. 19 f.
[66] Art. 10 L. 05.02.1934 Nr. 163, in: Gazz. uff., 20.02.1934, Nr. 41.
[67] G. *Stammati*, L'impresa nell'ordinamento corporativo, in: Dir. e prat. comm., 1940, I, S. 117 und 121.

vorweggenommen habe, legt das Verhältnis von Wirtschaft und Politik – handelt es sich nun um ein vom demokratischen Mechanismus vermitteltes Verhältnis oder nicht – allerdings keine gänzlich unterschiedlichen Ergebnisse fest.

Nun ist eine Betrachtung der Ereignisse, die in Kontinentaleuropa den Übergang von der Diktatur zur Demokratie charakterisiert haben, notwendig. Es ist bekannt, wie dieser mit dem Erlass von Verfassungen zusammenfällt, in denen Hinweise auf eine Ausweitung der wirtschaftlichen Freiheiten insbesondere in Bezug auf die Auswirkung solidaristischer Modelle auf vertikaler und horizontaler Ebene gegeben werden. Erstere betreffen die Befriedigung von Erwartungen, die mit der Anerkennung sozialer Rechte in einer Art und Weise verbunden sind, die den Aktionskreis des Marktes begrenzt. Letztere hingegen sind dazu bestimmt, den Markt anzupassen und damit die Bedingungen eines heteronomen, auf die Begrenzung der Privatautonomie gerichteten Eingriffs zu definieren.[68]

Aus ordoliberaler Sicht ist das Wesen der horizontalen und das der vertikalen Solidarität in der Formel „soziale Marktwirtschaft" zusammengefasst. Sie bezeichnet eine Situation, in der die Umverteilung des Reichtums – die Hauptform eines Eingriffs in soziale Schwäche – ein Ergebnis darstellt, das durch normative, direkt auf die Koordination der Produktionskräfte ausgerichtete Eingriffe nur vermittelt wird. Und tatsächlich soll die Anpassung des Marktes einzig und allein seinem Scheitern entgegenwirken[69] oder eventuell – notfalls mittels autoritärer Maßnahmen – den sozialen Frieden fördern, der unabdingbare Voraussetzung für die Akzeptanz des Systems und damit für seine Wirkungskraft ist.[70] Direkt auf die Umverteilung von Reichtum zielen hingegen Maßnahmen vertikaler Solidarität, die ihre Wirkung außerhalb der Marktgrenzen durch Eingriffe vorwiegend fiskalischer Natur entfalten.[71]

Eine solche Darstellung ist jedoch durch eine Neuinterpretation des von der Vergangenheit geerbten Zivilrechtssystems im Lichte verfassungsrechtlicher Werte und insbesondere des Prinzips horizontaler Solidarität zur Veränderung bestimmt. Auf diesem Wege wird das Vertragsrecht zum Instrument der Umverteilung von Reichtum nach Modellen distributiver Gerechtigkeit: nicht zugunsten des stärkeren Vertragspartners – wie es der Fall ist, wenn sich das Recht auf eine Berichtigung der

---

[68] Zitate in A. *Somma*, Diritto comunitario e patrimonio costituzionale europeo, in: Pol. dir., 2004, S. 263 ff.

[69] A. *Müller-Armack*, Wirtschaftslenkung und Marktwirtschaft (1946), Bern und Stuttgart, 1976, S. 116 ff.

[70] J. *Agnoli* e P. *Brückner*, Die Transformation der Demokratie, Frankfurt a.M., 1968, S. 45.

[71] A. *Müller-Armack*, (wie Fn. 69), S. 119.

durch das freie Spiel der Marktkräfte hervorgerufenen Vereinbarungen beschränkt – sondern zugunsten des schwächeren Vertragspartners.

Zu verdanken haben wir das dem Wirken der Gerichte, die in der Sache einem Schwäche-Modell Geltung verschaffen, dessen Bezugspunkt der typische Zusammenhang ist, in dem die Parteien handeln: ein Modell sozialer Schwäche struktureller Art, das nicht mit der Wiederherstellung der Fähigkeit zur Selbstbestimmung der Parteien auf dem Markt angegangen werden kann. Und im Übrigen ist das menschliche Bezugsmodell für solche Konstruktionen nicht mehr der den Wirtschaftswissenschaften entstammende homo oeconomicus. Man nimmt nunmehr auf die Soziologie Bezug, um die Bindungen des einzelnen gegenüber der Gesellschaft hervorzuheben: Bindungen, die eine Verhaltenserwartung betreffen, die von einem System sozialer, dem Abweichler drohenden Sanktionen kontrolliert wird. Das menschliche Bezugsmodell ist nun der homo sociologicus.[72] Es gibt zwar keinen Zweifel, dass die Idee, wonach die individuelle Selbstbestimmung hoffnungslos von äußeren Bedingungen behindert wird, eine Abstraktion darstellt. Das Gleiche gilt jedoch für die gegenteilige Idee privater von Bedingungen unabhängiger Handlungen, wenn sie nur auf dem Besitz ausreichender Informationen hinsichtlich der Umstände der zu treffenden Wahl basieren.[73]

Es wurde bereits gesagt, dass die Ausarbeitung des neuen Modells einer Neuinterpretation der Zivilgesetzbücher im Lichte verfassungsrechtlichen Werte durch die Gerichte zu verdanken ist. Eine beispielhafte Darstellung ermöglichen die in der italienischen Verfassung enthaltenen Formulierungen. Es handelt sich um Formulierungen, die zwar nicht immer in den anderen Verfassungen enthalten sind, die jedoch – wie beispielsweise in der deutschen Verfassung – anderen weniger eindeutigen Ausdrücken zu Ehren der in Bezug auf das Wirtschaftssystem angenommenen Neutralität der Verfassung entnommen werden können.

Das hier beschriebene Eingreifen in Schwäche zielt in der Tat darauf ab, dem demokratischen Spiel eine Wirkungskraft zu verleihen, die die Überprüfung der privaten Pflicht zur „politischen, wirtschaftlichen und sozialen Solidarität" (Art. 2) im Lichte der öffentlichen Pflicht „Hindernisse wirtschaftlicher und sozialer Natur, die durch die tatsächliche Begrenzung der Freiheit und Gleichheit der Bürger eine umfassende Entwicklung der menschlichen Person verhindern" (Art. 3) zur Folge hat. Dabei handelt es sich um Eingriffe, die auf den sozialen Konflikt durch eine gerechte Verteilung der Waffen der betroffenen Parteien einzuwirken beabsichtigen, nicht aber auch das Ergebnis der Gegenüberstellung lenken wollen. Dadurch wird die Verstaatlichung der marktrechtlichen

---

[72] Ein Muss ist der Verweis auf R. *Dahrendorf*, Homo sociologicus, Opladen, 1958.
[73] R. *Orestano*, Diritti soggettivi e diritti senza soggetto, in: JuS, 1960, insbes. S. 159.

Beziehungen zugunsten ihrer Vergesellschaftung überwunden:[74] erstere Grundlage eines Schutzes der bloßen jeweils verfolgten Erwartungen hinsichtlich des heteronomen Eingriffs der politischen Mächte, letztere Grundlage der Instanzen, die durch die Träger der schwächeren, von den Gerichten interpretierten Interessen verkörpert werden.

Eine Bezugnahme auf die in der italienischen Verfassung enthaltenen Formulierungen verstärkt die Weigerung etatistischer Visionen bzgl. der Konstruktion eines solidarischen Vertragsrechts, die das Eingreifen in Schwäche der Aufrechterhaltung bestimmter wirtschaftlicher Schemata unterordnen. Und tatsächlich ist insbesondere das Aufstellen von Pflichten zur Solidarität nicht Ausdruck der Absicht, die „generelle Unterordnung" des Individuums „unter die staatliche Macht" zu fördern, sondern vielmehr seine Bewertung als „Zentrum der Interessen, um die sich das gesamte System verfassungsrechtlicher Garantien dreht",[75] zu unterstützen. Außerdem vermeidet die Bezugnahme auf Angelegenheiten nicht nur wirtschaftlicher Natur – die „politische" und „soziale Solidarität" – produktivistische Visionen zum Vertragsrecht. Genauer gesagt ermöglicht sie die Hervorhebung des Umstands, dass sich die wirtschaftliche Situation eines Individuums notwendigerweise auf seine Möglichkeit, zu politischen und sozialen Bürgerrechten Zugang zu finden, auswirkt.[76]

An dieser Stelle muss betont werden, dass das beschriebene Modell durch Anschauungen ermöglicht wird, die das Zusammenleben – und somit das Vertragsrecht – als Konflikt begreifen. Natürlich ist es auch möglich, ein Vertragsrecht zu gestalten, das Ausdruck der durch den Sozialstaat verkörperten Philosophie und gleichzeitig Ausdruck der Kooperationsmodelle ist. Allerdings müsste ein solches Vertragsrecht unbedingt mit der Definition des gemeinsamen Ziels, dessentwegen die Parteien den Vertrag abgeschlossen haben, koordiniert werden. Und das führt – will man Fiktionen vermeiden – zur Einführung eines bestimmten Marktsystems durch die Rechtsordnung.

Der Übergang von einem ordoliberalen Eingriffsmodell zu Modellen solidaristischer Natur ist nicht immer klar und deutlich. Das zeigen beispielsweise die deutschen Entscheidungen, die sich mit der Zulässigkeit von Maßnahmen horizontaler Solidarität im Lichte der Koordination von Rechtsstaats- und Sozialstaatsprinzipien (Art. 20 GG) befassen. Als Beispiel ist hier das bekannte Urteil des Bundesverfassungsgericht zu nennen, in dem eine Bürgschaft, gegen die die zur Zeit der Unterschriftslei-

---

[74] M. *Weber*, Law in economy and society (1925), Cambridge Mass., 1966, S. 331 ff.

[75] A. *Barbera*, Art. 2, in: G. *Branca* (Hrsg.), Commentario della Costituzione, 1. Bd, Bologna und Rom, 1975, S. 98.

[76] Ähnlich D. *Kennedy*, The stakes of law, in: 15 Leg. Stud. Forum, 1991, S. 327 ff.

stung vermögenslose Bürgin rechtlich vorgeht, mit der Begründung für nichtig erklärt wird, dass die Ausübung der Privatautonomie in all den Fällen, in denen sie die Macht begründet, „den Vertragsinhalt faktisch einseitig (zu) bestimmen"[77] einzuschränken ist.

Ordoliberale Wurzeln hat in diesem Fall zum einen die Bezugnahme auf die Privatautonomie als ein Wert, der vor wirtschaftlichen Handlungen, die zu seiner Verneinung führen, zu schützen ist und zum anderen vor allem die Bedeutung, die der konkreten Situation, in der sich die Einigung vollzogen hat, zugewiesen wird: vor allem der Umstand, dass die Beschwerdeführerin gerade erst einmal einundzwanzig Jahre alt war und keinerlei berufliche Ausbildung hatte.

Und doch sind Teile der Entscheidung mit dem ordoliberalen Denken nicht vereinbar. Da ist zunächst die Bezugnahme auf Konfliktmodelle des sozialen Zusammenlebens, – die ihren Ausdruck vor allem in der Bemerkung findet, dass „am Zivilrechtsverkehr gleichrangige Grundrechtsträger teilnehmen", die „unterschiedliche Interessen und vielfach gegenläufige Ziele verfolgen" – wobei auf die Notwendigkeit, die Voraussetzungen für eine harmonische Entwicklung des Wirtschaftslebens zu schaffen, keinerlei Bezug genommen wird. Mit den ordoliberalen Theorien unvereinbar ist auch die Hervorhebung des typisierten Zusammenhangs, in dem die Vertragspartner handeln, und weniger der konkreten Situation des Vertragsschlusses: oder, mit anderen Worten, die bloße Zugehörigkeit zur Kategorie der Kunden einer Bank und weniger die fehlende tatsächliche Möglichkeit, die Vertragsfreiheit auszuüben. Zu dieser Folgerung verleiten die Hinweise auf „typisierbare Fallgestaltungen" und die „strukturelle Unterlegenheit des einen Vertragspartners".[78]

Anders gesagt stellt die Bezugnahme auf die individuelle Selbstbestimmung eine Technik dar, die auf bestimmte Werte zurückgeführt werden kann – nämlich die Förderung eines geordneten Marktsystems – die der ordoliberale Vertrag als Fixpunkt des heteronomen Eingriffs betrachtet. Ein Punkt, der jedoch von den solidarischen Modellen, die das Wesen des Marktes dem Gegenüberstehen sozialer Kräfte anvertrauen, die sich endlich auf einer Ebene tendenziell materieller Gleichheit befinden, wieder zur Diskussion gestellt wird. Genau das ist die Bedeutung der Betonung des typischen Zusammenhangs, in dem der Vertragsabschluss erfolgt – unabhängig von der konkreten Situation: die Bedeutung der Hervorhebung der vertraglichen Bindung unabhängig von der Handlung. Das muss das Ergebnis einer Rechtspolitik sein, die endlich den Prozess der Zerstückelung des einheitlichen Rechtssubjekts beendet, der von den Rhetorik zur Privatautonomie, die vom ordoliberalen Denken wieder ausgegraben und nur oberflächlich überarbeitet wird, immer noch behindert ist.

---

[77] BVerfG vom 19. September 1993, in: ZIP 1993, S. 1774 ff (1780).
[78] BVerfG vom 19. September 1993 (wie Fn. 77), S. 1780.

Solche Darstellungen charakterisieren nicht nur die deutsche Praxis. Sie finden sich auch in italienischem Zusammenhang und zwar insbesondere im Bereich der Anpassung des Arbeitsvertrags wieder, wo das Problem der fehlenden Selbstbestimmung auf dem Markt durch die Hervorhebung der sozialen Schwäche entwickelt wird, die sich aus der Zugehörigkeit zu einer Klasse ergibt – eine Vereinigung, in der „die Mitglieder konvergieren und schließlich auf der Grundlage des Einkommens, des ausgeübten Berufes, der formalen schulischen Bildung, des Viertels oder der Lokalität und der Art der Wohnung usw. zur Masse werden".[79] Und das insoweit, als man es als einen „Begriff allgemeiner Erfahrung" ansieht, dass sich „der Arbeitnehmer im Normalfall in einer Situation befindet, in der er nicht auf die Ausführung des Arbeitsvertrags verzichten kann" und dass deshalb „die Autonomie der vertragsschließenden Parteien" nicht „angemessen erscheint, zu einem ausgeglichenen Ergebnis der gegensätzlichen Interessen der Vertragspartner zu führen".[80] Auf skandinavischem Gebiet werden ähnliche Ergebnisse mithilfe der Theorie der „social force majeure" erzielt, die angewandt wird, um den von Krankheit oder Arbeitslosigkeit und daraus folgenden verminderten Einkommensmöglichkeiten getroffenen Schuldner zu befreien.[81]

Allerdings ist es nicht nur die typische Position des Arbeitnehmers – in Arbeitsverträgen und anderen Verträgen – und des Verbrauchers, die das solidarische Vertragsrecht zu stärken ermöglicht. Das geht beispielhaft aus der gerichtlichen Praxis in Deutschland bzgl. der „Schuldverhältnisse ohne primäre Leistungspflichten"[82] hervor. Man beschränkt sich in diesen Fällen nicht darauf, den Vertrag erneut zu verfassen – eine Situation, die noch durch den Rückgriff auf Fiktionen beschrieben werden kann, die die Hervorhebung der Einigung als Quelle der Bindung betreffen – sondern ihn direkt mit dem Ziel zu verfassen, einer von sozialer Schwäche gekennzeichneten Situation abzuhelfen. Das Ganze geschieht auf der Grundlage von Erwägungen, die nicht weit von denjenigen auf italienischem Gebiet entfernt sind, und die es ermöglicht haben, mit dem Begriff „sozialer Kontakt" das Verhältnis zwischen dem von einer öffentlichen Struktur abhängigen Arzt und dem Patienten, der Opfer eines ärztlichen Irrtums ist[83]

---

[79] F. *Ferrarotti*, Manuale di sociologia, 5. Aufl., Rom und Bari, 1995, S. 75.
[80] Cass. civ., 10. Juni 1993 n. 6487, in: Dir. e prat. lav., 1993, 2086 ss. Bzgl. der deutschen Entscheidungen, s. OLG Stuttgart, NJW 1988, S. 833.
[81] Darüber T. *Wilhelmsson*, Social force majeure – A new concept in Nordic consumer law, in: 13 J. Cons. Pol., 1990, S. 1 ff.
[82] Vor allem K. *Larenz*, Lehrbuch des Schuldrechts, Bd. 1, 14. Aufl., München, 1987, S. 104 ff.
[83] Cass. civ., 22. Januar 1999 n. 589, in: Corr. giur., 1999, S. 486 ff.

oder zwischen der öffentlichen Verwaltung und dem Bürger, der Empfänger einer durch diese ergehende rechtswidrigen Verfügung ist,[84] zu qualifizieren.

Wie wir sehen, gibt es zahlreiche und undefinierbare Fälle, in denen das solidarische Vertragsrecht eine Konkretisierung des Komplexes von Verhaltensnormen erlaubt, an die sich typischerweise starke Vertragspartner halten müssen, um zu vermeiden, dass Verhältnisse mit typischerweise schwachen Vertragspartnern zu einer bloßen Reproduktion der sozialen Hierarchie führen. Das ist unter anderem durch die wachsende Vertragsschließung in den Bereichen, die dem Markt früher entzogen waren, bedingt: insbesondere die Fälle, die traditionell mit den Institutionen des Sozialstaats angegangen wurden, werden heute angesichts des Privatisierungsprozesses des staatlichen Erhebungssystems der Privatautonomie anvertraut. Und das Gleiche gilt für den Prozess der Verschiebung der wirtschaftlichen Dynamik vom Massenverbrauch zur Börse, der Schwierigkeiten bzgl. der Individualisierung der jeweils betroffenen Interessenszentren hervorgerufen hat und damit die Dynamiken des sozialen Konflikts weniger transparent und stabil gemacht hat.[85]

---

[84] Z.B. Cons. Stato, 6. August 2001 n. 4239, in: *Urb. e app.*, 2002, S. 199 ff.
[85] Statt aller C. *Crouch*, Postdemocrazia, Rom und Bari, 2004, insbes. S. 41 ff.

Zwang und Ausbeutung beim Vertragsschluss

Thomas Gutmann (Münster)

I. Einführung

Die Rechtsdogmatik lebt, gerade auch im Vertragsrecht, zu einem erheblichen Teil von *incompletely theorized agreements*.[1] Wenn es um die Behandlung konkreter Fälle, spezifischer Rechtsfragen oder um dogmatische Grundsätze mittlerer Reichweite geht, erzielen wir unsere Konsense und herrschenden Ansichten meist ganz ungeachtet unserer oft unterschiedlichen und nicht selten kontroversen normativen Vorverständnisse und rechtstheoretischen Ausgangspositionen. Die konkreten Fälle und Probleme lassen sich in der Regel lösen (und müssen sich lösen lassen), ohne dass wir uns zuerst über die „letzten Dinge" einigen.

Andererseits kann die Rechtsdogmatik den Anspruch nicht aufgeben, ihren Gegenstand theoretisch zu systematisieren. In manchen Fällen tut sie zu diesem Zweck gut daran, einen Blick in ihre Nachbardisziplinen, in die Rechtstheorie, die praktische Philosophie und die analytische Philosophie zu werfen. Dort sind in den letzten drei Jahrzehnten erhebliche Anstrengungen unternommen worden, um die beiden Handlungsformen bzw. Konzepte von „Zwang" einerseits und „Ausbeutung" andererseits sowohl analytisch als auch normativ zu klären und auszudifferenzieren. Es wurde dabei klar, dass es sich bei Zwang und Ausbeutung um zwei in ihrer normativen Struktur grundlegend unterschiedliche Phänomene handelt. Im Substrat des Vertragsrechts, d.h. in der täglichen Realität der Vertragsschlüsse, finden wir beide vor. Die Ausgangsthese des folgenden Beitrags ist, dass eine adäquate Privatrechtsdogmatik – insbesondere eine adäquate Theorie des Vertrags – imstande sein muss, diesen Strukturunterschied nachzuvollziehen und rechtliche Normen und Institutionen bereitzustellen, in denen diese beiden Phänomene in ihrer Unterschiedlichkeit abgearbeitet werden können. Sowohl im deutschen Recht als auch im Bereich des Common Law besteht hier einiger Nachholbedarf.

---

[1] Zur Bedeutung und Funktion der *incompletely theorized agreements* im Recht siehe aus rechtspragmatischer Sicht C.R. Sunstein, Incompletely Theorized Agreements, *Harvard Law Review* 108 (1995), 1733 ff. und ders., *Legal Reasoning and Political Conflict*, New York/Oxford: Oxford University Press 1996, viii, 6 ff., 35 ff., 50 ff.

Ein „New Feature in Contract Law" ist darin zu sehen, dass seit einigen Jahren das Bewusstsein der Notwendigkeit dieser Aufgabe klarer hervortritt.

In methodischer Sicht stellt das Problem von Zwang und Ausbeutung beim Vertragsschluss ein Exempel dafür dar, wie die analytische Rechts- und Moralphilosophie als *ancilla juris* zu einer besseren, weil trennschärferen Rechtsdogmatik beitragen kann. Von der Rechtsgeschichte ist bei *dieser* Problematik Ähnliches nicht ohne weiteres zu erwarten. Jedenfalls ist dem heutigen Vertragsrecht, das auf der Ausdifferenzierung von Recht und Moral beruht und Privatautonomie in Form subjektiver Rechte garantiert, der Anschluss an die klassischen Theorien der Vertragsgerechtigkeit, etwa an das bis ins 18. Jahrhundert wirkende scholastische Postulat der Tauschgerechtigkeit und der materiellen Leistungsäquivalenz, im Wesentlichen versperrt. Dies ist gerade angesichts der durchaus zahlreichen Versuche zur Wiederbelebung dieser Tradition festzuhalten; zu nennen sind hier etwa James Gordleys Versuch, eine aristotelisch-scholastische Konzeption des Vertrages an das gegenwärtige Schuldrecht heranzutragen,[2] oder an die eigenwillige, sich formalistisch gebärdende, im Ergebnis aber ähnliche „Idee des Privatrechts" Ernest Weinribs.[3]

Der folgende Beitrag kann nicht mehr als eine grobe Skizze dieses Forschungsthemas bieten, in der auch sehr weitreichende Thesen nur knapp begründet werden und Details weitgehend ausgespart bleiben müssen.

II. Zwang und Freiwilligkeit

Dass eine Person „freiwillig" gehandelt hat, ist Voraussetzung dafür, ihr Verantwortung für ihr Handeln und dessen Folgen zuschreiben zu können und sie an ihr Handeln zu binden. Für die vertragliche Selbstbindung ist Freiwilligkeit konstitutiv. Ein Begriff der Freiwilligkeit, der diese Funktion der Verantwortungszuschreibung leisten soll, ist notwendigerweise durch zwei Eigenschaften gekennzeichnet.[4] Er stellt *erstens* ein *binäres*

---

[2] J. Gordley, *The Philosophical Origins of Modern Contract Doctrine*, New York/Oxford: Oxford University Press 1991; ders., Contract Law in the Aristotelian Tradition, in: P. Benson (Ed.), *The Theory of Contract Law. New Essays* (Cambridge Studies in Philosophy and Law), Cambridge: Cambridge University Press 2001, 265–334; ders., The Moral Foundations of Private Law, *The American Journal of Jurisprudence* 47 (2002), 1–23 und nunmehr ders., *Foundations of Private Law: Property, Tort, Contract, Unjust Enrichment*, Oxford: Oxford University Press 2006, 289 ff.

[3] E.J. Weinrib, The Idea of Private Law, Harvard: Harvard University Press 1995.

[4] Siehe zum Folgenden vertiefend und m.w.N. Th. Gutmann, *Freiwilligkeit als Rechtsbegriff*, München: C.H. Beck 2001.

Konstrukt dar – man hat entweder (hinreichend) freiwillig gehandelt oder nicht. Ein „bisschen freiwillig" im Rechtssinn gibt es nicht. Nicht die Art und die Zusammensetzung der unzählbaren, heterogenen, teils vorrationalen motivationalen Momente, die auf unsere Willensentschlüsse einwirken, sind von Interesse, sondern nur die *Abwesenheit* einer eng umrissenen Menge von Ausschlussfaktoren für Freiwilligkeit: Relevante Irrtümer und Täuschungen, Drohungen und *vis absoluta*.[5] Die Zurechnung ist am Ende immer eine ja/nein-Entscheidung. Dies ist deshalb zu betonen, weil in der Vertragstheorie mit Wendungen wie „je [...] *freiwilliger* [eine] vertragliche Pflicht übernommen worden ist, umso ..."[6] immer wieder gradualistische Freiwilligkeitskonzepte begegnen. Nähme man derlei ernst, würde der Satz *pacta sunt servanda* selbst verflüssigt. Die Geltung *jedes* Vertrages wäre eine Frage des mehr oder weniger. Das Vertragsrecht würde sich in einem Geflecht halb- und dreiviertelfreiwilliger Handlungen und Erklärungen der Rechtssubjekte verlieren.

Zweitens ist Freiwilligkeit ein *normatives Konzept*. Es gibt keine wertungsfreie, deskriptive, sozusagen „psychologische" oder handlungstheoretische Definition von Freiwilligkeit, die für moralische oder rechtliche Fragen von Interesse wäre. Diese Unterscheidung ist eine kategoriale. Freiwilligkeit ist ein immanent normativer Begriff insofern, als er nur sinnvoll mit Blick auf die Freiheitsrechte und rechtlich legitimen Erwartungen der Betroffenen bestimmt werden kann. Zwang in dem hier interessierenden Sinn kann nur von einem Handeln ausgehen, das in widerrechtlicher Weise die Zahl der dem Empfänger zur Verfügung stehenden (zumutbaren) Optionen verkürzt.

Dies bedeutet unter anderem, dass das Fehlen attraktiver alternativer Handlungsoptionen per se *keine* hinreichende Bedingungen für die Annahme ist, dass die betreffende Person in normativ relevantem Sinn nicht freiwillig handeln kann. Hinter dem Begriff der „Not-" oder „Zwangslage" verbergen sich zwei äußerst unterschiedliche Handlungskontexte. Eine solche Situation lässt sich unter entscheidungstheoretischen Gesichtspunkten als eine beschreiben, in der der Betroffene – außer dem Abschluss des zu beurteilenden Vertrags – keine anderen von ihm positiv bewerteten Möglichkeiten zu handeln hat. Er „muss" den Vertrag schlie-

---

[5] Plastisch die Entscheidung BGH NJW 1988, 2599 (2601), die betont, „daß nur eine durch widerrechtliche Drohung verursachte Zwangslage zur Anfechtung nach § 123 I BGB berechtigt. [...] Unter der freien Willensentscheidung, die § 123 I BGB allerdings schützt, ist nur die nicht rechtswidrig beeinflußte Willensentscheidung zu verstehen [...]. Die rechtsgeschäftliche Entscheidungsfreiheit des einzelnen wird also nicht allgemein gegen jede Art von Beeinträchtigung durch eine Zwangslage geschützt, sondern nur gegen die rechtswidrige Beeinflussung durch arglistige Täuschung und widerrechtliche Drohung".

[6] J. Hager, Grundrechte im Privatrecht, JZ 1994, 373–383, 383; Herv. T.G.

ßen, weil alle anderen Optionen relativ zu dieser aus seiner Perspektive noch schlechter scheinen.[7] Sich in einer Situation mit ausnahmslos schlechten Handlungsoptionen zu befinden, kann umgangssprachlich als „Schwächesituation" bezeichnet werden. Man kann auch ein „Machtgefälle", eine Situation der „Imparität" oder eine „Ungleichgewichtslage" (in Bezug auf die jeweils verfügbaren wählbaren Handlungsoptionen) konstatieren. Dieser Umstand kann als solcher freiwilliges Handeln in dem hier interessierenden Sinn jedoch nicht ausschließen. Die normative Beurteilung dieser Situation hängt – fasst man die intensive Diskussion über die Freiwilligkeitsthematik der vergangenen Jahrzehnte knapp zusammen – vielmehr davon ab, ob die Entstehung dieser „Zwangslage" beschränkter Optionen als solche *dem Vertragspartner zugerechnet werden kann oder nicht*. Ist dies der Fall – idealtypisch ist eine widerrechtliche Drohung im Sinne des § 123 Abs. 1 Alt. 2 BGB durch die andere Partei – liegt Zwang vor. Der Betroffene hat dann nicht freiwillig gehandelt.

Anders ist die Situation zu beurteilen, wenn die schwierige Situation („Zwangslage"), in der sich die Partei befindet, gerade nicht von dem Vertragspartner (oder von anderen Personen, deren Handeln diesem zurechenbar ist), herbeigeführt wurde, sondern von ihm nur vorgefunden und ausgenützt wird. Dies muss dann mit einer anderen Kategorie als der des Zwangs erfasst werden: mit der der *Ausbeutung* (bzw. des Wuchers). *Zwang* (Unfreiwilligkeit) und *Ausbeutung* (Wucher, „Ausnützen" einer „Zwangslage" des Ausgebeuteten) sind in ihrer normativen Struktur *kategoriell verschieden*.

III. Ausbeutung

„Ausbeutung" gehört zu den schwierigsten und umstrittensten Konzepten der analytischen Moral- und Rechtsphilosophie;[8] ihr Kernkonzept ist je-

---

[7] Er befindet sich m.a.W. in so ernsthafter Bedrängnis, dass der Vertrag „ihm als das ‚kleinere Übel' erscheint" (so *Münchener Kommentar* BGB–Mayer-Maly/Armbrüster, 4. Aufl. 2001, § 138 Rn. 149 m.w.N. zur „Zwangslage" im Sinne des § 138 Abs. 2 BGB.

[8] Einen illustrativen Überblick zum Stand der Diskussion gibt A. Wertheimer, Exploitation, in: E.N. Zalta (Ed.), *The Stanford Encyclopedia of Philosophy* (Summer 2005 edition), URL = http://plato.stanford.edu/archives/sum2005/entries/exploitation/. Siehe daneben vor allem ders., *Exploitation*, Princeton: Princeton University Press 1996; R. Bigwood, *Exploitative Contracts*, Oxford: Oxford University Press 2003 (mit abweichendem Konzept); R.J. Arneson, Exploitation, in: L.C. Becker/Ch. Becker (Eds.), *Encyclopedia of Ethics*, New York: Routledge 2001, 350–352; A.W. Wood, Exploitation, *Social Philosophy and Policy* 12 (1995), 136–158; J.L. Hill, Exploitation, *Cornell Law Review* 79 (1994),

doch klar. Der Unrechtsgehalt der Ausbeutung bzw. des Wuchers liegt darin, dass eine Partei eine individuelle Schwächesituation der anderen Partei dazu ausnützt, für ihre eigene Leistung eine deren Wert krass übersteigende Gegenleistung zu gewinnen.[9] Ausbeutung setzt sich mithin aus einem prozeduralen Moment (dem Ausnützen) und einem substantiellen Moment (der Inäquivalenz der Leistungen[10]) zusammen.

631–699; J. Feinberg, *Harmless Wrongdoing. The Moral Limits of the Criminal Law*, Vol. IV, New York/Oxford: Oxford University Press 1988; D. Zimmerman, Coercive Wage Offers, *Philosophy & Public Affairs* 10 (1981), 121–145; ders., More on Coercive Wage Offers. A Reply to Alexander, *Philosophy & Public Affairs* 12 (1983), 165–171 und D. Golash, Exploitation and Coercion, *Journal of Value Inquiry* 15 (1981), 319–328.

[9] Ausbeutung und Zwang haben deshalb unterschiedliche Foci: Zwang ist primär eine Funktion der Auswirkung eines Ansinnens auf die Optionen des Adressaten, Ausbeutung eine Funktion der Auswirkung des Ansinnens auf die Interessen dessen, der das Ansinnen ausspricht, vgl. Feinberg, a.a.O., 177 f., 203. Der Wortlaut des § 138 Abs. 2 BGB bringt das besonders deutlich zum Ausdruck. Darin werden typische Umstände bezeichnet, die zwangsläufig zur Verhandlungsunterlegenheit des einen Vertragsteils führen und zu denen auch dessen Unerfahrenheit gerechnet wird. Nutzt der überlegene Vertragsteil diese Schwäche aus, um seine Interessen in auffälliger Weise einseitig durchzusetzen, so führt das zur Nichtigkeit des Vertrages.

[10] Will man nicht die Marxsche Mehrwerttheorie übernehmen, entzieht sich insoweit auch der Terminus „Ausbeutung" einer einfachen Definition. Fraglich ist bereits, ob Ausbeutung, in der Tradition der Theorie des *pretium iustum*, über einen „Normalpreisansatz" (P bekommt um ein Bestimmtes mehr als den üblichen Preis) oder einen „Vergleichsansatz" (P bekommt aus dem Austausch sehr viel mehr als Q) oder mittels beidem definiert werden sollte (Zimmerman [1983], a.a.O.). Gegen den Vergleichsansatz spricht, dass es in nüchterner entscheidungstheoretischer Sicht und im Hinblick auf Grenznutzenüberlegungen sogar regelmäßig der Fall ist, dass der Bewucherte durch die Transaktion mehr gewinnt als der Wucherer. Um ein beliebtes Beispiel zur Illustration heranzuziehen: Ein Arzt, der für eine lebensrettende Operation einen wucherischen Betrag fordert, gewinnt, wenn er ihn erhält (und der Patient gerettet wird), unter Grenznutzenüberlegungen weniger als der bewucherte Patient (vgl. Wertheimer [2005], a.a.O., sub 3.). Die für die Ausbeutungssituation charakteristische Imparität liegt gerade darin, dass der Ausbeuter bzw. Wucher bei der fraglichen Transaktion weniger zu verlieren hat bzw. weniger gewinnen muss und deshalb eine größere „Verhandlungsstärke" (Bundesverfassungsgericht) hat. Die moralische oder rechtliche Bewertung der Angemessenheit einer Transaktion unter Ausbeutungsgesichtspunkten kann deshalb nicht (allein) durch einen Vergleich der relativen Vorteile erfolgen, die die Parteien aus dem Vertrag ziehen. Klar ist jedoch Folgendes: Würde man davon ausgehen, dass Markttransaktionen schon dann beiden Parteien Vorteile bringen, wenn beide in der konkreten Situation das Gut der

Ausbeutung bzw. Wucher einerseits und Zwang andererseits unterscheiden sich damit erstens dadurch, dass nur für den Unrechtsgehalt ersterer die *Unangemessenheit der Art oder der Höhe des Vorteils*, den der Ausbeuter aus der Zwangslage zieht (in der er sein Opfer vorfindet), wesentlich ist.[11] Zweitens – und vor allem – unterscheidet sich Ausbeutung von Zwang sowohl hinsichtlich ihrer Struktur als auch hinsichtlich ihres Unrechtscharakters[12] dadurch, *dass Ausbeutung und freiwilliges Handeln*

---

jeweils anderen Partei ihrem eigenen Gut vorziehen, und hierbei die Hintergründe ausblenden, die zur Bildung des subjektiven Werts der fraglichen Güter für die Parteien beitragen, wäre Ausbeutung definitorisch unmöglich. Insofern setzt der Begriff „Ausbeutung" notwendigerweise ein Konzept des „objektiven" Werts von Gütern, zumindest aber die Vorstellung einer fairen Spanne für das Verhältnis von Leistung und Gegenleistung voraus. „A transaction is exploitative only if it is unfair" (Wertheimer [2005], a.a.O., sub 1.; Arneson [2001], a.a.O., 515). Ausbeutung bzw. Wucher sind deshalb intrinsisch normative Konzepte. Gegenstand der Diskussion ist die Bestimmung einer „Grundlinie", von der aus die Unfairness oder Unangemessenheit des vom Ausbeuter erzielten Vorteils zu bemessen ist. In der theoretischen Analyse ist umstritten, inwieweit die Vorstellung eines idealen Marktpreises (d.h. eines auf einem hypothetischen idealen Markt gebildeten Preises) dies leisten kann (vgl. etwa Wertheimer 1996 vs. Arneson 1996). Zumindest zur Bestimmung des „auffälligen Mißverhältnisses" zwischen versprochenen oder gewährten Vermögensvorteilen einerseits und der Leistung andererseits im Sinne des § 138 Abs. 2 BGB stellt die deutsche Rechtsprechung auf deren objektiven Wert ab, der in der Regel durch einen Marktvergleich bestimmt wird, d.h., das vereinbarte Entgelt wird, soweit möglich, dem marktüblichen Preis, den die Mehrzahl der übrigen Anbieter für vergleichbare Leistungen fordert, gegenübergestellt, vgl. BGH NJW 2003, 1596 (1597) m.w.N; *Bamberger/Roth*-Wendtland, *BGB*, 2003 (Akt. 2005), § 138 Rn. 44 f. Ein auffälliges Missverhältnis wird i.d.R. (ebenso wie beim wucherähnlichen Geschäft des Abs. 1, vgl. unten, 6.2.1.3.) nach der alten laesio enormis-Größenordnung angenommen, wenn der objektive Wert von Leistung und Gegenleistung um etwa 100% oder mehr voneinander abweichen; nach der Rechtsprechung des BGH zum Mietwucher ist dort ein auffälliges Missverhältnis zu bejahen, wenn das übliche Entgelt um mehr als 50 % überschritten wird (BGHSt 30, 280, 281; vgl. BGHZ 135, 269, 277).

[11] Vgl. Feinberg, a.a.O., 211 ff. Siehe § 138 Abs. 2 BGB und § 291 StGB, nach denen sich die Partei bzw. der Täter Vermögensvorteile versprechen oder gewähren lassen muss, „die in einem auffälligen Mißverhältnis zu der Leistung" stehen.

[12] Auch moraltheoretisch liegt ein erheblicher Unterschied zwischen Ausbeutung einerseits und Zwang sowie Täuschung andererseits in der Art der Instrumentalisierung des anderen. Zwang sowie Täuschung unterminieren die Fähigkeit des anderen, als autonome, Entscheidungen treffende Person zu handeln, auf eine Weise, die von Ausbeutung nicht erreicht wird, vgl. C. Korsgaard, The Reasons We Can Share, *Social Philosophy and Policy* 10 (1993), 24–51, 40.

kompatibel sind. Man kann sich freiwillig ausbeuten lassen.[13] Wenn sich eine Person in einer Not- oder Zwangslage, d.h. in einer Situation mit ausnahmslos sehr schlechten Handlungsoptionen befindet, dann wird sich ihr die Option, ein immer noch schlechtes, relativ aber vorteilhaftes, ausbeutendes Angebot einer anderen Person anzunehmen, regelmäßig als die relativ beste Handlungsalternative darstellen. Es mag für sie – jedenfalls dann, wenn sie die Überwindung ihrer gegenwärtigen Notlage als ihr Hauptziel versteht, also mit einer hohen Präferenz versieht – deshalb subjektiv rational sein, ein solches Angebot anzunehmen und sich ausbeuten zu lassen. Tut sie es, handelt sie in jedem normativ relevanten Sinn freiwillig. Dies zwingt zugleich zu der Annahme, dass es – in einem bestimmten Sinn – Ausbeutungsrelationen gibt, die für beide Seiten vorteilhaft sind.[14]

Hiermit hängt das *Paradox des Ausbeutungsschutzes* zusammen. Während es immer im Interesse eines Opfers von Zwang liegt, von der erzwungenermaßen eingegangenen Verpflichtung befreit zu werden, ist dies bei von Ausbeutung betroffenen Personen nicht ohne weiteres der Fall. Gerade weil Ausbeutung freiwilligkeitskompatibel ist, greift der Versuch, jemanden vor (nicht erzwungener) Ausbeutung zu schützen, regelmäßig in dessen Freiheit ein. Zugleich kann Ausbeutung in Form des Zwangslagenwuchers für den Betroffenen relativ zu seinen sonstigen Optionen vorteilhaft sein. Das Ziel, mit Blick auf den Unrechtsgehalt des Verhaltens des Begünstigten ausbeuterisch erlangte Vorteile zu verhindern, darf die konkreten Interessen des Ausgebeuteten und seine Einschätzung der Situation jedenfalls im Regelfall nicht außer acht lassen. Soweit der Ausgebeutete mit dem ausbeuterischen Rechtsgeschäft seine „am wenigsten schlechte" Handlungsoption wahrgenommen hat, kann die Verhinderung der Durchführung des inkriminerten Rechtsgeschäfts dem Betroffenen schaden. Dies gilt jedenfalls dann, wenn ihm nicht zugleich anderweitig aus seiner Zwangslage geholfen wird. Ausbeutungsschutz ist deshalb keineswegs eo ipso gerechtfertigt. Er stellt vor gerech-

---

[13] Feinberg, a.a.O., 176, 195 f.; Wood, a.a.O., 148 f.; Wertheimer (1996), a.a.O., 247 ff. und ders. (2005), a.a.O., sub 3; Arneson, a.a.O., 515. Diese Erkenntnis ist nicht neu. Vgl. dazu, dass Wucher die Freiwilligkeit des Vertragsschlusses des Bewucherten nicht in Frage stellt, bereits Thomas von Aquin, *Summa Theologica*, Pars IIa IIae, q. 77 mit q. 66 a. 4 und q. 66 a. 9; sowie ihm (mit intensiverer Begründung) folgend, die spanische Spätscholastik, v.a. D. De Soto, *De Iustitia et Iure* [1556], Nachdruck Madrid: Instituto de Estudios Públicos 1968, lib. VI, q. III, a 1.

[14] Eine Differenzierung, die Wertheimer [1996, a.a.O., 207 und 2005, a.a.O., sub 2] als Differenzierung zwischen *harmful exploitation* und *mutually advantageous exploitation* systematisch herausgearbeitet hat. Dies bedeutet nicht, dass der Unrechtscharakter wechselseitig vorteilhafter, aber ausbeutender Transaktionen entfiele (Wertheimer [1996], a.a.O., 279; [2005], a.a.O., sub 4).

tigkeitstheoretisch komplexe Probleme und erfordert ein zielgenaues und folgenorientiertes Vorgehen.[15] Hierbei taugt der Hinweis darauf, dass Ausbeutungsschutz der *Gruppe oder Klasse* der Personen, denen der Ausgebeutete als Kreditnehmer, Käufer, Mieter etc. angehört, grundsätzlich nicht dazu, die individuelle und konkrete Interessenbeeinträchtigung des gegen seinen Willen vor Ausbeutung Geschützten zu überspielen. Die rechtsdogmatische Umsetzung des Schutzes vor Ausbeutung beim Vertragsschluss verlangt mithin, dem Subjekt dieses Schutzes Entscheidungsmöglichkeiten offenzuhalten. Hierauf ist zurückzukommen.

Auf der Grundlage dieser konzeptionellen Unterscheidung ist es im Übrigen in rechtstheoretischer Sicht schlechthin ausgeschlossen, mit einem Angebot[16] in die Freiheitsrechte des Adressaten einzugreifen.[17] Man kann ein Angebot – auch ein schlechtes oder auf Ausbeutung zielendes – entweder annehmen oder es ablehnen und damit in genau der Situation verbleiben, in der man gewesen wäre, wenn es nicht ausgesprochen worden wäre. Deshalb kann man durch ein Angebot keine Freiheitseinbuße erleiden.

Eine wichtige *normative* Wertung,[18] die diese strukturelle Analyse stützt, liegt in dem *Problem der Lastenverschiebung*: Wäre das Unfreiwilligkeitsverdikt bereits aus der bloßen Tatsache abzuleiten, dass eine Partei eine Wahl zwischen defizienten, unbefriedigenden Handlungsoptionen zu treffen hat (sich also dergestalt in einer „Zwangslage" befindet), so würde dies eine Verantwortungs- und Lastenverschiebung auf den Transaktionspartner bedeuten. Dieser würde, auch *ohne* dass ihm die Entscheidungssituation des anderen Teils zugerechnet werden könnte, das Risiko zu tragen haben, dass sich jener unter Rekurs auf das Vorliegen „unglücklicher" Entscheidungsumstände von gegebenen Erklärungen lösen oder gar die Nachbesserung des geschlossenen Vertrages durchsetzen könnte. Die Folgen sozialer Ungleichheit oder biographischer Notlagen (in die sich der Betroffene vielleicht sogar in zurechenbarer Weise selbst gebracht hat) – und zugleich alle wesentlichen Vertragsrisiken – würden so kurzerhand auch dann auf den rechtsgeschäftlichen Partner überwälzt, wenn in des-

---

[15] Siehe vor allem Wertheimer (1996) a.a.O., 75 ff., 298–309, daneben Feinberg, a.a.O., 212 ff. und passim.

[16] Der Begriff ist hier im rechtstheoretischen Sinn gemeint (hierzu Gutmann, a.a.O., 87 ff.). Er geht über den rechtstechnischen Begriff des Antrags bzw. Angebots im Sinne der §§ 145 ff. BGB hinaus und meint jedes (nicht mit Zwang verbundene) Ansinnen, das auf einen Vertragsschluss gerichtet ist, auch die Annahme eines solchen.

[17] Vgl. Gutmann, a.a.O., 149 ff., 206 ff.; Wertheimer (1996), a.a.O.

[18] Für das geltende Recht belegt der Umkehrschluss aus § 123 Abs. 1 und § 138 Abs. 2 BGB, dass eine „Zwangslage" in diesem Sinn alleine nicht freiwilligkeitsausschließend wirkt.

sen Person oder Verhalten keine besonderen Gründe vorlägen, die dies rechtfertigten. Die Annahme, eine Wahl unter unbefriedigenden Optionen sei unfreiwillig, hätte mithin zufällige und damit willkürliche, d.h. nicht normativ begründbare Verteilungswirkungen.

Hinzu kommt ein zweiter Umstand. Wäre das Unfreiwilligkeitsverdikt bereits aus der bloßen Tatsache abzuleiten, dass eine Partei sich dergestalt in einer „Zwangslage" befindet, dass sie eine Wahl zwischen defizienten, unbefriedigenden Handlungsoptionen zu treffen hat, dann würden Menschen in schwierigen Entscheidungssituationen entmündigt. Hierauf zielt die Kritik daran, dass mit der Vorstellung einer freiwilligkeitsausschließenden „Not-" oder „Zwangslage" qua „Imparität" oder „fehlenden Verhandlungsgleichgewichts" eine den §§ 104 ff. BGB widersprechende Einführung einer „wirtschaftlichen Geschäftsfähigkeit"[19] bzw. einer „Geschäftsfähigkeit minderen Grades", „zweiter Klasse"[20] und einer „verkürzten Privatautonomie"[21] verbunden wäre, die es den Betroffenen verunmöglichen würde, rechtswirksame Handlungen vorzunehmen.[22] Dies wäre in der Tat „mit den Grundanforderungen an eine Gesellschaft von Freien und Gleichen unvereinbar" (BGH),[23] die nicht zuletzt auch dem Prinzip Privatautonomie zugrundeliegen.

Dies alles bedeutet keineswegs, dass die Rechtsordnung ausbeutende Verträge, die in einer solcherart definierten „Not-", „Zwangs-" oder „Ungleichgewichtslage" geschlossen wurden, durchzusetzen hat. Es besagt nur, dass sich ein richterlicher Eingriff in das Vertragsgefüge *nicht* darauf berufen kann, die betroffene Partei habe *unfreiwillig* gehandelt, d.h. ihre Willenserklärung sei ihr normativ nicht zurechenbar. Eine solche Annahme wäre entscheidungstheoretisch falsch und normativ nicht begründbar.

---

[19] S. Lorenz, *Der Schutz vor dem unerwünschten Vertrag. Eine Untersuchung von Möglichkeiten und Grenzen der Abschlußkontrolle im geltenden Recht*, München: C.H. Beck 1997, 512; vgl. T. Barnert, *Die formelle Vertragsethik des BGB im Spannungsverhältnis zum Sonderprivatrecht und zur judikativen Kompensation der Vertragsdisparität*, Heidelberg: Mohr Siebeck 1999, 269 ff.

[20] D. Coester-Waltjen, Die Inhaltskontrolle von Verträgen außerhalb des AGBG, AcP 190 (1990), 1–33 (20).

[21] H.-P. Westermann, Die Bedeutung der Privatautonomie im Recht des Konsumentenkredits, in: D. Medicus/H.-J. Mertens/K.W. Nörr/W. Zöllner (Hg.), *Festschrift für Hermann Lange zum 70. Geburtstag*, Stuttgart u.a. 1992, 995–1016 (998, 1013); D. Medicus, Abschied von der Privatautonomie im Schuldrecht, Köln: Schmidt 1994, 33 f.; Th. Koch, *Der Grundrechtsschutz des Drittbetroffenen. Zur Rekonstruktion der Grundrechte als Abwehrrechte*, Tübingen: Mohr Siebeck 2000, 480 f.; vgl. noch BGH NJW 1991, 2015 (2017).

[22] *Umbach/Clemens-Hillgruber*, Grundgesetz, 2002, Art. 2 I GG Rn. 112.

[23] BGH NJW 1991, 2015 (2017); *Umbach/Clemens*-Hillgruber, a.a.O., Rn. 114.

IV. Dogmatische Umsetzung in Deutschland

Blicken wir von dieser Analyse aus auf einige Strukturen einerseits des deutschen Rechts und andererseits des angelsächsischen Rechtskreises, so wird schnell deutlich, dass die wesentlichen Probleme der Rechtsdogmatik mit diesen Phänomenen daraus resultieren, dass Freiwilligkeits- und Ausbeutungsschutz miteinander vermengt werden.

Der Kern des Freiwilligkeitsschutzes, der Schutz vor Zwang beim Vertragsschluss durch widerrechtliche Drohung, wird in der deutschen Rechtsordnung durch § 123 Abs. 1 Alt. 2 BGB auf grundsätzlich adäquate, nämlich die normative Natur des Zwangskonzepts spiegelnde Weise[24] vermittelt. Vor der Ausbeutung bestimmter Schwächesituationen schützt § 138 Abs. 2 BGB – eine Norm, die in der Praxis jedoch ein Schattendasein führt.

Auch eine skizzenhafte Analyse der deutschen Vertragsrechtsdogmatik kann nicht an der Überformung des Vertragsrechts durch das Verfassungsrecht vorbeigehen. Dieser Umstand bereitet dem hier verfolgten Ziel einer Privatrechtsdogmatik, die imstande ist, den Strukturunterschied von Zwang und Ausbeutung nachzuvollziehen und beide Phänomene in ihrer Unterschiedlichkeit abzuarbeiten, besondere Probleme. Diese resultieren daher, dass das Bundesverfassungsgericht in seinen Leitentscheidungen zur richterlichen Inhaltskontrolle von (Bürgschafts-) Verträgen bei starkem Übergewicht eines Vertragspartners[25] die beiden Konzepte Unfreiwilligkeit und Ausbeutung zu einem theoretisch ungenießbaren Zwitter vermengt hat. Die vertragsrechtsdogmatischen Diskussionen, die in der Folge dieser Entscheidungen geführt wurden, haben dies nicht zu korrigieren vermocht. Dies gilt vor allem für die Rechtsprechung des Bundesgerichtshofs.

Das Bundesverfassungsgericht hatte bekanntlich postuliert, dass bei typisierbaren Fallgestaltung, die eine *strukturelle Unterlegenheit* des einen Vertragsteils erkennen ließen, dann, wenn die Folgen des Vertrages für den unterlegenen Vertragsteil ungewöhnlich belastend seien, die Zivilrechtsordnung Korrekturen ermöglichen müsse. Dies folge insbesondere aus der grundrechtlichen Gewährleistung der Privatautonomie (Art. 2 Abs. 1 GG).

Dieser Ansatz ist im entscheidenden Punkt zu undifferenziert, da sich hinter „struktureller Unterlegenheit" sowohl Zwangs- als auch Ausbeutungssituationen verbergen können. (Der Unterschied zwischen beiden

---

[24] Vgl. Gutmann, a.a.O., 247 ff. sowie Th. Schindler, *Rechtsgeschäftliche Entscheidungsfreiheit und Drohung. Die englische duress-Lehre in rechtsvergleichender Perspektive*, Tübingen: Mohr Siebeck 2005, 22 ff.

[25] BVerfGE 89, 214 vom 19.10.1993. Vgl. daneben BVerfG (1. Kammer des Ersten Senats) NJW 1994, 2749 (2750) und NJW 1996, 2021.

Zwang und Ausbeutung beim Vertragsschluss 59

stellt rechtstheoretisch im übrigen selbst für die Einwirkung des Verfassungsrechts auf das Vertragsrecht eine entscheidende Weiche: Während sich aus der grundrechtlichen Gewährleistung der Privatautonomie unmittelbar ergibt, dass Verträge, die unfreiwillig geschlossen wurden, nicht durchgesetzt werden dürfen, berührt Ausbeutung als solche, wie dargelegt, die Freiwilligkeit einer vertraglichen Disposition nicht. Sie kann kein Freiheitsrecht des Ausgebeuteten, auch nicht das Freiheitsrecht der Privatautonomie verletzen. Aus diesem Grund ist der Schutz vor *Ausbeutung*[26] nicht durch die *Freiheits*grundrechte und die grundrechtliche Gewährleistung der Privatautonomie geboten, sondern allenfalls – und selbst dies erscheint sehr zweifelhaft – durch das Sozialstaatsprinzip. Dies bedeutet nicht weniger, als dass die Begründung der Bürgschaftsentscheidung des Bundesverfassungsgerichts für den zivilrechtlichen Umgang mit dem Phänomen „Ausbeutung" keinen Anspruch auf Geltung erheben kann.[27])

Der Bundesgerichtshof hat diese Strategie der Nichtdifferenzierung dadurch verschärft, dass er sich entschlossen hat, die gesamte Problematik der Nahbereichsbürgschaften unter die Rubrik des § 138 Abs. 1 BGB zu subsumieren, gleichzeitig aber darauf abzustellen, dass es hierbei um den Schutz einer „freien Entscheidung" sowie vor einer „Fremdbestimmung" einer Willenserklärung gehe.[28] Diese *systematische Vermengung von Zwang und Ausbeutung unter der Rubrik des sittenwidrigen Handelns* hat den Vorteil, dass im Rahmen der für das Sittenwidrigkeitsverdikt des § 138 Abs. 1 BGB anzustellenden „Gesamtbetrachtung" und freien Wertung divergente Fakten und Argumente wie auf einen großen Sandhaufen geschüttet werden können, ohne dass sie im Einzelnen auf ihre Struktur und ihre Kohärenz überprüft werden müssten. Dies ist die ideale Arbeitssituation für den moralisch sensiblen Richterkönig. Der Preis für dieses Vorgehen ist jedoch erheblich.

Er ist zunächst in der Form eines nur noch metaphorischen und damit dogmatisch unbrauchbaren Freiwilligkeitsbegriffs zu entrichten. Dieser lässt sich z.B. an dem offensichtlich verfehlten, aber ständig wiederholten Argument des Bundesgerichtshofs demonstrieren, demzufolge eine enge persönliche Beziehung zwischen Bürgen und Hauptschuldner, etwa in Form einer Ehe, eheähnlichen Partnerschafts-, engen Verwandtschafts-

---

[26] Das Bundesverfassungsgericht zielt in seiner Bürgschaftsentscheidung (E 89, 214) gerade auch auf Ausbeutungsschutz und hat insoweit darauf hingewiesen, dass in § 138 Abs. 2 BGB „typische Umstände bezeichnet [würden], die zwangsläufig zur Verhandlungsunterlegenheit des einen Vertragsteils führen".

[27] Hierzu näher künftig Th. Gutmann, *Iustitia contrahentium. Zu den gerechtigkeitstheoretischen Grundlagen des deutschen Schuldvertragsrechts*, Kap. 5, i.E.

[28] Vgl. hierzu nur BGH NJW 2002, 744 (745).

oder Freundschaftsbeziehung „einen freien Willensentschluss"[29] des Bürgen, also *freiwilliges Handeln*, grundsätzlich *ausschließe*.[30]

Ungeachtet der Rhetorik einer Beeinträchtigung der Entschließungsfreiheit geht es dem Bundesgerichtshof der Sache nach jedoch allein um Ausbeutungsschutz. Die Rechtsprechung ruht auf einer Interpretation des Abs. 1 des § 138 BGB, die sich, wie die Senate offen legen, eng an der Tatbestandsstruktur von Absatz 2 der Norm orientiert.[31]

Zu kritisieren ist an diesem Vorgehen dreierlei. Erstens: Mit dieser wertenden Fokussierung auf den Schutz vor Ausbeutung gerät die normativ vorrangig zu behandelnde Frage nach genuinen Freiwilligkeitdefiziten beim Vertragsschluss aus dem Blick. Dies ist deshalb bedeutsam, als es in einer Fülle von Entscheidungen, in denen das Gericht § 138 Abs. 1 BGB zur Anwendung gebracht hat, in der Sache darum ging, dass der Bürge durch dem Gläubiger zurechenbare Umstände *in einer freiwilligkeitstheoretisch grundsätzlich relevanten Weise in seiner Entscheidungsfreiheit beeinträch-*

---

[29] BGH NJW 2001, 815 (817).
[30] Zusammenfassend G. Nobbe/H.-P. Kirchhof, Bürgschaften und Mithaftungsübernahmen finanziell überforderter Personen, BKR 2001, 5–15, 7 f. (dort auch zum Gegensatz zwischen einer „emotionalen Beziehung zwischen dem Bürgen oder Mithaftenden und dem Hauptschuldner" und einer „davon weitgehend unbeeinflussten" und deshalb „autonomen Entscheidung" des Bürgen). Der Bundesgerichtshof betont noch in einer seiner jüngeren Leitentscheidungen, mit dem Kriterium des Handelns aus emotionaler Verbundenheit werde den Vorgaben des Bundesverfassungsgerichts Rechnung getragen, den Bürgen „vor der Abgabe fremdbestimmter [...] Willenserklärungen zu schützen", siehe BGH NJW 2002, 744 (745).
[31] Dies hat J. Naumann, *Sittenverstoß und Privatautonomie*, Baden-Baden: Nomos 2003, 2 ff., 25 ff., 12, herausgearbeitet. Insbesondere tritt bei der Prüfung der Sittenwidrigkeit im objektiven Bereich das Kriterium des „krassen Missverhältnisses zwischen dem Verpflichtungsumfang und der Leistungsfähigkeit des dem Hauptschuldner nahestehenden Bürgen oder Mithaftenden" an die Stelle des von § 138 Abs. 2 geforderten auffälligen Missverhältnisses von Leistung und Gegenleistung (vgl. Nobbe/Kirchhof, a.a.O., 7; *Staudinger*–Horn, BGB, 13. Auflage 1997, § 765 Rn. 161). Während der BGH in der Anwendung von § 138 Abs. 2 BGB jedoch das sogenannte „Sandhaufentheorem", welches besagt, dass die tatbestandlichen Voraussetzungen des § 138 Abs. 2 BGB variabel und auch dann erfüllt sein, wenn ein Tatbestandsmerkmal „übererfüllt", ein gleichfalls erforderliches anderes aber „untererfüllt" oder „in geringem Maße" erfüllt sei, ablehnt (BGHZ 80, 153, 159), legt er sich eine solche Beschränkung in seiner Bürgschaftsjudikatur im Rahmen des Abs. 1 der Vorschrift nicht auf; typisch insoweit die Entscheidung BGH NJW 2001, 2466 (2467).

*tigt worden ist.*³² Dieses dogmatische Vorgehen ist nicht adäquat. *Beeinträchtigungen der Freiwilligkeit des Vertragspartners haben eine normativ andere Qualität als bloße „Sittenwidrigkeit".* Ein „rechtlich unzulässige[r] Einfluss auf die Entschließungsfreiheit"³³ berührt das normative Basiskonzept des Vertragsrechts, das Gebrauchmachen von Privatautonomie selbst. Unfreiwilliges Handeln begründet keine vertraglichen Verpflichtungen, und dieses Urteil kann nicht erst vom Ergebnis einer „zusammenfassenden Würdigung" aller subjektiven und objektiven Umstände des Vertrages nebst der moralischen Qualität der inneren Einstellung und Beweggründe der Parteien abhängen, wie sie für die Prüfung des § 138 Abs. 1 BGB gefordert wird.³⁴ Steht Freiwilligkeit als Bedingung der Zurechenbarkeit einer vertraglichen Disposition in Frage, kommt es nicht darauf an, ob „die Entscheidungsfreiheit des Bürgen *in anstößiger Weise* beeinträchtigt"³⁵ wurde – was der Bundesgerichtshof fordert –, sondern nur darauf, ob sie *überhaupt* (hinreichend) beeinträchtigt wurde. Genauso wenig kann es darauf ankommen, ob eine rechtsgeschäftliche Verpflichtung, die nicht hinreichend freiwillig eingegangen wurde, „ungewöhnlich belastende Folgen" für die Partei hat oder nicht. Eine angemessene zivilrechtsdogmatische Umsetzung dieser Vorgabe verlangt deshalb zwingend, bei der Vertragskontrolle zunächst mögliche Freiwilligkeitsdefizite abzuarbeiten. Hierzu stehen vor allem § 123 BGB und unterhalb dieser Schwelle §§ 280 Abs. 1, 311 Abs. 2 BGB (culpa in contrahendo) zur Verfügung. Wenn man richtigerweise davon ausgeht, dass die Dispositions- oder Entscheidungsfreiheit in den Schutzbereich der culpa in contrahendo fällt, dann kann und muss dieses Institut das Gros der vom Bundesgerichtshof bisher dem § 138 Abs. 1 BGB zugeschlagenen Fälle erfassen.

Zweitens erschwert sich das Gericht den Weg zu einer „sauberen", trennscharfen Dogmatik des Ausbeutungsschutzes, indem es dieses Konzept, wie dargelegt, immer wieder mit Überlegungen zur Freiwilligkeit des Vertragsschlusses vermengt, die hierfür grundsätzlich³⁶ irrelevant sind.³⁷

---

³² Zur Kasuistik vgl. Nobbe/Kirchhof, a.a.O., 14 m.w.N. sowie Naumann, a.a.O., 12 ff.

³³ Nobbe/Kirchhof, a.a.O., 7; vgl. BGH NJW 1996, 513 (515 – „unzulässige Einflußnahme [...] auf die Willensbestimmung").

³⁴ Ständige Rechtsprechung, siehe etwa BGHZ 125, 206 (209).

³⁵ BGHZ 137, 329 (333, Herv. T.G.); *Palandt*–Heinrichs, *BGB*, 65. Auflage 2006, § 138 Rn. 38f.

³⁶ Eine Ausnahme sind Konstellationen, in denen das Kreditinstitut die geschäftliche Unerfahrenheit des Bürgen ausnutzt, BGH NJW 2002, 2634 (2635). Auch die parallelen Tatbestände des § 138 Abs. 2 BGB, ein mangelndes Urteilsvermögen oder eine erhebliche Willensschwäche der Partei, bilden Grenzphänomene zwischen Unfreiwilligkeit und Ausbeutung. Sie sind dem Konzept „Ausbeutung" zuzuschlagen, soweit sie Phänomene bezeichnen, die primär der Person der schwäche-

Drittens stellt das Vorgehen des BGH noch aus einem weiteren Grund kein sinnvolles dogmatisches Konzept für einen Schutz vor Ausbeutung beim Vertragsschluss dar. Ein angemessener Umgang mit dem oben erläuterten *Paradox des Ausbeutungsschutzes* wird durch die konstruktive Bewältigung der Problematik im Rahmen des § 138 Abs. 1 BGB gleich in zweifacher Hinsicht behindert – zum einen durch die mangelnde Flexibilität der Rechtsfolge der Norm (Nichtigkeit), und zum anderen durch ihre beschränkte Steuerbarkeit, die dem von Amts wegen zu beachtenden Sittenwidrigkeitscharakter von Rechtsgeschäften geschuldet ist. Dies hält der betroffenen Partei den Freiheitsgewinn vor, der (wie im Falle eines Anfechtungsrechts oder eines Schadensersatzanspruchs) in der Gewährung eines subjektiven Rechts bestünde, über dessen Geltendmachung der Betroffene selbstbestimmt und im Licht seiner eigenen Interesseneinschätzung entscheiden könnte.

V. Zum Common Law

Ähnlich wie im deutschen Recht wird der Kernbereich des Zwangs auch im angelsächsischen Rechtskreis, bei einigen Unschärfen am Rande, adäquat erfasst, nämlich durch die *duress*-Lehre. Insbesondere die Rechtsprechung zur Fallgruppe des *economic duress*, die vor allem Drohungen mit einem Vertragsbruch erfasst, wird in ihrem grundsätzlichen Abstellen auf die Widerrechtlichkeit bzw. Illegitimität der Drohung der normativen Natur des Konzepts „Zwang" zunehmend gerecht.[38]

Im Kontrast hierzu lassen sich weder das historisch gewachsene Institut der *undue influence* noch die *equity-doctrine of unconscionability* für das Pro-

---

ren Partei und nicht nur der konkreten Vertragssituation anhaften und dergestalt von der stärkeren Partei nicht erzeugt, sondern vorgefunden werden.

[37] Typisch die Zusammenfassung der Grundthese des XI. Senats in der Entscheidung BGH NJW 2002, 744 (745): „Je stärker dabei das Übergewicht des Kreditgebers ist, je gravierender die Belastungen und je enger die persönlichen Beziehungen zwischen Bürgen oder Mithaftenden sind, desto wahrscheinlicher ist es, dass es an einer nüchtern abwägenden, selbstbestimmten Entschließung des Bürgen oder Mithaftenden fehlt."

[38] Siehe hierzu vertiefend Schindler, a.a.O., 96 ff., 111 ff.; *Chitty on Contracts* (H.G. Beale), 29th Ed., London: Sweet and Maxwell 2004, 7–006 ff., 7–035 ff; Lord Goff of Chieveley/G. Jones, *The Law of Restitution*, 6th Edition, London: Sweet and Maxwell 2002, 10-033; G. Virgo, *The Principles of the Law of Restitution*, Oxford: Clarendon Press 1999, 193 f., 200 ff. (siehe jedoch 218 ff.); und insbesondere die Entscheidung des House of Lords *The Evia Luck* (1992) 2 AC 152. Aus philosophischer Sicht A. Wertheimer, *Coercion*, Princeton: Princeton University Press 1987, 30 ff.

jekt einer klaren rechtsdogmatische Unterscheidung von Zwang und Ausbeutung beim Vertragsschluss fruchtbar machen.

Einen hybriden Charakter hat die *doctrine of undue influence*. Sie zielt einerseits auf den Schutz der Entscheidungsfreiheit unterhalb des Zwangs i.e.S., d.h. auf den Schutz vor Überrumpelung, unangemessenem Druck und Manipulation *(improper persuasion)*.[39] Gerade in der Klasse der *presumed undue influence* – in der vermutet wird, dass Rechtsgeschäfte innerhalb bestimmter Nähe-, Abhängigkeits- und Vertrauensverhältnisse *(special relationships bzw. relationships of trust and confidence*[40]), die für eine Partei manifest nachteilig sind, dadurch zustande gekommen sind, dass die begünstigte Partei dieses Verhältnis *ausgenutzt* hat[41] – trägt das Institut jedoch zugleich auch Züge des Ausbeutungsschutzes.[42] Hier wird insbesondere die Unzulässigkeit der Instrumentalisierung emotionaler Bindungen und Näheverhältnisse zu dem Zweck, jemanden zu einem risikoreichen oder seinen Interessen offensichtlich abträglichen Vertragsschluss zu bewegen, thematisiert. Mit dieser Orientierung der *presumed undue influence* am Ausbeutungsschutz[43] verträgt sich jedoch wiederum nicht, dass die angesprochene Vermutung grundsätzlich durch den Nachweis widerlegbar sein soll, die betroffene Partei habe sich unabhängig und adäquat beraten lassen,[44] ist die Grundkonstellation von Ausbeutung in Form des Zwangslagenwuchers doch, wie oben ausgeführt, gerade beratungsresistent. Darüber hinaus läßt sich *undue influence* sogar primär unter dem Gesichtspunkt eines (§ 138 Abs. 2 BGB) verwandten Ausbeutungsschutzes begreifen, wie etwa § 1575 California Civil Code zeigt.[45]

---

[39] Lorenz, a.a.O., 453 ff. weist auf das Konzept der *undue influence* als Institut zur Sanktionierung unzulässiger exogener Einflussnahmen auf die Entscheidungsfreiheit des Vertragspartners hin – ein Institut, das auf den Willenbildungsprozess blickt, (in der Regel) weder die Vermögenslage des Betroffenen bewertet noch in wesentlicher Weise auf Vorstellungen von Vertragsparität abstellt und ein reiches kasuistisches Kriterienmaterial zur Erfassung der „Unzulässigkeit" bzw. „Unangemessenheit" von Einflussnahmen bietet. Siehe auch Chitty, a.a.O., 7–053 f.

[40] Goff/Jones, a.a.O., 11-008.

[41] Chitty, a.a.O., 7–058 ff.

[42] Virgo, a.a.O., ch. 10, fasst *undue influence* unter die Überschrift *exploitation*.

[43] So explizit auch A. Burrows, *The Law of Restitution*, London: Butterworths 1993, 193 ff.

[44] Chitty, a.a.O., 7–079 f.; vgl. *Royal Bank of Scotland v Etridge* (No 2) [1998] 4 All ER 705.

[45] "Undue influence consists: 1. In the use, by one in whom a confidence is reposed by another, or who holds a real or apparent authority over him, of such confidence or authority for the purpose of obtaining an unfair advantage over him; 2. In taking an unfair advantage of another's weakness of mind; or, 3. In taking a grossly oppressive and unfair advantage of another's necessities or distress."

Ähnlich hybrid ist die *equity-Doctrine of unconscionability/unconscionable bargaining*. Die *doctrine of unconscionability*, hinsichtlich derer durchaus erhebliche Unterschiede zwischen der englischen, amerikanischen und australisch/neuseeländischen Tradition bestehen,[46] entspricht in ihrem Kernbereich weitgehend der Regelung in § 138 Abs. 2 BGB. Es geht um Rechtsgeschäfte, durch die jemand unter Ausbeutung der Zwangslage, der Unerfahrenheit, des Mangels an Urteilsvermögen oder der erheblichen Willensschwäche eines anderen eine in krass unfairer Weise erhöhte Leistung erhält.[47] Die Entwicklung der Doktrin war jedoch schon früh dadurch belastet, dass in ihrem Rahmen zugleich die Sonderproblematik allgemeiner Geschäftsbedingungen – die nichts mit Ausbeutungsschutz zu tun hat – abgearbeitet wurde. Zudem sind auch im angelsächsischen Bereich einige Begriffsunklarheiten festzustellen; insbesondere wird *unconscionability* im case-law immer wieder in den Zusammenhang mit dem Schutz der Entscheidungsfreiheit im engeren Sinn gebracht und vielen Fällen – gerade in solchen, in denen es um den Schutz der Dispositionsfreiheit geht – verwendet, wo andere Doktrinen und Institute angemessen wären.[48] Nicht umsonst gilt die Doktrin deshalb allgemein als kaum definierbar, heterogen, „quecksilbrig",[49] „amorph",[50] und insgesamt als wenig brauchbares Konzept, das gerade durch Versuche zu seiner Kodifizierung nicht klarer geworden ist: So deutet § 2-302 des amerikanischen Uniform Commercial Code (der auf die Doktrin nur verweist), in seiner Begründung darauf hin, es gehe hierbei gerade *nicht* um Ausbeutungsschutz, sondern um Entscheidungsfreiheit, insbesondere im Hinblick auf das Problem allgemeiner Geschäftsbedingungen.[51] Soweit, zumal im amerikanischen Recht, mit der Figur der *procedural unconscionability* allein auf die Umstände des Vertragsschlusses und nicht auf den Inhalt des Vertrags geblickt wird, läßt *unconscionability* sich ohnehin kaum mehr von *duress* oder *undue influence* unterscheiden.[52]

---

[46] S.E. Enman, Doctrines of Unconscionability in Canadian, English and Commonwealth Contract Law, *Anglo-American Law Review* 16 (1987), 191–219; Chitty, a.a.O., 7–121.

[47] Chitty, a.a.O., 7–114; Goff/Jones, a.a.O., 12-002 mit Verweis auf *Alec Lobb Ltd v. Total Oil GB Ltd* [1983] 1 W.L.R. 87, 94–95.

[48] Enman, a.a.O., 211.

[49] Goff/Jones, a.a.O., 12-006.

[50] J.E. Murray, *Murray on Contracts*, Third Edition, Charlottesville: The Michie Company 1990, § 92, p. 461, vgl. 487, 490.

[51] "The principle is one of the prevention of oppression and of unfair suprise [...] and not of disturbance of the allocation of risks because of superiour bargaining power", cf. Murray, a.a.O., § 96, p. 488, 495 ff.

[52] Chitty, a.a.O., 7–121; Murray, a.a.O., § 96, p. 491 ("lack of voluntariness").

VI. New Features

Diese sehr knapp gehaltene Analyse sollte die These stützen, dass die wesentlichen Probleme der Rechtsdogmatik mit diesen Phänomenen in beiden Rechtskreisen daraus resultieren, dass Freiwilligkeits- und Ausbeutungsschutz miteinander vermengt werden.

Nun sehen wir allenthalben und seit langem das Bestreben der Rechtsprechung, sich dogmatisch möglichst wenig eingeengte Spielräume zur Verwirklichung von Einzelfallgerechtigkeit zu erhalten bzw. zu verschaffen. Im Bereich des common law und der equity-Rechtsprechung ist dies ohnehin Tradition;[53] in Deutschland wird man den Ausbau der Generalklauseln zum Instrument einer umfassenden Billigkeitsjustiz als eine Hauptentwicklungslinie der Rechtsprechung des Reichsgerichts und des Bundesgerichtshofs seit 1920 begreifen dürfen. Die Unschärfe der verwendeten dogmatischen Figuren kommt dem entgegen. Es könnte also sein, dass die Rechtsprechung kein institutionelles Interesse an einer deutlicheren Ausdifferenzierung der Konzepte von Zwang und Ausbeutung hat.

Dem entgegenwirkend ist ein *new feature in contract law* darin zu sehen, dass seit einigen Jahren das Bewusstsein der Notwendigkeit dieser Aufgabe sehr viel klarer hervortritt. Es häufen sich nicht nur die rechtstheoretischen Texte zu diesem Thema; auch die Bemühungen zur europäischen und internationalen Vereinheitlichung des Vertragsrechts geben Anlass zur Hoffnung.

So enthalten die *Principles of European Contract Law* nicht nur in ihrem Artikel 4:108 eine adäquate Formulierung der Problematik Drohung und Zwang, sondern umschreiben im folgenden Abschnitt 4:109 (*Excessive Benefit or Unfair Advantage*) auch ein durchdachtes Konzept des Ausbeutungsschutzes:[54]

Article 4:109:
(1) A party may avoid a contract if, at the time of the conclusion of the contract:
(a) it was dependent on or had a relationship of trust with the other party, was in economic distress or had urgent needs, was improvident, ignorant, inexperienced or lacking in bargaining skill, and
(b) the other party knew or ought to have known of this and, given the circumstances and purpose of the contract, took advantage of the first party's situation in a way which was grossly unfair or took an excessive benefit.

---

[53] Siehe auch J. Gordley, Common law und civil law: eine überholte Unterscheidung, ZEuP 1993, 498 (517 f.).
[54] Vgl. den ähnlichen Art. 3.10 der UNIDROIT-Grundregeln der internationalen Handelsverträge 2004.

(2) Upon the request of the party entitled to avoidance, a court may if it is appropriate adapt the contract in order to bring it into accordance with what might have been agreed had the requirements of good faith and fair dealing been followed.
(3) A court may similarly adapt the contract upon the request of a party receiving notice of avoidance for excessive benefit or unfair advantage, provided that this party informs the party who gave the notice promptly after receiving it and before that party has acted in reliance on it.

Dieser Artikel 4:108 zieht nicht nur – mit Blick auf den angelsächsischen Rechtskreis[55] – die ausbeutungsrelevanten Bestandteile der *undue influence* und der *unconscionability*-Doktrin zusammen und trennt diese sowohl vom Freiwilligkeitsschutz als auch von der Problematik unangemessener Bedingungen, die nicht individuell ausgehandelt wurden. Er löst – mit Blick auf das deutsche Recht – den Ausbeutungsschutz auch von seiner falschen Verortung in der Sittenwidrigkeitsklausel. Zudem hält die rechtsdogmatische Umsetzung des Schutzes vor Ausbeutung beim Vertragsschluss durch ein Anfechtungsrecht, wie oben gefordert, dem Subjekt dieses Schutzes Entscheidungsmöglichkeiten offen. Zugleich wird die zu starre Rechtsfolge des § 138 Abs. 1 BGB (Nichtigkeit) durch ein flexibles richterliches Anpassungsrecht ersetzt. Die Qualitäten dieses Vorschlags vermögen die Richtigkeit der eingangs aufgestellten These in Frage zu stellen, dass die Rechtsdogmatik, um ihre Arbeit zu leisten, bisweilen der Hilfe ihrer philosophischen Nachbardisziplinen bedürfe.

---

[55] Zum Kaleidoskop der nationalen Regelungsmodelle in Europa siehe O. Lando/ H. Beale, *Principles of European Contract Law, Parts I and II. Combined and Revised. Prepared by the Commission on European Contract Law*, The Hague: Kluwer 2000, 263 ff.

Diskriminierungsschutz und Vertragsrecht – Entwicklungstendenzen im Rechtsvergleich

Matthias Lehmann (Bayreuth)

I. Sind Diskriminierungsschutz und Vertragsrecht unvereinbar?

Der Diskriminierungsschutz im Vertragsrecht gehört seit Jahren zum gesicherten Bestand des Gemeinschaftsrechts. Dennoch wird seine Berechtigung in Politik und Wissenschaft immer wieder bestritten. Diese Einwände sind fundamentaler Art. Sie stellen in Zweifel, dass im Vertragsrecht überhaupt Diskriminierungsschutz gewährt werden sollte. Wegen der Grundsätzlichkeit, mit der diese Ansicht das Antidiskriminierungsrecht ablehnt, ist nicht auszuschließen, dass sie auch auf die Fragen der Rechtsanwendung Einfluss nehmen könnte. Daher kann man nicht umhin, sich mit ihr auseinanderzusetzen.

Gegen die Anwendung des Antidiskriminierungsrechts im Vertragsrecht wird insbesondere vorgebracht, der Schutz vor Diskriminierungen sei mit den Grundprinzipien des Privatrechts unvereinbar.[1] Dieser Einwand übersieht, dass Privatrecht im Kern antidiskriminierend ist. Ihm geht es nicht um die distributive Gerechtigkeit, die auf die Person des Berechtigten oder Verpflichteten Rücksicht nimmt, sondern in erster Linie um die kommutative Gerechtigkeit, welche von der jeweiligen Person abstrahiert. Jedes „bürgerliche" Recht, verstanden als das Recht aller Bürger ohne Rücksicht auf deren Stand, ist auf die Gleichbehandlung der Rechtssubjekte ausgerichtet. Ein Beispiel aus der Geschichte mag dies belegen: Als der *Code civil* im Jahre 1804 eingeführt wurde, diente seine gleichmäßige Anwendung auf alle *citoyens* dazu, die Privilegien des Adels unter dem *Ancien Régime* abzuschaffen. Zu ihnen gehörte etwa, dass Handelsgeschäfte für Angehörige des Adelsstandes nicht verpflichtend waren.

---

[1] In Deutschland wird diese Kritik besonders prononciert vorgetragen durch *Pikker*, JZ 2002, 880–882; ders., JZ 2003, 540–545; ders., in: Lorenz (Hrsg.), Karlsruher Forum 2004: Haftung wegen Diskriminierung nach derzeitigem und künftigem Recht, 2005, S. 13, 26–85. In Spanien finden sich ähnliche Gedanken bei *Díez-Picazo*, Sistema de Derechos fundamentales, 2. Aufl. 2005, S. 197. In Belgien wird die Freiheit zu diskriminieren als „fundamentalste Freiheit" bezeichnet von *Storme*, Vivat Academia 2005, Nr. 126, S. 3–27.

Der *Code civil* machte Schluss mit solcher Art von Begünstigungen. Ein umgekehrtes Beispiel für den nichtdiskriminierenden Charakter des Privatrechts ist die während des Dritten Reichs diskutierte Beschränkung der Rechtsfähigkeit im Sinne des BGB auf „Volksgenossen".[2] Sie zielte auf die Überwindung des Prinzip der Gleichheit ab, welches in der Zuerkennung der Rechtsfähigkeit an alle Menschen seinen Ausdruck findet. Schon in die erste Bestimmung des BGB sollte also eine Diskriminierung eingefügt werden. Dies stand mit der Idee eines „bürgerlichen" Rechts in eklatantem Widerspruch.

Auch wenn das Konzept des Privatrechts damit im Kern antidiskriminierend ist, wird dieselbe Eigenschaft jedenfalls dem Vertragsrecht abgesprochen. Denn der Vertrag ist ein Mittel zur Diskriminierung: Er eröffnet die Möglichkeit, zu einer Person in besondere Rechtsbeziehungen zu treten. Durch die Wahl eines Vertragspartners schließt man zugleich andere aus, zu denen man diese besondere Beziehung eben nicht haben will. Die Möglichkeit zu diskriminieren ist durch die Privatautonomie verbürgt. Wenn auch der Inhalt der abschließbaren Verträge in den letzten Jahrzehnten immer weiter beschränkt wurde, so doch nicht die Abschlussfreiheit, insbesondere die Freiheit, den Vertragspartner zu wählen. Das Verbot der Diskriminierung scheint auf den ersten Blick mit dieser Freiheit zu kollidieren, denn es untersagt, die Wahl des Partners an bestimmten Kriterien auszurichten. Daraus ziehen die Kritiker weitreichende Schlüsse: infolge der Anwendung des Antidiskriminierungsrechts im Vertragsrecht werde die *iustitia commutativa* durch die *iustitia distributiva* verdrängt; an die Stelle der dezentralen Steuerung durch individuelle Entscheidungen trete eine Verteilungsgerechtigkeit, die durch den Staat verordnet ist und durch die Gerichte durchgesetzt wird; der individualrechtliche Güteraustausch werde „sozialisiert".[3] Diese Auffassung prophezeit uns also eine neue Art der Planwirtschaft, die aus der Anwendung des Diskriminierungsrechts folge.

Ich will zur dargestellten Meinung an dieser Stelle noch keine Position beziehen. Stattdessen schlage ich vor, einige ausländische Rechtsordnungen zu betrachten, die seit langem Diskriminierungsverbote kennen, und zu untersuchen, wie sie diese mit dem Grundsatz der Vertragsfreiheit kombiniert haben. Der Blick über den Tellerrand des eigenen Rechts hinaus ist immer bereichernd. Im Falle der Diskriminierungsverbote ist er es aber besonders, weil er vor übertriebenen Befürchtungen bewahrt. Denn auch Rechtsordnungen, die wir grundsätzlich als liberal ansehen, kennen seit langem Diskriminierungsverbote im Vertragsrecht. Um dies

---

[2] Siehe *Larenz*, in: Dahm (Hrsg.), Grundfragen der neuen Rechtswissenschaft, 1935, S. 225, 241.

[3] *Picker*, in: Lorenz (Hrsg.), Karlsruher Forum 2004: Haftung wegen Diskriminierung nach derzeitigem und künftigem Recht, 2005, S. 13, 20.

zu erkennen, ist es hilfreich, die Untersuchung nicht nur auf europäische Staaten zu beschränken, sondern auch über den Atlantik zu schauen. Damit die Entwicklungstendenzen in den verschiedenen Rechtsordnungen klar nachgezeichnet werden können, ist es jedoch notwendig, den Rechtsvergleich nicht in klassischer Weise nach Rechtsordnungen oder Rechtskreisen geteilt vorzunehmen, sondern nach systematischen Kriterien vorzugehen. Diese folgen einem Ordnungsprinzip, welches sich im Antidiskriminierungsrecht seit langem als hilfreich herausgestellt hat: Zunächst wird nach dem Anwendungsbereich der jeweiligen Diskriminierungsverbote gefragt (II), dann nach den verbotenen Merkmalen unterschiedlicher Behandlung (III), im Anschluss nach der Rechtfertigung (IV) und schließlich nach den Sanktionen (V).

II. Anwendungsbereich der Diskriminierungsverbote

1. Wettbewerbsrecht

Die ersten Diskriminierungsvorschriften finden sich an unerwarteter Stelle: im Wettbewerbsrecht. Dieses untersagt seit langem die unterschiedliche Behandlung bestimmter Unternehmen. Die sachlich nicht gerechtfertigte Ungleichbehandlung eines Unternehmens gegenüber einem anderen kann den Tatbestand des Missbrauchs einer marktbeherrschenden Stellung erfüllen.[4] Allerdings ist dieses Diskriminierungsverbot besonderer Natur, denn es richtet sich nur an bestimmte Unternehmen, nämlich solche, die marktbeherrschend sind. Soweit die Voraussetzung einer marktbeherrschenden Stellung nicht vorliegt, ist jegliches diskriminierendes Verhalten erlaubt. Außerdem entsprechen die meisten der verbotenen Beschränkungen nicht dem klassischen Bild der Diskriminierung, weil sie sich vorwiegend im Wirtschaftsverkehr auswirken. Auch ist das Verbot des Missbrauchs der marktbeherrschenden Stellung nicht gerade auf den Abschluss von Verträgen bezogen, sondern erstreckt sich auf jegliche Form der Behinderung anderer Unternehmen im Verkehr. Es geht also hier vor allem um die Sicherung des Zugangs zu bestimmten Märkten. Dennoch zeigt schon das Wettbewerbsrecht, dass Diskriminierungsverbote dem Privatrecht nicht grundsätzlich fremd sind.

2. Arbeitsrecht

Das klassische Feld des Diskriminierungsschutzes im Vertragsrecht ist das Arbeitsrecht. Hier reicht der Schutz vor ungerechtfertigter Ungleichbe-

---

[4] Vgl. § 20 I GWB, Art. 81 S. 2 lit. c EG-Vertrag.

handlung am weitesten. Das liegt zweifellos daran, dass Arbeitsverträge für das persönliche Fortkommen und den Wohlstand von herausragender Bedeutung sind. Frühzeitig eingeführt wurde etwa das Verbot, Männern und Frauen unterschiedlichen Lohn zu zahlen.[5] Daneben gibt es aber seit langem auch andere Diskriminierungsverbote. Das deutsche Arbeitsrecht etwa kennt das aus Artikel 9 Abs. 3 GG abgeleitete Verbot, hinsichtlich der Gewerkschaftszugehörigkeit zu unterscheiden, oder das richterrechtlich ausgeformte Verbot, schwangere Frauen bei der Einstellung zu benachteiligen.

Die Fokussierung des Diskriminierungsverbots auf das Arbeitsrecht hat auch legislative Folgen: Häufig sind Bestimmungen über Diskriminierung in nationale Arbeitsgesetzbücher oder Arbeitsvertragsgesetze eingefügt.[6] Ihre Herausnahme aus dem Arbeitsrecht und Erstreckung auf andere Bereiche bereitet damit nicht selten gesetzgebungstechnische Schwierigkeiten. Soweit sie dennoch erfolgt, bleibt die Methode der arbeitsrechtlichen Regelung typenbildend auch für die Ächtung der Diskriminierung in anderen Bereichen. Man hat das Arbeitsrecht daher auch als „Oberhof" des Antidiskriminierungsrechts bezeichnet.[7]

3. Andere Vertragsarten

Vom Arbeitsrecht ausgehend wurden die Diskriminierungsverbote in andere Gebiete ausgedehnt. Dies ist zunächst der Fall für den mit dem Arbeitsrecht eng zusammenhängenden Bereich der Bildung. Bildung eröffnet die Möglichkeit zur Vorbereitung und Qualifizierung für den Arbeitsmarkt; daher ist ein arbeitsrechtliches Diskriminierungsverbot ohne ein vorgeschaltetes Verbot der unterschiedlichen Behandlung während der Ausbildung wertlos. Aus diesem Grund platziert zum Beispiel der britische *Sex Discrimination Act 1975* das Verbot, beim Zugang zu Bildungseinrichtungen nach dem Geschlecht zu differenzieren, in die Nähe des arbeitsrechtlichen Diskriminierungsverbotes.[8] Diese Regelung in einem der ersten Antidiskriminierungsgesetze war wegweisend für das Gemeinschaftsrecht, welches ebenfalls Diskriminierungsverbote im Bildungsbereich aufstellt.[9]

Doch außer in den mit dem Arbeitsrecht eng verbundenen Bereich der Bildung wurden Diskriminierungsverbote auch auf ganz anderen Gebieten

---

5 Vgl. Artikel 141 des EG-Vertrags (früher Art. 119 des EWG-Vertrags).
6 Siehe z.B. Art. 22–32 portugiesischer *Código do Trabalho*.
7 *Schmidt-Kessel*, in: Leible (Hrsg.), Diskriminierungsschutz durch Privatrecht, 2006, S. 53 (56).
8 Britischer *Sex Discrimination Act 1975*, section 22.
9 Siehe Art. 3 I lit. b und g Richtlinie 2000/43/EG.

vorgesehen. So sieht etwa der bereits erwähnte britische *Sex Discrimination Act 1975* das Verbot vor, Frauen beim Verkauf oder der Vermietung von Grundstücken zu benachteiligen. Diese Bestimmung kann man damit zu erklären versuchen, dass der Immobilienmarkt ebenso wie der Arbeitsmarkt wegen des Überhangs der Nachfrage auf einer Marktseite von einem starken Machtgefälle der Parteien gekennzeichnet ist. Sie steht allerdings in auffälligem Kontrast zur deutschen Regelung des Allgemeinen Gleichbehandlungsgesetzes (AGG), welches den Wohnungsbereich weitgehend von seinem Anwendungsbereich ausnimmt.[10] Eine einheitliche Tendenz des Antidiskriminierungsrechts lässt sich daher hinsichtlich der Immobilienverträge nicht ausmachen.

4. Öffentliche Angebote

Eine neue Qualität des Antidiskriminierungsrechts ist erreicht, wo der Anwendungsbereich der Diskriminierungsverbote nicht mehr auf bestimmte Vertragsarten beschränkt ist, sondern an die Art anknüpft, wie die Leistung angeboten wird. Die Richtlinie 2004/113/EG verbietet Diskriminierungen hinsichtlich von Gütern und Dienstleistungen, die der Öffentlichkeit ohne Ansehen der Person zur Verfügung stehen – man sollte vielleicht besser sagen: typischerweise zur Verfügung gestellt werden. Dass bei solchen öffentlich angebotenen Waren und Dienstleistungen nicht diskriminiert werden darf, hat in anderen Rechtsordnungen lange Tradition. In Großbritannien beispielsweise ist es bereits seit dem Jahr 1975 untersagt, im Fall eines *common calling*, das heißt eines an die Allgemeinheit gerichteten Angebots von Gütern, Einrichtungen oder Dienstleistungen, nach dem Geschlecht zu differenzieren.[11] Dasselbe Ergebnis wurde in Frankreich mit dem Verbot des *réfus de vente* erreicht, das allerdings einen sehr viel weiteren Anwendungsbereich hat. Das heute im *Code de la consommation* niedergelegte Verbot richtet sich gegen jegliche Ablehnung der Belieferung eines Verbrauchers, gleichgültig aus welchem Grund sie erfolgt.[12]

Beide Verbote haben eine ganz andere Richtung als die zuvor genannten: Sie sollen weder den Zugang zu notwendigen Einrichtungen noch die Versorgung mit bestimmten Gütern oder Dienstleistungen sicherstellen. Denn es ist gerade kein Kriterium, dass der Diskriminierte auf die Leistung des Anbietenden angewiesen ist. Es geht vielmehr darum, dass aus

---

[10] § 19 V 1 AGG. Allerdings werden Vermieter von mehr als 50 Wohnungen wieder in den Anwendungsbereich einbezogen, vgl. § 19 V 3 AGG.
[11] Section 29 britischer *Sex Discrimination Act 1975*.
[12] Art. L122-1 französischer *Code de la consommation*. Ein Vorläufer dieser Regelung war Art. 30–36 der *Ordonnance 86-1243* vom 1.12.1986.

der Ablehnung der Leistung eines ansonsten öffentlich gemachten Angebots gegenüber einer bestimmten Person oder Personengruppe eine negative Wirkung folgt. Man kann sie als „Gefühl des Diskriminiert-Seins" bezeichnen. Der Anbieter muss sich seinerseits den Vorwurf gefallen lassen, dass er sich in gewisser Weise zu seinem eigenen Verhalten in Widerspruch setzt: Er bietet eine Leistung an die Öffentlichkeit ohne Ansehen der Person an, nimmt dann aber bestimmte Gruppen von Personen aus. Es ist verständlich, dass diese Art von Verhalten als mit der Gleichheit unter den Bürgern unvereinbar angesehen wird.

Man sieht, dass das Verhalten im allgemeinen Zivilrechtsverkehr durchaus diskriminierende Wirkungen haben kann, die dem Gerechtigkeitsgefühl widersprechen. Dogmatisch lassen sie sich am besten in der Nähe der Verletzung des allgemeinen Persönlichkeitsrechts verorten. Denn durch die Ausnahme von einem öffentlich gemachten Angebot werden das Ansehen und die Würde der Person beeinträchtigt. Allerdings hat die konsequente Verbot dieser Beeinträchtigungen zur Folge, dass der Anwendungsbereich des Antidiskriminierungsrechts gegenüber dem ursprünglichen Ansatz in erheblichem Maße ausgeweitet wird: Da alle öffentlich angebotenen Güter und Dienstleistungen erfasst sind, fallen nun im Grundsatz alle Angebote von Gewerbetreibenden an Verbraucher darunter. Die Diskriminierungsverbote, die sich vorher nur auf bestimmte Vertragsarten bezogen, werden zum allgemeinen Standard für alle Verbraucherverträge.

5. Unbeschränkter Anwendungsbereich

Zweifellos seinen Höhepunkt erreicht das Antidiskriminierungsrecht in jenen Rechtsakten, die keinerlei Beschränkungen ihres Anwendungsbereichs kennen. Solche Bestimmungen finden sich insbesondere in den skandinavischen Rechtsordnungen. So ist etwa das dänische Gesetz zur Gleichstellung von Frau und Mann neben Arbeitgebern und staatlichen Stellen auf alle Unternehmen und sonstigen „öffentlichen Aktivitäten" anwendbar.[13] Das finnische Gesetz zur Gleichheit der Geschlechter erstreckt seinen Anwendungsbereich auf „alle gesellschaftlichen Bereiche", soweit sie nicht ausdrücklich ausgenommen sind.[14] Das norwegische Gesetz über die Gleichheit der Geschlechter ist nach seiner eigenen Regelung anwendbar auf „alle Gebiete", mit Ausnahme nur der „internen Angelegenheiten von Religionsgemeinschaften".[15] Alle übrigen Bereiche des

---

[13] Art. 2 I dänisches *lov om ligestilling af kvinder og mænd*.
[14] Art. 7 finnisches Gesetz zur Gleichheit der Geschlechter.
[15] Norwegisches Gesetz zur Gleichbehandlung der Geschlechter von 1978, § 2 I.

sozialen Lebens sind erfasst, soweit nicht ein Dispens durch den König erteilt wurde.[16]

Die genannten Gesetze gehen sehr weit. Ihr Anwendungsbereich ist weder auf bestimmte Vertragstypen noch auf bestimmte Arten des Angebots beschränkt. Sie unterwerfen beispielsweise eine Privatperson, die ihr Haus oder ihr Auto an einen Nachbar verkaufen möchte, den Diskriminierungsverboten. Ob solche weiten Antidiskriminierungsgesetze tatsächlich empfehlenswert sind, wenn man sie ernsthaft anwendet und durchsetzt, ist zweifelhaft und hängt insbesondere davon ab, welche Diskriminierungsmerkmale man verwendet.

III. Verpönte Diskriminierungsmerkmale

Neben dem Anwendungsbereich ist die entscheidende Frage jeglicher Diskriminierungsverbote, welche Merkmale untersagt werden. Nur aus dem Zusammenspiel des verpönten Merkmals mit dem Anwendungsbereich ergibt sich die reale Bedeutung des Diskriminierungsverbots.

1. Persönliche Eigenschaften

In Europa ist zuerst das Geschlecht als Diskriminierungsmerkmal anerkannt worden. Besondere Bedeutung hat das Verbot der Diskriminierung zwischen Mann und Frau bei der Bemessung des Entgelts für Arbeitsleistungen nach Artikel 141 des EG-Vertrages (früher Artikel 119 EWG-Vertrag). Durch die Entscheidung des EuGH wurde diese Bestimmung im Jahre 1976 für unmittelbar anwendbar erklärt.[17] Doch schon vorher enthielten die nationalen Rechtsordnungen entsprechende Verbote, die sich direkt im Zivilrechtsverkehr auswirkten. Bereits im Jahre 1970 wurde in Großbritannien der *Equal Pay Act* verabschiedet. Der irische *Antidiscrimination (Pay) Act* wurde 1974 angenommen. Die praktische Bedeutung des Verbots des Geschlechts als Differenzierungsmerkmal ist besonders groß, denn es waren gerade die Gesetze zur Gleichbehandlung von Mann und Frau, bei denen der Anwendungsbereich später über das Arbeitsrecht hinaus verallgemeinert worden ist.[18] Die Richtlinie 2004/113/EG vollzieht diese Entwicklung nach, indem sie die Ungleichbehandlung aufgrund des Geschlechts bei öffentlichen Angeboten von Gütern und Dienstleistungen verbietet.

---

[16] Norwegisches Gesetz zur Gleichbehandlung der Geschlechter von 1978, § 2 III.
[17] EuGH, Rs. 43/75, *Defrenne/Sabena*, Slg. 1976, 455.
[18] Siehe oben unter I 4 und 5.

Darüber hinaus wurde das Verbot der Geschlechterdiskriminieung besonders weit ausgestaltet, indem auch die Belästigung untersagt wurde.[19] Schon die Schaffung eines bestimmten Umfelds, das von Einschüchterungen, Anfeindungen, Erniedrigungen, Entwürdigungen oder Beleidigungen gekennzeichnet ist, kann eine Diskriminierung darstellen. Vorbild ist insoweit das „hostile work environment" des US-amerikanischen Rechts.

Das Geschlecht war das erste Merkmal, hinsichtlich dessen in Europa Diskriminierung im Zivilrechtsverkehr untersagt wurde. Alle nachfolgenden Gesetze nahmen dieses Verbot zum Modell. Daher lässt sich daher ohne Übertreibung sagen, dass aus historischer Sicht die Gleichheit von Mann und Frau die Keimzelle des europäischen Antidiskriminierungsrechts ist.

Ganz anders in den USA. Hier steht das Verbot der ungleichen Behandlung aufgrund der Rasse am Anfang der Tradition der Antidiskriminierungsgesetzgebung. Es wurde seit dem Bürgerkrieg in verschiedenen *Civil Rights Acts* ausgeformt. Für das Zivilrecht relevant wurde insbesondere der aus dem Jahre 1964. Er verbietet neben der Diskriminierung aufgrund der Rasse, Hautfarbe und nationaler Herkunft auch die Ungleichbehandlung aufgrund des Geschlechts und der Religion.[20] Das Gesetz ist im allgemeinen Zivilrechtsverkehr anwendbar, insbesondere bindet es Hotels, Motels, Restaurants, Theater und alle öffentlichen Unterkünfte. Außerdem sind die Diskriminierungsverbote nach dem praktisch sehr bedeutsamen *Title VII* des *Civil Rights Act 1964* auch bei Arbeitsverhältnissen zu beachten.[21]

In das europäische Recht ist die Rasse als verbotenes Diskriminierungsmerkmal durch die Richtlinie 2000/43/EG aufgenommen worden. Viele Vorbilder in den Rechtsordnungen der Mitgliedstaaten gab es nicht. In das niederländische Recht war 1994 ein Verbot eingeführt worden, wegen der Rasse zu diskriminieren,[22] allerdings erst nach langen Protesten.[23] In den anderen Mitgliedstaaten wenden sich die Verfassungen zwar meist ausdrücklich gegen die Diskriminierung aufgrund der Rasse, doch beziehen sich diese Vorschriften nicht speziell auf den Zivilrechtsverkehr. Die im Vergleich zu den Vereinigten Staaten späte Einfügung des Merkmals in das europäische Recht kann ohne weiteres damit erklärt werden, dass das Bedürfnis dazu in den europäischen Staaten erst in neue-

---

[19] Art. 2 lit. c, d der Richtlinie 2004/113/EG.
[20] Pub.L. 88-352, 78 Stat. 241, 2.7.1964.
[21] Später kodifiziert als 42 U.S.C. § 2000e.
[22] Aber siehe Art. 2 I i.V.m. Art. 1 I lit. b, c niederländisches *Algemene Wet Gelijke Behandling* aus dem Jahre 1994.
[23] Vgl. *Schieck*, Differenzierte Gerechtigkeit, 2000, S. 104.

rer Zeit verspürt wurde, ausgelöst durch die veränderten gesellschaftlichen Bedingungen der Multikulturalität.

Das Verbot, Behinderte im Zivilrechtsverkehr zu diskriminieren, ist überraschenderweise relativ jüngeren Datums. Es wurde zunächst in den USA mit dem *American with Disabilities Act 1990* eingeführt.[24] Dieser ist dem *Civil Rights Acts 1964* nachgebildet und verbietet Einrichtungen, die der Öffentlichkeit zugänglich sind, die Benachteiligung behinderter Menschen. Aus diesem Verbot folgt die Pflicht zur Schaffung eines einfachen Zugangs. Die zivilrechtlichen Ansprüche, die der *Act* für den Fall der Verletzung dieser Pflicht vorsieht, haben zur landesweiten Veränderung der Eingänge von Hotels, Restaurants, Transportmitteln und Geschäften geführt. In Europa war es wiederum die Gemeinschaft, welche die Benachteiligung im Zivilrechtsverkehr aufgrund einer Behinderung als Thema aufgegriffen hat. Die Richtlinie 2000/78/EG sieht ganz dem amerikanischem Vorbild folgend die Verpflichtung vor, für angemessene Vorkehrungen hinsichtlich von Menschen mit Behinderung zu sorgen.[25] Allerdings stellt das Merkmal der Behinderung die nationalen Gesetzgeber offenbar vor besondere Schwierigkeiten, da den Mitgliedstaaten eine Verlängerung der ansonsten geltenden Umsetzungsfrist um drei Jahre ermöglicht wurde.[26] Dennoch scheint die Ächtung der Diskriminierung Behinderter auf breiten Konsens in den Mitgliedstaaten zu stoßen. Denn obwohl sich das gemeinschaftsrechtliche Verbot nur auf das Arbeitsrecht bezieht, wurde es bei der Umsetzung etwa in Belgien, Finnland, Irland und Deutschland auch auf andere Bereiche des Zivilrechtsverkehrs ausgedehnt.[27] Augenscheinlich sind viele Gesetzgeber der Ansicht, dass der Schutz Behinderter vor Diskriminierung nicht auf das Arbeitsrecht beschränkt bleiben darf. Die Frage ist allerdings, wie eine Behinderung definiert wird; die nationalen Gesetze enthalten hierzu teilweise unterschiedliche Bestimmungen, durch die der Anwendungsbereich des Diskriminierungsverbots eingeschränkt wird. Doch gibt es auch die umgekehrte Tendenz zur Ausweitung auf geringere Beeinträchtigungen. Bemerkenswert ist etwa das belgische Recht, welches das Gebot der Gleichbehandlung Behinderter um ein Verbot der Diskriminierung wegen des gegenwärtigen oder künftigen Gesundheitszustandes ergänzt.[28]

---

[24] 42 U.S.C. § 12101.
[25] Art. 5 Richtlinie 2000/78/EG.
[26] Art. 18 II der Richtlinie 2000/78/EG.
[27] Siehe Art. 2 § 1, 4 des belgischen *Loi du 25 février 2003 tendant à lutter contre la discrimination et modifiant la loi du 15 février 1993 créant un Centre pour l'égalité des chances et la lutte contre le racisme*; das finnische *Antidiskriminierungsgesetz*; Art. 4 des irischen *Equal Status Act 2000–2004*; § 19 I des deutschen AGG.
[28] Art. 2 § 1 des belgischen *Loi du février 2003*.

Ein weiteres besonders heikles Diskriminierungsmerkmal ist das Alter, da die Rechtsordnung selbst an vielen Stellen aufgrund des Lebensalters differenziert. In vielen Fällen ist es sinnvoll, nach dem Alter zu unterscheiden; man denke etwa nur an die Geschäftsfähigkeit oder die Arbeitsmarktpolitik.[29] Dennoch wurde das Alter in die Reihe der verbotenen Diskriminierungsgründe aufgenommen. Tonangebend war auch insoweit wieder das U.S.-amerikanische Recht, welches heute im *Age Discrimination in Employment Act* Ungleichbehandlung aufgrund des Alters im Bereich des Arbeitsrechts verbietet.[30] In das europäische Antidiskriminierungsrecht ist das Alter durch die Richtlinie 2000/78/EG gelangt.[31] Doch sieht diese insoweit besonders weite Rechtfertigungsgründe vor.[32] Zudem wurde ebenso wie hinsichtlich der Behinderung den Mitgliedstaaten eine besonders lange Umsetzungsfrist erlaubt.[33]

2. Persönliche Einstellungen und Überzeugungen

Unter den persönlichen Einstellungen und Überzeugungen, aufgrund derer eine Diskriminierung verboten ist, ragt die Religion heraus. Sie wurde im Zivilrechtsverkehr zuerst durch den amerikanischen *Civil Rights Act 1964* verboten.[34] In den europäischen Staaten findet sich das Verbot der Diskriminierung aufgrund der Religion in den meisten Verfassungen, doch ist es auf das Vertragsrecht nicht unmittelbar anwendbar. Es wurde erst durch die Richtlinie 2000/78/EG eingeführt.[35] Allerdings bleibt den religiösen Gemeinschaften selbst ein gewisses Diskriminierungsrecht vorbehalten. Selbst die Rechtsordnungen, die den Anwendungsbereich ihrer Gesetzgebung zur Gleichstellung von Mann und Frau nicht beschränken, kennen eine Ausnahme für die inneren Angelegenheiten von Religionsgemeinschaften.[36]

Problematischer als das religiöse Bekenntnis ist die Weltanschauung. Das liegt zum einen daran, dass sich nur schwer definieren lässt, was unter

---

[29] Siehe z.B. Art. 7 I a und b des niederländisches *Wet Gelijke Behandling op grond van leeftijd bij de arbeit*, wonach unter bestimmten Umständen eine arbeitsmarktpolitisch motivierte Benachteiligung aufgrund des Alters erlaubt ist. Dazu *Asscher-Vonk/Schlachter*, RIW 2005, 505.
[30] 29 U.S.C. §§ 621 ff.
[31] Art. 1 Richtlinie 2000/78/EG.
[32] Art. 6 Richtlinie 2000/78/EG.
[33] Art. 18 II Richtlinie 2000/78/EG.
[34] Siehe oben 1.
[35] Siehe Artikel 1 der Richtlinie 2000/78/EG.
[36] So zum Beispiel das norwegische Gesetz zur Gleichbehandlung der Geschlechter, oben unter II 5.

einer Weltanschauung zu verstehen ist. Zum anderen überschneidet sich die Nicht-Diskriminierung aufgrund der Weltanschauung mit der politischen Gesinnung. Auf diese Weise gewinnt bei der Diskussion um das Merkmal oftmals die Erwägung Einfluss, bestimmten Parteien keinen erleichterten Zugang zu privaten Einrichtungen zu gewähren. Diese hat etwa in Deutschland zur Herausnahme der Weltanschauung aus dem Verbot der Diskriminierung im allgemeinen Zivilrechtsverkehr geführt. Vor diesem Hintergrund stellt sich die Frage der Verfassungsmäßigkeit solchen Vorgehens, auf die später einzugehen ist.[37]

Nicht ganz einfach unter die bisherigen Kategorien einzuordnen ist das Verbot, aufgrund der sexuellen Ausrichtung zu diskriminieren. Homosexualität als „persönliche Eigenschaft" zu bezeichnen, wäre an sich schon eine Diskriminierung. Daher wird sie hier unter der zugegebenermaßen etwas unbeholfenen Kategorie der „persönlichen Einstellung und Überzeugung" erörtert. Was mit der sexuellen Ausrichtung gemeint ist, lässt sich nicht einfach sagen. Das englische Recht hat insoweit einen Definitionsversuch unternommen, der nicht ganz unumstritten ist.[38] Das Verbot, nach der sexuellen Ausrichtung zu diskriminieren, existierte schon lange vor der Richtlinie 2000/78/EG. So wurde es etwa in den Niederlanden schon im Jahre 1994 in das *Algemene Wet Gelijke Behandling* eingefügt.[39] Ausnahmsweise ist das Vorbild dafür einmal nicht die USA. Ganz im Gegenteil wird dort versucht, die Einführung von Diskriminierungsverboten zugunsten Homosexueller durch Verfassungsänderung zu untersagen, mit anderen Worten ein „Verbot von Diskriminierungsverboten" zu erlassen.[40] Man geht also im Vergleich zu Europa in die umgekehrte Richtung. Das Verbot der Diskriminierung aufgrund der sexuellen Einstellung ist deshalb die einzige wirklich europäische Schöpfung des Antidiskriminierungsrechts.

3. Ausweitung

Andere Rechtsordnungen sehen weitere Diskriminierungsmerkmale vor, die in den europäischen Rechtsakten nicht genannt sind. Das portugiesische Arbeitsgesetzbuch sieht zum Beispiel ein Verbot der Ungleichbehandlung aufgrund des genetischen Erbguts und wegen des Personen-

---

[37] Siehe unten, 4.
[38] Vgl. *Bell*, (2004) 67 (3) Modern Law Review 465, 467 f.
[39] Art. 2 I i.V.m. Art. 1 I lit. b, c niederländisches *Algemene Wet Gelijke Behandling*.
[40] Der *Supreme Court*, der sich mit einer entsprechenden Zusatz zur Verfassung Colorados auseinanderzusetzen hatte, hat diesen als mit der Bundesverfassung unvereinbar verworfen, siehe *Rower v. Ewans*, 517 U.S. 620 (1996).

stands vor.⁴¹ Das französische Recht verbietet allgemein die Diskriminierung aufgrund der „Sitten" (*mœurs*) einer Person,⁴² ohne dass klar definiert ist, was unter dem Begriff in diesem Zusammenhang gemeint ist. Das belgische Gesetz nennt neben den bekannten Diskriminierungsmerkmalen auch die Abstammung, das Vermögen, die philosophische Überzeugung, den derzeitigen oder künftigen Gesundheitszustand sowie physische Merkmale.

Bemerkenswert ist ein slowenisches Gesetz, welches es unter anderem verbietet, aufgrund der Bildung oder des finanziellen Status' zu differenzieren.⁴³ Das erscheint aus verschiedenen Gründen bedenklich: Ist nicht der Bildungsstand eines Arbeitnehmers ein wesentliches und legitimes Merkmal für die Einstellung? Und ist nicht der finanzielle Status eines Kunden entscheidend, wenn diesem Kredit gewährt werden soll? In der Tat sind wir hier bei den Bedenken gegen die Antidiskriminierungsgesetzgebung angelangt, die ich am Anfang herausgestellt habe. Werden die Merkmale zu weit ausgedehnt, besteht die Gefahr, dass in Beurteilungen eingegriffen wird, die vernünftigerweise auf privatautonomer Ebene getroffen werden sollten. Das ist jedoch kein Einwand gegen den Diskriminierungsschutz im Vertragsrecht an sich, sondern nur gegen eine zu weit gehende Ausdehnung der verpönten Merkmale. Die Aufgabe, die jeweils verbotenen Merkmale in Bezug auf bestimmte Lebensbereiche festzulegen, obliegt dem Gesetzgeber. Er muss danach suchen, in welchen Bereichen eine bestimmte Eigenschaft typischerweise Anlass für Diskriminierungen bietet, wo sie also, in der Terminologie des amerikanischen Verfassungsrechts, eine „suspect classification" darstellt. Andererseits muss er auch beachten, ob mit einer Differenzierung nicht so häufig legitime Zwecke verfolgt werden, dass ein allgemeines Verbot mit rechtfertigungsbedürftigen Ausnahmen unangebracht wäre. Diese Fragen können Schwierigkeiten bereiten, da sie für verschiedene Verträge und abhängig von der Situation unterschiedlich zu beantworten sind. Insoweit wird man dem Gesetzgeber einen gewissen Gestaltungsspielraum zugestehen müssen.

---

41 Art. 23 portugiesischer *Código do Trabalho*.
42 Art. 225-1 französischer *Code pénal*.
43 Slowenisches Gesetz zur Umsetzung des Gleichbehandlungsgrundsatzes, Amtsblatt Nr. 50/2004, zitiert in: Europäisches Netz unabhängiger Sachverständiger im Bereich der Nichtdiskriminierung, Entwicklung des Antidiskriminierungsrechts in Europa, 2005, S. 21.

4. Verpflichtung zur Ausweitung?

Die meisten Verfassungen der Mitgliedstaaten enthalten allgemeine Gleichbehandlungsgrundsätze oder verbieten Diskriminierungen aus einzeln aufgezählten Gründen. Wird in diesen Staaten ein zivilrechtliches Antidiskriminierungsgesetz verabschiedet, dessen verbotene Diskriminierungsmerkmale enger gefasst sind, fragt sich, ob es mit der Verfassung übereinstimmt. Dass diese Frage nicht nur theoretischer Natur ist, zeigt ein interessantes Urteil des Verfassungsgerichtshofes Belgiens, der *Cour d'arbitrage*. Das belgische Gesetz vom 25.2.2003 zum Kampf gegen die Diskriminierung hatte die politische Überzeugung und die Sprache nicht als verbotene Merkmale aufgenommen. Dagegen richtete sich die Klage des „Vlaams Blok" und eines Juraprofessors. Die *Cour d'arbitrage* entschied, dass das Gesetz gegen das in Artikel 10 und 11 der belgischen Verfassung enthaltene allgemeine Diskriminierungsverbot verstoße, da kein rechtfertigender Grund bestehe, die politische Überzeugung oder die Sprache anders zu behandeln als die im Gesetz genannten Diskriminierungsmerkmale. Mangels entsprechender Rechtsgestaltungsbefugnisse konnte der Gerichtshof aber die gesetzlichen Merkmale nicht um die politische Überzeugung und die Sprache erweitern. Daher entschied er, dass die Beschränkung des Diskriminierungsverbots auf bestimmte Merkmale insgesamt gegen die Verfassung verstoße.[44]

Gleichgültig, wie man die Begründung dieser Rechtsprechung beurteilt, ihre Folge ist, dass dem Gesetzgeber die Möglichkeit zur Definition der verpönten Diskriminierungsmerkmale aus der Hand genommen ist. Das wird besonders bedeutsam dadurch, dass auch völkerrechtliche Abkommen weite Diskriminierungsverbote enthalten. Das belgische Verfassungsgericht hatte sich ausdrücklich auf Artikel 14 der Europäischen Menschenrechtskonvention sowie auf Artikel 26 des Internationalen Pakts über Bürgerliche und politische Rechte bezogen, um die partielle Aufhebung des belgischen Antidiskriminierungsgesetzes zu begründen.[45] Diese Bestimmungen verbieten als Gründe für Ungleichbehandlungen neben dem Geschlecht, der Rasse, der Hautfarbe, der Sprache und der Religion auch die politische oder „jede andere" Überzeugung, die nationale oder soziale Herkunft, die Zugehörigkeit zu einer nationalen Minderheit, das Vermögen, die Geburt oder „jede andere Situation". Macht man mit den dort genannten verbotenen Diskriminierungsmerkmalen ernst, so würden die verbotenen Diskriminierungsmerkmale grundlegend erweitert. Das würde nicht nur für das belgische Recht gelten, sondern für

---

[44] Belgische *Cour d'arbitrage*, Urteil Nr. 157/2004 v. 6.10.2004, S. 19 (unter B.15).

[45] Belgische *Cour d'arbitrage*, a.a.O., S. 18 (unter B 10).

alle Rechtsordnungen der an die völkerrechtlichen Texte gebundenen Staaten. Die enorme Sprengkraft der Entscheidung der belgischen *Cour d'arbitrage* für das allgemeine Zivilrecht ist offensichtlich.

IV. Rechtfertigungsgründe

1. Differenzierung nach Diskriminierungsmerkmalen

Die Verwendung eines verbotenen Diskriminierungsmerkmals beim Abschluss, der Durchführung oder Beendigung des Vertrags bleibt ohne Folgen, soweit sie gerechtfertigt ist. Alle Rechtsordnungen kennen Rechtfertigungsmöglichkeiten für Diskriminierungen, ob gesetzliche oder richterrechtliche. Allerdings lässt sich zunächst eine Beobachtung machen, die von besonderer Bedeutung ist: Nicht alle Diskriminierungsmerkmale sind in gleichem Maße für Rechtfertigungen offen. Zum Beispiel können für die Ungleichbehandlung von Mann und Frau wegen ihrer biologischen Verschiedenheiten durchaus gute Gründe bestehen.[46] Dagegen ist für eine Benachteiligung aufgrund der Rasse eine Rechtfertigung nicht vorstellbar, selbst wenn die entsprechende Richtlinie den Mitgliedstaaten Ausnahmen bezüglich eines mit der Rasse oder der ethnischen Herkunft zusammenhängenden Merkmals unter bestimmten Umständen erlaubt.[47] Die Rasse ist unabhängig von allen Umständen als Unterscheidungskriterium verpönt. In der Tat ist sogar zweifelhaft, ob es das Kriterium in objektiver Hinsicht überhaupt gibt; die Antidiskriminierungsgesetze distanzieren sich jedenfalls von jeder Art der Rassentheorie.[48] In jedem Fall sind Ungleichbehandlungen aufgrund der Rasse wesentlich schwerer zu rechtfertigen als solche aufgrund des Geschlechts. Es gibt also harte und weiche Diskriminierungsverbote.

Daraus folgt, dass die Rechtfertigungsgründe nicht für alle Unterscheidungsmerkmale gleich sein können. Das gilt selbst dann, wenn diese in einem Gesetz zusammengefasst sind. Ein Beispiel dafür liefert das niederländische *Algemene Wet Gelijke Behandling*. Es sieht in seinem Artikel 2 sehr differenzierte Rechtfertigungsgründe für die Benachteiligung aufgrund des Geschlechts, der Rasse und der Nationalität vor. Das niederländische Gleichbehandlungsgesetz ist eines der ältesten und am meisten diskutierten in Europa, so dass es durchaus als Messgröße für zukünftige

---

[46] Siehe z.B. section 7 britischer *Sex Discrimination Act 1975* oder Art. 2 VI der Richtlinie 76/207/EWG in der Fassung durch die Richtlinie 2002/73/EG.

[47] Artikel 4 der Richtlinie 2000/43/EG. Das deutsche AGG hat von dieser Ermächtigung keinen Gebrauch gemacht.

[48] Siehe Erwägungsgrund 6 der Richtlinie 2000/43/EG sowie Art. 2 § 1 des belgischen Gesetzes (oben Fußn. 27), der von „*une prétendue race*" spricht.

Entwicklungen in anderen Staaten dienen kann. Daraus folgt eine erste wichtige Schlussfolgerung für das Antidiskriminierungsrecht im Allgemeinen: Auch wenn die verschiedenen Diskriminierungsverbote zu einem Prinzip zusammengefasst werden, wird man nicht umhinkommen, für jedes spezifische Merkmal spezielle Rechtfertigungsgründe zu erarbeiten. Das kann entweder durch Gesetzes- oder durch Richterrecht geschehen. Die Tendenz des Antidiskriminierungsrechts geht damit zur Differenzierung hinsichtlich der Rechfertigung.

2. Aushöhlung der Diskriminierungsverbote

Eine weitere Schlussfolgerung hängt mit der oben festgestellten Ausweitung des Diskriminierungsrechts zusammen. Wenn der Anwendungsbereich der Diskriminierungsverbote immer weiter ausgedehnt wird und die untersagten Diskriminierungsgründe ständig vervielfältigt werden, wächst das Bedürfnis, entstehende Härten durch Rechtfertigungsgründe abzumildern. Das gilt etwa für die Benachteiligung aufgrund des Alters, die unter vielen Umständen legitim sein kann.[49] Damit ist eine Grenze für die Erweiterung der Antidiskriminierungsverbote vorgezeichnet: Diese lassen sich nicht unendlich ausweiten, ohne dass sie zugleich in gewisser Weise ihre strikte Durchsetzbarkeit zu verlieren. Der Preis der Ausdehnung des Antidiskriminierungsrechts ist die Vervielfältigung der Rechtfertigungsgründe. Ein generelles Diskriminierungsverbot müsste mit so vielen Möglichkeiten der Rechtfertigung ausgestattet werden, dass es ausgehöhlt würde. Daher wirken sich die Unterschiede zwischen den nationalen Rechtsordnungen hinsichtlich des Anwendungsbereichs der Antidiskriminierungsgesetze[50] in der Praxis viel geringer aus, als die gesetzliche Formulierung vermuten lässt. Die Ausdehnung des Antidiskriminierungsrechts limitiert sich damit in gewisser Weise selbst.

V. Sanktionen

Die Richtlinien zur Antidiskriminierung sprechen sehr allgemein von „Sanktionen", welche die nationalen Rechte im Falle der Verletzung von Diskriminierungsverboten vorsehen müssen. Nur ausnahmsweise werden die Mitgliedstaaten auch dazu verpflichtet, den Opfern von Diskriminierung die Möglichkeit zur Kompensation oder Reparation des bestehenden Schadens zu eröffnen, wie etwa in der Richtlinie 2004/113/EG;[51] anson-

---

[49] Siehe dazu oben unter III 1.
[50] Siehe vor allem oben, unter I 5.
[51] Z.B. Art. 8 II der Richtlinie 2004/113/EG.

sten ist dies in das Ermessen der nationalen Gesetzgeber gestellt. Gemeinsam ist allen Richtlinien nur die Forderung, die Sanktionen sollen „wirksam, verhältnismäßig und abschreckend" sein.[52] Welcher Art die Sanktionen aber sind, ist nicht näher beschrieben.

1. Straf- und verwaltungsrechtliche Sanktionen

Manche Staaten sehen als Rechtsfolge von Verstößen gegen das Diskriminierungsverbot auch strafrechtliche Sanktionen vor. Zum Beispiel enthält der französische *Code pénal* sehr drastische Strafdrohungen. Eine unerlaubte Diskriminierung kann mit Freiheitsstrafe von drei Jahren sowie mit Geldstrafe bis zu 45.000 Euro geahndet werden; ist die Tat in der Öffentlichkeit begangen, sind sogar fünf Jahre Freiheitsstrafe und bis zu 75.000 Euro Geldstrafe möglich.[53] Nach dem spanischen *Código Penal* ist die Verweigerung der Leistung durch einen Unternehmer oder sonstigen gewerblichen Anbieter wegen der Rasse oder der ethnischen Herkunft des Vertragsinteressenten strafbar, wenn dieser ein Recht auf die Leistung hat.[54] Ein Verstoß gegen diese Vorschrift kann unter anderem mit einem befristeten Berufsverbot geahndet werden.[55]

Andere Staaten bevorzugen dagegen verwaltungsrechtliche Mittel, um das Diskriminierungsrecht durchzusetzen. Teilweise sind zu diesem Zweck sogar spezielle Verwaltungseinrichtungen geschaffen worden. In den skandinavischen Staaten wird diese Aufgabe durch einen *Ombudsman* wahrgenommen.[56] Andere Länder ernennen sogenannte Gleichbehandlungsbeauftragte und daneben entsprechende Kommissionen sowie Kontaktpersonen.[57] Die Befugnisse dieser Verwaltungsstellen sind zum Teil sehr umfassend. Ein bemerkenswertes Beispiel ist das zypriotische Recht, nach dem der Gleichstellungsbeauftragte nicht nur Beschwerden hören kann, sondern auch Empfehlungen an die Einrichtung oder das Unternehmen richten darf, gegen welches sich die Beschwerde richtet.[58]

---

[52] Siehe z.B. Art. 15 S. 2 der Richtlinie 2000/43/EG.
[53] Art. 225-2 französischer *Code pénal*.
[54] Art. 510 f. spanischer *Código civil*.
[55] Vgl. *Köhncke*, Vertragsfreiheit in Deutschland und Spanien, 2006, S. 264.
[56] Z.B. ist in Norwegen für Fragen der Geschlechtergleichbehandlung der *likestillingsombudet* zuständig. In Finnland gibt es einen Ombudsman für Minderheiten (*Töihin tai työharjoitteluun*).
[57] Siehe z.B. §§ 21–36 österreichisches Bundes-Gleichbehandlungsgesetz.
[58] Siehe *Europäische Kommission, Generaldirektion Beschäftigung, Soziales und Chancengleichheit*, Rechtsbehelfe und Sanktionen im Antidiskriminierungsrecht der EG, 2005, S. 31.

2. Zivilrechtliche Sanktionen

Auch soweit die Staaten zivilrechtliche Sanktionen vorsehen, sind zum Teil erhebliche Unterschiede zu verzeichnen. Zum Beispiel wird die Höhe der Entschädigung für eine Diskriminierung durchaus unterschiedlich beurteilt. Während beispielsweise das belgische Recht für den Fall der Nichteinstellung eine Entschädigung des Arbeitgebers von sechs Monatsgehältern oder den Ausgleich des reellen Schadens vorsieht,[59] können nach österreichischem Recht höchstens drei Gehälter verlangt werden.[60] Manche Gesetzgeber beweisen hinsichtlich der Sanktionen besonderes viel Einfallsreichtum. Am meisten sticht insoweit das portugiesische Recht hervor, das eine ganze Liste von Folgen der Diskriminierung enthält. Dazu gehört nicht nur, dass der Diskriminierenden den Anspruch auf öffentliche Leistungen verlieren kann, sondern auch, dass er von der Vergabe öffentlicher Aufträge ausgeschlossen werden kann.[61]

Es würde den Rahmen dieses Beitrages sprengen, alle Sanktionen der nationalen Rechte im Detail miteinander zu vergleichen. Fest steht eines: Das Antidiskriminierungsrecht ist ein Beispiel derjenigen Rechtsgebiete, dessen Zwecke sowohl durch zivil-, straf- und verwaltungsrechtliche Sanktionen verwirklicht werden können. Welcher Weg am besten geeignet ist, wird vom nationalen Recht autonom entschieden. Dem Gesetzgeber steht die Wahl der Mittel offen, mit denen er die europäischen Diskriminierungsverbote durchsetzt. In den einzelnen Mitgliedstaaten ist man insoweit verschiedene Wege gegangen. Das Antidiskriminierungsrecht tendiert daher hinsichtlich der Sanktionen zur Diversifizierung.

Das Gemeinschaftsrecht stellt jedoch als Mindestanforderung, dass die Sanktionen wirksam, verhältnismäßig und abschreckend sein müssen. Ob eine rein zivilrechtliche Sanktion, wie sie etwa das deutsche Recht vorsieht, dem genügt, ist nicht sicher. Denn es kann mit guten Gründen bezweifelt werden, ob die Verpflichtung zum Schadensausgleich allein „abschreckend" wirkt, wenn man berücksichtigt, dass sich ihre Bemessung allein am Schaden des Verletzten ausrichtet. Wie der EuGH über diese Frage entscheiden würde, ist offen.

VI. Ausblick

Es ist schwer vorauszusagen, in welcher Richtung sich der Diskriminierungsschutz im Vertragsrecht entwickeln wird. Die vorausgehenden Erörterungen haben aber gewisse Tendenzen sichtbar werden lassen. Zum ei-

---

[59] Artikel 21 § 4 des belgischen Gesetzes (oben Fußn. 27).
[60] § 18 österreichisches Bundes-Gleichbehandlungsgesetz.
[61] Art. 11 I portugiesisches *lei n° 18/2004* vom 11.5.2004.

nen ist ein Hang zur Ausdehnung des Anwendungsbereichs des Antidiskriminierungsrechts erkennbar. Zum anderen ist eine Tendenz zur Ausweitung der verbotenen Differenzierungsmerkmale deutlich geworden. Gleichzeitig wurde gezeigt, dass mit der Verbreiterung des Antidiskriminierungsrechts eine Vervielfältigung und Ausdifferenzierung der Rechtfertigungsgründe einhergeht. Schließlich ist hinsichtlich der Sanktionen die Tendenz zur Diversifizierung auf der Ebene der mitgliedstaatlichen Rechtsordnungen zu Tage getreten. In der Summe kann man daher zur Schlussfolgerung gelangen, dass sich der Diskriminierungsschutz im Vertragsrecht zugleich ausweitet, differenziert und diversifiziert.

Unter diesen Umständen kann man den eingangs dargestellten pauschalen Vorwurf, Diskriminierungsschutz und Vertragsrecht seien miteinander unvereinbar, nicht teilen. Durch zunehmende Spezialisierung passt sich das Antidiskriminierungsrecht vielmehr den Besonderheiten der privatrechtlichen Autonomie immer besser an. Freilich ist man insoweit vor Auswüchsen und Fehlgriffen nicht gefeit. Aber das ist keine eigentliche Besonderheit des Diskriminierungsschutzes. Solchen Fehlentwicklungen lässt sich am besten vorbeugen, indem man eine engagierte wissenschaftliche und politische Diskussion führt, die nicht mit ideologischen Einstellungen vorbelastet ist. Werden diese Vorgaben beachtet, dann besteht kein Grund, dem sich entwickelnden Diskriminierungsschutz im Vertragsrecht pessimistisch gegenüberzustehen.

Das Antidiskriminierungsrecht in der Acquis-Gruppe und die fehlende Umsetzung von Antidiskriminierungsrichtlinien in das polnische Zivilrecht

Fryderyk Zoll (Krakau)

I. Der Entwurf der Acquis-Gruppe zum Antidiskriminierungsrecht

1. Die Methode der Acquis-Gruppe im Bereich des Antidiskriminierungsrechts

Es ist nicht mein Ziel, die gesamte Arbeitsmethode der Acquis-Gruppe darzustellen. Das Konzept der Acquis-Gruppe und die Idee der Sammlung von Prinzipien des geltenden europäischen Vertragsrechts wurde in der Literatur bereits dargestellt.[1] Zusammenfassend kann man hier nur sagen, dass die Acquis-Gruppe eine Art von „Restatement" des Gemeinschaftsprivatrechts vorzubereiten beabsichtigt hat.[2] Der erste Band soll im Frühjahr des nächsten Jahres erscheinen und wird vermutlich auch das Restatement des gemeinschaftlichen Antidiskriminierungsrechts beinhalten. Ganz grob gesagt, versucht die aus mehreren Wissenschaftlern zahlreicher juristischer Fakultäten Europas zusammengesetzte Acquis-Gruppe, aus der Vielzahl von geltenden Normen des europäischen Privatrechts ein kohärentes System des Vertragsrechts zu konstruieren. Solch eine Vorgabe verlangt es, Entscheidungen zu treffen, welche Normen des Gemeinschaftsrechts einen breiten europäischen Konsens über einzelne Institute des Vertragsrechts zum Ausdruck bringen und daher ausreichend generalisierungsfähig sind, um Bausteine eines allgemeinen Vertragsrechts zu

---

[1] Siehe z.B. C. Aubert de Vincelles/J. Rochfeld (red.), *L'Acquis Communautaire. Les sanctions de l'inexécution de contrat*, Paris 2006, S. 4–5.

[2] Die Frage, ob das Werk der Acquis-Gruppe als ein „Restatement" bezeichnet werden kann, habe ich in meinem Aufsatz *CISG und CFR im Bereich der Leistungsstörung* besprochen – ZEuP 1/2007 (im Druck); R. Schulze stellt dagegen die Methode der Acquis-Gruppe (die er als *Acquis-Approach* bezeichnet) als Alternative zur Restatements-Methode dar – R. Schulze, *European Private Law and Existing EC-Law*, European Review of Private Law 1/2005, S. 7.

werden. Der *Acquis Communautaire* ist bekanntlich zersplittert und an vielen Stellen weit von der Vollständigkeit entfernt.[3] Der Bereich des Antidiskriminierungsrechts weist aber im Verhältnis zu den anderen Bereichen des Privatrechts viele Besonderheiten auf. Das Antidiskriminierungsrecht ist im klassischen Zivilrecht eine relativ neue Entwicklung. Es steckt keine entwickelte juristische Tradition dahinter. Die Antidiskriminierungsrichtlinien[4] stellen ein relativ komplettes System dar, wenn auch Einzelfragen (wie z.B. die konkrete Gestaltung der Sanktionen) dem nationalen Gesetzgeber überlassen wurden. Die Antidiskriminierungsrichtlinien werden nach einem relativ einheitlichen Muster gebaut. Es bestehen zwar teilweise unvertretbare Unterschiede, die verwendete Methode ist aber jeweils vergleichbar. Daraus könnte entnommen werden, dass die Aufgabe des „Drafting Team"[5] relativ unkompliziert war. Man musste nur aus den zwei zivilrechtlichen Richtlinien eine einheitliche Regelung entwerfen, welche diese beiden Richtlinien auf einen gemeinsamen Nenner bringen würde. Die Aufgabe war jedoch komplizierter, als es auf den ersten Blick scheint. Die Aufgabe der Acquis-Gruppe beschränkt sich nicht nur auf eine bloße Wiedergabe des Gemeinschaftsrechts. Es geht dabei auch um eine Verbesserung des *Acquis* und eine notwendige Anpassung an das gesamte System der Prinzipien des gelten-

---

[3] E.-M. Kieninger/S. Leible, *Plädoyer für einen „Europäischen wissenschaftlichen Ausschuß für Privatrecht"*, Europäische Zeitschrift für Wirtschaftsrecht 2/1999, S. 37–39.

[4] Bisher wurden fünf Anti-Diskriminierungsrichtlinien erlassen – 2000/43; 2000/78; 2002/73; 2004/113 und 2004/54. Die letzte genannte Richtlinie wird am 15. August 2004 die Richtlinie 2002/73 ersetzen. Vier dieser Richtlinien befassen sich ausschließlich mit den Fragen des Arbeitsrechts. In dieser Bearbeitung werden zwei Richtlinien erfasst, welche das außerarbeitsrechtliche Vertragsrecht betreffen: Richtlinie 2000/43 zur Anwendung des Gleichbehandlungsgrundsatzes ohne Unterschied der Rasse oder der ethnischen Herkunft und die Richtlinie 2004/113 zur Verwirklichung des Grundsatzes der Gleichbehandlung von Männern und Frauen beim Zugang zu und bei der Versorgung mit Gütern und Dienstleistungen. Die Richtlinie 2000/43 umfasst eine ganze Reihe von Rechtsverhältnissen, überwiegend auf dem Gebiet des Arbeitsrechts, Sozialschutzes etc. Sie erfasst aber auch in Art. 3.1. lit. h. den Zugang zu und die Versorgung mit Gütern und Dienstleistungen, die der Öffentlichkeit zur Verfügung stehen, einschließlich dem Wohnraum. Nur dieses letzte Gebiet war für die Arbeiten der Acquis-Gruppe von Relevanz.

[5] Die Mitglieder des Drafting Team der Acquis-Gruppe waren: S. Navas Navarro (Barcelona), S. Leible (Bayreuth), Jerzy Pisuliński (Krakau), Fryderyk Zoll (Krakau).

den Europäischen Vertragsrechts (Acquis-Prinzipien).[6] Das System der Acquis-Gruppe sollte dabei Regeln in einer zur direkten Anwendung geeigneten Form enthalten. Die Antidiskriminierungsrichtlinien bieten den nationalen Gesetzgebern an einigen Stellen nur allgemeine Gebote.[7] Das Drafting Team musste bei solchen Fällen ähnlich vorgehen, wie es bei der Umsetzung von Richtlinien in die nationalen Rechtsordnungen erforderlich ist; dabei sollte die Idee der Richtlinie aber möglichst genau verwirklicht werden.

Das Drafting Team wurde mit der Aufgabe der Anfertigung eines Restatement des Antidiskriminierungsrechts der Gemeinschaft auf dem Gebiet des außerarbeitsrechtlichen Vertragsrechts beauftragt. Die Grundsätze der Acquis-Gruppe sollen sich im gegebenen Stadium auf das Vertragsrecht beschränken. Es besteht die Frage, ob das Antidiskriminierungsrecht mit dieser Vorgabe überhaupt zu vereinbaren ist. Die Funktion des Antidiskriminierungsrechts ist die Bekämpfung von gesellschaftswidrigen Verhaltensweisen. Das ist eine Aufgabe, die traditionell dem Strafrecht angehört. Das Vertragsrecht scheint auf den ersten Augenblick eine relativ ungeeignete Stelle dafür zu sein. Wenn schon eine derartige Regelung in eine zivilrechtliche Systematik aufgenommen werden müsste, würde man auf den ersten Blick eher das Deliktsrecht als geeignetes Rechtsgebiet ansehen. Die Tatsache, dass das Antidiskriminierungsrecht in das vertragsrechtliche System der Acquis-Gruppe aufgenommen wurde, ist vielleicht eher ein Zufall, der auf die genetische Verwandtschaft der Acquis-Grundsätze und des Gemeinsamen Referenzrahmens (CFR) zurückzuführen ist, bei welchen das Antidiskriminierungsrecht auch als ein Teil des Systems vorgesehen wurde.[8]

Es wäre aber übertrieben zu behaupten, dass die Regeln über den Schutz vor der Diskriminierung im System der Acquis-Gruppe einen Fremdkörper bildeten. Die Grundsätze der Acquis-Gruppe beruhen zu großen Teilen auf verbraucherrechtlichen Richtlinien. Das gemeinschaft-

---

[6] Die Grundregeln der Acquis-Gruppe haben bisher keine offizielle Bezeichnung. Ich verwende vorläufig die Bezeichnung „*Principles of Existing European Contract Law – PEECL*". Diese Bezeichnung wurde von R. Schulze vorgeschlagen. Es sieht aber so aus, dass eine andere Bezeichnung gewählt werden wird. Bis dahin verbleibe ich bei den „Grundsätzen des Geltenden Europäischen Vertragsrechts" oder Acquis-Prinzipien.

[7] Das ist vor allem im Fall der Sanktionen der Fall – siehe Art. 15 der Richtlinie 2000/43 und Art. 14 der Richtlinie 2004/113.

[8] Siehe aber K. Riesenhuber, *Diskriminierungsverbote im Europäischem Privatrecht* (in:) S. Leible/M. Schlachter, *Diskriminierungsschutz durch Privatrecht*, Sellier 2006, S. 127, der eine Zuordnung zum Vertragsrecht als gerechtfertigt sieht. Vgl. S. Leible, *Non-Discrimination*, ERA-Forum 2006, Special Issue – European Contract Law, S. 84.

liche Verbraucherrecht erfüllt auch auf dem Gebiet des Vertragsrechts eine Funktion der Erzwingung eines verbraucherfreundlichen Verhaltens der Parteien. Es ist auch eine Aufgabe, welche nach ihrem Zweck über die Grenzen des Vertragsrechts hinausgeht. Das gesamte Gebiet der vorvertraglichen Informationspflichten einschließlich der Sanktionen für ihre Verletzung erfüllt eine allgemeine Ordnungsfunktion. Einer derartigen Ordnungsfunktion dient ebenfalls das Antidiskriminierungsrecht, welches auch zum Ziel hat, bestimmte Verhaltensweisen in der vorvertraglichen und vertraglichen Stufe zu erfüllen.

2. Das Antidiskriminierungsrecht der Gemeinschaft auf dem Gebiet des Vertragsrechts (ohne Berücksichtigung des Arbeitsrechts)

Das Antidiskriminierungsrecht der Gemeinschaft findet seine Grundlage im Primärrecht der Gemeinschaft.[9] Art. 12 des EG-Vertrages verbietet jede Diskriminierung wegen der Staatsangehörigkeit und Art. 13 Abs. 1 EGV enthält eine Kompetenzgrundlage für den Rat für die Anwendung von notwendigen Mitteln, um jede Diskriminierung wegen der Rasse, des Geschlechtes, ethnischer Herkunft, der Religion, der Weltanschauung, der Behinderung und der sexuellen Orientierung zu bekämpfen. Es wurden zwei Richtlinien erlassen, welche das außerarbeitsrechtliche Vertragsrecht betreffen: die Richtlinie 2000/43 vom 29. Juni 2000 zur Anwendung des Gleichbehandlungsgrundsatzes ohne Unterschied der Rasse oder der ethnischen Herkunft (wobei diese Richtlinie einen umfangreicheren Anwendungsbereich hat – in dieser Bearbeitung behandele ich jedoch nur Fragen, die für das außerarbeitsrechtliche Vertragsrecht von Bedeutung sind) und die Richtlinie 2004/113 vom 13. Dezember 2004 zur Verwirklichung des Grundsatzes der Gleichbehandlung von Männern und Frauen beim Zugang zu und bei der Versorgung mit Gütern und Dienstleistungen.[10] Die beiden Richtlinien haben eine vergleichbare Struktur. Es wird unterschieden zwischen einer unmittelbaren und mittelbaren Diskriminierung.[11] Es bestehen Möglichkeiten, eine Ungleichbehandlung zu rechtfertigen, wobei im Fall der Richtlinie 2000/43 solche Möglichkeiten sehr bescheiden sind und praktisch auf bestimmte Fragen der beruflichen

---

[9] Siehe dazu: S. Leible, *Non-Discrimination*, S. 76–78; F. Stork, *Das Anti-Diskriminierungsrecht der Europäischen Union und seine Umsetzung in das deutsche Zivilrecht*, Peter-Lang Verlag, 2006, S. 47 ff.

[10] Für eine Darstellung der beiden Richtlinien siehe: F. Stork, *Das Anti-Diskriminierungsrecht*, S. 102 ff.

[11] Art. 2 Abs. 2 lit. a und b der Richtlinie 2000/43 und Art. 2 lit. a und b der Richtlinie 2004/113.

Tätigkeit eingeschränkt werden.[12] Beide Richtlinien sehen aber vor, dass die positiven Maßnahmen, welche eine Gleichstellung in der Praxis verwirklichen sollen, nicht gegen den Gleichbehandlungsgrundsatz verstoßen.[13] Die beiden Richtlinien erfassen durch den Begriff der Belästigung unerwünschte Verhaltensweisen, welche wegen der Eigenschaft, die eine Diskriminierung begründet, die Würde der Person betreffen (im Falle der Richtlinie 2004/113 fällt darunter auch die sexuelle Belästigung).[14]

Die beiden Richtlinien sehen auch vor, dass die Mitgliedstaaten entsprechende Sanktionen für Zuwiderhandlungen vorsehen. Die konkreten Sanktionen werden nicht genannt[15] – es wird lediglich erwähnt, dass sie auch Schadensersatzleistungen an die Opfer erfassen können. Es wird jedoch klargestellt, dass die Sanktionen wirksam, verhältnismäßig und abschreckend sein müssen.[16]

In beiden Richtlinien ist ferner die gleiche Beweislastregel vorgesehen.[17] Es wird ein *prima facie* Beweis zugelassen, eine Glaubhaftmachung von Tatsachen, welche eine mittelbare oder unmittelbare Diskriminierung vermuten lassen, reicht aus. Die weitgehende Ähnlichkeit der in beiden Richtlinien angewandten Regelungstechniken erlaubt eine weitgehende Vereinigung der beiden Regelungswerke, was im Entwurf der Acquis-Gruppe auch unternommen wurde.[18]

3. Die Struktur des Entwurfes der Acquis-Gruppe über den Schutz vor der Diskriminierung

Der Entwurf der Acquis-Gruppe bezüglich der Diskriminierung enthält momentan drei separate Abschnitte.[19] Der erste Abschnitt enthält ein allgemein formuliertes Verbot der Diskriminierung. Dieses Verbot sollte

---

[12] Art. 4 der Richtlinie 2000/43 (Minderung des Verbotes der Ungleichbehandlung im Fall der Beschäftigung); Art. 4 lit. 5, Art. 5 Abs. 2 der Richtlinie 2004/113 (im Falle von Versicherungsverträgen).
[13] Art. 5 der Richtlinie 2000/43; Art. 6 der Richtlinie 2004/113.
[14] Art. 2 Abs. 3 der Richtlinie 2000/43; Art. 4 Abs. 3 der Richtlinie 2004/113.
[15] Siehe dazu: S. Leible, *Non-Discrimination*, S. 84.
[16] Art. 15 der Richtlinie 2000/43; Art. 14 der Richtlinie 2004/113.
[17] Art. 8 Abs. 1 der Richtlinie 2000/43; Art. 9 Abs. 1 der Richtlinie 2004/113.
[18] Auch andere Antidiskriminierungsrichtlinien, welche außerhalb dieser Studie liegen, haben eine vergleichbare Struktur. Zur Frage der Übertragbarkeit der arbeitsrechtlichen Erfahrungen auf dieser Ebene siehe: S. Krebber, *Die arbeitsrechtlichen Diskriminierungsverbote als Regelungsvorbild* (in:) S. Leible/M. Schlachter, *Diskriminierungsschutz durch Privatrecht*, Sellier 2006, S. 93 ff.
[19] Eine frühere Fassung des Entwurfes wurde von S. Leible vorgestellt – S. Leible, *Non-Discrimination*, S. 88 ff.

in eine Liste von Grundsätzen des gemeinschaftlichen Vertragsrechts aufgenommen werden. Es ist aber noch nicht entschieden, ob das generelle Diskriminierungsverbot endgültig an dieser Stelle bleibt, oder doch in die Kategorie von Regeln (*rules*) zu verschieben ist.[20] Dann würde das Diskriminierungsverbot als eine Art Generalklausel fungieren. Der Grundsatz lautet: „Jede Diskriminierung wegen des Geschlechtes, der Rasse oder der ethnischen Herkunft ist untersagt". Der Entwurf hat das Diskriminierungsverbot eng gefasst.[21] Man hat sich nur auf die Eigenschaften beschränkt, die im Wortlaut der beiden Richtlinien, welche das außerarbeitsrechtliche Vertragsrecht betreffen, die unerlaubte Diskriminierung begründen. Dies hat einen einfachen Grund. Der Entwurf der Acquis-Gruppe ist als ein Restatement zu betrachten, was dazu verpflichtet, rein politische Entscheidungen – soweit möglich – nicht zu treffen. Die Erweiterung eines solchen Katalogs wäre eine rein politische Entscheidung. Art. 13 Abs. 1 des EG-Vertrages enthält zwar eine Grundlage für eine Rechtsetzung, die auch andere Gründe erfasst, der europäische Rechtsetzer hat davon im Bereich des außervertraglichen Vertragsrechts jedoch keinen Gebrauch gemacht. Dazu sollte man ihn in diesem Bereich vielleicht auch nicht voreilig bewegen, weil die zivilrechtlichen Instrumente für solche Zwecke nicht am besten geeignet zu sein scheinen.[22] Dazu komme ich noch später.

Im zweiten Abschnitt befinden sich die Definitionen der Diskriminierung. Diese Definitionen finden naturgemäß ihren Ursprung in den Richtlinien und versuchen, die beiden Texte zu vereinheitlichen. Der Entwurf verzichtet aber auf die Verwendung der Begriffe der „direkten" und „indirekten Diskriminierung". Die Definition der Diskriminierung erfasst jedoch in ihrem Kern zwei Tatbestände – die Ungleichbehandlung einer Person im Verhältnis zur Behandlung (oder vermutlichen Behandlung) einer anderen Person in einer vergleichbaren Lage, aber auch die Anwendung einer scheinbar neutralen Vorschrift, eines Kriteriums oder eines Verfahrens, wodurch eine Person auf Grund der bestimmten Eigenschaft (welche die Diskriminierung veranlasst) einen Nachteil im Vergleich zu einer anderen Person erleidet. Das entspricht zwar der Unter-

---

[20] In der ersten Veröffentlichung der Acquis-Prinzipien, welche im Frühjahr 2007 auf den Markt kommen sollen, hat das Redaction Committee der Acquis-Gruppe beschlossen, diesen Grundsatz vorläufig als eine *rule* zu verorten. Das wird vielleicht noch den Inhalt der Antidiskriminierungsregeln der Acquis-Gruppe beeinflussen müssen, was aber bei der endgültigen Fassung des gesamten Projekts berücksichtigt werden kann.
[21] Siehe dazu: S. Leible, *Non-Discrimination*, S. 81–82.
[22] Über Pläne der weiteren Ausdehnung des Diskriminierungsverbotes durch die Kommission siehe: F. Stork, *Das Anti-Diskriminierungsrecht der Europäischen Union*, S. 36 f.

scheidung nach der mittelbaren und unmittelbaren Diskriminierung, ein Verzicht auf die Verwendung der begrifflichen Unterscheidung hat aber seine Folgen. Die beiden Arten der Diskriminierung werden dadurch gleichgestellt. Dies ergibt sich aus einer Überzeugung, dass aus der Perspektive des Zivilrechts die indirekte Diskriminierung als eine Umgehung der direkten Diskriminierung betrachtet wird. Es bestehen dann keine Gründe dafür, unterschiedliche Rechtsfolgen an die direkte und indirekte Diskriminierung zu knüpfen. Das spielt vor allem bei der Möglichkeit der Legitimierung einer Ungleichbehandlung einer Person wegen einer eine Diskriminierung begründenden Eigenschaft eine Rolle. Der Entwurf sieht im Abschnitt, der die Definitionen enthält, auch eine Regel vor, die besagt, dass eine Ungleichbehandlung, die durch einen legitimierten Zweck gerechtfertigt ist, nicht als Diskriminierung zu qualifizieren ist, dies gilt jedoch nur dann, wenn die angewandten Mittel für die Erreichung des Zweckes notwendig und verhältnismäßig sind. Diese Möglichkeit der Rechtfertigung einer Ungleichbehandlung ist dann nach dem Wortlaut des Entwurfes für die mittelbare und unmittelbare Ungleichbehandlung in gleicher Weise möglich. In den Richtlinien ist die Technik der Rechtfertigung der Ungleichbehandlung etwas anders konstruiert. Beide Richtlinien verwenden bei der Definition der mittelbaren Diskriminierung eine zusätzliche Wertung. Die Verwendung von scheinbar neutralen Kriterien, Vorschriften oder Verfahren, die aufgrund einer der genannten Eigenschaften benachteiligend wirken, erwächst nur dann nicht zu einer Diskriminierung, wenn diese Kriterien, Vorschriften oder Verfahren durch ein rechtmäßiges Ziel sachlich gerechtfertigt und die Mittel zur Erreichung dieses Ziels angemessen und erforderlich sind. Zugleich gelten auch für die mittelbare Diskriminierung die allgemeinen Legitimierungsmöglichkeiten einer Ungleichbehandlung (Art. 4 und 5 der Richtlinie 2000/43 und Art. 4 Abs. 5 der Richtlinie 2004/113). Eine derartige Notwendigkeit der Doppelwertung mag zwar zu ganz feinen theoretischen Differenzierungen führen,[23] ist aber wenig praktikabel. Solch eine Wertung muss sowieso in einem Denkvorgang durchgeführt werden – kann eine Ungleichbehandlung durch einen höheren Zweck als zulässig betrachtet werden? Ein Doppelvorgang bei der mittelbaren Diskriminierung ist eine komplizierte Ausdrucksweise eines simplen Gedankens – bei der mittelbaren Diskriminierung sollte es einfacher sein, eine Ungleichbehandlung als begründet einzustufen. Im Fall der Ungleichbehandlung wegen der ethnischen Herkunft oder der Rasse ist die Legitimierung der Ungleichbehandlung stark eingeschränkt. Die rechtfertigenden Wertungsmöglichkeiten im Fall der mittelbaren Diskriminierung wegen der Rasse oder ethnischen Herkunft sollen nur im Rahmen von Art. 4 bzw. 5 der Richtlinie möglich sein. Im Entwurf der Acquis-Gruppe ist die Formulie-

---

[23] Siehe z.B. K. Riesenhuber, *Diskriminierungsverbote*, S. 133.

rung zwar auf den ersten Blick abstrakter und weniger ausdifferenziert. Das führt aber grundsätzlich zu keinen anderen Ergebnissen, obwohl es ein bisschen mehr Spielraum für die Durchführung von Wertungen lässt. Jedoch müssen auch bei der abstrakten Formulierung des Entwurfes die Rechtfertigungsmöglichkeiten im Fall der Ungleichbehandlung aus Gründen der Rasse und der ethnischen Herkunft auf Grund der historischen Erfahrungen Europas extrem eng verstanden werden – im Bereich der Versorgung mit Gütern und Dienstleistungen kann man sich eine Rechtfertigung einer derartigen Ungleichbehandlung kaum vorstellen.

Der Entwurf erweitert, den Richtlinien getreu, den Begriff der Diskriminierung auf die Belästigung und die sexuelle Belästigung.[24] Hiermit entfernt sich der Entwurf von den ordentlichen vertragsrechtlichen Instrumentarien. Man kann sich aber auch im Anwendungsbereich des Entwurfes, vor allem bei Dauerschuldverhältnissen, solche Verhaltensweisen vorstellen. Sie können beispielsweise im vorvertraglichen Stadium vorkommen. Dies eröffnet den Weg für die Anwendung von Rechtsbehelfen, z.B. eine vorzeitige Kündigung des Mietvertrages durch den Mieter und Schadensersatz. Im Fall des Tatbestandes der Belästigung ist aber die deliktische Funktion dieser Regelungen besonders offenkundig.

Umso mehr spiegelt sich die deliktische Funktion des Antidiskriminierungsrechts in der ebenfalls richtliniengetreuen Erfassung der Anstiftung (bzw. Anweisung) zur Diskriminierung wider, die ebenfalls als ein selbständiger Diskriminierungstatbestand qualifiziert wird. Da ein solcher Tatbestand ein Teil des vertragsrechtlichen Entwurfes wird, ist er dem Gebot der Kohärenz unterworfen. Bei der gesamten Regelung ist die Linie zwischen dem Vertrags- und Deliktsrecht unscharf.

Die Definitionen verweisen nicht auf die Gründe der Diskriminierung. Die Definition ist geeignet, alle Arten der Diskriminierung zu erfassen. Die Beschränkung durch die Erwähnung der Gründe der Diskriminierung ergibt sich bloß aus dem genannten Hauptgrundsatz. Die Gründe der Diskriminierung werden auch in den Regeln erwähnt, die die Rechtsbehelfe und Sanktionen der Diskriminierung bestimmen. Eine derartige Konstruktion wurde aus Praktikabilitätsgründen angenommen. Falls neue Richtlinien erlassen werden, würde das keinen Einfluss auf die Struktur der Definition haben. Die Änderungen der anderen Vorschriften wären in dieser Hinsicht einfacher vorzunehmen. Die gewählte Lösung hat aber auch eine andere mögliche Folge. Sie schließt nicht aus, dass die Diskriminierungen aus anderen Gründen (z.B. der Religion oder der sexuellen Orientierung) die Merkmale der Leistungsstörung erfüllen oder eine Verletzung bestimmter vorvertraglicher Pflichten begründen können.

Der dritte Abschnitt enthält die Regelung von Rechtsbehelfen und die Fragen der Beweislast. Die Materie ist auf drei Artikel verteilt. Der erste

---

[24] Siehe dazu auch S. Leible, *Non-Discrimination*, S. 83 ff.

bestimmt, welche Rechtsbehelfe überhaupt zur Verfügung stehen, im zweiten wird ihr Inhalt bestimmt. Der dritte ist ausschließlich der Frage der Beweislast gewidmet. Als grundsätzliches Rechtsmittel wird vom Entwurf der Schadensersatz (*compensation*) vorgesehen, der sowohl materielle als auch immaterielle Schäden erfasst.[25] Der Entwurf bestimmt aber, dass die diskriminierte Person von allen möglichen Rechtsbehelfen Gebrauch machen kann, wenn dies verhältnismäßig ist und diese Rechtsbehelfe dazu geeignet sind, die Folgen einer Diskriminierung zu beseitigen oder eine weitere Diskriminierung zu verhindern. Der Entwurf bestimmt ferner, dass neben dem Grundsatz der Verhältnismäßigkeit in Bezug auf die erlittene Verletzung auch die abschreckende Funktion solcher Rechtsmittel berücksichtigt werden soll. Die beiden Richtlinien verlangen, dass die Sanktionen für die Diskriminierung abschreckend wirken sollen. Der Entwurf erwähnt im Fall von Schadensersatz für Vermögensschäden diese Funktion nicht. In diesem Fall soll die Höhe des Schadensersatzes der Höhe des erlittenen Schadens entsprechen. Für einen Abschreckungseffekt gibt es hier keinen Raum.[26]

In der gesamten Acquis-Gruppe war es umstritten, ob ein offener Katalog von Rechtsbehelfen gegen die Diskriminierung eine begrüßenswerte Lösung sein kann. Es wurde in der Diskussion auf die Missbrauchsgefahr hingewiesen. Die Richtlinien geben hier keinen eindeutigen Hinweis darauf, wie die Rechtsbehelfe im Einzelnen ausgestaltet werden sollen.[27] Jeder Katalog von Rechtsbehelfen bzw. Sanktionen würde dann die Grenze des Restatements überschreiten, da er nur das Ergebnis der „freien Schöpfung" sein müsste. Es gibt aber auch sachliche Gründe für eine derartige Entscheidung. Die Diskriminierung kann ganz unterschiedlichen Formen annehmen und das vertragliche oder vorvertragliche Verhältnis ganz unterschiedlich beeinflussen. Es kann daher kaum vorhergesehen werden, welche Sanktionen oder Rechtsbehelfe tatsächlich die Folgen der Diskriminierung beseitigen können. Der Entwurf sieht jedoch eine Hierarchie von Rechtsbehelfen vor. Der Schadensersatz (für den materiellen sowie immateriellen Schaden) gilt als das grundsätzliche Rechtsmittel. Die anderen Rechtsmittel stehen der Partei nur dann zu, wenn dies angemessen ist (*if appropriate*). Das heißt, dass sie nur dann angewendet werden sollen, wenn ein Schadensersatz die Folgen der Diskriminierung nicht beseitigen kann und zugleich keine präventive Wirkung entfaltet. Diese Funktionen bestimmen überdies die Schranken für die Auswahl des zustehenden Behelfes.

---

[25] S. Leible, *Non-Disrimination*, S. 85.
[26] So auch S. Leible, *Non-Discrimination*, S. 85.
[27] K. Riesenhuber betont aber überzeugend, dass die Sanktion des Schadensersatzes nach dem Gemeinschaftsrecht verpflichtend ist – K. Riesenhuber, *Diskriminierungsverbote*, S. 135.

Der Entwurf regelt, ebenso wie die Richtlinien, die Frage der Beweislast. Nach der gemeinschaftsrechtlichen Vorgabe führt er einen *prima facie* Beweis ein. Nach dem Wortlaut dieser Vorschrift reicht es aus, dass die Person, welche behauptet, diskriminiert worden zu sein, die Tatsachen begründet, welche es erlauben, eine Diskriminierung zu vermuten, um eine Diskriminierung anzunehmen, es sei denn, dass der potentielle Täter das Gegenteil beweist. Es ist aber mehr als nur eine Vorschrift, die sog. faktische Vermutungen regelt. Dadurch sollte eine weitgehende Erleichterung der Beweisführung zum Ausdruck gebracht werden. Es sollte ausreichen, dass die betroffene Partei glaubhaft macht, dass Umstände gegeben sind, welche erfahrungsgemäß in den gegebenen gesellschaftlichen Verhältnissen zu einer Diskriminierung führen können.[28] Das kann z.B. der Fall sein, wenn der Abschluss des Mietvertrages dem Vertreter einer ethnischen Minderheit verweigert wird, und es allgemein bekannt ist, dass in der Gesellschaft die Vertreter dieser Gruppe benachteiligt werden, es sei denn, dass der potentielle Vermieter beweisen kann, dass andere Gründe als die ethnische Herkunft hier entscheidend waren.

4. Die Einbindung des Entwurfs in das System des Vertragsrechtes der Acquis-Gruppe

Der Entwurf der Acquis-Gruppe über die Diskriminierung ist relativ autonom. Er bildet ein kleines System für sich selbst. Dies ist deswegen verständlich, da das Diskriminierungsrecht – wie bereits erwähnt – ganz stark durch die deliktsrechtlichen Elemente geprägt wird. Aus diesen Gründen bilden die Vorschriften über die Diskriminierung eine volle normative Regelung. Der Entwurf bestimmt selbständig den Tatbestand der Diskriminierung und ihre Sanktionen. Für die Anwendung seiner Regeln ist es

---

[28] Im Ergebnis gibt es, wie ich glaube, keinen Unterschied zwischen meinem Verständnis der Beweislastregeln und der Auffassung von F. Stork, der eine Annahme des *prima facie Beweises* hier als unausreichend ansieht – *Das Anti-Diskriminierungsrecht*, S. 240. Es handelt sich vielleicht um durch unterschiedliche Rechtstraditionen geprägte diverse Verständnisse der Formulierung *prima facie* Beweis. Ich bin aber der Meinung, dass die Richtlinien keine Beweislastumkehr anordnen. Siehe auch die Formulierung in der englischen Sprache der entsprechenden Motive zu den Richtlinien (Nr. 21 der Richtlinie 2000/43; Nr. 22 der Richtlinie 2004/113), wo die Formulierung des „*prima facie* case" verwendet wird. Siehe auch die von M. Schmidt-Kessel zitierte Entscheidung des englischen *Court of Appeal* in der Sache Karen Lily King v. Great-Britain-China Center (1992), I.C.R. 516 – M. Schmidt-Kessel, *Fremde Erfahrungen mit zivilrechtlichen Diskriminierungsverboten* (in:) S. Leible/M. Schlachter, *Diskriminierungsschutz durch Privatrecht*, Sellier 2006, S 69.

nicht nötig, sich mit anderen Teilen der gesamten Acquis-Prinzipien zu befassen. Die einzige Ausnahme betrifft vielleicht die Regeln, die den Umfang des Schadens bestimmen. Abgesehen davon sind alle Voraussetzungen der Haftung für eine Diskriminierung bereits dem Antidiskriminierungsentwurf zu entnehmen. Dies schließt aber nicht aus, dass eine diskriminierende Handlung allein aus der Perspektive des Diskriminierungsentwurfs zu beurteilen ist. Sie kann z.B. auch die Voraussetzungen einer Leistungsstörung erfüllen (oder Verletzung vorvertraglicher Pflichten). In den meisten Fällen ist aber diese zusätzliche Bestimmung unnötig, da der Entwurf durch seinen offenen Katalog der Sanktionen auch diese Sanktionen der Leistungsstörung bzw. der Verletzung vorvertraglicher Pflichten erfasst. Sie kann aber dann von Bedeutung sein, wenn es sich um die anderen Gründe der Diskriminierung nach Art. 12 oder Art. 13 Abs. 1 des EG-Vertrages handelt. Solche Arten der Diskriminierung können durch die allgemeinen Rechtsbehelfe der Leistungsstörung sanktioniert werden. Im Falle der Diskriminierung wegen der Staatsangehörigkeit kann es auch zu einer direkten Anwendung des Art. 12 des EG-Vertrages kommen, wobei sich die Sanktionen allerdings aus dem Leistungsstörungsrecht ergeben müssen.

5. Die Rolle des Entwurfes

Der Entwurf des Antidiskriminierungsrechts der Acquis-Gruppe bildet einen Teil des gesamten Systems der Acquis-Prinzipien. Er sollte auch in den Gemeinsamen Referenzrahmen (CFR) als Beitrag der Acquis-Gruppe in dieses Projekt aufgenommen werden. Dadurch wird eine Synthese der zwei Richtlinien vorgestellt, die vielleicht einen bescheidenen Vorschlag der Rechtsvereinheitlichung in Europa darstellt. Der Entwurf soll jetzt mit dem Band I der Acquis-Prinzipien veröffentlicht werden und dann dem wissenschaftlichen Diskurs zur Verfügung stehen. Er gibt aber nicht nur Anlass zu einer Diskussion von Vor- und Nachteilen einer solchen Regelung, sondern erlaubt überdies, erneut zur Diskussion zu stellen, ob privatrechtliche Mittel tatsächlich für die Bekämpfung der Diskriminierung geeignet sind.

II. Das Antidiskriminierungsrecht in Polen

1. Das Schweigen des polnischen Gesetzgebers im Bereich der Umsetzung des Antidiskriminierungsrechts im außerarbeitsrechtlichen Vertragsrecht

Obwohl die Frist für die Umsetzung der Richtlinie 2000/113 bereits abgelaufen ist[29] und für die Umsetzung der Richtlinie 2004/43 bald abläuft,[30] hat es der polnische Gesetzgeber bisher unterlassen, die beiden Richtlinien im Bereich des außerarbeitsrechtlichen Vertragsrechts in das polnische Recht umzusetzen. Im Arbeitsrecht wurden dagegen die arbeitsrechtlichen Antidiskriminierungsrichtlinien umgesetzt (Art. 1813a-Art. 1813e des Arbeitsgesetzbuches). Das Fehlen der Umsetzung des Antidiskriminierungsgemeinschaftsrechts in das polnische Zivilrecht eröffnet zahlreiche Fragen, die die europarechtliche Verantwortung Polens für die Unterlassung einer Umsetzung der Richtlinie in diesem Bereich und eine eventuelle Staatshaftung betreffen. Diese Fragen werden in dieser Bearbeitung jedoch nicht erörtert. Für die hiesige Analyse bleibt die Fragestellung, wie man mangels Umsetzung das geltende Recht richtlinienkonform anwenden soll und wie die Richtlinien am besten umgesetzt werden sollten, um die bestehende Struktur des Zivilrechts am wenigsten zu verletzen.

Die Gründe für das Schweigen des polnischen Gesetzgebers in diesem Bereich sind eher unklar. Abgesehen von vereinzelten Pressemeldungen und einem Vortrag, der noch nicht veröffentlicht wurde, wurde dieses Thema unter den polnischen Zivilrechtlern gar nicht diskutiert.[31] Dass

---

[29] Die Umsetzungsfrist der Richtlinie 2000/43 ist am 19. Juli 2003 abgelaufen (Art. 16).

[30] Die Richtlinie 2004/113 soll bis zum 21. Dezember 2007 umgesetzt werden (Art. 17 Abs. 1).

[31] Auf der Tagung der zivilrechtlichen Lehrstühle Polens im September 2006 in Wisła wurden die Antidiskriminierungsrichtlinien von R. Trzaskowski auf dem Gebiet des Zivilrechts vorgestellt. Eine entsprechende Veröffentlichung des Tagungsbandes befindet sich im Druck. In der arbeitsrechtlichen Literatur ist die Lage etwas besser. Siehe z.B. I. Boruta, *Zakaz dyskryminacji w zatrudnieniu. Nowa regulacja prawna* (*Diskriminierungsverbot bei der Beschäftigung. Neue rechtliche Regelung*), Praca i Zabezpieczenia Społeczne, 2/2004, S. 2 ff.; J. Król, *Nowelizacja Kodeksu pracy dotycz¹ca równego traktowania w zatrudnieniu na tle regulacji wspólnotowych* (*Eine Novelle des Arbeitsgesetzbuches betreffend der Gleichbehandlung bei der Beschäftigung auf dem Hintergrund des Gemeinschaftsrechts*), Radca Prawny 4/2004, S. 94 ff.; T. Liszcz, *Równoœæ kobiet i mê¿czyzn w znowelizowanym kodeksie pracy* (*Gleichheit von Frauen und Männern im novellierten Arbeitsgesetzbuch*), Praca i Zabezpieczenia Społeczne, 2/2002, S. 2 ff.; P. Czarnecki, *Rozk³ad*

ein Bedarf bestünde, auch das klassische Vertragsrecht an das Antidiskriminierungsrecht der Gemeinschaft anzupassen, war bisher nicht bewusst geworden. Der Grund dafür steckt zum Teil noch im zu geringeren Interesse der Wissenschaft an der europäischen Rechtsentwicklung. Hier ändert sich die Lage aber glücklicherweise ganz entscheidend und hoffentlich wird das europäische Privatrecht bald auch in Polen zu einem der wichtigeren Untersuchungsfelder werden. Man kann das Schweigen der privatrechtlichen Lehre in diesem Bereich aber auch dadurch erklären, dass man einfach nicht damit gerechnet hat, dass die Antidiskriminierungsrichtlinien das klassische Zivilrecht überhaupt betreffen könnten. Man kann auch sagen, dass das vielleicht (zwar eher unbewusst) keine falsche Einstellung ist. Vielleicht ist der zivilrechtliche Weg der Umsetzung dieser Richtlinien nicht die richtige Lösung. Vielleicht sollte diese Aufgabe eher den Strafrechtlern anvertraut werden. Dazu komme ich noch am Ende meiner Ausführungen.

2. Die richtlinienkonforme Auslegung der Vorschriften des polnischen Zivilgesetzbuches

Obwohl auf dem Gebiet des Zivilrechts keine Umsetzung der Antidiskriminierungsrichtlinien stattgefunden hat, liefert das polnische Zivilgesetzbuch genügend Spielraum, um mittels einer gemeinschaftsrechtskonformen Auslegung die Ziele der Richtlinien auf dem Gebiet des Zivilrechts zu erreichen. Dem polnischen Zivilgesetzbuch aus dem Jahre 1964 war ein Antidiskriminierungsgedanke von vornherein nicht fremd. Art. 543 ZGB bestimmt, dass eine öffentliche Zurschaustellung einer Sache am Verkaufsort unter Angabe des Preises als Verkaufangebot gilt. Dahinter steht der Grundgedanke, dass für den Verkäufer die Möglichkeit der Auswahl seiner Kunden einschränkt wird. Der Verkäufer ist durch das öffentliche Recht gezwungen, die Sachen samt dem Preis auszustellen,[32] und das führt automatisch zu einer Offerte. Jeder kann dieses Angebot annehmen, selbst wenn der Verkäufer diese Person aus unterschiedlichen Gründen (z.B. der Rasse, ethnischer Herkunft oder auch anderen Eigenschaften) nicht mag und sich normalerweise weigern würde, mit solch einer Person einen Vertrag abzuschließen.[33] Diese Vorschrift reicht sicherlich nicht

---

ciężaru dowodu w sprawach na tle dyskryminacji (*Beweislast in den Diskriminierungssachen*), Praca i Zabezpieczenia Społeczne, 3/2006, S. 11 ff.
[32] Siehe Art. 12 Abs. des Gesetzes vom 5. Juli 2001 über Preise (o cenach).
[33] Die antidiskriminierende Funktion dieser Vorschrift wird durch die abdingbare Natur dieser Vorschrift eingeschränkt. Zu dem nicht zwingenden Status dieser Vorschrift siehe J. Jezioro (in:) E. Gniewek, *Kodeks cywilny. Komentarz* (*Zivilgesetzbuch. Kommentar*). C.H. Beck 2006, S. 935, Rn 4.

aus, um die Vorgaben der Richtlinien zu erfüllen. Sie kann aber auch eine Funktion erfüllen, die von diesen Richtlinien beabsichtigt ist. Eine Grundlage für die weitere Berücksichtigung von Antidiskriminierungsrichtlinien liefern die Vorschriften von Art. 23–24 und Art. 415 und 448 ZGB. Art. 415 ZGB ist eine nach dem französischen Modell konstruierte deliktische Generalklausel (wer einem anderen schuldhaft einen Schaden zugefügt hat, ist zum Schadensersatz verpflichtet). Art. 23 ZGB stellt die persönlichen Güter der Menschen unter Schutz. Diese Vorschrift nennt beispielhaft einige dieser Güter, wie Gesundheit; Freiheit; Ehre; Gewissensfreiheit; Name; Pseudonym; Recht am eigenen Bild; Briefgeheimnis; Unverletzlichkeit der Wohnung, wissenschaftliche, künstlerische, erfinderische Schöpfung etc. Wie gesagt, ist dieser Katalog aber offen und auch andere Güter können davon erfasst werden.[34] Art. 24 ZGB regelt die Folgen der Verletzung der geschützten persönlichen Güter. Nach dieser Vorschrift kann jeder, dessen persönliches Gut durch eine fremde Handlung bedroht wird, eine Unterlassung dieser Handlung verlangen, es sei denn, dass keine Rechtswidrigkeit gegeben ist. Wenn eine Verletzung bereits stattgefunden hat, kann der Verletzte eine Handlung verlangen, die die Folgen der Verletzung beseitigt. Art. 448 ZGB ist eine Grundlage für Schmerzensgeld im Fall der Verletzung eines persönlichen Guts.

Es stellt sich die Frage, ob eine Diskriminierung als Verletzung eines persönlichen Guts im Sinne von Art. 23 ZGB verstanden werden kann. Stellt jede nach dem Gemeinschaftsrecht unerlaubte Diskriminierung zugleich eine Verletzung eines persönlichen Guts dar oder muss durch die Diskriminierung ein anderes Gut, wie z.B. die Ehre, verletzt werden? Eine gemeinschaftskonforme Auslegung[35] soll zur Bejahung der Frage führen, ob jede Diskriminierung wegen des Geschlechts, der Rasse und der ethnischen Herkunft zugleich eine Verletzung des persönlichen Guts bedeute.[36] Eine derartige Auslegung des Art. 23 ZGB führt zu einer Ausformulierung des „negativen" persönlichen Guts, das darin besteht, beim Abschluss, bei der Ausführung und bei der Beendigung von Verträgen nicht aus diesen Gründen diskriminiert zu werden. Ein derartiges „negatives" Gut ist mit anderen durch Art. 23 ZGB geschützten Gütern verwandt. Durch die Diskriminierung nutzt man eine persönliche Eigenschaft der Person, um sie in der Gesellschaft schlechter zu stellen. Die Auswahl einer derartigen

---

[34] Siehe dazu: A. Cisek (in:) E. Gniewek, *Kodeks cywilny. Komentarz* (*Zivilgesetzbuch. Kommentar*). C.H. Beck 2006, S. 56, Fn. 1.

[35] Zur gemeinschaftsrechtskonformen Auslegung des Rechts im Diskriminierungsbereich siehe: R. Streinz, *Verwirklichung des Gleichbehandlungsgrundsatzes* (in:) S. Leible/M. Schlachter, *Diskriminierungsschutz durch Privatrecht*, Sellier 2006, S. 32 f.

[36] Zur Diskriminierung als Verletzung des Persönlichkeitsrechts siehe: F.J. Säcker, *Vertragsfreiheit und Schutz vor Diskriminierung*, ZEuP 1/2006, S. 4.

Eigenschaft ist durch die Richtlinien und auch die Werte, welche man unterstützen oder in der Gesellschaft etablieren möchte, als unzulässig anzusehen. Das Recht sollte hier die Entwicklung der bestimmten Ethik unterstützen, wonach eine Diskriminierung wegen derartigen Eigenschaften *ipso facto* als Verletzung der menschlichen Würde zu qualifizieren ist. Eine Erfassung dieser „negativen Güter" von Art. 23 ZGB ist konform mit dem Geist der Antidiskriminierungsrichtlinien. Falls diese Prämisse stimmt, würde die Anwendung des polnischen Rechts trotz der fehlenden (und weiterhin nach dem Gemeinschaftsrecht erforderlichen Umsetzung) zu denjenigen Ergebnissen führen, welche von den Richtlinien postuliert werden. Art. 24 ZGB enthält einen offenen Katalog an Sanktionen, welche entsprechend der Art der Verletzung und dem Bedürfnis der Beseitigung entsprechen können. Durch Art. 448 ZGB kann dann auch ein Schmerzensgeld zugesprochen werden. Nach Art. 415 ZGB kann der Täter ferner zum Schadensersatz verpflichtet werden, falls Schäden entstehen. In den beiden letzten Fällen wäre es erforderlich, ein Verschulden nachzuweisen, was aber normalerweise allein im Tatbestand der Diskriminierung enthalten ist. Da alle diese Vorschriften Generalklauseln enthalten, hat das Gericht viel Spielraum, die nicht direkt ausgesprochenen Inhalte der Richtlinien dort zu hineinzulesen. Die Natur der Generalklausel erlaubt auch eine Rechtfertigung der Ungleichbehandlung, wenn diese der Erreichung legitimer Zwecke dient und dafür notwendig ist. Die unterschiedlichen Maßstäbe der Richtlinien können im Rahmen der gemeinschaftskonformen Auslegung entsprechend berücksichtigt werden.

Eine derartige Auslegung führt aber zur Frage, ob schon dadurch im Rahmen des internen polnischen Rechts alle Arten der Diskriminierung, die in Art. 12 und 13 Abs. 1 des EG-Vertrages genannt sind, unter Art. 23 ZGB fallen. Das ist zumindest keine notwendige Schlussfolgerung. Die Frage hängt vom Ergebnis der gemeinschaftskonformen Auslegung ab. Das „negative" persönliche Gut, nicht diskriminiert zu werden, kann als solches bei der heutigen Rechtslage nur in Verbindung mit dem Gemeinschaftsrecht erschaffen werden. Das Gemeinschaftsrecht liefert hier eine erforderliche Wertung, welche es erlaubt, ein derartiges „Gut" unter den Schutz des Rechts zu stellen, wenn durch die Diskriminierung aus einem anderen Grund keine anderen schützenswerten Güter wie die Menschenwürde, die Ehre, die Privatsphäre etc. verletzt werden. Die Verwendung einer Generalklausel kann nicht zu einer völlig freien Einschränkung der Privatautonomie führen. Die unscharfen Konturen der Generalklausel brauchen eine stärkere Unterstützung, als nur die bloße ethische Wertung, dass eine Diskriminierung als moralisch „schlecht" zu beurteilen ist. Das Gemeinschaftsrecht liefert hier zusätzlich eine rechtliche Stütze, durch sich welche mittels einer gemeinschaftskonformen Auslegung die Generalklausel konkretisieren lässt. Da der europäische Rechtsetzer die anderen Gründe der Diskriminierung nach Art. 13 des EG-

Vertrages in dem hier relevanten Rechtsbereich bisher nicht durch Akte des Sekundärrechts verboten hat, reichen sie allein nicht aus, um unter Art. 23 ZGB subsumiert werden zu können.[37] Die Frage der Diskriminierung wegen der Staatsangehörigkeit nach Art. 12 des EG-Vertrages ist mit dem Problem verbunden, ob diese Vorschrift horizontal direkte Anwendung finden kann.[38] Die Bedeutung dieser Frage ist im Bereich der der Versorgung mit Gütern und Dienstleistungen dienenden Verträge aber marginal, und in praktischen Fällen würde dies zugleich eine Diskriminierung wegen der ethnischen Herkunft bedeuten.

3. Eine Variante der Umsetzung der Antidiskriminierungsrichtlinien ins polnische Zivilrecht

Bisher wurde der Öffentlichkeit kein Entwurf für die Umsetzung vorgelegt, und es sind bisher auch keine privaten Vorschläge zur Diskussion gestellt worden. Deswegen kann ich nur mein Konzept der Umsetzung kurz schildern. Wenn man sich dafür entscheidet, die Diskriminierung wegen der Rasse, der ethnischen Herkunft und des Geschlechts mit zivilrechtlichen Mitteln zu bekämpfen, scheint eine Änderung des Art. 23 ZGB die günstigste Variante zu sein. Man sollte einfach einen § 2 beifügen mit dem Inhalt, dass als Verletzung des persönlichen Guts auch eine Diskriminierung wegen der Rasse, der ethnischen Herkunft und des Geschlechts beim Zugang zu und bei der Versorgung mit Gütern und Dienstleistungen, die der Öffentlichkeit zur Verfügung stehen, einschließlich Wohnraum, zu betrachten ist. Diese sparsame Änderung würde grundsätzlich den Vorgaben der Richtlinien genügen. Solch eine Lösung würde praktisch die Resultate der obig dargestellten gemeinschaftskonformen Auslegung kodifizieren. Um eine volle Umsetzung zu erreichen, müsste man noch überlegen, ob nicht zusätzlich eine Novelle des Zivilverfahrensgesetzbuches erforderlich wäre, um ausdrücklich den *prima facie* Beweis im Bereich der Diskriminierung zu bestimmen. Der Bedarf nach einer solchen Vorschrift ist zumindest fraglich. Das ZVGB enthält in Art. 231 eine Bestimmung, welche es dem Gericht erlaubt, die Tatsachen als bewiesen anzunehmen, wenn eine solche Schlussfolgerung auf Grund anderer Tatsachen zu treffen ist. Diese sog. faktischen Vermutungen sind

---

[37] Art. 13 Abs. 1 hat keine direkte horizontale Wirkung – siehe R. Streinz, *Verwirklichung*, S. 23; F. Stork, *Das Anti-Diskriminierungsrecht*, S. 48 mit Hinweisen auf die vereinzelt vertretenen anderen Positionen. Siehe aber auch EuGH C-144/04, Mangold vs. Helm.

[38] Siehe dazu: S. Leible, *Non-Discrimination*, S. 77; R. Streinz, *Verwirklichung des Gleichbehandlungsgrundsatze*, (in:) S. Leible/M. Schlachter, *Diskriminierungsschutz durch Privatrecht*, Sellier 2006, S. 16 ff.

zwar nicht gleich mit dem *prima facie* Beweis der Richtlinien, sie erlauben es aber, die gleichen Ergebnisse zu erzielen. In diesem Fall besteht kein dringender Umsetzungsbedarf.[39]

III. Das Problem der Eignung zivilrechtlicher Mittel für die Bekämpfung der Diskriminierung

1. Der Regelungsbedarf hinsichtlich des Zugangs zu Gütern und Dienstleistungen im Falle einer diskriminierenden Ungleichbehandlung

Man könnte behaupten, dass diese (bereits am Anfang angekündigte) Frage nicht im letzten, sondern bereits im ersten Kapitel dieser Ausführungen hätte erörtert werden müssen. Da sie aber erst am Ende kommt, ist sie vielleicht ein Ausdruck des bestimmten Fatalismus. Die Rahmenstrukturen sind teilweise vorgegeben. Man hat durch die europäische Rechtsentwicklung relativ wenige Chancen, noch im Vorfeld die grundsätzlichen Fragen zu diskutieren. Eher hat man mit schon gewachsenen Effekten zu tun, welche nur optimal umgesetzt werden sollten. Die beiden Richtlinien betreffen ganz tief greifend eine der wichtigsten Säulen der privatrechtlichen Ordnung – die Privatautonomie und beschäftigen sich mit dem Prozess der Willensbildung, also mit einem eigentlich der äußeren Welt nicht zugänglichen Vorgang. Aus diesem Grund ist die Konstruktion des *prima facie* Beweises einer der Kernpunkte der beiden Richtlinien. Im reinen Vorgang der Willensbildung würde ohne eine solche Regel fast keine Chance bestehen, eine Diskriminierung zu beweisen. In den heutigen abendländischen Gesellschaften ist es eher selten, mit einer nach außen manifestierten Diskriminierung konfrontiert zu werden. Es werden keine Schilder ausgehängt, die eine bestimmte Gruppe ausschließen oder bevorzugen, wenn es sich um an die Öffentlichkeit gerichtete Einladungen zum Vertragsabschluss handelt. Selten wird zugegeben, dass der wahre Grund für die Verweigerung des Abschlusses eines Mietvertrags die ethnische Herkunft des Bewerbers ist. Solche Vorgänge müssen nicht begründet und nicht dokumentiert werden. Man kann „nein" sagen, ohne es rechtfertigen zu müssen. Ein fester Bestandteil der Privatautonomie ist als Element der Vertragsfreiheit die Abschlussfreiheit. Die Konstruktion des *prima facie* Beweises versucht, die absolut internen Denkprozesse von

---

[39] Vgl. aber die Auffassung von F. Stork, *Das Anti-Diskriminierungsrecht*, S. 240 (vermutlich würde dieser Autor meine Auffassung in dieser Hinsicht nicht teilen können).

Menschen einer Kontrolle zu unterziehen.[40] Die Anwendung zivilrechtlicher Mittel hat, selbst wenn die Sanktionen „abschreckend" wirken sollten, den Reiz, der Schärfe eines Strafverfahrens zu entkommen und so die schwierigen, wenn nicht gar nicht nachweisbaren Ereignisse als bewiesen zu fingieren. Warum man dies tut, ist aber auch nachvollziehbar. Wir leben in einer immer weniger homogenen Gesellschaft. Man wird immer öfter mit anderen Kulturen, Lebensweisen, Werten etc. konfrontiert. Es ist eine Aufgabe der Rechtsordnung, ein harmonisches Zusammenleben der Gesellschaft trotz dieser Zersplitterung zu gewährleisten. Es ist auch einsehbar, dass zum großen Teil eine Ungleichbehandlung im Zugang zu den Dienstleistungen und Gütern, besonders im Bereich des Wohnraums eine tatsächliche Integrationsschranke darstellen kann. Die Tendenz, das Recht auch in diesem Bereich zur Erzwingung der Gleichbehandlung von Mitbürgern anzuwenden ist verständlich. Ist es aber überhaupt denkbar, wirklich reale Instrumente auf diesem Gebiet zu etablieren, ohne die Grundlagen eines Vertragsmechanismus zu zerstören? Da man auch versucht, flächendeckend die unscharfen und selten völlig nachvollziehbaren Vorgänge zu kontrollieren, droht der ganzen Regelung eine gefährliche Ineffizienz. In solchen feinen Bereichen schwächt eine solche Ineffizienz des Rechts nicht nur das Ansehen des Rechts selbst, sondern droht auch, eine Gegenreaktion zu bewirken – es entsteht ein Anlass, sich noch stärker gegen bestimmte Minderheiten zu positionieren. Um das Antidiskriminierungsrecht effektiv zu machen, muss man darauf verzichten, alle Vorgänge zu regeln – man sollte sich nur auf krasse und transparente Fälle beschränken. Eine Kontrolle von internen Motiven einer menschlichen Handlung scheint reine Utopie zu sein.

2. Das Problem der unscharfen rechtlichen Kriterien am Beispiel der Rasse und der ethnischen Herkunft

Eine von den Richtlinien erfasste Diskriminierung muss sich auf die genannten Eigenschaften der Person beziehen, wie die Rasse, die ethnische Herkunft oder das Geschlecht. Die erste Eigenschaft – die Rasse – ist aufgrund der europäischen Geschichte und Erfahrung von besonderer Bedeutung. Es bleibt das Problem der Feststellung, was eigentlich eine Rasse im Sinne der Richtlinien sein soll? Welche Diskriminierung sollte eigentlich in diesem Zusammenhang bekämpft werden? Der Begriff der Menschenrasse in einem anthropologischen Sinne ist zeitlich sehr stark über-

---

[40] Vgl. K. Riesenhuber, *Europäisches Vertragsrecht*, De Gruyter 2006, S. 188, Rn. 423.

holt.⁴¹ Eine typologische Erfassung von Menschenrassen und damit verbundene Klassifizierungen spielen in der Wissenschaft eigentlich keine Rolle. Auch ein Versuch, die Menschenrassen als „genetisches System mit unscharfen Grenzen und wechselndem Bestand" zu verstehen, wurde wegen der genetischen Veränderbarkeit im Rahmen einer Population bei Seite gelassen.⁴² Der Begriff der Rasse gilt heute nur als „ein Synonym einer Lokalpopulation, ohne jegliche Bedeutung für die Taxonomie, welcher aus überwiegend traditionellen Gründen bei einer immer kleineren Minderheit von Anthropologen fungiert".⁴³ Das betont auch die Richtlinie 2000/43 selbst, wenn sie im Motiv 6 ausdrücklich besagt, dass „die Europäische Union [...] Theorien, mit denen versucht wird, die Existenz verschiedener menschlicher Rassen zu belegen, zurück[weist]. Die Verwendung des Begriffs „Rasse" in dieser Richtlinie impliziert nicht die Akzeptanz solcher Theorien". Es bleibt dann aber ein Problem, wenn ein Begriff zum Tatbestandsmerkmal wird, objektiv aber keine Designate hat, welche in der Wirklichkeit bestehen. Es handelt sich in der Richtlinie offensichtlich um ein anderes Verständnis der Menschenrasse – es geht um kein objektives, wissenschaftliches Kriterium, sondern um ein subjektives Kriterium der Person, die diskriminierend handelt. Das, was bekämpft werden soll, ist eine Ungleichbehandlung wegen eines Kriteriums, das in einer primitiven Volksauffassung als Rasse gilt.⁴⁴ Durch diese Feststellung wird die Sache aber nicht viel einfacher. Weiterhin weiß man nicht genau, wie einzelne Sachverhalte abzugrenzen sind. Es droht die Gefahr, dass jede Verweigerung des Abschlusses eines Vertrages, die sich nicht durch klare Umstände, wie z.B. die Zahlungsunfähigkeit, rationalisieren lässt, als eine Verweigerung wegen einer Eigenschaft angesehen wird, die eine Diskriminierung begründen kann. Jeder Mensch hat bestimmte Eigenschaften, die ihn von anderen Menschen unterscheiden. Wenn Menschenrassen in einem objektivierbaren Sinne nicht bestehen, kann man eigentlich kein Urteil treffen, ob eine Diskriminierung wegen der Rasse stattgefunden hat. Die Richtlinie 2000/43 verwendet neben dem Begriff der Rasse auch die ethnische Herkunft als ein Kriterium, das eine Diskriminierung begründet. Die ethnische Gruppe ist auch ein Begriff, der durch relativ unscharfe Kriterien bestimmt wird. Es handelt sich dabei um eine gesellschaftliche Gruppe, welche durch die eigene Sprache

---

41 J. Strzałko, *Rasy ludzkie (Menschenrassen)*, *Wielka Encyklopedia* PWN (*Große Enzyklopädie*), Bd. 23, 2004, S. 145; dazu auch F. Stork, *Das Anti-Diskriminierungsrecht*, S. 87; vgl. K. Riesenhuber, *Diskriminierungsverbote*, S. 131.
42 J. Strzałko, *Rasy ludzkie (Menschenrassen)*, S. 145 f.
43 J. Strzałko, *Rasy ludzkie (Menschenrassen)*, S. 146.
44 Siehe: F. Stork, *Das Anti-Diskriminierungsrecht*, S. 88 f. Der Autor beschreibt den sog. sozialwissenschaftlicher Begriff und formuliert plastisch, dass „ein Rassist [...] gleichsam zum Schöpfer der Rasse [wird]".

bzw. Dialekt, die gemeinsame Herkunft, das Bewusstsein der Geschichte und Kultur, das Wertesystem, Symbole, die Religion und ein Gemeinsamkeitsgefühl zusammen mit einem Abgrenzungsgefühl gegenüber anderen solchen Gruppen gekennzeichnet wird. Dabei müssen all diese Eigenschaften aber nicht gleichzeitig vorliegen oder gleichmäßig bewusst werden.[45] Es ist aber sehr schwierig, bei solch unscharfen Kriterien im konkreten Fall festzustellen, ob tatsächlich eine Diskriminierung wegen der Rasse oder der ethnischen Herkunft im Sinne der Richtlinie stattgefunden hat. Nehmen wir als Beispiel den Fall eines Antisemiten, der sich weigert, einen Mietvertrag mit einer Person abzuschließen, weil er dieser Person etwa wegen der dunkleren Hautfarbe die jüdische Herkunft zuschreibt. Abgesehen davon, ob ein solcher Denkvorgang von außen überhaupt feststellbar ist, stellt sich die Frage, ob hier eine Diskriminierung wegen der Rasse oder der ethnischen Herkunft überhaupt gegeben ist. Man muss das vielleicht bejahen – es geht eher um eine subjektive Erfassung der Dinge durch den Täter. Man müsste diese Regelung dann eher auf alle Fälle von „Fremdenhass" erstrecken (obwohl der Begriff „Fremde" auch in diesem Fall nicht der Realität entspricht).[46] Dann aber wäre es höchst schwierig, eine Abgrenzung zu ziehen, wenn eine irrationale Ungleichbehandlung, die z.B. wegen einer Körpereigenschaft vorgenommen wird (etwa: Ich vermiete nicht an Personen mit einer Körpergröße von über 1,90 m) anzunehmen ist, die jedoch nicht mehr als eine Diskriminierung wegen der Rasse oder ethnischen Herkunft zu verstehen ist. Da diese Kriterien so unpräzise und wissenschaftlich unfundiert sind, führt das zu einer notwendigen Einzelfallrechtsprechung. Man hat zwar ein klares Bild der Hautfarbe vor Augen, es ist jedoch zu befürchten, dass eine praktische Anwendung auf enorme Schwierigkeiten stoßen wird.

3. Das Antidiskriminierungsrecht im Dienste des Schutzes von Allgemeininteressen

Nehme man ein rein hypothetisches Beispiel, dass ein Reiseunternehmen eine bestimmte ethnische Gruppe nicht bedienen will und dies (um den Fall simpel zu halten) ganz offen legt. Sollen alle Mitglieder dieser Gruppe (manchmal mehrere Millionen von Menschen) z.B. zum Ersatz vom immateriellen Schaden berechtigt sein? Vielleicht ist es gar nicht notwendig, dass sie einen Vertragsschluss anstreben, umso mehr, da eine Erfolglosigkeit solchen Bestrebens von vornherein ersichtlich ist? Wäre jeder berechtigt, wäre dies tatsächlich ein Fall, der vom Zivilrecht geregelt

---

[45] *Wielka Encyklopedia PWN (Große Enzyklopädie)* – Stichwort: *grupa etniczna (ethnische Gruppe)*, Bd. 10, 2002, S. 498.
[46] Siehe: F. Stork, *Das Anti-Diskriminierungsrecht*, S. 89.

sein sollte? Es geht hier doch um die klaren Interessen der Allgemeinheit. Ich glaube, dass das Zivilrecht eigentlich nicht die strafrechtliche Funktion ersetzen sollte. Man tut dies, um der Strenge des Strafrechts auszuweichen und die Schwäche der Norm mit unscharfen Grenzen den milden Auslegungsmethoden des Zivilrechts zu unterwerfen. Das ist kein richtiger Weg. Die strafrechtlichen Typen sollen ausreichend präzise formuliert werden und an die Stelle der unklaren zivilrechtlichen Mittel treten, die ohnehin wenige Chancen auf eine effiziente Wirkung haben. Die Richtlinien schließen diesen Weg nicht aus.

IV. Schlussfolgerung

Der Entwurf der Acquis-Gruppe über das Antidiskriminierungsrecht ist ein Versuch, die bestehenden zwei Richtlinien in einer knappen Regelung zu vereinheitlichen und in das System von Grundregeln des geltenden Europäischen Rechts einzubauen. Das Vertragsrecht des Acquis soll so eine Regelung erfassen, da die Idee eines von den Gespenstern des Aberglaubens, des Hasses und der Vorurteile befreiten Vertragsrechts im heutigen Acquis verwurzelt ist. Dies ist aber nur ein Beginn der Überlegungen, mit welchen Mitteln eine Diskriminierung im Bereich des Vertragsrechts bekämpft werden soll, und der Weg zur Lösung dieses Problems scheint noch sehr lang zu sein.

A Special Private Law for B2C?
Silver Bullet or Blind Alley?

Barbara Dauner-Lieb * *(Cologne)*

I. Relevant Issue

The following contribution addresses the role of consumer protection within the context of Europeanization of private law. The project for a "European Civil Code" is currently on the political agenda and is to be realized within the framework of discussions between jurisprudence and practice. It is the greatest challenge to confront European lawyers thus far, and the final outcome is not yet clear. Politicians are currently referring to a Common Frame of Reference. However, there can be no doubt that this Common Frame of Reference is only to be the first stage in a step-by-step plan ending in a "text which is both binding and convincing in terms of form and content".[1]

In view of the gigantic dimensions of the project, the complexity of the task and the turgescent flood of paperwork, there is a considerable risk of the focus of discussion being diverted into finer details and consequently central points being neglected.[2] In particular, there has thus far been no

---

* Professor Dr. *Barbara Dauner-Lieb*, Chair of Civil, Commercial and Corporate Law, Labour Law and European Private Law, Director of the Institute for Labour Law and Commercial Law and Judge at the Constitutional Court of NRW – Caroline Parker, LL.M. is hereby thanked for her support with the translation.

[1] Cf. *von Bar*, Die Mitteilung der Europäischen Kommission zum Europäischen Vertragsrecht, ZEuP 2001, 799, 804.

[2] Cf. *Schulze*, ZRP 2006, 137; K. Schmidt, Verbraucherbegriff und Verbrauchervertrag – Grundlagen des § 13 BGB, JuS, 2006, 1; see for an overall analysis *Heiderhoff*, Grundstrukturen des nationalen und europäischen Verbrauchervertragsrechtes – Insbesondere zur Reichweite europäischer Auslegung, 2004; see also *Enders*, Neuerungen im Recht der Verbraucherdarlehensverträge, 2004; *Riesenhuber*, System und Prinzipien des europäischen Vertragsrechts, 2003; *Ring*, Wertminderung infolge bestimmungsgemäßer Ingebrauchnahme nach § 357 Abs. 3 BGB – Unternehmerschutz statt Verbraucherschutz?, in: Dauner-Lieb/Konzen/K. Schmidt (eds.), Das neue Schuldrecht in der Praxis, 2003, p. 347 ff.; *Reuter*, Die Integration des Verbraucherschutzrechts in das BGB, in:

adequate discussion on whether the provisions of a "European Civil Code" should apply in equal measure to all contractual parties, or whether a distinction should be made between B 2 B contracts and B 2 C contracts. Such distinction would ultimately lead to the development of a "special private law" for consumers.[3] On no account is this question of a purely technical nature. It concerns the fundamental principles of European private law and could have considerable effects on a common "legal identity" in Europe.

II. Consumer protection from a German perspective

1. Consumer protection as alien element

Consumer protection in civil law, in a nutshell, means that contractual freedom is restricted if one of the contractual parties concludes the contract for private purposes, i.e. as private person rather than as a business (sec. 13 German Civil Code – BGB).[4] This principle represents an alien element in the traditional German legal system. The standards of the German Civil Code were in principle applicable to all legal subjects, without any distinction on the basis of neediness, financial standing or economic role. In principle such provisions were optional. The contractual parties were free to decide with whom they wished to conclude contractual agreements and the content of such agreements. Civil law consumer protection undermines the principle of formal abstract equality and

---

Eckert/Dellbrück (eds.), Reform des deutschen Schuldrechts, 2003, p. 99; *Lurger*, Grundfragen der Vereinheitlichung des Vertragsrechts in der Europäischen Union, 2002, p. 301; *Hamarthy*, Marktwirtschaft und Zivilrecht, ZEuP 2001, 548; *Grundmann*, Privatautonomie im Binnenmarkt, JZ 2000, 1133; *Reich*, Das Phantom "Verbraucherrecht" – Erosion oder Evolution des Privatrechts?; *Dreher*, Der Verbraucher – Das Phantom in den Opera des europäischen und deutschen Rechts?, JZ 1997, 167; *Heiss*, Europarecht, Verbraucherrecht und allgemeines Privatrecht, JZ 1997, 83; *Tonner*, Die Rolle des Verbraucherrechts bei der Entwicklung eines europäischen Zivilrechts, JZ 1996, 533.

[3] Cf. *Lieb*, Sonderprivatrecht für Ungleichgewichtslagen, AcP 178 (1978), 196; *Westermann*, Sonderprivatrechtliche Sozialmodelle und das allgemeine Privatrecht, AcP 178 (1978), 150.

[4] Cf. *Dauner-Lieb*, europäisches Verbraucherschutzrecht als Motor der Veränderung des deutschen Privatrechts, in: Hopt/Tzouganatos (eds.), Europäisierung des Handels- und Wirtschaftsrechts, 2006; for discussion of basic aspects, *Dauner-Lieb*, Verbraucherschutz durch Ausbildung eines Sonderprivatrechts für Verbraucher – systemkonforme Weiterentwicklung oder Schrittmacher der Systemveränderung, 1983.

the principle of private autonomy. This is the real reason why the German economy remains so unequivocally sceptical of the perspective of a European Civil Code. After two decades of restricting private autonomy by mandatory consumer protection legislation, there are fears that the development of a European Civil Code could restrict contractual freedom even further, and thus impinge on flexibility and innovation.[5]

2. The focus of private law: the homo oeconomicus

Formal abstract equality and private autonomy are based on a liberal "model of society".[6] The main role is played by the "homo oeconomicus". Homo oeconomicus is in a position – within the scope of his financial possibilities – to ensure that his various requirements are satisfied, irrespective of social circumstances, financial standing, professional and personal know-how. Market paradigms are based on this assumption, that all individuals partaking in commercial transactions are capable of and prepared to systematically seek their own economic uses, and to use their available, albeit scarce, funds in a reasonable manner: since individuals engaging in commerce will make a reasonable selection from the numerous goods on offer, any supplier offering the best price for goods appropriate to satisfy such requirements will benefit from increased sales and thus increased profits. Consequently, competition arises between the suppliers of the relevant market. This competition results in constant innovation and improved quality, with a simultaneous attempt to achieve the lowest prices possible. At the same time it guarantees that economic resources are optimally used and that ultimate consumers are amply supplied with the required and desired goods.[7] For this social model, the barely comparable starting positions of individual legal subjects, differences in income, commercial experience and professional training are irrelevant. The functioning of this model exclusively depends on whether the legal subjects make reasonable, i.e. competition-related use, of their more or less scarce financial resources. All persons with legal capacity are deemed equally able and willing to find an appropriate use for their financial resources, irrespective of whether this occurs within the course of private consump-

---

[5] *Jahn*, Rettet das BGB vor Brüssel, Frankfurter Allgemeine Zeitung – FAZ, 18.10.06.
[6] Cf. *Wieacker*, Das Sozialmodell der klassischen Privatrechtsgesetzbücher und die Entwicklung der modernen Gesellschaft (1953), in: Industriegesellschaft und Privatrechtsordnung, 1974, p. 9.
[7] See *Jörges*, Verbraucherschutz als Rechtsproblem, 1981, p. 18 et seq., 31 et seq.; for an economic analysis of the law. *Eidenmüller*, Der homo oeconomicus und das Schuldrecht, JZ 2005, 216.

tion or commercial purposes with the conclusion of the agreement: to this extent all legal subjects are considered "abstractly equal". The liberal social model is clearly no reflection of reality, which could be empirically investigated with the help of social science, but a model containing highly fictitious, or even normative elements. The instrument of private autonomy is directly based on the theory of formal-abstract equality; as, in principle, parity between the parties is assumed with respect of their ability to conduct themselves reasonably in the market, it is correct to leave it up to the contractual parties to decide whether, and with whom, they wish to conclude a contractual agreement, as well as whether the principal performances are proportional to one another and the finer details.[8]

3. The criticism of the liberal social model

The liberal social model of the German Civil Code (BGB) was strongly attacked in an early phase of the consumer protection movement.[9] The BGB was qualified as an expression of the class dominance of the bourgeoisie at the end of the 19th century; the abstraction of equality and private autonomy was said to exclusively serve the interests of the capitalist and, consequently, could no longer be deemed applicable under the dominance of the social state.[10] The need to protect consumers was derived from the fact that a consumer has no alternative than to consume, and therefore cannot exert pressure on the powerful "other side" of the market by refraining from consumption. Therefore, the homo oeconomicus was considered fictional from the very start. This criticism was accompanied by the development of social consumer protection models – sweeping mandatory provisions were demanded as central instruments for the protection of the consumer.[11]

The objections to consumer protection concepts based on the consumer's reliance on consumption are well-known: mandatory standards in private law are not sufficient. What is necessary is the parallel development of dirigiste structures; the reasonableness of contracts must be decided by state institutions rather than sovereign consumers. In the event

---

[8] Detailed discussion: *Heiderhoff* (n. 2), p. 295 et seq.
[9] Cf. *Raiser*, "Die Zukunft des Privatrechts", Vortrag gehalten vor der Berliner Juristischen Gesellschaft am 21. April 1979, in: Aufsätze zum Privat- und Wirtschaftsrecht aus drei Jahrzehnten, 1977; *Reich*, Zivilrechtstheorie, Sozialwissenschaften und Verbraucherschutz, ZRP 1974, 187.
[10] *Reifner*, Alternatives Wirtschaftsrecht am Beispiel der Verbraucherverschuldung – Realitätsverleugnung oder soziale Auslegung im Zivilrecht, 1979, p. 31.
[11] *Reifner* (n. 10); Criticism *Dauner-Lieb*, Verbraucherschutz (n. 4), p. 133 et seq.

of the feared withdrawal of private capital, the only way of accommodating such "reliance on consumption" would be by stipulating a legal compulsion to enter into contracts, investment control and state production of particular goods. That these fears are realistic can also be seen from the fact that it is currently being openly discussed in Germany whether the mandatory protective standards of tenancy law and employment law have led to counterproductive effects and must thus be radically reduced. Against this background, it is not surprising that social or even socialist aspects in the legal political discussion concerning the future developments of consumer law no longer play an appreciable role.

III. The information model

1. The renaissance of the homo oeconomicus

The liberal social model is experiencing a considerable renaissance in economic and legal policies, *itner alia* as a consequence of the collapse of the socialist economic systems. Within the scope of recalling the rewards of the market and competition, we once again find a use for the homo oeconomicus: over the last few years the principle of the mature and responsible consumer has asserted itself on both a national and European level; it being assumed that such a consumer can regulate his affairs sensibly and reasonably on the basis of adequate information. Under current consumer protection concepts, the so-called information model dominates.[12] The approach of this model is to regard the consumer as primarily protected by functioning competition, and as a result to emphasise the importance of effective competition. In particular, however, this model specifies that adequate information and market transparency are further, essential preconditions for the functioning of contractual freedom and the market mechanism. The necessity to protect consumers by restricting contractual freedom is derived from a structural inferiority of the consumer, in the form of a typical deficit of information vis-à-vis the other side of the market. This is compatible with the liberal social model and thus in conformity with the free market economy. It is, admittedly, questionable whether this approach can justify the creation of special rules for consumers. The problem of sufficient information not only affects con-

---

[12] For a discussion of homo oeconomicus within the scope of an economic analysis, see e.g. *Eidenmüller*, Der homo oeconomicus und das Schuldrecht: Herausforderungen durch Behavioral Law and Economics, JZ 2005, 216, 221; *Grundmann* (n. 2), JZ 2000, 1136; for a detailed discussion of liberal information model, *Dauner-Lieb* (Verbraucherschutz, n. 4), p. 62 et seq.

sumers, but all legal subjects who engage in legal transactions without having professional expert knowledge of the particular agreement to be concluded.

2. Compensation instruments

As possible legal instruments for compensating information deficiencies, a first point for consideration is the stipulation of information duties.[13] Consumer advice centres or "Stiftung Warentest" (a German comparative consumer information body), for example, are aimed at increasing the level of available information and creating "information markets". Establishing civil law duties of information and disclosure can ensure that consumers have the key information necessary to make a prudent choice with respect to the conclusion of specific contracts. If such information duties are violated, the contractual partner should be granted a right of cancellation or revocation.

Furthermore, a control on the content of standard terms and conditions is compatible with the assumptions underlying the information model. That the user of standard terms and conditions is better informed about the market than the other party can be readily accepted. In particular, the consumer is overtaxed by the comprehensive provisions of typical standard terms. They are aimed at covering all conceivable situations and risks relevant for a particular type of transaction, and are thus inevitably complicated and incomprehensive for the layman. While the offer side can include comprehensive experience and know-how in the formulation of the standard terms, due to its commercial and organisational concentration on particular types of business, the market side is confronted with a pre-formulated contractual text, the content and scope of which are totally unclear. For this reason alone, the market side does not have the possibility of influencing the content of the agreement. Therefore, there would be no point in stipulating information duties, as these would not usually be effective. Even a legally trained person would find it difficult to fully comprehend the situation, even if the contractual text were read out and explained to him. Furthermore, standard terms and conditions often play a subordinate role in the creation of an intention to enter into a contract. This may explain why there is hardly any competition in this area. Against this background, it appears justifiable, on the basis of an

---

[13] There is no room here to discuss the disadvantageous consequences of an information overload for the consumer; see e.g. *Eidenmüller* (n. 12), JZ 2005, 216, 221.

information model, to balance the unilateral exploitation of private autonomy exercised by a user of standard terms, by way of judicial control.[14]

3. Evaluation of applicable consumer contract law

If one examines existing European consumer contract law, as well as its transposition into national law, in terms of whether it is compatible with the information model, this gives a nuanced result: the numerous information duties ordered for the protection of the consumer conform to the system and are thus, in principle, unobjectionable. This also applies to a right of withdrawal in the event of the required information not being disclosed. The German law of withdrawal for consumer agreements (sec. 355 BGB) also covers constellations under which the binding effect of contracts is relaxed, irrespective of information deficits. This can be justified – still in conformity with the system – on the basis of a selective, situation-related need for protection. This particularly applies to the right of withdrawal for door-to-door sales (sec. 312 BGB). A further relaxation of the principle *pacta sunt servanda* would no longer be compatible with an information model of the free market economy – despite the elaborate attempts at constructing a "competitive contract law".[15] The control mechanism pursuant to secs. 305 et seq. BGB can – as presented – easily be justified in an information model.

One aspect which is clearly problematic within the context of an information model is, however, the Consumer Sales Directive. The mandatory nature of the Directive is stipulated in Art. 7, and this restricts private autonomy in large parts of sales law. Accordingly, the optional warranty law previously applicable to the purchase of consumer goods, as set forth in the BGB, has now largely been replaced by mandatory provisions (secs. 474, 475 BGB). This cannot be justified on the basis of a structural information disparity between business and consumer. It is not clear why parties to a contract are no longer entitled to exclude the warranty for a used good, in return for a corresponding price discount. Against this background, it is not surprising that possible structural information deficits between business and consumer are not even mentioned in the recitals of the Consumer Sales Directive.

---

[14] See *Dauner-Lieb*, p. 72 et seq., ultimately also *Eidenmüller*, JZ 2005, 216, 222.
[15] *Micklitz*, Perspektiven eines Europäischen Privatrechts, ZEuP 1998, 243; for criticism see *Heiderhoff* (n. 2), p. 376 et seq.

IV. Consumer protection as an answer to "legitimate expectations" on the part of the consumer?

1. Does European consumer protection lack an underlying concept?

The conclusion of our considerations thus far, i.e. that the Consumer Sales Directive is not compatible with the principles of the liberal information model, gives rise to critical questions. It is necessary to explain the ostentatious contradiction, that commitments to the market, competition and homo oeconomicus dominate in the legal and economic manifestos, whilst – at the same time – rigorously restricting what is probably the most important element of private law philosophy: private autonomy. There are two possible interpretations. The first possibility is the attempt at a veiled, perhaps even unconscious relapse into social or even socialist consumer protection models – in the light of the fact that the legislative bodies of the European Community and the relevant personalities are on no account comprised in a politically homogenous manner. The other possibility is that the Consumer Sales Directive reflects a largely unmethodical and excessive desire for political action.

2. The consumer model of the Directives: the easygoing consumer

Heiderhoff has developed a totally different interpretation.[16] She believes that the question of imbalance between the contractual parties, for the purpose of legitimizing interventions in private autonomy, is a traditionally German approach which is unknown to European law. On a European law level, consumer protection is, from a market political perspective, regarded as a confidence-boosting measure which particularly serves to encourage consumers to engage in cross-border consumption. Consumer protection under civil law allows the consumer to conduct himself comfortably and perhaps even fugaciously in the marketplace – without this having any negative consequences. European law therefore sees no problem in upholding the alleged interests of the consumer as mandatory contractual content, and granting consumers far-reaching rights of withdrawal. As a consequence of the consumer's "legitimate expectations" being fulfilled, the consumer acquires increasing confidence and thus becomes more active in cross-border commerce. European consumer contract law is thus aimed at "improving the market". The central politi-

---

[16] *Heiderhoff* (n. 2), p. 281 et seq., 289 et seq.

cal aim is to persuade the consumer to make more use of his contractual freedom to conclude contracts abroad by considerably restricting the freedom of contractual formcontent?.

3. Doubts

Proceeding from the assumption that European consumer contract law is actually based on the concept of "strengthening and improving the effectiveness of freedom to contract by extensively restricting the freedom of contractual content", a number of questions arise. Particularly problematic is whether the consumer is thereby actually persuaded to engage in increased cross-border consumer activities. Within the discussion of the control of standard terms and conditions, until now the assumption has been that for the average contracting party (and not only the consumer), the contractual conditions presented to him will hardly play any role in the formation of his intention to enter into a contract. However, on the basis of a liberal information model, this is precisely the justification given for subjecting contracts to subsequent judicial content control. The consumer's reluctance to engage in cross-border transactions could be due to totally different reasons, particularly the – not wholly unjustified – fear that a legal dispute with a distant partner in another country could give rise to practical problems. A causal connection between a mandatory unification of laws and a willingness to engage in cross-border legal transactions has at any rate not yet been empirically proven.

The concept of promoting cross-border activities by mandatory consumer protection law throws up still more serious problems. It is based on the assumption that the consumer must be protected in his "legitimate expectations", to the extent that – in the event of a disruption in performance – he can be confident of finding corresponding, favourable legal framework conditions in other countries. Admittedly, this can only function if the typical problems are covered by the relevant regulatory framework. However, precisely this is not the case with respect to the Consumer Sales Directive. The problem of possible damages claims on the part of the purchaser has been omitted: there is thus no reason for confidence on the part of the consumer. Also the minimum uniform standard expressly mentioned in the recitals of the Consumer Sales Directive and set forth in Art. 8 cannot be reconciled with a postulate to the effect that the consumer can assume that beyond the national borders he will encounter provisions whose level of protection equate to that of domestic law. The generous application of mandatory law is particularly opposed by the fact that this would cement the current status quo of the legal and political situation to a considerable extent and usually for a considerable length of time.

V. Lessons learned from the reform of the German law of obligations

The determination of the status quo by an application of mandatory law is extraordinarily problematic from a legal political perspective. This is vividly illustrated by the problems experienced within the reform of the German law of obligations.[17] Many explosive problems, also important in practice, are due to the fact that the Consumer Sales Directive is not convincing in all its aspects – despite intensive preliminary work. Particular mention should be made of the consumer's right to demand that the seller effects repair work free of charge: the new right to subsequent performance (sec. 439) which the German legislator supplemented with a corresponding right of the seller to render performance a second time, gives rise to a number of complex problems.[18] The right to subsequent performance is closely connected with a further complex change, the so-called recourse to the final seller, which is based on Art. 4 of the Consumer Sales Directive. This provision creates more problems than it solves.[19]

Experiences with the German law of obligations show that within the context of the far larger project of Europeanizing the law of obligations, caution and a sense of proportion are required with respect to consumer law provisions. It is already clear that European consumer contract law has got out of hand in so many points that meanwhile it is necessary to ask whether consumers should not be protected against insufficiently researched consumer protection provisions. At present there is no convincing overall concept for the relationship between consumer law and general civil law. For this reason, the necessary theoretical basis required to set the course between a generally applicable European law of obligations and a differentiation between B to B and B to C contracts is lacking. Within the scope of the necessary basic considerations, the focus must return to the concept of private autonomy. If one wishes to take up the cause of market orientation and deregulation in the European Community, it is necessary to consider that contractual freedom is a central com-

---

[17] See for a most informative overview *Zimmermann*, The New German Law of Obligations – Historical and Comparative Prospectives, Oxford University Press, 2005.

[18] See *Dauner-Lieb*, Viereinhalb Jahre Gesetz zur Modernisierung des Schuldrechts, AnwBl 2006, 430.

[19] See *Schumacher*, Der Lieferantenregress gemäß §§ 478, 479 BGB, 2004; *Dauner-Lieb*, Der Letztverkäuferregress in der Praxis, in: Abels/Lieb (eds.), AGB und Vertragsgestaltung nach der Schuldrechtsreform, 2005.

ponent of a liberal private law based on the free market economy, and accordingly any intervention in contractual freedom must be legitimate on convincing grounds.

A European private law focussing on the responsible and mature homo oeconomicus needs no, or only very few, provisions for B 2 C contracts.*

---

* Translation by Caroline Parker LL.M, Linklaters.

Consumer Concepts for a European Code?

Geraint Howells (Lancaster)

I. Introduction

It is not disputed that the largest part of the European contract law *Acquis* derives from the consumer context. Those who wish to use the *Acquis* as the foundation for a more ambitious European intervention into contract law might point to significant laws outside the consumer context, like the Late Payments Directive[1] and the Commercial Agents Directive,[2] but undoubtedly the consumer law directives form the bulk of the *Acquis*. Opinions differ about the extent to which these rules can be generalised. Some fear the infection of general contract law with alien consumer-welfarist values.[3] Others, like myself, are concerned that the consumer rules might be watered down if they are generalised to cover all contracts and when combined with increased use of maximal harmonisation there will be a loss in consumer protection.[4] This of course leaves open the question whether the general contract law should be modernised and infused to some greater or lesser extent with consumer-welfarist values. Others are indeed more positive and believe the *Acquis* contains some desirable modern rules which can improve national legal orders and ensure a fairer contract law.[5] Many would at least welcome some of the consumer rules being extended to small and medium sized enterprises.

However, my task is to see whether the consumer concepts found in the *Acquis* are fit for purpose to be extrapolated to a European legal instrument dealing with general contract law. In this paper I am less concerned with the legal status of the instrument than with its substantive content. It could be a tool kit, handbook, optional instrument or full blown Code. To avoid unnecessary politicalisation, I will use the term

---

[1] OJ 2000 L 200/35.
[2] OJ 1986 L382/17.
[3] This is the fear of many commercial lawyers, particularly form the common law tradition.
[4] My opinion can be found in 'Consumer Protection and European Contract Law Harmonisation' Special Issue ERA-Forum on European Contract Law 45.
[5] R. Schulze, 'European Private Law and Existing EC Law (2005) 13 *European Review of Private Law* 3.

CFR to fudge the status of the instrument. This may be cowardly, but like the Commission I have found it is a convenient term. It does raise a problem, however, for the desired content of the rules may indeed be different depending upon the purpose the instrument is seeking to perform. However, we shall gloss over this for the most part.

If the consumer *Acquis* is to be taken as the basis of the CFR this seems to presume that the rules in the consumer Acquis have some value; that the consumer rules are good rules that could usefully be applied in a wider range of contexts. Of course it does not always follow that good consumer rules are the same as good general rules. There can be 'good consumer rules that are bad general rules' or 'bad consumer rules that are good general rules'. However, in part this paper at least wants to reflect on the assumption that the existing consumer *Acquis* provides good consumer rules. Good in this European context has at least two dimensions covering both the substantive content of the rules (a matter of judgment in many cases) and their effectiveness at promoting convergence (something which at this early stage of the development of EC law has still to be fully tested). For the most part I will restrict myself to evaluating them as concepts promoting convergence and stay away from controversy about specific areas of policy. The development of European consumer rules also needs to be related to the national context within Member States. Finally the desirability of using these consumer concepts as a model for a CFR will be explored.

This paper was presented at a conference showcasing the results of a very impressive project looking at terminology in European private law. As the project demonstrated there are many terms used in the *Acquis*;[6] I will simply pick out a few of the central concepts that help highlight my argument which is that European consumer law and policy is still at an embryonic stage and whilst some concepts have the potential to help convergence at the European level, equally many of the concepts serve the aim of European integration rather than consumer protection. As European consumer law is still in its infancy, it seems premature to use its concepts necessarily as the foundations of the CFR. This is not an argument against harmonisation, just an argument against over reliance on consumer concepts as the basis of that harmonisation merely because they are found in the existing *Acquis*.

The concepts chosen for evaluation are 'consumer'; 'information obligation'; 'cancellation'; 'unfair terms', 'non-conformity'; those related to remedies; 'defect/safety'; and 'unfair commercial practices.' It will be noted that not all of these are contract law concepts. Some like 'defect/safety' and 'unfair commercial practices' relate to tort or administrative consumer protection law. Yet such concepts can assist with the gen-

---

[6] See web-site http://www.uniformterminology.unito.it.

eral arguments. Moreover some of these concepts define terms ('consumer', 'unfairness', 'rescission', 'damages') whilst others reflect policy choices ('information', 'cancellation'); although naturally underlying any choice of definition there of course lies a policy choice. Further it should not be overlooked that consumer law is not necessarily treated as a discrete topic with general rules applying to all consumer contexts. Sometimes concepts have developed in relation to very particular forms of consuming affecting particular products or services (timeshare, package travel, consumer credit etc) or forms of selling (doorstep, distance selling). It may even be more natural to take stock of the state of European consumer law and to look for scope for rationalisation there,[7] rather than using it as the springboard for broader contract law reform. Nevertheless it seems sensible to look at these central terms to see if European consumer law concepts have a coherency that merits their consideration as the basis for wider law reform.

II. Evaluating European Consumer Concepts

1. Consumer

Although there are several variations, most of the EC directives use a definition of consumer based on a consumer being 'a natural person who is acting for purposes which are outside his trade, business or profession.' It is well known that the European Court of Justice has refused to extend this protection beyond consumers proper[8] or to include contracts where there are mixed private and business purposes, unless the trade or professional purpose is so limited as to be negligible in the overall context of the supply.[9] This is very restrictive. Member States' laws in many cases provide for broader protection, for example, extending protection to

---

[7] See the Commission study co-ordinated by Hans Schulte-Nölke at Bielefeld into the eight contract law directives available at http://ec.europa.eu/con sumers/cons_int/safe_shop/acquis/comp_analysis_en.pdf. Indeed several proposed generalisations of the law seem finally to restrict themselves to the consumer context, or at least feel safest when proposing general rules in that field. See recently the *Green Paper on the Review of the Consuemr Acquis* available at http://ec.europa.eu/consumers/cons_int/safe_shop/acquis/green-paper_cons_acquis_en.pdf.

[8] *Criminal proceedings against Patrice di Pinto* Case C-361/89 [1991] ECR I 1189.

[9] *Johann Gruber v Bay Wa AG* Case C-464/01 [2005] ECR I-439.

small businesses,[10] businesses generally,[11] buyers not in the same speciality as the seller,[12] and when goods are bought for mixed purposes.[13] The variety of national definitions is too varied to do justice to in this paper, but it is clear that if the European definition became the norm it would reflect a significant change in policy at Member State level, which would no doubt be unacceptable to many. Of course the restrictive interpretation of the European concept of 'consumer' has been made in the knowledge that in many cases this reflects the minimum standards required to be imposed by European law, with Member States retaining the freedom to introduce more protective rules. Thus at the very heart of any new European CFR we find the European concept of 'consumer' to be of little assistance in drawing the line between consumer rules and the rules of general contract law. The European concept was fashioned in a very particular context of punctual consumer protection legislation introduced on a narrow constitutional foundation which the European Court of Justice has been keen to confine within narrow boundaries. When devising the CFR a far more complex set of factors has to be taken into account in drawing this divide if it is to become the norm rather than the minimum protection in European legal systems.

2. Information obligations

It is well known that a central element of European consumer policy has been to encourage consumer confidence by providing consumers with information about products and services. This is not the place to list all the information obligations found in European consumer law directives.[14]

---

[10] For example, in the United Kingdom the Consumer Credit Act can potentially protect partnerships of two or three persons, see s.1(a) Consumer Credit Act 2006 (definition of individual).

[11] This is the case with many continental laws governing unfair competition: see VIEW, *The Feasibility of a General Legislative Framework on Fair Trading* available at http://europa.eu.int/comm/consumers/cons_int/safe_shop/fair_bus_pract/green_pap_comm/studies/sur21_sum_en.pdf. and R. Schulze and H. Schulte-Nölke *Analysis of National Fairness Laws Aimed at Protecting Consumers in Relation to Commercial Practices* available at http://europa.eu.int/comm/consumers/cons_int/safe_shop/fair_bus_pract/green_pap_comm/studies/unfair_practices_en.pdf.

[12] As in French controls on exclusion clauses, see S. Whittaker, *Liability for Products* (Oxford, 2005) at p. 95.

[13] *R & B Custom Brokers Co Ltd v United Dominions Trust* [1988] 1 WLR 321.

[14] See, S. Weatherill, 'The Role of the Informed Consumer in European Community Law' (1994) 2 *Consumer Law Journal* 49, G. Howells and T. Wilhelms-

One telling example however is Directive 2002/65 concerning the distance marketing of consumer financial services.[15] This imposes obligations to inform the consumer of around forty pieces of information. The length of the list is partly explained by the Commission's attempt to produce a maximal harmonisation directive; a goal that was not achieved, because even with such a long list of information obligations, Member States wanted to retain the right to add to it.

The principle of information obligations is well settled in European consumer law. It fits in with a policy of reducing substantive controls to ease cross border trade and also aligns itself with national policies in several Member States which increasingly focus on the informed consumer agenda.[16] However although the principle is well settled the implementation of it is subject to much criticism at the EC level and Member States still are nervous about relying entirely on EC legislation. Moreover that EC legislation does not appear to be underpinned by clear rationales and policies concerning the amount of information that should be communicated, when and in what form (especially in the context of internet shopping). In other words even within the context of European consumer law the application of the information obligations needs to be revised.[17]

When it comes to extending information obligations beyond consumer contracts to general contract law the matter is problematic given the different traditions within Europe as regards pre-contractual disclosure.[18]

---

son, *EC Consumer Law*, (Dartmouth, 1997) at pp. 306–315, S. Grundmann, G. Kerber and S. Weatherill (eds.), *Party Autonomy and the Role of Information in the Internal Market* (de Gruyter, 2001) and G. Howells, A.Janssen and R. Schulze (eds.) *Information Rights and Obligations – A Challenge for Party Autonomy and Transactional Fairness* (Ashgate, 2004) and T. Wilhelmsson and C. Twigg-Flesner 'Pre-contractual information duties in the *Acquis communautaire*' *European Review of Contract Law* 2006, pp. 441–470.

[15] OJ 2002 L 271/16.

[16] In the UK see Department of Trade and Industry, *Extending Competitive Markets: Empowered Consumers, Successful Business* (July 2004).

[17] See, A. Nordhausen, ' Information Requirements in the E-Commerce Directvie and the Proposed Directive on Unfair Commercial Practices' in Howells, Janssen and Schulze (eds.), *op.cit* who has tried to provide a better framework for information rules in the e-commerce context based around the core information rules contained in the Unfair Commercial Practices Directive and B. Wendlandt, 'EC Directives on Time-Sharing and for self-employed commercial agents – Apples, Oranges and the Core of the Information Overload Problem' also in Howells, Janssen and Schulze , *op. cit.*, who reviews the information rules in the Timeshare Directive in light of the Commercial Agents Directive.

[18] R. Sefton-Green (ed.) *Mistake, Fraud and Duties to Inform in European Contract Law* (Cambridge 2005).

Suggested approaches have ranged from that of Schulze, who cautiously focuses rather on first providing a general provision in the consumer context[19] to the relatively bolder efforts of Wilhelmsson and Twigg-Flesner.[20] Yet even Wilhelmsson and Twigg-Flesner have to place a lot of emphasis on the Consumer Sales Directive,[21] which allows traders to affect the appreciation of conformity by disclosing information about the goods. It seems a big step to move from the benefits that might indirectly be derived from disclosure in the specific context of sales law to supporting a general duty to disclose and it is noticeable that outside the consumer context the authors resist the temptation to develop general principles other than in the context of assessing the quality of goods and services. Such a general principle may be a welcome step, but it is one that needs to be openly debated and the central issues analysed rather than trying to introduce it on the back of a specific provision, which in European law is in any event limited to consumers sales. My argument is not necessarily against the principle of duty to disclose – that needs to be discussed – but rather with using the consumer *Acquis* as support for that principle.

3. Right of withdrawal

Alongside information duties, another hallmark of the developing European consumer law has been the right of withdrawal which is found in many consumer contract directives either where the consumer enters contracts in situations where he or she may be subject to rash decision-making (timeshares sold on holiday or door-step sales) or without an adequate opportunity to inspect the goods (distance sales). Again this is not the place to explain the *Acquis* in full.[22] Schulze has convincingly set out some principles which can be derived from the *Acquis* and yet place it on a more rational basis.[23]

---

[19] R. Schulze, 'Pre-contractual Duties and Conclusion of Contract in European Law' (2005) 13 *European Review of Private Law* 841.

[20] T. Wilhelmsson, 'European Rules on Pre-Contractal Information Duties?' Special Issue ERA-Forum on European Contract Law 16 and Wilhelmsson and Twigg-Flesner, *op. cit.*

[21] OJ 1999 L171/12.

[22] See G. Howells, 'The right of withdrawal in European Consumer Law' in *European Contract Law* R. Schulze and H. Schulte-Nölke eds (ERA, 2002); and R. Schulze, 'Pre-contractual Duties and Conclusion of Contract in European Law' (2005) 13 *European Review of Private Law* 841.

[23] R. Schulze, 'Pre-contractual Duties and Conclusion of Contract in European Law' (2005) 13 *European Review of Private Law* 841.

Most obviously harmonisation of the withdrawal periods is desirable. The periods currently run from 7 to 30 days in EC directives. 14 days seems to be emerging as a consensus harmonised period in any future harmonisation. In a number of other areas (such as the need for communication of withdrawal, no need to provide reasons for withdrawal, notification of right of withdrawal, time when declaration of withdrawal becomes effective, and effects of withdrawal[24]) Schulze shows that greater clarity can and needs to be introduced.

One interesting area is the question of maximum time periods when the information on the right of withdrawal is not supplied. Two policies are evident. The Doorstep and Distance Selling of Financial Services Directives have no maximum duration. The right of withdrawal period does not even commence until the appropriate information has been provided. This policy has been supported by the European Court of Justice in the context of doorstep selling.[25] Other directives, such as the Timeshare and Distance Selling Directives delay the cancellation period by a maximum of three months. Particularly the difference in approach between the two distance selling directives is startling. This needs to be harmonised and any divergences from the standard approach explained on policy grounds. Moreover as became obvious at a CFR stakeholder meeting on this topic, consideration might need to be given to whether the extended withdrawal period only applies when there has been a failure to inform of the right of withdrawal or should continue to apply to a failure to supply a broader range of information. Clearly policy issues are at stake here and a lot may depend upon the extent to which Member States' courts take account of the enjoyment consumers have had of products when exercising their right of withdrawal.[26]

What is important for the present moment is that even within the consumer field the principles of withdrawal need to be clarified and rationalised. It may even be possible to use the set of principles developed by Schulze to introduce rules in the CFR that apply whenever legislation (not just related to consumers) provides for a right of withdrawal. However, few people argue that the right of withdrawal can be a generalised principle in all consumer contracts, yet alone on all of general contract law. That would cause too much uncertainty and all contracts do not possess the characteristics of imbalance that justify the punctual rights of withdrawal European consumer law gives consumers in particular con-

---

[24] I would probably argue for even greater precision of the effects of withdrawal.

[25] *Heininger v Bayrische Hypo unde Veriensbank*, Case C-481/99 [2001] ECR I-4781.

[26] On an Austrian decision requiring the consumer to pay for the use of the product before returning the goods see P. Rott, 'Ein teurer Widerspruch! – Besprechung von OGH, 27.9.2005, Az. 1 Ob 110/05s' *VuR* 2006, 218.

texts. Schulze has argued that the right of withdrawal is better classified as a general contract law principle than a consumer law rule, because its rationale is based on structural imbalance, which whilst not found in business-to-business contracts can be found in other sectors.[27] Yet when he comes to formulate general principles his most general principle, linked to contracts made away from business premises, is restricted to consumer contracts.

To some extent whether the CFR should include a general statement on the right of withdrawal depends on the nature of that instrument. If it is truly a toolkit or handbook whose purpose is to remind legislators to consider the desirability of introducing a right of withdrawal whenever there is a structural imbalance the inclusion of such a general rule would be unobjectionable. However, it is not possible to develop a general hard law rule out of the present *Acquis*. Such extensions will involve important policy debates and the present examples of such a right can only form the background to developments which are inevitably going to be sector or situation specific.

4. Unfair Terms

The last two sections have focussed on policies of information provision and the right of withdrawal which can be viewed as the hallmarks of European consumer legal policy. We now come to consider some concepts that try to concretise some substantive standards within European consumer law and assess the extent to which they represent a successful harmonisation policy.

The Unfair Terms in Consumer Contracts Directive[28] defines a term as unfair 'if, contrary to the requirement of good faith, it causes a significant imbalance in the parties' rights and obligations arising under the contract, to the detriment of the consumer.' [29] The reference to good faith is what excites many (especially common) lawyers about this provision.[30] It is indeed true that some elements of the directive espouse social cohesion and it adopts a continental approach, only including in a subsidiary way concepts based on the English reasonableness criteria. Nevertheless as

---

[27] R. Schulze, 'Pre-contractual Duties and Conclusion of Contract in European Law' (2005) 13 *European Review of Private Law* 841, *op cit* at p. 857.

[28] OJ 1993 L 95/29.

[29] Art. 3(1).

[30] See H.Collins, 'Good Faith in European Contract Law (1994), 14 *Oxford Journal of Legal Studies* 229 and M. Tenreiro, 'The Community Directive on Unfair Terms and National Legal Systems: the Principle of Good Faith and Remedies for Unfair Terms' (1995) 3 *European Review of Private Law* 273.

Elise Polliot noted during the debates at the conference it is far from being good faith in its full scale continental (French) sense. Indeed even if it should not be read as producing a fully cumulative procedural and substantive test[31] given that good faith also represents a substantive control – the final inclusion of good faith can be viewed as a symbolic victory for the supporters of good faith as a general principle but a practical hindrance to consumer redress. Unlike earlier drafts, in the final Directive good faith no longer stands as an independent test of unfairness, but is an additional requirement to significant imbalance.

The House of Lords in *Director General of Fair Trading v First National Bank*[32] has been criticized for failing to understand the substantive control implicit in good faith.[33] This seems unfair, but maybe that is because I too am a common lawyer. The judgments certainly show an understanding of the interplay between procedural and substantive control implicit in the test and in truth it comes across as a 'good faith' attempt to apply the test. The treatment of the debtor in that case can certainly seem harsh at first glance. He paid off the debt by agreed installments and then was faced with a bill for the interest on the outstanding debt which he thought he had cleared. This had been set out in a letter by the bank. Understandably perhaps this had apparently not registered with the debtor. The demand came as a surprise and a shock. But what else was the bank to do? The need for such a clause allowing interest to be charged on debts can only be understood if one appreciates that the English court rules prevent interest being included on judgment debts in respect of regulated consumer credit agreements. The unfairness has to be assessed in the light of the background national law rules. A clause of this nature may be unfair in one state and fair in another depending on the background legal context. This was appreciated by the European Court of Justice in *Freiburger Kommunalbauten v Hofstetter*[34] when it said questions of unfairness were for the appreciation of the national court and refused to become involved.

This does not mean that the impact of European law is not helping convergence. English lawyers are certainly now more familiar with the concept of good faith. This case study might nevertheless cause one to

---

[31] R. Brownsword, G. Howells and T. Wilhelmsson, 'Between Market and Welfare : Some reflections on Article 3 of the EC Directive on Unfair Terms in Consumer Contracts' in *Fairness in Contract*, C. Willett ed. (Blackstone Press, 1996).

[32] [2002] 1 AC 481.

[33] H.-W. Micklitz, 'Zum Verständnis von Treu und Glauben im Englischen Vertragsrecht – eine Besprechung von House of Lords' *Office of Fair Trading v First National Bank*, ZEuP 2003, 865.

[34] C-237/02 [2004] 2 CMLR 13.

question whether those who advocate harmonization on economic grounds of reducing litigation costs might not be frustrated due to the continued national variations in application. Others might applaud this diversity.

Turning to the question whether this concept of unfairness can be applied more generally in contract law, this again seems to be a matter for debate. The Directive is limited to consumer contracts and in fact only to non-negotiated terms in consumer contracts. Whether a CFR should adopt similar rules for a wider range of contracts is obviously a matter for debate, but the European legislator's choice in relation to consumer contracts is only background information to that policy decision. Certainly an integrated regime for unfair term control might be desirable. The English Law Commission has proposed extending similar controls as apply to consumers to small businesses. It also proposes clarifying the law for consumers by consolidating both the Unfair Terms in Consumer Contract Regulations[35] and the Unfair Contract Terms Act 1977. Those who see good faith in the Unfair Terms in Consumer Contracts Directive as a precursor to its general adoption will be disappointed to find that the Law Commission prefers a new test of whether a term is 'fair and reasonable' to the 'complex and unfamiliar phrases' of the Directive.[36] This would not seem to be a good omen for broader harmonisation.

5. Non-conformity

At first glance the non-conformity principle introduced by the Consumer Sales Directive[37] is perhaps the must successful example today of a harmonised concept. It benefited from being based on the Vienna Convention on Contracts for the International Sale of Goods, which was familiar to lawyers in all Member States and formed the law of all states bar the United Kingdom. It was not problematic to obtain agreement on the core concept of non-conformity because non-conformity sounded familiar to French lawyers and the criteria expanding on the principle resembled the implied terms relating to quality familiar to common lawyers. The major legal system that needed most reform was the German and it recognised that its rules were in need of an overhaul.[38]

---

[35] Law Commission, *Unfair Terms in Contracts*, (Cm 6464, 2005).
[36] See explanatory notes to draft Bill at p. 145.
[37] OJ 1999 L171/12 , art.2.
[38] See, S. Grundmann, D. Medicus and W. Rolland (eds.). *Europäisches Kaufgewährleistungsrecht: Reform und Internationalisierung der deutschen Schuldrechts* (Hallesche Schriften zum Recht, Band 13, 2000).

The German experience is very positive from an integrationist perspective, for not only did the German legislator willingly embrace the new European model in the consumer context, but also used it as a springboard for the reform of Bürgerliches Gesetzbuch that embraced general sales law.[39] However, the experience of France and the United Kingdom tell a more complex and worrying tale for those who favour the development of common principles. Implementation in the United Kingdom was fairly straightforward with additional rights for consumers being grafted on to the existing Sale of Goods Act 1979. One result of this, however, was that the differences between consumer sales law and general sales law actually became more pronounced.[40] In France, the initial proposals were positive for European integration favouring using the principle of non-conformity in the Directive to remove the complex distinctions between the rules on *obligations de conformité* and the *garantie légale*.[41] This produced a fierce debate at the centre of which was the question of whether France should modernise its laws and try to influence the movement towards European harmonisation to adopt French rules (which seems to reflect the German approach) or rather see European law as an alien force threatening the traditional principles of French law.[42] The latter view seems to have prevailed, for rather than a wholesale reform of the Civil Code, the Directive was instead introduced by reform of the consumer code. Again the difference between consumer and general sales law was in fact emphasised and the impact of Europe minimised.

The non-conformity principle caused upheaval in Germany, but elsewhere seems to have been relatively easy to implement because it can be all things to all people. It allows national traditions to remain undisturbed (partly because of the minimum character of the Directive). The German experience shows that European concepts can be embraced as

---

[39] R. Zimmermann. 'Liability for non-conformity: the new system of remedies in German sales law and its historical context' (2004) 39 *Irish Jurist* 1; H. Schulte-Nölke, The New German Law of Obligations: An Introduction available at http://www.iuscomp.org/gla/literature/schulte-noelke.htm.

[40] See, G. Howells and C. Twigg-Flesner, 'Much Ado About Nothing? UK Implementation of the Consumer Guarantees Directive' in *Verbraucherkauf in Europa* M. Schermaier (ed.) (Sellier, 2003) and R. Bradgate and C. Twigg-Flesner, *Blackstone's Guide to Consumer Sales and Associated Guarantees* (Oxford UP, 2003).

[41] *Rapport général du groupe de travail sur l'intégration en droit français de la directive 1999-44 du Parlement européen et du Conseil du 25 Mai 1999 sur certains aspects de la vente et des garanties des biens de consommation*, available at http://www.justice.gouv.fr/publicat/RappGTIDF.htm.

[42] In more detail see Whittaker, *op. cit.* at pp. 574–583.

part of a reform of the general law of contract. Equally this requires a political will to achieve this, which is clearly lacking in some Member States.

6. Remedies

It is widely acknowledged that remedies are one of the least developed parts of the *Acquis*. True, the concept of damages has been interpreted by the European Court of Justice[43] and the Consumer Sales Directive[44] contains provisions on remedies, but even these concepts remain to be fully crystallised in European jurisprudence. For the most part the European legislator has been happy to leave remedies and sanctions to Member States national laws so long as, to borrow a phrase from many directives, they are 'effective, proportionate and dissuasive.' Certainly the *Acquis* will not be very influential in drafting this part of the CFR.

7. Defect/safety

Perhaps unsurprisingly concepts relating to safety appear to have been the easiest to obtain convergence around. This is partly because, whilst safety is a socially and culturally relative concept, nevertheless Western Europe is sufficiently homogenous to agree on core safety values. It is also because the safety related terms were either new or replacing fairly recent concepts in the Member States' legal order. There was no competition with long-standing national traditions. Both the terms studied under this heading and the next relating to unfair competition are not directly related to contract law, but are included for the lessons they can provide us about both harmonisation and extrapolation from the consumer to the general law.

The Product Liability Directive[45] has introduced strict liability for defects in products. Defect is commonly defined in all Member States. This acceptance of a strict liability standard based around a common understanding of defectiveness has been assisted by the continued availability of traditional contractual and non-contractual remedies and pre-existing special liability schemes, like that for drugs in Germany.[46] However, within its field the European Court of Justice has been keen to ensure the

---

[43] Simone Leitner v. TUI Deutschland GmbH & Co. KG C-168/00 [2002[ECR 1-2631.
[44] OJ 1999 L171/12, art. 3.
[45] OJ 1985 L210/29.
[46] Lovells, *Product Liability in the European Union*, (2003).

European rules remain the sole source of general strict liability.[47] Nevertheless, the application of this concept has been far from harmonious. One might contrast the way the development risks defence provided a defence for the suppliers of contaminated blood in *Scholten v The Foundation Sanquin of Blood Supply*,[48] but not in *A v National Blood Authority*.[49] In fact the way the defectiveness concept is applied seems to differ between the common law and some continental traditions, due to the need for the common law judge not merely to apply the principles, but also to give a detailed explanation to justify his decision.[50] This makes his function less like an assessor of facts, performing the function of a jury member, and more judicial so that the concept takes on more of the character of a legal than a factual test.

In the regulatory field the General Product Safety Directive's[51] concept of safety seems to have been easily assimilated into the Member States' legal systems. Few Member States had their own concept of safety in regulatory law and those that existed were not greatly different from the Directive's Moreover in this regulatory context the concept serves more as an organizing principle to guide actors than a term whose content is tested in the courts. Indeed there are few court judgments to assess whether the term is consistently applied across Europe.

8. Unfair commercial practices

Apart from highlighting the problems of harmonizing the application of concepts even once common terminology is established at the European level, the last section also demonstrated a contrast between the ease with which common European safety concepts were accepted compared with the hand wringing that has gone on in many areas of contract law. In

---

[47] See, Commission v France, Case C-52/00, [2002] ECR I-3827 paras 17–20 Commission v Greece, C-154/00 [2002] ECR I-3879 paras 13–16; González Sanchez v Medicina Asturiana SA Case C-183/00, [2002] ECR I-3901 paras 26–29 and Skov v Bilka Case C-402/03{2006] 2 CMLR 16.
[48] 3 Feb. 1999.
[49] [2001] 3 All ER 289.
[50] See G. Howells, 'Product Liability- A History of Harmonisation' in *Towards a European Civil Code (3ed.)* and also in *Product Liability in Comparative Perspective*, D. Fairgrieve (ed.) (Cambridge UP, 2005). It would be wrong for a common lawyer to categorise all continental systems together and this comment seems most pertinent to the French based legal systems where judgments are terse and as Whittaker notes assessment of 'defect' is within the 'sovereign power of assessment' of the *juge du* fond, *op. cit.* at p. 75.
[51] OJ 2002 L11/4.

large part this might be explained by the fact that the safety concepts were newer and therefore less burdened by the need to accommodate national traditions.

In this respect the general unfairness clause in the Unfair Commercial Practices Directive[52] makes a nice comparison. It was also surprisingly easily adopted. In part this was because most continental systems had such a general clause and felt their regimes would be largely undisturbed. It was not seen as a threat to their legal culture, but rather an endorsement of it. Whether this is correct is a matter for debate since the European unfairness clause should have an autonomous content which may not map on directly in all respects to national understandings of fairness and as it is a maximum harmonisation directive it may in time yet come to challenge national legal systems. At the other extreme the United Kingdom lacked such a general clause and had identified this as a weakness in its legal structures.[53] Like the German law of sales, the English law of fair trading was ripe for reform and the European Directive provided the momentum and direction for change. Again it was therefore easily accepted. Yet only experience will reveal if English trade practice law can adapt to the general clause, although as the Australians have done so successfully this should be possible.[54] Yet one might suspect that even once the common standard is introduced there may be differences in application given the fact that consumer values in marketing practices still vary throughout Europe.[55] Only time will tell. What we can learn from the unfair commercial practices experience is that European concepts are likely to be most acceptable to national legal systems if they replicate national standards (although there is the risk that national lawyers too readily equate the European standard to their own) or provide a welcome model for reform.

When it comes to generalising from the consumer context to all commercial practices and not just those aimed at consumers one sees the same sort of tensions that will emerge in the contract field. Some states will certainly be keen on this as that is reflects their national traditions of having such general clauses available for both business-to-consumer and business-to-business practices. Indeed some states were upset the Directive was limited to consumers and had pressed for its extension. However, often the general clause is applied with different nuances in consumer

---

[52] OJ 2005 L149/22, on which see G. Howells, H.-W. Micklitz and T. Wilhelmsson, *European Fair Trading – The Unfair Commercial Practices Directive* (Ashgate, 2006).

[53] DTI, *Comparative Report on Consumer Policy Regimes*, (October 2003).

[54] See Trade Practices Act 1974.

[55] T. Wilhelmsson, 'Harmonising Unfair Commercial Practices Law: The Cultural and Social Dimensions' *Osgoode Hall Law Journal*, forthcoming.

and business contexts and there may need to be some refinements and added complexity on account of this. However, other states may object to suggestions that applying the principle to consumer transactions should be seen as a first step inevitably leading to the principle's general application.

III. Conclusions

Section II.1. showed that the European *Acquis* defining consumer is likely to be too restrictive to represent the position in Member States. The narrow European definition serves the purpose of the European legislator which is restricted on constitutional grounds to dealing with consumers *stricto sensu*. This is acceptable only so long as minimal harmonisation preserves the scope of Member States to offer broader protection.

Sections II.2 and II.3. considered the two hallmark polices of European consumer protection – information and right of withdrawal – and showed that whilst the broad contours of these policies were well established they still needed refining and there was no obvious reason why they should simply be applied to contract law in general without there being an independent policy choice being made.

Sections II.4. and II.5. illustrate two of the core concepts of European law that have become widely accepted as cornerstones of consumer law in the Member States – contractual unfairness and non-conformity. These examples illustrate that even formal uniformity can hide different national traditions[56] and that moreover the step from acceptance as a concept for consumer law to adoption for general contract law still requires a policy decision. This is even more clearly the case in relation to remedies discussed in section II.5. given the limited *Acquis* on this topic. Sections II.6. and II.7. looked at consumer concepts related to safety and commercial practices unrelated to contract law, but they nicely illustrated some of the more general points about how difficult it can be to achieve practical as well as formal harmonisation.

Moreover, from the range of examples it can be seen that European concepts are most easily assimilated when they either seem to resemble national concepts, or there was little pre-existing national tradition or national law was recognised as being in need of reform. In many areas of contract law there are strongly held national traditions which local lawyers will be reluctant to abandon. The lessons derived from the experience of consumer harmonisation are relevant to the general question of

---

[56] In similar vein and looking at the role of the European Court of Justice in reducing divergences see P. Rott, 'What is the Role of the ECJ in EC Private Law' (2005) 1 *Hanse Law Review* 6.

adopting a general contract law for Europe. My concluding remarks return, however, to the central issue in this paper of whether the consumer concepts should be taken as the basis for the CFR .

My fundamental problem is to see why the policy choice in the consumer context should *necessarily* guide the choice for other contexts. To do so may well risk imposing on the business community inappropriate rules in the same way as consumers were forced to work with ill-suited commercial law until consumerism developed new legislative tools and influenced judicial attitudes from the 1960's. It may well be that the consumer concepts are very good ones which could be useful in other contexts, perhaps particularly in relation to small and medium sized businesses. But this is a matter for debate and there should be no automatic presumption that what suits the consumer context is good for all contracts.

Moreover, unlike some other well respected commentators,[57] I am less enthusiastic about using the present *Acquis* as one of the primary inspiration for a CFR. The consumer *Acquis* has been the product of much well intentioned legislative reform, but those rules have had to be fashioned around political compromise and constitutional constraints and the results, on many occasions, have only been acceptable because they represented minimum levels of harmonisation that Member States could improve upon.[58] It may be politically convenient if the desired choice for a CFR also reflects the *Acquis*. However, it would be rash to rush to adopt the *Acquis*, which is itself recognised as being in need of review and reform,[59] as a blueprint for a general contract law in the CFR. This is not to deny the *Acquis* contains some useful building blocks, or even gems, that might form part of the mosaic that will be the CFR. It is merely to argue that in the case of something as potentially important as the CFR the principles should be based on their inherent value rather than their provenance.

Undoubtedly one should not ignore the *Acquis* and there is good sense in trying to co-ordinate it better and seek to derive general principles in the consumer context. My point is that there is no necessary logic in using it as the starting point for the CFR. Indeed the Commission has now become less ambitious and DG-SANCO is itself only seeking to use the CFR within the consumer field. Indeed it always seemed a somewhat random selection of DG SANCO as the lead directorate on a project that

---

[57] R. Schulze, 'European Private Law and Existing EC Law (2005) 13 *European Review of Private Law* 3.

[58] G. Howells and T. Wilhelmsson, 'EC Consumer Law – Has it Come of Age?' (2003) 28 *European Law Review* 370.

[59] See the Commission study co-ordinated by Hans Schulte-Nölke at Bielefeld into the eight contract law directives.

avowedly had a broader ambit that just consumer protection. It may indeed be better if the CFR project came under the umbrella of a different directorate-general, possibly DG- Justice.[60]

However, I also suspect one's attitude to the integration of consumer principles into the CFR and the general law of contract depends upon one's national perspective. It is hard not to view European law through pragmatic national eyes. The common law has traditionally a very hard nosed laissez-faire approach to contract law. However, this has been tempered by legislative interventions and for the most part the judiciary has been sympathetic to consumer concerns and applied the general rules flexibly to assist deserving consumers. Thus the bifurcation between consumer and commercial law seems to work for consumers in the United Kingdom. By contrast my sense is that in some civilian traditions, it is hard, notwithstanding good faith clauses, to relieve the consumer of the burden of some of the harder edged rules in say the German Bürgerliches Gesetzbuch. Thus the general law needs to be softened and European law provides a means to achieve this. This is only an hypothesis which needs detailed testing, but might explain why lawyers with similar mentalities and objectives might take a different view of the relationship between European consumer and general contract law.

European consumer and contract law is certainly weaving a rich tapestry of interlinking principles and rules. Whether the CFR becomes an all-embracing cover is yet to be determined. It will need to survive in the competition between legal systems and to do so will need to be equipped with the principles best suited to the parties' needs. Some, but not all, of these are likely to be found in the European consumer *Acquis*.

---

[60] See K.-H. Lehne, 'European Contract Law – The European Parliament's Perspective' Special Issue ERA-Forum on European Contract Law 12.

Part II
Preparation and Formation of the Contract

The Function of Letters of Intent and their Recognition in Modern Legal Systems

*Giuditta Cordero Moss** (Oslo)

I. Introduction

A contract is traditionally understood as the result of the exchange of an offer and of a conforming acceptance. If the acceptance does not conform with the offer, it will be considered as a counter-offer. Until there is full conformity, a contract is not deemed to have been entered into (the "mirror-image doctrine"). Acceptance does not necessarily need to be express, it can also be made tacitly; if the offeror starts performing the contract, the offeree's non-conforming acceptance/counter-offer will be thereby tacitly accepted, and the terms therein contained will be deemed to be the terms of the contract ("last-shot doctrine").

The picture of a contract as an exchange of offer and acceptance no longer reflects the reality of contract formation in a large number of commercial transactions. It is long since recognized that this idea is representative of only part of contractual practice, and has consequently been challenged by legal theory, as well as in judicial practice and in legislation. Thus Norwegian theory[1] and court decisions,[2] for example, refer to a "gradual formation of consent" and see the contract as growing during the negotiations, as long as the essential terms are agreed, without being subject to a formalization of a "meeting of the minds" or to a full agreement on all terms of the transaction. Also German legislation[3] has

---

* Dr. juris (Oslo), PhD (Moscow), Professor, University of Oslo, Norway.
[1] Hagstrøm, V., *Avtalebundenhet ved forhandlinger i kommersielle forhold*, in Lov og Rett,1995, pp. 595ff., Woxholt, G., *Avtalerett*, Oslo 2003, pp. 149ff.
[2] Among the recent Supreme Court decisions on this matter see Rt 1998 s 946.
[3] BGB § 155; a battle of the forms results in a binding contract, but without the non-conforming terms, as long as there is no doubt about the parties' intention to be bound by the essential terms of the deal, see §§ 154.1 and 306.1, as interpreted in *Staudingers Kommentar zum Bürgerlichen Gesetzbuch*, Book 1, *Allgemeiner Teil 4*, Berlin 2003, § 150 note 18, § 155 note 12, and id., Book 2, *Recht*

recognised that a contract may be considered entered into even if not all the terms have been agreed upon, as long as these terms are not essential, and the "knock-out" doctrine in case of so-called "battle of the forms" is a manifestation of this.

In the context of larger commercial contracts with long-lasting and complicated negotiations, a wide-spread practice is to sign various documents in the course of the negotiations, usually named "Letters of Intent", „Heads of Agreement" or "Memoranda of Understanding". In the traditional picture of contract formation, a Letter of Intent is hard to categorize: it is not an offer, it is not an acceptance, it is not the final contract text. It is a pre-contractual document with an unclear function. A letter of intent is not necessarily easier to define under the more modern understanding of contract formation.[4] Can it be considered as an element in the growing consent? If so, what legal effects would it have? What will be addressed here is the question of the function of Letters of Intent, and whether adjustments in the law of contract formation may be desirable in order to ensure it an appropriate recognition.

II. Some types of Letter of Intent and their functions

The legal effects of a Letter of Intent cannot be conclusively assessed, mainly because the content and function of Letters of Intent vary considerably from case to case. Three typical versions of Letter of Intent will be considered here, their respective functions will be explained and some of the interesting aspects connected with their legal effects will be highlighted. In order to distinguish the three types from each other, the first one will be defined as "Letter of Intent", the second one as "Heads of Agreement", and the third one as "Memorandum of Understanding". These definitions, however, are used here only for convenience and are not suggested as the only or the most appropriate definitions for the respective types. The names for pre-contractual documents are numerous and seem to be used interchangeably, without any specific legal effects being attached to the name that is used at any specific time. Moreover, the various types described herein do not necessarily appear only in their

---

der Allgemeinen Geschäftsbedingungen, Berlin 2006, § 306 note 4, with further references to case law and literature.

[4] Although Letters of Intent have been receiving increasing attention in legal doctrine in the past decade or two, they seem to be still surrounded by a certain aura of mystery: see, for example, the comments made in Fontaine, M. and De Ly, F., *Drafting International Contracts*, Ardsley, New York, 2006, p. 6. See also Lake, R. and Draetta, U., *Letters of Intent and Other Precontractual Documents*, London 1994 and Lutter, M., *Der Letter of Intent*, Köln, Berlin, etc., 1998.

pure form; thus, pre-contractual documents may present elements of various types and be described with yet another name. For the purpose of simplicity, each individual type will be considered separately here.

1. Letter of Intent as a "preview" of the final contract

Sometimes Letters of Intent are written in a way that resembles the final contract that is being negotiated by the parties. A Letter of Intent of this type might, for example, contain articles stating that "the parties shall establish a jointly owned company for the purpose of manufacturing and selling the products (the "Newco")", "party A shall own 51% of the share capital of Newco and party B shall own 49%", "party A shall contribute to the share capital of Newco partly in kind, by transferring the technology related to the manufacturing of the Products, as herein defined, and partly in cash", "party B shall contribute to the share capital of Newco in kind, by transferring the ownership of the production facility located in XX". The Letter of Intent may continue with articles regulating the envisaged role of the parties in the future company ("party A shall be in charge of the technical production management, the financial management and the marketing strategy of Newco", "party B shall be in charge of the relations with the authorities and the human resources of Newco"). Until its last article, the Letter of Intent may, thus, be mistaken for being a binding contract between the parties. Not only the purpose of their cooperation, also its form and the parties' related rights and obligations are regulated in the Letter of Intent, maybe not in the finest details, but sufficiently to be determinable. The last article of the Letter of Intent, however, testifies that the document does not represent the final contract between the parties: the last article usually says something like "This document is a Letter of Intent and is not binding on the parties".

Apart from the apparent contradiction between the content of the text and its final negation in the last article, it seems difficult to understand the function of such a document.

a. No commitment to execute the contract

The parties seem to have quite clear ideas about the form of their cooperation (incorporation of a company), the respective areas of responsibility, even the split in the share capital: why did they sign a Letter of Intent and not a binding contract? The obvious answer is that the parties have not yet negotiated all the specific aspects of their cooperation and therefore are not in a position to write the contract in the degree of detail that they would feel comfortable with. Because details may have a significant impact on the evaluation of the transaction, it is understandable that the parties do not want to be bound until all technical, financial, commercial, etc. elements are finally agreed upon.

The document is said to be not binding, therefore the parties have not committed themselves to establish the joint company. Each of the parties can walk away from the deal if it loses interest in the cooperation.

b. An uncommitted description of terms

If the parties do not, and with good reason, want to be bound until they have agreed on all aspects of their cooperation, why do they describe their cooperation in such a precise way in the Letter of Intent and what is this document meant to achieve? The document is said to be not binding not only in respect of the freedom not to finalise the cooperation, but also in respect of the content of the cooperation: should party B during the negotiations decide that it is prepared to proceed with the cooperation only if it obtains 50% of the share capital of Newco (as opposed to the 49% set forth in the Letter of Intent), it would not be in breach of contract, because the document is not a binding contract. During the detailed negotiations, numerous issues may arise that impact upon the parties' respective evaluation of their own and the other party's contribution to the cooperation, and this may have consequences relating to the split of the share capital between themselves (for example, the technology to be transferred by A may turn out not to be the most modern or the most appropriate for the envisaged production). It is, therefore, understandable that the parties do not want to be bound to some items of the deal as long as the others are unclear.

While it may from a legal point of view be possible to argue that a certain parameter (for example, 49% of the share capital) was not binding, its disregard may create practical difficulties during the negotiations, and a sudden change of position in such an important respect might undermine the mutual trust that is necessary for a successful cooperation.

Therefore, the Letter of Intent may be seen as an attempt to convey a certain moral pressure against unjustified modifications to the terms contained therein, sometimes coupled (possibly unconsciously) with a malicious thought that this might restrict the other party's freedom, while its own freedom remains unaffected due to the non-binding character of the document. Sometimes the moral pressure is expressed in the same clause determining the non-binding character of the document, that continues with a provision according to which "the parties shall continue negotiations in good faith", or "the parties shall use their best efforts to reach an agreement". Often these clauses are not considered to be particularly binding, and they are defined as being "only" best effort obligations, therefore without any binding content. The legal effects of these obligations will be touched upon in section III.3 below.

c. Exclusion of liability

What other reasons may the parties have to sign a Letter of Intent in this form? It is not unusual for one party to emphasise the last article of the Letter of Intent, about the parties not being bound. In these cases a party may deem that the most important function of a Letter of Intent consists in establishing that the parties are not bound. A party may, for example, wish to keep all possibilities open to start a similar cooperation with a third party, or to enter that specific market on its own. A Letter of Intent specifically stating that the parties are not bound may create the illusion that any break off of the negotiations is acceptable. If the parties want to maintain full liberty in respect of the negotiations, why do they execute a document describing in relative detail the result that the negotiations are supposed to achieve? Sometimes the explanation may be found in a malicious use of the ambiguity of this document. The non binding character will be invoked if one party wishes to break off the negotiations or to modify the terms set forth in the Letter of Intent, whereas the moral commitment will be invoked if it wishes to prevent the other party from doing so. In other situations the Letter of Intent may be executed out of contractual habit, because it is customary to execute this kind of document during complex negotiations. If the parties do not have specific matters that should be regulated in the pre-contractual phase (which would lead them to adopt one of the two types of pre-contractual documents that will be described below), but want to comply with the contractual habit of executing a pre-contractual document, they may end up drafting a Letter of Intent without a clear function, such as the one described here.

d. Regulation of the parties' conduct during the negotiations

If the Letter of Intent contains clauses regulating the relationship between the parties during the negotiations, it may have an important function: for example, a clause according to which the parties commit not to negotiate with third parties for a determined period of time, a clause according to which the parties commit to keep any information exchanged during the negotiations confidential, a clause submitting any disputes arising out of the Letter of Intent to a certain governing law and to arbitration. These commitments may be of crucial importance to the parties.

The effectiveness of these clauses, however, may be questioned, if the final article ("This document is not binding on the parties") is deemed to cover these provisions also. Also, the effectiveness of a choice of law and of an arbitration clause may be questioned, if the document is not considered to be a contract, since in various systems choice of law and arbitration are restricted to contractual questions. This can be avoided by a proper drafting, for example by stating that certain clauses are intended to be binding. A Letter of Intent of this kind would be the hybrid between a document purporting not to have a legal effect and a contract regulating specific rights and obligations, similar to the one described in section II.3 below.

e. Unclear Function

In summary, a Letter of Intent drafted as if it was the final contract, with a qualifying clause that it is not binding, seems to have a highly unclear function: it is not a commitment to finalise the cooperation, it is not a commitment to apply certain criteria or parameters in case the cooperation is finalized, it may not even be a commitment to certain conduct during the negotiations. As long as the function of the document remains so unclear, it is not surprising that it is not easy to find appropriate regulation for such documents in the law of formation of contract. To what extent the goals of a Letter of Intent of this type may be achieved will be discussed in section III.2 below.

2. Letter of Intent (Heads of Agreement) as a confirmation of partial agreement

Sometimes the parties to a Letter of Intent wish to record a partial agreement that they have reached in the negotiations of a complicated matter. The parties may, for example, have discussed and reached an agreement on the technological and commercial aspects of their envisaged cooperation, while the financial and legal aspects thereof still remain to be discussed. In such a situation, the parties may wish to formalize their agreement on the aspects that have already been negotiated, while maintaining an uncommitted approach to the execution of the contract. In other words, the parties are still unbound, but they agree that some terms of the prospective deal are firm and shall be incorporated in the final contract, if there will be a final contract. In such a situation, the parties may want to sign a form of Letter of Intent, that will be defined here, for convenience, as Heads of Agreement. As opposed to the form of Letter of Intent that was discussed above, the Heads of Agreement do not purport to constitute a non binding document. However, their effect does not extend to committing the parties to the final cooperation. Should the parties resolve to proceed to the cooperation, they will have to incorporate the parameters that were set forth in the Heads of Agreement.

The function of the document is easier to see in the Heads of Agreement than in the Letter of Intent as described above: in complicated transactions the negotiations may go on over several years, and numerous teams from each of the parties may be involved, each with its own specialization. Even if each party has a project manager maintaining overall control over the negotiations, the convenience of recording and rendering firm the specific terms to which each of the teams arrived in the course of the months and years of negotiations is evident. At the same time, it is understandable that the parties desire to maintain the freedom not to finalise the deal, until all the elements have been agreed upon and the transaction in its totality can be evaluated. The Heads of Agreement allow the parties freedom not to commit executing the contract, and at the same time prevent the re-opening of already negotiated elements over and over again. Sometimes this is coupled with an expressed obligation to negotiate the remaining terms of the contract in good faith. The legal effectiveness of this mechanism, however, deserves a more extensive comment, that will be made in section III.3 below.

3. Letter of Intent (Memorandum of Understanding) as a tool for structuring negotiations

Sometimes the parties to a Letter of Intent, that in this context will be referred to as a Memorandum of Understanding, wish to utilize the document for the purpose of structuring the negotiations and regulating their relationship during the pre-contractual phase. The parties may, for example, need to proceed with various feasibility studies of different aspects of the prospective cooperation (geological, technical, financial, etc.), they may need to arrange with third parties the terms of the financing and the insurance, they may need to assess with third parties the terms for supply of utilities or raw materials, and many other aspects might need assessment before a comprehensive contract may be drafted. Many of the activities required in connection with such extensive assessments are expensive and time-consuming; the parties may wish to allocate the responsibility and the costs for these activities between each other. Some of these activities may be initiated only after others have been concluded (for example, the negotiation of the financing may take place only after the various parameters for the fixed costs, such as the supply of utilities and energy, have been determined); therefore, the parties may wish to regulate the timetable for each of these activities.

In addition to the regulation of this extensive activity, the parties may wish to regulate the question of exclusivity in negotiations, for example fixing a time period within which each of them commits not to negotiate with any third parties, as well as confidentiality provisions in respect of the information obtained or developed during this activity.

The Memoranda of Understanding have the function of regulating these rights and obligations between the parties in the phase of negotiations. They have the function and the legal effect of a contract, and they may well contain a choice of law and an arbitration clause. They create an enforceable commitment between the parties: not a commitment to execute the future contract, to incorporate therein some specific terms, or to negotiate in good faith, as seen in respect of the Letter of Intent or the Heads of Agreement above, but a commitment to carry out certain activities during the phase of negotiations, to bear some costs, to refrain from negotiating with other parties for a certain period, not to disclose certain information, etc. The fact that they are called Letter of Intent or Memorandum of Understanding or some other name that refers to the pre-contractual phase in which they are employed does not deprive them of their binding legal effects, as long as the content is described with sufficient certainty.

III. Some observations on the legal effect of pre-contractual documents

As seen above, it may be difficult to identify the functions of some of the described pre-contractual documents. Once the functions are identified, moreover, they might turn out not to be effective means to achieve the desired goals. Some interesting aspects related to the legal effects in selected legal systems will be discussed below.

1. No commitment to execute the contract

As long as the will of the parties not to be bound is expressed with sufficient clarity, then without question it seems that the final contract cannot be deemed to be formed, even if it is described in full detail in the Letter of Intent.

The matter may be evaluated differently, however, if some time has elapsed following execution of the Letter of Intent. If the parties have continued negotiations, have added further details of the envisaged transaction, if one party has started costly preparations for performance without the other party pointing out that no final contract has been formed, or even if both parties have started performance of the transaction, their conduct may be interpreted as a manifestation of their will to be bound to the result of the negotiations, or as a waiver of the clause according to which the document was not binding. If the Letter of Intent contains all the essential elements of a contract, such an interpretation is certainly possible, depending on the factual circumstances. That a Letter of Intent may be considered to constitute the final contract, therefore, is not completely unlikely, but will depend on the factual circumstances.

This interpretation might, to a certain extent, be influenced by the degree of loyalty that the parties owe to each other according to the governing law. As will be seen in more detail below, traditionally legal systems of the Civil Law, particularly those influenced by the Germanic tradition, assume that the parties are under a duty of loyalty even during the phase of negotiations of a contract,[5] whereas the systems of the Common Law, particularly English law, are more based on the freedom of the parties to assess their own risks and take care of their own interests.[6] Breach of the duty of loyalty (if any) in the example given above, where a party has started costly preparations in the legitimate expectation that the contract will be concluded and the other party has not pointed out that no binding contract exists between the parties nor is likely to be signed, is primarily likely to result in a liability to reimburse damages, rather than considering the contract as entered into. However, it cannot be excluded that the existence of a duty of loyalty might affect the interpretation of the parties' conduct and lead to the conclusion that the parties intended to be bound.

---

[5] The pre-contractual liability, or *culpa in contrahendo*, was introduced in the German legal system by Jhering, R., "Culpa in contrahendo, oder Schadenersatz bei nichtigen oder nicht zur Perfektion galangten Verträgen", in *Jahrbücher für die Dogmatik des heutigen römischen und deutschen Privatrechts*, vol. 4, 1861, pp. 1 et seq. The BGB reform of 2002 has now codified it in § 311, but case law already had established, following Jhering, that by starting negotiations the parties enter into a special relationship creating a duty of loyalty to each other according to § 241, para. 2, the breach of which entitles the other party to reimbursement of damages (in the reformed BGB, according to § 280). In Norwegian law pre-contractual liability has been extensively analysed in Simonsen, L., *Prekontraktuelt ansvar*, Oslo 1997, who considers the general principle of fair dealing and mutual trust in the negotiations as a basis, see pp. 122 et seq. and 151 et seq. See also Hagstrøm, V. and Aarbakke, M., *Obligasjonsrett*, Oslo 2003, p. 86.

[6] English law, in particular, is quite restrictive in allowing interference with the parties' freedom in the pre-contractual phase, as will be seen below. In other systems belonging to the Common Law, the concept of good faith and fair dealing is considered to be more relevant already in the phase prior to the conclusion of contract.

The Letter of Intent as such, therefore, does not constitute the final contract or create an obligation to execute the final contract. In the legal systems that assume a duty of loyalty in the phase of negotiations, however, a Letter of Intent might be considered as creating, or rather as enhancing, an already existing duty to negotiate in good faith, as will be seen in the sections below.

2. Uncommitted description of terms

As long as the pre-contractual document, as seen in the Letter of Intent described in section II.1 above, specifically aims at avoiding any binding legal effects, it is justifiable to hold that the parties intended that no legal effects should arise out of the document. One can however wonder what exactly the parties wanted to achieve with it: that the function of such a document is unclear, has already been mentioned above, and will not be repeated here. Since a document describing the envisaged transaction has been drafted and signed, however, it is worthwhile investigating whether the execution of this document creates some legal effects in spite of the parties' explicit intention to avoid any such effects. The question is whether the existence of a Letter of Intent creates a special duty of care between the parties, or enhances an existing duty of loyalty or duty to negotiate in good faith. If this were the case, the Letter of Intent would turn out to have unexpected legal effects and even be counterproductive.

The answer varies according to the law governing the legal relationship. As will be explained more in detail below, the approach of Common Law systems (particularly, of English law) and of Civil Law systems differs considerably in respect of the pre-contractual phase. While English law is based on the freedom of the parties to structure the negotiations as they please and on the principle that each party is to assess its own risks and to negotiate the contract in such a way that it takes care of its own interests, the Civilian systems are based on an underlying principle of good faith, that extends even to the pre-contractual phase and may create liability in the case of disloyal conduct. A negotiating party does not incur liability under English law if it changes the terms of the deal during the negotiations or if it decides not to enter into the negotiated contract. Also under German or Norwegian law a party is free to change the terms of the deal under negotiation or to decide not to execute the final contract; however, if this conduct is carried out contrary to good faith and has caused damages to the other party, there may be a basis for invoking pre-contractual liability.

Would the execution of a Letter of Intent add to or modify these approaches to pre-contractual liability?

Under English law, it seems that the primary means of grounding pre-contractual liability would be to assume a duty of care between the parties. Where such a duty exists, negotiations must be carried out in good faith. A duty of care in the negotiations normally exists only where there is a relationship of a fiduciary nature, such as in employment contracts, counselling relationships or where a party is performing functions in the public interest within a statutory framework,[7] circumstances that do not normally occur in the context of commercial contracts. Would the execution of a Letter of Intent create such a duty of care? There is no authority to suggest so; in fact, the aversion of English courts against agreements to agree, famously manifested by the House of Lords in *Walford v. Miles*, is well known: "A duty to negotiate in good faith is as unworkable in practice as it is inherently inconsistent with a position of a negotiating party. [...] [W]hile negotiations are in existence either party is entitled to withdraw from these negotiations, at any time and for any reason. [...] Accordingly, a bare agreement to negotiate has no legal content."[8] Therefore, even if the Letter of Intent contained a clause explicitly requiring the parties to negotiate in good faith, it would not be enforceable. This seems to confirm that a Letter of Intent is not capable of creating any duty between the parties, even more so if it does not contain any clause on good faith negotiations.

Would the execution of a Letter of Intent enhance the duty of loyalty already existing in the Civilian systems? The requirement of good faith increases progressively as the parties get closer to each other's position under the negotiations and the expectation that a contract will be concluded becomes stronger.[9] The execution of a Letter of Intent, as such, is not an occurrence that has automatic effects in this context; however, depending on its content and on the phase of the negotiations in which the document is signed, and particularly when the Letter of Intent describes in some detail the final result of the negotiations, it may be considered as evidence of the closeness of the parties' relationship. That the parties negotiated, drafted and executed a document describing their common goals certainly seems to testify to a closer relationship than if only loose communications had taken place. In itself the process of drafting and negotiating the Letter of Intent is likely to have brought the parties closer to each other's position within the aim of formulating the common goals. When the Letter of Intent contains an extensive description of the deal it may be considered as evidence of a quite advanced

---

[7] *Re Debtors (nos 449 and 450 of 1998)* 1 All E.R.(comm.) 149, at p. 158, and see *Chitty on Contracts*, vol. I, 2004, 2-134. See also *Chandler v. Crane, Christmas & Co*, [1951] 2 K.B. 164.
[8] *Walford v. Miles* [1992] 1 All E.R. 453, 461.
[9] For Norwegian law see Simonsen, *op.cit.*, 242 et seq.

status of the negotiations, and therefore it can be used as a basis for arguing that the duty of good faith owed to each other is enhanced. This would be even more so if the Letter of Intent contained a clause referring to negotiations in good faith. The consequences of the breach of such duty will be seen below in sections III.3 and III.4.

3. Confirmation of partial agreement

The confirmation of partial agreement characteristic of the pre-contractual document that was defined as Heads of Agreement in section II.2 has, *prima facie*, a clearer function than the Letter of Intent. The parties do not claim to be completely uncommitted; they register that they agreed on certain terms of the envisaged transaction, and they agree to insert these terms in the future final contract. The parties, however, do not commit themselves to the final contract or to the other terms of the envisaged transaction. They remain free to negotiate other terms, to introduce new ones, to withdraw others, or to resolve that they will not enter into the final contract.

The legal effects of the Heads of Agreement have to be assessed in light of this combination of commitment and freedom. The direct legal effects consist in the commitment to incorporate the agreed terms in the final contract, if the parties resolve to execute a final contract. Therefore, a party will be in breach of the Heads of Agreement (and incur liability for breach of contract) if it insists on executing the final contract without the agreed terms. It does not seem very realistic, however, that a party should openly violate the Heads of Agreement: if it does not intend to execute the contract, it remains free to do so without violating the Heads of Agreement, and if it is interested in the final contract but wishes to change the agreed terms, in many situations it will be possible to propose new terms complementar to those already agreed that will have the effect of indirectly modifying the agreed terms without directly violating the Heads of Agreement. The Heads of Agreement, therefore, seem not to be a very efficient instrument.

Therefore, it is worth investigating whether the Heads of Agreement have some further legal effects, beyond the commitment to incorporate the agreed terms. These effects could possibly consist of an obligation to negotiate the remaining terms of the contract in such a way that they do not contradict or affect the terms already agreed. This would not be an obligation to achieve a certain result, because the parties do not know, prior to the negotiations, what result they will achieve, if they will achieve any result at all. It would be an obligation to conduct the negotiations taking due account of the terms of the Heads of Agreement, to negotiate in such a way that the terms contained in the Heads of Agreement are not deprived of their intended meaning. Put differently, this would be an obligation referring not to the result of the negotiations, but to the conduct of the negotiations. It would be an obligation to use best efforts to reach an agreement incorporating the terms of the Heads of Agreement. Sometimes the Heads of Agreement may contain a clause explicitly referring to a duty to continue negotiations in good faith, which may be considered as equivalent.

Would this obligation have any legal effects? Under English law, as already pointed out, an obligation to agree or to negotiate in good faith is not enforceable. Would a best effort obligation to reach an agreement be enforceable? A best effort obligation differs from a result obligation in that it does not guarantee a result, but it guarantees that measures will be undertaken in order to reach a certain result. If the result is not reached there is no breach, as long as the measures were properly taken. Best effort obligations are enforceable under English law, as long as the promised conduct is sufficiently certain. Thus, best effort obligations to obtain an export licence are enforceable (and breach thereof can be basis for liability), because it is sufficiently clear what would constitute best efforts: apply for a licence, comply with the authorities' requirements, etc.[10] A best effort obligation to reach an agreement, on the other hand, could be considered as equivalent to an obligation to negotiate in good faith, and would not meet the requirements of certainty:[11] what would exactly be expected of the parties is unclear, given that the parties are not subject to any duty of loyalty or other restrictions during the pre-contractual phase and are free to assess their own interests during the negotiations. Therefore, violation of any such best effort obligation would not be considered as a basis for liability under English law.

In the Civilian systems, generally, the obligation to negotiate in good faith arises out of the already mentioned duty of loyalty between the parties. As already seen above, this obligation may be enhanced by the fact that the parties have negotiated and executed a Letter of Intent laying down the main terms of their negotiations; the obligation may be even further entrenched by the Heads of Agreement, especially if they purport to be binding. It seems, therefore, without question that the Heads of Agreement are accompanied in many Civilian systems by an obligation to continue the negotiation of the terms still outstanding in such a way that the meaning and purpose of the agreed terms is not affected. If one takes a closer look, however, the question is raised of how a violation of this

---

[10] *Chitty, op cit.*, 2-135 and footnote 549.
[11] *Ibid.* and footnote 550, interpreting *Walford v. Miles*, cir. However, this interpretation is not completely uncontroversial, see for example *Anson's law of contract*, 28th ed., Oxford 2002, pp. 64 et seq., interpreting the same case as if it considered best endeavours to agree as enforceable.

best effort obligation could be established and what would be the consequences of breaching such an obligation.

There will likely be considerable evidential difficulties in establishing that negotiations have not been carried out in good faith, or that a party has not employed its best efforts to reach an agreement, if the disagreement relates to specific substantial aspects of the transaction. The evaluation of the parties' respective contributions, the organisation of the envisaged activity, the allocation of costs and profits depend on the totality of the envisaged transaction, on how the transaction fits into each of the parties' business concept, marketing strategy, procurement arrangements, etc. Each party evaluates all these aspects according to its own criteria and interests, and it might be very difficult to argue that a certain evaluation is not made in good faith.

Should it nevertheless be possible to argue that a party did not use its best efforts to reach an agreement, it seems that the only remedy that would be available is reimbursement of losses incurred by the other party as a consequence of this violation.

The classical Civilian remedy for breach of obligation, specific performance, does not seem to be available in the case of an obligation to negotiate in good faith. An imaginable circumstance in which specific performance might be possible is if the object of the obligation were the result of the negotiations, i.e. to execute the contract. Since the object of the obligation is the process of the negotiations, however, it seems impossible to obtain specific performance by forcing one party to be cooperative. It is possible to imagine a situation in which the Heads of Agreement were very detailed and extensive, and then during the further negotiations one party presented all the other outstanding terms to the other party; if all these terms were accepted in full by the other party, and then the first party had introduced new elements to engineer a disagreement in the negotiations that did not really exist, the possible result of the negotiations might appear to be easier to identify. Even in such a far-fetched case, however, it does not seem possible to perform the obligation to negotiate in good faith by specifically disregarding the last introduction of terms and considering the contract as formed on the basis of the Heads of Agreement and the terms that have been proposed by one party and accepted by the other. Such a specific performance would render the proposal of terms during negotiations as equivalent to an offer that becomes binding if it is accepted. During negotiations, however, the parties are not making offers; they are following their respective strategic lines towards a complex consensus, and this might well entail the willingness to move closer to the other party on some areas but not on others, introducing new elements for balancing other concessions, and so on. It is in the nature of complex negotiations, even if they are carried out in good faith, that the total picture acceptable to each of the parties is not known until the end of the process. A remedy of specific performance that crystallizes the negotiations prior to the conclusion of the process would not correspond to the function of the negotiations. The only possible remedy to a breach of the obligation to negotiate in good faith seems, therefore, to be the reimbursement of damages. Because the terms of the final contract are not determinable, it is not possible to assess the loss incurred by the other party in relation to the expected gains that the negotiated contract would have created if it had been entered into. The reimbursable damages, therefore, would have to be the costs and losses incurred as a consequence of the failed negotiations. This seems to coincide with the regime in the legal systems that regulate pre-contractual liability.[12]

Even assuming, therefore, that a breach of the obligation to negotiate in good faith may be proven in respect of the substance of the negotiations, which seems to be quite difficult, the Heads of Agreement do not seem to add considerably to the already existing regime of pre-contractual liability.

4. Exclusion of liability

One of the most important clauses of pre-contractual documents is deemed to be the clause specifying that no party shall be considered liable for the failure to reach an agreement and that each party shall bear its own costs and shall not seek compensation from the other party for any losses or damages that it might incur as a consequence of the negotiations or their failure. Letters of Intent and most other pre-contractual documents often are intended to emphasise the parties' full freedom during the negotiations.

As seen in section III.3, the freedom of each party to form its own business evaluation of the envisaged transaction and to decide whether the negotiated terms are acceptable or not does not seem to be restricted by an obligation to negotiate in good faith or a best effort obligation to reach an agreement, whether they are explicitly contained in a pre-contractual document or implied by the governing law.

It is possible to identify at least two further elements in the desired freedom during the negotiations: freedom in respect of the reasons (beyond the substantial reasons described above) for initiating, continuing or breaking off the negotiations, and freedom in respect of the way in which the negotiations are conducted. In respect of these two elements, the parties might incur a liability, particularly under many Civilian laws, that a

---

[12] See *Staudinger, op cit., Allgemeiner Teil 4*, cit., §§ 145–156, notes 28 d) and 50, with further references. For an extensive analysis under Norwegian law see Simonsen, *op.cit.*, pp. 320 et seq.

pre-contractual document is not necessarily capable of excluding and that, on the contrary, might be enhanced by such a document that seems apt to increase the duty of loyalty existing between the parties.

The former element relates to good faith in the initiation or continuance of negotiations. A party may initiate negotiations knowing from the outset that it will not enter into the final contract; the negotiations may be started for many reasons, such as, for example, to prevent the other party from entering into a contract with a third party, or to develop its own knowledge about that type of transaction, or to have some terms with which to compare the terms of another negotiation that is being carried on in parallel. Alternatively, the negotiations might have started in good faith, but at a certain point in time one party may have resolved not to enter into a contract with that counterparty, and yet might have continued the negotiations, for example for the reasons just mentioned. The negotiations might then be brought to an end either because the party that did not intend to finalize the contract executed a similar contract with a third party, or because it arranged its business in such a way that the contract is not necessary or possible, or because for other reasons it lost interest, even in the real grounds for continuing the negotiations. The break off of the negotiations may be open or disguised by some substantial impossibility to reach an agreement, wilfully created by that party. This conduct does not seem to ground liability under English law;[13] it would, though, represent a breach of the obligation to negotiate in good faith existing under many Civilian laws.[14]

The latter element would consist, for example, of withholding material information relevant to the other party's evaluation of the negotiated transaction, thus inducing the other party to continue negotiations that otherwise would have been of no interest. As long as this conduct does

---

[13] According to the rule expressed by the House of Lord in *Walford v. Miles, op cit.* See also *Regalian Properties v. London Dockland Development Corp.*, [1995] W.L.R.212. A partial remedy against this conduct is represented by the doctrine of restitution; however, restitution aims at recovering a benefit gained by the party which walked away from the negotiations, not at compensating the losses suffered by the other party, see *Chitty, op cit.*, paras. 29-001 et seq. In some cases a restitutionary obligation may arise even if no benefit was gained, but this is primarily so if the other party has rendered services at the request of the party breaking off: see *Chitty, op cit.*, paras. 29-012 et seq., 29-020 et seq., and *Anson,op cit.*, p. 67.

[14] As long as the party breaking off the negotiations has created an expectation in the other party as to the seriousness of the negotiations, there is a breach of the duty of loyalty provided for in § 241, para. 1 BGB; see Staudinger, *op cit*, Book 2, *Vertragsschluss*, Berlin 2005, § 311 Notes 109 et seq. For Norwegian law, see Hagstrøm, Aarbakke, *op.cit.*, p. 86, and Simonsen, *op.cit.*, pp. 195 et seq.

not result in giving false information to the other party, it does not seem to be able to ground liability under English law: silence is not deemed to be a misrepresentation.[15] It would represent a violation of the duty to negotiate in good faith existing in many Civil Law systems.[16]

What would be the remedies for this breach of the duty to conduct the negotiations in good faith? As already seen, it does not seem possible to obtain specific performance in this case, as there is no obligation to conclude a contract and, even if there was one, the terms of the contract would not be determined or determinable with sufficient certainty. The available remedy would be the reimbursement of damages, and the damages would be measured in accordance with the so-called negative interest, i.e. the losses connected with having relied on the failed negotiations. A liability in this respect would be an exception to the general principle that each party bears its own costs in connection with negotiations and preparations of contracts, and is based on the theory of the *culpa in contrahendo*.

Would it be possible to exclude liability for such conduct with a pre-contractual document? A document emphasising that the parties are free to withdraw from the negotiations at any moment and for any reason is certainly sufficient under English law to exclude any liability for, e.g., costs incurred by the other party for the specific purpose of preparing the performance of the negotiated contract, since there is no such liability under English law in the first place.[17] The answer is less certain in Civilian systems. An agreement to exclude liability for gross negligence or wilful misconduct does not seem to be enforceable,[18] therefore the legal effects of the exclusion of pre-contractual liability must be regarded from a different perspective: not as an acknowledgement of one party's possibility to act contrary to good faith, but as an acknowledgement that the other party is aware of the first party's position and that therefore conduct in accordance with that position would not be considered contrary good faith. If, for example, a party discloses in the pre-contractual docu-

---

[15] Chitty, *op cit.*, para. 6-013.
[16] Information duties are among the classical duties of loyalty arising out of § 241 BGB; Staudinger, *op.cit.*, Book 2, *Einleitung zum Schuldrecht, Treu und Glauben*, Berlin 2005, § 241, notes 429 et seq.; specifically for the pre-contractual phase, see Staudinger, *op.cit.*, Book 2, *Vertragsschluss, op cit.*, § 311 note 107. In respect of Norwegian law, see Simonsen, *op.cit.*, 47 et seq., 192 et seq.
[17] See footnote 13 above.
[18] The principle of good faith (Treu und Glauben) is contained in § 242 and is considered to be mandatory, see Staudinger, *op.cit.*, Book 2, *Einleitung zum Schuldrecht, Treu und Glauben*, cit., § 242 notes 107 et seq. For an extensive analysis of Norwegian theory and case law on the subject matter, see Hagstrøm, Aaarbakke, *op.cit.*, pp. 624 et seq.

ment that it is carrying out parallel negotiations with a third party, failure to finalize the contract because it was concluded with the third party cannot be deemed to be a violation of the duty to negotiate in good faith. Assuming, however, that the pre-contractual document does not mention anything in respect of parallel negotiations, that the negotiations are quite advanced, and that the other party, relying on an imminent conclusion of the final contract, starts to prepare the performance of the contract by initiating, for example, a costly reorganization of its activity; if the party that does not intend to conclude the contract does not inform the other party of the uncertainty connected with the finalization of the contract and silently lets the other party incur these costs, a clause in the pre-contractual document excluding liability generally does not seem to be sufficient.

5. Regulation of the parties' conduct

The regulation of the parties' conduct during the negotiations, typical of the document that was defined here as Memorandum of Understanding (and that obviously could be present also in the other types of pre-contractual documents), is a contractual regulatory instrument aimed at allocating risk between the parties, defining obligations, as well as remedies for their breach. A Memorandum of Understanding, therefore, does not create particular interpretative or structural problems: it is a binding and enforceable contract, even if it is concluded in connection with the negotiations of another contract.

IV. Developments in the legal systems for a more effective use of Letters of Intent?

The law of contract formation does not seem to pay express attention to the phenomenon of pre-contractual documents. Are adjustments possible or desirable, to ensure that this wide-spread contractual practice finds a proper recognition?

1. Unclear function

Many of the difficulties in identifying a legal regime for pre-contractual documents are probably a consequence of the unclear function of some of these documents, as seen above. As long as the parties draft a document that purports to have no legally binding effects but some sort of moral commitments, and they possibly count on the ambiguity of the document to invoke full freedom or moral commitment according to what is more advantageous on a particular occasion, it is not surprising and not problematic that Letters of Intent do not enjoy a direct recognition in the law of contract formation.

2. Contrasting legal traditions

Other difficulties in identifying an adequate regulation of pre-contractual documents may be the consequence of the different approaches in different legal traditions that the documents might be connected with.

Should the Letter of Intent or Heads of Agreement contain a clause obliging the parties to negotiate in good faith, or to use their best efforts to reach an agreement, that clause would be considered as not enforceable under English law, because it is not sufficiently certain, and it would not add considerably to the Civilian regimes. In neither case would this clause have a considerable impact on the parties' freedom to evaluate the substance of the envisaged transaction and to decide whether the negotiated terms are acceptable or not.

Letters of Intent, however, are often written in a way that seems to assume the regime of freedom to negotiate existing under English law: the parties specify that they are not committed to execute the contract, that they are not bound to incorporate in any final contract the terms contained in the Letter of Intent, that they are not liable for any of their conduct during the negotiations. Under English law, the parties would not really have needed to write all this in the Letter of Intent, because this freedom would follow by operation of law. This is not the only example of redundant contractual practice, so it should not be too surprising that the parties spell out in the Letter of Intent a freedom that they enjoy anyway under the law. Under a Civilian law, the parties might not achieve the described freedom in full; on the contrary, by executing a Letter of Intent they run the risk of increasing or specifying the duty of loyalty that in turn reduces their freedom under the negotiations. This is not the only example of contractual practice borrowed from the Common Law tradition and clashing with principles of the Civil Law.

Contractual practice, therefore, seems to have taken a direction, with the wide-spread use of Letters of Intent, not compatible with the prevailing principles in many Civil Law systems. Would it be possible, *de lege ferenda*, to reconcile these two dimensions, so that the acknowledged practice of executing Letters of Intent obtains an adequate recognition also in the Civil Law systems?

3. Trans-national models

It is tempting to look for inspiration in the restatements of principles for international contracts, the UNIDROIT Principles and the Principles of European Contract Law. Is their regulation of pre-contractual liability more adequate than the traditional Civilian approach, to regulate the practice of executing Letters of Intent?

At first sight, the regime of the UNIDROIT Principles and of the PECL seems to substantially correspond with the Civil Law tradition: the principle of good faith is said to underlie the whole of the restatements,[19] the parties are under a duty of loyalty to each other with various manifestations under the negotiations,[20] and they are liable for unjustified break-off of negotiations.[21] This approach does not seem to be very compatible with the full freedom under the negotiations, the absence of a duty to negotiate in good faith and the unenforceability of an agreement to agree characteristic of the English system and assumed by the drafters of a typical Letter of Intent.

A more careful analysis of the matter, however, makes the resemblance between the restatements and the Civil tradition less evident: this is because the standard of good faith, against which the restatements measure the pre-contractual liability, is expressly to be established not on the basis of a national legal tradition, but on the basis of the standard generally recognised in international trade.[22] One of the most important sources of generally acknowledged principles of international trade is international contract practice; and the wide-spread contract practice of writing Letters of Intent seems to indicate that the parties do not expect to be bound by a mutual duty of loyalty when they write that they shall remain uncommitted and that any liability for break-off of negotiations or otherwise shall be excluded. Therefore, it does not seem correct to construe the principle of good faith in the restatements as if it imposed obligations or duties in clear contradiction with contract practice, which is one of the most important sources that shall be used to precisely establish the content of the principle of good faith. On the other hand: the principle of good faith is undoubtedly given a central role in the restatements; therefore, it does not seem logical to construe it, albeit in accordance with in-

---

[19] See article 1.7 of the UNIDROIT Principles of International Commercial Contracts and article 1:201 of the PECL.

[20] See article 2.1.15(2) of the UNIDROIT Principles of International Commercial Contracts and article 2:301(2) of the PECL.

[21] See article 2.1.15(3) of the UNIDROIT Principles of International Commercial Contracts and article 2:301(3) of the PECL.

[22] See article 1.6 of the UNIDROIT Principles of International Commercial Contracts and article 1:106 of the PECL.

ternationally recognised contract practice, in such a restrictive way that it is deprived of any significant role. This paradox renders the regime of the restatements quite unpredictable in its application, and therefore not fully adequate to regulate commercial relationships, where the foreseeability of the legal positions and of the remedies is deemed to be very important.

4. Conclusion

In conclusion, it seems that the most appropriate way to recognise the practice of executing Letters of Intent would be to adopt an approach close to that of English law, with minimal interference by duties of loyalty or of good faith in the pre-contractual phase. The principles of loyalty and good faith, however, are fundamental principles of the Civilian traditions, even if in varying degrees in different countries, and even if the application of these principles might be more restricted in the context of commercial transactions between professional parties, where Letters of Intent may be more common. The use of Letters of Intent, therefore, seems to be doomed to clash to a certain degree with the Civil Law tradition. Also, in view of the unclear function of some Letters of Intent, that seems to invite malicious use of their ambiguity, it seems questionable, to what extent this contract practice deserves such an acknowledgement as to induce modification to fundamental principles of the legal systems.

The parties are advised to carefully evaluate the legal effects of the documents that they execute, and to avoid documents with an unclear function. The use of pre-contractual documents for allocating between the parties duties connected with the pre-contractual phase, for regulating rights and obligations during the negotiations, for establishing confidentiality or other obligations is advisable and does not create interpretative or structural problems. The use of pre-contractual documents for describing envisaged but uncommitted obligations, for creating moral but non binding obligations, for maintaining or creating a total freedom in connection with the described object, as seen above, is more uncertain in respect of the legal effects, and may even turn out to achieve a result opposite to the desired.

New Mechanisms for Concluding Contracts

Thomas Pfeiffer (Heidelberg)

I. Offer and Acceptance

When I was asked by the organizers of this conference to give a speech on "New Mechanisms for Concluding Contracts", I was a bit unsure whether they had the same in mind as I have. It may be helpful, therefore, at the outset, to clarify that I am not going to speak about new technological developments, such as the conclusion of contracts via the internet. In that respect, questions may arise concerning computers generating declarations of legal intent. Those questions, however, do not relate to the legal mechanism for the conclusion of contracts, which is what I am going to speak about.

At the outset, one may wonder whether the legal mechanism for the conclusion of contracts deserves any special attention. More or less all legal systems recognize that a contract can be concluded by an exchange of offer and acceptance. In an international perspective, this principle is, e.g., embedded in articles 14–24 CISG or in articles 2:201–2:211 PECL.

However, it is a well known fact that a mere exchange of offer and acceptance – "I offer you this contract. Do you accept?"/"I do." – is limited to take-it-or-leave-it situations and that, in many cases, the parties negotiate their contracts, which is likely to result into a more complicated exchange of statements and declarations. Again, all legal systems recognize therefore that the real issue is more complicated: It is about the existence of sufficient consent, which may emerge during longer periods of contact or a longer process of contractual negotiations.

Moreover, consent depends, to some extent, on its definition: A legal system may either follow the so-called "mirror image rule" requiring that an acceptance exactly matches the offer, or it may (under certain circumstances) allow that the acceptance deviates from the offer (see e.g. article 19 para 2 CISG or article 2:208 paras 2 and 3 PECL).

In the present transitory situation of European contract law, it is therefore necessary to take a closer look at some new phenomena of contract law in order to understand better what the conclusion of contracts is about.

II. New phenomena

Such new phenomena can be observed in the context of both consumer contracts and business transactions:

1. Consumer law

a. Information, formation, withdrawal

Sometimes, the "new" mechanism for the conclusion of consumer contracts is analyzed as a process comprising three stages: information, exchange of declarations, and a cooling-off period with a right to withdraw from the contract for the consumer.[1]

In this context, information requirements form an essential part of various European consumer law directives. They apply to situations that place the consumer at a significant informational disadvantage because of the technical medium used for contracting, the physical distance between business and consumer, or the nature of the transaction, and require the supplier to provide information about certain circumstances which in particular include the main characteristics of the goods or services, the price including delivery charges, taxes and other costs, the address and identity of the business with whom the consumer is transacting, the terms of the contract, the rights and obligations of both contracting parties, and any available redress procedures (Principles of Existing EC Contract Law – "Acquis Principles", article 2:203, forthcoming).

Whereas information duties can be analyzed as derivative (and extensions) of the general obligation to negotiate in good faith,[2] withdrawal

---

[1] For this problem see *Thomas Pfeiffer*, Der Vertragsschluss im Gemeinschaftsrecht, in: Reiner Schulze/Martin Ebers/Hans Christoph Grigoleit (eds.), Informationspflichten und Vertragsschluss im Acquis communautaire, 2003, pp. 103–115, at 110 et seq.

[2] It is clear though that the information duties in EC consumer law go beyond a mere obligation to act honestly insofar as they are used as a means to equip the consumer for the market, *Thomas Wilhelmsson*, ERA-Forum 2006 – Special Issue European Contract Law, pp. 16–25, at 19 et seq. However, information duties in consumer law are limited to situations where the consumer is at a significant informational disadvantage (which the business is aware of) so that information duties do not only serve market needs but can be a part of the obligation of the business to provide the information needed for negotiations in good faith.

rights directly affect the binding nature of contractual consent.[3] Again they can be understood best if seen against the background of traditional contract law:

According to traditional contract law, offer and acceptance are a method of expressing consent, or of determining the existence of consent. But again, all legal systems agree that consent may have defects, and some defects, especially serious cases of fraud and error, may invalidate consent or, at least allow a party to successfully challenge its binding effect. The "new" withdrawal rights in European consumer law extend this concept.[4] They can be seen as a reaction to problems which may affect the substantive validity of the consent. This has frequently been analyzed so that only a brief restatement of this analysis is necessary:

In the case of the Door-step Selling Directive 85/577, the consumer may be caught unawares by the door-step seller (supplier prepared to negotiate, consumer not prepared; consumer may sign contract only to get rid of sales agent; consumer cannot compare different offers). In the case of the Distance Selling Directive 97/7, the consumer cannot inspect the product in advance. One may, of course argue that this can also be the case outside of organized distance marketing systems; however, this is the rationale stated in recital (14) of the directive. In the case of the Distance Marketing of Financial Services Directive 2002/65, recital (23) refers to the general argument that the consumer deserves optimum protection. In other words: if a mere mouse-click constitutes consent to contract having far reaching effects, a cooling-off period is a safeguard against premature statements of consent by the consumer. In the case of the Consumer Credit Directive 87/102 and the Timesharing Directive 94/47, the rationale is similar: Both address complicated transactions which appear persuasively attractive for the consumer.[5]

Seen against the background of traditional doctrines concerning fraud and error, the withdrawal rights in consumer law are different from these doctrines insofar as the former do not require that there is an actual error or mistake in the person of the consumer. Instead, it is sufficient that, according to the situation or the nature of the contract, there is a significant danger that the consumer has not or could not reflect thoroughly

---

[3] Technically, the withdrawal is independent from the way in which consent has been reached; it may may be construed as a revocation of the offer or of the acceptance or as a withdrawal from the contract as such, see *Stefano Troiano*, Formation of Contracts under EC-Directives, in Hans Schulte-Nölke/Reiner Schulze (eds.), Europäisches Vertragsrecht im Gemeinschaftsrecht – European Contract Law in Community Law, 2002, pp. 97–109, at 102.

[4] *Thomas Pfeiffer* (footnote 1 *supra*) at 110.

[5] *Thomas Pfeiffer*, in: Wolfgang Ernst/Reinhard Zimmermann, Zivilrechtswissenschaft und Schuldrechtsreform, 2001, pp. 481–525, at 496.

enough about a contract before stating contractual consent. Yet, in a broader perspective, both serve similar purposes, and it can be said that withdrawal rights are a (mere) extension of known doctrines.

b. Open questions

Although modern consumer law has provided for these withdrawal rights, there are still open questions. In discussions about the effectiveness of these rights, one immediately faces the questions: Is this sufficient? Although these rights exist, consumers still sign contracts which reasonable persons would not sign.

I give one example: Withdrawal rights require the consumer to act so that a hesitant consumer may refrain from withdrawing although he is dissatisfied with a contract after he has signed it. As a consequence, in time sharing cases, it has been discussed whether there should be cooling-off period before signing of the contract.[6]

My personal attitude towards such discussions is nevertheless sceptical: You can make the conclusion of a contract as complicated as you wish – there will always be some deals that are better and others which are less advantageous for the consumer. This problem cannot be solved by the law on formation of contract. And as far as doubling the cooling-off period is concerned: Two cooling-off periods are too complicated. If the alternative is either a cooling-off period before and or one after the conclusion of the contract: it is still better to have such a right after the conclusion of the contract.

Another aspect concerns standardized contracts as an instrument for a more adequate contract law. The idea is that, from the consumer perspective, standardized contracts add more transparency to the market: It is easier to compare product and price if all other aspects of a contract are identical. To some extent, we do already follow this concept. The whole concept of mandatory consumer law, as provided e.g. by the Consumer Sales Directive 1999/44, is based on the idea that, in an internal market, a limitation on the parties' rights to determine the content of their con-

---

[6] *Thomas Pfeiffer/Burkhard Hess/Martin Gebauer/Boris Schinkels/Peter Boos*, Analyse verbraucherpolitischer Defizite beim Erwerb von Teilzeitnutzungsrechten – Studie im Auftrag des Bundesministeriums für Verbraucher Ernährung und Landwirtschaft, 2006, http://www.ble.de/download/pdf/04HS058.pdf, 31.1.2007, pp. 155–161.

tract may strengthen the willingness of consumers to actually engage in cross-border transactions.[7]

However, there are limits to this concept. Again, the Consumer Sales Directive is an example of this: Its mandatory rules prevent the seller from restricting the consumer's rights in respect of defective goods. The effect of this, however, is that everything becomes a problem of information and of the pre-contractual statements of the supplier.[8] It is still possible to sell a "lemon" to the consumer if the information given makes sufficiently clear to the consumer that the sold good actually is a "lemon". Since the consumer's capacity to handle and to understand information is limited, mandatory law and standardized contracts do not necessarily help to solve any problems. In certain cases, they may even function as an obstacle if a supplier wants to present a new service concept – unless the standard is not a mandatory one (in this case, however, the standards do not operate as legal standards but as standards building on information and reputation[9]). And most importantly, they do not solve the problem that the consumer may regret the conclusion of a contract because of the price.

In this respect, there will always be limits to the effectiveness of the law of contract formation as an instrument of consumer protection, and "new mechanisms" can change this only to a small extent.

2. Business transactions

"New mechanisms" are a phenomenon not limited to consumer contracts. In business transactions, we see such new mechanisms inparticular where long-term contracts or complicated transactions are concerned.

In the case of contracts on the construction of industrial sites, in M&A transactions, in contracts on research and development or on fence-to-fence production, the general rule, according to the personal experience of the speaker, is that there is virtually no contract without a pre-contractual agreement or instrument. These include letters of intent, memoranda of understanding, instructions to proceed or some other pre-

---

[7] *Bettina Heiderhoff*, Grundstrukturen des nationalen und des europäischen Verbrauchervertragsrechts – Insbesondere zur Reichweite europäischer Auslegung, 2004, p. 330.

[8] For the role of pre-contractual statements see e.g. *Reiner Schulze*, Conclusion of Contract, in ERA-Forum 2006 – Special Issue European Contract Law, pp. 25–34, at 30 et seq.

[9] See e.g. *Gralff-Peter Calliess*, Grenzüberschreitende Verbraucherverträge, pp. 314 et seq.

liminary statement of what a party intends and how, or that both parties intend to negotiate or to conclude a contract and how.

These pre-contractual agreements typically include a schedule of negotiation (determined e.g. by the planned start of production), procedures of negotiation, rules on confidentiality, on liability during the negotiations, a prohibition of head-hunting among the other side's staff, a list of information and of goods and services to be rendered or provided by the parties during negotiation, and of issues already agreed on by the parties.

The effect and the significance of such pre-contractual agreements may be far reaching. They may, in some cases replace the actual contract. In the automotive industry, it is rather common that no formal contract between the assembler and the supplier is signed but only a "Letter of Nomination" based on the negotiations is issued by the assembler and addressed to the supplier. Sometimes, even this does not happen since the start of production has occured without any document being signed.

If the subject of the contract is complicated, the contract needs to be capable of later change. Sometimes these changes occur in a formalized manner, i.e. in a formalized amendment to an existing contract, sometimes they do not. This again is not as new as it may seem. In the construction industry, this has always been the situation. Since no building is built exactly in the way it was planned, no offers are made in this industry without stating the price for man-hours of additional work.

Another aspect in this context is whether a duty to negotiate should be recognized. Article 6:111 PECL as well as article 6.2.2 UPICC give an affirmative answer, which is probably adequate for certain cases of long term contractual relationship. However, it remains to be seen to what extent controversies about the sufficiency of contractual negotiation will effectively enrich the world of contract law.[10]

III. Reasons

With these phenomena, contract law reacts to certain changes in the world of transactions. Seen in a general perspective, the following aspects are relevant for a more complicated world of contract formation:

Firstly, the world has become more international. We experience more cultural diversity between contract parties. This means that there are fewer standards which can be taken for granted. Consequently, there is a

---

[10] See e.g. *Thomas Pfeiffer*, Die Beendigung des Vertrages wegen schwerwiegender Störung: Wegfall der Geschäftsgrundlage und Kündigung aus wichtigem Grund, in: Oliver Remien (ed.), Schuldrechtsmodernisierung und Europäisches Vertragsrecht – Zwischenbilanz und Perspektiven, forthcoming.

greater need for more detailed legal rules providing for the necessary framework for negotiating and concluding contracts.

Secondly, the world has become technically more complicated. In a world of knowledge, the protection of trade and business secrets at the stage of contract negotiations is more relevant than it used to be. The variety of goods and services is much greater and the design of goods and services itself is more complex so that it is more complicated to negotiate a contract. And by the way: this also includes legal knowledge so that we simply know more about how to conceive a framework for negotiating and concluding contracts.

Thirdly, the world has become richer. Although this statement may apply to parts of the world only, it is relevant. Where it applies, e.g. in the western world, there is simply more time left and there are more resources available, which can be invested into a more elaborated way of negotiating and concluding contract.

Fourthly, there is word processing and email exchange. It has become much easier to write and rewrite lengthy documents again and again and to exchange them with potential business partners. Not surprisingly, contract lawyers have made use of these new opportunities.

IV. Assessment

Bearing all this in mind, the question is whether the world of contract formation has really changed. This again is, to a large extent, a question of perspective. After all, everything is still about consent and avoiding defects. The question we have to answer is whether these new phenomena require new rules for the formation of contracts or a new understanding of their function.

This is certainly not the case on an abstract level. The rule that "Consent makes contract" is still valid and legitimate. What I like to call the "magical moment" (i.e. when a contract acquires binding force) still exists.[11] This does not exclude that parties can agree to amendments of a contract at a later stage or that the law states that later events have an influence on the contract. Such an influence has always existed, as e.g. the rules on force majeure or hardship demonstrate. It is certainly more difficult to determine such a magical moment, and it is also possible that this moment is not identical for the parties to a contract. The fact, however, that it has become more difficult to determine this moment by no means supports the assumption that there is no such moment.

As far as business transactions are concerned, concluding a contract may be more difficult but that does not necessarily result in new questions

---

[11] *Thomas Pfeiffer* (footnote 1 *supra*) p. 110.

on the level of law making. The parties can agree about how they intend to proceed during the negotiation of a contract, and they actually do so if necessary.

In consumer law the situation is different: There is a need for rules to ensure that actual informed consent of consumer exists if a contract has been signed. Meanwhile such rules exist in EC consumer law. Seen against the background of traditional contract law, these rules still look unfamiliar for a continental civil lawyer. They follow a rather casuistic detailed technique of law making in order to secure a uniform practice in all Member States.

It is not unlikely that this situation will change in the future course of legal development. In the process of discussing a Europeanization of contract law, based on legal practice concerning existing EC-contract law and the forthcoming Common Frame of Reference, a common culture of contract law in Europe – or at least (maybe more realistically) some aspects of a common contract law culture – will emerge. As far as this is the case, more abstract and less detailed rules will be possible despite the complications of modern contract formation. I am certain that this conference and the Uniform Terminology Project can contribute to this goal.

The Binding Effects of Advertising

Peter Møgelvang-Hansen* (Copenhagen)

I. Scope

In practice, the first commercial communications aimed at initiating the conclusion of contracts often take the form of advertisements published in different types of media, i.e. mass communication, that is not addressed to specified individuals, but to the public at large, special segments of the public or other groups of individuals whose identity is not known to the advertiser at the time of the advertisement.

Sometimes, as for instance in connection with e-commerce, all phases of commercial communication leading to a contract are entirely mass communication, in so far as the information given and statements made to prospective customers are standardized and not at all individualized.

Although advertising has been a not insignificant part of the process of concluding contracts for some considerable time, most legal systems seem to have been rather reluctant to deal with advertising (and other forms of mass communication) within the law of contract. To a large extent the issue of counteracting misleading advertising and other questions concerning the legal effects of advertising seem to have been considered not as a concern of contract law but a matter that should be dealt with solely or primarily by the special acts concerning marketing and fair trading.[1]

However, to some extent the general principles of contract law may work as tools giving violations of marketing practices law a contract law remedy[2] and legal practice and consumer legislation both at the national

---

* *Professor Peter Møgelvang-Hansen, Law Department, Copenhagen Business School.* The article is based on a lecture given in Münster, May 22nd, 2006 as part of the series: New Features in Contract Law.

[1] Directive 2005/29/EC concerning unfair business-to-consumer commercial practices in the internal market and amending to be deleted [the "Unfair Commercial Practices Directive"] is without prejudice to contract law and, in particular, to the rules on the validity, formation or effect of a contract [art. 3 (2)].

[2] Thomas Willhelmsson: European Rules on Pre-contractual Information Duties in ERA-Forum, scripta juris europaei, Special Issue 2006, European Contract Law p. 24 (concerning The Unfair Commercial Practices Directive).

and the European level have addressed some of the contract law implications of the ever more significant role played by advertising in the process of contract formation.

In the following I shall deal with some of the questions concerning the contract law implications of advertising. The main question is to what extent and how the contract law remedies supplement the law of marketing and fair trading in protecting the legitimate expectations based on advertising and in counteracting misleading advertising.

I concentrate on two different types of questions concerning the binding effect of advertising according to contract law. The first group concerns advertising as binding information. The second group concerns advertising as a binding promise. The questions are dealt with primarily on the basis of the *acquis communautaire* and Nordic law.

II. Advertising as binding information

1. When a contract is concluded

Under this heading fall cases where it is evident that a contract has been entered into and where the question is in what way prior advertising made by the commercial party to the contract affects the interpretation and content of the contract.

First of all, the advertisement may influence the content of the contract in so far as it can constitute a breach of contract if the goods or services delivered under the contract do not conform to the advertisement.

Positive statutory rules to this effect are found in the Consumer Sales Directive,[3] art. 2 (2)(d) and (4):

»2. Consumer goods are presumed to be in conformity with the contract of sale if they:
[...]
(d) show the quality and performance which are normal in goods of the same type and which the consumer can reasonably expect, given the nature of the goods and taking into account any public statements on the specific characteristics of the goods made about them by the seller, the producer or his representative, particularly in advertising or on labelling.
[...]
4. The seller shall not be bound by public statements, as referred to in paragraph 2(d) if he:

---

[3] Directive 1999/44/EC on certain aspects of the sale of consumer goods and associated guarantees.

shows that he was not, and could not reasonably have been aware of the statement in question,

shows that by the time of the conclusion of the contract the statement had been corrected, or

shows that the decision to buy the consumer goods could not have been influenced by the statement.«

and in the Package Travel Directive,[4] art. 3(2):

"The particulars contained in the brochure are binding on the organizer or retailer, unless:
- changes in such particulars have been clearly communicated to the consumer before conclusion of the contract, in which case the brochure shall expressly state so,
- changes are made later following an agreement between the parties to the contract."

In Nordic consumer sales law rules equivalent to the consumer sales directive art. 2 (2)(d), were introduced i 1970s.[5] Similar rules on the effect of public statements are found in the Finnish, Norwegian and Swedish acts on consumer services contracts.[6]

In Nordic law there seems to be no doubt that the "the precontractual, public statement rule" can be regarded a general principle of contract law applicable also outside the scope of the positive statutory rules.

An example is found in a Danish Supreme Court decision from 1984[7] which established that a contract for the supply of oil to a weekend cottage would have to be interpreted in the light of the marketing material of the oil company in question. According to the marketing material the delivery system of the oil company would ensure that at all times there would be oil in the tank so that the customers would not have to worry about the risk of running dry. When the oil tank did run dry and the furnace consequently went out, this was due to the fact that the oil company had disregarded its contractual obligations. Therefore, the company was

---

[4] Directive 90/314/EEC on package travel, package holidays and package tours.
[5] They are now found in the Danish Sales of Goods Act § 76 (1); The Finnish Consumer Protection Code chapter 5, § 13; the Icelandic Consumer Sales Act § 16 (1)(c) and (2); the Norwegian Consumer Sales Act § 16 (1)(c) and (2); Swedish Consumer Sales Act § 19 (2) and (3).
[6] The Finnish Consumer Protection Code chapter 8, § 13, Norwegian Act (63/1989) on Craftsmen's Services § 18 and the Swedish Consumer Services Act (1985:716) § 10.
[7] Reported in Ugeskrift for Retsvæsen 1984 p. 392.

considered liable in damages to the customer for his loss incurred by water damage after the water pipes froze and burst.[8]

The pre-contractual public statement rules of the Consumer Sales Directive and the Package Travel Directive deal with rather specific situations and they are the result of special legislative efforts made to protect consumer buyers and package tour travellers. Nevertheless, also at the European level they should not be regarded only as special protective measures but rather as an expression of a general principle of interpretation, primarily in cases where a contract does not deal explicitly with certain questions which have been dealt with by one of the parties in a pre-contractual statement, be it addressed directly to specified individuals or to the public at large.

In such cases it is a reasonable expectation of the other party to the contract that the terms are in accordance with the pre-contractual statement made by a party to the contract, also when it is given in an advertisement, brochure etc.

If the rule of the Consumer Sales Directive is regarded rather as a principle of interpretation protecting the reasonable expectations of a party to a contract as opposed to a special rule protecting consumers it is not easy to understand why it should be restricted to apply to consumer sales only and not to business-to-business sales or to transactions other than contracts than sale, for instance service contracts.

According to § 434(1), 2nd and 3rd sentence BGB, the public statement rule similar to the one found in the Consumer Sales Directive is not limited to consumer sales. Also the "pre-contractual public statement rule" found in art. 6:101(1) and (2) PECL applies beyond consumer relations. Furthermore, the PECL rule is not limited to sales contracts but also applies to contracts concerning services etc.

---

[8] The 1984 Supreme Court decision interpreted the contract in the light of the marketing material concerning a question not dealt with explicitly by the contract. The principle may also apply in special cases where the marketing material promises more than the contract actually gives the party, cf. e.g. a decision of July 5th 2004 (case no. 62.786) made by the Danish Insurance Complaints Board. The Board interpreted an insurance contract (a so-called "extended warranty") concerning a laptop computer in accordance with the statements in a sales brochure so that the insurance covered all forms of theft and not only burglary (as the coverage was defined in the terms of the insurance contract). The Board found that the question concerning coverage of theft other than burglary was important to the buyer's decision to take out the insurance and that the insurance company when mentioning the theft coverage in the brochure should have specified in the brochure that the theft coverage included burglary only.

Also the Acquis Group considers "the pre-contractual public statement rule" of the Consumer Sales Directive and the Package Travel Directive a general principle of the *acquis communautaire*.[9]

The public statement rule of the Consumer Sales Directive applies not only to public statements made by the seller but also to public statements made by "the producer or his representative". However, according to the directive the seller is not bound by a 3rd party statement if the seller shows that "he was not and could not reasonably have been aware of the statement".

The PECL-rule and the Nordic consumer law rules equivalent to art. 2, (2) Consumer Sales Directive define the scope of the 3rd party public statement rule so that it applies to all prior links in the business chain and not only "the producer and his representative".

The Icelandic, Norwegian and Danish rules on consumer sales also have a somewhat wider scope than the rule of the Consumer Sales Directive in that the seller is bound even if he did not know of the public statement given by a previous link in the business chain. The point seems to be that the seller profits from the advertising made by for instance the producer or the importer and that, therefore, it is reasonable that the seller has to take also the negative consequences when the advertisement is misleading.[10]

According to the Acquis Group also the 3rd party public statement rule is considered a general principle of the Acquis but so far it has not been specified which 3rd parties are to be taken into account.

2. When a contract is not concluded

The pre-contractual public statement rule deals with the situation where a contract is concluded by way of making the public statement part of the contract.

Advertising regarded as part of the process leading to the formation of a contract can also be considered legally "binding" information in so far as it raises the question whether a party is entitled to damages for costs incurred in concluding a contract whereby he relies on advertising that turns out to be misleading.

In view of the increased importance of advertising and other mass-communication as a part of the process leading to the conclusion of con-

---

[9] *Reiner Schulze* in ERA-Forum: scripta juris europaei, Special issue 2006: European Contract Law pp. 26–32.
[10] The seller is bound only by advertising made by a previous link in the same chain of distribution and not by advertising made by competitors, parallel importers etc.

tracts such liability may naturally be seen as a modern version of the principle of *culpa in contrahendo*.

In Denmark and Sweden it has not been necessary to elaborate on the principle of *culpa in contrahendo* since both countries have explicit statutory rules to the effect that violations of the Marketing Practices Act, including misleading advertising, can trigger liability for damages in accordance with the general rules of tort law.[11]

However, in practice the possibility to claim damages in such cases on the basis of misleading advertising is more theoretical than real, at least as far as consumers are concerned, primarily because it is very difficult for consumers to demonstrate that the misleading advertising caused any significant economic loss. During the preparation of the new Danish Marketing Practices Act (1389/2005) attempts were made to bring about a rule authorizing non-pecuniary damages for the inconvenience of consumers relying on misleading advertising in order to counteract *inter alia* so-called bait-advertising, i.e. advertisement for a product at a favourable price whereby the seller cannot reasonably believe that he will be able to meet the expected demand.[12] The attempts were not successful and there are still no rules allowing non-pecuniary damages in such cases.

3. Advertising as binding promise

The pre-contractual public statement rule mentioned above deals with the construction of the contract in cases where the question of the advertiser being bound by a public statement is not raised until after a contract has been made between the parties. In such cases the question is not whether the advertisement is in itself an offer, but only what impact the information advertised has on the content of the contract.

---

[11] § 20 (2), Danish Marketing Practices Act (1389/2005); § 29 Swedish Marketing Practices Act (1995:450).

[12] Betænkning (1457/2005) om markedsføring og prisoplysning p. 243. The rule proposed by a minority of the commission preparing the act was identical to the tentative rule suggested in a Nordic Report (TemaNord 2001.549 by Kai Krüger and Peter Møgelvang-Hansen):

"Misleading commercial advertising incurs liability on the advertisor according to general principles of tort law when the consumer was justified in assuming that the advertised statements would form part of an offer to conclude a contract. If the consumer has suffered substantial inconvenience, the consumer is in addition entitled a reasonable compensation even if no financial loss or expenses has been inflicted on him."

Normally, the advertiser is interested in selling the goods in question on the terms advertised. This fact is in itself a factor creating expectations.

However, the situation may be different when the purchase of goods appears more advantageous to the customer than intended by the advertiser, either due to an error in the advertisement or in order to attract customers – in the case of misleading advertising[13]. The question here is whether the advertisement is in itself an offer or merely an invitation to treat.

If the advertisement is an invitation to treat, the advertiser is simply entitled to refuse to sell on the terms advertised; in that case it is the customer reacting to the advertisement who has the role of an offeror whose offer the advertiser can refuse to accept. If the advertisement is considered an offer, it is in itself binding according to Nordic contract law and cannot be revoked once it has become known to the offeree and it remains binding if it is accepted.

The traditional approach in most Member States seems to be that an offer must be addressed to one or more specific persons and that a declaration addressed to the public, that would otherwise be considered an offer, is an invitation to make an offer. However, the traditional approach also seems to recognize that in some special situations, such as for instance the announcement of rewards, a declaration addressed to the public can have the same effect as an offer. Also, in recent decades the courts in at least some Member States have become more willing to qualify statements addressed to the public as offers (e.g. display of goods with price indication).[14]

---

[13] Directive 2005/29/EC concerning unfair business-to-consumer commercial practices in the internal market and amending to be deleted ("Unfair Commercial Practices Directive") Annex I contains a list of commecial practices which are in all circumstances considered unfair, including

"5. *Making an invitation to purchase products at a specified price without disclosing the existence of any reasonable grounds the trader may have for believing that he will not be able to offer for supply or to procure another trader to supply, those products or equivalent products at that price for a period that is, and in quantities that are, reasonable having regard to the product, the scale of advertising of the product and the price offered (bait advertising).*

6. Making an invitation to purchase products at a specified price and then:

(a) refusing to show the advertised item to consumers;or

(b) refusing to take orders for it or deliver it within a reasonable time;or

(c) demonstrating a defective sample of it,

with the intention of promoting a different product (bait and switch)."

[14] Principles of European Contract Law Parts I and II (ed. *Ole Lando and Hugh Beale*), Kluwer Law International. 2000 p. 161–163.

In a case from 1985[15] the Danish Supreme Court had the opportunity to address the question in a case concerning the window display of TV sets with a price tag of DKK 1,695. Stating that by a mistake the price tag had been placed on the wrong TVsets, the shop refused to sell at a price lower than DKK 5,421.

The Supreme Court held that the price-tagging of goods on display is an offer and not merely an invitation to bargain. However, in the concrete case the shop was not bound by the offer since it was voidable, due to a mistake of which the offerees were or ought to have been aware. In order to prove their point the offerees had taken a snapshot of the display (thereby indicating that they were aware of potential problems).

In another case, from 1991[16], the Supreme Court reached a similar result based on an interpretation of the promise made. The case involved a discount store advertising chocolate bars at prices below the wholesale price. It was promoted by a door-to-door leaflet drop and on signs in the store. The owner of a chocolate shop wanted to buy the discount store's entire stock of 4,000 bars of chocolate. But the discount store refused to sell. Again the Supreme Court based its decision on the fact that the display in the shop was an offer. However, six judges were of the opinion that it should have been clear to the chocolate shop owner that the advertising for the chocolate bars was aiming at the ordinary clientele consisting of private consumers and that the discount store had not intended the sale of large quantities of the chocolate bars to competitors, for them to sell on. Three judges, however, did not want to interpret the offer in this restrictive way and decided in favour of the chocolate shop owner.

The two cases mentioned cannot safely be taken to mean that advertisements in printed media in themselves can be considered binding offers according to Danish law. Although such a rule is supported by both the traditional viewpoint concerning reasonable expectations and the views relating to the enforcement of marketing practices, recent Danish appellate court practice still seems to proceed from the presumption that advertisements in the media are not in themselves considered binding offers.[17]

---

[15] Reported in Ugeskrift for Retsvæsen 1985 p. 877.
[16] Reported in Ugeskrift for Retsvæsen 1991 p. 43.
[17] During the preparation of the new Danish Marketing Practices Act (1389/2005) attempts were made by a minority of the commission to introduce a rule giving binding effect to advertising. The attempt was unsuccessful. Cf. Betænkning (1457/2005) om markedsføring og prisoplysning p. 243. The proposal of the minority was identical to the tentative rule suggested in a Nordic Report (TemaNord 2001.549 by Kai Krüger and Peter Møgelvang-Hansen):
"An advertisement in the context of marketing of products and services to the public is considered a legally binding offer if a consumer, in view of the con-

In the case reported in Ugeskrift for Retsvæsen 2002.631 (Western High Court) a DIY store distributed a promotion newspaper presenting several "Queue-offers" on the front page. One of the "queue offers" concerned a Stiga rotor lawn-mower, Turbo 530 SE. According to the ad the lawn-mower would be for sale at a price of 2,995 DKK (regular price 4,995 DKK) on Saturday May 6th at 9 o'clock. According to the advertisement this "Queue-offer" concerned one and only one lawn-mower. A consumer (who later became the plaintiff) joined the queue at 7:30 on May 6th; he was number 5 but found out that the four persons before him in the queue were not interested in the lawn-mower. While he waited in the queue the store manager addressed him in order to know what queue-offer he was interested in. The consumer said that he wanted the lawn-mower and the store manager wrote it down. Shortly before 9 o'clock the consumer was told by the store manager that the lawn-mower advertised had been sold by mistake a couple of days before at the regular price and that the store had no similar lawn-mower left. Information to this effect was in fact displayed on a sign near the entrance.

The consumer brought the case before the Consumer Complaints Board claiming 2,000 DKK (the price difference) arguing that he had been entitled to buy the lawn-mower for the price advertised. The majority of the Board stated that an advertisement in newspapers etc. containing price indications is generally only an invitation to make an offer and not a legally binding offer. The majority saw no reason to make an exception in the case at issue.

The High Court agreed with the majority of the Consumer Complaints Board in so far as it stated that price indications in advertisements are generally only invitations to make offers. However, the High Court decided the case in favour of the consumer with reference to the special circumstances of the case, especially the fact that the store manager, by writing down the wish of the consumer to buy the lawn-mower, had given him the impression that it was for sale. The consumer had not seen the sign near the entrance and neither the sign nor the qualification in the promotion newspaper in respect of sold out items could justify a different result.

However, analogous with the Supreme Court cases concerning window displays with price tags it seems to be the general Danish view that the

---

tents of the statement, its framing or other circumstances reasonably had the impression that the statement was meant to be a binding offer. Statements of the kind dealt with in the preceding paragraph are considered to have been revoked when a similar statement has been made to the public."

display of goods on websites to be ordered online at a fixed price are binding offers to sell at the price indicated.[18]

Under art. 14(2) CISG a proposal other than one addressed to one or more specific persons is considered merely an invitation to make an offer, unless the contrary is clearly indicated by the person making the proposal. In contrast, the PECL in art. 2:201(3) expressly extends the concept of offer to proposals made to one or more specific persons and to the public and specifies the conditions for a public advertisement to constitute an offer, cf. art. 2:201(3). The difference between the CISG and PECL here concerns the starting point. Thus, the PECL rule is a presumption rule that the advertiser can easily avoid simply by indicating that the proposal is not meant to be a binding offer but merely an invitation to treat: But by doing so the seller may make the advertisement appear less convincing. Also the CISG rule is a rule of presumption, not a rule excluding offers to the public as a matter of principle.

As mentioned above some of the consumer protection directives contain rules on the binding effect of advertisements, brochures and other public statements. In addition to the rules already mentioned art. 6 of the Consumer Sales Directive states that product guarantees in advertisements shall bind the guarantor. While this rule, in cases where the seller is the guarantor, can be seen as a rule concerning the construction of the sales contract, between the same parties it seems to be an example of the binding effect of a promise made to the public in so far as it concerns guarantees given by a party other than the seller of the product, for instance the producer or the importer.

The rules of the directives mentioned above appear to be founded upon a general assumption that public statements have a major role to play in the process of contract formation and that public statements actually influence the decision to enter into a contract. Thus, in a contract law context the rules can be seen as concrete manifestations of a general principle of protecting the reasonable expectations of individual consumers based upon public statements. Why should a statement which expresses an apparent intention to be bound when it is read in its normal context lose the status of being an offer just because it is made to the public?

Regarded in a broader context, the rules of the directives can also be seen as concrete examples of contract law rules counteracting misleading advertising by allowing the reasonable understanding of the statement as it appears to prevail over the true intention of the person who made a misleading or ambiguous statement.

From a traditional contract law point of view this interpretation may seem far-fetched; it is based upon an instrumental understanding that

---

[18] *Benedikte Holberg et al.*: Forbrugeraftaleloven, Jurist- og Økonomforlagets forlag (2006) p. 121.

may seem unfamiliar to traditional contract law, as opposed to public law. From the EU-law point of view, however, a pragmatic, instrumental approach to the choice and combination of marketing law and civil law instruments seems to be consistent with the *effet utile* and the effective remedies approach and can hardly be surprising. Based on this approach, the rules on the binding effect of public statements can (also) be regarded as examples of rules based upon a general principle of contract law to counteract misleading advertising etc. by protecting reasonable expectations held by consumers and created by public statements.

Even if at this stage of the development the acquis may not have a sufficient basis for formulating a general principle of contract law to this effect it seems reasonable to at least assume that the development is moving in this direction and that accordingly the acquis does not exclude the possibility of public statements being considered offers.

In addition to this it should be noted that generally offers made to the public are subject to the same contractual principles as offers made to specific persons. This includes the general principles of interpretation according to which, for instance, a professional seller's offer made to the public to sell goods is normally to be understood with the reservation that it concerns only a stock of goods necessary to meet a demand that could reasonably be expected at the time the offer was made.

Furthermore, a revocation of an offer to the public can be effected by a public statement similar to the one containing the offer. This is in accordance with the principle in Art. 2(4) of the Consumer Sales Directive concerning the neutralisation of the effects of public pre-contractual statements.

Part III
Performance and Remedies

Remedies for Breach of Contract in European Private Law – Principles of European Contract Law, Acquis Communautaire and Common und Frame of Reference

Martin Schmidt-Kessel (Osnabrück)

The topic "Remedies for Breach of Contract in European Private Law" implies two major prior elements for the following analysis of that part of European Contract law: The first concerns: "Breach of Contract" which is the starting point of our analysis. This starting point has to be explained before dealing with remedies. The second prior element that confronts us concerns the concept of remedy. Remedy, as a concept, is by no means a uniformly established notion in all European legal orders. This umbrella concept (which, in a way, negates the different types of remedies under consideration) needs to be developed subsequent to the discussion on breach of contract. The third part of my paper is then devoted to the system of the different remedies, if indeed it can be said that there is such a system, in European Private Law. While this idea of remedies focuses on the perspective of the aggrieved party, the final part of this paper will deal with the other side of that coin: the mechanism of the right to cure of the party in breach. One of the questions most discussed in this field within the preparatory works for the academic Draft Common Frame of Reference on European Contract Law is the question of broadening Article 8:104 PECL and developing from it a complete section within the chapter of remedies for breach of contract.

I. Avant propos: Breach of Contract

Viewed from a comparative perspective breach of contract is a rather vague concept to say the least. While it can be said that there is basically a common understanding of what a breach of contract connotes, as this notion emanates from a core of cases, the views of what denotes an "inexécution", a "Pflichtverletzung" or a "breach of contract" differs significantly when that core of common understanding is more closely examined. European Community Law has not developed a generally accepted notion of breach of contract in any of its legal instruments either. Furthermore if one traces back the notion of breach of contract to its origins in Common Law, especially in English Common Law, it is difficult to find any attempt to define or even explain what is meant by breach of contract.

The same holds true when one tries to bring the several cases of breach of contract into a logically convincing order: the former German Law of Obligations organized the rules on breach of contract following a "cause approach", i.e. delineating the different types of breach of contract into cases of impossibility, of delay and of defective performance or the so-called "positive Vertragsverletzung". A similar tendency can be drawn from a statement in the Late Payment Directive of the European Community where delay is referred to as a type of breach of contract.[1] At the other end of the spectrum of possible approaches of systemizing breach of contract one finds systems which are based on a uniform notion of breach of contract. At least, the English Common Law seems to be predominantly based thereon. "Breach of contract" there simply characterizes a deviation of the party's performance from the contractual scheme, i.e. the non-performance of one of its duties.[2] Between these two extremes, several systems are to be found which start from a uniform notion of breach of contract but then differentiate as to the several aspects of breach. The Dutch Civil Code e.g. draws a line between the excused non-performance and non performance which is not excused ("niet-nakoming" as the umbrella term encapsulating both cases, and the "tekortcoming in de nakoming" which concerns the case of the non-performance not excused).[3]

More convincing is a system which distinguishes between different types of duties or obligations of the parties, namely because the respective categories take account of the content of the contract, and thereby incorporate the primary idea of the enforcement of contracts: namely the realization of the parties' intention. However, even here one needs to be careful not to replace intent by dogmatic concepts. The German distinction between "Leistungspflichten" (duties to render a performance) and "Schutzpflichten" (duties to protect parties' interests) e.g. only works as long as none of the characteristic obligations under the contract is di-

---

[1] See *Schmidt-Kessel*, Verzug, in: *Gebauer/Wiedmann* (eds.), Zivilrecht unter Europäischen Einfluß, Stuttgart 2005, para. 13 and *Riesenhuber*, System und Prinzipien des Europäischen Vertragsrechts, Berlin 2003, 537.

[2] *Schmidt-Kessel*, Standards vertraglicher Haftung nach englischem Recht, Baden-Baden 2003, 4–7; see *Lando*, in: Hartkamp et al. (eds.), Towards a European Civil Code, 3rd Ed. 2004, 505, 506.

[3] See *Lando*, in: *Hartkamp* et al. (eds.), Towards a European Civil Code, 3rd Ed. 2004, 505, 506, 508, 512.

rected to the protection of the other party. The most promising differentiation is therefore the French distinction between "obligations de moyens" and "obligations de résultat" which René Demogue came up with in the 1920s and which is nowadays part of several legal systems including the UNIDROIT Principles on International Commercial Contracts. The basic idea of this distinction is to draw a line between duties which include an undertaking to achieve a specific result and those duties which may be directed to such a result but which only force the debtor to deploy certain methods and thereby meet the required standard of behaviour.

In line with Article 8:108 PECL, however, this idea of the major difference between "obligations moyens" and "obligations de résultat" will probably not be adopted explicitly in the Draft Common Frame of Reference.[4] Instead, the central idea encapsulates organizing the cases of breach of contract along the lines of excused non-performance and the non-performance which is not excused (Article III-3:101 DCFR). In the former case the party aggrieved by breach of contract may resort to any of the remedies set out in the Principles of the Draft CFR (specific performance, withholding performance, termination of contract, price reduction, damages and interest – Article 8:101(1) PECL; Article III-3:101(1) DCFR). In the latter case of the debtor's excused non-performance the creditor may resort to all these remedies except when seeking specific performance and damages (Article 8:101(2) PECL; Article III-3:101(2) DCFR).

What is meant by "excused" is made clear under PECL by a cross reference to Article 8:108 PECL which does not appear in Article III-3:101 DCFR. Article 8:108 PECL (and Article III-3:104 DCFR) contains a classical force majeure clause referring to an impediment beyond control. In most respects this clause comes close to a mere reflection of Article 79 CISG. This type of a force majeure clause, implied by law in every contract, is useful. However, it is primarily directed at restricting liability for the breach of an obligation to achieve a specific result ("obligation de résultat"). In the case of an "obligation de moyens" the question of excuse is dealt with in an entirely different way: certainly, in cases of force majeure, the debtor is excused. However, the debtor is not excused on the grounds of the force majeure but due to the fact of his meeting the requirements of behaviour and of due care which substantiate his duty of performance. In this respect the system of PECL is, in a way, lacking.

In the view of the drafters the same, i.e. the (exclusive) applicability of the force majeure clause, holds true for, without a doubt, Article III-3:101 and III-3:104 DCFR. There is however a slight change in the wording: Article III-3:101 no longer contains a cross reference to Article III-3:104.

---

[4] But see *Smits*, in *Busch/Hondius* et al., Commentary, The Hague 2002, Art. 8:101 No. 2.

The conclusion can be drawn therefrom that the excuse due to an impediment is not the only way of excusing the debtor's non-performance and one may therefore develop a separate rule of excuse for the case of an "obligation de moyens". Generally such gap filling is helpful but it should be expressed in a much clearer way by not striking out the cross reference to the force majeure clause but by supplementing the formula "is not excused under Article X" with the words "or otherwise".

II. The Concept of Remedy

Neither the numerous EC directives nor the Principles of European Contract Law nor the Draft Common Frame of Reference (as it currently stands) really make explicit what the term remedy in the sense of the respective legal instruments connotes. In academic literature one finds the circumscription of "consequences of non-performance"[5] or the most sophisticated definition of remedy as a "mechanism to allocate detrimental consequences to the defaulting party if that party is in fault or carries the risk".[6]

The fact that Article 3 of the Consumer Sales Directive is construed along the lines of the remedies in the CISG for defects in the goods sold shows, however, that this – obviously undefinable – idea of remedy is accepted in the same way by these instruments as it is under the Principles of European Contract Law and the Draft Common Frame of Reference. What is a remedy then? It is not necessarily a claim because under the concept of the Principles termination is effective by a simple notice of the creditor and not by an action against the debtor. It is therefore no *actio* in the *ius commune* sense either. The chapters on remedies in PECL and the DCFR contain the following claims, namely those relating to specific performance, those relating to damages and those following from a price reduction or termination of contract. The same claims can be found in Article 3 of the Consumer Sales Directive. The set of remedies named in these provisions also contains, what in German is known as "Gestaltungsrechte", i.e. rights which have to be exercised by notice and normally within a particular period of time. Moreover the right to withhold performance is difficult to bring under one of these categories of claims and Gestaltungsrechte. European Contract Law in its different manifestations therefore follows a pragmatic approach which does not distinguish between different types of remedies like Ansprüche, Gestal-

---

[5] Lando, in: Hartkamp et al. (eds.), Towards a European Civil Code, 3rd Ed. 2004, 505.

[6] Lando, in: Hartkamp et al. (eds.), Towards a European Civil Code, 3rd Ed. 2004, 505, 506.

tungsrechte and Einreden. Organising the consequences of a breach of contract in this manner obviates the need for the rather old-fashioned dogmatic categories under which these consequences are dealt with in some Continental legal systems. European Contract Law, therefore, turns back to the more practical question: What is the position of the party aggrieved by a breach of contract?

III. The System of Remedies

In dealing with the system of remedies the first question of which remedies are available needs to be addressed. When answering this question, by outlining the several remedies available, one has to take into account that it is by no means self-evident that all consequences of a breach of contract are qualified as a remedy. At a later stage, the interplay and the relationship between the available remedies will fall to be considered, namely is there a hierarchy among these remedies and does the possibility exist of combining the various remedies or may only a selection of these remedies be combined?

1. Remedies available

a. Right to Specific Performance

It is a truism that the claim for specific performance is the obvious remedy in continental legal systems[7] while it is the exception in Common Law, as that equitable remedy lies within the discretion of the judiciary. However, when one subjects the continental rules of the specific performance to closer examination especially in the cases where that remedy is not available, it becomes apparent that the differences between both approaches are limited.[8]

Apart from the rather special questions on monetary obligations (Article 9:101 PECL) the difference between the two approaches is essentially confined to cases of indeterminate obligations. In these cases the aggrieved party may normally obtain performance from another source and is, therefore, under Article 9:102(2)(d) PECL barred from its claim for specific performance. Thus far under PECL the Common Law approach

---

[7] Lando, in: Hartkamp et al. (eds.), Towards a European Civil Code, 3rd Ed. 2004, 505, 506, 509.
[8] Cf. Neufang, Erfüllungszwang als "remedy" bei Nichterfüllung, Baden-Baden 1998; Remien, Folgen von Leistungsstörungen, in: Schulte-Nölke/Schulze (eds.), Europäisches Vertragsrecht im Gemeinschaftsrecht, Bonn 2002, 139, 142.

prevails. In the DCFR the respective exception to the specific performance claim will presumably be struck out. Thereby the pendulum falls back to the concept prevailing in continental legal systems. This is, in my view, a regrettable development but the new rule is in line with the cases where specific performance is provided for by the Community Law namely as regards the claims for substitute performance, reparation and alternative arrangements for the consumer under the Consumer Sales Directive and the Package Travel Directive.[9] Providing the creditor with the broad option of claiming specific performance needlessly strengthens a remedy of insignificant practical importance. This approach is also questioned on the continent. The academic Draft Common Frame of Reference therefore should abstain from such an infiltration of consumer law ideas into the general law of contracts and therefore stick to the exclusion of specific performance where the creditor may reasonably obtain performance from another source.

b. Right to withhold Performance

The right of the debtor to withhold performance is twofold. On the one hand the time of performance is identified. In this respect the right to withhold performance is dealt with, e.g. in Article 58 CISG. On the other hand it works as a remedy against the creditor who is in breach and in this respect the right to withhold performance may re-arrange the content of the contractual duties. However, a closer analysis of the function of this re-arrangement shows that the right to withhold performance only restricts duties of the aggrieved party.

While the right of withholding performance is basically a concept which is foreign to Community Law,[10] the Principles of European Contract Law and the academic Draft Common Frame of Reference do recognise it: see for example Article 9:201 PECL and Article III-3:401. Without mentioning any idea of a synallagma, those Articles are restricted to duties which derive from the same contract. The much broader Commercial Law Concept of the right to withhold performance which leads to a

---

[9] See *Remien*, Folgen von Leistungsstörungen, in: *Schulte-Nölke/Schulze* (eds.), Europäisches Vertragsrecht im Gemeinschaftsrecht, Bonn 2002, 139, 141 et seq.; *Schmidt-Kessel*, Arbeitskampf und Vertragserfüllung im Europäischen Privatrecht, Festschrift Löwisch, sub I 1 a (to appear Munich 2007).

[10] But see Article 3 I lit. c No. i Late Payment Directive; *Remien*, Folgen von Leistungsstörungen, in: *Schulte-Nölke/Schulze* (eds.), Europäisches Vertragsrecht im Gemeinschaftsrecht, Bonn 2002, 139, 142 et seq. (refering to No 1 lit. o of the annex to Article 3 Unfair Contract Terms Directive); *Schmidt-Kessel*, NJW 2001, 97, 99.

kind of lien or pledge in the objects withheld is not dealt with in the Principles of European Contract Law. The Draft Common Frame of Reference will only mention the consequences of such a right of retention in its principles on Proprietary Security Rights (Article IX-2:108). The scope of the right to withhold performance is broadened in both texts and embraces cases in which it becomes clear that the other party will not perform when that other party's performance becomes due (Article 9:201 PECL) or covers cases where it is uncertain whether the creditor will be able to render its own performance (Article 8:105(1) PECL).

c. Termination of the Contract

Where the breach of the contract seriously disturbs the performance of the contract the creditor regularly has a right to terminate. The terminology used to describe the creditor's rights to terminate is debated and debatable in most legal orders. The respective provisions of Community Law[11] and the rules in the Principles of European Contract Law as well as in the Draft Common Frame of Reference opted for a rather vague terminology giving more importance to the decisions of substance rather than to the dogmatic debates. European Contract Law therefore does not provide a sharp line between "Rücktritt" and "Kündigung", i.e. between a termination leading to, basically, a restitution of the performances rendered which in functional terms means a retroactive effect and the termination which only works *ex nunc* releasing both parties from their obligations to effect future performance but absent any kind of restitution.[12] The regime of the consequences of termination under the Principles of European Contract Law covers both constellations and apart from the necessity of implementing some minor corrections seems to provide for a well founded solution.

The remedy of termination is open to the creditor in case of a fundamental breach by the debtor (Article 9:301(1) PECL). This category of fundamental breach is defined in Article 8:103 PECL and is well-known to many legal systems. To cite a few examples the concept is anchored in Article 25 CISG, Article 16 Commercial Agents Directive or §§ 281 (2),

---

[11] See *Remien*, Folgen von Leistungsstörungen, in: *Schulte-Nölke/Schulze* (eds.), Europäisches Vertragsrecht im Gemeinschaftsrecht, Bonn 2002, 139, 143 et seq.; *Schmidt-Kessel*, Arbeitskampf und Vertragserfüllung im Europäischen Privatrecht, Festschrift Löwisch, sub I 1 b (to appear Munich 2007).

[12] To narrow therefore *Remien*, Folgen von Leistungsstörungen, in: *Schulte-Nölke/Schulze* (eds.), Europäisches Vertragsrecht im Gemeinschaftsrecht, Bonn 2002, 139, 144 et seq.

314 (2), 323 (2) BGB.[13] The most general case in the definitions contained in Article 8:103 PECL and Article III-3:502 DCFR is the one where the non-performance substantially deprives the creditor of what he was entitled to expect under the contract unless the other party did not foresee and could not reasonably have foreseen that result. This general definition is flanked by the cases of necessity of strict compliance and intentional (or reckless) non-performance. The basis of the right to terminate is rounded off by three special cases, that of anticipatory breach (Article 9:304 PECL), the case of the defence of insecurity (Article 8:105(2) PECL) and the special rule on dividable contracts in Article 9:302 PECL. On the other hand neither the damage caused to the aggrieved party nor the fault of the debtor are taken into account.[14] Articles 9:301(2), 8:106(3) PECL contain a "Nachfrist"-mechanism and thereby flank the general clause of fundamental breach by a more technical tool which helps the parties to bring the contract to the necessitated end.[15] Where a right to terminate is available for the aggrieved party it is usually executed by notice (Article 9:303(1) PECL) which is even dispensable in the case where the non-performance is excused through impediment which is total and permanent (Article 9:303(4) PECL).[16]

The termination of the contract under the Principles of European Contract Law releases both parties from their obligations to effect future performance but it has generally no retroactive effect (Article 9:305(1) PECL). However, there are three exceptions to that rule. The first concerns obligations in the liquidation of the contract which mainly include the restitution of things lent to the other party for the time of the contract and in the special case of the Package Travel Directive at least the duty to transport the traveller back. Much more significant is the second exception, i.e. the recovery of performances for which the counter-performance is not received (Article 9:307, 9:308 PECL). This exception

---

[13] See *Schlechtriem*, Abstandnahme vom Vertrag, in: *Basedow*, Europäische Vertragsrechtsvereinheitlichung und deutsches Recht, Tübingen 2000, 159, 163.

[14] The first question was discussed under Article 25 CISG, see *Schlechtriem*, Abstandnahme vom Vertrag, in: *Basedow*, Europäische Vertragsrechtsvereinheitlichung und deutsches Recht, Tübingen 2000, 159, 163.

[15] Cf. *Schlechtriem*, Abstandnahme vom Vertrag, in: *Basedow*, Europäische Vertragsrechtsvereinheitlichung und deutsches Recht, Tübingen 2000, 159, 167 et seq.

[16] Attaching this rule to the force majeure-clause (cf. Article III-3:104(4) DCFR) seems worth reconsidering: Not the impediment beyond control as a yardstick for the excuse of the debtor should be the basis of the extinguishing of the contract but the fact that specific performance can no longer be claimed for reasons of unlawfulness or impossibility under Article 9:102(2)(a) PECL or Article III-3:302(3)(a) DCFR.

brings the consequences of termination very close to a retroactive effect of the termination where one of the parties did not perform at all. It is, obviously, based on the Common Law doctrine of failure of performance. The third exception is strictly speaking a special category of the second one: Article 9:304, 8:105(2), 9:302 PECL deal with special cases of fundamental breach. The Draft Common Frame of Reference will most probably contain a separate chapter on unwinding contracts. The latest draft in the first line changes the order of priorities and starts with the general rule that restitution takes place (Article III-8:101(2) DCFR). The case of the termination in the sense of a "Kündigung" for breach, which only takes effect ex nunc, is now part of an exception to that rule (Article III-8:103 DCFR).

d. Price Reduction

The remedy of price reduction is very common to European Private Law. Article 3(5) of the Consumer Sales Directive and Article 4(6) Denied Boarding Regulation both contain mechanisms to reduce the price.[17] Article 9:401 PECL contains a general right to reduce the price. This remedy is by no means self-evident in many legal orders. While some continental legal systems recognise only several descendants from the Roman *actio quanti minoris* which are confined to some special contracts, a general remedy of price reduction is an even more unknown concept in a Common Law system. However, the basic idea of having such a possibility of reducing the price is very useful provided that it is possible to avoid a claim for damages by proving impediment beyond control or other reasons to excuse non-performance. The right to reduce the price is in those cases the only way to exclude the equivalence between performances of both sides.

e. Damages and Interest

Where non-performance is not excused European Private Law provides for a claim for damages. First of all, as in most legal orders, there is no general fault principle laid down in Article 9:501(1)[18] but the rules of the Principles of European Contract Law and the envisaged rules of the Draft

---

[17] See *Remien*, Folgen von Leistungsstörungen, in: *Schulte-Nölke/Schulze* (eds.), Europäisches Vertragsrecht im Gemeinschaftsrecht, Bonn 2002, 139, 145.

[18] *Medicus*, Voraussetzungen einer Haftung für Vertragsverletzung, in: *Basedow* (ed.), Europäische Vertragsrechtsvereinheitlichung und deutsches Recht, Tübingen 2000, 179, 187.

Common Frame of Reference do not provide for a strict contractual liability regime. The same holds true for the several provisions for damages under European Community Law.[19] The previously mentioned, as far as the Principles are concerned, somewhat obscure distinction between "obligation de moyens" and "obligation de résultat" leads firstly to the result that in the former case liability will be avoided by observing the standard of due care; in this case there simply will be no non-performance. In the alternative case of an "obligation de résultat" the force majeure clause of Article 8:108 PECL has its proper field of application.[20] Here lies the major difference between the general fault principle and the solution found in the Principles of European Contract Law and which is provided for in the Draft Common Frame of Reference which is generally in line with the standard of liability under the Package Travel Directive: In the case of an obligation to achieve a specific result the debtor will be excused only in the case of an event beyond his control. Distortions stemming from a source internal to the sphere of the debtor are not beyond his control and therefore do not provide the debtor with an excuse, whereas under a fault principle such internal impediments may provide the debtor with a defence.[21]

The contractual liability in the Principles of European Contract Law will lead to a complete reparation including the loss the aggrieved party has suffered and the gain of which it has been deprived (Article 9:502 PECL).[22] Article 9:501(2)(a) PECL makes it clear that damages in this sense include non-pecuniary loss and therefore cover *Simone Leitner* type cases like Article 5(2) Package Travel Directive.[23] Similar to many legal

---

[19] See *Schmidt-Kessel*, Arbeitskampf und Vertragserfüllung im Europäischen Privatrecht, Festschrift Löwisch, sub I 1 c (to appear Munich 2007).

[20] *Lando*, in: *Hartkamp* et al. (eds.), Towards a European Civil Code, 3rd Ed. 2004, 505, 508, 511.

[21] See *Schmidt-Kessel*, Arbeitskampf und Vertragserfüllung im Europäischen Privatrecht, Festschrift Löwisch, sub I 1 c (to appear Munich 2007); *Medicus*, Voraussetzungen einer Haftung für Vertragsverletzung, in: *Basedow* (ed.), Europäische Vertragsrechtsvereinheitlichung und deutsches Recht, Tübingen 2000, 179, 187 et seq.

[22] Cf. *Koziol*, Europäisches Vertragsrechtsvereinheitlichung und deutsches Schadensrecht, in: *Basedow* (ed.), Europäische Vertragsrechtsvereinheitlichung und deutsches Recht, Tübingen 2000, 195, 196.

[23] Contra as to the content of the Directive *Remien*, Folgen von Leistungsstörungen, in: *Schulte-Nölke/Schulze* (eds.), Europäisches Vertragsrecht im Gemeinschaftsrecht, Bonn 2002, 139, 146. See the criticism on Article 9:503 PECL by *Koziol*, Europäisches Vertragsrechtsvereinheitlichung und deutsches Schadensrecht, in: *Basedow* (ed.), Europäische Vertragsrechtsvereinheitlichung und deutsches Recht, Tübingen 2000, 195, 198.

orders, Article 9:503 PECL provides for a foreseeability criterion to avoid compensation for damages which at the time of the conclusion of the contract were not in the contemplation of the parties.

Two special types of damages are dealt with separately in Article 9:506 and 9:507 PECL: Where the aggrieved party wishes to get compensation for the cost and expenses of a substitute transaction, damages measured on this basis are available if the aggrieved party has terminated the contract. The same holds true where the aggrieved party wishes to refer for the purpose of calculation to the current price. Both rules will give rise to the same discussions which occurred in the examination of Articles 74 to 76 of the CISG. The pertinent cases begin with substitute transactions realized before notice of termination or without any later notice of termination. The practical experience with the said provisions of the CISG shows that it will be necessary to overcome the main purpose of that connection between termination and damages of that type, namely the avoidance of speculation by the aggrieved party, at least in some of those cases.[24] The Black Letter rules of PECL therefore urgently need to be refined before transposed lock stock and barrel into an academic Draft Common Frame of Reference.

The same is true as regards the consequences of a delay in payment of money. In this instance Article 9:508 PECL and Article III-3:708 DCFR do not meet the standards set by the Late Payments Directive. Here again further refinement of the PECL provision is needed before the provision can be utilised as part of a Common Frame of Reference.

2. Hierarchy of Remedies

Neither Community Law nor the Principles of European Contract Law accept a general hierarchy of remedies, according to which one of them would prevail.[25] There is no priority of the claim for specific performance, which is mostly accepted under German Law. Furthermore there is also no priority of a claim for damages in the case of non-performance. Such a general rule of priority is neither formulated explicitly nor can it be implied from the requirements of the several remedies.[26]

---

[24] See *Stoll/Gruber* in: *Schlechtriem/Schwenzer*, CISG Commentary 2nd English Ed., Art. 75 No. 5 and Art. 76 No. 3.

[25] The opposite does not follow from the fact, that the Consumer Sales Directive does not deal with damages, cf. *Remien*, Folgen von Leistungsstörungen, in: *Schulte-Nölke/Schulze* (eds.), Europäisches Vertragsrecht im Gemeinschaftsrecht, Bonn 2002, 139, 145 et seq.

[26] *Smits*, in *Busch/Hondius* et al. (eds.), Commentary, The Hague 2002, Art. 8:101 No. 4. But see for the Community Law *Remien*, Folgen von Leistungsstörungen,

There are, however, some exceptions. The most important exception applies in the event that two or more remedies are simply incompatible which each other regarding their consequences. For instance, following a successful termination of a contract the claim for specific performance is excluded.[27] A further exception is the above mentioned requirement of termination for the availability of some kinds of damages. A third exception leading to a priority of the specific performance claim, seems to be exceptionally included in the debtor's right to cure under Article 8:104 PECL: This right to cure, however, forecloses a priority for the claim of specific performance and merely gives the debtor the possibility to exclude certain remedies by its own activities.

3. Cumulation of Remedies

While several legal systems have their own mostly dogmatic based difficulties with the cumulation of several remedies of breach of contract the Principles of European Contract Law and the Draft Common Frame of Reference in contrast opt for a rather pragmatic approach. Article 8:102 provides that the only bar to a cumulation of remedies is their incompatibility.[28] Remedies which are not incompatible may be cumulated. This is particularly apt as regards the relationship between termination and damages and the relationship between specific performance and damages. For the latter case there is a specific rule in Article 9:103 PECL which amends the general rule of compatibility of both remedies by adding the stipulation that the barriers to specific performance do not preclude a claim for damages.

The incompatibility of remedies is in most cases not explicitly spelt out. The first exception to this can be found in Article 9:401(3) PECL whereby the Principles make clear that price reduction excuses damages for reduction in value of the performance owed by the debtor. The second noteworthy instance is hidden in Article 9:508(2) PECL where in the case of delay in payment of money the Principles provide that any *further* loss is recoverable beyond the sum of interest the debtor has to pay. Both rules represent the more general principal that double recovery is excluded under the Principles of European Contract Law. However even

---

in: *Schulte-Nölke/Schulze* (eds.), Europäisches Vertragsrecht im Gemeinschaftsrecht, Bonn 2002, 139, 147, who points to the difference between the Consumer Sales Directive and the Overbooking Regulation.

[27] Further exceptions of this kind will be dealt with under section III.3 concerning the possibility of cumulation of remedies.

[28] As to the question of a later change of choice of remedies see *Smits*, in *Busch/Hondius* et al., Commentary, The Hague 2002, Art. 8:102 No. 2.

IV. Remedies and Right to Cure

An aspect which has only lately come up for discussion is the question of whether a general right to cure restricts the remedies of the creditor. The several community directives do not provide for a general defence of the debtor. Several elements of the concept of curing defects by the debtor are included in the Package Travel Directive and the Consumer Sales Directive. Article 5(4) of the Package Travel Directive establishes a duty of the consumer to communicate any failure in the performance of the contract but this duty, which obviously aims to open a possibility of curing the defective performance, does not provide any remedies for the case of breach of duty. On the other hand there are several remedies of the consumer in existence, i.e. the right to withdraw from the contract under Article 4(5) and the claim for damages under Article 5(2) of the directive, which are not restricted by any requirement. Therefore it seems doubtful whether the national legislature may restrict those remedies by a right to cure. However, the idea of a right to cure was broadly discussed in the preparatory works for the Consumer Sales Directive, in which several hints on the existence of an implied right to cure can be ascertained. For instance the optional duty to inform the seller of the lack of conformity in Article 5(2) and furthermore, when compared to the remedies of repair or replacement, the additional prerequisites of the price reduction and the termination of the sales contract under Article 3(5) of the directive also indicate an implied right to cure. The purpose of this additional requirement is namely to open the possibility for the seller of curing the defect. This can be drawn from the fact that the buyer can resort to price reduction and termination in the event that both rights of specific performance are not available to the buyer. In those circumstances the opportunity of the seller to cure will depend on possible inconveniences to the consumer and on the fact that he cures within a reasonable time. However even these implications which are supported by the very purpose of the rule to promote a cure of the damage, do not provide the seller with a distinct right to cure.

The Principles of European Contract Law on the other hand do provide for such a right to cure. The right to cure is available under Article 8:104 where, in the case of non-conformity of the performance tendered, the debtor may make a new and conforming performance, in the event that the time for rendering performance has not yet occurred or the delay would not be such as to constitute fundamental non-performance. This right to cure is strengthened by the rules on fixing additional periods for performance in Article 8:106. Paragraph 2 of that Article excludes any remedy apart from the right to withhold performance and the claim for damages (for late performance) during an additional period allowed by the creditor. The system spanned by these two provisions leads to the main rule that where the defect in the performance rendered is not to be qualified as a fundamental breach of the contract there is a right to cure restricting the claim for damages, the right to reduce price and the right to terminate the contract. If the creditor fixes (or allows) an additional period of time for performance the situation changes. During that period the party in breach is protected from invocation of the several remedies. The aggrieved party may only withhold performance of its own reciprocal obligation and claim damages for the delay and other damage which has occurred in the meantime. This immunization from the claim for specific performance, for full compensation, for price reduction and for termination ends when the period ends or earlier if the aggrieved party receives notice from the other party that the latter will not perform within the period. At the end of the period fixed or allowed the aggrieved party may terminate the contract even if the breach is not a fundamental one.

This idea of a general right to cure is elaborated on in a more detailed way in a new section of the chapter "Remedies for Breach of Contract" in the Draft Common Frame of Reference as it stands at the moment. This idea leads to the question of whether it is really necessary to have such an explicit right to cure, restricting damages claims and termination and to give so much weight to the position of the debtor in breach. There is some doubt about such a strengthening of that position which derives from the restrictive approach to the principles which is prevalent in most European legal systems regarding the implementation of duties to cooperate. To force an innocent creditor to accept performance by curing a defective performance deviates from the concepts which are to be found in the rules on specific performance. The final version of the academic Draft Common Frame of Reference should show some more consistency in that respect.

V. Conclusion

Remedies for breach of contract are a useful category for the unification of European Private Law. The main task of that unification is to build up a common technical language of the law in order to promote a common understanding amongst the various legal orders. Some decades ago, *Ole Lando* and his Commission began their work by refraining systematically from entering any dogmatic debate and by restricting their work to the rules of substance. If there is an ideal way to unify European Private Law and to bring together a real European theory of Civil Law this must be the appropriate approach to follow.

La proposition de réforme des sanctions de l'inexécution du contrat dans l'Avant-projet de réforme du Code civil français et l'influence européenne

Judith Rochfeld (Paris)

A l'orée du bicentenaire du Code civil, en 2004, une trentaine d'universitaires français, spécialistes du droit civil, se sont attelés à proposer une réforme de la partie du Code consacrée au droit des obligations et de la prescription. Ce projet s'est concrétisé, sous l'égide du Professeur Catala, par la rédaction d'un Avant-projet de réforme, remis au Ministre de la Justice, le 22 septembre 2005.[1] L'une des motivations de ce travail était de confronter l'état du droit français en la matière aux principes du droit européen des contrats issus des travaux de la Commission Landö, ainsi qu'aux autres travaux d'harmonisation et aux droits des pays européens voisins. Il paraissait ressortir de la comparaison que si, sur certains points, le droit français était ou pouvait entrer en convergence avec la trame proposée pour l'Europe, sur d'autres points, des divergences importantes existaient.

Parmi ces dernières, le droit français de l'inexécution se caractérisait par une grande spécificité. Pour avoir reçu la tâche d'y réfléchir au sein de ce groupe de travail et de proposer des évolutions, je présenterai dans les lignes qui suivent le cheminement suivi à cet effet, en partant de l'état des textes existants et de leurs lacunes (I), pour en arriver à éclairer les propositions de réforme et les hésitations sous-jacentes (II). Je voudrais avertir immédiatement qu'il s'agit de faire partager un parcours de doutes, d'hésitations, qui ne prétend nullement à une vérité et ne tend qu'à ouvrir à critique et discussion, notamment au regard des traditions et pratiques juridiques voisines.

---

[1] Cet avant-projet est disponible sur le site du Ministère de la justice français, à l'adresse : www.justice.gouv.fr/publicat/rapport/RAPPORTCATALASEPTEMBRE2005.pdf ; il est actuellement soumis à la discussion par les professionnels du droit.

I. L'état des textes existants et leurs lacunes

Le travail de réflexion a pris comme point de départ la seule disposition de la matière traitée, certes célébrissime en droit français, à savoir l'article 1184 du Code civil :

« *La condition résolutoire est toujours sous-entendue dans les contrats synallagmatiques, pour le cas où l'une des deux parties ne satisfera point à son engagement.*

Dans ce cas, le contrat n'est point résolu de plein droit. La partie envers laquelle l'engagement n'a point été exécuté, a le choix ou de forcer l'autre à l'exécution de la convention lorsqu'elle est possible, ou d'en demander la résolution avec dommages et intérêts.

La résolution doit être demandée en justice, et il peut être accordé au défendeur un délai selon les circonstances. »

Cet article se caractérise par plusieurs particularités. Il précise tout d'abord qu'une condition résolutoire est toujours sous-entendue dans le contrat synallagmatique, « pour le cas où l'une des parties ne satisfera point à son engagement ». Il ajoute ensuite que, dans ce cas, le créancier se trouve investi d'une option entre une demande d'exécution forcée et une demande de résolution, chacune éventuellement accompagnée de l'octroi de dommages et intérêts.

Si, enfin, le créancier opte pour la résolution, le texte lui enjoint de la demander en justice, un délai pouvant être accordé au défendeur « selon les circonstances ».

Le fondement, les conditions, et la philosophie censés porter cette disposition sont particulièrement intéressants. Quant à son fondement, il est explicite : la résolution est assise sur le mécanisme de la condition résolutoire (par fidélité à l'idée d'autonomie de la volonté faisant de la bonne exécution du contrat la condition du consentement) ; elle s'inscrit comme implicite dans tous les contrats synallagmatiques. Quant à ses conditions de mise en œuvre, on note le caractère judiciaire de la mesure. Quant à la philosophie sous-jacente du texte, deux idées l'irriguent. En premier lieu, le juge intervient pour assurer la défense du principe de la force obligatoire, qui voudrait que le contrat soit exécuté quelles que soient les circonstances et les difficultés rencontrées ; et qu'en conséquence, il ne soit anéanti que dans les seuls les cas d'inexécution très grave, par décision du juge contrôlant ce seuil de gravité. En second lieu, le juge intervient pour garantir une protection minimale au débiteur, celui-ci ne devant pas subir une sanction, trop vite assénée et sans contrôle, de la part de son partenaire si son inexécution n'est pas la conséquence d'un fait volontaire ou si elle revêt un caractère minime. La première idée relève du moralisme contractuel, la seconde de l'humanisme contractuel. Elles donnent toutes deux leur spécificité au droit français.

En effet, si l'on synthétise l'ensemble de ces précisions, ces idées induisent, dans la tradition française, que la résolution soit conçue comme une sanction, d'une part ; étroitement surveillée dans son application par le juge et prononcée par ce dernier, d'autre part ; en dernière extrémité, enfin.

Plusieurs conséquences en découlent. Tout d'abord, la résolution est entourée d'un halo de méfiance et ne doit intervenir que dans les cas extrêmes de faillite irrémédiable du contrat. Ensuite, quand bien même une inexécution serait constatée, un grand pouvoir d'appréciation, dit « pouvoir modérateur », est laissé au juge, qui lui permet de choisir la mesure la plus appropriée. Par exemple, il pourra refuser de prononcer la résolution, préférant laisser une chance au débiteur de s'exécuter pendant un délai déterminé ; il pourra remplacer la résolution par des dommages et intérêts ; il pourra prononcer une résolution aux torts réciproques ; ou encore une résolution assortie de dommages et intérêts.[2]

Par ailleurs, hormis cet article fondamental, des lacunes importantes marquent le Code civil actuel. Elles relèvent de trois domaines.

En premier lieu, elles touchent les prévisions initiales. La résolution est, en effet, la seule mesure prévue pour l'ensemble des contrats. Les autres mesures ne sont évoquées que dans des textes, épars, dédiés aux contrats spéciaux, que ce soit l'exception d'inexécution, prévue pour la vente, l'échange ou le contrat d'assurance par exemple,[3] ou la théorie des risques (inexécution pour cas de force majeure), construite par la doctrine, sur le fondement de textes relatifs au bail et au contrat d'entreprise, notamment.[4]

En deuxième lieu, des lacunes marquent les conditions d'application des mesures. L'article 1184 ne précise pas celles entourant la résolution : rien n'est dit, notamment, sur le seuil d'inexécution propre à l'entraîner, cette disposition se contentant de viser le « cas où l'une des parties ne satisfera point à son engagement ». La jurisprudence en appelle tradition-

---

[2] Cf. J. Fischer, *Le pouvoir modérateur du juge en droit civil français*, préf. P. Le Tourneau, PUAM, 2004, n° 171 et s., p. 160 et s.

[3] Article 1612 C. civ. (vente) : « le vendeur n'est pas tenu de délivrer la chose, si l'acheteur n'en paye pas le prix et que le vendeur ne lui ait pas accordé un délai pour le payement » ; Article 1704 (échange) : « Si l'un des copermutants a déjà reçu la chose à lui donnée en échange, et qu'il prouve ensuite que l'autre contractant n'est pas propriétaire de cette chose, il ne peut être forcé à livrer celle qui est promise en contre-échange, mais seulement à rendre celle qu'il a reçue » ; art. L. 113-3 C. ass. (contrat d'assurance).

[4] Article 1722 (bail) : « si, pendant la durée du bail, la chose louée est détruite en totalité par cas fortuit, le bail est résilié de plein droit » ; Article 1788 (contrat d'entreprise) : « si la matière fournie par l'ouvrier vient à périr de quelque manière que ce soit avant sa livraison la perte est pour l'ouvrier ».

nellement au « manquement suffisamment grave ».[5] Le constat peut être étendu à l'exception d'inexécution.

Enfin, des lacunes intéressent les effets des différentes sanctions de l'inexécution. L'article 1184, toujours, ne précise rien quant à l'étendue de ceux de la résolution : rétroactifs ou non ; touchant ou non l'ensemble du contrat. Certes, la référence en son sein à la « condition résolutoire » a orienté vers la rétroactivité. Mais, doctrine et jurisprudence n'en ont pas moins créé une variante, la « résiliation » ou résolution pour l'avenir, qui l'écarte. Pour autant, le critère de la distinction des contrats résolus et des contrats « résiliés » n'est ni très explicite ni indiscutable.[6] Par ailleurs, rien n'est dit, des suites de l'application des diverses mesures, notamment de l'organisation des restitutions et du fondement de ces dernières.

Enfin, au-delà de ces lacunes, la réflexion devait prendre en considération les évolutions de la jurisprudence et de la pratique, ainsi que les influences européennes.

Du côté de la jurisprudence, et pour ne citer que les principales mutations, des nuances au caractère judiciaire de la résolution ont été introduites. Après avoir exceptionnellement admis la rupture unilatérale dans des hypothèses circonscrites,[7] les juges, spécialement la première chambre civile de la Cour de cassation, par deux arrêts importants du 13 octobre 1998 et du 20 février 2001, se sont plus radicalement prononcés pour l'admission d'une rupture, mise en œuvre par l'un des contractants. La Cour de cassation a ainsi énoncé que « la gravité du comportement d'une partie à un contrat peut justifier que l'autre (partie) y mette fin de façon

---

[5] Le critère n'est cependant pas unique. Les juges peuvent également prononcer une résolution, en l'absence de manquement « suffisamment grave », dans les cas d'inexécution intentionnelle ou de confiance perdue par le cocontractant.

[6] Cf. Cass. civ. 1e, 3 nov. 1983, *Bull. civ.* I, n° 252, p. 227, *Defrénois* 1984, art. 33368, p. 1014, obs. J.-L. Aubert, *RTD civ* 1985, p. 166, obs. J. Mestre, et 13 janv. 1987, *Bull. civ.* I, n° 11, p. 8, JCP G 1987, II, 20860, note G. Goubeaux : « la résolution pour inexécution partielle atteint l'ensemble du contrat ou certaines de ses tranches seulement, suivant que les parties ont voulu faire une convention indivisible ou fractionnée en une série de contrats ».

[7] Celles-ci étaient au nombre de trois : l'urgence ; l'« état de nécessité ; la « situation devenue intolérable », par exemple, une perte de confiance lorsque celle-ci est particulièrement nécessaire à la relation contractuelle ; sur ces admissions, R. Encinas de Munagorri, *L'acte unilatéral dans les rapports contractuels*, préface A. Lyon-Caen, LGDJ, 1995, n° 145 et s., p. 139 et s. ; J. Ghestin, M. Billiau, C. Jamin, *Traité de droit civil. Les effets du contrat*, LGDJ, 3e éd., 2001, n° 423 et s., p. 433 et s.

unilatérale à ses risques et périls »,[8] « peu important que le contrat soit à durée déterminée ou non ».[9]

Du côté de la pratique, on relève le renversement du principe de la compétence du juge par l'insertion très fréquente de clauses résolutoires.[10]

Enfin, l'influence des travaux d'harmonisation européens et des modèles juridiques voisins, majoritairement habités par le système de la résolution unilatérale pesait sur le droit national en le menaçant d'isolement.

Pour toutes ces raisons, on pouvait légitimement tenter de réordonner la matière et de proposer une réforme.

II. Les propositions de réforme : l'influence européenne et la mutation profonde du droit français

Au travers de l'Avant-projet, divers changements sont proposés. Ils font l'objet de la section V (cf. annexe n° 1). Après les avoir évoqués dans leur ensemble, on discutera, en priorité, de la mesure phare relative au choix du mode de résolution, passant de judiciaire à unilatérale. Celui-ci démontre, en effet, l'influence de l'harmonisation européenne et les bouleversements qu'elle peut entraîner dans les conceptions nationales.

Quant aux principaux changements, on remarquera tout d'abord les consécrations textuelles des mécanismes de l'exception d'inexécution (art. 1157, cf. annexe n° 1), de la résolution conventionnelle (ainsi que de certaines des conditions de sa mise en œuvre : exigence de précision des inexécutions ouvrant à résolution ; mise en demeure ; le contrôle de la bonne foi tel que pratiqué par la jurisprudence restant, lui, implicite ; art. 1159).

On relèvera également la reconstruction d'une certaine unité des sanctions de l'inexécution. Elles s'ordonneraient désormais autour d'une idée objective, détachée de toute référence à la faute. Elles s'appliqueraient en conséquence aux cas de force majeure ou de cause légitime empêchant l'exécution (la théorie des risques, construite par la doctrine, s'y intégrerait donc ; la référence n'est explicite que pour l'exception d'inexécution

---

[8] Cass. civ.1ᵉ, 13 oct. 1998, D. 1999, p. 197, note C. Jamin et Somm., p. 115, obs. P. Delebecque, Defrénois 1999, p. 374, obs. D. Mazeaud, JCP G, 1999, II, 10133, note N. Rzepecki.

[9] Cass. civ.1ᵉ, 20 février 2001, D., 2001, p. 1568, note C. Jamin et Somm., p. 3239, obs. D. Mazeaud, RTD civ. 2001, p. 363, obs. J. Mestre et B. Fages, Defrénois 2001, p. 705, obs. E. Savaux.

[10] Elles ne sont toutefois pas autorisées dans tous les contrats, par exemple elles sont interdites dans le bail d'habitation.

mais s'étend à la résolution[11]). La jurisprudence est, déjà, en ce sens. La suppression de la condition résolutoire, en tant que fondement de la résolution, en outre, permettrait à cette mesure de prendre place dans le chapitre de celles relatives à l'inexécution, tout en conservant l'alternative avec l'exécution forcée. Les différentes sanctions de l'inexécution du contrat seraient donc réunies dans un chapitre cohérent, alors qu'avant elles étaient éparpillés à divers endroits du Code.

Par ailleurs, au titre des effets des mesures, le moment de prise d'effet de la résolution serait fixé (cf. *infra*), tandis que serait refusée la résolution anticipée (on peut se reporter à l'article 1158, cf. annexe). Par ailleurs, en conformité aux PDEC,[12] le droit français abandonnerait le principe du caractère rétroactif de la résolution, sauf critère départageant les hypothèses où il est nécessaire d'anéantir tous les effets passés (c'est l'objet des articles 1160 et suivants, cf. annexe).

Si l'on en vient maintenant au problème central qui concentre les principaux enjeux de la matière, la réforme a tranché la question du choix du caractère judiciaire ou unilatéral de la résolution.

En effet, une fois admise l'idée de ne pas en rester au *statu quo ante*, que ce soit pour ne pas ignorer les revendications d'évolution ou pour considérer la différence entre la France et ses voisins européens, deux directions étaient envisageables.

Une première orientation pouvait prôner une approche binaire et objective : il s'agissait d'ouvrir une alternative entre résolution unilatérale et résolution judiciaire, le domaine de chacune ne dépendant pas d'un choix de l'une des parties – le créancier – , mais d'un critère objectif tenant en la gravité du manquement.

Ainsi, la résolution unilatérale, parce qu'elle revient à investir le créancier d'un pouvoir unilatéral de rompre, pourrait ne se justifier que si un seuil d'inexécution manifeste est atteint (cf. les fondements français traditionnel et la méfiance à l'égard des pouvoirs exercés par l'un des contractants sur l'autre) : l'idée, ici, serait que, pour se passer du juge et abandonner l'appréciation à l'une des parties, il faut que le manquement soit facile à caractériser, qu'il soit manifeste, et que sa constatation ne donne pas lieu à contestation sérieuse ; il le faudrait d'autant plus, toujours dans cette première conception, que la charge du procès est inversée et pèse sur le débiteur, s'il estime que la résolution a été mise en œuvre de façon illégitime. En conséquence, alors que l'on pouvait se contenter, antérieurement, c'est-à-dire au sein de la résolution judiciaire, du seuil du « manquement suffisamment grave », il pourrait sembler nécessaire de

---

[11] Cf. art. 1157, al. 2 : « *Lorsque l'inexécution résulte d'une force majeure ou d'une autre cause légitime, le contrat peut être pareillement suspendu si l'inexécution n'est pas irrémédiable* ».

[12] Art. 9 : 305.

caractériser un manquement d'une particulière gravité, pour le jeu de la résolution unilatérale.

C'est pourquoi, dans cette première orientation, la résolution unilatérale n'était prévue que dans les hypothèses d'inexécution totale, conçues comme celles d'un contrat totalement inexécuté ou exécuté avec retard lorsque le délai a été stipulé, ou apparaît, comme essentiel.

A l'inverse, la résolution restait judiciaire, dans les autres cas, c'est-à-dire dans les hypothèses d'exécution partielle, défectueuse ou tardive, pour lesquelles il est nécessaire d'apprécier la gravité du manquement, voire de moduler la sanction.

On parvenait ainsi à la proposition suivante, sous forme d'alternative :

« Une partie peut résoudre le contrat s'il y a inexécution totale de la part de l'autre partie (suivent les conditions reprises dans la version définitive proposée, cf. art. 1158, annexe).

Dans l'hypothèse où l'inexécution n'est pas totale, le juge prononce la résolution si l'intérêt au contrat ne peut plus être satisfait. Il peut également octroyer au défendeur un délai pour exécuter. A défaut, le juge prononce le maintien du contrat et alloue, le cas échéant, des dommages et intérêts au demandeur ... »

Au titre des avantages de cette proposition, ou de ce que d'aucuns pourraient considérer comme tels (mais tout le problème est là), on relèverait que le système restait objectif, au sens où il n'investissait pas le créancier de la possibilité discrétionnaire de choisir le mode de sanction, et qu'une considération du seuil de gravité du manquement intervenait en amont.

Au titre de ses inconvénients, on pouvait, non seulement noter la difficulté de qualifier les manquements, et le possible contentieux pouvant en naître, mais également la perpétuation de la particularité française, les autres droits européens ne connaissant pas ce type d'alternative objective.

C'est pourquoi, après arbitrage, une deuxième orientation, celle des articles 1158 et 1158-1 des textes proposés, a consisté à rejeter cette alternative pour retenir une option, maniée par le créancier, entre résolution judiciaire et résolution unilatérale.

L'alinéa 2 de l'article 1158 prévoit ainsi que, « *quand il opte pour la résolution, le créancier peut soit la demander au juge, soit, de lui-même, mettre en demeure le débiteur défaillant de satisfaire à son engagement dans un délai raisonnable, à défaut de quoi il tiendra le contrat pour résolu* ».

Au titre des avantages de cette seconde direction, on compte l'absence de seuil problématique entre résolution unilatérale et judiciaire. Mais, surtout, et ces arguments ont été très forts dans l'option choisie, elle permettait la mise en conformité du droit français avec celui de ses voisins, plus précisément d'ailleurs avec le droit néerlandais qui connaît cette même option, la méthode unilatérale faisant, là, figure d'hypothèse normale (article 267 du Livre 6 du nouveau C. civ. néerlandais). L'impact politique et psychologique d'une mesure conçue comme marquée du sceau d'une certaine modernité, parce qu'adoptée assez généralement, a ainsi beaucoup joué.

Par ailleurs, les préoccupations d'efficacité économique de la sanction ont également pris l'avantage : la résolution unilatérale permettrait une plus prompte ré-allocation des ressources, ainsi que, plus globalement et par voie de conséquence, une préservation optimale de l'intérêt du marché. L'exécution devrait ainsi être « efficace », ou le contrat devrait disparaître.

Au titre des inconvénients des mesures proposées, néanmoins, on peut compter, l'absence de seuil précis autorisant le créancier à se prévaloir de la résolution.[13]

Surtout, le juriste français aura tendance à relever la « subjectivation » du droit de rompre, une telle disposition réalisant, en effet, l'octroi d'une véritable prérogative unilatérale au créancier.

En conséquence, l'adoption de l'article proposé, au-delà de son aspect technique, réaliserait une totale inversion de la conception française actuelle. Celle-ci évoluerait d'une résolution-accident – maniée par le juge, entourée d'un halo de méfiance et ne devant intervenir que dans les cas extrêmes de faillite irrémédiable du contrat, après exercice d'éventuel pouvoirs modérateurs –, vers une résolution-prérogative, maniée par le créancier, binaire, et faisant disparaître tout pouvoir modérateur.[14]

Le texte concrétiserait également l'inversion, lourde, de la charge du procès, sur les épaules du débiteur.

Néanmoins, ce choix s'entourerait des précautions requises par le changement de modèle et l'introduction d'un pouvoir unilatéral sans intervention du juge. Celles-ci tiennent en l'organisation de la considération minimale des intérêts du débiteur lors de la mise en œuvre de la prérogative par le créancier, d'une part, et en l'exigence d'éléments permettant l'exercice d'un éventuel contrôle *a posteriori* de cette dernière par le juge, d'autre part.

Tout d'abord, la considération minimale des intérêts du débiteur est visible à l'alinéa 2 de l'article 1158 proposé qui précise que, quand il opte pour la résolution unilatérale, le créancier

---

[13] Sur cette critique, cf. H. Beale, « La réforme du droit français des contrats et le « droit européen des contrats » ; perspective de la *Law Commission* anglaise », in *La réforme du droit des contrats : projet et perspectives*, Rev. Droit des Contrats, 2006, p. 135 et s.

[14] Sur cette évolution, sous l'influence des principes de droit européens des contrats, cf. notre article, « Résolution et exception dinexécutio ... », in *Les concepts contractuels français à l'heure des principes européens des contrats* (Dir.) P. Rémy-Corlay et D. Fenouillet, Dalloz, 2003, p. 213 et s., p. 217.

doit « *mettre en demeure le débiteur défaillant de satisfaire à son engagement* ». Cette mise en demeure intervient comme une condition, traditionnelle, destinée à parvenir à l'exécution (dernière tentative pour obtenir cette dernière) et à assurer un respect minimal des intérêts du débiteur, dans un souci d'humanisme : la mesure est informative au sens où elle évite de surprendre le partenaire contractuel[15] ; elle se veut également comminatoire, le créancier manifestant par son biais sa volonté de voir l'obligation exécutée.[16]

Par ailleurs, le créancier doit octroyer un délai raisonnable d'exécution (alinéa 2 de l'article 1158).

On se reportera ensuite à l'alinéa 3 du même article, qui prévoit que « *lorsque l'inexécution persiste, le créancier notifie au débiteur la résolution du contrat et les raisons qui la motivent* ». En effet, on trouve ici, sur le modèle des travaux d'harmonisation européens,[17] l'exigence de notification. Celle-ci répond au besoin d'information du débiteur de la fin du contrat et à la nécessité de constater la volonté du créancier de rompre.[18] Elle fixe précisément la date de la rupture à sa réception par l'autre partie[19] et

---

[15] Cf. B. de Coninck, « La mise en demeure. Rapport belge », *in* Les sanctions de l'inexécution des obligations contractuelles, Etudes de droit comparé, sous la dir. de G. Viney et M. Fontaine, Bruylant, LGDJ, 2001, p. 165.

[16] On peut s'interroger, si les propositions devaient être retenues, sur le sort qui serait réservé à cette mise en demeure, dans les hypothèses où l'exécution serait d'ores et déjà impossible. Dans ce cas, dans le système actuel, la jurisprudence a allégé l'exigence qui l'entoure, la demande en justice du créancier pouvant valoir mise en demeure. On peut imaginer que ce raisonnement pourrait valoir également ici et que la notification puisse valoir mise en demeure. Cf., sur cette évolution, J. Ghestin, C. Jamin et M. Billiau, Les effets ..., op. cit., nn° 452, pp. 512 et s. ; Cass. civ.1e, 23 mai 2000, D. 2000, IR, p. 203.

[17] Cf. Art. 9 : 303 : Notification de la résolution :
« (1) *La résolution s'opère par notification au débiteur* ;
(2) *Le créancier est déchu du droit de résoudre le contrat s'il n'adresse pas notification dans un délai raisonnable à partir du moment où il a eu, ou aurait dû avoir connaissance, de l'inexécution* ».
Sur cet article, I. de Lamberterie, G. Rouhette, D. Tallon et C. Witz, *Les principes du droit européen du contrat. L'exécution, l'inexécution et ses suites*, version française, Doc. française, 1997, p. 206.

[18] Cf., déjà, l'article L. 114-1 C. cons. qui enjoint au consommateur, dont le produit ou la prestation n'a pas été livré ou exécuté sept jours après la date prévue, de notifier par lettre recommandée la « dénonciation » du contrat.

[19] En lieu et place de l'incertitude et des hésitations du droit français antérieur, cf. J. Ghestin, C. Jamin et M. Billiau, *op. cit.*, n° 543 et s., p. 598 et s., un flou existant dans la jurisprudence ; par ex., Cass. civ. 3ᵉ, 13 mai 1998, *Bull. civ.* III, n° 98, p. 66, la fixant au jour du jugement, constitutif.

s'intègre dans la catégorie des actes réceptifs. A cette date, les effets de la rupture ne se développent alors que pour l'avenir, conformément à la suppression de la condition résolutoire comme fondement de la résolution et au modèle européen.[20]

Par ailleurs, l'exigence de motivation de cette notification intervient en prévision du contrôle postérieur du juge.

Celui-ci est prévu par l'art. 1158-1, alinéa. 1er, sur le fondement de l'idée que la mise en œuvre d'une prérogative unilatérale justifie un tel contrôle, les pouvoirs du juge allant, alors, « *selon les circonstances* », de la validation de la résolution à la condamnation à l'exécution du contrat, avec octroi éventuel « d'un délai au débiteur ».

Ce contrôle ne va toutefois pas sans difficultés. Deux directions sont possibles, selon le degré de discrétion du droit ainsi reconnu au créancier. Soit le juge disposera d'un véritable pouvoir de contrôle et il sera un « juge contrôleur ». Soit il ne fera qu'entériner une décision prise par le créancier, se changeant en « juge homologateur ».[21]

Dans la première direction, où le juge exercerait un contrôle véritable en tant que juge-contrôleur, il pourrait porter une appréciation réelle de la mise en œuvre et de l'opportunité de la prérogative unilatérale de décider de la résolution, quand bien même le contrôle interviendrait *a posteriori*.[22]

Deux types de critères pourraient ici être utilisés. En premier lieu, on peut imaginer un contrôle de l'abus du droit : l'exercice par le créancier de sa prérogative de résoudre unilatéralement le contrat pourrait être jugée abusive si elle apparaît particulièrement injustifiée ou brutale pour le débiteur ou sans qu'il y ait véritablement un intérêt. Plus avant et en second lieu, un contrôle de proportionnalité pourrait être conduit : il s'agirait de mettre en balance les intérêts respectifs des parties, à savoir l'intérêt du créancier à la mise en œuvre de la mesure et la défaillance et/ou les moyens du débiteur (par exemple, au vu du coût, financier, hu-

---

On relèvera que cette date est la plus à même d'introduire un équilibre entre les intérêts de chacune des parties (par exemple, elle est appliquée en droit du travail en matière de licenciement, cf. art. L. 122-14-1, al. 1er).

[20] Art. 9 : 305 : Effets de la résolution en général :

« *(1) La résolution du contrat libère les deux parties de leur obligation d'effectuer la prestation ou de la recevoir dans le futur ; mais sous réserve des articles 9 : 306 à 9 : 308, elle est sans effet sur les droits et obligations qui avaient pris naissance au moment où elle est intervenue* ».

[21] Selon les expressions de J. Normand, « Conclusions », *in Le conventionnel et le juridictionnel dans le règlement des différends*, P. Ancel et M.-C. Rivier, (dir.), Economica, 2001, p. 148.

[22] C'est le cas, plus largement, pour l'exercice de toutes les prérogatives unilatérales, telle la mise en œuvre des clauses résolutoires.

main ou social, de la résolution).[23] Ces critères pourraient d'ailleurs s'entremêler, l'approche en termes de proportionnalité pouvant fonder le constat d'un abus de droit.[24] Au soutien de cette première direction, on peut relever, dans la proposition de réforme, l'exigence de notification des motifs de la rupture.

Dans cette direction toujours, la sanction la plus adéquate serait le prononcé du maintien du contrat dans les cas où la décision de rompre serait intervenue de façon illégitime. Cette possibilité est ouverte à l'article 1158-1 alinéa. 2 proposé.[25]

Au soutien de la seconde direction, néanmoins, celle d'un juge ne faisant qu'homologuer la décision du créancier et d'un contrôle minimal, plusieurs arguments peuvent être avancés.

Tout d'abord, on remarquera que l'exigence du seuil traditionnel du « manquement suffisamment grave », qui impliquait un contrôle de proportionnalité de la mesure, ou la précision d'un seuil quelconque, n'a pas été reprise ou effectuée. Ce seuil pourrait cependant être réintégré *a posteriori*.

Surtout, le renversement du temps et de la charge du procès, sur les épaules du débiteur du fait de l'intervention *a posteriori* du juge, induit non seulement que le champ du contrôle soit réduit en pratique, au sens où peu de contractants prendront le risque et supporteront le coût d'une telle entreprise, mais également que, la décision ayant d'ores et déjà déroulé ses conséquences, le juge soit placé devant un état de fait qui lui laisse peu de marge de manœuvre, si ce n'est l'octroi de dommages et intérêts. On ajoutera à cet égard qu'il existe des doutes, en droit français, sur la compétence du juge des référés pour prononcer le maintien du contrat. Or, il est le juge de l'urgence, le seul qui puisse efficacement intervenir afin d'ordonner à un contractant, en temps utiles, de continuer l'exécution de son contrat alors que celui-ci veut illégitimement en sortir

---

[23] Cf. l'opposition entre « droit » à la résolution, véritablement absolutiste, et « intérêt » à la résolution, intégrant une mise en balance avec l'intérêt d'autrui, entendu en priorité comme celui du débiteur, éventuellement des tiers, Y.-M. Laithier, *Etude comparative des sanctions de l'inexécution du contrat*, préf. H. Muir Watt, LGDJ, 2004. n° 219 et s., p. 304 et s., spéc. n° 227 et s., p. 311 et s.

[24] Comp. le contrôle entourant la mise en œuvre des clauses résolutoires, fondé sur la bonne foi mais non sur la proportionnalité ; cf., par ex., Cass. civ.1e, 16 fév. 1999, Bull. civ. I, n° 52, qui reproche à celui qui se fonde sur une telle disposition d'avoir attendu plusieurs années d'inexécution avant de se prévaloir brutalement de la clause.

[25] Art. 1158-1 : « *Il est loisible au débiteur de contester en justice la décision du créancier en alléguant que le manquement qui lui est imputé ne justifie pas la résolution du contrat ... Le juge peut, selon les circonstances, valider la résolution ou ordonner l'exécution du contrat, en octroyant éventuellement un délai au débiteur* ».

en alléguant une résolution. Le juge du fond, quant à lui, n'interviendra que face à une exécution d'ores et déjà été interrompue et une rupture consommée, de sorte que toute idée de maintenir le contrat pourra sembler illusoire. Dans cette situation, seuls des dommages et intérêts pourront être ordonnés et il risque de se produire un déplacement, d'un contrôle de la légitimité de la mesure de résolution vers celui de la responsabilité civile.[26]

Plus profondément, on peut alors soulever une interrogation plus cruciale, tenant aux répercussions que pourraient avoir ces propositions sur la conception même que le droit français a forgé du lien contractuel, la conception que l'on adopte des pouvoirs du créancier ne pouvant lui être étrangère.

Or, on notera que cette partie se trouve, dans une certaine mesure, privilégiée dans la relation, au nom de l'efficacité de la sanction : certes, chaque contractant détient cette faculté de résoudre le contrat, mais la résolution unilatérale favorise le créancier qui se libère rapidement, quitte à être attaqué pour abus, mais *a posteriori* et de façon limitée comme nous l'avons vu. Il y a ici basculement de la charge et du sens du procès et « subjectivation » du rapport contractuel, dans sa phase d'exécution, au sens où on donne à chacun des contractants un droit subjectif de rompre.

Ce constat peut appeler, pour un juriste français, deux réserves, tenant, d'une part, à la répartition des pouvoirs entre les parties et le juge et, d'autre part et par voie de conséquence, au rôle du juge. Entre les parties, tout d'abord, on peut penser que reconnaître au créancier le droit de rompre unilatéralement le contrat revient, dans un mouvement déjà largement démontré, à valoriser l'unilatéralisme dans la relation contractuelle et à concevoir cette dernière, non plus comme une situation objective régie par le droit, sous contrôle du juge, mais comme un agencement de pouvoirs et de devoirs de chacune des parties envers l'autre.[27] Cela revient également à entériner, certes pour des raisons qui peuvent paraître légitimes, la déjudiciarisation. Plus avant, dans le cas spécifique de la résolution, on peut se demander si cela n'équivaudrait pas à attribuer au créancier non seulement une forme de *jurisdictio*, mais également d'*imperium* (la notion est ici entendue largement) au sens où tout se pas-

---

[26] Cf. l'idée de glissement du contentieux vers celui de la responsabilité civile, notre article, « Résolution et exception d'inexécution ... », art. préc. (n° 14), p. 229 et s.

[27] Cf. R. Encinas de Munagorri, Rafael *L'acte unilatéral dans les rapports contractuels*, préf. A. Lyon-Caen, LGDJ, 1995 ; D. Mazeaud et C. Jamin (dir.), *L'unilatéralisme et le droit des obligations*, Economica, 1999 ; pour une comparaison sur ce point, du droit français et du droit anglais, cf. S. Whittaker, « Un droit à la prestation plutôt qu'un droit à l'exécution? Perspectives anglaises sur l'exécution en nature de la réparation », RDC 2005, p. 54.

serait comme si le créancier endossait les pouvoirs de décision, de commandement et d'imposition de cette décision, tous pouvoirs relevant antérieurement du juge. Il se produirait ainsi une sorte d'introduction de la juridiction dans le contrat, ou du moins d'une justice privée provisoire, en lieu et place de celle déléguée par l'Etat. A l'égard du juge, par voie de conséquence, nous avons vu que les interrogations sur l'étendue de ses pouvoirs et sa marginalisation n'étaient pas minces.

En conclusion, on le voit, sous l'influence européenne, le droit français s'applique à opérer des mutations profondes qui touchent des fondements très ancrés de sa philosophie juridique et pourraient atteindre jusqu'à la conception même du lien contractuel. Celle-ci évoluerait d'un lien de droit sous contrôle du juge,[28] d'un lien d'obligation entre deux individus, pour devenir celle d'un « lien fonctionnel », finalisé vers la seule satisfaction et le seul avantage du créancier.[29]

III. Annexe Textes proposés

1. Textes proposés (version française)

AVANT-PROJET DE REFORME DU DROIT DES OBLIGATIONS
(Articles 1101 à 1386 du Code civil)
ET DU DROIT DE LA PRESCRIPTION (Articles 2234 à 2281 du Code civil)
Rapport à Monsieur Pascal Clément Garde des Sceaux, Ministre de la Justice 22 Septembre 2005
SECTION 5. DE L'INEXECUTION DES OBLIGATIONS ET DE LA RESOLUTION DU CONTRAT (ARTICLES 1157 A 1160-1)

Article 1157
Dans un contrat synallagmatique, chaque partie peut refuser d'exécuter son obligation tant que l'autre n'exécute pas la sienne.

Lorsque l'inexécution résulte d'une force majeure ou d'une autre cause légitime, le contrat peut être pareillement suspendu si l'inexécution n'est pas irrémédiable.

A l'exception d'inexécution, l'autre partie peut répliquer en prouvant en justice que la suspension du contrat n'est pas justifiée.

Article 1158
Dans tout contrat, la partie envers laquelle l'engagement n'a pas été exécuté, ou l'a été imparfaitement, a le choix ou de poursuivre l'exécution de l'engagement ou de

---

[28] S. Whittaker, art. préc., p. 54, qui rattache cette conception à l'héritage du droit romain.
[29] Sur cet aspect, Y.-M. Laithier, « La prétendue primauté de l'exécution en nature », RDC 2005, p. 161.

provoquer la résolution du contrat ou de réclamer des dommages intérêts, lesquels peuvent, le cas échéant, s'ajouter à l'exécution ou à la résolution.

Quand il opte pour la résolution, le créancier peut soit la demander au juge, soit, de lui-même, mettre en demeure le débiteur défaillant de satisfaire à son engagement dans un délai raisonnable, à défaut de quoi il sera en droit de résoudre le contrat.

Lorsque l'inexécution persiste, le créancier notifie au débiteur la résolution du contrat et les raisons qui la motivent. Celle-ci prend effet lors de la réception de la notification par l'autre partie.

Article 1158-1
Il est loisible au débiteur de contester en justice la décision du créancier en alléguant que le manquement qui lui est imputé ne justifie pas la résolution du contrat.

Le juge peut, selon les circonstances, valider la résolution ou ordonner l'exécution du contrat, en octroyant éventuellement un délai au débiteur.

Article 1159
Les clauses résolutoires doivent expressément désigner les engagements dont l'inexécution entraînera la résolution du contrat.

La résolution est subordonnée à une mise en demeure infructueuse, s'il n'a pas été convenu qu'elle résulterait du seul fait de l'inexécution. La mise en demeure n'est efficace que si elle rappelle en termes apparents la clause résolutoire.

En toute hypothèse, la résolution ne prend effet que par la notification qui en est faite au débiteur et à la date de sa réception.

Article 1160
La résolution peut avoir lieu pour une partie seulement du contrat, lorsque son exécution est divisible.

Article 1160-1
La résolution du contrat libère les parties de leurs obligations.

Dans les contrats à exécution successive ou échelonnée, la résolution vaut résiliation ; l'engagement des parties prend fin pour l'avenir, à compter de l'assignation en résolution ou de la notification de la résolution unilatérale.

Si le contrat a été partiellement exécuté, les prestations échangées ne donnent pas lieu à restitution ni indemnité lorsque leur exécution a été conforme aux obligations respectives des parties.

Dans les contrats à exécution instantanée, elle est rétroactive ; chaque partie restitue à l'autre ce qu'elle en a reçu, suivant les règles posées à la section 6 ci-après du présent chapitre.

2. Textes proposés (version anglaise)

SECTION 5. OF THE NON-PERFORMANCE OF OBLIGATIONS AND OF THE RESOLUTION OF CONTRACTS

Article 1157
In a synallagmatic contract, each party may refuse to perform her obligation should the other party fail to perform her own obligation.

When the non-performance is a consequence of force majeure or any other justified cause, the contract may likewise be suspended if the non-performance is not irreversible.

Except in the case of non-performance by one party, the other party may counter by proving before a court of law that the suspension of the contract is not justified.

Article 1158
In all contracts, the party for whose benefit the performance of an obligation was not carried out, or was poorly carried out, may either seek performance of the obligation or cause the dissolution of the contract or ask for the payment of damages that may be added, depending on the circumstances, to the performance or the dissolution.

When electing to have the contract dissolved, the creditor may either petition the court that dissolution be granted, or, on his own, put the debtor in default to perform within a reasonable time, failing which he will have the right to dissolve the contract.

When the non-performance continues, the creditor notifies the debtor that the contract is rescinded and of the grounds for the resolution. The latter is effective upon receipt of the notification by the other party.

Article 1158-1
The debtor is permitted to challenge the creditor's decision in court and argue that the imputation that he failed to perform does not justify the resolution of the contract.

The court may, according to the circumstances, uphold the resolution or order that the contract be performed, potentially granting an additional time to the debtor.

Article 1159
Resolutory clauses must expressly identify the commitments the non execution of which will lead to the resolution of the contract.

The resolution is contingent upon an unsuccessful putting in default, if it had not been agreed that it would occur by the mere fact of the non-performance.

In any case, it is effective only upon notification made to the debtor and from the time of its receipt.

Article 1160
The resolution may take place with respect to a part of the contract only, when its performance is divisible.

Article 1160-1
The resolution of the contract releases the parties from their obligations.

In contracts to be performed in successive stages or over a period of time, the resolution amounts to resiliation ; the commitment of the parties is terminated prospectively, from the time of the filing for resolution or from the notification of the unilateral resolution.

If the contract was performed in part, the performances that were exchanged do give rise neither to restitution nor to indemnification when they were carried out in conformity with the respective obligations of the parties.

In contracts of instantaneous performance, it is retroactive; each party returns to the other what she received from the latter, according to the rules stated in section VI below of this chapter.

Third Party Questions: The Privity Problem[1]

John N. Adams[2] *(Sheffield)*

I. Introduction

This paper addresses the question of the standing of third parties to a contract. Is it possible for a third party to sue on a contract made for its benefit? Can a person be burdened by the obligations under a contract to which it was not a party? Up to the nineteenth century, English law was essentially about the enforcement of *promises* and in consequence the former problem did not arise, because the law had no concept of *parties* to a contract, the only question being whether the person seeking to enforce a contract was a promisee.[3] In the nineteenth century, however, largely borrowing from the writings of the French jurist Pothier[4] the English law of contract was remodelled, and a contract came to be perceived as a bilateral transaction. This was a logical concomitant of Pothier's view that a contract must involve a meeting of minds. As a consequence, the doctrine of consideration, which until the nineteenth century had had close affinities to the canon law doctrine of *causa*,[5] assumed its modern form, which roughly corresponds to the 'price for which a promise is bought'.[6] A view adopted by the House of Lords in the important case of *Dunlop v Selfridge*.[7]

---

[1] This paper owes much to the discussions my former colleague Professor Roger Brownsword (now of King's College, University of London), and I have had over the last thirty years or so, beginning with the classification of privity questions, which we devised one afternoon in the summer of 1977.
[2] Professor Emeritus of Law, University of Sheffield; Adjunct Professor, University of Notre Dame London Law Centre.
[3] See A.W.B. Simpson *History of the Common Law of Contract* Oxford University Press. 1975. pp. 475–85. This older doctrine survived in the United States – see *Lawrence v Fox* 20 NY 258 (1859).
[4] *Traité des Obligations*.
[5] Certainly, the doctrine of *causa* seems to have been *one* of the possible sources of the doctrine. See Simpson op. cit. p. 384 *et seq.*; Barton (1969) 85 LQR 372.
[6] Pollock on Contracts 13th ed. p. 133.
[7] [1915] AC 847.

The beginnings of the privity doctrine can be traced back to *Williams v Everett*,[8] but the leading case of the nineteenth century is *Tweddle v Atkinson*.[9] In that case, the plaintiff's father, and his prospective father-in-law, mutually agreed to pay sums of money to the plaintiff on his marriage. The plaintiff duly married, but the father-in-law died before his portion of the money had been paid. It was held that the plaintiff could not recover the money, even though the agreement had expressly provided that the plaintiff should have the right to sue on it. Wightman J said:

'It is now established that no stranger to the consideration can take advantage of a contract, although made for his benefit'[10]

To the extent that the court in *Tweddle v Atkinson* assumed that the privity doctrine was a corollary of the consideration requirement, its reasoning was open to challenge, for whilst the consideration doctrine determines which class of *promise* is enforceable, the privity doctrine determines *who* can enforce a promise.[11] Since these are distinct questions, it does not follow that a third party's failure to provide consideration should preclude it from enforcing a promise. However, in *Tweddle v Atkins* counsel conceded that the privity doctrine represented the rule in English contract law.[12] This being the case, it might have been expected that the authority of *Tweddle v Atkinson* would be quite short-lived. However, in *Dunlop v Selfridge*[13] the House of Lords in effect declared that the privity doctrine was one of the cornerstones of English contract law.

II. The privity questions

Although *Dunlop v Selfridge* seemed to treat all privity questions as being one, there are in fact four distinct questions:
1. can a person enforce a contract to which he is not a party? (We will call questions of this sort P_1)
2. can a person set up a defence based on the terms of a contract to which he is not a party in order to answer a claim brought by a person who is a party to the relevant contract? (P_2)

---

[8] (1811) 4 East 582.
[9] (1861) 1 B & S 393.
[10] Ibid at p. 398.
[11] See Collins *The Law of Contract* 4th ed. Butterworths. 2006. p. 315.
[12] Flannigan *Privity: the End of an Era (Error)* (1987) 103 LQR 564.
[13] Above.

3. can a contracting party set up a defence based on the terms of his own contract in order to answer a claim brought by a person who is not a party to the relevant contract? (P_3)
4. can a contracting part enforce his own contract against a person who is not a party to the relevant contract? (P_4)

According to the doctrine of privity as laid down in *Dunlop v Selfridge*, each of these questions must be answered in the negative. To answer P1 and P2 questions in the affirmative would be to allow a third party to take the benefit of a contract to which it was not a party; to answer P3 and P4 questions in the affirmative would be to involve burdening a person with a contract to which it was not a party.

III. Exceptions to the privity rule

1. Introduction

As explained above, the privity rule was quite a modern innovation. It had to live alongside rules already well-established at the time, such as the liability of the drawer of a bill of exchange to the ultimate holder. Moreover, it did not put an end to developments in related fields of law, such as tort. Here are some examples.

2. The law of negligence

This is a body of law which developed *after* the introduction of the privity doctrine. The key case was *Donoghue v Stevenson*.[14] In relation to P1 questions, there is a tension between the principle laid down in *Dunlop Pneumatic Tyre Co Ltd v Selfridge Ltd*[15] and the 'neighbour' principle laid down in *Donoghue v Stevenson*.[16] In the latter case a friend bought a bottle of ginger beer for the pursuer at a café. She drank some of it, then refilled her glass, at which point a decomposing snail allegedly popped out of the opaque bottle. As a result, she became ill, and sued the manufacturers.

---

[14] [1932] AC 562.
[15] [1915] AC 847: see above.
[16] Above. See Jaffey *Sub-contractors – Privity and Negligence* [1983] CLJ 37; Holyoak *Tort and Contract after Junior Books* (1983) 99 LQR 591; Jaffey *Contract in Tort's Clothing* (1985) 5LS 77; Markensinis *An Expanding Tort Law – The Price of a Rigid Contract Law* (1987) 103 LQR 354; Lorenz and Markensinis *Solicitors Liability towards Third Parties: Back into the Troubled Waters of the Contract/Tort Divide* (1993) 56 MLR 558.

Now, assuming the ginger beer to have contained a snail,[17] the manufacturers would clearly be liable to the person to whom they supplied it under a contract of sale. But the pursuer was a third party to that contract of sale (as, indeed, she was a third party to the contract of sale between the cafe proprietor and the pursuer's friend).[18] According to the *Dunlop* principle, the pursuer could acquire no benefit under that contract because she was a third party to it. Yet according to the principle laid down in *Donoghue*, the pursuer might recover against a manufacturer in respect of physical injuries suffered as a result of the manufacturer's negligence. So long as *Dunlop* is restricted to claims for purely economic loss, and *Donoghue* is restricted to claims other than for purely economic loss[19] (and, we might add, so long as a rational distinction can be drawn between the two kinds of loss),[20] the principles do not compete with one another. However, once third parties are permitted to recover in tort in respect of economic losses, as they are in the case of negligent misstatements,[21] the question of the relationship between contractual and tortious principles is raised.

---

[17] It was later found that it did not, but that finding of fact does not affect the legal principles laid down in the case.

[18] Courts have on occasion fudged this point in restaurant sales – see *Lockett v A & M Charles Ltd* [1938] 4 All ER 170.

[19] *Simaan General Contracting Co v Pilkington Glass Ltd (No 2)* [1988] QB 758.

[20] This question has been much discussed in relation to third parties in connection with the development of strict product liability in the United States. See Restatement 2d para 402A and Uniform Commercial Code 2–318. See eg *State v Tyanek Timber Inc* 680 P 2d 1148 (1984); *Miller v US Steel Corpn* 902F 2d 573 (7th Circ, 1990). Remedial building work having to be carried out by the plaintiffs, to a building occupied by them, as a result of the defendant's negligent performance under a contract to which the plaintiff was not a party is considered to be pure economic loss, see eg *Department of the Environment v Thomas Bates & Son Ltd* [1989] 1 All ER 1075; *D & F Estates Ltd v Church Com" for England* [1989] AC 177; *Greater Nottingham Co-operative Society Ltd v Cementation Piling & Foundations Ltd* [1989] QB 71. The policy considerations underlying these decisions may be summed up in a formal way by saying that no duty of care is owed to the plaintiffs (claimants): *Smith v Littlewoods Organisation Ltd* [1987] AC 241 (vandals started fire in building adjoining the plaintiff's which had been left vacant by defendants). These cases mark a move away from *Junior Books Ltd v Veitchi Ltd* [1983] 1 AC 520. On the other hand, direct physical damage to goods or other property to which the plaintiff third party had title, or of which it was possessed, generally gives rise to liability.

[21] The seminal case is *Hedley Byrne & Co Ltd v Heller and Partners* [1964] AC 465.

3. Vicarious immunity

The problems which this doctrine seeks to resolve were very much to the fore after the development of the railways in the first half of the nineteenth century. These problems can be resolved by a semi-fictitious use of the doctrine of agency, but the principle of vicarious immunity has developed as a separate way to resolve them. Briefly, the issue is this: if carrier (1), who has entered into a contract containing a limitation of damages clause with the consignor, transfers the goods to carrier (2), does that second carrier (or other bailee) get the benefit of the limitation of damages clause in the first contract?

The principle of vicarious immunity is illustrated by the case of *Elder, Dempster Ltd v Paterson Zochonis & Co Ltd*.[22] In that case the House of Lords held that the owners of a vessel were entitled to rely on the limitations contained in a bill of lading issued pursuant to a contract between the cargo owners and the charterers of the vessel, when they (the owners of the vessel) were sued by the cargo owners in respect of damage caused by bad stowage. In other words, a P3 question was answered in the affirmative.[23] However, this decision appears to be inconsistent with *Scruttons Ltd v Midland Silicones Ltd*,[24] in which the task of extracting a ratio from the case was described as 'unrewarding'.[25] An alternative explanation of the case is that what was involved was a bailment on terms.[26]

4. Special acceptances in the law of bailments

The English law of bailments is almost entirely derived from Roman law, and is quite separate from the law of contract,[27] and the doctrine of special acceptance in bailments long predates the emergence of the modern

---

[22] [1924] AC 522.
[23] See also *Mersey Shipping & Transport Co Ltd v Rea Ltd* (1925) 21 Lloyd's Rep 375; *Pyrene Co Ltd v Scindia Steam Navigation Co Ltd* [1954] 2 QB 402 It is unclear how the Contracts (Rights of Third Parties) Act 1999 applies to P$_3$ situations: see below.
[24] See below.
[25] [1962] AC 446 per Lord Reid at 479. See also *Johnson Matthey & Co Ltd v Constantine Terminals Ltd* [1976] 2 Lloyd's Rep 215; *The Forum Craftsman* [1985] 1 Lloyd's Rep 291.
[26] See the speech of Lord Sumner in *Elder, Dempster & Co Ltd v Paterson Zochonis & Co Ltd* [1924] AC 522, 564. See also *K H Enterprises (cargo owners) v Pioneer Container, The Pioneer Container* [1994] 2 AC 324, 339-340; *The Mahkutai* [1996] 3 All ER 50.
[27] See *Coggs v Bernard* (1703) 2 Ld Raym 909.

law of contract and the privity principle.[28] In *Morris v C W Martin & Sons Ltd*[29] Lord Denning MR said:

> 'Now comes the question: can the defendants [sub-bailees] rely, as against the plaintiff [the owner of a mink stole deposited with a furrier for cleaning] on the exempting conditions [in the contract between the plaintiff and the furrier] although there was no contract directly between them and her? There is much to be said on each side. On the one hand, it is hard on the plaintiff if her just claim is defeated by exempting conditions of which she knew nothing and to which she was not a party. On the other hand, it is hard on the defendants if they are held liable to a greater responsibility than they agreed to undertake ... The answer to the problem lies, I think, in this: the owner is bound by the condition if he has expressly or impliedly consented to the bailee making a sub-bailment containing those conditions, but not otherwise.'[30]

The particular privity questions posed in *Morris v Martin* were both P2 and P3: could the sub-bailees rely on the terms either of the head contract between the plaintiff and the furrier, or of the sub-contract between the furrier and themselves, to limit their liability? Lord Denning's dictum is equally applicable to both of these questions, and answers them in the affirmative.

5. Covenants running with personal property

So far as P4 questions are concerned, although *Port Line*[31] represents the orthodox approach that a person cannot be held to the terms of a contract to which he is not a party, there is contrary authority of some respectability. In *De Mattos v Gibson*,[32] Knight Bruce J said:

> Reason and justice seem to prescribe that, at least as a general rule, where a man by gift or purchase acquires property from another, with knowledge of a previous contract lawfully and for valuable consideration made by him with a third person to use and employ the property

---

[28] It derives primarily from Coke's notes to *Southcote's Case* (1601) 4 Co Rep 83b. See Adams *The Standardisation of Commercial Contracts or the Contractualisation of Standard Forms* (1978) 7 Anglo-Am LR 136.
[29] [1966] 1 QB 716.
[30] Ibid at 729.
[31] *Port Line Ltd v Ben Line Ltd* [1958] 2 QB 146.
[32] (1858) 4 De G & J 276.

for a particular purpose in a specified manner, the acquirer shall not, to the material damage of the third person, in opposition to the contract and inconsistently with it, use and employ the property in a manner not allowable to the giver or seller.[33]

Attempts to rely on the *De Mattos* principle have been made in a variety of contractual contexts, most famously (and most successfully) in *Lord Strathcona Steamship Co v Dominion Coal Co*, where the Privy Council apparently applied the principle in holding that the defendant was not free to ignore the terms of a charterparty of which he was aware when he bought the vessel. Although it is possible to reconcile the decision in this case with that in Port Line, on the basis that at the relevant time the defendant in the latter case had no knowledge of the plaintiff's rights under the charterparty, the authorities clearly evince differing approaches to P_4 questions.

This is unfortunate, because a pressing problem at the moment arises out of the growing practice of taking outright assignments of copyrights.[34] Thus, in *Barker v Stickney*[35] the plaintiff had assigned his copyright to a company in return for a royalty. The company went into liquidation, and the copyright was sold on to the defendant third party. It was held that the defendant was not bound to pay the royalties to the plaintiff. The manifest injustice of this is becoming quite widespread, because more and more publishers insist on outright assignments, and also film and sound programme production companies. Outsourcing the production of television and radio programmes by the BBC and other broadcasting organisations is now very general. Many of these production companies are small, and liquidations are frequent. The copyrights are then sold on, frequently to large US companies. A consequence of this has been that some quite well-known authors have lost their right to payment, as well as a host of minor authors. It is regrettable, therefore, that the Law Commission did not see fit to deal with what we have charactised as 'P4' problems.[36] Is there any possible solution through the case law?

In *Barker v Stickney* the earlier case of *Werderman v Société Général d'Elecricité*[37] was distinguished. In that case, the plaintiff, a patentee, had assigned his patent to A and B who had covenanted to use their best endeavours to license it. A and B then formed a company and assigned the patent to it. The plaintiff sued this company for an account of profits,

---

[33] Ibid at 282.
[34] As will be seen, the P_4 question can also arise in relation to other types of intellectual property.
[35] [1919] 1 KB 121.
[36] See below.
[37] (1881) 19 Ch D 246. See also *Dansk Rekylriffel Syndicat Aktieselskat v Snell*.

which was granted. In *Barker v Stickney* Bankes LJ cited with approval Vaughan Williams LJ's explanation in *Bagot Pneumatic Tyre Co v Clipper Pneumatic Tyre Co*[38] of cases such as *Werderman*. Vaughan Williams LJ said:

> If the judgments in *Werderman v Société Général d'Elecricité* are looked at carefully, I think it will be seen that all that is decided by that case is this, that if you had notice of a contract between the person under whom you claim property, real or personal, and a former owner of the property, whereby a charge or incumbrance was imposed upon the property of which you thus take possession and have the enjoyment, you take the property subject to the charge or incumbrance, and can only hold it subject thereto.

Bankes LJ suggested that the interest of the plaintiff was closely analogous to a vendor's lien.[39] All that existed in the present case, however, was a mere assignment showing no intention to create a charge or vendor's lien. It must be said that in the analogous case of the collateral contract, stricter proof was required in the first part of the twentieth century, than became the case later,[40] so that it may be that courts would be prepared to imply a charge. In any event, it is now clear that a vendor's lien arises by operation of law, and is not dependent on the intention of the parties.[41]

A further possibility was suggested by Diplock J in *Port Line Ltd v Ben Line Ltd*.[42] After discussing the *De Mattos v Gibson* principle as enunciated by Knight Bruce J,[43] he pointed out that it was a treated as a doctrine applicable to both real and personal property, dependent on notice alone up to the end of the nineteenth century. Indeed, the doctrine of restrictive covenants in relation to land had been understood in this way for 20 years after *Tulk v Moxhay*.[44] The doctrine of the restrictive covenant had developed along the lines of a negative easement, however.[45] As a doc-

---

[38] [1908] 2 Ch 127.
[39] Which are binding on third parties: see *Barclays Bank v Estates & Commercial Ltd* [1997] 1 WLR 415.
[40] See *Heilbut Symons & Co v Buckleton* [1913] AC 30, 47, and below.
[41] See *Barclays Bank v Estates & Commercial Ltd* [1997] 1 WLR 415.
[42] [1958] QB 146.
[43] See above.
[44] (1848) 2 Ph 774.
[45] See *Swiss Bank Corpn v Lloyds Bank Ltd* [1979] Ch 548 per Browne-Wilkinson J. Under the doctrine of retrictive covenants in its modern form, the covenantee is not seeking to stop the third party from interfering with the contract be-

trine dependent purely upon notice, it was discredited in *LCC v Allen*.[46] He suggested that a possible ratio of *Lord Strathcona Steamship Co v Dominion Coal Co*[47] was that the purchaser of the vessel had used expressions which amounted to a trust in favour of the charterers. This could provide an explanation of *Werderman v Société Général d'Elecricité*, for after all, the plaintiff was only asking for an account of profits. In other words, it is plausible that the royalties as they came in were impressed with a trust in favour of the plaintiff. Arguably, *Barker v Stickney*, in which the court looked only for evidence of a charge or incumbrance, ignored this separate possibility, and to this extent was wrongly decided. We can agree, therefore, with Hoffmann J in *Law Debenture Trust Corpn plc v Ural Caspian Oil Corpn Ltd*,[48] that the principle of *Lord Strathcona Steamship Co v Dominion Coal Co* 'does not provide a panacea for outflanking the doctrine of privity of contract' – but understood in the way we have suggested, *Werderman* might provide a modest remedy for a great injustice.

6. Agency

English law's treatment of agency, is seen as an exception to the privity rule. Whilst in English law when an agent contracts for a named principal within the scope of the agent's authority it can be argued that the agent is merely an instrument or extension of the principal, who is the real contracting party. This is certainly the way in which agency tends to be treated in many civil law systems. The difference, however, lies in the fact that in English law a principal may be bound in circumstances that go far beyond situations where there is an agent acting for a named principal. French law actually forbids making a contract in one's own name except for oneself.[49] By contrast in English law an undisclosed principal can be bound, and sue on a contract to which it was a third party, and in circumstances where the agent is acting within its ostensible or apparent authority, but not actual authority. An agent can also bind a principal by an act within its ostensible or apparent authority. It is this which justifies the treatment of agency as an exception to the privity principle.

The law of agency is a well-established exception to the rule that a person cannot confer benefits, nor impose burdens, on a third party. Under

---

tween the covenantor and the coventantee, but to perform the contract entered into between the covenantor and the covenantee.
[46] [1914] 3 KB 642 (in which Scrutton LJ listed the cases in which he considered the doctrine to have been buried).
[47] [1926] AC 108.
[48] [1993] 2 All ER 355, 362.
[49] Code Code Civil Art. 1119.

the law of agency the third party (the principal) may both be benefited and burdened. The existence of the principal does not have to be known to the party with whom the agent is contracting. It should be noted that an agent may be the agent of both contracting parties. Thus insurance brokers are both agents of the insured, and of the insurer.[50]

Once an agent is clothed with apparent or ostensible authority, no private instructions prevent its acts within the scope of that authority from binding the principal.[51]

7. Implied collateral contract

The collateral contract has proved a fruitful way of circumventing the privity rule in other situations. In *Shanklin Pier v Detel*[52] the plaintiffs had employed contractors to paint their pier, and instructed them to use a paint made by the defendants. The instruction was given in reliance on a representation made by the defendants to the plaintiffs that the paint would last seven years. It lasted for only three months. It was held that the defendants' representation gave rise to a collateral contract that the paint would last seven years.

8. Confidential information and trade secrets

A person who is employed owes a duty of good faith to his or her employer, and disclosure of the employer's confidential information or trade secrets[53] to a third party is a breach of that duty.[54] The rule extends to other situations in which a duty of confidentiality may be implied,[55] but it should be noted that an employee's duty of confidentiality is wider during the term of the contract of employment, than it is afterwards when the rule is that an employee should be free to use the skills learned during the

---

[50] See eg *Touche Ross & Co v Colin Baker* [1992] 2 Lloyd's Rep 207; *Siu Yin Kwan v Eastern Insurance* [1994] 1 All ER 213.
[51] *Watteau v Fenwick* [1893] 1 QB 346.
[52] [1951] 2 KB 854; folld in *Wells (Merstham) Ltd v Buckland Sand and Silica Co Ltd* [1965] 2 QB 170.
[53] As to what amounts to a trade secret see Coleman *The Legal Protection of Trade Secrets* Sweet & Maxwell. 1992. Ch. 2.
[54] See eg *Thomas Marshall v Guinle* [1979] FSR 208; *PSM International v Whitehouse* [1992] IRLR 279.
[55] See *Seager v Copydex Ltd* [1967] RPC 349; *Coco v A N Clark (Engineers) Ltd* [1969] RPC 41.

course of employment.[56] Third parties who acquired the information from the party owing the duty of confidentiality are bound to respect the obligation of confidentiality.[57] It is not clear if the action for breach of confidence is founded on a purely equitable right (in which case the claimant ought in principle to fail against a bona fide purchaser for value without notice), or a property right, or if the remedy is restitutionary in nature or tortious: the case law is not satisfactory on this point, as support can be found for each of these four possible bases, and each exhibits certain anomalies if it is the basis of the action.[58] For example, there is authority that the basis is purely equitable, but third parties do not appear to be subject to the bona fide purchase for value rule.[59]

Accordingly, to the extent that the existence of a contractual restraint may extend the scope of confidential information over and above the situation where an employee discloses information in breach of his or her duty of good faith, this would appear to be another exception to the rule that a contract between two parties cannot affect a third party. It must be said, however, that this is a difficult and obscure area.

9. Bankers documentary credits

It is unclear whether or not bankers' documentary credits form an exception to the privity rule. Is it a case of a third party being able to enforce a contract made for its benefit, or an exception to the rule that unilateral promises are not enforceable?[60] Such instruments, unlike negotiable instruments,[61] are not excluded from the provisions of the Contracts

---

[56] *Stevenson Jordan and Harrison v MacDonald and Evans* (1951) 68 RPC 190.
[57] *Distillers Co (Biochemicals) Ltd v Times Newspapers* [1975] QB 613; *Schering Chemicals v Falkman* [1982] QB 1. If the recipient is at the outset innocent, it seems that liability will only be imposed from when notice of the breach of confidence is received: *Stephenson Jordan v MacDonald & Evans* (1951) 68 RPC 190; *Printers & Finishers v Holloway* [1965] RPC 239; *Malone v Metropolitan Police Comr (No 2)* [1979] 2 All ER 620.
[58] See Coleman *Legal Protection of Trade Secrets* (1992) Ch. 3.
[59] See Coleman op. cit. para 3.9.
[60] There is authority for the view that a confirming bank is contractually liable to the beneficiary in the speech of Lord Diplock in *United City Merchants v Royal Bank of Canada* [1983] 1 AC 168, 183, but he cited no cases in support of his proposition.
[61] Contract (Rights of Third Parties) Act, s.6(1). To the extent that negotiable instruments are used in connection with documentary credits, as in negotiation credits, they are clearly unaffected by the Act. See also *Mahonia Ltd v West LB AG* 2004 WL 1808816.

(Rights of Third Parties) Act 1999.[62] But if we ask what promise the beneficiary of the credit might enforce under the Act, it can only be that of the advising or confirming bank. The buyer and the issuing bank merely mandate the advising bank. Section 1(1) might be read literally as making unilateral promises enforceable, but s 1(2) refers to 'parties' and it seems that what s 1 is intended to do is to permit a third party to sue on a bilateral contract provided the conditions laid down in the Act are satisfied. Accordingly, the better view would seem to be that documentary credits are not an exception to the privity rule, but rather they are an exception to the consideration requirement. However, they are often listed as an exception to the privity rule, and we include them here for completeness.

Documentary credits are issued under contracts between the issuing bank and its customer, to which the beneficiary of the credit is a third party. Once the beneficiary of the credit has been notified, it can insist on payment under the credit according to its terms, against presentation of the specified documents.[63] If the credit is unconfirmed and revocable, such presentation must take place before any revocation.[64] The only exception to the right of the beneficiary to insist on payment, is where there is clear evidence of fraud on its part.[65] Fraud on the part of a third party does not relieve the bank from its duty to pay.[66] The Law Commission in its Report 'Privity of Contract: Contracts for the Benefit of Third Parties'[67] did not specifically deal with this as an exception to the privity rule, but if they are, documentary credits operate according to international rules which are well understood around the world. Parties who have arranged payment by documentary credit must abide by their agreement, and are not permitted to short-circuit the credit by making direct claims on each other.[68]

---

[62] See below.
[63] See eg *Hamzeh Malas & Sons v British Imex Industries Ltd* [1958] 2 QB 127; *Discount Records Ltd v Barclays Bank Ltd* [1975] 1 WLR 315; *European Asian Bank AG v Punjab and Sind Bank* [1982] 2 Lloyd's Rep 356. The practice on documentary credits is laid down in the Uniform Customs and Practice for Bankers' Documentary Credits issued by the International Chamber of Commerce.
[64] See *Cape Asbestos Co v Lloyds Bank Ltd* [1921] WN 274.
[65] *Steijn v J Henry Shroder Banking Corp* 31 NYS 2d 631 (1941).
[66] *United City Merchants (Investments) Ltd v Royal Bank of Canada* [1983] 1 AC 168.
[67] Law Com No 242 (Cm 3329, July 1996) – which resulted in the Contracts (Rights of Third Parties) Act 1999, as to which see below.
[68] *Soproma SpA v Animal By-Products Corpn* [1966] 1 Lloyd's Rep 367, 385. There are exceptions to this rule, eg if the intermediary bank becomes insolvent (ibid at p. 386).

10. Performance bonds and guarantees

These work in a somewhat similar way to documentary credits, and are closely related to the standby credit.[69] They are commonly used in connection with international construction contracts. In the event of defective performance by the contractor, the client beneficiary becomes entitled to call on the bond according to its terms, for payment by way of compensation. Typically, the amount would be up to 10% of the contract price. Whilst the traditional form requires the beneficiary to establish default on the part of the contractor, in recent times it has become customary where the client has a strong enough bargaining position, for it to insist on 'on-demand' guarantees, which oblige the issuer to pay against written demand, irrespective of default. In these situations, unjustified calls have become something of a problem in recent times, but the courts have taken the view that if the contractor chooses to place itself at the mercy of the beneficiary in this way, it must take the consequences.[70] What was said above in relation to documentary credits and the Law Commission Report is also applicable in this context.

11. Bills of exchange, promissory notes and other negotiable instruments[71]

The Bills of Exchange Act 1882 (BEA) codified the long-established rules on negotiable instruments, under which holders might enforce the obligations on the bill against drawers and other signatories to the bill. A person signing as drawer, indorser or acceptor of a bill makes the engagement set out in BEA 1882, ss 54 and 55, and is liable on such engagement notwithstanding the absence of privity of contract. The C(RTP)A 1999 provides that it confers no rights on a third party in the case of a contract contained in a bill of exchange.[72]

---

[69] Ie an undertaking by a bank to make payment to a third party, or to accept bills of exchange drawn by it, provided it tenders the specified documents in time. In ordinary documentary credits, the documents to be tendered relate to the underlying sales transaction, and include a transport document such as a bill of lading. By contrast, a stand-by credit may be triggered simply by a statement that the other party to the underlying contract is in default.
[70] See *Edward Owen Engineering Ltd v Barclays Bank International Ltd* [1978] QB 159.
[71] Contract (Rights of Third Parties) Act 1999, s.6(1) excludes these contracts from its application.
[72] C(RTP)A 1999, s 6(1); LC No 242 para 12.17.

IV. Contracts (Rights of Third Parties) Act 1999 (C(CRTP)A 1999[73]

1. Introduction

Five years after the publication of its provisional recommendations in favour of reforming the privity rule in English contract law,[74] the Law Commission confirmed its view and, indeed, the view of a considerable body of judicial[75] and academic[76] opinion, as well as that of the vast majority of the Commission's consultees[77] – that the privity doctrine was ripe for reform. In its central recommendation, the Commission proposed that third parties (subject to being expressly identified) should have the right to enforce contractual provisions where either (i) the contracting parties intend to confer such a *right* upon the third party (the so-called 'first limb' of the test of enforceability) or (ii) the contracting parties intend to confer a benefit on the third party (the so-called 'second limb' of the test of enforceability) – provided that the contracting parties do not also intend that the third party beneficiary should *not* have the right to enforce the contract. The first limb of the test of enforceability would apply to a case such as *Tweddle v Atkinson*[78] (where the contracting parties expressly provided for the third party to have the right to enforce the

---

[73] The C(RTP)A 1999 largely follows the draft Bill to be found at the end of the Law Commission's Report *Privity of Contract: Contracts for the Benefit of Third Parties* Law Com No.242 (Cm 3329, July 1996) (hereafter, 'the Report'), on which see Adams, Beyleveld and Brownsword *Privity of Contract – the Benefits and the Burdens of Law Reform* (1997) 60 MLR 238.

[74] Privity of Contract: Contracts for the Benefit of Third Parties (Law Com Consultation Paper No 121) (1991).

[75] The Report opens with Steyn LJ's critical observations on the injustice of the privity principle in *Darlington Borough Council v Wiltshier Northern Ltd* [1995] 1 WLR 68, 76 – particularly to the effect that 'there is no doctrinal, logical, or policy reason why the law should deny effectiveness to a contract for the benefit of a third party where that is the expressed intention of the parties'. For further examples of judicial calls for reform, see paras 2.64–2.69 of the Law Commission's Report.

[76] In para 2.63 (at note 163) of the Report, the Commission cites some 16 examples, starting with Corbin *Contracts for the Benefit of Third Persons* (1930) 46 LQR 12. The majority of the academic calls for reform to English law, however, lie in the last ten years (including Adams and Brownsword *Privity and the Concept of a Network Contract* (1990) 10 Legal Studies 12 and Beyleveld and Brownsword *Privity, Transitivity and Rationality* (1991) 54 MLR 48).

[77] See para 1.6 of the Report.

[78] (1861) 1 B & S 393.

contract); and the second limb would apply to a case such as that of *Beswick v Beswick*.[79] In the latter case, Peter Beswick carried on business as a coal merchant. He contracted to sell the business to his nephew John in consideration, *inter alia*, that he should pay Mrs Beswick £5 weekly for the rest of her life following his death. Following Peter's death, John paid Mrs Beswick for one week and refused to pay anymore. The Court of Appeal held that, as her husband's administratrix she was entitled to enforce the contract.[80]

The Report, thus, signalled a decisive break from the orthodoxy of the privity doctrine which, in the earlier part of the century, was identified by Viscount Haldane LC as one of the fundamental principles of English contract law.[81]

The task of reforming such an inconvenient doctrine as the privity rule, however, was far from straightforward. It is one thing to condemn the doctrine as unfair and inconvenient, but how was reform best to be effected? Essentially, there were two models of the way to proceed.[82] According to the first model, in a climate that is no longer rigidly formalistic,[83] reliance may be placed on the judiciary to relax orthodox privity restrictions where they give rise to concern (so that a simple enabling provision – for example, of the kind proposed by the Ontario Law Reform Commission[84] – explicitly authorising the courts to exercise such a discretion is all that is required). The Commission, however, preferred a second model, concluding (as in its Consultation Paper) that a detailed legislative scheme was required. The practical advantage of laying down a clear legislative scheme for third party rights was obvious; moreover, the Commission feared that it could be accused of ducking out of its respon-

---

[79] [1968] AC 58.
[80] Two of the judges, Denning and Danckwerts L.JJ held that she was also entitled to enforce the contract in her own right by virtue of ss 56(1) and 205(1)(xx) Law of Property Act 1925.
[81] *Dunlop Pneumatic Tyre Co v Selfridge and Co Ltd* [1915] AC 847, 853. See para 6.7.
[82] A third model invites incremental relaxation of the rule in specific contexts – for example, as was done with bills of lading (see the Bills of Lading Act 1855 now replaced by the Carriage of Goods by Sea Act 1992: and see the Report, paras 2.59 and 12.7–12.11). However, if the reform of privity is to be of a general nature, the incremental model is not appropriate.
[83] See, eg Steyn *Does Legal Formalism Hold Sway in England?* (The 1996 Presidential Lecture to the Bentham Club, University College, London); Stevens *Judges, Politics, Politicians and the Confusing Role of the Judiciary* (Hardwicke Building Lecture, London, 21 May, 1996); and, generally, see Adams and Brownsword *Understanding Law* (4th ed. Sweet and Maxwell, 2006) Chs 4 and 5.
[84] For discussion, see the Report, paras 5.5–5.6.

sibilities if it left major questions of principle to be settled by the courts.[85] However, even in an ideal world, free of the pressure to deliver a politically 'sellable' package, the challenge, as Professor Andrew Burrows put it, is the familiar one of striking the right balance between the interests of certainty (calculability) and flexibility (fairness in the individual case).[86] As might already be apparent, the centrepiece of the proposed scheme, the test of enforceability, was an heroic attempt to compromise the needs of contractors to be able to predict and to plan with the need to reserve some degree of flexibility (conspicuously so in the proviso to the second limb of the test set out above). This test is used in the C(RTP)A 1999.

Even if we agree that a detailed legislative scheme was the right way ahead, there remained controversial questions about how far, and how fast, we should proceed. For example, should legislation make special provision for consumer contractors along the lines currently being adopted in the European Union?[87] Or, should the legislation tackle the vexed question of whether sub-contract exclusions or restrictions should bind a third-party head-contractor?[88] In both instances, the Commission preferred to keep these questions at arm's length. Generally, the Commission favoured a cautious approach, putting to one side 'more radical possibilities ... for fear that the central reform would otherwise be endangered' – advancing, instead, a package of what it perceived to be 'relatively conservative and moderate measure[s]'[89] calculated to modify the privity doctrine in a way that would enjoy widespread support.[90] Accordingly, whilst some might think that the Commission's proposals were a bit unexciting, the progressive view is that they should be seen as initiating, in the shape of the C(RTP)A 1999, rather than as placing final limits upon, a programme of modification to the privity doctrine.

---

[85] See the Report, para 5.6.
[86] Burrows *Reforming Privity of Contract: Law Commission Report No 242* SPTL Annual Conference, Cambridge, 11 September, 1996, esp pp 1 and 9.
[87] See Directive 1999/44/EC on certain aspects of the Sale of Consumer Goods and Associated Guarantees implemented in the UK by SI 2002/3045. See also European Commission, Green Paper on Guarantees for Consumer Goods and After-Sales Services, COM (93) 509 final, 1993; on which, see Weatherill *Consumer Guarantees* (1994) 110 LQR 545.And, for discussion of whether there should be a special test of enforceability for consumers, see the Report, paras 7.54–7.56.
[88] See eg *Morris v CW Martin and Sons Ltd* [1966] 1 QB 716; *K H Enterprise v Pioneer Container, The Pioneer Container* [1994] 2 All ER 250 (noted by Phang (1995) 58 MLR 422); see discussion in text below.
[89] The Report, para 5.10.
[90] See, eg the Report, para 1.9: 'Our general approach has been to devise moderate reform proposals which can be expected to gain wide support.'

2. Scope of the reform

It is trite law that the privity doctrine has two dimensions, one preventing someone not party to a particular contract from taking its benefit, the other protecting someone not party to a particular contract from burdens purportedly imposed upon them by the agreement of the contractors. Generally, the Commission seemed to think that the latter aspect, while not altogether satisfactory, was less urgently in need of reform.[91] In line with this view, the Commission declared that its proposed reforms did not seek to amend the burden side of the privity doctrine;[92] and, in various sections of the Report, the Commission stopped short of proposing reform precisely because it saw itself in danger of crossing the line between the benefit and the burden side of the doctrine. Hence, for example, the Commission 'reluctantly' decided that arbitration and jurisdiction clauses lay beyond the scope of the reform because such clauses 'do not lend themselves to a splitting of the benefit and the burden' (the third party being 'burdened' by such clauses).[93]

How, though, should the distinction between benefits and burdens be made? As the Commission noted in its Consultation Paper, privity questions (which, of course, might arise in single-contract or multiple-contract – chains and network – settings) typically arise in one or more of the four forms set out at the beginning of this chapter.[94] P1 is the paradigm form of the benefit question; and, since *Scruttons Ltd v Midland Silicones Ltd*,[95] P2 can be thought of as an extension of this same question. P4 is the paradigm form of the burden question (certainly in a case such as *Lord Strathcona Steamship Co v Dominion Coal Co*).[96] But, where does this leave P3? In the Commission's Consultation Paper, it was not en-

---

[91] A view with which we would strongly disagree.
[92] See the Report, para 2.1. For contracts for the international carriage of goods by road and rail, or cargo by air, where the governing international conventions involve both third party benefits and burdens, see the Report, paras 12.12–12.15 and clauses 6(2)(b) and 6(3)(b) of the draft Bill.
[93] The Report, para 14.18 (and paras 14.14–14.19), drawing on Lord Goff's reasoning in *The Mahkutai* [1996] AC 650, PC. Similarly, see paras 8.12 (the Commission's 'recognition that a company's right under a pre-incorporation contract may be conditional should not be misconstrued as permitting obligations under a pre-incorporation contract to be imposed on the company') and 10.10 (defences, set-offs, and counterclaims).
[94] This typology was adopted by the Commission in its Consultation Paper (note 1 above). See Adams and Brownsword *Privity and the Concept of a Network Contract* (1990) 10 LS 12.
[95] [1962] AC 446.
[96] [1926] AC 108.

tirely clear how (or whether) the dual intention test (the Commission's earlier test of enforceability) should be applied to P3 questions; and, in the Report, the Commission again is less than explicit in dealing with this question.

At first impression, the logic of the Commission's approach appeared to be that P3 questions should fall outside the proposals because they seem to raise burden issues.[97] However, in a later, extended discussion of the boundary between benefits and burdens, the Commission distinguishes between 'imposing a burden on the third party' and 'conferring a conditional benefit'.[98] Here, the thrust of the discussion is that a contracting party can set up a (burdensome) condition as a defence to a third party claim, but not as a cause of action in its own right. For example, if a contract confers a right of way on a third party on condition that the third party keeps it in repair, failure by the third party to meet the repairing condition would be a defence for a defendant contractor but it would not be a ground for action against the third party.[99] Significantly, the Commission continued:[100]

A very important example of a condition being attached to the benefit enforceable by the third party (C) is where in the contract between A and B benefiting C, there is a clause excluding or limiting A's liability to C. C's right to enforce A's promise under our proposed Act must be subject to the exclusion or limitation clause.

These remarks receive no further elaboration. In principle, the example could fit with a single-contract P1 situation (and such situations certainly tend to bulk large in the Commission's thinking); or, it could fit with a multiple-contract P3 situation. Again, in principle, multiple-contract P3 situations might arise where A brings a claim against C in tort, or (if privity is relaxed) where A brings a claim against C for breach of the contract between B and C. Given that the Commission intends to avoid disturbing third party burden questions, it must be assumed that the proposals do not cover P3 situations where A brings a claim against C in tort. However, this leaves P3 situations where A's claim is based in contract and, here, the Commission's remarks imply that, say, a sub-contractor could set up a sub-contract exclusion or limitation as a condition of a third party head-contractor taking the benefit by suing on the sub-contract, and that a third party consumer might only be able to enforce a manufacturer's supply contract subject to the manufacturer's ex-

---

[97] See eg para 2.1 of the Report and footnote 6 thereto. And, in correspondence, Professor Burrows has intimated that the proposals are concerned purely with P_1 and P_2 questions, not with P_3 or P_4.
[98] The Report, para 10.25
[99] The Report, paras 10.26–27.
[100] The Report, para 10.30.

clusions or limitations. Perhaps, then, the proposals should be understood as converting P3 situations of this kind to P1 situations, with the relevant exclusions or limitations being treated as conditions to which the benefit is subject.[101] Whether such exclusions or limitations would then be subject to regulation under the Unfair Contract Terms Act 1977 is an important question which is dealt with below.

3. Extension of reform

C(RTP)A 1999, s 7(1) provides that the new test of enforceability 'does not affect any right or remedy of a third party which exists or is available apart from this Act'. This preserves the many existing statutory and common law exceptions to the privity doctrine, including those discussed above; and, crucially, it opens the way to judicial development of third party rights.

We should emphasise that we do not wish our proposed legislation ... to hamper the judicial development of third party rights. Should the House of Lords decide that in a particular sphere our reform does not go far enough and that, for example, a measure of imposed consumer protection is required or that employees (even though not mentioned in the contract) should be able to rely on exclusion clauses that protect their employers under a doctrine of vicarious immunity, we would not wish our proposed legislation to be construed as hampering that development.[102]

4. Key provisions

Implementation of the Law Commission's key proposal[103] is effected by C(RTP)A 1999, s 1 –

(1) Subject to the provisions of this Act, a person who is not a party to a contract (a 'third party') may in his own right enforce a term of the contract if

(a) the contract expressly provides that he may, or

(b) subject to subsection (2), the term *purports [emphasis supplied]* to confer a benefit on him.

(2) Subsection (1)(b) does not apply if on a proper construction of the contract it appears that the parties did not intend the term to be enforceable by the third party.

---

[101] C (RTP) A 1999 s.1(6).
[102] The Report para 5.10.
[103] In para 7(6) of their Report.

(3) The third party must be expressly identified in the contract by name, as a member of a class or as answering a particular description but need not be in existence when the contract is entered into.

(4) This section does not confer a right on a third party to enforce a term of a contract otherwise than subject to and in accordance with any other relevant terms of the contract.

Where the test of enforceability is satisfied, the third party has the full range of remedies available to a claimant contracting party, with the normal rules relating to remoteness and mitigation, and the like, applying by analogy.[104] Finally, s 1(6) makes it clear that references to a third party enforcing a contract include the third party 'availing himself' of exclusions or limitations of liability.

At first glance, the import of these provisions looks pretty straightforward. As noted at the outset, in a case such as *Tweddle v Atkinson*,[105] where the contractors expressly provide for a named third party to have the right to enforce the contract, the first limb of the test (C(RTP)A 1999, s 1(1)(a)) applies – and this is so even if, unlike in *Tweddle v Atkinson*, the contract does not purport to confer a benefit on the third party.[106] If the contractors do not expressly provide for the third party having the right to enforce the contract, but clearly intend to confer a benefit on the third party (as, say, in *Beswick v Beswick*),[107] then under the second limb of the test (s. 1(1)(b)) the third party will have the right to enforce the contract – at any rate, the third party will have this right subject to the proviso in s 1(2). Similarly, in more complex contractual situations of the kind encountered in such leading cases as *Scruttons Ltd v Midland Silicones Ltd*,[108] and *The Eurymedon*,[109] the defendant stevedore third parties will be able to rely on exclusions or limitations in the carriage contract if the right to enforce[110] is expressly granted (under the first limb) or if the relevant provisions of the carriage contract are designed to confer a benefit on the stevedores and, on its proper construction, the

---

[104] See C(RTP)A 1999, s 1(5).
[105] (1861) 1 B & S 393.
[106] For discussion, see the Report, paras 7.12–7.16.
[107] [1968] AC 58.
[108] [1962] AC 446.
[109] *New Zealand Shipping Co Ltd v A M Satterthwaite and Co Ltd* [1975] AC 154. See para 6.20.
[110] The idea of 'enforcing' an exemption or limitation clause might seem a strained use of the language. However, as the explanatory notes to the Law Commission's draft Bill state, the purpose of s 1(5) (C(RTP)A 1999, s 1(6)) is to make 'it clear that the Act is to apply so as to entitle a third party to take advantage of an exclusion or limitation clause, as well as to enforce 'positive' rights'.

carriage contract does not negative the third party having a right to enforce the terms (under the second limb and the s 1(2) proviso).

It might also be thought that s.1 gives, via the second limb of the test, a right in a *White v Jones* type of situation,[111] to give to a disappointed third party legatee a right to sue a solicitor for breach of contract who has negligently drafted a will. This, however, was not the Commission's intention. In an extended discussion of this matter, the Commission explained that it regarded it as something of a distortion to characterise a contract between a testator and a solicitor as one intended to confer a benefit on a third party – and, of course, given the House of Lords' opening up of a tortious line of relief in *White v Jones*, the Commission saw no pressing practical urgency to encourage such distortion.[112] Thus:

It is our view, therefore, that the negligent will-drafting situation ought to lie ... just outside our proposed reform. It is an example of the rare case where the third party, albeit expressly designated 'as a beneficiary' in the contract, has no presumed right of enforcement. Indeed it is arguable that, by merely adjusting the wording of the second limb to include promises that are 'of benefit to' expressly designated third parties, rather than those that 'confer benefits on' third parties, we would have brought the negligent will-drafting situation within our reform. But we believe that these words draw a crucial distinction between the situation where it is natural to presume that the contracting parties intended to confer legal rights on the third party and the situation where that presumption is forced and artificial.[113]

Now, this is instructive. To block the third party's right in the negligent will-drafting situation, the Commission might have been expected to have relied on the proviso written into s 1(2) – on the basis that, normally, the presumption is that a testator and his solicitor do not intend the contract for professional legal services to be enforceable at the suit of a beneficiary (a presumption that the contracting parties might seek to reinforce by explicit declaration). Instead, however, the Commission preferred to deal with this by indicating that the phrase 'purports to confer a benefit' in s.1(1)(b) has been carefully chosen specifically to exclude *White v Jones* type cases. In this way, the Commission not only avoided any doubt; it avoided provoking the reservation that, where contracts are made for the benefit of third parties, the principle of respecting contractual intention should not operate as an unqualified licence to exclude the third party's right to enforce.

As the somewhat oblique exclusion of *White v Jones* claimants reveals, the application of the test of enforceability is not entirely straightforward.

---

[111] [1995] 2 AC 207, and see paras 6.9ff.
[112] See the Report, paras 7.19–7.27.
[113] The Report, para 7.25.

For one thing, as suggested above,[114] there are bound to be problems with the application of a distinction between contracts that purport to confer a benefit on a third party and those contracts that simply are of actual or potential benefit to a third party. To some extent, the problem is lessened by the requirement that the third party must be expressly identified; and the Commission classified contracts for professional services (at least, in the context of negligent will-drafting) as merely of potential benefit to a third party. Nevertheless, difficult cases surely will arise for decision;[115] and it will be interesting to see not simply how such difficulties are resolved in particular cases, but also how far the courts are able to maintain a clear line between the question of whether the contract purports to confer a benefit on a third party and the question of whether the contractors intended to create legally enforceable rights in favour of a third party – the point being that draftsmen might attempt to signal that a contract is not intended to confer a benefit on a third party by providing that it is not intended that third parties should have a right to enforce the contract.

This fairly obvious difficulty apart, there are, it may be suggested, three major aspects of the test of enforceability that need clarification. First, in relation to C(RTP)A 1999, s 1(2), how significant is it that the contracting parties did not draft the contract in a way that gave the third party beneficiary a direct right to enforce under the first limb of the test? Secondly, what precisely is the default position under s.1(2) in relation to the rebuttal of the presumption of enforceability (and, concomitantly, which features of the contractual matrix might be material for the purposes of rebutting the presumption)? And, thirdly, where reliance is placed on standard head contract exclusions and limitations of liability for the benefit of sub-contractors, are we to treat this as an argument under the first or the second limb of the test of enforceability?

5. The contractors' right to vary or cancel their contract (and the crystallisation test)

The question of whether contractors, having conferred a right to enforce upon a third party, should then be able to vary or cancel their agreement (to the detriment of the third party) was one to which the consultation

---

[114] Para 6.56.

[115] See the Report, para 7.41 for the distinction between (in text) a contract of sale in which goods are to be delivered to a third party (arguably a contract to confer a benefit on a third party) and (in footnote 31 thereto) such a contract without delivery to a third party (arguably merely a contract of potential benefit to a third party).

exercise produced no agreed answer. At one extreme, the Commission rejected the view that contracting parties should be allowed to vary or cancel at any time:[116]

At the core of this issue is a conflict between preserving the freedom of the contracting parties to implement their intentions as they see fit at any particular time, and allowing the creation of effective third party rights so that a third party can arrange its affairs with some certainty. We consider that the former policy is outweighed by the latter.

At the other extreme, the Commission rejected as too restrictive the view that the contracting parties should be denied any right to vary or cancel – after all, the third party might not even be aware of the original contract.[117] In the event, the compromise between the contractors' freedom to change their minds and the third party's interests is struck in C(RTP)A 1999, s 2. According to s 2(1), where a contract is enforceable by a third party, the contractors may not without the third party's consent vary or cancel in the following three situations:

(a) [if] the third party has communicated his assent ['assent' being defined in s 2(2) as covering both words and conduct] to the contract to the promisor];
(b) [if] the promisor is aware that the third party has relied on the contract; or
(c) [if] the promisor can reasonably be expected to have foreseen that the third party would rely on the contract and the third party has in fact relied on it.

The strength of initial contractual intent, however, is preserved by s 2(3), which reserves to the contractors the right expressly to provide:
(a) the contract may be capable of being cancelled or varied without the consent of the third party; or
(b) the consent of the third party is required in circumstances specified in the contract instead of those set out in subsection (1)(a)–(c).

Seemingly, the Commission's intention was that the exercise of an express right to vary or cancel without the consent of the third party (under s 2(3)(a)) should be effective even though the third party was unaware of the reservation (or, quaere, the exercise of the right).[118] On the other hand, in the absence of express reservation, if the contracting parties cannot reasonably ascertain whether or not the third party has in fact relied on the contract, s 2(5) authorises the court to dispense with the third party's consent – and similar authorisation is given by s 2(4), where the

---

[116] The Report, para 9.8.
[117] The Report, para 9.10.
[118] The Report para 9.39.

third party's consent is required but where it cannot be obtained either because his whereabouts cannot reasonably be ascertained or he is mentally incapable of giving consent. Where a court dispenses with consent, s 2(6) provides that 'it may impose such conditions as it thinks fit, including a condition requiring compensation to the third party'. This jurisdiction is exercisable both by the High Court and the County Court.[119]

Put simply, the 'crystallisation test' proposed by the Commission was third party acceptance or reliance,[120] but this was qualified by express reservation. Although some will favour different features of this compromise, it is unclear quite how it fits with the Commission's aspiration to reconcile the third party's reasonable expectations with the contractors' intentions. The Report goes out of its way to emphasise that the third party's reliance need not be detrimental.[121] For example, the third party may have 'relied' by making investments in anticipation of contractual performance in its favour, which investments prove so profitable that the third party is better off even if the contractual performance does not materialise. As the Commission rightly stated, if the requirement is detrimental reliance, then this 'tends to shift the focus away from protecting the claimant's expectation interest to protecting the claimant's reliance interest'.[122] However, if the intention is to protect the third party claimant's expectation interest, it is unclear why actual reliance of any description should be required.[123] Indeed, in so far as the Commission's proposed crystallisation test turns on acceptance (the third party communicating assent), there need be no reliance, so why insist upon actual reliance (albeit not detrimental reliance) where there has not been acceptance?

The protection of legitimate expectation is surely the cornerstone upon which the law of contract, including the doctrine of privity, should be based.[124] If A and B are in no sense indebted to C, there is no reason why A and B should contract for the benefit of C. To this extent, it is in line

---

[119] C (RTP) A 1999 s.2(7).

[120] Drawing on the analogy of promissory estoppel (where the party seeking the protection of the estoppel has the burden of proving reliance), the Commission argues that the burden of proving reliance should lie with the third party (see The Report, para 9.34). However, the Commission also remarks that it would be unfair to expect the contracting parties to prove that the third party has not relied (The Report, para 9.34) – although the difficulty of proving a negative does not seem to have troubled the Commission so much in formulating its proposals in relation to the test of enforceability.

[121] See eg the Report, paras 9.14 and 9.19.

[122] The Report, para 9.19.

[123] Although, no doubt, actual reliance could be pleaded as evidence of expectation.

[124] See Adams, Beyleveld and Brownsword *Privity of Contract – the Benefits and Burdens of Law Reform* [1997] 60 MLR 238.

Third Party Questions: The Privity Problem 237

with the protection of legitimate expectation to treat the intentions of A and B as decisive. However, once A and B have freely chosen to contract for the benefit of C, the position is materially altered. As we have said already, if the purpose of a contract is to confer a benefit on a third party, this cannot be nullified by simple denial (non-performance) or by contrary (contradictory) declarations of intent. Equally, whether A and B are now free to change their minds and cancel or vary the contract depends on the expectations that C legitimately has in the altered situation. Where A and B have not expressly reserved the right to vary or cancel the contract, and where C is aware of the contract (with the authorisation of A and B), then it is plausible to reason that C has a right to hold A and B to the contract (ie to bar cancellation or variation of the contract).

Putting together these observation, it may be suggested that a crystallisation test based on awareness is the most direct way of protecting the legitimate expectations of the third party; that, if (taking the Commission's line) mere awareness is to be rejected as the test[125] then mere acceptance or communicated acceptance (as per the Commission) is perhaps the next best test; and that, once the crystallisation test turns on actual reliance (albeit not necessarily detrimental reliance), then the link with the protection of the third party's legitimate expectation, if not broken, is certainly attenuated.[126]

---

[125] See the Report, para 9.12, for the Commission's rejection of a 'mere awareness' test. The Commission first cited the case of a third party who 'while aware of the terms of the contract, has no wish to take advantage of them or who does not believe that the promise will be performed or that he or she has an entitlement to performance'. But this is a case of waiver or non-expectation. The acid test is a third party with a legitimate expectation. The Commission then suggested that mere awareness will not do because there might be a dispute where the third party encourages or acquiesces in a variation or cancellation of the contract and then decides that it wants performance after all. Again, though, in a legal regime organised around the idea of protecting the legitimate expectations of all participants in a situation (including the contractors), this is less than convincing.

[126] In defence of the Commission's proposals, it may be argued that the combination of tests based on acceptance and reliance satisfies evidential concerns about the reality of the third party's expectation, and ensures that third parties who actually rely (on the basis of their expectation of benefit) are not prejudiced by not knowing that a communicated acceptance will protect their expectation. Cf the Report, para 9.24, where the Commission argued along these lines in rejecting a single test based on acceptance (but, notice the way in which the possibility of detrimental reliance was used to give persuasive force to this argument).

6. The availability of defences (including defences which might be open to challenge under the Unfair Contract Terms Act 1977)

Giving effect to one of the Commission's most contentious recommendations, C(RTP)A 1999, s 7(2) provides that Unfair Contract Terms Act 1977, s 2(2) (restriction on exclusion etc. of liability for negligence) is not to apply where the negligence consists of the breach of an obligation arising from a term of a contract and the person seeking to enforce it is a third party acting in reliance on s.1. The disapplication of UCTA 1977, s.2(2) must be set alongside three other doctrinal elements: first, that (exceptionally) UCTA 1977, s.2(1) will be available to a claimant making a third party contractual claim;[127] secondly, that the Commission's general approach was to leave UCTA 1977 unamended and, as presently understood, unavailable to third party contractual claimants (s2(1) apart); and, thirdly, that UCTA 1977, s.2(2) will remain available to claimants who plead their action in the tort of negligence.

7. Defences

As elsewhere in its Report, the Commission's approach to defences[128] centred on establishing a default position that the contractors should be free to modify by express provision. The default position is provided for by C(RTP)A 1999, s.3(2), according to which the defendant promisor (contractor) is to have available by way of defence or set-off (against a third party who satisfies the test of enforceability) any matter that:
(a) arises from or in connection with the contract and is relevant to the term,[129] and
(b) would have been available to him by way of defence or set-off if the proceedings had been brought by the promisee.

---

[127] See the Report, para 13.12. *Sed quaere*: why would such a claim be pleaded in contract rather than in negligence?.

[128] By 'defences', the Commission intends to cover 'matters which render the contract void (for example, fundamental mistake) or voidable (for example, the promisee's misrepresentation, duress or undue influence) or that have led to the contract being discharged (for example, frustration or serious breach by the promisee)' (see the Report, para 10.2). Once an agent is clothed with apparent or ostensible authority, no private instructions prevent its acts within the scope of that authority from binding the principal.

[129] See para 10.12 of the Report and C(RTP)A 1999, s 7(2)(b).

This position takes a middle path between two positions – either allowing only such defences as affect the existence or validity of the contract or the particular contractual provision purporting to benefit the third party (which the Commission rejected as too narrow), or allowing all defences, set-offs, and counterclaims that would have been available against the contractual promisee (which the Commission rejected as too wide).[130] However, s.3(3) of the Act reserves to the contractors the right to narrow or widen the defences or set-offs otherwise available under s.3(2). Similarly, s.3(4) specifies the default position with regard to defences, set-offs, and counterclaims that are specific to the third party (rather than arising from the contract) – the default position being that such defences are available – but s.3(5) reserves to the contractors the power expressly to provide for a less inclusive range of defences, set-offs, and counterclaims.

8. Respect for contractual intention

For two principal reasons, it can be argued that the exclusion of UCTA 1977 betrays a misplaced respect for the intentions of the contracting parties. First, the principle of respect for contractual intention implies respect only for the joint intentions of the contractors. By disapplying (not extending) UCTA 1977, the Commission exposes third parties to the risk of being denied a remedy by a contractor who unilaterally relies on otherwise bad defences – and all for the sake of respecting supposedly joint contractual intention. Secondly, even if a particular contractual exclusion does represent the joint intentions of the parties, the Commission's proposal exposes third parties to the risk of a contractor being allowed to defend against a third party claim in a way that violates the integrity of the constitutive purpose of the contract (thereby violating the principle of respect for contractual intention).

9. Exceptions

Some of these have been mentioned in the text above. For convenience, I am going to set out the relevant provisions of the Act in full here.

6. (1) Section 1 confers no rights on a third party in the case of a contract contained in a bill of exchange, promissory note or other negotiable instrument.

---

[130] See the Report, paras 10.8–10.12.

(2) Section 1 confers no rights on a third party in the case of any contract binding on a company and its members under section 14 of the Companies Act 1985.
(3) Section 1 confers no right on a third party to enforce –
  (a) any term of a contract of employment against an employee,
  (b) any term of a worker's contract against a worker (including a home worker), or
  (c) any term of a relevant contract against an agency worker.
(4) In subsection (3) –
  (a) 'contract of employment', 'employee', 'worker's contract', and 'worker' have the meaning given by section 54 of the National Minimum Wage Act 1998,
  (b) 'home worker' has the meaning given by section 35(2) of that Act,
  (c) 'agency worker' has the same meaning as in section 34(1) of that Act, and
  (d) 'relevant contract' means a contract entered into, in a case where section 34 of that Act applies, by the agency worker as respects work falling within subsection (1)(a) of that section.
(5) Section 1 confers no rights on a third party in the case of –
  (a) a contract for the carriage of goods by sea, or a contract for the carriage of goods by rail or road, or for the carriage of cargo by air, which is subject to the rules of the appropriate international transport convention, except that a third party may in reliance on that section avail himself of an exclusion or limitation of liability in such a contract.
(6) In subsection (5) 'contract for the carriage of goods by sea' means a contract of carriage –
  (d) contained in or evidenced by a bill of lading, sea waybill or a corresponding electronic transaction, or
  (e) under or for the purposes of which there is given an undertaking which is contained in a ship's delivery order or a corresponding electronic transaction.
(7) For the purposes of subsection (6) –
  (a) 'bill of lading', 'sea waybill' and 'ship's delivery order' have the same meaning as in the Carriage of Goods by Sea Act 1992, and
  (b) a corresponding electronic transaction is a transaction within section 1(5) of that Act which corresponds to the issue, indorsement, delivery or transfer of a bill of lading, sea waybill or ship's delivery order.
(8) In subsection (5) 'the appropriate international transport convention' means –
  (a) in relation to a contract for the carriage of goods by rail, the Convention which has the force of law in the United Kingdom under section 1 of the International Transport Conventions Act 1983,

(b) in relation to a contract for the carriage of goods by road, the Convention which has the force of law in the United Kingdom under section 1 of the Carriage of Goods by Road Act 1965, and
(c) in relation to a contract for the carriage of cargo by air –
  (i) the Convention which has the force of law in the United Kingdom under section 1 of the Carriage by Air Act 1961, or
  (ii) the Convention which has the force of law under section 1 of the Carriage by Air (Supplementary Provisions) Act 1962, or
  (iii) either of the amended Conventions set out in Part B of Schedule 2 to the Carriage by Air Acts (Application of Provisions) Order 1967.

10. Conclusion

In some respects, the Commission's work on privity could be regarded as carrying forward the project initiated by the Law Revision Committee's pre-war Second World War recommendation that the doctrine of privity should be relaxed to enable third parties to enforce contracts expressly purporting to confer a benefit upon them.[131] Yet, the Law Revision Committee's proposals failed to materialise in legislation – and, in this sense, the Commission was in a way having a second bite at the cherry.[132] To avoid any doubt, therefore, I should emphasise that, whatever criticisms I might have of the Commission's proposals, the instinct that the privity rule is in need of reform was surely correct and it is important that the C(RTP)A 1999 survived the parliamentary process to put a legislative seal of approval on this overdue reform.

What, then, should be the overall assessment of the Commission's proposals on which the C(RTP)A 1999 is based? Basically, the Commission was guided (quite rightly in our view) by two principles: one principle is that we should respect the intentions of contracting parties; the other principle was that we should protect the (legitimate) expectations of parties who are potential beneficiaries of transactions. However, it is certainly strongly arguable that the former principle needs to be understood in the light of the purpose of any particular transaction – a matter of con-

---

[131] See Law Revision Committee, Sixth Interim Report, Statute of Frauds and the Doctrine of Consideration (1937) Cmd 5449. The Commission also broadly follows the Law Revision Committee in allowing a contractor to raise defences that would have been available against a fellow contractor and in allowing the contractors some right to vary or cancel their agreement. For discussion, see the Report, paras 4.2–4.4.

[132] See Beatson *Reforming the Law of Contracts for the Benefit of Third Parties: A Second Bite at the Cherry* (1992) 45 CLP 1.

siderable importance where we are considering the possible rebuttal of, or restriction upon, a third party's presumptive right to enforce – and, in the final analysis, it has to be squared with the principle of protection of legitimate expectation (this principle applying both to third parties and to the contractors themselves). It is true that, in many cases, the outcome is not affected by the priority set between these two principles, because they each point to the same result. Nevertheless, as argued previously, it sometimes does matter whether legitimate expectation or contractual intention is taken as the criterion – and, certainly, in contractual networks, where main contracts and sub-contracts jointly serve a unifying purpose, it is as much a matter of logic as expectation to treat the transacting parties as contractually joined.[133] The failure to give expectation its due weight was apparent, too, in the Commission's treatment of the contracting parties' right to vary or cancel (where the link between the proposed crystallisation test and protection of the third party's legitimate expectation is at least attenuated); and, in displacing (not extending) the applicability of the Unfair Contract Terms Act 1977, the Commission not only fails to give legitimate expectation its proper weight, it distorted the principle of respect for contractual intention. On the other hand, the Commission's readiness to review the enforceability of gratuitous promises is a welcome indication of a renewed concern with protecting legitimate expectation.

Having resolved to base its proposals on respect for the contracting parties' intentions, the Commission's principal difficulty was to strike the right balance between calculability and flexibility. This balancing exercise is at its most sensitive in the second limb of the test of enforceability. Although the design of this limb of the test (including the proviso) is not without precedent – in fact, it is very closely modelled on the test laid down by s. 4 of the Contracts (Privity) Act 1982 in New Zealand – the adoption of a two-limbed test of enforceability gives rise to uncertainties that make no positive contribution to the desired element of flexibility. In a sense, the Commission has substituted a dual-track approach for its earlier dual intention test without altogether eliminating unproductive uncertainty. As we have suggested, the conjunction of the two limbs invites litigation about the precise relationship between the first and the second limb (particularly, where the defendant contractor seeks to rebut the presumption under the proviso); and, where a third party seeks to rely on exclusions or other protective terms, there is scope for argument in relation to whether such terms fall under the first or the second limb. Moreover, although the proviso is intended to allow for flexibility, the

---

[133] See the argument in Beyleveld and Brownsword *Privity, Transitivity, and Rationality* (1991) 54 MLR 48; and Adams and Brownsword *Key Issues in Contract* (1995) ch 5.

Act could offer more assistance (through indicative guidelines) in relation to the way in which the discretion that accompanies this flexibility is structured – is there any reason, for example, why guidelines should not have indicated that the availability of a direct contractual recourse is normally to be taken as counting against the third party having a right to enforce, and indicating that exclusions drawn by an employer in favour of his third party employees should be treated normally as enforceable by the employees? Or, even better, for the avoidance of doubt, why should such exclusions not be treated as giving employees a right to enforce under the first limb? Or, even better, for the avoidance of disputes such as that in *London Drugs Ltd v Kuehne and Nagel International Ltd*.[134] In this case, pursuant to a warehousing contract, London Drugs delivered a transformer to the defendants for storage. Clause 11(b) of the contract provided as follows:

The warehouseman's liability on any one package is limited to $40 unless the holder has declared in writing a valuation in excess of $40 and paid the additional charge specified to cover warehouse liability.

Instead of making the declaration and paying the appropriate charge, London Drugs included the transformer in its all risks insurance cover. When London Drugs gave the order for the transformer to be loaded for delivery to their new factory, two of the defendant's employees negligently damaged it by allowing it to topple over. The amount of damage was $34,000. London Drugs sued both Khehne and Nagel, and the two employees in negligence. The Supreme Court held that there should be a general relaxation of the privity doctrine where –
(i) a limitation of liability clause, either expressly or impliedly, extends its benefit to the employees (or employee) seeking to rely on it; and
(ii) the employees (or employee) seeking the benefit of the limitation of liability clause were (was) acting in the course of their (his) employment and were performing the very services provided for in the contract between their (his) employer and the plaintiff (customer) when the loss occurred.

The two employees were therefore held to be covered by the limitation of liability clause. Accordingly, why could the C(RTP)A 1999 not have been provided that exclusions drawn by employers are to be construed as giving employees a right to enforce even if the employees are not expressly designated?

---

[134] [1990] 70 DLR (4th) 51; affd. 97 DLR (4th) 261.

It is also regrettable that the Commission failed to address P4 problems, which probably give rise to at least as many problems in commercial contexts[135] as the other three privity problems.

In conclusion, for the reform of the privity doctrine as evinced by the Act is to be applauded. The benefit is that it promises to break the stranglehold of the privity orthodoxy – not simply in the ad hoc way achieved by the existing statutory exceptions to the doctrine,[136] but across the board through the general application of the test of enforceability. However, the burden of implementing these proposals, of ironing out any difficulties that emerge, and of developing more radical regimes of third party rights, has been handed back to the courts. As is apparent from this paper, the present situation is riddled with anomalies, many of which the Act does little to remove.

---

[135] See above. In some circumstances, as noted above, the distinction between a benefit and a burden may not be as obvious as it seems – see *Andromeda Marine SA v O W Bunker & Trading A/S* 2006 WL 1078890. The problem was noted by the Law Commission when they decided only to deal with the benefit side of the privity problem – see The Report 6.17.

[136] C(RTP)A 1999, s 7(1), it will be recalled, preserves the existing statutory exceptions to the third party rule.

Part IV
Legal Pluralism and
International Challenges

Political Economy and Contract Law

John C. Reitz[1] (Iowa)

I. Introductory Example: "At Will" Employment Contracts

The way in which the contract law of different countries reflects distinctive political economies was dramatically revealed by riots in the spring of 2006. The riots took place in France and were directed against the government's proposal to alter the law concerning employment contracts by introducing at will employment for young, first-time workers. In France, employers may terminate most employment only for certain reasons. Such employment contracts are said to be terminable only "for cause." Most employment contracts in the United States, by contrast, can be terminated by the employer for any reason or no reason as long as the employer does not terminate for certain prohibited reasons. We call this arrangement employment "at will." Reactions to the French strikes on both sides of the Atlantic revealed a rather stark difference in assumptions about the degree to which the state should intervene in employment markets to limit or eliminate at will employment. The French were passionate in their support for government intervention; in the United States, employment at will evokes very little protest. Employment contracts thus illustrate my general thesis that views about the desirable level of state intervention in markets – an ideological feature I refer to as "political economy" – is an important design principle of legal systems and that many major differences among legal systems correspond to differences in the overall political economies of the respective countries. We will begin our investigation of the role political economy plays in the

---

[1] Edward L. Carmody Professor of Law, Associate Dean for International and Comparative Law Programs, University of Iowa College of Law. The author would like to thank Professor and Dean Reiner Schulze of the law faculty of the University of Münster, Germany, for the invitation to speak in the series of lectures that gave rise to this volume; Dean Carolyn Jones and the University of Iowa Law School Foundation for financial support for the researching and writing of this paper; Matthew Morriss for research assistance; and faculty colleagues at Münster and Iowa who attended presentations of the paper for their helpful questions, comments, and suggestions. Unless otherwise noted, all translations are by the author.

contract law of France, Germany, the United Kingdom, and the United States with a closer look at the French riots over at will contracting.[2]

In April-May, 2006, French students and labor unions, joined by teachers, the jobless, and even retirees, took to the streets in an escalating series of actions to protest government proposals to amend the labor laws to give employers a limited right to terminate young, first-time permanent employees on an at will basis[3] The proposed law would have created a new two-year labor contract (the so-called *contrat première embauche* or C.P.E.) for businesses with over twenty workers and for workers younger than twenty-six employed for their first job. The new contract would have permitted employers to terminate without notice, severance pay, or the obligation to show that the employee has violated the contract.[4] Over a two-month period of disruptions, the protestors managed to "shut down universities, threatened to hurt tourism and economy, and brought violent clashes between young people and police."[5] Eventually,

---

[2] Comparative analysis has to start with a clear focus on a manageable number of specific jurisdictions. The focus on these four countries is justified because, as the following discussion will show, these four countries alone provide sufficient contrasts in political economy to test the thesis, because they are such economically and politically significant countries that their legal systems have exercised great influence on the development of law elsewhere, and because they have especially well documented and analyzed systems of law. It is also only fair to admit additional practical reasons for this focus. These are the four countries I have spent the most time studying, I read their chief languages fluently, and I have access at Iowa to a magnificent library collection for the law of these four countries. In any event, to the extent that it is necessary to discuss how European Union law has forced a modification of the contract law of the European countries in this group, the paper's coverage will actually be considerably broader.

[3] Elaine Sciolino, "Not '68, but French Youths Hear Similar Cry to Rise Up," *New York Times*, March 17, 2006, at A6; Craig S. Smith, "Opponents of New French Labor Law Step Up Protests," *New York Times*, March 21, 2006, at A9.

[4] Corinne Maier, "French Twist," *New York Times*, March 31, 2006, at A19. Another specially terminable first-time employment contract, the C.N.E., created in 2005 already covered smaller businesses. Id. See also Smith, *supra* n.3.

[5] Elaine Sciolino, "Chirac Will Rescind Labor Law That Caused Wide French Riots," *New York Times*, April 11, 2006, at A1. Opinion polls reported very substantial opposition within the French public to the proposed new C.P.E labor contract. Smith, *supra* n. 3 (two out of three people); Sciolino, *supra* n. 3 (68 percent).

the French political leaders bowed to public opposition and rescinded the law that promulgated the C.P.E. contract.[6]

German law and French law both protect workers by eliminating "at will" employment for most regular employees. In Germany, employees are protected both by statutory notice periods and by general statutory restrictions on dismissal. Thus an employer can generally terminate contracts of employment for an indefinite period of time only after statutorily specified notice periods, which vary with the length of service from four weeks to seven months.[7] In addition, the Dismissal Protection Act [*Kündigungs-schutzgesetz*] prohibits terminations in establishments over a certain, rather small size[8] and for employees who have worked for more than six months as "socially unjustified" [*sozial ungerechtfertigt*] unless they are for certain specific reasons. Reasons that "socially justify" a termination include serious employee illness that would prevent the employee from fulfilling his obligations, employee misconduct or incompetence-- reasons that U.S. law would view as "material breach" or "cause" by the employee sufficient to excuse termination of an employment contract in the United States.[9] Such reasons would generally also permit the employer to avoid the statutory notice periods and terminate immediately.[10] Reasons sufficient to take the termination outside the protection of the Dismissal Protection Act also include "compelling operational requirements" [*dringende betriebliche Erfordernisse*],[11] but these operational requirements have to make it "virtually impossible for the employer to retain the employee."[12] Similar grounds of severe economic circumstances may excuse the employer from the statutory notice provisions.[13] But the

---

[6] After the French Constitutional Council upheld the constitutionality of the law passed to implement the proposed contract, Craig S. Smith, "French Law Is Affirmed as Protests Snarl Traffic," *New York Times*, March 31, 2006, at A4, President Chirac agreed to rescission of the law. Sciolino, *supra* n. 5.

[7] § 622 BGB.

[8] The Dismissal Protection Act originally applied to establishments employing no more than five employers, but it has been amended to apply only to firms with more than ten employees. Manfred Weiss, Labor Law, in Introduction to German Law 299, 330 (Joachim Zekoll & Mathias Reimann, eds., 2005).

[9] Stefan Lingemann, et al., Employment & Labor Law in Germany 28–30 (2003); Weiss, *supra* n. 8, at 330–332. The courts have generally required that employers give wayward employees at least one warning before discharge for cause. S. Lingemann, et al., *op. cit.*, at 28.

[10] § 626 BGB (termination without notice for good cause (*aus wichtigem Grund*)); Weiss, *supra* n. 8, at 330.

[11] § 1(2) KSchG.

[12] Weiss, *supra* n. 8, at 331. See also § 1(2)1.b) KSchG.

[13] § 626 BGB; Weiss, *supra* n. 7, at 330.

economic ground of excuse does not secure employers a wide field of discretion in firing. In particular, dismissal is not justified if there is any reasonable possibility of transferring the employee to another job; re-training may even be required.[14] Moreover, if the company has a works council, it has to be consulted prior to any dismissal.[15]

The French protection against at will contracts is similar but appears to apply to all employers without regard to size. In France, most employees work under contracts for an indeterminate period, and these contracts may be terminated by the employer only for a "real and serious ground of dismissal" – serious breach or incapacity such as would be regarded as "cause" in the United States[16] – or, as in the case of Germany, for economic reasons, but as in Germany the employer can use this reason to justify termination of employment only if the employer can show that business pressures have caused it to restructure its workforce in such a way that the employee in question can no longer fill any possible position for the employer. Retraining may have to be offered because the Court of Cassation has repeatedly held that an employee may not be terminated just because he lacks the qualifications for or cannot adapt himself to the technical requirements of the restructured job.[17] Except in the case of serious breach by the employee that compromises the future of the employer, the termination cannot take effect immediately and in any case must be accompanied by notice and an opportunity for a hearing by the personnel office.[18] From the beginning of these protections in 1945 up to 1975, there was, in addition, "a fairly rigid system requiring administrative authorization from the Ministry of Labour for [economic] dismissals although the employers were in the private sector."[19] Since 1975, the French state has relinquished the strict form of state control of economic dismissals, but employers still have to give notice to the state administration so that it can monitor the required discussions with the workforce, and employers with more than 50 employees have to produce a "social plan" showing how they will restructure their workforce, indicating what opportunities there are for employment in new positions, and justifying the need for any proposed terminations for those employees who cannot

---

[14] Id. at 331–332; accord S. Lingemann, et al., supra n. 9, at 31.
[15] Works Councils Constitution Act, Section 102 I [BetrVG § 102 I]. See generally S. Lingemann, et al., supra n. 9 at 26–27; Weiss, supra n. 8, at 332–333.
[16] John Bell, et al., Principles of French Law 473–474 (1998); Frédéric-Jérôme Pansier, Droit du travail 207–208 (2d ed. 2000).
[17] J. Bell, et al., supra n. 16, at 472–474; F-J. Pansier, supra n. 16, at 223–225.
[18] F-J. Pansier, supra n. 16, at 201–203, 207, 226.
[19] J. Bell, et al., supra n. 16, at 473.

take up a new position. The state administration has the authority to review these social plans.[20]

These employee protections are of long standing in both German and French law[21] and are but aspects of the many ways in which German and French law have developed special protections for employees.[22] Even

---

[20] Id.; F-J. Pansier, *supra* n. 16, at 228–234.

[21] German notice protections appear to go back at least to amendments introduced into the German Commercial Code [*Handelsgesetzbuch* or HGB] in 1897–98 to protect clerks of commercial enterprises by requiring both employer and employee to give at least six weeks notice to terminate a clerk's contract of employment for an indefinite term and prohibiting express agreements from shortening the notice period to less than one month or imposing unequal notice periods on the parties. See §§ 66–69 HGB; RGZ 68, 317 (decision of the German Federal Supreme Court [*Reichsgericht*], 3rd Civ. Div., May 1, 1908). For English translations of these materials, see Rudolf B. Schlesinger, *et al.*, *Comparative Law* 654–660 (6th ed. 1998). The German Supreme Court's 1908 opinion interpreted the legislative history to show an intent to protect clerks, not employers. Therefore, the court construed Section 67's rule against unequal notice periods as prohibiting a shorter notice period for the employer, but not for the employee. Section 68 of the Commercial Code at that time limited the coverage of the rule governing express agreements to clerks whose annual salary was no more than 5000 Marks, an amount that would have covered clerks up to the level of at least junior executives. R. Schlesinger, *et al.*, *op. cit.*, at 655 n.57. The provisions were abrogated in 1969 and similar rules covering a broader class of employees were incorporated into Section 622 of the German Civil Code [*Bürgerliches Gesetzbuch* or BGB]. Id. at 654 n.55. The rule allowing express agreements to give the employee, but not the employer, the benefit of a shorter notice period has been retained in current law. § 622(6) BGB; Weiss, *supra* n. 8, at 330. See generally, Otto Mühl, *et al.*, 4/1 Soergel, *Bürgerliches Gesetzbuch* § 622, Randnummern (Rndnr.) 1–5 (1997)(history, especially more recent history, of notice rule).

The Dismissal Protection Act goes back to rules that were developed, originally on a collective basis, in Germany in connection with demobilization of the German Army in the wake of World War I, which is also the period when the notice periods for discharge were increased for employees with substantial seniority. 1 Reinhard Richardi, *et al.*, *Münchener Handbuch zum Arbeitsrecht* § 3 Rndnr. 8 (2000).

French controls on dismissals date to Liberation in 1945, as indicated above in the text. *See also* Jean-Claude Javillier, *Droit du travail* 298–300 § 317 (2d ed. 1981).

[22] These include the special protections for and encouragement of collective bargaining, rules on minimum wages and working conditions, rules against discrimination in employment, workers' councils to represent workers in issues

though both French and German law permit an employer to discharge an employee for cause, as well as for certain economic reasons, the employer's invocation of any of those reasons can be subjected to judicial review in a suit for wrongful termination. Employers in those countries fear the difficulties and associated litigation risk of having to prove their claims in the special labor courts to such an extent that they regard it as next to impossible to discharge a worker covered by the anti-discharge protections. By contrast, the at will employment regime secures a wide berth for employer discretion in terminating employees that cannot be challenged in court. The idea behind the French proposals in the spring of 2006 was to introduce at will employment for young, first-time employees as a way to encourage employers to give jobs to young people, by reducing the risk for the employer that once it had given someone the status of employee, it would be stuck with that person for the duration of their working lifetime, even if they turned out to be unsuitable.[23] The protestors, however, saw this proposal as a first step toward dismantling all legal protections for employees.[24]

In the United States, most employers are not protected by statutory notice provisions or restrictions on termination. The common law therefore controls, and at common law, contracts of employment for indefinite terms which do not expressly address termination procedures – by far the most common type of employment contract in the United States – are interpreted to be contracts which both sides can terminate at any time. As a result, most people in the United States work under at will employment contracts.[25] Common parlance uses the word "firing" to refer to all employment terminations. This usage seems at least to recognize the hardship and pain that can be associated with termination of employment. Nevertheless, at will employment appears to be well accepted in the United States.

---

concerning the workplace, co-determination (in Germany), and the special labor courts. J. Bell, *et al., supra* n. 16; Nigel Foster & Satish Sule, *German Legal System and Laws* 528–546 (3d ed. 2002).

[23] Maier, *supra* n. 4.

[24] Sciolino, *supra* n. 3; Sciolino, *supra* n. 5. The French students also objected to being singled out for unequal treatment since the proposed labor contract would have applied only to young, first-time workers. Maier, *supra* n. 4.

[25] *See generally* 2 Mark A. Rothstein, *et al., Employment Law* 401–506 (3rd ed. 2004); David J. Walsh & Joshua L. Schwarz, *State Common Law Wrongful Discharge Doctrines: Up-Date, Refinement, and Rationales*, 33 Am. Bus. L.J. 645 (1996); Charles J. Muhl, *The Employment-at-will Doctrine: Three Major Exceptions*, 124 Monthly Lab. Rev. 3 (2001) (updating the study by Walsh and Schwarz through October 1, 2000). Only Arizona and Montana have adopted comprehensive legislation limiting at will employment. *Id.* at 11 n.3.

It should be clear that at will contracting is the unregulated form of the labor contract. Employers prefer at will contracting over the kind of employee protections one sees in France and Germany because at will contracting gives the employer maximum flexibility with regard to the size (and cost) of the workforce. The employment regimes in France and Germany are the product of statutes. In the absence of state intervention into the employment market, the employers' preference for at will employment will generally control. One can think of several explanations. One would be that the employers are the repeat players in the relevant employment markets to a much greater extent than individual employees and generally have greater resources to devote to contract drafting (or the avoidance of written employment contracts). Another would be that employers have the market leverage in times of labor surplus and it is precisely in times of labor shortages, when workers might have the bargaining leverage to eliminate at will employment by contract, that they also have weaker economic incentive to do so.

U.S. law does, however, generally impose some limits on employer terminations, even under at will contracts. The principal limitations are the result of a tort the courts have gradually come to recognize where the firing is determined to violate or frustrate important public policy. Thus, for example, in most states the employer commits a tort, and can be liable for substantial damages, if it discharges the employee in retaliation for the employee's refusal to commit perjury,[26] filing a workmen's compensation claim,[27] engaging in union activity,[28] or serving jury duty.[29] By virtue of this tort--whose exact boundaries are quite disputed today in the United States--and court expansion of some related contract doctrines, U.S. law has in effect said that even in at will contracts some reasons for firing an employee are impermissible.[30] But that position is quite far from the gen-

---

[26] Petermann v. Int'l Brotherhood of Teamsters, 344 P.2d 25 (Cal. App. Ct. 1959).

[27] Frampton v. Central Indiana Gas Co., 297 N.W.2d 425 (Ind. 1973); Sventko v. Kroger Co., 245 N.W.2d 151 (Mich. App. Ct. 1976); Brown v. Transcon Lines, 588 P.2d 1087 (Or. 1978).

[28] Glenn v. Clearman's Golden Cock Inn, Inc., 13 Cal. Rptr. 769 (Cal. App. Ct. 1961).

[29] Nees v. Hocks, 536 P.2d 512 (Or.1975); Reuther v. Fowler & Williams, Inc., 386 A.2d 119 (Pa. Super. Ct. 1978).

[30] *See generally* Muhl, *supra* n. 25, at 4–7 (describing debate among state courts over whether "public policy" can be found only in state constitutions and statutes or whether the courts can base the policy on broader grounds; 43 states had adopted some form of public policy tort by October 1, 2000). *See, e.g.*, Sheets v. Teddy's Frosted Foods, Inc., 427 A.2d 385 (Conn. 1980)(majority gives protection of tort to quality control director who claimed that he had

eral French and German rule that a regular employee may not normally be discharged except for serious breaches of contract or specific, restricted economic grounds, even if the employer made no such promise or representation. Despite the folk expression of concern inherent in the term "firing," people in the United States are so used to the system of employment at will that they viewed the reasons for the French protests with varying degrees of derision and incomprehension.[31]

---

been discharged for his efforts within company to ensure that employer's products complied with applicable laws concerning labeling and licensing; dissent would limit the tort to dismissal in retaliation for employee's refusal to commit clear violation of statute).

Courts in many states have been willing to hold employers to express promises of job security, including especially promises that employees will be discharged only for just cause or only after certain procedures. In some states these promises may be oral and not reflected in any writing, and in many states they may be contained in employee manuals or handbooks that were given to the employee outside of, and often long after, whatever bargaining or offer and acceptance lead to the employee's being hired, even if the employee was hired on an oral agreement. Muhl, *op. cit.*, at 7–10 (38 states by October 1, 2000). This method of limiting at will contracting would significantly reduce the number of employees subject to discharge at will, but it applies only to those employers who make express representations about job security or the process to be followed in terminations. Also, some states permit employers to defeat this claim easily by putting disclaimers in their employee manuals, and the law in this area is in many states at least as unsettled as the law on the public policy tort. Walsh & Schwarz, *supra* n. 25, at 651–53.

A much smaller group of mainly western state courts have recognized an implied covenant of good faith and fair dealing in employment contracts generally. Muhl, *supra* n. 25, at 10–11 (11 states by October 1, 2000). While this basis for limited at will employment may sound expansive, "it tends to be limited to proscription of certain "bad faith" terminations (as opposed to those undertaken for insufficient cause or no cause) that have the effect of denying employees benefits and payments already earned ... " Walsh & Schwarz, *supra* n. 25, at 647. Thus in the few states that have adopted this approach, the doctrine of good faith and fair dealing essentially adds a few reasons to the list of forbidden reasons for firing an employee created by the public policy tort.

[31] *Baltimore Sun* reporter Jay Hancock summarizes American attitudes about at-will contracting as follows: "Americans, ... have accepted [the employer's broad layoff authority] with barely a whimper. People complain about layoffs, and many victims are devastated, but there has been nothing like the manifest outrage of France." Jay Hancock, "Ideas: Tales of the free market's forgotten losers; France seethes over a plan to allow layoffs, but Americans have quietly

The transatlantic standoff on the issue of employment terminations illustrates a more general contrast in political economies. I have elsewhere published more detailed accounts of what I mean by political economy and how I justify the characterizations I use for the political economies of different countries to be discussed here.[32] So for this paper, drawing on those earlier publications, I will just say enough to make my usage understandable and plausible.

By the term "political economy," I mean simply the role that the state is expected to play and does play in assuring the general welfare–in other words, the degree to which the state is expected to and does intervene in the market by regulating and providing welfare payments. I thus mean to invoke the standard spectrum that runs from the now virtually extinct socialist command economies on the extreme left or state-centered end of the spectrum to the mythical "laissez-faire" country on the extreme right or market-centered end. While there may be no actual country that has a truly laissez-faire economy, I do not hesitate to label the United States as

---

accepted them for years," *Baltimore Sun*, April 9, 2006, at 1F (review of Louis Uchitelle, *The Disposable American: Layoffs and their Consequences* (2006)).

The primary reaction by Americans to the French riots has been derision for the apparent disregard by the French rioters of the laws of economics. As Robert Samuelson of *Newsweek* put it, "[a]ll these [job] protections perversely–but predictably–stifle job creation." Robert J. Samuelson, "The Politics of Make-Believe: The student protesters in France think that if they march long enough or burn enough cars, they can make the future go away. No such luck," *Newsweek*, April 3, 2006, at 29. *See also* Thomas Sowell, "Legislating a 'right' to a job does not work. Raising costs usually results in fewer purchases," *Charleston Daily Mail*, March 22, 2006, at 4A ("Student riots in Paris remind us that education at elite academic institutions is not enough to teach either higher morals or basic economies ... [the students rioting] are too ignorant of economics to realize that [job protections] cost them jobs"). For similar opinions, see Cal Thomas, "Socialism Coming Home to Roost," *Augusta Chronicle*, March 31, 2006, at A5 (also published as "Capitalism will solve French job funk," *Buffalo News*, April 1, 2006, A7, and as "The French job funk," *Tulsa World*, April 2, 2006, at G5); Claire Berlinski, "As always, the mob governs France. Economic ignorance causes widespread misery," *Charleston Daily Mail*, March 29, 2006, at 4A (also published as "The French riots: They're, oh, so 18th century," *Pittsburgh Tribune Review*, April 2, 2006).

[32] *See, e.g.*, *Doubts about Convergence: Political Economy as an Impediment to Globalization*, 12 Transnat'l L. & Contemp. Probs. 139–159 (2002); *Political Economy as a Major Architectural Principle of Public Law*, 75 Tul. L. Rev. 1121–1157 (2001); *Political Economy and Abstract Review in Germany, France, and the United States*, in *Constitutional Dialogues in Comparative Perspective* 62–88 (Sally J. Kenney, William M. Reisinger and John C. Reitz, eds., 1999).

the most market-centered nation in the world. It would be incorrect, of course, to label it as laissez-faire. On some issues the U.S. state regulates quite significantly and effectively. But the United States also has a long history of ambivalence and skepticism about reliance on state organs to provide general welfare. The countries of continental Western Europe are usually described as "social welfare states." They fall somewhere in the middle of the spectrum. They believe in free markets, but they also believe that markets require significant government intervention to prevent unfairness and to ensure social solidarity. By contrast with the United States, their political economies are considerably more state-centered.

On the issue of protection of employers from firing without cause, French law and German law are similar, reflecting similarly state-centered or interventionist political economies, but we have already noted that French law imposes a somewhat more intensive scheme of regulation on private employment relationships. The protections against at will terminations apply to all employers, not just those with a certain minimum number of employees, as in Germany. In the post-World War II period, the French government adopted an even more obviously state-centered form of control, regulating terminations directly by requiring government approval. Even today, the French government plays a role in monitoring large employers' social plans, and the French state is involved in the termination talks between employer and employees' representatives. In its regulation of employment at will, France thus appears somewhat more state-centered than Germany. Because I am going to make similar arguments at several points in the paper, let me say a bit more about the differences between the French and German forms of a state-centered political economy.[33]

Much of the difference has to do with the way in which the state is organized. For example, while both Germany and France manifest considerable evidence of corporatism, much more than in the United States, there are rather different degrees of corporatism in the two countries. By "corporatism," I mean the melding of state structures with civil society through de jure or de facto state recognition of certain umbrella groups representing specific interests or sectors of the economy, such as employers, workers, craftsmen, merchants, or specific industries. In effect, corporatism builds umbrella interest groups, established as self-governing groups within civil society, into the official governing structure of the country. Germany seems to make extensive use of such corporatist structures to help in the formation of public policy. France appears to use corporatist structures to a lesser degree and relies to a greater extent on government officials to determine what the public interest is. French

---

[33] The following paragraph again draws on the publications listed in the previous footnote.

corporatist umbrella groups are much more likely to split along political lines, making them less capable to serve as representatives for a whole set of economic interests, and France has a long tradition of an administrative elite that has wielded power in France in a way that is more impervious to influence by civil society than is the case in Germany. Some commentators therefore label France a "statist" polity and Germany a "corporatist" polity. These are useful labels as long as we understand that they reflect tendencies, not hard and fast distinctions. I wish to use "statism" as a label for the slightly more state-centered form of interaction between private interests and public officials that one finds in France and which depends somewhat less on corporatist forms of interaction.

Political economy is not a feature that corresponds neatly with the distinction between civil law and common law. The issue of employment at will makes this point clear because on this issue, English law appears to be quite close to French and German law.[34] Perhaps reflecting its somewhat more liberal traditions, England adopted its legislation protective of employees only in the 1960s and 1970s, well after Germany and France had begun to put their protective regimes in place in the inter-war period.[35] This time difference is, however, rather slender evidence of a difference in political economy. Better evidence will emerge from a consideration of other contracts rules of the common law that exhibit a more liberal outlook. My argument, therefore, is that the United Kingdom is an intermediate case, neither as state-centered as France and Germany, for example, nor as market-centered as the United States. One symbol of this intermediate status is the fact that Britain has been the country of liberal political philosophers like John Locke and John Stuart Mill, but also of Thomas Hobbes, the apologist for state power. Britain has had a strong free

---

[34] Dismissal legislation now protects the employee in Britain in much the same way the employee is protected in France and Germany. Simon Deakin & Gillian S. Morris, *Labour Law* 386 (4th ed. 2005)("the UK follows a pattern well established in the systems of mainland Europe"); J. Bell, *et al.*, *supra* n. 16, at 473 (the French law "produces a treatment of economic dismissals which is recognizably similar to that of British employment law, though ... its present state is rather more formally managerialized, via the social plans, than is the case in the United Kingdom. The situation and development with regard to personal dismissals [for cause] resembles somewhat more closely that in the United Kingdom."); N. Foster & S. Sule, *supra* n. 22, at 536–537 (compelling business grounds sufficient under German law to justify economic terminations "cover the usual sorts of reasons why redundancies are justified in the UK"). *See generally*, S. Deakin & G. Morris, *op. cit.* The qualifying period for employment before the legal protections against firing take effect has been changed from time to time and in 1997 was reduced to one year. *Id.* at 392.

[35] *Id.* at 386.

market, but also socialized medicine and, to an ever changing extent, government ownership of substantial means of production, including, at times, coal mines and railways.[36]

It is clear that the values embodied in political economy figure prominently in the different reactions to at will employment in Europe and the United States. In one of his reports on the French employment at will protests, Craig Smith, a reporter for the *New York Times*, captured the contrast between the relevant political economies on the issue of employee termination protection. The right to fire workers, he wrote, "may sound like basic market economics to Americans, but while most of the world struggles to cope with the shifting threats and opportunities of an increasingly global economy, much of Europe, and France in particular, remains devoted to a quasi-socialist ideal."[37] To help a U.S. public accustomed to at will employment understand the conflict in France, Smith quotes a French writer who says, "In France, when people work, ... they say they have a 'situation,' which they expect to endure for life."[38] He quotes the director of a French polling company who opines that "[t]he role of the state isn't to liberalize the market, but, on the contrary, to make sure that workers are taken care of. In France, what we ask for is not

---

[36] By the eighteenth century, the British had developed a more liberal political economy than any European continental state, but the British experience as an island economy which, unlike the newly minted United States in the eighteenth and nineteenth centuries, had relatively little undeveloped land, led it to be influenced by rather different economic theories. Herbert Hovenkamp, *Enterprise and American Law, 1836–1937* 183–192 (1991). Since the post-war period, Britain has undergone waves of nationalization and privatization of industry, sometimes engaging in both at the same time. John F. McEldowney, *Public Law* 424–461 (1998); Andrew Le Sueur, et al., *Principles of Public Law* 86 (1999). Since the mid-twentieth century, the European Union has exerted strong political, economic, and legal pressure on the United Kingdom to accept the more regulatory approaches to the market. A good illustration of this process concerns the Social Charter of 1989 and the Social Protocol of the Maastricht Treaty, which called for special protections for labor. The UK opposed both of these documents and as a result was exempted in the Maastricht Treaty from coverage of the Protocol or any EU legislation adopted pursuant to it. But after the May 1997 victory of the Labour Party, the UK accepted both the Protocol and EU directives promulgated for all the other EU Member States pursuant to the Protocol, and Treaty of Amsterdam eliminated the "two-tier" nature of the EU on these social policy issues. George Bermann, et al., *Cases and Materials on European Union Law* 1297–1299 (2d ed. 2002).

[37] Craig S. Smith, "French Unrest Reflects Old Faith in Quasi-Socialist Ideals," *New York Times*, April 9, 2006, at A8.

[38] *Id.* (quoting Philippe d'Iribarne, author of *French Strangeness*).

that the state withdraws, but that it be as present as possible."[39] Alain Duhamel, a leading political commentator, characterized the French as "passionate in their distrust of market forces ..."[40] We can thus see strong differences between the political economies of France, Germany, Great Britain, and the United States, and we can see further that the at will employment contract in the United States is the product of the tendency toward leaving matters to an unregulated or minimally regulated market[41] while the protection against at will employment in Europe is the product of a much stronger impetus toward state regulation of the employment market.

---

[39] *Id.* (quoting Jean-Daniel Levy, director of a French polling company).

[40] Sciolino, *supra* n. 3.

[41] Since the regulation of employee terminations in the United States comes primarily in the form of tort law and, to a lesser extent, through expansive contract doctrine, developed by court decision, *see supra* note 30, one might argue about whether or not the employment contract is "regulated" in the United States with respect to the issue of at will contracting. In one sense, the tort rules and the implied contract and good faith doctrines adopted by some courts are a form of state regulation, but because they are the product of decisions in private law cases and not legislation, they may not have the political salience that legislative and administrative regulation has. U.S. opponents of state regulation tend to overlook the fact that judicial expansion of protection offered by tort law and other aspects of private law is the vestigial form of regulation that necessarily accompanies a market economy under a meaningful rule of law. To eliminate, for example, tort law entirely without providing an alternative remedy for those injured by market activity would be to permit market participants to escape liability for the costs they impose on others, a position which judges of all political stripes will eventually find untenable. The lack of universal health care exacerbates the situation. But the only alternatives to remedies provided by the market in combination with the common law of tort and other aspects of the common law are remedies provided by the state through public law, either against the market participants who create the costs or against the state itself as a form of state insurance or welfare payment. If none of those alternatives are developed, the crush of cases brought by injured parties eventually moves the judges to expand private law to provide remedies in at least the most egregious cases. Thus I would argue that in the United States regulation especially by tort law has been fostered by the deliberate choice not to regulate by statute or administrative rule, coupled with the decision not to provide universal health care. In effect, I argue that a market-centered political economy, like that of the United States, will tend to develop especially robust tort law, but that is a subject for a paper on political economy and tort law.

II. Other Obviously "Regulatory" Aspects of European Contract Law

Termination of employment contracts is hardly the only issue of contract law which tends to be regulated more strictly in Europe than in the United States. Another example which highlights the somewhat more state-centered political economy of France involves price controls. Despite the strong liberalism that influenced the drafting of the French Civil Code at the beginning of the nineteenth century,[42] significant price controls, especially over basic food stuffs and wages, have been a major feature of French life.[43] Wage and price controls are the very antithesis of free markets. The fact that price controls are not as generally or continuously found in the U.S., the U.K., or Germany suggests a greater degree of state-centeredness in France. Price and wage controls are another feature I point to justify the "statist" label for France.

There are undoubtedly many other contract law examples of a lesser degree of regulation in the United States and a greater degree of regulation in Europe. I should like to review briefly two more examples of contracts regulation: (1) consumers' rights of cancellation and (2) the treat-

---

[42] Jean Carbonnier wrote that "[i]n proclaiming the liberty of work, of commerce, and of industry ... in abolishing all forms of corporation ... the Revolution appears as a project of massive deregulation." 4 Jean Carbonnier, Droit civil § 74 at 151 (22d ed. 2000). However, after surveying the ways in which the French state has intervened in contractual freedom, starting with the many control measures adopted during and right after the French Revolution as control measures for a wartime economy, Dean Carbonnier pronounced one of the many epigrams for which he is noted: "France, when she is not socialist, is Colbertist, and often both at the same time." Id. § 75 at 153.

[43] Wages in France are subject to what is in effect "a universal hourly minimum wage system," the SMIC (or *salaire minimum interprofessionnel de croissance*), which was put into place in 1970 to replace an earlier minimum wage system that was not as "dynamic" in the sense that it was not subject to as effective a regime for annual adjustment to reflect economic and political factors. J. Bell, et al., supra n. 16, at 477. The SMIC represents the high water mark of governmental intervention in the labour market in France; it is fixed at a high enough level to be a major determinant of actual wage levels and relativities between wages, and although the rate-fixing decisions have to be taken *après avis de* (meaning, roughly, on the advice of) the tripartite National Commission for Collective Bargaining, the decisions are basically political ones. Id.

Prices have been fixed in France primarily for sale of commodities and agricultural and residential leases. 4 J. Carbonnier, supra n. 42, at 121; J. Bell, et al., op.cit., at 309 ("while over the last 10 years or so this ordre public de direction has been somewhat in retreat, its influence is still considerable.").

ment of standardized terms in what Americans call "contracts of adhesion." Both of these areas have been subject in Europe to harmonization pressures by the European Union, and even to the extent not fully harmonized, the rules of the three European countries being examined here are quite similar to each other and quite different from those of the United States.

1. Cancellation Rights

On both sides of the Atlantic, concern about the potential for unfairness in door-to-door consumer sales and certain other types of sales to consumers that are conducted at locations other than the regular business premises of the seller has led to recognition of a limited consumers' right to cancel those contracts. In the United States, current law is dominated by federal regulations issued by the Federal Trade Commission (FTC),[44] but those regulations leave room for a welter of state and local rules to apply, as well, unless they "are directly inconsistent" with the federal rules.[45] The FTC rules give consumers three days in which to cancel any covered consumer sale.

The cancellation right is a major departure from general principles of contract law. In effect, from the point of view of the seller of such a contract; the contract is not really a contract until the expiration of the cancellation period. I readily concede that the FTC rule is a substantial form of U.S. regulation touching consumer contracts. My argument is that the European rules constitute a more comprehensive regulation of the general problem. The first development in EU law in this area was Directive 85/577/EEC,[46] which required the Member States to adopt rules similar to the FTC rules in the United States for contracts negotiated with consumers away from the seller's premises. Subsequent EU directives expanded that aspect of consumer protection beyond the boundaries of U.S. law by providing similar consumer cancellation rights with respect to time-share contracts, insurance, and distance contracts.[47] German law goes beyond its duty to implement the Directive by also providing a cancellation right in the case of contracts for distance learning and consumer credit agreements.[48] The cancellation periods are also longer in Europe than in the United States. The EU directives generally require that the consumer be given a minimum of a seven-day cancellation period while German law

---

[44] 16 C.F.R. Part 429 (2006).
[45] 16 C.F.R. § 429.2 (b) (2006).
[46] 1985 O.J. L372/31.
[47] Basil S. Markesinis, et al., *The German Law of Contract* 265–267 (2d ed. 2006).
[48] Id. at 267

provides two-week cancellation periods, and in the UK, the Timeshare Act of 1992 expands the cancellation right to fourteen days.[49] Thus we can see that European regulation of this problem covers more than the sales outside regular business premises covered by the corresponding U.S. regulation, and it provides the consumer longer cancellation periods.

2. Regulation of Standard Terms

The regulation of standard terms or contracts of adhesion is intertwined with consumer protection issues but goes beyond consumer protections in all of the countries discussed here. Whether standard terms result from inequality of market power or from a rational attempt to realize savings from standardization of transactions, they are argued to be problematic because they do not result from a process of bargaining. They do not come therefore with the same guarantee of fairness that results from a process of bargaining. The problem is not, of course, limited to consumers because businesses make extensive use of standardized contracts among themselves, as well.[50]

My argument is that the regulation of standard terms is also stricter and more comprehensive in Europe than in the United States.[51] I think the argument is complicated, but not defeated, by the fact that the operative law in each of the countries in this comparison starts with similar broad authorizations to courts to invalidate contractual terms that are very unfair. In French and Germany law, I am referring to the good faith or *boni mores* provisions in the codes[52] which at least historically were related to

---

[49] *Id.* at 266.

[50] See the excellent general discussion in B. Markesinis, *et al.*, *supra* n. 47, at 164–169. It can be objected of course that, at least in a competitive market, the party that is asked to agree to a standardized contract may be able to bargain indirectly by refusing to contract on standardized terms to which it objects. In other words, there may be bargaining by "exit" rather than by "voice." But that argument assumes that the competition offers different contract terms. If it does not, "exit" does not produce a type of bargaining over the standard terms.

[51] For EU, German, and U.K. law on the point and comparisons to U.S. law, see generally, *id.* at 163–180; James R. Maxeiner, *Standard-Terms Contracting in the Global Electronic Age: European Alternatives*, 28 Yale J. Int'l L. 109 (2003) (arguing that Europe regulates standard terms more than the U.S.).

[52] C. civ. arts. 1133 (a contract's *cause* is illicit when contrary to good morals), 1134 (contracts must be performed in good faith); BGB §§ 138 (juristic act void if *contra bonos mores*), 157 (contracts interpreted according to good faith), 242 (performance subject to good faith).

the ancient idea of invalidating in the name of "lesion" or *laesio enormis* contracts characterized by gross unfairness in the exchange; in the U.S., to the unconscionability doctrine,[53] which covers some of the same ground. In theory, under these broad standards, courts could come to the same results in each country. But at least at the level of the rhetoric of legal doctrine, there is quite a significant difference because contract law in Europe supplements the general clauses with much more detailed legislation that addresses the specific issues posed by standard terms.

All the European countries are now required to conform their law to the minimum standards of the EU Directive on consumer protection (Directive 93/13/ECC),[54] Article (3)(1) of which states:

> A contractual term which has not been individually negotiated shall be regarded as unfair if, contrary to the requirement of good faith, it causes a significant imbalance in the parties' rights and obligations arising under the contract, to the detriment of the consumer.

Borrowing the technique from German law, the Directive also contains in an annex a list of suspect or presumptively prohibited contract terms.[55] The Member States are free to adopt more stringent controls, and German and U.K. law both contain statutes on standard terms that cover more than consumer contracts and appear to go beyond the standards of the Directive.[56] In addition to a general clause much like Article (3)(1) of the EU Directive, the German statute promulgates two lists of contract provisions, one list of suspect terms that may be prohibited, but only if further analysis shows that remedy to be warranted, and one list of terms that are prohibited per se. England decided to implement the EU directive by adopting a "carbon copy" of the directive as statute.[57] However, the British approach has been characterized by a reliance on administrative enforcement. As one set of scholars has remarked, "By far the most significant role with regard to the UK application of the Directive has so far been played by the Office of Fair Trading and its Unfair Contract Terms Unit . . . rather than through private enforcement of the regula-

---

[53] U.C.C. § 302; Restatement (Second) of Contracts § 208.
[54] 1993 O.J. L 95/29.
[55] The listed terms are not automatically deemed unfair, but are to be subjected to further analysis.
[56] *See generally* B. Markesinis, *et al.*, *supra* n. 47, at 166–180 (comparing U.K., German, and EU law). The applicable German law was originally a freestanding statute, *Das Gesetz zur Regelung des Rechts der Allgemeinen Geschäftsbedingungen* (ABG-Gesetz) of 1977, but since 2002, it has been incorporated in §§ 305–310 BGB. Maxeiner, *supra* n. 51, at 149–150.
[57] B. Markesinis, *et al.*, *supra* n. 47, at 168.

tions in the courts."⁵⁸ The British approach in this case is thus considerably more state-centered than the German approach which relies primarily on private enforcement.

French law implemented the Directive in 1995 by amending its Consumer Code to supplement the ancient and general idea of lesion with the principle of protection against "the abuse of economic power with the effect of obtaining an excessive advantage." In standard European style, the amended Consumer Code contains a long annexed list of suspect or presumptively invalid types of clauses, which the courts are invited to review under statutory criteria. Like the United Kingdom, however, France has adopted a rather state-centered model for implementing this law. New types of standard clauses are not invalidated under this new principle of consumer protection unless the French Government issues a decree to that effect. The Government is informed by, but not bound by, recommendations of a commission on abusive clauses composed of representatives from relevant professional groups and from consumer associations. Thus, the principal application of the Directive in France has been through the mechanism of administrative decree.⁵⁹

U.S. law has simply not produced any such detailed body of law, in part because U.S. law has not treated 'standard terms' as a formally separate category of contract terms."⁶⁰ But it has also not done so because U.S. judges have not in general shown much enthusiasm for policing contractual agreements under the general doctrine of unconscionability. While the German law on standard contract terms has produced a voluminous case law,⁶¹ Section 302 of the U.C.C. has not.⁶² U.S. courts have tended to confine unconscionability to procedural unfairness and are especially "reluctant to invalidate a term based on substantive unconscionability alone."⁶³ It thus appears reasonable to conclude that European law

---

⁵⁸ *Id.*

⁵⁹ 4 J. Carbonnier, *supra* n. 42, at 161–168. It appears somewhat uncertain what the judges' power is to void clauses which have not yet been the subject of administrative decree.

⁶⁰ B. Markesinis, *et al.*, *supra* n. 47, at 171.

⁶¹ Maxeiner, *supra* n. 51, at 149 (German Supreme Court alone decided more than 1500 cases between 1977 and 1999).

⁶² Maxeiner cites one study that counted just fourteen cases in a ten-year period in which a court found a contract or contract clause invalid under the doctrine of unconscionability. *Id.* at 121. "The actual number of cases [in which the courts have invalidated a contract or contract clause for unconscionability] is debated, but the fact that the number is in the tens or hundreds rather than in the thousands or higher seems clear." *Id.* at 121. n. 69.

⁶³ *Id.* at 119. My colleague Professor Steven Burton identifies and critiques a recent line of cases that has invoked unconscionability to invalidate arbitration

regulates the use of standard clauses much more strongly than U.S. law does.

As Markesinis, Unberath, and Johnson conclude in their comparative study of standard terms, the German courts have used the German law on standard terms to bind parties more tightly to the basic rules of contract law set forth in the Civil Code:

> The combined effort of these provisions is that the law of contract as contained in the Code is, to a certain degree, strict. ... by using standard terms (pre-formulated contracts) it is quite difficult to derogate from or contract out of those provisions of the Code, which are regarded as essential by the courts. This basic stance ... is clearly some way from the default position in English law ...[64]

It is even farther from the U.S. position, which – in line with its more pro-market political economy – tends to honor efforts to contract out, even in contracts of adhesion.

The thinking behind the development of the European law on this subject shows quite a different approach to political economy. Already in a 1958 law journal article Professor Raiser described a body of German case law that had instituted a process of openly evaluating the fairness of standard contract terms. He praised this abandonment of judicial "neutrality" towards contractual bargains as a "heroic deed of the German courts."[65] Markesinis, Unberath, and Johnson comment that it is "difficult to imagine in England statements ... encouraging the courts to abandon their 'neutrality' towards contracts terms."[66] In the U.S., it seems well-nigh unthinkable.

---

agreements included in employment contracts, on both procedural and substantive grounds. Steven J. Burton, *The New Judicial Hostility to Arbitration: Federal Preemption, Contract Unconscionability, and Agreements to Arbitrate*, 2006 J. Disp. Resol. – (forthcoming) (manuscript in possession of author). This development is quite new (most of the cases he cites are no older than the late 1990s) and concerns only one specific type of clause in one specific type of contract.

[64] B. Markesinis, *et al.*, *supra* n.47, at 178.
[65] '*Ruhmesblatt der deutschen Rechtspreching.*' JZ 1958, 1, 7 (cited in B. Markesinis, *et al.*, *supra* n. 47, at 164).
[66] B. Markesinis, *et al.*, *supra* n. 47, at 166.

III. Deeper, Non-Regulatory Impact of Political Economy on Contract Law

Perhaps at this point you may begin to fight with my categories. Perhaps you are thinking that of course some aspects of some contracts are subject to state regulation, and you will concede that more state-centered political economies will tend to favor stricter regulation than more market-centered political economies. That contrast follows after all tautologically from my definition of political economy. But what, you may be asking, does that tell us about contract law? Regulation is an aspect of public law; contracts is a subject of private law. By suggesting that political economy is an important element of each country's contract law, am I not simply confusing fundamental legal categories?[67] If we leave aside instances of direct economic regulation, which include regulation of labor and consumer issues, should we not find that contract law itself in every country is based on the same political economy because contracts in every legal system are primarily tools for market transactions? Does political economy really affect the deeper substance of contract law? I will give you three brief examples having to do with consideration theory and contract remedies.

1. The "Bargain" Theory of Consideration

There is nothing more characteristic of the common law's approach to contract law than "consideration" doctrine. In a common law contract between A and B, we say that A's contract promise to B is not enforceable unless it is "supported by consideration." That consideration can either be a performance or promise by B. According to Professor E. Allen Farnsworth, the term "consideration" was first used by the common law in such a technical sense in the sixteenth century. At that time, consideration doctrine required that B's performance or promise must either confer a benefit on A or impose some detrimental restriction on B's freedom of

---

[67] Professor René David reflects this point of view when he describes the many reasons why French jurists regard labor law as a type of law quite distinct from civil law. In fact, he says that "the civilist is thus shocked by various accepted labor law rules. He does not regard labor law as a branch of civil law; rather he considers it a new branch of the law that has been developed in opposition to the principles of civil law." René David, *French Law* 141–142 (translator, Michael Kindred, 1972). Dean Carbonnier also notes the conflict between the civil law's individualist orientation and the technocratic and interventionist spirit of modern consumer protection law. 4 J. Carbonnier, *supra* n. 42, at 168.

action.[68] This emphasis on material inducements appealed to the commercial spirit of the age in England.[69] But by the end of the nineteenth century in the United States, the requirement of benefits and detriments "had begun to be replaced by a requirement that the consideration be 'bargained for.'"[70] Thus was born the "bargain" theory of consideration, and it agreed even more with the prevailing "trust in free enterprise and in the dignity and creativity of the individual."[71] As a result of the consideration doctrine, promises to make gifts are not enforceable under U.S. law.

Both German and French law recognize and enforce promises to make gifts.[72] The concept of *cause*, which French law inherited from Roman law, has never been interpreted to invalidate promises to make a gift; it does not require a bargain or an exchange. In fact, in order to accommodate gift promises, *cause* has been formulated in a way that makes it primarily about the psychological motivation of the promisor.[73] German law does not use the concepts of consideration or *cause*. By including gift

---

[68] 1 E. Allen Farnsworth, *Farnsworth on Contracts* § 1.6 at 22 (3d ed. 2004).

[69] *Id*. Farnsworth quotes Fifoot as writing: "The large commercial interests of the new age sought a general sanction not for charitable gifts but for business enterprise. In such an environment it is not surprising that the judges should have required some material inducement to the defendant's undertaking." C. Fifoot, *History and Sources of the Common Law: Tort and Contract* 399 (1949) (quoted in 1 E. Farnsworth, *supra* n. 67, at 22).

[70] 1 E. Farnsworth, *supra* n. 68, §2.2 at 78. Farnsworth notes that the first Restatement of Contracts, which was promulgated in 1933, defines consideration exclusively in terms of bargain. *Id*.

[71] *Id*. at 79. British contracts treatises may appear not to emphasize the idea of bargain quite as much as the U.S. contract doctrine–they still feature the language of detriment or benefit to a greater extent than in the U.S.–but the approaches are not really distinct because British law insists that the benefit to A or the detriment to B must be given in return for A's promise. So the idea of bargain is merely expressed in other terms. *See, e.g., Anson's Law of Contract* 88–90 (28th ed. 2002) (J. Beatson, ed.); *Chitty on Contracts* §§ 3-004 to 3-013, at 217–224 (29th ed., 2004)(H.G. Beale, gen'l ed.).

[72] Subject, however, to some form requirements, such as notarial form. See the classic discussion of consideration as a "form" requirement and the possible analogues in French and German law in Arthur Taylor von Mehren, *Civil-Law Analogies to Consideration: An Exercise in Comparative Analysis*," 72 Harv. L. Rev. 1009 (1959).

[73] Arthur Taylor von Mehren & James Russell Gordley, *The Civil Law System* 914, 1028 (2d ed. 1977). *See generally* Barry Nicholas, *The French Law of Contract* 124–125 (2d ed. 1992); 4 J. Carbonnier, *supra* n. 42, at 125–141.

promises within the notion of contract, contracting under German and French law is not only about market transactions.

In the United States, by contrast, the bargain theory of consideration teaches students that contract law is all about bargained for exchange. It is of course true that most contracts in most countries are about bargained for exchanges. But the bargain theory of consideration not only puts the action of individuals and companies trading in the market in the foreground of contract law; it restricts contract law to deal-making in the market. U.S. contract law does not have to accommodate gift transactions. They are not contracts.

The bargain theory of contracts fits the basic neo-liberal argument against regulation and for the enforcement of contracts quite well. The basic argument is that parties are in the best position to determine how best to use their productive assets, keeping what they can profitably use and selling what they cannot so they can buy assets they can make better use of. Leaving price to the market, the argument goes, will result in productive goods coming into the hands of the parties who can make the best use of the assets because those parties will be able to pay the highest price for the assets. The productive capacity of the whole economy will therefore be increased, and contract law–so this theory suggests–plays the noble purpose of protecting and encouraging economic growth.[74] Promises to make gifts do not fit this logic. Enforcement of gift promises cannot be relied upon to bring goods into the highest use because they are not the product of a bargain. By celebrating the bargain in fundamental contract doctrine, U.S. contract law reinforces its market-centered political economy. The bargain theory of consideration becomes a "poster

---

[74] See, e.g., Marvin A. Chirelstein, *Concepts and Case Analysis in the Law of Contracts* 1–2 (3d ed. 1998)(a popular study aid for law students designed to supplement most of the standard contracts casebooks); Anthony T. Kronman & Richard A. Posner, *The Economics of Contract Law* 1–2 (1979)(a more scholarly treatment of the same idea, aimed at teachers of contract law). *See also* Richard Hillman, *The Richness of Contract Law: An Analysis and Critique of Contemporary Theories of Contract Law* 214 (1997)(summarizing the neo-liberal argument and critiquing it). Farnsworth's influential contracts treatise presents this view of exchange and contract law's role in promoting such exchanges, essentially without critical commentary. E. Farnsworth, *supra* n. 68, §§ 1.2–1.3, at 6–11. For a treatise that takes a more openly critical view of all rationales for contracts, including the neo-liberal one, see Joseph M. Perillo, *Calamari and Perillo on Contracts* § 1.4, at 6–13 (5th ed. 2003).

child" for the U.S. political economy and provides almost invisible reinforcement of market-centered values among U.S. lawyers and law students.[75]

But does the theoretical difference really make any practical difference? It is true that despite the unique features of consideration theory, most contracts enforceable at civil law are also enforceable at common law and vice versa. The major category of promises that are not enforceable at common law are promises to make a gift, and although they are not rendered entirely unenforceable by basic contract doctrine in the civil law world, they may not be enforceable if they do not conform to special form requirements.[76] Inconveniently and ironically–at least from the point of view of my thesis–there are some commercially important promises that are rendered unenforceable by consideration theory: the option contract, the requirements or output contract, and the exclusive dealing arrangement. But in the case of options (a one-sided promise to sell something up to a certain date in the future at a set price), common law lawyers simply provide as part of the bargain a modest payment for the option to satisfy the consideration requirement. In the case of requirements, output, and exclusive dealing contracts, the common law has found ways to accommodate itself to the needs of business without abandoning consideration theory.[77] So perhaps it is fair to say that the bargain theory of consideration is not a doctrine that makes a big practical difference in the world. But it affects the categories with which the common law lawyer confronts reality and it therefore makes a difference in how common law lawyers formulate their contract arguments and even how they set up some of their transactions. And this of course is what lawyers do; they formulate arguments and counterarguments and set up transactions. So it does make a significant difference to what lawyers do and may influence how they think about issues of political economy.

---

[75] I am not accusing contracts casebook editors necessarily of promoting neo-liberal ideology in this way. Many contracts casebooks suggest a critical stance toward the neo-liberal justifications for contract law, at least through a discussion of standard terms and the problems of adhesion contracts, if not more directly. But my point is that the central symbolic significance for contract law of the bargain theory of consideration subtly conveys to the student the centrality of the neo-liberal view. In this way, it appears to reinforce the American predisposition toward a market-centered political economy.

[76] See *supra* text at nn. 72–73.

[77] See U.C.C. § 2-306 (imposing duties of good faith and, in the case of exclusive dealing, best efforts to satisfy the consideration doctrine). The common law had already come to the same solution for exclusive dealing arrangements. Wood v. Lucy, Lady Duff-Gordon, 118 N.E. 214 (N.Y. 1917).

2. Contract Remedies

Another deeper, theoretical difference between the civil and common law of contracts has to do with the system of remedies for breach of contract. At common law, the primary remedy is damages, in which money is paid in substitution for the promised performance. Specific performance (or primary performance or performance *in specie*) is available only upon a showing that the award of damages would be insufficient to accomplish the purpose for which contract remedies are given; namely, to put the non-breaching party in the position it would have been in had the breaching party performed its promise. In the civil law, by contrast, the primary remedy for contract breach is specific or primary performance, if it is possible, and it is generally for the non-breaching party, not the court, to choose damages instead.[78]

The common law's rule making specific performance secondary represents the settlement in the late Middle Ages and early modern period of a "long jurisdictional struggle" between the common law courts and the courts of equity.[79] If damages were an adequate remedy, then the common law courts had jurisdiction because that was the primary remedy they could grant. As Professor Farnsworth explains:

> Equity would stay its hand if the remedy of an award of damages at law was "adequate." To this test was added the gloss that damages were ordinarily adequate – a gloss encouraged by the philosophy of free enterprise with its confidence that a market economy ought to enable the injured party to arrange a substitute transaction.[80]

The preference for damages thus presupposes a vigorous, smoothly functioning market where substitutes for the promised performance will be readily available, and the settlement between law and equity fit the emerging liberal order in England. A preference for specific performance does not necessarily make sense only if there is no smoothly functioning market, but it should be noted that it does make a great deal of sense if there is no dependable market for substitutes. This observation helps us understand the fact that contract penalties to enforce specific performance were the primary remedy under the command economy of the So-

---

[78] For a general discussion with extensive citations, see R. Schlesinger, *et al.*, *supra* n. 21, at 738–158. For German law, see B. Markesinis, *et al.*, *supra* n. 47, at 380, 387–388.

[79] 3 E. Farnsworth, *supra* n. 68, at § 12.4, at 163–164.

[80] *Id.* at 164 (footnote omitted).

viet Union.[81] The preference for the remedy of specific performance fits the more state-centered political economies.

Again, the practical effect of this difference may not seem very large because (1) countries like France and Germany have large, well-functioning markets covering many sectors of the economy and the victims of breach in these sectors almost always want the substitutional remedy of damages (who wants to deal with the breaching party right after his breach?); (2) the right to demand specific performance is hedged around with conditions and defenses that reduce the situations in which the remedy can actually be obtained, the most important of which is that if the performance can be done by another party, the creditor's remedy is limited to reimbursement for the cost of hiring that other party to perform;[82] and (3) the developing right to cure in the common law gives breaching parties a way at common law to avoid termination (though not damages for delay) and thereby also to avoid the non-delay portion of the damages that could come due if the contract is terminated because of the breach (in effect, the non-breacher may have a right only to cured performance and delay damages).[83] Still, as in the case of the bargain theory of consideration, I argue that the rhetorical or symbolic difference is large and reinforces the preference for the market-based political economy in the mind of the common law lawyer every time he or she works through the remedy system to make arguments or arrangements for a specific contract problem.

3. Termination of Contract for Serious Breach in French Law

My last example also concerns remedies for contract breach. This example also illustrates the greater degree to which French law appears to fit a more state-centered political economy.

In U.S. and U.K. law, but also in German law,[84] one contracting party's breach gives the other party the right to terminate the contract, at least if the breach is serious. The termination rules are not identical in these conditions, but they all differ from the French rule, which requires the non-breaching party to sue in court before he is released from his con-

---

[81] R. Schlesinger, et al., *supra* n. 21, at 757–758.
[82] For German law, B. Markesinis, et al., *supra* n. 47, at 388, 404 (discussing § 887 I ZPO).
[83] *See, e.g., id.* at 388–389.
[84] *Id.* at 388 (discussing § 323 BGB). But creditors must normally give extra time to perform, especially in German law. *Id.*

tinuing future obligations.[85] By comparison with the French rule, the rule allowing a party to terminate his performance because of the other side's breach obviously privatizes the management of breach situations. The French rule is based on the notion that the state may have an interest in the performance of the contract independent of the parties' interests. Therefore, a court has to authorize termination of a contract. For both of these reasons, the French rule fits a more state-centered political economy. It seems especially revealing that the French-style rule has remained attractive to a country like the Russian Federation, which while emerging from the socialist command economy of the former Soviet Union, has nonetheless not yet been able to liberalize and privatize its economy to the same extent as the Western European social welfare states. The parts of the Russian Civil Code adopted in the mid-1990s preserve the French-style rule requiring court-ordered termination.[86]

The presence of the state-centered version of the rule in French law, but not in German law, suggests a somewhat greater degree of state-centeredness in France than in Germany and therefore fits my argument that the French polity is somewhat more state-centered or "statist" than Germany. However, again the difference may be largely symbolic. After all, both French law and modern Russian law provide that a breach that amounts to a unilateral refusal to perform may give the other party the right to suspend performance unless the breaching party cures its repudiation by offering guarantees of performance.[87] Nonetheless, again I argue that the rhetorical differences are strong and they cause lawyers in the different legal systems to speak and act differently, and may well reinforce whatever predilections they have on the subject of political economy.

IV. What Should We Make of the Differences in Political Economy?

By this point, I hope I have established that differences in political economy relate to differences on at least some points of contact law. I am not

---

[85] B. Nicholas, *supra* n. 73, at 241–246 (discussing art. 1184 C. civ.); 4 J. Carbonnier, *supra* n. 42, §§ 185–190, at 339–347.

[86] Art. 450(2) *Grazhdanskii Kodeks* [Civil Code] RF (GK RF). *See also* A.L. Makovsky & S.A. Khokhlov, *Introductory Commentary to the Civil Code*, in The Civil Code of the Russian Federation lvi, xcvi (P. Maggs & A.N. Zhiltsov, eds. & trans., 1997)(explaining the state-centered policy behind Article 450).

[87] For French law, see B. Nicholas, *supra* n. 73, at 213–216 (referring to arts. 1612, 1613, 1253, 1704, & 1948 C. civ., but noting that the French courts have generalized the principle beyond the limits of those code sections). For Russian law, see Art. 328 GK RF; Makovsky & Khokhlov, *supra* n. 86, at xc.

arguing that the American political economy and its related contract law is better. Personally, I find much that is attractive in the continental European approach. But I am also not arguing that that approach is in any objective sense better, either. I don't believe that it is. Rather, I believe that each political economy is the product of that country's history. I am just trying to explain each legal culture to the other.

What follows from the connection with political economy, if I am right? First, some good news for the European project. If I am right that the United Kingdom has a political economy somewhere between that of the U.S. and that of continental Europe and that intermediate position is reflected in its legal system, including contract law, then it is much more conceivable that the U.K. can fully become part of the European Union than that the U.S. could. This argument suggests that we should not be misled by the labels "civil" and "common" law. The U.K. already has the same employee and consumer protections, roughly speaking, that Germany and France have. I have pointed to some aspects of contracts which show that in some fundamental ways – having to do with remedies and basic contract theory – the common law is more liberal than the civil law. I could point to many more examples. But these differences at the level of concept and basic theory do not necessarily create differences in practical result and to the extent that is true, the old fault line between civil and common law need not be a barrier to integration and harmonization of law.

But what about the more obvious differences in direct regulation that really do lead to different results, as in the difference between the approaches to the at will contract in the U.S. and in Europe? My second point is simply a plea for understanding; but *real* understanding, not just a loose and patronizing tolerance ("it may be alright for you, but not for us") that so often masks a complete lack of understanding or even outright derision.[88]

The problem is that political economy, while quite different from religion, nevertheless appears to be an aspect of our identity and personality that functions in an analogous way. There are no persuasive logical or empirical proofs that any particular point on the political economy spectrum is the best point. There are historical and philosophical reasons to think that the extreme points of the spectrum (the command economy or a completely laissez-faire regime) are not attractive.[89] But at least within the larger middle field from the more state-centered French model to the

---

[88] *See* n. 31 *supra* (U.S. reactions to French riots in the spring of 2006).

[89] I explore some of these limits on the degree to which the extreme points in the spectrum of political economy are compatible with democracy and the rule of law in *Export of the Rule of Law*, 13 Transnat'l. L. & Contemp. Probs. 429, 444–446 (2003).

more market-centered U.S. model and perhaps further in both directions, the choice comes down to a matter of belief. What is needed, therefore, as in instances of conflict over religious beliefs, is dialogue that is based on serious attempts to see the world through the eyes of the Other.

Consider, for example, the issue of at will employment. The U.S. position in favor of at will employment makes a great deal of sense if you believe that leaving employment markets unregulated will generally result in strong demand for workers. While no worker likes to be laid off, workers do not generally feel abused in a system of at will contracting if jobs are plentiful because if they lose one job, they are likely to find another on roughly the same terms. Employers like at will contracts under any market conditions because it gives them much more flexibility than they have under a regime where discharge is limited to cause, however defined. Many Americans argue that the unregulated approach can best be counted on to create new jobs because the regulated approach discourages employers from creating new jobs. The at will system, by contrast, encourages employers to experiment with hiring new employees to see if it can boost output and sales or otherwise take advantage of new market opportunities. If the new positions do not pay for themselves after a reasonable time, the employer can without cost discharge those employees and thus reduce its overall labor costs in a way that can prevent it from having to make undue sacrifice of profits.[90]

But critics of at will contracting can raise serious objections to this form of employment contract. Older workers in all countries have reason under an at will regime to fear that employers will fire older workers as soon as their wages rise under any system of seniority so that they can be replaced by younger, cheaper manpower. Moreover, all the arguments in favor of at will contracting depend on a rosy view of the power of the market to create jobs. Employees do not see their interests served by at will contracting if there are high joblessness rates so that laid off workers have poor job prospects; or if the relevant job markets are overwhelmed by guest workers; or if business loans are not readily available and stock markets do not function smoothly so that companies have difficulty raising capital and consequently are not really free to try new ventures that might create new jobs. Each of these factors is arguably a bigger matter of concern in some European countries than in the United States.

Similarly, one may doubt the power of the market to create new job opportunities if they are controlled by monopolies or oligarchies. Other more indirect factors may affect perceptions of the power of the markets to create new jobs. For example, how easy is it to move house and family

---

[90] This was the argument that French political leaders made to justify their ill-fated proposal to adopt at will employment for young, first-time employees on a limited basis. See text *supra* at n. 23.

for a new job? In the United States it appears to be in general easier to find a new apartment or to sell one's house and buy one in another city. In the United States, we have a long tradition, starting with patterns of westward movement to clear and settle new land, of letting the market move people around in great numbers. In Europe, people have not been as willing to let the market move them around. There appears to be, for many people, a greater attachment to the soil, or to city or village or family or *Stammtisch*. It does appear to be more difficult to find new apartments or to buy and sell housing in Europe. Under such conditions, the at will contract does not look so fair to employees, and it is perfectly understandable why they have fought for state regulation to eliminate at will employment.

It all comes down to the question: Whom or what do you trust? Do you tend to trust the creative force of business leaders and the markets or do you tend not to trust the market and therefore to prefer to trust in intervention in the market by various agents of the state? Most likely you do not trust anyone, but then the question is whom do you trust less? One has to choose some position on the political economy spectrum, and the position we choose probably tends to be the product of our people's history, personal experience, and the political economy of the institutional structures (including the law) under which we have lived.

I do not believe that we can all come to accept the same political economy, nor would such homogenization necessarily be a good thing. It may be a very good thing for the future of democratic governance in the world that there be maintained a spectrum of different political economies so that we can see in the different experiences of different countries the strengths and weaknesses of each type. But we can at least engage in respectful dialogue with each other about issues of political economy.

Dialogue can help us learn from each other. Through dialogue we can certainly identify aspects of our differences that are not impediments to cooperation or even harmonization. As I have already argued, the seemingly fundamental differences over consideration doctrine or contract remedies may not really be very difficult to bridge over because the differences are important more on the symbolic level than on the practical level. Picking apart differences to find common ground is always a valuable exercise.

Perhaps we can even borrow from each other in small ways without changing our overall political economy. France can experiment with the C.P.E. without abandoning its generally statist political economy. Without abandoning the at will contract, the U.S. can develop the public policy tort or the concept of the covenant of good faith and fair dealing to prevent employers from firing older employees in order to replace them with cheaper, younger workers. But there are limits to this approach. In general, it is not possible, I believe, to take only the good things about a particular political economy without also taking the bad things. To the extent at will employment is allowed, it leaves the employee unprotected. To the extent at will employment is prohibited by state regulation, the employer's flexibility is curtailed in a way that may inhibit new job formation. At the end of the day, we must accept that different nations will retain different political economies.

With respect to the significant differences in the degree of regulation that cannot be homogenized, the main way in which dialogue can help is simply by strengthening understanding. But this can happen only if dialogue is undertaken with a measure of modesty. In order to treat the Other's position with respect, one has to entertain seriously the notion that the other position may be at least as rational as one's own. It does not mean that you have to doubt your own position, but you have to avoid such pride that you refuse to consider the serious arguments and the different, but rational premises which might lead one to accept the other position. Only then can we talk of true understanding, on issues of religion or political economy. And if we do that, I claim that we can come to a much better understanding – a truly sympathetic understanding – of each other's legal systems, as well as of each other's overall political economies.

Remarques sur la proposition de règlement de la Commission européenne sur la loi applicable aux obligations contractuelles (Rome I)[*]

Paul Lagarde (Paris)

La proposition présentée par la Commission européenne le 15 décembre 2005[1] d'un règlement « Rome I » destiné à se substituer à la convention de Rome du 19 juin 1980 sur la loi applicable aux obligations contractuelles était attendue depuis longtemps,[2] particulièrement, après la publication en janvier 2003 d'un livre vert sur le sujet et les nombreuses réponses qui lui ont été apportées et que l'on a pu découvrir sur le site de la Commission.[3] Cette proposition apparaît cependant au moment où viennent d'entrer en vigueur les protocoles du 19 décembre 1988 relatifs à l'interprétation de la convention par la Cour de justice[4] et où vient de disparaître de ce fait l'un des principaux arguments en faveur du reformatage de la convention en règlement.

---

[*] Article publié dans la *Revue critique de droit international privé* (ci-après *RCDIP*), 2006.331 et reproduit avec l'aimable autorisation de celle-ci.
[1] Document COM(2005) 650 final, 2005/0261 (COD).
[2] Cf notre article « Vers une révision de la convention de Rome sur la loi applicable aux obligations contractuelles », *Mélanges Yves Guyon*, Dalloz, 2003, p. 571–586.
[3] Les deux réponses de caractère académique dans lesquelles la Commission semble avoir le plus volontiers puisé, avant ou après le livre vert, sont celle du GEDIP (consultable sur son site et, pour certains de ses éléments, *RCDIP*, 2000.929 et 2001.774) et celle du Max-Planck-Institut de Hambourg (*RabelsZ*, 2004.1-118).
[4] Après la ratification par la Belgique du second protocole, le premier protocole est enfin entré en vigueur le 1er août 2004. En vertu de ce protocole, les juridictions suprêmes des Etats membres ainsi que les juridictions statuant en appel peuvent demander à la Cour de justice de statuer à titre préjudiciel sur une question d'interprétation de la convention, alors qu'en vertu de l'article 68 du traité CE, seules les juridictions nationales « dont les décisions ne sont pas susceptibles d'un recours juridictionnel de droit interne » pourront interroger la Cour sur l'interprétation du règlement, pris sur la base de l'article 65 du traité.

La base juridique de la proposition est l'article 65 b du traité CE, combiné avec l'article 67 § 5 second tiret (issu du traité de Nice), permettant l'adoption par la procédure de codécision des mesures visant à « favoriser la compatibilité des règles applicables dans les États membres en matière de conflits de lois et de compétence », « dans la mesure nécessaire au bon fonctionnement du marché intérieur ». Sans reprendre ici la discussion, on notera avec satisfaction que la Commission, dans un souci de sécurité juridique, a choisi la voie du règlement et non celle de la directive. On appréciera également que la notion de bon fonctionnement du marché intérieur ait été entendue largement et n'ait pas conduit la Commission à limiter, sauf exceptions sur lesquelles on reviendra[5] sa proposition aux conflits de lois intracommunautaires.[6] Les rapports commerciaux avec des entreprises établies dans des Etats tiers peuvent évidemment affecter le marché intérieur et il est logique que la règle de conflit soit la même dans toutes ces situations.[7]

Dès lors que la décision était prise de remplacer la convention par un règlement, la question se posait de savoir quelles modifications lui apporter quant au fond. Il allait de soi que devaient disparaître les dispositions prévoyant la possibilité pour les Etats contractants de faire des réserves (art. 22) ou d'adopter pour une catégorie particulière de contrats des règles de conflit dérogatoires (art. 23), ainsi que les clauses finales liées à la nature conventionnelle de cet instrument. Il était bon également de combler certaines lacunes laissées ouvertes par les négociateurs de la convention, faute d'avoir pu trouver un accord entre eux, peut-être parce que la réflexion n'avait pas encore suffisamment progressé. Il était sans doute également opportun de corriger certains défauts de la convention, au demeurant mineurs, de l'adapter aux développements technologiques survenus depuis sa conclusion, principalement à l'expansion du commerce électronique, et de mettre le nouveau texte en harmonie avec le règlement Bruxelles I[8] et le futur règlement Rome II.[9] Sur ces points, la Commission n'a pas failli à la tâche.

Mais fallait-il aller plus loin et reconsidérer les bases mêmes d'une convention qui avait fait ses preuves et qui a servi de modèle hors de

---

[5] *Infra*, p. 13 et 20.

[6] La proposition reprend l'article 2 de la convention. La loi désignée par le règlement s'appliquera même si elle n'est pas celle d'un Etat membre.

[7] On peut observer, parallèlement, que le règlement Bruxelles I s'applique même si le demandeur est domicilié dans un pays tiers (CJCE 13 juil. 2000, *Group Josi*, aff. C-406/92, *Rec.* I-5925, concl. Fennelly, *Rev. gén. dr. ass.* 2000.931, note V. Heuzé, JDI 2002.623, obs. F. L).

[8] Règlement n° 44/2001 du 22 déc. 2000, *RCDIP*, 2001.188.

[9] Proposition présentée par la Commission le 21 février 2006, document COM(2006)83 final 2003/0168(COD).

l'Union à un nombre impressionnant de textes législatifs ? La Commission a cru pouvoir le faire, en invoquant certes de bonnes raisons, comme le souci de renforcer la sécurité juridique ou, dans un ordre d'idées différent, l'autonomie de la volonté. Prises une par une, chacune des innovations de la proposition peut être défendue avec de bons arguments et certaines mêmes avec de très bons arguments. Mais si l'on considère la proposition de règlement dans son ensemble, on ne voit plus très bien à quelle idée directrice il obéit, on décèle même quelques contradictions de méthode et l'on ne retrouve pas ce qui faisait la cohérence de la convention de Rome du 19 juin 1980. C'est ce que l'on voudrait faire apparaître en parcourant successivement les nouveautés affectant le champ d'application du règlement, la détermination de la loi applicable, le domaine de la loi applicable et les dispositions générales.

I. Champ d'application

Quelques retouches intéressantes sont apportées à l'article 1er de la convention. A l'instar de l'article 1er de la proposition modifiée Rome II et du règlement Bruxelles I, il est précisé au premier paragraphe que le nouveau règlement s'appliquera en matière civile et commerciale, à l'exclusion des matières fiscales, douanières et administratives. Il faudra s'attendre à certaines difficultés de qualification, à propos notamment des contrats de travail de l'Administration, pour lesquels la jurisprudence française admet l'application de la convention de Rome, mais refuse depuis peu la compétence des tribunaux administratifs.[10]

La liste des exclusions (§§ 2 et 3) est reconduite, à l'exception du pouvoir de représentation de l'intermédiaire, qui fait désormais l'objet d'une règle de conflit spéciale,[11] et des contrats d'assurances, pour lesquels subsiste néanmoins le renvoi, en annexe, aux indigestes règles de conflit contenues dans les directives assurances de la seconde génération[12]. L'exclusion des obligations contractuelles découlant des relations de famille est étendue aux obligations découlant des « *relations qui, conformé-*

---

[10] Cons. d'Etat 19 nov. 1999, *Tegos*, RCDIP, 2000.409, concl. Arrighi de Casanova, note S. Lemaire, JDI 2000.742, note J.F. Flauss ; Trib. Confl. 22 oct. 2001, *Bull.*, n° 20, p. 29, RCDIP, 2002.Som.822. V. Mathias AUDIT, « Les contrats de travail conclus par l'Administration à l'étranger », RCDIP, 2002.39 et s.

[11] Article 7, *v. infra*, p. 15.

[12] Deuxièmes Directives modifiées « assurance non vie » et « assurance vie », respectivement du 22 juin 1988 et du 8 novembre 1990, RCDIP, 1989.144 et la note, 1991.204.

ment à la loi qui leur est applicable, produisent des effets similaires ».[13] Cette terminologie se réfère évidemment aux partenariats enregistrés. Telle qu'elle est formulée, cette exclusion ne paraît toutefois pas couvrir les partenariats-contrats, comme le PACS français, la cohabitation légale belge ou le partenariat luxembourgeois, qui ne produisent pas d'effets similaires au mariage.[14] Est-ce bien le résultat cherché ? Veut-on vraiment, comme cela fut un moment proposé,[15] soumettre les obligations découlant du PACS, voire sa conclusion, à la convention de Rome, alors que progresse en droit comparé l'idée d'un rattachement à la loi de l'Etat d'enregistrement ? Une clarification serait ici hautement souhaitable.

L'innovation la plus remarquable est l'exclusion formelle des « *obligations résultant d'une relation précontractuelle* » (art. 1er § 2 i). La solution, discutée en droit comparé,[16] est en harmonie avec la jurisprudence intervenue à l'occasion des articles 5-1 et 5-3 de la convention de Bruxelles sur la notion d'obligation contractuelle.[17] Elle est globale, en ce qu'elle exclut du domaine du règlement tous les cas de responsabilité précontractuelle, que celle-ci soit encourue pour rupture de pourparlers, violation de

---

[13] Art. 1er, § 2 b et c. Le texte correspondant de la proposition modifiée Rome II emploie l'adjectif « comparables » à la place de « similaires ».

[14] Les textes récents de droit international privé marquent bien l'opposition entre les partenariats-mariages et les partenariats-contrats. Alors que la loi néerlandaise du 6 juillet 2004 sur les conflits de lois en matière de partenariat enregistré (*RCDIP*, 2005.538) ne prévoit la reconnaissance d'un partenariat enregistré à l'étranger que s' « il crée entre les partenaires des obligations qui correspondent en substance à celles qui découlent du mariage » (art. 2 § 5 c), ce qui exclut le PACS, le code belge de droit international privé (loi 16 juillet 2004, *RCDIP*, 2005.154) précise au contraire en son article 58 que « les termes 'relation de vie commune' visent une situation de vie commune donnant lieu à enregistrement par une autorité publique et ne créant pas entre les cohabitants de lien équivalent au mariage », ce qui exclut cette fois les partenariats-mariages.

[15] V. M. REVILLARD, « Le pacte civil de solidarité en droit international privé », *Defrénois*, 2000, art. 37124. Dans la 6ème édition (2006) de *Droit international privé et communautaire. Pratique notariale*, Mme Revillard semble se rallier à la loi de l'Etat d'enregistrement (n° 169).

[16] V. des éléments de droit comparé dans la note Rémy-Courlay sous CJCE 17 sept. 2002, *RCDIP*, 2003.668, spéc. p. 676.

[17] CJCE 17 septembre 2002, *Tacconi*, aff. C-334/00, *RCDIP*, 2003.668, note P. Rémy-Corlay, *IPRax* 2003.143 et note Mankowski, p. 127. Selon cet arrêt, en l'absence d'engagements librement assumés par une partie envers une autre, la responsabilité précontractuelle invoquée à l'occasion des négociations visant à la formation d'un contrat pour violation de l'obligation d'agir de bonne foi dans le cadre de ces négociations relève de la matière délictuelle ou quasi-délictuelle au sens de l'article 5, point 3 de la convention de Bruxelles.

l'obligation précontractuelle de renseignement, divulgation d'informations confidentielles obtenues au cours des négociations, etc. Le Max-Planck-Institut avait proposé d'exclure de l'exclusion les conséquences légales de la rupture de pourparlers et de les soumettre à la loi du contrat envisagé.[18] La Commission n'a pas voulu dissocier sur ce point la solution du conflit de lois et celle du conflit de juridictions et l'on peut approuver ce souci de simplification.

II. Détermination de la loi applicable

Si l'on met de côté les contrats de consommation et le contrat de travail qui appelaient des solutions particulières en vue d'assurer la protection de la partie faible, on peut dire que l'originalité de la convention de Rome était de poser des règles générales de conflits de lois reposant sur deux principes cardinaux, l'autonomie de la volonté et le principe de proximité. La proposition de règlement rompt cet équilibre. Le principe de l'autonomie de la volonté subsiste, quelque peu aménagé, mais privé de son complément. En effet, au principe de proximité succède une liste de solutions particulières, dont le lien de cohérence n'est pas évident.

1. Le remodelage de l'autonomie de la volonté (art. 3)

L'autonomie de la volonté reste le « principe clé » de la proposition, mais l'article 3 de la convention est modifié sur trois points importants.

a. Le choix tacite de la loi applicable

Les auteurs de la proposition ont voulu renforcer la sécurité juridique en posant la présomption que le choix par les parties du tribunal ou des tribunaux d'un Etat membre implique également le choix de la loi de cet Etat. Cette solution, soutenue en Allemagne,[19] est à notre sens très contestable. Les parties qui prennent la peine de choisir un for savent normalement qu'elles auraient pu choisir aussi la loi applicable. Si elles ne l'ont pas fait, l'interprétation de volonté la plus vraisemblable est qu'elles s'en remettent au droit international privé de l'Etat dont relève le tribunal élu. Plutôt que d'insérer cette présomption source de confusion,

---

[18] *RabelsZ* 2004, p. 89 ; dans le même sens, P. Rémy-Corlay, note préc., p. 679 et s.; H. STOLL, *Festschrift Apostolos Georgiades*, 2006, 941 et s., 950.
[19] MARTINY in *Münchener Kommentar zum BGB*, t. 10, 4ème éd. 2006, *ad* Art. 27 EGBGB, n° 48, p. 1696.

il aurait été plus opportun de réduire les divergences linguistiques bien connues de la convention de Rome sur le degré de certitude requis du choix tacite de la loi applicable. On est tout de même surpris que les trois versions connues de la proposition continuent à diverger. La seconde phrase de l'article 3 § 1er de la proposition mentionne, en français, un choix résultant « de façon certaine » des dispositions du contrat, du comportement des parties[20] ou des circonstances de la cause. Les mots entre guillemets se lisent dans la version anglaise « *with reasonable certainty* » et dans la version allemande « *mit hinreichender Sicherheit* », ce qui est à l'évidence fort différent.

b. Le choix d'un droit non étatique

Répondant aux souhaits exprimés par certains,[21] la proposition permet aux parties de choisir également « *comme loi applicable des principes et règles de droit matériel des contrats, reconnus au niveau international ou communautaire* ». Et elle ajoute, en reprenant les termes de l'article 7 § 2 de la convention de Vienne sur la vente internationale de marchandises, que « *les questions concernant les matières régies par ces principes ou règles et qui ne sont pas expressément tranchées par eux seront réglées selon les principes généraux dont ils s'inspirent ou, à défaut de ces principes, conformément à la loi applicable à défaut de choix en vertu du présent règlement* » (art. 3 § 2). Il s'agit là d'un choix délibéré de politique juridique, effectué avec une certaine modération,[22] dont nous voudrions seulement examiner ici comment il peut fonctionner.

Selon l'exposé des motifs, cette formulation « vise à autoriser notamment le choix des Principes UNIDROIT, des *Principles of European Contract Law* ou d'un éventuel futur instrument communautaire optionnel, tout en interdisant le choix de la *lex mercatoria*, insuffisamment précise, ou de codifications privées qui ne seraient pas suffisamment reconnues par la communauté internationale ». Si l'intention est à peu près claire, la formulation l'est beaucoup moins et l'on peut légitimement se demander quel est le critère qui permettra d'affirmer que les principes ou

---

[20] La mention du comportement des parties, qui ne figure pas dans la convention de Rome, pourrait permettre au juge de conclure à un accord procédural concernant la loi applicable.

[21] V. notamment en France, J.-P. BERAUDO, « Faut-il avoir peur du contrat sans loi? », *Mél. P. Lagarde*, 2005, p. 93 et s.

[22] Cette ouverture sur un droit non étatique est limitée à l'hypothèse d'un choix de loi par les parties et ne déborde pas sur la détermination du droit objectivement applicable. La proposition se garde des excès à cet égard de la convention interaméricaine de Mexico du 17 mars 1994 (*RCDIP*, 1995.173).

règles de droit matériel choisis sont reconnus par la communauté internationale et qui en décidera.[23]

On peut aussi se demander quelle est la portée de cette liberté nouvelle donnée aux parties. La convention de Rome ne considérait pas comme illicite le choix d'un droit non étatique. Elle considérait simplement qu'un tel choix n'était pas un choix de droit international privé et qu'il appartenait donc à la loi objectivement applicable de définir la place qu'elle pouvait accorder aux règles non étatiques choisies par les parties.[24] Les Principes UNIDROIT paraissaient bien confirmer cette vue, puisque, selon leur article 1-4, « Ces Principes ne limitent pas l'application des règles impératives d'origine nationale, internationale ou supranationale, applicables selon les règles pertinentes du droit international privé ». C'est donc qu'ils ne valent que dans les limites du droit impératif de la loi étatique objectivement applicable. Si désormais ces règles non étatiques pouvaient être choisies « comme loi applicable », il faudrait les détacher de l'emprise de la loi objectivement applicable, mise hors jeu par ce choix de droit international privé, et n'en limiter l'application que dans le cas de contrariété manifeste à l'ordre public international de la loi du for.[25] Dans un ordre d'idées un peu différent, si le choix des parties portait sur une convention internationale de droit matériel, comme par exemple en matière de connaissement la convention de Bruxelles non révisée de 1924, qui ne prévoirait pas une telle désignation et qui ne serait pas applicable *in casu* en vertu de ses propres dispositions, ce choix devrait l'emporter sur les dispositions impératives de la loi objectivement applicable.[26]

c. La réserve des lois de police et des dispositions impératives du droit communautaire

La proposition maintient opportunément à l'article 8 la réserve des lois de police, dans une rédaction très proche de celle de l'article 7 de la convention de Rome. Elle en donne même une définition, qui reprend à la fois leur justification de fond, dans les termes mêmes de Francescakis[27] et leur mode unilatéral d'application. Il est heureux que la limitation un instant

---

[23] V. la même interrogation sous la plume de P. MANKOWSKI, « Der Vorschlag für die Rom-Verordnung », *IPRax* 2006.101 et s., 102.

[24] V. nos observations, *RCDIP*, 1991.300–301.

[25] Comp. J.-P. BERAUDO, art. préc., n° 17, p. 104.

[26] C'est l'hypothèse de la clause *Paramount*, v. Com. 4 fév. 1992, *Karkaba*, *RCDIP*, 1992.495 et la note.

[27] Ph. FRANCESCAKIS, « Quelques précisions sur les 'lois d'application immédiate' et leurs rapports avec les règles de conflits de lois », *RCDIP*, 1966. 1 et s.

envisagée[28] de ne donner effet qu'aux lois de police d'un Etat membre ait été abandonnée, car le problème auquel répond cette disposition est le même, qu'il s'agisse des lois de police d'un Etat membre ou de celles d'un Etat tiers.

La proposition ajoute une autre limite, celle-ci nouvelle, à l'autonomie de la volonté en prévoyant que « le choix par les parties de la loi d'un Etat non membre ne peut pas porter atteinte à l'application des dispositions impératives du droit communautaire lorsqu'elles seraient applicables au cas d'espèce » (art. 3 § 5). Cette disposition viserait, selon l'exposé des motifs, à prévenir la fraude au droit communautaire. La formule est excessive, car il n'y a pas fraude à éluder une disposition simplement impérative du droit objectivement applicable, en faisant choix d'une loi qui ne la connaît pas. En réalité, cette disposition revient à ériger toute disposition simplement impérative du droit communautaire,[29] dès lors qu'elle serait objectivement applicable, en une disposition internationalement impérative, autrement dit en une loi de police. C'est ce qu'avait fait naguère la Cour de justice dans un arrêt controversé, en imposant l'application de la directive sur les agents commerciaux à un contrat liant un agent du Royaume-Uni à un commettant de Californie, malgré le choix par les parties de la loi californienne.[30] On peut regretter cette orientation. Autant il est légitime, dans un contrat intracommunautaire, d'imposer aux parties l'application des règles impératives du droit communautaire, par extension de la règle posée à l'article 3 § 3 de la convention de Rome, car un contrat intracommunautaire est un contrat interne au regard du droit matériel communautaire, autant il est contestable, dans les relations extracommunautaires, de refuser toute coordination avec le droit des Etats tiers en imposant unilatéralement l'application du droit communautaire. Un auteur averti a vu dans cette attitude de fermeture aux droits des pays tiers la caractéristique d'un ordre juridique encore « immature ».[31]

---

[28] Et dont la trace subsiste dans l'exposé des motifs.

[29] C'est-à-dire toute disposition à laquelle les parties ne peuvent déroger par contrat. V. par ex. l'article 19 de la directive agents commerciaux n° 86/653 du 18 déc. 1986.

[30] CJCE 9 nov. 2000, *Ingmar*, RCDIP, 2001.107, note L. Idot. *Adde* L. Bernardeau, « Droit communautaire et lois de police. A la suite de l'arrêt CJCE, 9 nov. 2000, Ingmar, aff. C-381/98 », JCP 2001.I.328 ; Wilderspin et Lewis, « Les relations entre le droit communautaire et les règles de conflit de lois des Etats membres », RCDIP, 2002, p. 1 et s., 289 et s., spéc. 295 et s.

[31] H. GAUDEMET-TALLON, *Le pluralisme en droit international privé. Richesses et Faiblesses, Cours général de droit international privé*, Rec. Cours La Haye, 2005, n° 274, p. 269 et les nombreuses références. V. également, redoutant l'érection en lois de police de l'ensemble des directives de rapprochement des législations,

La règle proposée par la Commission n'est pas destinée à s'appliquer aux contrats de consommation, sauf à la marge, puisque l'article 5 de la proposition prévoit déjà pour eux un rattachement impératif, mais elle pourrait limiter le choix de loi en tout domaine contractuel où intervient le droit communautaire, notamment, pour ne prendre qu'un exemple, pour les contrats de garantie financière.[32]

2. L'émiettement du rattachement objectif (art. 4 à 7)

a. La règle de principe (si l'on peut dire) de l'article 4

Dans la convention de Rome, sauf pour les contrats de consommation qui obéissent à une logique de protection de la partie faible, le rattachement objectif repose sur le principe de proximité. Ce principe est proclamé au § 1er de l'article 4, il est concrétisé par des présomptions dont la plus importante désigne la résidence habituelle de la partie débitrice de la prestation caractéristique (§ 2) et il est enfin rappelé au § 5 sous la forme de la clause d'exception. Ainsi avait-on cherché à concilier sécurité juridique et flexibilité, afin de parvenir à la justice du résultat. On a pu reprocher à cette insistance mise sur le principe de proximité au début et à la fin de l'article 4 d'affaiblir les présomptions contenues aux paragraphes 2 à 4 et d'inciter les juges à rechercher directement la loi du pays avec lequel le contrat présentait les liens les plus étroits.[33] C'est pourquoi le GEDIP avait proposé de supprimer le § 1er de l'article 4, d'indiquer directement que le contrat est régi, à défaut de choix, par la loi du pays où est située la résidence habituelle de la partie qui doit fournir la prestation caractéristique, éventuellement dans un souci pédagogique d'indiquer pour certains grands contrats quelle est la prestation caractéristique, et de conserver la clause d'exception.

La proposition de la Commission s'engage dans une tout autre voie. Elle répudie toute flexibilité au nom de la sécurité juridique. L'article 4 § 1 édicte une règle de rattachement fixe pour huit contrats nommés,

---

L. IDOT, note précitée sous l'arrêt *Ingmar*, RCDIP, 2001, p. 115 ; E. PATAUT, « Lois de police et ordre juridique commuautaire » in *Le conflit de lois et le système juridique communautaire*, Dalloz, 2004, p. 117 et s., 121.

[32] V. la directive 2002/47 du 6 juin 2002, art. 9, RCDIP, 2002.880.

[33] Comme l'a fait bien à tort, en matière de transport maritime, Com. 4 mars 2003, RCDIP, 2003.285 et la note, spéc. p. 292–293, DMF 2003.556, obs. Ph. Delebecque, JCP 2004.II.10071, note A. Sinay-Cytermann. Sur la critique mentionnée au texte, v. DICEY-MORRIS, *The Conflict of Laws*, 13ème éd., 2000, n° 32-123 et s.

supprime la clause d'exception[34] et ne recourt au critère de la prestation caractéristique et au principe de proximité qu'à titre très subsidiaire, pour les contrats non nommés (§ 2). Cette fixité n'est pas satisfaisante et donne l'impression, sur le plan de la méthode, d'un retour aux années soixante, à l'époque de la rédaction des lois de droit international privé de Tchécoslovaquie et de Pologne.

En premier lieu, les rattachements retenus ne sont pas tous fondés sur la même idée et peuvent de ce fait paraître arbitraires. Les plus nombreux reposent heureusement sur l'idée de proximité, concrétisée soit par la résidence habituelle du débiteur de la prestation caractéristique (lettres a,b,c, e et f[35]), soit par la localisation de l'immeuble objet du contrat (lettre d). Mais on comprend moins bien que les contrats de franchise et de distribution (lettres g et h) soient rattachés aux lois respectives du franchisé et du distributeur, contrairement à la solution qui avait fini par prévaloir en France.[36] L'exposé des motifs justifie ce rattachement par le souci de « protéger le franchisé et le distributeur en tant que parties faibles ». La généralisation paraît bien hâtive, quand on connaît la puissance économique de certains distributeurs.

En second lieu, le rattachement fixe de ces huit contrats à une loi déterminée, sans les possibilités d'adaptation que donne la clause d'exception, risque de conduire à des solutions malencontreuses. Prenons l'exemple de la vente. La convention de La Haye du 15 juin 1955 ne comporte pas de clause générale d'exception, mais les exceptions qu'elle apporte à la compétence de principe de la loi du vendeur remplissent la même fonction. Par exemple, les ventes en bourse ou les ventes aux enchères sont soumises, selon l'article 3, dernier alinéa de cette convention, à la loi du

---

[34] Qui subsiste cependant pour le contrat de travail, v. art. 6.

[35] Respectivement les contrats de vente, prestation de services, transport, location temporaire d'immeuble et contrat portant sur la propriété intellectuelle ou industrielle. Pour le transport, personne ne regrettera la présomption alambiquée et lacunaire de l'article 4 § 4 de la convention de Rome. Pour la location temporaire, le texte reprend opportunément la formulation du règlement Bruxelles I (art. 22 , point 1, al. 2).

[36] Pour le contrat de distribution, Com. 15 mai 2001, *Optelec*, RCDIP, 2002.86 et la note, JDI 2001.1121, note A. Huet, JCP 2001.II.10634, note J. Raynard , D. 2002.198, note C. Diloy et 1397, obs. B. Audit, *Lamy Dr. Des affaires*, fév. 2002, n°2898, p. 5, note H. Kenfack; 25 nov. 2003, RCDIP, 2004.102 et la note, JDI 2004.1179, note M.-E. Ancel, D.2004.474, note H. Kenfack, JCP 2004.II.10046, note J. Raynard. Approuvant la solution de la proposition de règlement, v. H. KENFACK, « Rome I et contrats de distribution : protéger les intérêts des distributeurs sans léser les fournisseurs », JCP éd. G , 25 janv. 2006, act. 31.

pays où se trouve la bourse ou dans lequel sont effectuées les enchères.[37] Faudra-t-il désormais renoncer à ces solutions de bon sens au nom de la sécurité juridique ? Et, plus généralement, faut-il avoir peur de la vie et des situations inattendues qu'elle réserve, en bloquant par avance toute possibilité d'adaptation des règles posées, notamment dans les situations bien connues de contrats liés à d'autres ? Le GEDIP comme le Max-Planck-Institut de Hambourg avaient l'un et l'autre proposé simplement de renforcer la formulation de la clause d'exception, afin de dissuader les juges d'y recourir par facilité. Une telle solution serait en effet préférable.[38]

En troisième lieu, le confinement du principe de proximité à un rôle subsidiaire a pour effet de supprimer, au moins formellement, un autre élément de souplesse qu'est actuellement la possibilité de dépeçage du contrat par le juge, dans le cas où une partie du contrat est séparable du reste du contrat et présente un lien plus étroit avec un autre pays.[39]

b. Règles spéciales à certains contrats

La proposition consacre, comme la convention de Rome, un article aux contrats de consommation et un autre au contrat de travail. Elle y ajoute un article sur les contrats de représentation.

aa. Contrats de consommation

L'article 5 de la convention de Rome repose sur une limitation de l'autonomie de la volonté, qui ne peut avoir pour effet de priver le consommateur des dispositions protectrices de la loi du pays de sa résidence habituelle, et sur un rattachement objectif à cette même loi. Le texte, élaboré à une époque où la protection juridique du consommateur était encore à ses débuts, était imparfait, en ce qu'il se limitait à certains contrats et que la protection n'était assurée que si le contrat avait été conclu dans certaines circonstances énumérées limitativement.

---

[37] Ces exceptions sont au contraire prévues à l'article 7 pour les contrats d'intermédiaires.
[38] Comp. les observations dans le même sens, à propos de la suppression de la clause d'exception dans la proposition de règlement Rome II, de C. NOURISSAT et de E. TREPPOZ, *JDI* 2003.28 ; H. GAUDEMET-TALLON, *Le pluralisme en droit international privé, richesses et faiblesses*, Cours général, Rec. Cours La Haye, 2005, p. 337 et s.
[39] Convention de Rome, art. 4, § 1, 2ème phrase.

La proposition s'efforce de remédier à ces défauts, mais au prix d'un bouleversement du système de la convention et d'une réduction critiquable du domaine de la règle.

La proposition précise opportunément que le cocontractant du consommateur[40] agit dans l'exercice de son activité professionnelle, ce qui a pour effet d'écarter du champ de l'article 5 les contrats entre particuliers.[41] Tout aussi heureusement, elle élargit le domaine de l'article 5 quant aux contrats auxquels il s'applique. Concrètement, cet élargissement permettra de protéger le consommateur qui contracte un crédit, même si ce crédit n'est pas lié au financement d'une fourniture de marchandises ou de services, ou qui procède à des investissements en valeurs mobilières proposés par sa banque,[42] ou qui contracte une assurance. Mais on peut regretter que la proposition maintienne une importante liste de contrats auxquels l'article 5 ne s'appliquera pas : ce sont d'abord les contrats de fournitures de services lorsque les services dus au consommateur doivent être fournis exclusivement dans un pays autre que celui de sa résidence habituelle. Mais pourquoi le consommateur ayant sa résidence habituelle à Paris qui loue à l'agence parisienne d'une chaîne étrangère une voiture à prendre et à rapporter à un aéroport étranger ne serait-il pas protégé au même titre que s'il prenait livraison de la voiture en France ? Sont également exclus les contrats de transport,[43] ce qui ne peut s'expliquer que par la pression des professionnels de la branche. Enfin, si l'on comprend l'exclusion des ventes d'immeubles, car il s'agit là d'opérations lourdes et soumises à un formalisme en lui-même protecteur, on doit regretter que l'exclusion couvre les baux immobiliers, notamment à usage d'habitation, qui affectent le consommateur dans sa vie quotidienne. On pourrait objecter que le bail immobilier sera normalement régi par la loi de situation de l'immeuble (art. 4 § 1 d de la proposition) qui correspondra à celle de la résidence habituelle du locataire, en tout cas dans le futur, mais pourquoi priver ce locataire de la protection que lui assure la loi de l'Etat où est située sa résidence habituelle au moment de la conclusion du contrat ?

La proposition abandonne l'énoncé des trois circonstances décrivant le consommateur passif digne de protection. La pratique, notamment en Al-

---

[40] Lequel agit « pour un usage pouvant être considéré comme étranger à son activité professionnelle ».

[41] Solution souhaitée par la doctrine, v. pour le règlement Bruxelles I, H. GAUDEMET-TALLON, *Compétence et exécution des jugements en Europe*, 3ème éd. 2002, n° 283.

[42] Cf rapport Giuliano-Lagarde, *ad* art. 5, n° 2, selon qui les ventes de titres sont exclues du domaine de l'article 5.

[43] Sauf les voyages à forfait au sens de la directive 90/314 du 26 octobre 1994.

lemagne les affaires de la Grande Canarie,[44] en avait montré les insuffisances. Pour tenir compte du commerce électronique, le texte proposé par la Commission reprend à juste titre celui de l'article 15 § 1 c du règlement Bruxelles I.[45] Il réserve cependant le cas où le professionnel ignorait, sans imprudence de sa part, le lieu de la résidence habituelle du consommateur.[46]

En dehors de ces aménagements, la proposition apporte deux bouleversements à l'économie générale de l'article 5. Le plus spectaculaire est de supprimer complètement l'autonomie de la volonté en la matière et de rattacher impérativement les contrats de consommation à la loi de l'Etat de la résidence habituelle du consommateur, à la manière de l'article 120 de la loi suisse de droit international privé. Mais, comme un auteur suisse a pu le remarquer, « il n'est pas sûr qu'une interdiction aussi absolue [de l'autonomie de la volonté] serve nécessairement et toujours les intérêts du consommateur »[47]. L'exposé des motifs de la proposition semble considérer comme un mal absolu ce qu'elle appelle le dépeçage, c'est-à-dire l'application simultanée de la loi choisie par les parties et de la loi de la résidence habituelle du consommateur.[48] Et, pour l'éviter, elle préfère l'application d'une seule loi, qui est celle du consommateur, réputée lui être plus favorable. Si l'objectif de l'article 5 est, comme on l'avait cru jusqu'ici, de protéger le consommateur, on ne peut échapper à un système de comparaison des législations. Encore faut-il que les termes à comparer soient judicieusement déterminés. L'article 5 de la convention de Rome mettait en concurrence la loi choisie et celle de la résidence habituelle du consommateur. Si celle-ci était peu protectrice du consommateur, l'intérêt du fournisseur était de ne faire aucun choix de loi. Pour éviter cette situation, le GEDIP avait proposé de laisser s'appliquer la règle de droit commun des articles 3 et 4 (loi choisie ou loi du fournisseur) et de la mettre en concurrence avec la loi éventuellement plus favorable de l'Etat de la résidence habituelle du consommateur. Il est regrettable que ce système efficacement protecteur n'ait pas été retenu.

Le second bouleversement, celui-ci très étonnant, apporté par la proposition est de limiter la protection au consommateur qui a sa résidence ha-

---

[44] Cf BGH 19 mars 1997, RCDIP, 1998.610 et la note.

[45] « Contrat conclu avec un professionnel qui exerce des activités commerciales ou professionnelles dans l'Etat membre de la résidence habituelle du consommateur ou qui, par tout moyen, dirige ses activités vers cet Etat membre ou vers plusieurs pays dont cet Etat membre » (art. 5 § 2, al. 2).

[46] Le texte français de la proposition comporte ici une disgracieuse faute de syntaxe, en faisant suivre de l'indicatif la locution « à moins que ».

[47] B. DUTOIT, *Droit international privé suisse. Commentaire de la loi fédérale du 18 décembre 1987*, 4ème éd. 2005, ad art. 120, n°7.

[48] Dépeçage qu'elle maintient pourtant sans état d'âme pour le contrat de travail.

bituelle dans un Etat membre. L'exposé des motifs ne fournit aucune explication à ce sujet.[49] Comment comprendre cette règle à caractère unilatéraliste[50] peu en harmonie avec les autres dispositions de la proposition ? Si le consommateur a sa résidence habituelle dans un Etat tiers, veut-on, en raisonnant de manière unilatéraliste, laisser s'appliquer la loi de celui-ci si elle se veut applicable ? Veut-on plutôt, l'article 5 étant écarté, laisser s'appliquer les articles 3 et 4, donc la loi choisie par les parties (c'est-à-dire par le professionnel) ou la loi du professionnel ? On le voit, cette discrimination selon la résidence habituelle du consommateur n'a pas de justification. Il serait facile de la corriger, mais alors le rattachement impératif à la loi de la résidence habituelle du consommateur révèlerait sa face sombre en privant de protection les consommateurs ayant la mauvaise fortune de résider dans un Etat non protecteur.

bb. Contrat de travail

Par contraste avec l'article 5, l'article 6 de la proposition maintient intégralement, tout en l'améliorant, la structure de l'article 6 de la convention de Rome. Le système de la comparaison des législations (entre la loi choisie et la loi objectivement applicable) et la clause d'exception, rejetés plus haut, sont ici confirmés. L'autonomie de la volonté, limitée par les dispositions impératives de la loi objectivement applicable est donc maintenue. La loi objectivement applicable est encore, comme dans la convention de Rome et sous réserve de la clause d'exception, la loi du pays où le travailleur accomplit habituellement son travail ou, s'il n'accomplit pas habituellement son travail dans un même pays, la loi du pays où se trouve l'établissement d'embauche du travailleur.

Les améliorations apportées au texte sont celles qui avaient été suggérées tant par le GEDIP que par le Max-Planck-Institut[51] et doivent être approuvées. Le texte assimile au lieu d'accomplissement habituel du travail le lieu « à partir duquel » le travailleur accomplit habituellement son

---

[49] L'hypothèse d'une copie inattentive de l'article 15 § 1 du règlement Bruxelles I, où la limitation aux consommateurs d'un Etat membre va de soi, s'agissant d'un règlement de la compétence juridictionnelle, a été émise par MANKOWSKI, *IPRax*, 2006.106, 1ère col.

[50] Qu'on pourrait formuler ainsi : la loi de l'Etat membre dans lequel un consommateur a sa résidence habituelle régit les contrats conclus par celui-ci avec un professionnel.

[51] V. pour de plus de détails nos explications, cette *Revue*, 2001.774 et notre article précité, *Mélanges Yves Guyon*, p. 584.

travail, ce qui règle au moins partiellement[52] le cas des personnels navigants rattachés à une base fixe.[53] Il donne une définition assez précise du détachement temporaire pendant lequel le contrat de travail reste soumis à la même loi. Le détachement est temporaire « *lorsque le travailleur est censé reprendre son travail dans le pays d'origine après l'accomplissement de sa tâche à l'étranger* ». C'est donc *ex ante* que ce caractère temporaire est apprécié, lorsqu'il est limité à une certaine mission dont la durée n'est pas fixée précisément, et non *ex post* en fonction de la durée écoulée. Et en cas de contrats de travail conclus successivement par un même salarié avec des sociétés du même groupe, le texte n'exclut pas le caractère temporaire du détachement, ce qui permet la permanence de la loi applicable au rapport de travail.[54] Toujours à propos du détachement, la proposition réserve explicitement l'application de la directive 96/71 du 16 décembre 1996 sur le détachement des travailleurs dans le cadre d'une prestation de services[55]. Enfin, la loi du lieu de l'établissement d'embauche du travailleur s'applique non seulement lorsque le travailleur n'accomplit pas habituellement son travail dans ou à partir d'un même pays, mais également, selon la proposition, lorsqu'il accomplit habituellement son travail dans un espace sans souveraineté. Cette utile précision donne une solution satisfaisante au rattachement des travailleurs employés sur une plate-forme pétrolière en haute mer.

cc. Contrats conclus par un intermédiaire

Dans un article 7 entièrement nouveau, la proposition prévoit le rattachement des contrats d'intermédiaires. Les règles retenues sont les mêmes que celles de la convention de La Haye du 14 mars 1978[56] et ne devraient

---

[52] V. les observations plus critiques de MANKOWSKI, art. préc., *IPRax* 2006, p. 108, 1ère col.

[53] Sur les difficultés de détermination de la loi applicable au contrat de travail des pilotes, v. l'affaire *Air Afrique* et notamment les arrêts d'une chambre mixte de la Cour de cassation du 28 février 1986, *RCDIP*, 1986.503 et la note ; cf. H. GAUDEMET-TALLON, « Sur l'affaire *Air Afrique* », *Dr. Social*, 1986.406.

[54] L'appréciation se fera au cas par cas. Comp., pour l'application de l'article 5-1 de la convention de Bruxelles, CJCE 10 avr. 2003, aff. C-437/00, *Rev. Trim. Dr. Europ.*, 2003.535, obs. P. Rodière, *IPRax* 2004.336 et note Krebber, p. 309.

[55] V. art. 22, litt. a, et annexe I.

[56] Sur cette convention, ratifiée au sein de l'Union européenne par seulement trois Etats, la France, les Pays-Bas et le Portugal, v. notre chronique, *RCDIP*, 1978.31 et « La convention de La Haye du 14 mars 1978 sur la loi applicable aux contrats d'intermédiaires et à la représentation revisitée en 1994 », in *Eser-*

pas dérouter les juristes français. Les rapports internes et externes sont centrés sur la loi de l'Etat d'établissement de l'intermédiaire, avec des exceptions bien définies en faveur de la loi du lieu d'activité de l'intermédiaire lorsqu'elle coïncide avec celle de l'établissement du représenté ou, pour les relations externes, du tiers.

L'existence d'une règle spéciale pour les contrats d'intermédiaires n'ira cependant pas sans poser des problèmes de qualification. La proposition ne reprend pas la définition très étudiée de l'intermédiaire donnée par la convention de La Haye, qui incluait dans cette notion notamment le courtier.[57] On peut penser qu'elle y renvoie implicitement, ce qui serait raisonnable mais n'est pas évident. La proposition ne mentionne pas non plus le cas de l'intermédiaire salarié. On peut penser que, pour les relations entre celui-ci et son employeur, l'article 6 l'emportera sur l'article 7.[58] Pour le pouvoir de représentation de l'intermédiaire salarié, l'article 7 doit en revanche s'appliquer. Enfin, la proposition n'a pas repris la disposition de la convention sur les contrats mixtes (article 7), qui pourrait également être utilisée à titre de *ratio scripta*.

III. Domaine de la loi applicable

Sur toutes les questions qu'on peut grouper sous cette rubrique, la proposition maintient le plus souvent sans les modifier les dispositions de la convention de Rome. Elle apporte cependant ici ou là des précisions non dépourvues d'intérêt.

L'article 10 sur la forme[59] ajoute une troisième branche à la règle de conflit alternative de la convention de Rome (loi régissant le contrat quant au fond ou loi du lieu de la déclaration de volonté). Le contrat sera également valable en la forme s'il satisfait aux prescriptions de la loi de la résidence habituelle de l'une ou de l'autre des parties. Cette addition, suggérée tant par le GEDIP que par le Max-Planck-Institut, a en vue les contrats conclus par voie électronique, pour lesquels le lieu où le contractant a exprimé par un « clic » son consentement est souvent inconnu et dépourvu en lui-même de signification.

---

cizio di poteri gestori nel contesto internazionale (sous la direction de T. Ballarino et S. Tondo), Milan, 1996.3-24.

[57] Cf. pour une agence matrimoniale la note sous Civ. 1ère 12 juillet 2005, *RCDIP*, 2006.94, spéc. 97 et s.

[58] L'article 10 de la convention de La Haye écarte l'application du chapitre sur les relations internes « lorsque le contrat créant le rapport de représentation est un contrat de travail ».

[59] Rebaptisé « validité formelle du contrat », bien qu'il règle également la loi applicable à la forme d'un acte juridique unilatéral.

Les modes de transmission et d'extinction des obligations font l'objet de compléments utiles. L'article 13, qui correspond à l'article 12 de la convention de Rome, regroupe en un seul article la cession de créances et la subrogation conventionnelle.[60] Son apport le plus important est de combler la lacune concernant la loi applicable à l'opposabilité aux tiers de la cession de créance en donnant compétence, conformément à une opinion largement dominante et dans la ligne de la convention des Nations Unies du 12 décembre 2001 sur la cession de créances dans le commerce international, à la loi du pays où le cédant (ou le subrogeant) a sa résidence habituelle (art. 13, § 3).[61]

La proposition a conservé pour cet article le style simple de la convention de Rome. Il subsiste cependant quelques difficultés, tenant à la fois à la persistance dans le texte proposé de discordances entre les versions linguistiques de la convention et au mode de rédaction très « anglo-saxon » de la convention des Nations Unies.[62] Là où les textes français et allemand soumettent à la loi de la créance cédée le « caractère cessible » ou la « cessibilité » (*Übertragbarkeit*) de la créance, le texte anglais, plus restrictif, ne soumet à cette loi que « *the effectiveness of contractual limitations on assignment*[63] », ce qui élimine notamment certaines limitations légales à la cessibilité, comme celles frappant les créances alimentaires ou les créances de salaires, qui étaient les exemples le plus souvent donnés lors de la négociation de la convention de Rome.[64]

L'article 15 de la proposition, intitulé « pluralité de débiteurs », explicite la règle qui figure déjà à l'article 13 § 2 de la convention de Rome sur la subrogation légale du codébiteur *solvens* dans les droits de l'*accipiens* contre les autres codébiteurs. Le recours subrogatoire du *solvens* contre ses codébiteurs dépend de la loi qui régissait sa propre obligation envers le créancier. La seconde phrase de l'article 15 ajoute cependant une règle

---

[60] En ce sens déjà D. PARDOEL, *Les conflits de lois en matière de cession de créance*, Paris, LGDJ, 1997, n° 653 et s., 663. Au § 2 de l'article 13 de la proposition, un lapsus a fait écrire « subrogeant » au lieu de « subrogé ».

[61] V. sur l'ensemble de la question P. LAGARDE, « Retour sur la loi applicable à l'opposabilité des transferts conventionnels de créances », *Mélanges Jacques Béguin*, Litec, 2005, p. 415 et s.

[62] Pour une étude très fouillée de ces difficultés, v. M.-E. ANCEL, E.-M. KIENINGER ET H. C. SIGMAN, « La proposition de Règlement Rome I et les effets sur les tiers de la cession de créances », *Banque & Droit*, 2006, n°107, p. 39–46 .Les auteurs se prononcent substantiellement pour un alignement du futur règlement sur la convention des Nations Unies. *Adde* FLESSNER et VERHAGEN, *Assignment in European PIL*, 2006, favorables à la loi choisie par les parties, à défaut à la loi de la créance cédée.

[63] Même rédaction à l'article 29 de la convention des Nations Unies.

[64] *Adde, infra*, p. 19.

nouvelle, ainsi conçue : « *lorsque la loi applicable à l'obligation d'un débiteur envers le créancier prévoit des règles destinées à le protéger contre des actions en responsabilité, il peut également les invoquer à l'encontre des autres débiteurs* » Cette règle est peu éclairée par l'exposé des motifs, qui se borne à indiquer qu'elle « vise à préciser la situation d'un débiteur qui bénéficierait d'une protection particulière ». Elle paraît tirer son origine des réponses du Max-Planck-Institut au livre vert de la Commission sur Rome I et que l'Institut de Hambourg avait déjà présentées avec plus de détails dans ses observations sur la proposition de la Commission d'un règlement sur la loi applicable aux obligations non contractuelles (Rome II).[65] Le texte[66] présuppose donc que les obligations des codébiteurs envers le créancier originaire sont régies par des lois différentes. L'idée semble être que le recours subrogatoire du *solvens* ne doit pas avoir pour effet de rendre la situation du codébiteur poursuivi par ce dernier plus mauvaise qu'elle ne l'aurait été en application de la loi régissant sa propre obligation. Il faut donc permettre à ce codébiteur d'opposer au demandeur des exceptions qu'il aurait pu opposer au créancier, par exemple la compensation avec une dette de ce dernier. Sans doute pourrait-il aussi invoquer des règles de la loi régissant son obligation, relatives aux recours entre coobligés et plus favorables que celles prévues par la loi régissant l'obligation du *solvens*.[67]

L'article 16 comble une lacune importante de la convention de Rome concernant la compensation légale. Les négociateurs de la convention n'avaient pu départager la solution française, qui n'admet la compensation légale que si elle est prévue par les deux lois régissant les obligations à compenser, et la solution allemande, qui écarte le cumul de lois et retient la loi de l'obligation à laquelle est opposée la compensation. La proposition de règlement a choisi la solution allemande.[68] Elle est en cohérence avec le droit matériel allemand, selon lequel le débiteur poursuivi qui invoque la compensation avec une créance qu'il possède contre le demandeur doit faire une déclaration. Il est alors logique que le défendeur puisse invoquer la loi régissant sa propre obligation pour contester les ef-

---

[65] *RabelsZ*, 2003.1 et s., spéc.46 et s.

[66] Qui, curieusement, n'a pas été repris dans l'article correspondant de la nouvelle proposition de règlement Rome II, COM(2006)83 final, présentée par la Commission le 21 février 2006.

[67] On songe ici à la règle de l'article 1214 du code civil français qui oblige le codébiteur d'une dette solidaire, qu'il a payée en entier, à diviser son recours contre ses codébiteurs pour leur part respective.

[68] Cette solution semble avoir été retenue également par l'article 6 § 1 du règlement 1346/2000 du 29 mai 2000 sur les procédures d'insolvabilité, mais la Cour de justice avait au contraire paru retenir la solution cumulative dans un arrêt du 10 juillet 2003 (aff. C-87/01 P, *Commission c. Conseil des Communes et Régions d'Europe*).

fets de la déclaration de compensation faite par l'autre partie. Au contraire, si « la compensation s'opère de plein droit par la seule force de la loi, même à l'insu des débiteurs » (art. 1290 c. civ. français), il n'y a pas de raison de privilégier la loi de l'une ou de l'autre obligation et le système cumulatif s'impose. Mais en réalité, même en droit français, la mise en jeu de la compensation légale appelle toujours une manifestation positive de volonté de celui qui l'invoque.[69] La compétence donnée à la loi de l'obligation passive, selon la terminologie allemande (*die Passivforderung*) est donc acceptable. Le GEDIP avait fait observer dans sa réponse au livre vert que le résultat pourrait être injuste « car il crée une inégalité entre les créanciers lorsqu'une des deux créances seulement est protégée par une interdiction de compensation, par exemple une créance de salaire. Dans une telle hypothèse, celui dont la créance est protégée pourra, s'il est demandeur, invoquer la loi régissant sa créance pour empêcher son adversaire de lui opposer la compensation, tandis que ce dernier, s'il est lui-même demandeur, ne pourra pas le faire, parce que la loi régissant sa créance ne fait pas obstacle à la compensation. C'est vrai, mais ce résultat tient au contenu des règles protectrices des lois régissant respectivement les obligations croisées. L'important, dans l'exemple donné, est que le salarié puisse invoquer sa créance sans se voir opposer la compensation avec la créance de son débiteur contre lui et le système retenu garantit ce résultat.

IV. Autres dispositions

Sous cet intitulé résiduel, le chapitre III de la proposition rassemble un certain nombre de règles, dont certaines sont reprises purement et simplement de la convention de Rome : exclusion du renvoi (art. 19), ordre public (art. 20), systèmes non unifiés (art. 21).[70] Ce chapitre ne reprend pas la disposition de la convention sur son interprétation uniforme (art. 18), qui, dans l'esprit des négociateurs, aurait pourtant conservé son utilité même après l'attribution à la Cour de justice d'une compétence d'interprétation de la convention.[71]

---

[69] V. GHESTIN-BILLIAU-LOISEAU, « Le régime des créances et des dettes », *in* Traité de droit civil de J. Ghestin, LGDJ, 2005, n°1021; TERRÉ-SIMLER-LEQUETTE, *Droit civil. Les obligations*, Précis Dalloz, 9ème éd., 2005, n° 1406.

[70] A l'exclusion du § 2 de l'article 19 de la convention de Rome, qui ne fait pas obligation aux Etats contractants à système non unifié d'appliquer la convention aux conflits de lois intéressant uniquement leurs unités territoriales. Pourquoi cette omission, alors que ce § 2 est maintenu dans la nouvelle proposition de règlement Rome II (art. 22)?

[71] V. rapport Giuliano-Lagarde, *ad art.* 18.

L'article 18 de la proposition précise ce qu'il faut entendre par résidence habituelle pour les personnes morales, notamment lorsque le contrat est conclu par un établissement secondaire ou que la prestation doit être fournie par un tel établissement, et pour les personnes physiques agissant dans l'exercice de leur activité professionnelle. Ces dispositions se trouvaient déjà à l'article 4 § 2 de la convention de Rome et il s'agit ici surtout d'une clarification de forme bienvenue,[72] sauf toutefois pour l'article 13 § 3 soumettant l'opposabilité aux tiers de la cession de créances à la loi de l'Etat de la résidence habituelle du cédant.[73] Il est nécessaire que le conflit entre les tiers, par exemple les cessionnaires successifs d'une même créance, soit tranché en application d'une loi unique.[74]

La convention de Rome réservait dans son article 20 la priorité du droit communautaire qui, dans le domaine des conflits de lois en matière de contrats, était alors embryonnaire. L'article 22 de la proposition réserve sous le point a l'application de quatre directives opportunément énumérées dans une annexe I du futur règlement, ce qui est bien, mais la clarté en résultant est passablement atténuée par les points b et c. Est-il utile de réserver au point b les actes communautaires qui « *régissent les obligations contractuelles et qui, en vertu de la volonté des parties, s'appliquent dans les situations comportant un conflit de lois* »? Si l'on vise par là le futur code européen optionnel des contrats, le problème n'est-il pas déjà réglé par l'article 3 § 2 de la proposition, qui permet aux parties de choisir des règles de droit matériel des contrats reconnues au niveau communautaire? Et la sauvegarde, au point c, des règles destinées à favoriser le bon fonctionnement du marché intérieur, n'est-elle pas suffisamment garantie à la fois par l'article 3 § 5 [75] et par l'exception d'ordre public?

La convention de Rome réservait également l'application des conventions internationales (art. 21), ce qui visait principalement les conventions de La Haye du 15 juin 1955 sur la vente et du 14 mars 1978 sur les contrats d'intermédiaires. Prolonger cette solution eût été maintenir une non uniformité des solutions pour ces deux contrats. Plutôt que d'inciter les Etats membres qui sont parties à ces conventions à les dénoncer, la

---

[72] L'article 18 de la proposition a également l'avantage d'éviter le détour que l'article 4 de la convention fait par le « principal établissement » de la partie agissant dans le cadre de son activité professionnelle. La nouvelle proposition Rome II rétablit pourtant cette référence au principal établissement (art. 20 § 2).

[73] V. *supra*, p. 16.

[74] La convention des Nations Unies (art. 5 h) retient en cas d'établissements du cédant dans plus d'un Etat, celui où s'exerce son administration centrale et, à défaut d'établissement, sa résidence habituelle. V. en ce sens, les auteurs cités *supra*, note 62.

[75] V. *supra*, p. 7 et s.

proposition a choisi une solution intermédiaire[76] consistant à faire prévaloir le futur règlement « *lorsque tous les éléments de la situation sont localisés au moment de la conclusion du contrat dans un ou plusieurs Etats membres* » et à ne réserver l'application des conventions que dans les relations extracommunautaires. C'est sans doute la moins mauvaise des solutions, même si la distinction entre les situations purement intracommunautaires et les autres risque d'être parfois difficile à tracer.

L'article 24 et dernier de la proposition comporte une disposition transitoire difficile à interpréter. Le futur règlement s'appliquera aux obligations contractuelles nées après son application, ce qui est la répétition de l'article 17 de la convention de Rome et ne surprend pas. Mais le texte ajoute que, pour les obligations contractuelles nées antérieurement, le règlement s'applique « *lorsque ses règles conduisent à la même loi que celle qui aurait été applicable en vertu de la convention de Rome de 1980* ». L'exposé des motifs ne fournit aucune explication de cette étrange règle. Les obligations contractuelles anciennes sont par hypothèse soumises à la convention de Rome, et elles le restent si cette convention conduit à une solution différente de celle du règlement. Si la convention de Rome conduit au même résultat que le règlement, elle cesse de s'appliquer et laisse la place au règlement. A quoi cela sert-il, puisque le résultat doit être le même ? Si les protocoles du 19 décembre 1988 n'étaient pas entrés en vigueur, le texte de la proposition aurait permis de soumettre une question préjudicielle d'interprétation à la Cour de justice. Maintenant qu'ils sont entrés en vigueur, l'application du règlement à la place de la convention aura pour effet de réduire au contraire les possibilités de recourir à la Cour de justice.[77] Est-ce le but recherché ? Il nous semble, sauf preuve rapportée de son utilité, que cet article 24, § 3 pourrait être supprimé sans inconvénient.

V. Conclusion

La proposition de la Commission améliore sur de nombreux points la convention de Rome et il faut lui en savoir gré. Ainsi en est-il, sous certaines réserves indiquées, de la clarification concernant les relations précontractuelles, de la définition du consommateur et de la formule trouvée pour tenir compte du commerce électronique, de la nouvelle rédaction de l'article 6 sur le contrat de travail, des compléments apportés aux règles sur la cession de créance et la subrogation, du nouvel article sur la com-

---

[76] Une solution analogue est retenue par la nouvelle proposition Rome II pour les conventions de La Haye du 4 mai 1971 sur les accidents de la circulation routière et du 2 octobre 1973 sur la responsabilité du fait des produits.

[77] V. *supra*, note 4.

pensation, des précisions données concernant la résidence habituelle et de la solution apportée au conflit avec les conventions de La Haye.

En revanche, il serait souhaitable que la Commission apporte des précisions, corrige quelques malfaçons et reconsidère certaines solutions de fond, comme l'article 250 § 2 du traité CE lui en donne le pouvoir, tant que le Conseil n'a pas statué. Des précisions sont nécessaires sur l'inclusion ou l'exclusion des partenariats enregistrés du type contractuel, les critères de reconnaissance au niveau international des règles de droit matériel non étatique, la notion de droit impératif communautaire à l'article 3 § 5, la notion d'intermédiaire et les points b et c de l'article 22 sur la priorité du droit communautaire. Les principales malfaçons à corriger concernent le maintien des divergences linguistiques sur le choix tacite (art. 3) et sur la cessibilité de la créance (art. 13), la limitation de l'article 5 aux consommateurs ayant leur résidence habituelle dans un Etat membre et, semble-t-il, la disposition transitoire finale de l'article 24, al. 3. Les règles de fond à reconsidérer – et c'est pour nous le plus important – sont la suppression malheureuse de la clause d'exception à l'article 4 et l'abandon à l'article 5 du système de la comparaison des législations.

Time to Slice and Dice in the Contractual Kitchen?

Simon James[1] *(London)*

I shall start with three related observations on the nature of contract law and the progress so far made with codification. I shall then turn to the conclusions that can be drawn from these observations.

I. Three points

1. The unity of contract law

The first observation is as to the unity of contract law. It is convenient for lawyers to think of contract law as a single topic – the same law applying to all contracts. And, indeed, there may still be a unifying overall structure within each legal system – perhaps even internationally – but once discussion passes beyond generalities, contract law fragments into smaller pieces. This fragmentation occurs both at a practical level and at a theoretical level.

In practical terms, a loan agreement looks nothing like a building contract, which in turn looks nothing like an intellectual property licence. This is not remotely surprising. The demands of different industries and subject matters and not the same, and the drafting of the contracts reflect his.

Further, the manner in which contracts are entered into varies enormously. Some contracts – commercial loan agreements, corporate acquisitions etc – are written down, often at great length, and negotiated line by line. This contrasts starkly with a typical consumer contract, even where it concerns the purchase of a relatively expensive item, like a washing machine or a camera. There might be something in writing (though often not), but if consumers tried to negotiate the terms of their contracts, most shop assistants would look at them with incredulity. Shop assistants have no authority to negotiate; that is not their job. For consumers making purchases online, there is no individual on the other end of the line with whom to try to negotiate.

---

[1] Partner, Clifford Chance LLP, London.

Further, even if consumers could find someone with whom to negotiate, in most situations it would not be economic to do so. If consumers sought to negotiate the detail of their purchases, transaction costs would soar. The resulting price rises would mean that all consumers paid far more than is currently the case. The benefits of low prices far outweigh those of individual negotiation.[2]

Fragmentation also occurs at a theoretical level, typically from rules that restrict the parties' freedom of contract. There are, of course, some general rules that have this effect, but increasingly there are specific rules that apply to specific contracts. As with the drafting and entry into of particular contracts, the law that applies to a particular contract may not be the same as the law that applies to another contract. An obvious historical example of this is land law. Much of land law is concerned with contracts – a contract is, for example, usually how land is sold and how leases are granted. But contracts concerning land are subject to numerous formalities that do not apply to other contracts.[3] As a result of this, land law has for centuries been treated as a separate topic because of its distinct subject matter.

More recently, employment law has effectively become a separate area into which the general contract lawyer dare not tread. A contract of employment is, in principle, a contract like any other, but the wide variety of EU and domestic legislation[4] has made employment law a highly specialised topic. The contract has its place, but it is so entrammelled by rules and regulations as to what it can and cannot contain, and how it can and cannot be terminated, that most of the traditional principles of contract law have little part to play. Seeking to apply these general principles of contract law will lead to error.

More recently still, consumer law has, in my view, gone the same way as employment law.[5] Article 153(1) of the EC Treaty commits the EU to providing a high level of consumer protection,[6] which has been provided

---

[2] This is not to mention the frustration, not to say riots, that would be caused by the queues in shops.

[3] Eg section 2 of the UK's Law of Property (Miscellaneous Provisions) Act 1989.

[4] For example, Council Directive 93/104/EC on working time, Council Directive 96/34/EC on parental leave, Council Directive 98/59/EC on collective redundancies, and so on and so forth.

[5] See Sir David Edward's *Concluding Remarks* in *The Harmonisation of European Contract Law: Implications for European Private Laws, Business and Legal Practice* by Vogenauer and Weatherill (Editors), Hart Publishing, 2006, page 251.

[6] The EU provided this protection even before it had a treaty base for doing so: see Weatherill, *Constitutional Issues – How Much is Best Left Unsaid* in *The Harmonisation of European Contract Law: Implications for European Private Laws,*

in, for example, Directive 1999/44/EC on the sale of consumer goods and associated guarantees, Council Directive 93/13/EEC on unfair terms in consumer contracts and Council Directive 85/577/EC on contracts negotiated away from business premises. These regulations and directives again make consumer law an area that the general contract lawyer must approach with caution. Freedom of contract has little part to play. Legislation has balanced the rights and obligations of businesses and consumers, and it is usually the result of this balancing exercise that dictates the parties' principal rights and obligations – at least those that might lead to any contention – rather than any terms the parties have agreed.

2. Existing non-national codifications of contract law

My second observation is as to the success, or otherwise, of the private enterprise codifications of contract law.[7] There are, most notably, UNIDROIT's *Principles of International Commercial Contracts*[8] and, more recently, *Principles of European Contract Law*,[9] prepared by the Lando Commission and now taken on by the Study Group on a European Civil Code. These codifications have, however, had relatively little impact on the commercial world. For example, it has been said that only 0.8% of the cases handled by the ICC used transnational laws of this sort.[10]

Business and Legal Practice by Vogenauer and Weatherill (Editors), Hart Publishing, 2006.

[7] I am not bothered by terminology – transnational, international or non-national law. By non-national or transnational law, I mean only a "law" that is not tied to a particular national legal system, whether or not it seeks legitimacy by international usage or supposed observance by the merchant community (see, for example, Sir Roy Goode, *Usage and its Reception in Transnational Contract Law* (1997) 47 ICLQ 1, pages 2–3).

[8] Adopted first in 1994 and revised in 2004. See, for example, Basedow, *The UNIDROIT Principles of International Contract Law and German Law* at http://www.jura.uni-Freiburg.de/einrichtungen/gfr/Bristol/Basedow/basedow.PDF.

[9] *Principles of European Contract Law*, by Lando and Beale (Editors), Kluwer Law International, 2000.

[10] Cited by Magnus and Mankowski at page 14 of their *Joint Response to the Green Paper on the Conversion of the Rome Convention of 1980 on the Law Applicable to Contractual Obligations into a Community Instrument and its Modernisation*, available at http://ec.europa.eu/consumers/cons_int/safe_shop/fair_bus_pract/cont_law/comments/index_en.htm. Outside arbitration, these codes can only take effect as standard terms because the Rome Convention does not allow parties to chose a non-national law. Arbitration commonly does permit this (eg section 46 of the UK's Arbitration Act 1996).

This lack of impact is not surprising. As I have said, different contracts have different needs. A highly generalised and somewhat academic construction is unlikely to be of any great interest to commercial parties. The practical issues that arise on a contract require practical solutions relevant to the needs of the particular contract in question. A solution that works for a building contract will not necessarily work for a loan agreement or a securitisation contract.

Perhaps the most successful transnational codification of this kind is the Vienna Convention on the International Sale of Goods, also the work of UNCITRAL. The degree to which it has succeeded is because it focuses on the detailed needs of one particular kind of transaction, rather than trying to be all-encompassing.

Interestingly, one of the most successful private codifications is UCP 500[11] on *Uniform Customs and Practice for Documentary Credits*, published by the ICC, which is invariably used to govern documentary credit transactions.[12] This success is undoubtedly because its scope is limited to one specific type of transaction and because it meets the needs and expectations of the industry that carries out that type of transaction, not least because the industry was involved in its preparation.

UCP 500 is used to govern documentary credit transactions as if it were a system of law, even though documentary credits seldom have arbitration agreements.[13] As a result, the Rome Convention requires that UCP 500 be treated as a set of standard terms only, contrary to the apparent wishes of the parties. This means that, when considering any legal issues arising on a documentary credit transaction, it is necessary first to identify a national governing law of the transaction, then to be satisfied that this national governing law will accept the incorporation of UCP 500 into the contract, then to consider the principles of interpretation of that national law and construe UCP 500 accordingly, and finally to consider the impact of any mandatory laws that might affect UCP 500 (eg good faith). That is not what the parties generally have in mind when stating that their transaction is governed by UCP 500.

3. The demand for transnational law

My final observation is as to the commercial demand for transnational law. Clifford Chance's survey in early 2005 demonstrated that business in

---

[11] UCP 500 does, of course, have its predecessors and successors – UCP 600 will take effect on 1 July 2007.
[12] There are, of course, other private codifications which are routinely adopted for particular kinds of transactions. I take UCP 500 as an example only.
[13] Letters of credit very rarely include the choice of a national governing law.

Europe does like the idea of a European contract law.[14] This was a survey of 175 businesses across eight member states of the EU. 83% of businesses viewed favourably or very favourably the concept of a harmonised European contract law (see Table 1 below). Further, 82% said that they would be likely or very likely to use an optional European contract law in cross border transactions.

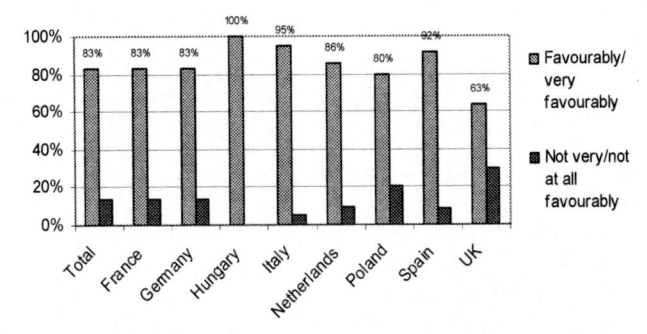

Table 1: How favourably do you view the concept of a harmonised European Contract Law?

There is, therefore, demand from business for a European contract law. However, that demand is not for a single European contract law that replaces existing national laws. 83% considered that it is important to be able to choose the governing law of a contract, and 61% were of the view that the ability to choose from different contract laws across Europe is an advantage. The Rome Convention enshrines the principle of party autonomy in the choice of the law governing a contract, whether that law comes from within or without the European Union.

Further, the Clifford Chance survey shows that businesses would be prepared to use a European contract law if one were available. 92% said that if an optional European contract law were to be established, they would be likely or very likely to use it in connection with cross-border transactions. This is not surprising. Business life would be easier if a neutral contract law were available within the Europe Union, rather than

---

[14] The results of the survey can be found at http://www.cliffordchance.com/expertise/publications/details.aspx?FilterName=@URL&contentitemid=8354. The results are also set out and discussed by Professors Vogenauer and Weatherill in *The Harmonisation of European Contract Law: Implications for European Private Laws, Business and Legal* Practice by Vogenauer and Weatherill (Editors), Hart Publishing, 2006. The survey covered both SMEs and larger businesses; there was, in the main, no material difference in the responses between SMEs and other businesses.

merely 25 nationally based laws.[15] Fewer lawyers might be needed, and legal spend might be reduced.

This willingness to use a transnational contract law does, however, contrast with the very limited use of the existing transnational laws. Again, that is perhaps not surprising. The Clifford Chance survey could only test the theoretical willingness to use a European law. The willingness to do so in practice will depend upon the content of the law in question. The general transational laws that exist now are, it would appear, not considered satisfactory; if they were considered satisfactory, they would be used more.[16]

II. The needs of international business

So what conclusions can one draw from these three observations? Once it is accepted that consumer law is, like employment law, different, contract law becomes much less complicated. There is no need to protect a business party in the way required if a consumer is involved.[17] This makes contract law more straightforward because the overriding principle becomes freedom of contract, which is not the case with consumers. A whole raft of social and other concerns is removed. The tier of mandatory laws can be stripped down, perhaps even stripped away.

In the light of this, how can the needs of business be met? I suggest that the way forward is two-fold: first, a recognition that a non-national law can be the governing law of a contract; and, second, a concentration on smaller scale codifications governing particular types of contract rather than a single all-encompassing contract law.

---

[15] The figure is in fact higher than 25 (or, soon to be, 27) in view of the federal nature of the legal systems of some member states, such as the United Kingdom.

[16] It should be added that, in a legal timeframe, these transnational laws are still relatively new.

[17] In paragraph 4 of its resolution of 23 March 2006 on European contract law, the European Parliament reminded the Commission "that the term "business" covers more than just large corporations and includes small – even one-person – undertakings which will often require contracts that are specially tailored to their needs and that take account of their relative vulnerability when contracting with large corporations." Some SMEs are undoubtedly vulnerable, but so are some large corporations. I see no basis upon which a practical or principled distinction can be made between different sizes of businesses.

1. Non-national law as contractual governing law

This first point seemed at one time recently to be uncontroversial.[18] The European Commission's proposed Rome I Regulation offered recognition to non-national laws (article 3(2)), and the European Parliament's draft report accepted this.[19] However, the Finnish Presidency's most recent draft of the Rome I Regulation has removed this provision,[20] and Member States are reported to have agreed unanimously with this removal of article 3(2).

It is, perhaps, unsurprising that member states should show a lack of enthusiasm for non-national laws. Allowing the choice of a non-national law permits parties to opt out of the mandatory laws of the members states whose laws would otherwise be the governing law of the contract. However, I see no problem with this.[21] Indeed, it seems to me that this has already been conceded in principle. Arbitrators in many countries are allowed to apply a law other than a national law:[22] why should courts be any different? Courts are, of course, called upon by the New York Convention to enforce arbitration awards.

Further, the mandatory laws of any particular country represent the social, economic and other values of that country. Why should, for example, a Polish company dealing with a Portugese company be obliged to chose the values of Portugal, Poland or of some third country? What legitimate interest has any of these countries in imposing its values on international contracting parties? The principle of freedom of choice is now

---

[18] Cf *The Case Concerning the Payment of Various Serbian Loans Issued in France*, Perm Ct of Int Justice, Series A, No 20 (1929): "Any contract which is not a contract between States in their capacity as subjects of international law is based on the municipal law of some country."

[19] European Parliament's Committee on Legal Affairs' draft Report dated 22 August 2006 (Provisional 2005/0261(COD), by Maria Berger (Rapporteur)).

[20] Council of the European Union, Interinstitutional File 2005/0261 (COD), document 13853/06, Justciv 224, Codec 1085, dated 12 October 2006.

[21] P Nygh observed in *Autonomy in International Contracts*, OUP, 1998, that "[n]o state can hope effectively to control international contracts. National laws can be made by express provision or necessary implication, to extend to international transactions and national courts can be compelled by such mandatory laws of international application to apply them. But normally a plaintiff has several fora available and can avoid such national restrictions by choosing a more favourable forum ... Any attempt therefore to restrict the autonomy of the parties beyond internationally accepted parameters would be worthy of King Canute." (page 2).

[22] Eg section 46 of the UK's Arbitration Act 1996.

widely accepted;[23] it should not be restricted by limiting that choice to national laws. Equally, if there are circumstances when a state does have a legitimate interest in contractual terms, that situation is adequately protected by article 3(4) of the Rome Convention, which does not allow parties to opt out of a country's mandatory law if all the circumstances of the case are connected with that country only, and by public policy.[24]

But this approach is not entirely free from its critics. The responses to the European Commission's consultation on a possible Rome I Regulation identify three primary objections.[25] These are: first, codifications do not provide a complete legal system; secondly, they are not sufficiently certain; and, thirdly, they are not balanced.

a. Lack of completeness

Dealing with the first of these points, since codifications are, currently, only allowed to take effect as a set of standard terms, it is hardly an objection to elevating their status to argue that no one has drafted one that is as complete as an entire domestic legal system. There was limited point in doing so, as it would be trumped in the courts by the mandatory rules of a domestic legal system. (Though, it should be said, PECL and UNIDROIT look tolerably complete to most people.)

In any event, if there is an obvious gap, it can be filled by the appropriate national laws. The concept of deçepage is nothing new.[26] Nor is the concept of contractual obligations being governed by one law, but non-contractual obligations being subject to a different law.

---

[23] For example, article 3(1) of the Rome Convention.

[24] Cf *Ingmar GB Ltd v Eaton Leonard Technologies Inc* (ECJ), Case C-381/98 per Advocate General Léger. One might wonder whether, within the EU at least, so many tiers of mandatory laws are required. The Rome Convention does, and any successor Regulation probably will, continue to impose the mandatory rules of the governing law, of the forum, of countries with which a transaction is closely connected and so on, not to mention public policy.

[25] See the responses to the European Commission's initial consultation paper on Rome I (COM(2002) 654 final),which are published on its web site.

[26] Rome Convention, article 3(1) (last sentence). Indeed, article 23 of the Brussels Regulation has also been said by the European Court of Justice to provide a code, outside the rest of the contract, that governs the validity of jurisdiction clauses (*Benincasa v Dentalkit*, European Court of Justice, Case C-269/95). Even in *The Case Concerning the Payment of Various Serbian Loans Issued in France*, Perm Ct of Int Justice, Series A, No 20 (1929), the court said that "it should be observed that even apart from rules of public policy, it is quite possible that the same law may not govern all aspects of the obligation."

UCP 500, which I have mentioned, offers a good example. Lawyers would seldom think of it as a "law" because it is not, and does not aspire to be, a complete system answering all possible questions that might arise. It does, however, deal with virtually all issues that arise in the documentary credits transactions it governs. Why should it not be considered to be a law, even if on a small number of occasions, it needs to be supplemented by rules drawn from another law?

b. Lack of certainty

The second objection is lack of certainty. This is a somewhat curious objection given the trend now to what the EU euphemistically calls a "margin of discretion",[27] ie built-in uncertainty to allow judges to do what they consider to be the right thing in the case before without being forced into one particular answer by prescriptive rules.

Be that as it may, a well-drafted law could provide every bit as much certainty as existing national laws. PECL and UNIDROIT certainly cannot be criticised any more than domestic laws on that ground. The stronger point, however, is that it is for the parties to decide how much certainty they want. If they choose to govern their relations by lex mercatoria, commercial principles common to civilised nations[28] or whatever, why should they not be able to do so? Alternatively, If parties wish to place certainty above the growing trend amongst judges and legislators to discretionary justice, so be it.

---

[27] Eg, in paragraph 11 of its resolution of 23 March 2006 on European contract law, the European Parliament said that it "[n]otes that with over-detailed legal provisions on individual aspects of contract law there is a danger of being unable to react flexibly to altered legal circumstances, and therefore favours the adoption of general regulations including legal concepts which are not precisely defined, thus giving the courts the necessary margin of discretion in arriving at their judgments."

[28] For example, the contract for the construction of the Channel Tunnel was to be "governed by and interpreted in accordance with the principles common to both English law and French law, and in the absence of such common principles by such general principles of international trade law as have been applied by national and international tribunals. Subject in all cases, with respect to the works to be respectively performed in the French and in the English part of the site, to the respective French or English public policy (ordre public) provisions" (see *Channel Tunnel Group Ltd v Balfour Beatty Construction Ltd* [1993] 1 AC 334, 347 (UK House of Lords). Whatever the political and other merits of this choice, it does not offer certainty.

c. Lack of balance

The final objection is lack of balance. Again, there is no reason why there should be a lack of balance if a transnational law is properly prepared. In any event, lack of balance really means a lack of mandatory laws, removing from the parties the ability to achieve their own balance. In business to business transactions this paternalistic approach has little role to play. The essence is, and should be, freedom of contract. The balance should be set by the parties, not a third force with no knowledge of the particular circumstances in which the parties find themselves. If the parties choose a law with extensive mandatory rules, that is fine. If they do not do so, that is also fine.

But in more general terms, if it is acceptable for the parties to choose a non-national law accompanied by an arbitration clause, why can they not do so if accompanied by a choice of court? Even if a law is incomplete, uncertain and lacking in balance, why do we suppose that judges cannot deal with a situation that apparently causes arbitrators few problems?

Similarly, if, as most ritually incant, the key is freedom of contract, that freedom must include the right to do things that others consider unwise. In truth, that already happens: parties make bargains others would not contemplate; they draft contracts badly; they forget bits. Judges are well-used to sorting through the detritus left by the contracting parties' failures – that is, after all, an essential aspect of the judicial process. There is no reason why judges cannot perform the same function when faced with a choice of law that is not a national law.

2. Smaller scale transnational laws

Turning to my second point, the need for smaller scale, industry based, transnational laws, there are a number of reasons, both theoretical and practical, why this represents the way forward.

I have spoken of the fragmentation of contract law. In the light of this, there is no reason why a specific contract law designed to be applicable to the building industry, loan agreements or whatever should not be drafted. If, say, it is appropriate in a particular industry for a contract only to be concluded in writing, so be it. If it is appropriate for drafts of a contract to be taken into account, or not taken into account, as an aid to interpretation, again so be it.

The first practical reason for this approach lies in the preparation and acceptance of any private transnational law. As I have said, the existing major transnational laws are largely academic projects. They have not, so far at least, had much success in the practical world. Contract law is, above all other aspects of the law, a practical subject – it is the lifeblood of commerce, and it must meet the needs of commerce. A transnational law will only succeed if it is produced by academics, practitioners and business people working together.[29] Practitioners and business people will in most cases not become involved if the product is too general, too large scale and too remote from their daily work. They want to see some practical benefit from the participation. That can, in my view, only be realistically achieved by dealing with matters on a smaller scale, addressing practical issues that arise in a particular industry. It is because UCP 500 does this that it has been so much more successful than the grander scale efforts.

The second practical benefit is speed. Codifiying contract law is a long, difficult task within one country.[30] Seeking to prepare a transnational law, crossing borders, is many times more difficult and lengthy.[31] Cutting it down into smaller, practical segments is a means of achieving something that might not otherwise be achieved. Transnational laws would not be prepared in isolation; they would build on each other, taking the best bits, the bits that work for them. From smaller parts, it might be ultimately be possible to come up with a general law, but even before that stage, it would encourage different legal traditions across Europe to speak to each other more freely.

This does, of course, all beg the question as to what criteria a non-national law must meet in order to move beyond a set of standard terms. The European Commission's draft Rome I Regulation says that a non-national law must be "recognised internationally or in the Community" (article 3(2)). The Commission's notes say that PECL and UNIDROIT meet these aims, but lex mercatoria does not because it is not sufficiently precise. The Commission is right that lex mercatoria is not at all precise,[32] but otherwise the Commission seeks to place the bar too high. The key should not be international recognition, but recognition by the parties of some independent third party product. For example, ISDA's Master Agreement is invariably used to govern derivatives transactions: why should ISDA not be able to expand the terms of that agreement and ele-

---

[29] Although contact between academics and practitioners in England (I cannot comment on the position elsewhere) has certainly improved in the last quarter of a century, it still does not go anything like far enough.

[30] At least, without the dictatorial powers of a Justinian or a Napoleon.

[31] Professor Basil Markesinis described such European codification as "utopic at best, ludicrous at worst" (*The Gradual Convergence*, Markesinis (Editor), page 15).

[32] "There is ... a tendency to romanticise the law merchant and to treat it as an integrated corpus of universally applied law akin to canon law, when in truth it was never an organised body of legal rules at all" (Sir Roy Goode, *Usage and its Reception in Transnational Contract Law* (1997) 47 ICLQ 1, page 5).

vate it into a law? Why should other bodies not be able to draft their own laws? I might not consider a particular law prepared in this way to be a satisfactory law, and I might think that parties who chose it are unwise. I might also think that the choice of some national laws is similarly imprudent, but what I think is not the point. If parties wish to do something injudicious, ever reckless, the principle of freedom of contract allows them to do so. Competition between different laws might actually improve the quality of those laws, ensuring that only the best survive.[33]

The existing non-national laws also have overt political aims. For example, PECL was drafted with the longer-term objective of "bringing about the harmonisation of general contract law within the EU".[34] The originator of PECL, Professor Lando, also commented that "there is cultural value in having Europeans live under the same laws".[35] Whatever may be the merits of that viewpoint, its expression makes it harder to achieve what business wants. It raises the hackles of all sorts of constituencies, whether Euro-sceptic, legal conservative, or simply those who are happy with the way things are. Though lacking the attraction of a grand vision,[36] the pragmatic benefits of a smaller scale approach are potentially huge. Something might be achieved that would promote trade and genuinely remove obstructions to the internal market within the EU.

---

[33] This does depend upon there being a competitive market so that one party cannot impose its will on all others, creating an imbalanced situation.

[34] *Principles of European Contract Law*, by Lando and Beale (Editors), Kluwer Law International, 2000, Introduction, page xxiv.

[35] Professor Ole Lando, in Barrett and Bernardeau (Editors), *Towards a European Civil Code – Reflections on the Codification of Civil Law* (2002), page 43.

[36] To the English, always something to be viewed with suspicion.

Variations on the Concept of Contract in a European Perspective: Some Unresolved Issues

Michele Graziadei (Alessandria)

I. Introduction

The ongoing debate over the development of private law in Europe is currently characterised by certain tensions among the different national legal traditions.[1] These tensions also involve the field of contract law, traditionally considered to be one of the most cosmopolitan areas of the law. In the sphere of fundamental rights law, European law has grown under the umbrella of the European Convention on Fundamental Rights. The Nice Charter of Fundamental Rights paves the way to further developments in this respect. As far as contract is concerned, European fundamental rights law provides a first answer about what is common among the Member States.[2] The complexity of the law regulating transactions outside the sphere of influence of the European law on fundamental rights, at the level of national legal orders, as well across national legal orders and at the EC level, seems to be more difficult to dominate in intellectual terms.[3]

---

[1] P. *Legrand*, A Diabolical Idea in A. *Hartkamp et al.* (eds.), Towards a European Civil Code (3rd ed. Nijmegen 2004) 245 is eloquent on this point.

[2] A. *Colombi Ciacchi*, 'The Constitutionalization of European Contract Law: Judicial Convergence and Social Justice', (2006) 2 European Review of Contract Law 167; H. *Collins*, 'European Social Policy and Contract Law', (2005) European Review of Contract Law 114, esp. 116–117; O. *Cherednychenko*, 'Fundamental Rights and Contract Law', (2006) 2 European Review of Contract Law 489; M. R. *Marella*, 'The Old and the New Limits of Freedom of Contract in Europe', (2006) 2 European Review of Contract Law 257 (a brilliant critical assessment of the present situation).

[3] There is growing attention of the circumstance that this difficulty is compounded by the fact that Europe is a multilingual language: e.g. V. *Jacometti*, B. *Pozzo* (eds.), Multilingualism and European Law (2006); G. *Ajani*, M. *Ebers* (eds.), Uniform Terminology for European Contract Law (Baden-Baden 2005); R. *Sacco* (eds.), L'interprétation des textes juridiques rédigés dans plus d'une langue (Torino, Paris, 2002).

As European lawyers, these features of the present European landscape are opportunities, rather than difficulties. Therefore my reference to 'unresolved issues' in the title of this paper is not intended as a pessimistic remark about the future, but it is simply a note about where we stand. So far, there is no common vision of what private law will be in Europe in the years to come, despite the growing numbers of contributions that are dedicated to this topic across Europe and the initiatives of the EC in this field. With respect to the subject of the present paper – contract law – one could carve out an exception for the consumer law aspects of the topic.[4] The law relating to contracts with consumers does not have such a long history as the rest of the law of contracts. Therefore it is less conditioned by the rich and complex legacy of the past out of which the general law of contracts emerges. Furthermore, European directives have played a large role in its recent development. The major challenge in terms of developing a European outlook on the law of contracts is clearly constituted by the general landscape of private law with respect to contracts. It is here that it is difficult to find a bridge among competing visions of contract law. The European Principles of Contract Law and the European Contract Code prepared by the Academy of European Private Lawyers are brave efforts in this respect. They try to overcome the problem – as professors sometimes do – by assuming that we all know what a contract is. We do, of course, and yet we also have different approaches to that key notion. Each major national legal tradition has evolved its own notion(s) of contract in this respect. Therefore, we can all say we know what contracts are. On the other hand, these notions differ. Hence, though we all know what a contract is, we all differ in approaching the subject. It is this difference among conceptions of contracts that should be addressed now.[5] It is remarkable that this difference also raises signifi-

---

[4] The measure in which this is possible is the object of the enlightening contribution by G. *Howells* to this volume.

[5] The are several comparative works well worthy of consultation on this point: J. Gordley, Foundations of Private Law: Property, Contract, Unjust Enrichment (Oxford, 2006); R. *Sacco*, G. *De Nova*, Il contratto (3rd ed. Torino, 2003) (I am much indebted to this work); H. *Beale*, A. *Hartkamp*, Hein *Kötz*, D. *Tallon*, Contract Law: Cases, Materials and Text (Oxford, 2001), (therein the contributions by B. *Rudden* and C. *Jauffret Spinosi*); J. *Gordley* (ed.), The Enforceability of Promises in European Contract Law (2001); H. *Kötz*, European Contract Law, I, (trans by T. *Weir*, Oxford, 1997); R. *Zimmermann*, Law of Obligations, Roman Foundations of the Civilian Tradition (Oxford 1996); J. P. *Dawson*, Gifts and Promises: Continental and American Law Compared (New Haven and London, 1980); A.T. *von Mehren*, Contracts in General, in International Encyclopedia of Comparative Law, ch. 1, 9, 10, (Tubingen, The Hague, Boston, London, 1982, 1992, 1998); R. *Schelsinger* (gen. ed.) Formations of Con-

cant and unexpected problems in the field of consumer law, which are seldom discussed.[6] Bearing this difference in mind, the proposal to resort to European Standard Contract Terms to facilitate transactions across the European space requires careful evaluation also.[7] To make progress in our field the general issue should therefore not be sidestepped. To be sure, the existing Acquis communautaire provides sources that are relevant to the analytic exercise undertaken in the following pages.[8] Nevertheless, these sources allow us to catch only glimpses of what is at stake here. The following pages are an effort to cast light on this point. I will not try do more than to sketch the general argument, as it is proper for a short essay. Hence, I will not address several issues that would need coverage by a lenghtier treatment of the topic. I am thinking, first of all, to general issues of contract law, such as the interests protected by the law of contracts and the relationship contracts and contract remedies, as well as to related points such as whether promises should be accepted to become binding, or the extent to which an agreement is necessary to bring about a contract.[9] If my effort is fruitful, the analysis could be developed with respect to other aspects of the same general question. Why, for example Directive 2002/47/EC is entitled "les contrats de garantie financière" in its French version (similar expressions are employed in the Italian version as well), while both the English and the German versions of this instrument avoid references to the concept of contract?

---

tracts (Dobbs Ferry, N.Y. 1968); G. *Gorla*, Il contratto. Problemi fondamentali trattati con il. metodo comparativo e casistico (Milano, 1955). So far, no general meta-analysis of this rich literature is available. *D. Kennedy*, 'From the Will Theory to the Principle of Private Autonomy: Lon Fuller's Consideration and Form', 100 Colum. L. Rev. 94 (2000) prvides an excellent example of what than meta-analysis could achieve.

[6] As pointed out by S. *Whittaker* 'Unfair Terms, Public Services and the Construction of a European Conception of Contract' (2000) 116 Law Quarterly Review 99–107; P. *Nebbia*, Unfair Contract Terms in European Law: A Study in Comparative and EC Law (Oxford and Portland, Or. 2006), 95 et seq. See also G. *Cavalier, F. Upex*, 'The Concept of Employment Contract in European Union Private Law' (2006) 55 International and Comparative Law Quarterly 587.

[7] S. *Whittaker*, 'On the Development of European Standard Contract Terms' (2006) 2(1) European Review of Contract Law 51.

[8] For an excellent guide to it see R. *Schulze*, 'European Private Law and Existing EC Law' (2005) 1 European Review of Private Law 3.

[9] On this point I refer the reader to the brilliant analysis developed by R. *Sacco, Formation of Contracts*, in A. Hartkamp et al. (eds.), *Towards a European Civil code* (fn1, above), 353 et seq. and J. Gordley, The Philosophical Origins of Modern Contract Doctrine (Oxford, 1991).

II. Three notions of contract

1. Contract as the voluntary assumption of an obligation

National systems of contract law in Europe can be arranged along an ideal line which links two opposite poles. At one extreme, contract is the voluntary assumption of an obligation by a manifestation of intent. Well known examples of this conception are provided by German law and Scots law. Both highlight the role of individual will in identifying the category of contractual obligations. Both do not stipulate causa and consideration as prerequisites for the validity of contracts,[10] though both require specified forms for the validity of specific contracts.[11]

The European Court of Justice adopted a similar idea when it was called upon to clarify the special grounds of jurisdictions for contractual and extracontractual claims under the Brussels Convention on Jurisdiction and the Enforcement of Judgments in Civil and Commercial Matters of 1968 (now replaced by the EC Council Regulation No 44/2001). In several cases, the Court held that: "… the expression matters relating to contract within the meaning of Article 5(1) of the Brussels Convention is not to be understood as covering a situation in which there is no *obligation freely assumed by one party towards another*".[12] The most recent case of this kind is *Fonderie Officine Meccaniche Tacconi SpA v Heinrich Wagner Sinto Maschinenfabrik GmbH (HWS)*.[13] The question submitted to the Court was whether an action for precontractual liability (as a result of the unlawfully breaking off of negotiations) falls within the scope of the *forum delicti* (Art. 5(3)) or within the scope of the *forum contractus* (Art. 5(1)), or within the general criterion of the domicile of the defendant. The Court held that the action did not involve 'matters relating to a contract' and fell instead within the scope of the *forum delicti* because in the circumstances there was no obligation freely assumed by one party towards another on the occasion of negotiations with a view to the formation of a contract.[14]

---

[10] On causa and consideration see see below §§ 2 and 3.

[11] On the form of promises to make gifts in German law: BGB §518; in Scots law: Requirements of Writing (Scotland) Act 1995, s. (1)(2)(a)(ii).

[12] Case C-26/91 *Handte v Traitements Mécano-chimiques des Surfaces* [1992] ECR I-3967, §15; *Réunion Européenne and Others v. Spliethoff's Bevrachtingskantoor BV*, [1998] ECR I-6511, § 17 (emphasis added).

[13] 2002] ECR I, 7357, at § 19.

[14] For critical comments on this decision see P. Mankowski, 'Die Qualifikation der culpa in contrahendo – Nagelprobe für den Vertragsbegriff des europäischen IZPR und IPR, Anmerkung zu: EuGH, U. v. 17.09.2002 – Rs. C-334/00' IPRax 2003, 127–135; G. Afferni, Case Note, (2005) European Review of Contract

The Rome Convention on the Law applicable to Contractual Obligations of 1980, which is also part of the *acquis communautaire*, points in the same direction. The Convention does not define the notion of 'contractual obligation' (Art. 1). Nonetheless, the European Court of Justice holds that the Convention applies where there is a voluntary assumption of an obligation.[15] The choice to have an autonomous notion of contract for the purposes under the Convention helps once more to promote a uniform application of the Convention in Europe. The step in this direction was clearly facilitated by the circumstance that, at the national level as well, the concepts used by private international law do not reflect purely national concerns.[16] But, of course, the autonomous notion that the Convention adopts (just like that emerging from the Brussels Convention on jurisdiction and judgments) is functional for the purposes of the Convention. It does not tell us much about the ethos and the structure of the notions of contract emerging at the national level, nor about their implications or corollaries.

2. Contract as a bargain

At the other extreme of the aforementioned ideal line there is the pole represented by English law (Irish law shares the same basic features of English law, as far as I can tell). English law rejects the idea that the voluntary assumption of an obligation is enough to produce a contract. A contract requires a *bargain* between the parties. The constellation of different rules that make up the doctrine of consideration – applicable to all contracts not made by deed – sanctions this conclusion. Lacking the ele-

---

Law, 96. Though the conceptual argument about the absence of an obligation freely assumed by one party towards another party in this case is prominent in the decision of the Court, the contractual qualification of the litigious issue was also rejected on the basis of the functional consideration relating to the difficulty of establishing ex ante where a (contractual) obligation of good faith in the negotiations should be performed (cf. para. 22 of the decision).

[15] *Soc. Handte et Cie Gmbh V. Tm CS* [1993] ECR I 3967. There are opinions to the effect that such a voluntary assumption of responsibility must result out of agreement (see e.g., R. *Plender*, The European Contracts Convention (2nd ed., London, 2001), § 3-09, 3-10). But this does not appear to be settled and one may wonder why an obligation resulting out of a unilateral promise would be excluded from the scope of application of the Convention.

[16] See, e.g., *In Re Bonacina, Le Brasseur v. Bonacina* [1912] 2 Ch. 394 (a voluntary agreement lacking consideration may be invalid under the applicable lex fori, but it can still be considered as a contract from the point of view of choice of law rules).

ment of reciprocity that is characteristic of a bargain, the relationship between the parties is not a contract. Hence, a gratuitous mandate, or a gratuitous deposit are not contracts under English law. Trusts and gifts are not contracts under English law either, of course. If a promise not supported by consideration is made in the form of a deed, the existence of the required form will render the promise binding, despite the lack of consideration. But, absent this form, the promise will be a nullity, even if it is accepted.

Are there traces of this notion of contract in the acquis communautaire? This idea features in the decision of European Court of Justice in the famous *Dietzinger* case.[17] That case concerned the question whether a contract of guarantee or suretyship that is concluded (under German law) between a financial institution and a natural person who is not acting in the course of his trade or profession, to secure a claim by the financial institution against a third party in respect of a loan, is covered by the words "contracts under which a trader supplies goods or services to a consumer" of art. 1(1) of the doorstep selling directive (85/577/EEC). The Court answered the question with the following statement:

"it is apparent from the wording of Article 1 of Directive 85/577 and from the ancillary nature of guarantees that the directive covers only a guarantee ancillary to a contract whereby, in the context of 'doorstep selling', a consumer assumes obligations towards the trader with a view to obtaining goods or services from him."[18]

In other words, the Directive applies to guarantees, but only where the main debt itself constitutes a consumer transaction. In the case of Herr Dietzinger and of the guarantee he had signed for the benefit of his parents the credit in question was a business credit for a building firm. Hence, Herr Edgar Dietzinger could not invoke the German legislation implementing the Doorstep Selling Directive. For present purposes, the case is remarkable not so much because of the conclusion it reached,[19] but because the Belgian, Finnish, French and German Governments *rely-*

---

[17] *Bayerische Hypotheken- und Wechselbank AG v Edgar Dietzinger Environment and Consumers* Case C-45/96 [1998]ECR 1998, I-1199.
[18] Ibid., § 22.
[19] C Joerges, 'The Bright and the Dark Side of the Consumer's Access to Justice in the EU', (2001) Global Jurist: Vol. 1: Iss. 2 (Topics), Article 1; Id., 'Interactive Adjudication in the Europeanisation Process? A Demanding Perspective and a Modest Example, (2000) 8 European Review of Private Law, 8 (2000).

ing on the English text of the directive[20] argued that the guarantee was not a contract for the purpose of the directive:

> "because the consumer receives no consideration, or, in other words to the same effect, because the guarantee is not a synallagmatic contract – namely a bilateral agreement involving mutual and reciprocal obligations or duties – but a unilateral undertaking from the point of view of the guarantor."[21]

3. Contract as the voluntary assumption of an obligation supported by a sufficient cause

French and Italian law fall in between the opposite poles of this field. Both French and Italian law link the notion of a contract to the element of *cause*, or *causa*, which can be onerous or gratuitous. Hence the category of contracts includes a wide range of gratuitous transactions (including gifts and promises of gifts, which must be notarized), alongside onerous transactions. Yet the requirement of causa operates to exclude the validity of abstract promises, contrary to what happens under German and Scots law. This requirement has often been attacked because of its ambiguity or indeterminacy. Nonetheless, the recent French project of reform of the civil code maintains the notion of cause as a requirement for the validity of a contract.[22]

III. Coming to terms with different notions of contract

1. The limitations of a functional approach

How have the aforementioned differences among conceptions of contracts been understood in a wider European perspective, i. e. in a perspective that includes the relevant parts of the national laws? The answer may

---

[20] R. Sacco, 'L'interprète et la règle de droit européenne', in R. Sacco (ed.), 226 et seq.
[21] Opinion of Advocate General *Jacobs* delivered on 20 March 1997, Case C-45/96. [1998] ECR, 1998, I-1199, § 14, summarizing the submission of the aforementioned Governments. The UK government did not submit arguments to the effect that the guarantee was not covered by the directive.
[22] *Avant-Projet de reforme du droit des obligations(Articles 1101 à 1386 du Code civil) et du droit de la prescription (Articles 2234 à 2281 du Code civil)*, Rapport à Monsieur *Pascal Clément Garde des Sceaux*, Ministre de la Justice. On the other hand, the Dutch Civil Code has abandoned this requirement.

lie in the comparative works that have addressed the point. To simplify my analysis I will concentrate on the treatment of the English law of contracts by one of the few textbooks that aim to map the entire field of contracts in a comparative perspective and that has been virtually mandatory reading for comparative lawyers across Europe, namely, Zweigert and Kötz's *Introduction to Comparative Law*.[23] The title of the relevant chapter of the book is: 'Indicia of Seriousness'.[24] The topic is approached from the following perspective. There are some requirements of contracts distinct from form – such as consideration under English law – introduced by the law to make sure that the intention to enter into a binding contract is serious.[25] Let me make clear that this view of consideration is not eccentric at all. It retrieves a theory that has a long historical pedigree. A major study of the history of English contract law notes that this view of consideration was familiar at least to some medieval interpreters of the common law who held that consideration was a way to check whether promises were seriously made.[26] From the contemporary point of view, it is common to find statements that ventilate the opinion that consideration serves an evidential and formal function and that the requirement of consideration may also ensure that a promisor has deliberately decided to contract.[27] Yet, this reconstruction of the function of consideration is still missing something. As a rule, English lawyers – contrary to their Scottish or German colleagues – are still unable to say that *a seriously intended gratuitous promise is binding without more, even when it is not a promise of gift.* There is a gap, or rather a mismatch, in the analysis of the law that I am discussing here. True, in England (as elsewhere) a promise or an agreement made without the intention to be legally bound will not be binding in principle. But this doctrine belongs to a separate chapter of the English

---

[23] K. Zweigert, H. Kötz, Introduction to Comparative Law (3rd ed. trans. By T. Weir, Oxford, 1998).

[24] Ibid., pp. 388–409. This way to frame the question raises a general problem, i.e. why deliberation in making the promise is so important to the law. On this point see J. Gordley, *Foundations of Private Law*, p. 355.

[25] See, e.g., at p. 390: "In the common law of England and the United States an informal promise is treated as serious only if it is made against a 'consideration', that is some counterpart from the promisee."

[26] Cf. A.W.B Simpson, *A History of the Common Law of Contract. The Rise of the Action of Assumpsit* (Oxford, 1975), p. 322 (on Christopher St. Germain's Doctor and Student).

[27] See., e.g., J. Beatson, *Anson's Law of Contract* (28th ed. Oxford 2002), pp. 88–89. As to the latter function, the author cites *Pillans v. van Mierop* (1765) Burr.1663, per Willmot J. at 1670. But before turning to these functions Beatson makes clear that the idea of reciprocity is the 'distinguishing mark' of consideration. On this point see below.

law of contracts nowadays.[28] The doctrine of consideration cannot be understood only as a way to check the seriousness of the relevant intention, apartfrom a broad functional perspective. Indeed, some of the statements of that leading *Introduction* contradict – as they should – the opening line that the requirement of consideration can be understood as a way to ensure that the intention to enter into a contract was a deliberate one.[29] In the twentieth century opinions have been advanced in England to suggest that the doctrine of consideration could as well be abandoned as a mere technicality. These proposals have never been put on the legislative agenda, but the approach to that requirement today in England is less rigid than in the past precisely because by now it is clear that this requirement may actually *defeat* the fulfilment of the deliberate intention of the parties, as it was pointed out by Russel LJ in *Williams v. Roffey Bros. & Nicholls (Contractors) Ltd*[30] with respect to agreements that introduce contractual modifications:

"I do not believe that the rigid approach to the concept of consideration [...] is either necessary or desirable. Consideration there must still be but, in my judgment, *the courts nowadays should be more ready to find its existence so as to reflect the intention of the parties to the contract* where the bargaining powers are not unequal and where the finding of consideration reflects the true intention of the parties."[31]

---

[28] The historical path to the present approach is traced by *A. W. B. Simpson*, 'Innovation in Nineteenth Century Contract Law' (1975) 91 LQR. 247 to the influence of continental writers on the common law; *D. Ibbetson*, A Historical Introduction to the Law of Obligations (Oxford 1999), 236 et seq. casts light on the tension between a will theory of contract from which the doctrine originates and the model of contract as exchange.

[29] Cf. *K. Zweigert, H. Kötz*, Introduction to Comparative Law, p. 391: "The promise may be the result of mature reflection, it may be actuated by the most praiseworthy motives, and the promisor may be morally bound to honour his word, but the Common Law requires more than this. It requires that the parties have made a 'bargain' with each other and that the promise in question be part of this 'bargain': 'An Englishman is liable not because he has made a promise, but because he has made a bargain' " (the citation featuring in this passage is from the book on the law of contract by *Cheshire Fifoot* and *Furmstone*). If I am not wrong, *H. Kötz*, European Contract Law, I, (trans by *T. Weir*, Oxford, 1997), shows a remarkable change of heart on treating consideration as an indicia of seriousness. See also below, III.4.

[30] [1991] 1 Q.B. 1.

[31] [1991] 1 Q.B. 1, at 18 (emphasis added). The court held that, under the circumstances, the modification of the contract had provided 'practical benefit' to the claimant, and that the agreement to modify the contract was therefore sup-

Though consideration has been functionally approached (inter alia) as a tool to check if the promise or the agreement was seriously intended, an attempt to account for it from this perspective only is partial and limited. It strips the English notion of contract of some features that we should rather take into account to understand it on its own terms. What are these features? It is time to take a closer look at them.

2. Understanding foreign law notions in their own terms

The quintessential idea lurking behind the notion of consideration is that of 'self interest'. Contracts are binding because each contracting party advances its own interest by entering into the contract. From an English perspective contracts and promises are not altruistic acts. They are utilitarian ventures rooted in reciprocity. Lacking this element – reciprocity – the expression of the intention to be legally bound is simply not enough. Since contracts are made in the name of self-interest, it follows that each party is supposed to look after its own interest. The idea that consideration should be adequate to have a binding promise is not part of the English law either, according to the orthodox view of the matter. Courts do not interfere with the parties' assessment of the value of what is exchanged, provided that the intention to enter into the contract is not vitiated. Even if the requirement of consideration were to be abrogated tomorrow, this utilitarian shape of the English law of contract would not change as rapidly. The doctrine of consideration may be a technicality, but it is a technicality that tells us a lot about the English law of contracts, about its formative ideas and principles.[32]

3. Getting the full picture

What are we to make of this last remark? For the sake of discussion, here I will sketch two possible reactions to the analysis I have developed so far. The first reaction is, in my view, naïve and tends to stress difference. The second reaction looks more carefully at the implications of a law of contract that puts reciprocity on its coat of arms. By doing so, this alternative reaction unveils the hidden side of a law of contract squarely based on the notion of reciprocity.

---

ported by consideration. This view is criticised by E. McKendrick, Contract Law (Houndsmill, Basingstoke 5th ed. 2003), 96–98.

[32] Compare on this point H. Kötz, European Contract Law, I, p. 58.

The first reaction that I am introducing goes more or less like this. English law is truly at odds with legal systems belonging to the Romanistic world. It is definitely at odds with German law, possibly the most coherent illustration of the Romanistic legal tradition. German law, faithful to the immortal teaching of Kant, honours the idea that persons are moral agents by enforcing promises as manifestations of free will. True, in Germany also promises of gifts require the notarized form prescribed by the Civil Code to ensure genuine consent. But outside this special case, the binding force of individual will is recognized without more. English law, on the contrary, puts promises and contracts in the service of commerce. No wonder that the English law of contracts has a distinctive adversarial flavour which, incidentally, explains its traditional resistance to 'good faith'. No wonder that Scottish law – being faithful to its civilian roots – rejects the English requirement of consideration. I need not labour the point further: English contract law would still be – according to this view – the creation of a country under the spell of a 'vil ésprit de commerce'.[33] The reaction I am picturing takes for granted that the English legal tradition is a monolith, like the other legal traditions that are played up against it. It thus dramatizes the differences existing between these various traditions but, in doing so, it is rather naïve. It is naïve at two levels. First of all, in historical terms, the English law of contract has been part of a European wide movement of *ideas and practices* long before the establishment of the European Community.[34] What are we to make of this part of the history of English law? But it is also rather naïve because it fails to grasp and make sense of other aspects of English law, which are no less important than those discussed so far. To be sure, English law considers the pursuit of self-interest the dominant motive in the field of contracts. But in England, as elsewhere, the range of (informal) inter vivos transactions that actually occurs is by no means limited to self-interested transactions. Consider the following instance. Undertakings to act *in the interest of another* in English law are not considered contractual in nature – for obvious reasons, at this point – yet they originate in obligations that are enforceable against the person who is acting in such capacity (i.e.

---

[33] The expression was used during the works for the preparation of the French civil code by no less than J.M. *Portalis* to stigmatise the English law because it provided for life insurance contracts ('l'homme est hors de prix' !). The French Council of State, nonetheless, allowed them as well. On this interesting episode: F. *Drosso*, 'Le viager ou les ambiguïtés du droit de propriété dans les travaux préparatoires du Code civil' Droit et Société, 2001, p. 895, esp. p. 909.

[34] This is a topic for another day, of course. But, to return briefly to good faith, let's at least keep in mind at least that it found its place in insurance law in England law long before the establishment of the European Community and the impact of its directives on the national contract laws.

as a fiduciary). Here is a concise definition of the obligations that bind a person who is in a fiduciary position:

> "A fiduciary must act in good faith; he must not make a profit out of his trust; he may not act for its own benefit or for the benefit of a third person without the informed consent of his principal."[35]

Once a fiduciary relationship is in place, there are no obstacles to reach the conclusion that it involves duties of loyalty and of good faith. These duties are indeed the gist of a fiduciary relationship. Fiduciary relationships are not contractual in nature under English law, yet fiduciary duties intersect contract law and provide important supplements to it. The typical instance of this complex configuration is provided by the law of agency.[36] To denote the expression of intent that originates fiduciary obligations English lawyers speak of 'undertaking', rather than of 'promise'. This terminological shift reflects the idea that fiduciary obligations and contractual obligations belong to different compartments of the law. Nonetheless, as far as inter vivos transactions are concerned, there are undertakings which are promises in terms of operative facts. With respect to them, the line drawn between 'promise' and 'undertaking' marks a distinction without difference.[37]

4. The ironic side of self interest

The ironic side of a law of contract rigorously based on the pursuit of self interest emerges as soon as this branch of the law is considered in the wider context of English law. In that wider context, reference to self-interest appears under a different light. Rather paradoxically, the egoistic edge of the law of contracts provides a frame for marking off transactions that do not conform to the stringent logic of self interest. These are transactions that bring in the risk of disadvantageous consequences due to the possible presence of elements of overreaching. Since the ambit of contract law in England is defined through the idea of reciprocity, any transaction lacking this element is comprised within the domain of those transactions that must be strictly scrutinized under this theory.

---

[35] *Bristol and West B.S. v. Mothew* [1998] 1 Ch. 1, at p. 18, per Millet LJ (as he then was).
[36] F.M.B. *Reynolds*, Bowstead and Reynolds on Agency (18 ed. London, 2006).
[37] A. *Burrows* 'We Do This At Common Law But That in Equity' (2001) 22 Oxford Journal of Legal Studies 1.

Probably the best illustration of this aspect of English law is offered by the law relating to the granting of security.[38] Consider the typical case in which a wife grants a security to a lender over her share of the matrimonial home in order that her husband (or the husband's company) could obtain further finance from a bank for the purposes of his business. The transaction 'calls for an explanation' if it cannot be explained in commercial terms. In such cases, the bank will have to show that the wife acted independently of undue influence and with full appreciation of the practical implications of the transaction to avoid the rescission of it.[39] The bank usually discharges the burden of proof in this matter by showing that the person providing the security obtained independent and competent advice, in accordance with guidelines set out by the House of Lords in *Royal Bank of Scotland v. Etridge (No 2)*.[40] If the bank hires a solicitor to provide the wife with proper advice, the solicitor's duties are owed to the wife and to the wife alone. As a core minimum, a solicitor advising the wife can be expected to give advice relating to the nature of the documents submitted to her and the practical consequence these will have for her, the seriousness of the risks involved, the purpose of the facility, the amount of the facility, the fact that the amount and terms might be changed without reference to her. The advice should be given in a face-to-face meeting in the absence of the husband. The solicitor should also make clear that is her choice whether to enter into the transaction or not and that it is not a formality.[41]

All these consequences flow from the fact that a transaction of this kind does not clearly advance the interest of the person granting the security.

Can the language of the cases relating to this problem be translated into a language that is more familiar to civil lawyers? In the law of Scotland, the rules applicable in these cases are held to be a manifestation of the principle of good faith: "Lying behind these examples of situations where the creditor is obliged to take steps in the interest of the cautioner

---

[38] For a wider approach to the theme see A. *Colombi Ciacchi*, Non-Legislative Harmonisation of Private Law under the European Constitution: The Case of Unfair Suretyships, (2005) European Private law Review 285.

[39] The notion of undue influence that is deployed to sanction the possibility of abuse of trust and confidence is not to be considered a peculiarity of English law. Cf. S. *Wer*, Undue influence – mögliche Einflüsse des Civil law von Ende des 16. bis Anfang des 19. Jahrhunderts?, ZSS Rom. Abt., 2006, 248.

[40] *Royal Bank of Scotland v Etridge* (No 2) [2001] 1 AC 773.

[41] Ibid., per *Lord Nicholls*. The bank must provide the solicitor with the financial information that he needs for the purpose of advising the wife and bank should take steps to check directly with the wife the name of the solicitor she wishes to act for her.

is the basic element of good faith."[42] But is the test under which these transactions are reviewed in England and in Scotland actually the same? Though with some hesitation, the Scottish Court of Session did not commit itself to this conclusion.[43] Apparently, one of the reasons of its reluctance to adhere to it, is the circumstance that the type of detailed guidance provided to lenders by the House of Lords in the *Etridge* case is not fully consonant with the flexible approach favoured under a good faith test.

IV. Conclusions

There are several unresolved issues on the road to the further development of a European dimension of private law. Many of these unresolved issues concern the assessment of the utility of more European Community law in the field of private law and to the redistributive effects of such a move. Answering the questions raised in this respect may involve more empirical research as well as decisions that have a broad political nature. Clearly, European integration through private law cannot be only considered as an academic exercise. There is, however, one aspect of this story which raises an uncomfortable point for all those involved in this research field. That is the difficulty produced by the fact that foreign law is sometimes approached with the wrong questions in mind. To ask the wrong questions is the most successful recipe to get the wrong answers. It may well be that some of the unresolved issues that complicate today's contract law landscape in Europe have their source in this original sin.

---

[42] *Smith v. Bank of Scotland* 1997 S.L.T. 1061, at 1066 per *Lord Clyde*.
[43] *Clydesdale Bank plc v. Black* 2002 S.L.T. 764 (Extra Division of the Inner House). Cf. M. Higgins, A Break From the Old Routine: The Doctrine in *Smith* (2002) S.L.T. 173.

Standard terms in International Commercial Law – the example of documentary credits

Christian Twigg-Flesner[*] (Hull)

I. Introduction

This paper focuses on the role of standard terms in the context of international commercial law. Although in many ways not a altogether new feature of contract law, the abortive attempt by the European Commission to promote European-wide action in this area as part of its general initiative on a European Contract Law[1] has provided a fresh impetus for examining this topic. The decision by the Commission to scale back its activities in this regard[2] is welcome – but not because the cross-border development of standard contract terms is undesirable: for many years, standard contract terms for international commercial transactions have been developed at a transnational level with considerable success, and action confined to the territory of the European Union (EU) would probably not have added much of value. However, that is not to say that the widespread use of standard terms in international commerce is without its own challenges, and national legal systems will have to cope with trying to ensure that such standard contract terms are given full effect, even when faced with the difficulty of reconciling such terms with principles and doctrines of domestic law. In order to illustrate that this can be done successfully, this paper will highlight one of the arrangements for international trade finance, documentary credits, based largely on a set of internationally-agreed standard terms. The next section will explore the relevance of standard terms in International Commercial Law, followed

---

[*] Senior Lecturer in Private Law, University of Hull, UK.
[1] Communication from the Commission to the European Parliament and the Council, A More Coherent European Contract Law. An Action Plan, COM (2003) 68 final, paras 81–88 and Communication from the Commission to the European Parliament and the Council, European Contract Law and the revision of the *acquis*: the way forward, COM(2004) 651 final ('*The Way Forward*'), pp. 6–8.
[2] Although it is not entirely clear if all activities in this field have now been abandoned: see *First Annual Progress Report on European Contract Law and the Acquis Review* COM (2005) 456 final, 23 September 2005, page 10.

by an overview of the rules regarding documentary credits. The role of standard terms in the general debate about the *lex mercatoria* raises interesting questions, which are briefly alluded to. A final section then comments on the EU's activities in this area.

II. Standard terms in International Commercial Law – General Observations

1. Developing International Commercial Law

The development of an International Commercial Law[3] has occupied scholars and international organisations alike for some time now, and the ever-increasing globalisation of commerce ensures that this trend continues. International Commercial Law is made up of a diverse range of components, including international conventions on aspects of commercial law, general principles of law, uncodified and codified usages, and, indeed, standard terms.[4] These activities are motivated by a concern about the differences in national commercial laws and the impact this may have on the smooth operation of international commerce. The fact that national laws vary will require the parties to an international contract to seek legal advice on the possible consequences for their transaction.

Removing such differences would reduce a potential obstacle towards international commerce. The overarching objective is therefore to create a harmonised, or even uniform, set of rules within which international commerce can operate. Thus, conventions are adopted to create a formal legal framework that will deal with specific legal matters, such as the sale of goods or agency. Agreeing on a convention that is acceptable to as many nations as possible is a major challenge, because consensus between different legal traditions is often elusive. Indeed, there is scepticism regarding the use of conventions for the harmonisation of commercial law save in respect of matters where international action is really needed (such as the protection of property interests across borders).[5] Model laws, which are not intended to have the same binding force and are conse-

---

[3] Or Transnational Commercial Law – this paper will use the term International Commercial Law.

[4] There may be some overlap between these components. Leading examples include the United Nations Conventions on the International Sale of Goods (CISG) and the UNIDROIT Principles of International Commercial Contracts.

[5] See e.g., Hobhouse, "International Conventions and Commercial law: the pursuit of uniformity" [1990] *Law Quarterly Review* 530.

quently more flexible, are easier to adopt, and individual states are often free to adapt such laws to their own legal system.[6]

Whatever method is chosen, it should be appropriate to the objective pursued. In the context of international commercial law, that objective should be facilitating commerce and respecting, as much as possible, the methods developed by commerce for organising its dealings. Care needs to be taken that commerce is promoted, rather than stifled, by the action taken.

2. The significance of standard terms

In this regard, an important tool for promoting international commerce is the development of standard terms, or international trade terms.[7] Standard terms are sets of contract terms drafted independently of any specific contractual negotiation, and are used for transactions which occur frequently. The use of standard terms has obvious benefits, particularly in terms of efficiency – little time needs to be spent on developing and negotiating terms and conditions, and this will produce cost savings. Such contracts may be drafted by individual businesses for use in transactions with their customers, but this can lead to problems when two businesses have their own conflicting sets of standard terms. Because of this, standard terms developed by commerce-related organisations (whether domestic or international) will be of more use, because such organisations will be neutral with regard to the relationship between prospective contracting parties. This is particularly important for international commerce. For certain categories of transactions which occur frequently in international commerce, there will be advantages to having available a set of standard terms that can be used, irrespective of where the contracting parties are located and which law might govern their contract. Standard terms which are developed at the international level by an organisation which commands the respect of the international commercial community, could significantly facilitate international commerce.

Standard terms of this type benefit from being drafted by those with expertise in the relevant sector of international commerce. The drafting procedure can be less formal than would be the case with international conventions, because there will be less concern about the impact on an established national legal framework than there would be with a conven-

---

[6] L. Del Duca "Developing Transnational Harmonisation Procedures for the Twenty-first Century", in R. Cranston and R. Goode (eds.), *Commercial and Consumer Law: National and International Dimensions* (Oxford: Clarendon Press, 1993).

[7] This paper will continue to use the term 'standard term'.

tion. Moreover, there is an speed advantage: if new terms are needed, they can be developed more quickly, and if it subsequently transpires that the standard terms do not work as well in practice as hoped, they can be amended more easily than, for example, a convention.[8]

The leading organisation in this field is the International Chamber of Commerce (ICC),[9] which has developed model contracts and clauses designed for international commerce (INCOTERMS). The ICC seeks to avoid any particular national bias, but instead concentrates on drafting terms which seek to protect both parties' interests. This should make their model contracts widely attractive. The work of the ICC includes drafting the *Uniform Customs and Practice for documentary credits*, which are dealt with below.

Standard terms only take effect if they are incorporated by the parties into their contract. Because standard terms need to be incorporated, they have no free-standing legal effect, which makes them unsuitable for issues which require a clear legal framework.

The success of standard terms in promoting international commerce depends on whether they are adopted by parties to international contracts. If the standard terms do not properly reflect commercial practice, then their adoption is unlikely.[10]

Disputes arising in respect of contracts based on standard terms will often be heard by international arbitrators. However, courts do become involved, and, in the absence of a system of international commercial courts, the task of interpreting such standard terms will fall on the domestic courts. Indeed, the bulk of the work of the English commercial court involves the construction of standard terms.[11] With contracts based on international standard forms and not necessarily relying on legal terms of art, a court faces the dual challenge of construing the contract correctly and of ensuring that its decision does not conflict with the intentions of those who drafted the standard terms.

A difficulty with standard terms is that all contracts, including international commercial contracts, depend for their effectiveness on a particular national law of contract. There may be points of conflict between the relevant standard terms and domestic laws, particularly with regard to

---

[8] Generally, R. Goode, "Reflections on the Harmonisation of Commercial Law" in R. Cranston and R. Goode (eds.), *Commercial and Consumer Law: National and International Dimensions* (Oxford: Clarendon Press, 1993).

[9] See http://www.iccwbo.org/.

[10] R. Goode, "Reflections on the Harmonisation of Commercial Law" in R. Cranston and R. Goode (eds.), *Commercial and Consumer Law: National and International Dimensions* (Oxford: Clarendon Press, 1993), p. 9.

[11] R. Goff, "Commercial Contracts and the Commercial Court" [1984] *Lloyds Maritime and Commercial Law Quarterly* 382, p. 387.

rules which are mandatory (including rules on the incorporation of standard terms and the controls regarding unfair terms). This problem might affect the effectiveness of such terms, but it also poses a challenge for those jurisdictions which make the use of certain standard terms unattractive or impossible to avoid, thereby potentially stifling commerce through rigid adherence to rules which may not be suitable for international commercial contracts.

III. The Uniform Customs and Practice for Documentary Credits – Successful Standard Terms

An important aspect of any international commercial transaction is that one party will be required to pay the other for the goods or services supplied. The obvious risks in any commercial contract are financial, but these are exacerbated in the international context. However, commerce – banks, in this instance – has developed a system for international payments which reduces many of the risks: documentary credits. The interesting feature of this is that the framework that governs documentary credits does not rely on international conventions, but is based entirely on a set of standard terms developed by commerce without regulatory intervention.

1. Documentary Credits

One of the obvious risks in international commerce for a seller is that he may not receive payments for goods after they have been despatched, particularly if there is a risk that the buyer may become insolvent. At the same time, a buyer may be unwilling to make payment until goods which are in conformity with the terms of the contract have been received. It is obvious that neither party can insist on receiving performance from the other party before commencing its own performance, and both will have to find a middle ground. The documentary credit system has developed to resolve this impasse. A documentary credit, or letter of credit, is an undertaking given by a bank to a seller of goods to pay the price due for the goods if specific conditions are met, generally the presentation of shipping documents and other documents as stipulated. The advantage for the seller is that payment will be promised by the bank which is far less likely to be unable to pay. The buyer will have some assurance that the seller has performed his obligations, although, as will be seen shortly, the risk of obtaining an inadequate performance of the contract is higher for the buyer than the seller.

2. Documentary Credits and the UCP

Documentary credits are governed by the *Uniform Customs and Practice for documentary credits*, or UCP. The first version was published in 1933,[12] and there have been regular revisions since then – the most recent version are the UCP600.[13] They are developed by the Commission on Banking Techniques and Practice of the International Chamber of Commerce (ICC), whose membership comprises representatives from the commercial community. The UCP600 are therefore not created by legislators, but rather by the commercial community that will actually apply them. Their wide-spread use by banks for global commerce has lead to the suggestion that the UCP "represent the most successful attempt at harmonisation of international commercial law."[14]

One of the interesting features of the UCP is the fairly recent establishment by the ICC of a dispute resolution procedure to assist with the application of the UCP (in 1997). This involves a panel of experts dealing both with disputes and questions of application regarding the UCP.[15] This procedure is intended to be swift, and the presumption is that its decisions are not binding on the parties. In view of the expertise of the panel and the direct involvement of the ICC, any decisions are likely to be accepted by the parties. The existence of this procedure is somewhat unusual, because it is one of the rare instances in the field of International Commercial Law where there is a central authority that can assist with the application of internationally-agreed rules.[16]

The UCP are one example of standard terms in international commerce. To describe the UCP as "terms" might be regarded as a misnomer,

---

[12] With subsequent revisions in 1951, 1962, 1974, 1983 and 1993. The 1993 version is known as the UCP500.

[13] The UCP600 were adopted in late October 2006 and due to come into effect on 1 July 2007. The previous version was the UCP500 from 1993. The United Nations Commission on International Trade Law has endorsed the UCP500 and previous versions, but at the time of writing, the new UCP600 had not yet been endorsed. References to specific provisions in this paper are still to the UCP500.

[14] R. Bradgate, *Commercial Law*, 3rd edition, Oxford: Oxford University Press, 2000, p. 797.

[15] See *ICC Rules for Documentary Instruments Dispute Resolution Expertise* (DOCDEX), 2002.

[16] The EU has the benefit of its Court of Justice, whose jurisdiction entails the ability to give binding views regarding the interpretation of EU legislation (Art. 234 EC).

and some prefer to refer to the UCP as "guidelines".[17] However, the UCP will only apply if incorporated expressly into the relevant contract, because they have no independent legal status.[18] It is certainly the case in English law that the UCP are ultimately contractual in nature and are treated as a set of contractual terms.[19]

It is debatable how easily they could be incorporated by implication – this may be a matter for the domestic law applicable to the transaction. Therefore, although the UCP by their name are described as a custom and one might therefore expect implication into any relevant contract by implication, it does seem that a more deliberate step by the parties is required to conduct a transaction on the basis of the UCP. For example, Horn argues that express incorporation is a precautionary step for the protection of bank customers because the UCP favour banks rather than bank customers, and that the UCP should not be regarded as trade usages.[20] In contrast, Dalhuisen takes the view that incorporation is not necessary because of the UCPs' customary nature.[21] In practical terms, the documentation used by a bank will almost certainly include a direct reference to the UCP in any event, thereby ensuring their incorporation.[22]

3. UCP – A brief outline

For present purposes, it will be sufficient to give a brief overview of the system operated under the UCP.[23] The contract of sale between buyer and seller will require the buyer to pay by documentary credit. The buyer will instruct his bank (the *issuing* bank) to set up a documentary credit which will promise payment to the seller once the conditions specified by the buyer have been met. It is possible that a documentary credit may be *revocable*, i.e., subject to revocation by the issuing bank before payment is due, but since the UCP500, there is a presumption that documentary

---

[17] E.g. E. P. Ellinger, "Use of some ICC guidelines" [2004] *Journal of Business Law* 704.
[18] See Article 1 UCP500.
[19] See R. Goode, *Commercial Law*, 3rd edition (London: Penguin, 2004), p. 970.
[20] N. Horn in "The Use of Transnational Law in the Contract Law of International Trade and Finance" in K. P. Berger (ed.), *The Practice of Transnational Law*, The Hague: Kluwer Law International, 2001.
[21] J. Dalhuisen, *Dalhuisen on International Commercial, Financial and Trade Law*, 2nd edition, Oxford: Hart Publishing, 2004, p. 150.
[22] Cf. Bradgate, note 14 above, p. 798.
[23] A key practitioner text is J. Raymond, A. Malek and D. Quest, *Documentary Credits* 4th edition, Tottel Publishing, 2007 (forthcoming).

credits are *irrevocable*.[24] This means that the issuing bank is under an irrevocable obligation to pay, provided that the seller presents the correct documents.

The issuing bank will also make arrangements with another bank in the seller's country to act as *advising* bank to inform the seller that a documentary credit has been opened. The advising bank may simply act as an agent for the issuing bank in communicating the opening of the credit and for paying the seller, in which case the credit will be regarded as *unconfirmed*. The advising bank may, however, agree to assume a separate obligation to pay the seller, and where this occurs, the credit is *confirmed*. A confirmed credit will, of course, provide a stronger assurance of payment to the seller, and a subsequent failure by the advising bank (which is then also referred to as the *confirming* bank) to make payment in respect of a credit it has confirmed would enable the seller to sue a bank in his own jurisdiction.

An important feature of documentary credits is that they are *autonomous*,[25] i.e., the credit and the related sales contract are separate transactions. A failure by the seller fully to comply with the terms of the contract of sale would consequently not entitle the buyer or one of the banks involved in the documentary credit to refuse to pay the seller, provided that all the requirements for gaining the entitlement to be paid under the credit are met by the seller.

In addition, the documentary credit system relies entirely on documents (which no longer have to be paper documents[26]), and the parties to the credit will only deal with each other on the basis of documents.[27] The buyer therefore needs to specify clearly not only the conditions that need to be met by the seller before payment should be made, but also the documents that need to be presented by the seller to demonstrate compliance with such conditions. In the UCP, there are four categories of documents: transport documents, insurance documents, invoices, and other documents (e.g., warehouse receipts, certificates of origin, certificates of quality etc.).[28] The seller, having been advised of the opening of the credit and having shipped the goods, will submit the documents required under the credit to the advising/confirming bank. The bank is re-

---

[24] Art. 6 para (c) UCP500.
[25] Art. 3 UCP500.
[26] A modified version of the UCP500, known as the eUCP, came into effect from April 2002. The new UCP600 will incorporate these modifications, with one UCP applying both to paper and electronic documents.
[27] Art. 4 UCP500.
[28] See Arts. 23–38 UCP500.

quired to check within a reasonable time[29] that the documents submitted by the seller comply, on their face, with the terms and conditions of the credit. In carrying out this process, banks should take "reasonable care", and compliance is to be determined by international standard banking practice.[30] In the English literature, this is generally known as the principle of 'strict compliance'. There is some uncertainty as to how strictly the documents tendered by the seller must comply with the terms of the credit, although it is generally accepted that the standard is a high one. If there are discrepancies, the bank may consult with the buyer about waiving these, if it so decides. There is no obligation to do so, however, and the bank can decide instead to refuse the documents and give notice to the seller that the documents do not comply.[31] The risk of non-compliance of the documents tendered by the seller with the conditions of the credit is a high one – indeed, in the majority of cases, documents are rejected by banks when first presented by the seller.[32] The most recent version of the UCP seeks to reduce the instances of finding non-compliance by clarifying that the information in the documents need not be identical to that in the credit provided that it does not conflict with it, which should reduce the number of discrepancies.[33]

4. Challenges for domestic courts

As mentioned earlier, the UCP have no independent force of law and take effect through incorporation into the contract between the buyer and the issuing bank. The legal effectiveness of the UCP therefore may depend on their fit with the relevant principles of contract law governing the particular contract. This may throw up a number of challenges, depending on the doctrinal requirements of a particular jurisdiction. English law, for example, with its requirement that a contract requires consideration,[34] might be expected to have difficulties with the fact that the pay-

---

[29] Art. 13 para (b) UCP500; in the UCP600, the reference to a "reasonable time" will be replaced with a maximum period of five banking days.
[30] Art. 13 para (a) UCP500.
[31] Art. 14 UCP500.
[32] See M. Bridge, "Documents and Contractual Congruence in International Trade" in S. Worthington (ed.), *Commercial Law & Commercial Practice*, Oxford: Hart Publishing, 2003, p. 227; Bradgate, *Commercial Law*, p. 810.
[33] P. Taneja, "UCP600: a document restoring the credibility of L/Cs" [2006] *DC Insight* Oct-Dec. [http://www.iccbooks.com/Home/CredibilityofLCs.aspx] (last accessed 8 January 2007).
[34] See generally G. H. Treitel, *The Law of Contract*, 11th edition, London: Sweet and Maxwell, 2003, ch.3.

ment undertakings of the issuing and/or confirming banks are intended to be enforceable by the seller. It seems that the seller provides no consideration to either bank in return for the undertaking to pay the seller on presentation of the relevant documents, and applying the doctrine of consideration strictly could lead a court to conclude that a seller would be unable to enforce this undertaking in legal proceedings. Such a conclusion would obviously undermine the effectiveness of the UCP, and various attempts have been made to justify the enforceability of the banks' obligations towards the seller.[35] However, to date, no attempt has been made to challenge documentary credits on this basis, and it is extremely unlikely that, if an English court was asked to address this issue head-on, it would be held that documentary credits are unenforceable for want of consideration. Indeed, the courts have been sensitive to the fact that "an elaborate commercial system has been built up ... and ... it would be wrong to interfere with that established practice".[36]

As the UCP are terms of a contract, the courts will essentially be involved in the interpretation of that contract when it comes to resolving disputes regarding documentary credits. Here, the courts need to tread carefully and avoid interpretations that could undermine the operation of the UCP. This may be particularly challenging when a matter comes before a court which is not addressed directly in the UCP. This poses the risk of letting domestic rules infiltrate the framework established by the UCP which – even with the best of intentions – could create serious difficulties. However, the English courts have generally responded well in such circumstances, but there are instances where attempts to come to an interpretation which matches commercial expectations have run into difficulties. A somewhat controversial example is *United City Merchants (Investments) Ltd v Royal Bank of Canada (The American Accord)*.[37] In this case, a fraudulently issued bill of lading showing the wrong shipping date of manufacturing equipment was presented by the seller (who was unaware of the fraud) to the confirming bank. The bank refused to pay because it was aware that the goods had not been shipped on the date stated in the bill of lading. The question eventually resolved by the House of Lords was whether in these circumstances, the bank was justified in its refusal to pay. It was held that because the seller had not been fraudulent himself and was unaware that the date was incorrect, the bank was obliged to honour its commitment to pay on presentation of the documents. Underpinning the reasoning of Lord Diplock, who gave the only speech, is the fundamental principle that documentary credits are

---

[35] See e.g., the summary in Bradgate, *Commercial Law*, p. 802.
[36] *Per* Jenkins LJ in *Hamzeh Malas & Sons v British Imex Industries Ltd.* [1958] 2 QB 127 at p. 129.
[37] [1983] 1 AC 168.

autonomous and that the parties only deal with each other on the basis of the documents. If the documents, on their face, are in order, then the bank is obliged to pay. The House of Lords had to consider the argument that the obligation to pay should not arise if the documents, whilst on their face in order, contain a material inaccuracy. This proposition was firmly rejected by Lord Diplock, because accepting it "would, in my view, undermine the whole system of financing international trade by means of documentary credits".[38] Moreover, the UCP themselves state that neither the issuing nor the confirming bank assume any responsibility for the accuracy or genuineness of the documents,[39] provided that the banks have examined the documents with reasonable care. A different conclusion would be "strange from the commercial point of view".[40] The only situation in which a court should permit a bank to refuse to pay is where there the seller fraudulently presents documents which he knows contain inaccuracies or wrong information.[41]

On the one hand, this judgment is remarkable because it seeks to resolve the question before the court on the basis of the UCP and the needs of commerce.[42] On the other, the reasoning has been heavily criticised both for misunderstanding the relevant provisions of the UCP and for its assumptions regarding the various obligations owed by the bank. In particular, Goode argues that the bank is not under an *obligation* to pay, but is *entitled* to pay if it has concluded after reasonable examination of the documents that they are in order.[43] He states that this is in effect a rule to protect a bank which has paid out, rather than a positive obligation to pay out once apparently conforming documents have been presented. However, according to the UCP, the bank has to undertake to pay if the seller presents the relevant documents, and the courts have certainly treated this as a binding obligation.[44] Irrespective of the correctness of the reasoning or outcome in this case, it does illustrate the difficulties for the courts in resolving disputes based on standard terms such as the UCP.

Overall, therefore, courts need to ensure that their involvement in disputes involving standard terms such as the UCP does not undermine the effectiveness of terms which have evolved from commercial practice and are therefore best suited to the particular transaction.

---

[38] [1983] 1 AC 168, p. 184.
[39] Art. 15 UCP500.
[40] [1983] 1 AC 168, p. 184/5.
[41] [1983] 1 AC 168, p. 183.
[42] D. Irvine, "The law: an engine for trade" (2001) 64 *Modern Law Review* 333, p. 341.
[43] See R. Goode, *Commercial Law*, 3rd edition (London: Penguin, 2004), p. 994.
[44] *Hamzeh Malas & Sons v British Imex Industries Ltd.* [1958] 2 QB 127 at p. 129.

IV. International Commercial Law, the *lex mercatoria*, and Standard terms

It was noted above that one of the hallmarks of the UCP, and the possible reason for their success, is the fact that they are drafted by experts in banking and are based on banking practice. It is therefore plausible to suggest that the UCP are a good example of the kind of non-legal commercial practice known as the *lex mercatoria*. A perennial debate in the International Commercial Law field is about its constituent parts, particularly the existence and relevance of the *lex mercatoria*. Historically, the *lex mercatoria* was the system of rules that governed mercantile trade in mediaeval times. These rules were separate from other laws, and dispute resolution was a matter for merchants' courts. But slowly, the old *lex mercatoria* was taken over by the common law courts in England, and overtaken by national codification movements during the rise of the strong nation states. The wide range of instruments which can, in one way or another, be included within the scope of International Commercial Law, has by some been regarded as the new *lex mercatoria*.[45] Others, however, take a much more narrow view of what constitutes the *lex mercatoria*, confining its scope to international trade practice.[46] In its purest form, therefore, the *lex mercatoria* is continuously evolving and changes spontaneously,[47] although attempts are made to develop some sort of hierarchy.[48]

An obvious concern about the narrow view of the *lex mercatoria* is that it is impossible to identify what its substance is. It is therefore not surprising that conventions such as the CISG, the UNIDROIT Principles of International Commercial Contracts, or standard terms developed by international organisations have been described as codifications of the *lex mercatoria*, but that view is not uncontroversial.[49] With regard to standard terms, Goode, having noted that standard terms cannot have independent legal force because of their dependence on incorporation into particular contracts, suggests that they are at best "evidence of existing usage or

---

[45] E.g., A. Goldstajn, "The new Law Merchant" [1961] *Journal of Business Law* 12.

[46] R. Goode, "Rule, Practice and Pragmatism in Transnational Commercial Law" (2005) 54 *International and Comparative Law Quarterly* 539, pp. 546–547.

[47] Ibid.

[48] See e.g., J. Dalhuisen, *Dalhuisen on International Commercial, Financial and Trade Law*, 2nd edition, Oxford: Hart Publishing, 2004.

[49] O. Lando, "The Lex Mercatoria in International Commercial Arbitration" (1985) 34 *International and Comparative Law Quarterly* 747; R. Goode, "Usage and its reception in Transnational Commercial Law" (1997) 46 *International and Comparative Law Quarterly* 1.

fashioners of new usage."⁵⁰ Thus, he states that the UCP "*may* be evidence of pre-existing usage but this will not be true of all the terms, since there will inevitably be some departures in order to improve current practice" – after all, the function of standard terms is to provide a degree of harmonisation to facilitate international commerce.⁵¹ So even the UCP, codified and improved practice as they are, designed by the banking experts for banks, may not be part of the narrow *lex mercatoria*.

However, such reservations about the status of standard terms should not detract from the fact that such contracts can be of more immediate use in promoting international commerce than conventions, because they are created by those who best understand the needs of commerce.

V. The European Commission and Standard Contract Terms

Following the launch of its (on-going) activities in the field of European Contract Law in 2001,⁵² the Commission proposed to promote the establishment of standard contract terms, particularly by offering guidance on the constraints set by European law regarding the use of standard terms and conditions.⁵³ The Commission was concerned that standard terms had generally been developed only at the national level, and were therefore ill-suited to cross-border transactions.

The Commission was keen to support the creation of sectoral standard contract terms that could then be used throughout the EU. It initially suggested that it would establish a website that could be used by businesses for exchanging information that would assist in the drafting of standard contract terms, but that was abandoned. The reasons for this seemed to be predominantly of a practical nature, particularly in keeping the site up-to-date and ensuring the accuracy of the information placed on it. Substantive concerns were based on the fact that EU-wide standard contract terms would have to be compatible with the most restrictive national rules.⁵⁴

---

⁵⁰ Goode, n. 8 above, p. 26.
⁵¹ R. Goode, "Rule, Practice and Pragmatism in Transnational Commercial Law" (2005) 54 *International and Comparative Law Quarterly* 539, p. 550
⁵² Communication from the Commission to the Council and the European Parliament on European Contract Law, COM (2001) 398 final.
⁵³ *Action Plan*, paras 81–88.
⁵⁴ *First Annual Progress Report on European Contract Law and the Acquis Review* COM (2005) 456 final, 23 September 2005, p. 10.

There are additional reasons for shying away from pursuing EU-wide standard contract terms:[55] first, there is the general difficulty of language (and terminology), particularly with regard to translating a set of standard terms from one language into another. Secondly, there are variations in the domestic contract laws of the Member States regarding the default rules applicable to certain types of contract.[56] Thirdly, the approach to interpreting contracts varies between jurisdictions, and that, too could reduce the effectiveness of such terms.[57]

These are all good reasons for being cautious about developments in this regard; yet, in view of the success of international standard terms (and not just the UCP, which deal with a particular aspect of banking practice, but also things such as the INCOTERMS), it does seem feasible to push ahead with standard terms generally. Curiously, the Commission seems to be ignorant of the activities of various international organisations,[58] including the ICC.[59] Had their activities been considered as part of the debate, it might have become apparent that it is possible to succeed in developing standard terms for cross-border use. It might, however, also have created the impression that European initiatives in this regard are not needed – the international (global) level has probably pre-empted this issue. The Commission has rightly been criticised for failing to recognise the significant work that has already been done in the field of international standard terms, and this failure might be the primary reason for the lack of support from businesses for the Commission's proposals in this regard.[60]

One might even go one step further and suggest that the real problem for the European level could perhaps be the fact that the concern about the normative framework within which standard terms would be developed is too great, and identifying the needs of commerce in respect of cross-border trade has been given insufficient emphasis.

---

[55] S. Whittaker, "On the Development of European Standard Contract Terms" (2006) 2 *European Review of Contract Law* 51.
[56] *Ibid.*, pp. 61–63.
[57] *Ibid.*, pp. 63–67.
[58] The only reference is to an organisation called Orgalime, which is cited as an example of an organisation that has managed to produce standard terms for cross-border transactions.
[59] Cf. E. McKendrick, *The Creation of a European Law of Contracts – The Role of Standard Form Contracts and Principles of Interpretation* (The Hague: Kluwer, 2004).
[60] U. Bernitz, "The Commission's Communications and Standard Contract Terms" in S. Vogenauer and S. Weatherill (eds.), *The Harmonisation of European Contract Law* (Oxford: Hart Publishing, 2006).

It remains to be seen whether the Commission has abandoned this issue altogether; in particular, the identification of legislative obstacles to the use of standard contract terms on an EU-wide basis, with a view to reducing or eliminating them,[61] could be a worthwhile endeavour.

VI. Conclusion

This contribution highlighted the importance of standard terms for international commerce, and the challenges they present for domestic courts. The example of the UCP on documentary credits shows that such terms can be hugely successful. Internationally developed standard terms reflecting commercial practice are of significant benefit in facilitating trade. The European Commission's attempt to support work on EU standard terms was abandoned, which, in view of the long-established activities at the international level is not to be regretted. This is not because the development of standard terms is too difficult a task – but because it is primarily for commerce to develop standard terms which will be of use.

---

[61] First Annual Progress Report, pp. 6–8.

Part V
National Experience and
Supranational Law

The Common Frame of Reference in general – a resumé of the current status

Hugh Beale[1] *(Warwick)*

In this paper I give an account of progress on the project to create a Common Frame of Reference, and offer a personal view of what may happen over both the next few months and in the longer term.

I. The background[2]

Readers will know that for some time the European Community has had a project to develop a "European" contract law in some shape or form. For present purposes we may begin the story in 2001 with the European Commission's *Communication on European Contract Law*.[3] This asked first whether there was any evidence that differences between the legal systems were hindering trade within the internal market. It then set out four options. These were:
1. No action
2. To promote the development of common contract law principles, leading to more convergence of national laws.
3. To improve quality of the legislation already in place and
4. To adopt new comprehensive legislation at the EC level.

---

[1] Professor of Law, University of Warwick; Law Commissioner for England and Wales (Commercial and Common Law). I was a member of the Commission on European Contract law 1987–2000 and am a member of the Study Group on a European Civil Code. Thus in my personal capacity I am one of the 'researchers' for the CFR project. The views expressed here are purely personal. Contact address: Hugh.Beale@lawcommission.gsi.gov.uk.

[2] This is a shortened version of an account published in H Beale, 'The Development of a European Private Law and the European Commission's Action Plan on Contract Law' (2005) X Juridica International 4.

[3] COM (2001) 398 Final.

The Communication produced a very large number of responses, which can be found on the Commission's website.[4] There was certainly evidence that in some sectors differences between the legal systems were indeed causing additional costs in trade between Member States, though the degree of the hindrance was estimated very differently by different respondents. As to the options, there were very few who said nothing should be done. Almost everyone agreed that the quality of the existing legislation should be improved. Many people supported the development of common contract law principles though some, including our government, doubted whether convergence of national laws should be seen as an end in itself. As to the question of comprehensive legislation at EC level, there was wide variety of opinion from those who wanted a civil code as soon as possible to those, again like the United Kingdom government, who were opposed to option 4 "in any of its forms".

There were also differing reactions also among the European institutions, varying from a cautious response on the part of the Council of Ministers[5] to a very enthusiastic one, with a detailed and ambitious plan of action, from the Parliament.[6] There was also an interesting reaction from the Economic and Social Committee. This said it would prefer to see a European contract law in the form of a Regulation.[7] This would not replace national laws, however. It would be on a set of rules that the parties could choose to govern their contract in place of national law. It would contain consumer protection measures, since ECOSOC sees the new law as being particularly valuable to consumers and SME's.

In 2003 the Commission published its *Action Plan on a more coherent European Contract Law*.[8] This proposed, in essence, combining the second and third options. It proposed that the existing *acquis communautaire* should be improved and future legislation should be drafted by using a Common Frame of Reference ('CFR').[9] The CFR is in effect the restatement referred to in the second option of the earlier paper. The CFR would not have independent legal force but would be a guide or tool-box for legislators. The paper also suggested promoting European Community-wide contract terms (the Commission's involvement was to be limited providing a website on which information about contract terms could be exchanged); and that there should be 'further reflection' on the need for an optional instrument.

---

[4] http://europa.eu.int/comm/consumers/cons_int/safe_shop/fair_bus_pract/cont_law/comments/summaries/sum_en.pdf.
[5] http://register.consilium.eu.int/pdf/en/01/st12/12735en1.pdf.
[6] COM(2001) 398 final, C5-0471/2001 – 2001/2187(COS) (OJ C 140 E, 13.6.2002 p. 538.
[7] Ecosoc INT/117 European contract law (OJ C 241, 7.10.2002, p. 1).
[8] COM (2003) final, OJ C 63/1 ('AP').
[9] AP para 72.

Further details of the Commission's plans were set out in a document in 2004, *European Contract Law under the Revision of the Acquis: the way forward*.[10] This suggested that the Common Frame of Reference should contain common fundamental principles of contract law, definitions and some model rules. An annex to the document suggested the possible content of the CFR. The Commission seemed to envisage that the CFR will cover the general parts of contract law (the annex reads very much like the table of contents to the Principles of European Contract Law) plus provisions on consumer law. That is an important addition since the PECL deliberately did not cover consumer law. Further, there might be provisions on specific contracts, sales and insurance being mentioned. Meanwhile, it was announced that eight consumer directives are to be reviewed and these can then be revised in the light of the CFR.[11]

The core of the project thus seemed to comprise three things: development of a Common Frame of Reference to act as a legislator's guide or tool-box; the promotion of EU-wide standard terms; and the possible Optional Instrument. I will not say anything more about the second idea, which has since been dropped by the Commission.[12] Instead I will concentrate on the CFR as legislator's guide and the possible Optional Instrument.

II. The Common Frame of Reference as a tool-box for Legislators

1. Principles, definitions and model rules

What would the CFR 'as a tool-box for legislators' contain, and what purposes would it serve? The *Way Forward* paper stated:

The structure envisaged for the CFR ... is that it would first set out common fundamental principles of contract law, including guidance on when exceptions to such fundamental principles could be required. Secondly, those fundamental principles would be supported by definitions of key concepts. Thirdly, these principles and definitions would be completed by model rules, forming the bulk of the CFR.[13]

---

[10] Communication from the Commission to the European Parliament and the Council, COM(2004) 651 final, 11 October 2004.
[11] Directives 85/577, 90/314, 93/13, 94/47, 97/7, 98/6; 98/27, 99/44. See WF para 2.1.1.
[12] See First Annual Progress Report on European Contract Law and the Acquis Review, COM(2005) 456 final, para 4.
[13] WF para 3.1.3, p. 11.

Annex I to *The Way Forward*, in which the Commission sets out a possible structure for the CFR, envisaged three separate chapters for Principles, Definitions and Model Rules respectively.

As examples of the "Principles" to be included in Chapter I of the CFR, the Annex listed 'the principle of contractual freedom', 'the principle of the binding force of contract' and 'the principle of good faith.'[14] Thus Principles seem to be simply the most general provisions of contract law.

"Definitions" seemed to be meant in a broad sense, to include not only definitions of particular terms such as "consumer" but also broader concepts. The Annex gave as examples:

'Examples: definition of contract, damages. Concerning the definition of a contract, the definition could for example also explain when a contract should be considered as concluded.'

In practice, a definition of "damages" or of "when a contract is concluded" is really a reference to a set of principles by which the matter is to be determined. So it is not at first sight clear how "principles" and "definitions" are different from "model rules". This seems to be confirmed by the Annex to *The Way Forward*. The model rules that were envisaged by the Annex seemed to be the equivalent of the rules of the Principles of European Contract Law ('PECL').[15] Sections I and III-VII follow very closely the scheme of PECL, not only Parts I and II but also Part III. Part III deals with a number of topics that either are applicable not only to contract claims but others,[16] or were omitted from the earlier work.[17] Annex I of *The Way Forward* included most of the former but not the latter. However, there would be at least one major difference from PECL. The CFR would be used to help revise the consumer *acquis* and would cover with consumer contracts,[18] whereas PECL had deliberately not dealt with consumer contracts specifically.[19]

---

[14] AF Annex I, p. 14.

[15] See *Principles of European Contract Law, Parts I and II* (ed O. Lando and H. Beale) (Kluwer, 2000); *Part III* (ed. O. Lando, E. Clive, A. Prüm and R. Zimmermann) (Kluwer 2003).

[16] Plurality of parties, Assignment of claims, Substitution of new debtor – transfer of contract, Set-off and Prescription. The annex includes all but Set-off.

[17] Illegality, Conditions and Capitalisation of interest. The annex does not refer to these, save that 'interest' is mentioned in the remedies section without indicating whether simple or compound interest is meant.

[18] See e.g. WF para 3.1.3, p. 11.

[19] See the Introduction to *Parts I & II*, xxv.

2. Purposes of a legislator's guide

It seems to me that the division between principles, definitions and model rules is not so much about the form of the CFR as about its possible functions. To explain this it may be easier to take them in the reverse order.

a. Model rules

The Commission will be reviewing, and possibly revising, eight consumer directives. Part of the review will be concerned with how the Directives have been implemented in the Member States, and in particular whether the 'minimum harmonisation' provisions have hindered achievement of the elimination of internal market barriers caused by differences between the laws of the Member States.[20] But it seems that the review is also concerned with the coherence and substance of the consumer *acquis*. If the Directives are to be revised, the Commission would obviously find it useful to have "model" rules which it could use or adapt to replace the existing articles of the various Directives. For example, the CFR might contain model rules showing how principles that underlie the various sectoral provisions might be given a wider application, so as to eliminate current gaps and overlaps. This might be done by a more "horizontal approach". The proposed rules might go beyond the existing consumer *acquis* to reflect what the authors of the CFR think are the "best solutions found in Member States' legal orders".[21] This might reflect what is to be found in those Member States that give consumers more than the minimum protection required by current Directives – an issue that will become particularly important if there is to be a move towards more "full" (at one time called "maximal") harmonisation.

b. Definitions

However, model rules will not be enough. Directives frequently employ legal terminology and concepts that they do not define. The classic example, referred to in the Commission's papers, is the *Simone Leitner* case.[22] The ECJ had to decide whether the damages to which a consumer

---

[20] WF para 2.1.1, p. 3. The Commission has commissioned a study of the implementation of the Directives, being carried out by a group headed by Professor Hans Schulte-Nölke.
[21] WF para 2.1.1, p. 3.
[22] Case C-168/00 *Simone Leitner v TUI Deutschland* [2002] ECR I-2631.

was entitled under the provisions of the Package Travel Directive must include compensation for non-pecuniary loss suffered when the holiday was not as promised. This head of damages is recognised by many national laws but was not recognised by Austrian law. The ECJ held that 'damage' in the Directive must be given an autonomous, "European", legal meaning – and in this context is to be interpreted as including non-pecuniary loss. A CFR containing definitions would be useful for questions of interpretation of this kind. National legislators seeking to implement the Directive and national courts would be able to consult the CFR to see what may have been meant – and, if comparative Notes are included, as they are in PECL, these will tell them how, if at all, the CFR definition differs from their existing national law.

The definitions would be even more valuable if they were adopted by the European institutions, preferably by an inter-institutional agreement or something equivalent, as a guideline for legislative drafting. The legislator could then employ these words and concepts, confident that the meaning will be clear without them having to be defined – or, if the legislator so chooses, they can vary or exclude the agreed meaning by particular provisions in the legislation. In other words, at the heart of the CFR as "toolbox" should be a set of agreed definitions of legal terms and concepts for use in drafting or revising European legislation.[23]

c. Principles

"Principles" would be different again. I think they would be rather abstract but nonetheless useful reminders to the legislator, for example that they should start with an assumption of freedom of contract that should be qualified (for example, by adopting mandatory rules for consumer protection) only when the case for such protection has been clearly made out. They might also include general principles of more-or-less universal application, such as the principle of good faith. But here we come to a problem and a further possible purpose for the CFR.

---

[23] This means that the CFR as tool-box would NOT be legislation in itself. This goes most of the way to meeting the criticisms made by the Study Group on Social Justice in European Law in their Manifesto "Social Justice in European Contract Law: a Manifesto", European Law Journal, Vol 10, No 6, November 2004, pp. 653–674.

d. 'Essential background' information

The problem is that if the CFR is to include general principles such as 'good faith', we need to be absolutely clear what the CFR (as legislator's guide) is actually telling the legislator. The principle of good faith is not known in the laws of all the Member States – in particular, in the common law jurisdictions. It is true that even the common law systems contain many particular rules that seem to be functionally equivalent, in the sense that they are aimed at requiring the parties to act in good faith.[24] However the legislator cannot assume that whatever requirements it chooses to impose to protect consumers will always be supplemented by a general requirement that the parties act in good faith. If it wants this to be the case in the common law jurisdictions, it will have to incorporate the requirement into the directive – as of course it did with the Directive on Unfair Terms in Consumer Contracts.[25] Alternatively, it will need to insert into the directive specific provisions to achieve the results that in other jurisdictions would be reached by the application of the principle of good faith.

In other words, the legislator needs to have accurate information about the different laws in the various Member States. European legislators need to know what is a problem in terms of national laws and what is not.

Take another example. In drafting or revising a directive dealing with pre-contractual information, legislators will want to know what they need to deal with and what is already adequately covered, and in a reasonably harmonious way, by the law of all Member States. Thus the general rules on incorporation of standard terms are relevant to unfair terms. The general principles on mistake, fraud and provision of incorrect information form essential background to the consumer *acquis* on pre-contract information. In this sense, even a "legislator's toolbox" needs statements of the "common principles" that are found in the different laws, and a note of the variations. These would not be intended as model rules to be included in the *acquis*, but as information about what is "out there" and what can be omitted from the *acquis* because, in one form or another, all Member States already have it.

This implies that, in addition to principles, definitions and model rules, the CFR could usefully contain what I term essential background material. This would group information about the different laws under headings with which the legislator will be familiar.

---

[24] See the Notes to PECL art. 1:201.
[25] Council Directive 93/13/EEC, art. 3(1).

III. A possible Optional Instrument

It is worth noting what is meant by "optional instrument". At least in informal discussion, some commentators on the *Communication* of 2001 seemed to suggest that, as not all countries would agree to a European Contract Code to replace national laws, there might instead be a new treaty adopting an optional code to which countries could adhere if they wished. In other words the situation might be a bit like adoption of the common currency, with another two-speed Europe. But this is not what the *Communication* referred to explicitly[26] nor what the *Action Plan* or *Way Forward* envisages.[27] They speak of a set of contract rules that the parties might choose to govern their contract, rather as now parties in the countries that have ratified CISG can choose to use it for international sales. This, of course, is what seemed to be envisaged by ECOSOC.[28]

There is not space here to discuss all the possible forms and contents of an optional instrument. Later in the paper I will return to the question whether or not the idea should be pursued. For the moment it is enough to remark that both the Commission and many of those involved in discussion of the project seemed to envisage that it might be a set of principles, based on the CFR, [29] that the parties might opt to use[30] in place of national law.[31] The Commission envisaged that it might be general or sector-specific.[32] It should certainly apply to business-to-business ('B2B') contracts but might also apply to consumer contracts.[33]

IV. Production of the CFR

1. The 'Network of Excellence'

As to how the CFR will be produced, the *Action Plan* referred to the research that is on-going,[34] and stated explicitly that it did not wish to re-

---

[26] See para 66.
[27] See WF para 2.3. WF Annex II contains a very full discussion of the possibilities.
[28] Above, note 7.
[29] WF Annex II p. 19.
[30] WF Annex II p. 18 states that most respondents favoured an opt-in model.
[31] WF Annex II p. 19.
[32] WF Annex II p. 20.
[33] WF Annex II p. 20.
[34] For a description of some of the research projects see H Beale, 'The Development of a European Private Law and the European Commission's Action Plan on Contract Law' (2005) X Juridica International 4, 5–6.

invent the wheel; further research projects should be started only where on-going research leaves a gap. However, DG Sanco (which was the leading DG in producing the Action Plan) did not offer to fund research itself, possibly because of uncertainty over whether it would have a legal base for so doing. Instead, the *Action Plan* suggested that research funds would be made available to research groups via the Sixth Framework Programme, which specifically included a call for research in this area. The result has been that a number of the groups have been combined into a single 'Network of Excellence'[35] that has been given a grant to produce a draft CFR or, to use the terminology of the bid, "Common Principles of European Contract Law", by the end of 2007. Three groups will be involved in drafting rules – these groups are termed, somewhat ambiguously in English, the "Principle Drafting Groups". These are the European Research Group on Existing EC Private Law (Acquis group) (which is looking particularly at the principles of the existing *acquis*),[36] the Project Group on a European Restatement of Insurance Law[37] and the Study Group on a European Civil Code (including its various teams).[38] Other groups will be providing "evaluation" of the draft CFR. These include the Common Core of European Private Law (or Trento) Project (which looks at how typical cases would be resolved in the various national systems, and will apply the same approach to the draft CFR),[39] the Association Henri Capitant[40] (which will address the underlying moral, philosophical and political foundations of each country's legal rules and point out the differences in the legal systems which have solid justifications and the ones that do not) and the Research Group on the Economic Assessment of Contract Law Rules (which will do as its name suggests). There will be two "Support Groups". The Database Group of the Institut Charles Dumoulin will create a database on the national case-law in the field of private law, organised according to the structure of the draft CFR. Relevant case law will be summarised in English or/and French and made available in full in its original language. The Academy of European Law (ERA) in Trier will organise conferences on the project.

---

[35] It appears that the relevant DG prefers to deal with networks of researcher groups rather than with the groups individually.
[36] See http://www.acquis-group.org.
[37] See http://www2.uibk.ac.at/zivilrecht/restatement.
[38] See http://www.sgecc.net. The Lando group that produced PECL has been subsumed into this larger Study Group.
[39] See e.g. R Zimmermann and S.Whittaker (eds.) *Good Faith in European Contract Law* (Cambridge UP, 2000). See http://www.jus.unitn.it/dsg/commoncore/home.html.
[40] See http://membres.lycos.fr/HenriCapitant/sommaire.htm.

The content was determined by what the researchers sought to bid for rather than by what DG Sanco may have thought it would need for the CFR, and it is a very wide project, including not only specific contracts such as sales, services, long-term contracts (commercial agency, distribution and franchise) and personal security but also topics such as tort, restitution, benevolent intervention and security over moveable property.

2. Stakeholder and expert meetings

The Way Forward made it clear that the Commission does not wish to rely on a wholly academic product. "Stake-holder participation" is essential. The Commission has established a network of stakeholder experts to engage with the academic researchers; and there were to be regular workshops "to enable stakeholders to identify practical issues to be taken into account and give feedback."[41] Working groups of experts from Member States were also set up.[42]

The original plan for the stakeholder meetings was that they should cover almost all the topics to be included in the draft CFR to be produced by the researchers under the FP6 contract. Thus there would have been about 30 stakeholder meetings. I have described the progress of these stakeholder meetings, and the first of a series of conferences on the project held in London,[43] in detail elsewhere.[44] It is enough to note that they encompassed a wide range of topics, including ones that are not of direct relevance to the consumer *acquis*. In other words, it seems that the Commission wanted to discuss the draft CFR both as a draft legislator's guide to help with revision of the consumer *acquis* and as the possible basis for an optional instrument applying at least to B2B contracts.

3. "Re-focussing" of the project

Since the start of the project, and particularly since the London conference, the Commission has sought to re-focus the project to concentrate on material that is relevant to revision of the consumer *acquis*. At first we thought that this would mean merely eliminating workshops on topics

---

[41] WF para 3.1.2, p. 10.
[42] Ibid.
[43] The first "European Discussion Forum", hosted by the British Presidency. It was to have taken place in London in July 2005 but because of the London bombings it was postponed until 26 September 2005.
[44] See H Beale, 'The European Commission's Common Frame of Reference Project: a progress report' (2006) 2 ERCL 303.

The Common Frame of Reference in general 353

such as tort and benevolent intervention that have almost no connection to issues covered by the consumer *acquis* or are unlikely to be relevant to EU legislation in the foreseeable future. Both the Commission and stakeholders seemed to think that the workshops should cover, and probably the final CFR should include, general principles of contract law along the lines suggested by Annex I o the *Way Forward* document.

However, at the end of 2005 it became clear that the Commission had something much more radical in mind. It held discussions with researchers on how the workshops could be organised in order to prioritise the work relevant to the consumer *acquis*, and what material should be presented to the stakeholders. The workshops would need to be completed by mid-2006 so that the Commission could use the researchers' texts, as amended after stakeholders' comments, by the start of 2007. Otherwise the *acquis* could not be revised by the Commissioner's deadline of 2009. Within this time frame there could be no discussion of general contract law as such. Any question of discussing the material as the basis for an optional instrument was put on one side. This would not affect the contract with the Network of Excellence: the researchers would still be obliged to deliver the full range of work originally undertaken. But it would affect drastically the workshops for 2006, and possibly the ultimate content of the CFR.[45]

To help the Commission, the researchers agreed to a revised plan of workshops under which the meetings for the first half of 2006 would focus on the principal topics relevant to revision of the consumer *acquis*. The next 6 meetings would cover:
- Pre-contract information
- Cancellation rights
- Unfair Terms
- Sales 1: conformity and "commercial"[46] guarantees
- Sales 2: remedies and transfer of risk
- Consumer rights to damages

This seems a very narrow focus. It is really dealing only with what the revised directives should include, "model rules" for consumer directives.

However, after some discussion, it was agreed the material to be presented for each workshop should be wider than this. It should include not just proposals for revision of the directives but also definitions of terms that may be used in the directives and not defined by them (such as "damages" or "when a contract is included"). It should also include, for

---
[45] It was emphasised that no final decision on the content would be made before the end of the project in 2007.
[46] I.e. guarantees voluntarily offered by the seller or producer to the consumer: see Directive 1999/44 art. 6.

information purposes, a statement of the general principles of contract law to be found in the Member States.

Thus in the first half of 2006, six workshops were held, and the definitions and rules were presented in three groups: (1) the model rules ('acquis revision' rules), (2) the definitions ('directly relevant principles of general contract law') and (3) the principles that the researchers consider to be 'essential background' to the *acquis* under discussion. (1) and (2) were to be discussed in the workshops but there would not be time to discuss (3). Instead, stakeholders would be invited to send in written comments on (3).

The workshops in 2006 were chaired the official in charge of the team within DG Sanco responsible for revision of the consumer *acquis*, Mr Giuseppe Abbamonte. It has to be said that they were rather successful. There was lively participation from many stakeholders, particularly from consumer organisations and organisations representing businesses that deal with consumers. The Chairman and the other Commission officials present were actively and constructively involved in the discussion. Mr Abbamonte said that he had found the workshops helpful.[47] On the other hand, those stakeholders who were not so concerned with consumer legislation but were interested in discussing the draft CFR as the basis for an optional instrument for B2B contracts naturally felt that the workshops were of less interest to them, and several previously active participants stopped coming.

4. Future workshops?

The question is, what should happen now? Some of us had hoped that the Commission might give some indication at the second conference on the project, held in Vienna in May 2006,[48] but this was not the case.

At the last workshop, held on 6 July 2006, the Commission official in charge of the Action Plan as a whole, and who had chaired most of the workshops in 2005, came to speak briefly. He appeared to indicate that he regarded the workshops needed for purposes of revision of the consumer *acquis* as having been completed. He indicated that, although no decisions had yet been made, it was likely that there would be no more work-

---

[47] Mr Abbamonte outlined some of the possibilities for revision of the consumer acquis in a paper given at a conference on 'The Review of the Consumer Acquis and the CFR – progress, key issues, perspectives, held in Vienna under the Austrian Presidency on 25–26 May 2006. His paper is available at http://ec.europa.eu/consumers/cons_int/safe_shop/fair_bus_pract/cont_law/conference052006/giuseppe_abbamonte.pdf .

[48] See previous note.

shops unless other DGs were interested in taking up the CFR for their purposes.

This came as something of a disappointment. First, it seems to be based on a misunderstanding of what it had been possible to achieve in the workshops. Although the 'directly relevant principles of general contract law' and the 'essential background' material had been given to stakeholders, there had usually been little or no chance to discuss them, because of the time taken to discuss the 'acquis revision' rules. Thus I would argue that if we are to have a CFR that will be a useful tool-box even just for the purposes of the revision of the consumer *acquis*, we need to have workshops on the topics of general contract law that have not yet been discussed so far. These should include:
1. General provisions (including the ever-controversial good faith clause) and Interpretation
2. Formation of contracts
3. Validity and Illegality
4. Performance
5. Remedies for non-performance (this might be sub-divided)
6. Prescription (this is of considerable practical importance e.g. in consumer sales and product liability)

Further topics could be agreed by the workshops as work progresses and as the scope of the revised *acquis* becomes clearer.

Secondly, this seems to be an abandonment by DG Sanco of any idea of an optional instrument.

Fortunately, however, it may be that other Directorates-General will find some interest in the idea. At the same time as this narrowing of the CFR, another development has opened up once more the question of an optional instrument. In December 2005 the Commission, through a different DG (Freedom, Security and Justice, formerly known as Justice and Home Affairs) produced a proposal for a new regulation on the law applicable to contractual obligations (Rome I).[49] This follows a Green Paper of 14 January 2003.[50] One of the principal changes would be in Article 3, which is designed to ensure freedom of choice. The introduction to the proposal explains:

To further boost the impact of the parties' will, a key principle of the Convention, paragraph 2 authorises the parties to choose as the applicable law a non-State body of law. The form of words used would authorise the choice of the UNIDROIT principles, the *Principles of European Contract Law* or a possible future optional Community instrument, while excluding the *lex mercatoria*, which is not precise enough, or private codifi-

---

[49] Brussels, 15.12.2005; COM(2005) 650 final (2005/0261 (COD)).
[50] COM (2002) 654 final.

cations not adequately recognised by the international community. Like Article 7(2) of the Vienna Convention on the international sale of goods, the text shows what action should be taken when certain aspects of the law of contract are not expressly settled by the relevant body of non-State law.[51]
Article 3(2) of the draft provides:

> 2. The parties may also choose as the applicable law the principles and rules of the substantive law of contract recognised internationally or in the Community.

However, questions relating to matters governed by such principles or rules which are not expressly settled by them shall be governed by the general principles underlying them or, failing such principles, in accordance with the law applicable in the absence of a choice under this Regulation.

Were this to be adopted, PECL and the Unidroit principles would become an optional instrument quite apart from the CFR. The same would be true of an optional instrument based on the CFR if only it could obtain Community recognition.

I do not know what chance this proposal has of being taken forward. It depends very much, I suspect, on the reaction of the Member States, and this in turn may depend on the reaction of the legal profession in each State. But at least the DG responsible for revision of the Rome Convention may have an interest in discussing with stakeholders the Principles which it is suggesting might be adopted by contracting parties in place of a national law.

It is possible that other DGs may also have some interest in the CFR. For example, one finding from the responses to the Commission's Communication of 2001 was that differences between the laws of the Member States caused considerable hindrances in the fields of insurance and financial services. These fall within the responsibility of the DG for the internal market.

The organisers of the Joint Network of Excellence have submitted to the Commission a paper outlining the workshops that they would like to see held over the next few months. They are as listed above. We await developments.

---

[51] COM(2005) 650 final, page 5.

5. An end to the CFR as legislator's guide for drafting the consumer acquis?

We have to ask whether, from DG Sanco's point of view, there is no longer perceived to be a need for a CFR that should provide either definitions or essential background information to legislators. We were told that no decision has been made, and none will be made for some time. However the attitudes of some officials towards general contract law sometimes seemed distinctly hesitant. The officials at the workshops seemed to be concentrating on the substance of the Directives, the model 'acquis revision' rules. That is of course perfectly sensible. I am not sure whether the apparent reluctance to organise workshops to discuss general principles of contract law is because DG Sanco's 'institutional view' is that these have been discussed adequately already (which, as I have said, would be a misapprehension), or whether really they think the CFR should not contain, for instance, definitions. Since definitions are at the heart of the CFR, that would amount really to abandoning the idea at least as far as consumer *acquis* is concerned.

I very much hope that DG Sanco will not abandon the idea that the CFR should contain general principles of contract law, at least so far as is needed to provide definitions of terms that will be used in the revised Directives. It is quite true that considerable improvements in the *acquis* could be made without the need for these definitions. As several stakeholders have pointed out, you don't need a CFR to sort out the differences in withdrawal periods, or to apply rights to pre-contractual information and rights of withdrawal in a more "horizontal" manner so as to eliminate gaps in coverage. Nor do we need it to identify variations in the way the Directives have been implemented in the Member States. That, as I have said, is the subject of a separate study.[52] I can therefore understand why general contract law is not felt to be crucial at this stage. But when it comes to fixing the precise contents of new directives legislators will need the essential background information that I think the CFR should provide. Even more importantly, for the actual drafting of the revised directives, if we are to reduce the uncertainty over what is meant by concepts which are not defined and which are not understood in the same way in every Member State, we will need definitions of the terms employed. I believe that some Commission officials are at least sympathetic to this view. I hope it becomes Commission policy.

---

[52] See note 20 above.

V. The CFR as basis for an Optional Instrument

I think that the doubt over the future of the CFR as a legislator's guide makes it even more important to consider seriously the idea of an Optional Instrument. This is for two reasons. The first is that I think it could be quite useful for cross-border transactions of relatively low value. Secondly, it could be a substitute – albeit a poor substitute – for the CFR as tool-box.

It might also be of some value way of protecting small business. At the Vienna conference, Diana Wallis MEP, who is a very active member of the Parliament's Committee on Legal Affairs, gave a paper in which she called for greater protection for other groups in addition to consumers. She said:

> There are other weaker parties (employees, trustees, franchisees, commercial agents, and small business) who also need EU level protection.[53]

I consider below whether the Optional Instrument would help small businesses in this respect. However, like her, I conclude that this kind of protection is more likely to be achieved by "horizontal instruments."

1. The Optional Instrument as an alternative to national law

It is evident that when parties from different member states are contracting with each other, differences between the laws can add to the transactions costs of the deal. Neither party may know very much about the law of the other party's country, and to find out may be quite expensive. True, these costs do not prevent cross-border contracts being made, and when the contract (or series of contracts being contemplated) is of high value, the cost of finding out about the other party's law may be comparatively insignificant. When the transaction is relatively small, however, the cost may be an important factor, especially if there is thought to be a significant risk that one or other party may default so that law matters. For such contracts, neither party may be happy about adopting the other party's law to govern the contract. I suggest that this is particularly the case for small and medium-sized enterprises ('SMEs'). Their contracts are not likely to be so large that the cost of legal advice is unimportant, but on occasion the legal risks may be significant.

---

[53] Available at http://www.dianawallismep.org.uk/articles/recent.html.

2. A law for the risk-averse

Thus the parties may wish to find a neutral 'third law' with which each is familiar. As my English colleagues are fond of emphasising, for many international contracts English law is often the "law of choice" for international contracts although neither party has any close connection to England. Why then, some colleagues ask, do we need a non-national law such as an Optional Instrument? Why not just encourage everyone to use English law?

There may be several answers to this. One is very simple. English law is very suitable for some kinds of transactions, such as commodity sales, charter-parties, and many financial transactions. However for others it is less suitable. This is because of the highly individualistic nature of English contract law. For instance, English contract law does not know any duty of good faith, any duty of disclosure[54] or any duty to point out that your contracting party is labouring under a mistake of fact, even when you know full well that they would never enter the contract if they knew the truth.[55] Moreover, some of the protection that is available in 'domestic contracts' does not apply to international contracts.[56] I suspect that SMEs are likely to be risk averse and, if properly advised, would choose to contract under a law under which the other party does have to act in good faith and under which unfair terms will be struck down. An Optional Instrument – or indeed PECL in their published form – would provide this kind of alternative.

3. Protection for small businesses?

Would creating an Optional Instrument of this kind give the kind of protection for small businesses that Diana Wallis seems to envisage? For example, should they benefit from protection against unfair contract terms in the same way as consumers?[57]

I wholly agree that at least "micro-businesses" (fewer than 9 employees) need this kind of protection. In the UK the Law Commissions have recommended that provisions equivalent to those of the Directive on Unfair Terms in Consumer Contracts should apply in favour of micro-

---

[54] Other than in insurance contracts, which are 'of the utmost good faith': see *Chitty on Contracts* (29th ed, 2004), para 6-140 and ch 41.
[55] See Chitty para 5-006.
[56] Unfair Contract Terms Act 1977 does not apply to contracts under which the law applicable is English law "only by choice of the parties (and apart from that choice would be the law of some country outside the UK)": s 27(1).
[57] See Directive 93/13/EEC.

businesses.[58] I am glad to be able to report that the Government has accepted the recommendation in principle, though subject to further consideration of the detail and to an impact assessment.[59] PECL already contains such a provision.[60] An Optional Instrument could also contain one, and could go further and give small businesses the same protection as consumers when they make purchases at a distance and so on.

Moreover, the provisions could be made mandatory.[61] This may seem a bit odd: how can a provision of an optional instrument be mandatory? The answer is that for small businesses, and likewise were the Optional Instrument is to be made applicable to consumer transactions, it should not be possible to choose to have the contract governed by the Optional Instrument without also accepting the consequence that certain provisions would thereby become mandatory. Any other rule would not protect the small business or consumer: they might choose the Optional Instrument because they think it offers protection, only to find that the small print of the contract disapplied the relevant articles. That should not be permitted. As far as any mandatory rules for small businesses or consumers are concerned, it would have to be an "all-or-nothing" system.

I would like to see protection for small businesses built into any optional instrument. However, I do not think that this would be sufficient. I think that we need to consider a directive that would require Member States to give this kind of protection. There are two reasons why I do not think an optional instrument alone would do the trick for small businesses.

The first reason is simple. Small businesses are very unlikely to have either the sophistication to know that they should seek to have the contract governed by the Optional Instrument or the bargaining power to insist on it.

The second reason is that while strengthening the private law affecting small businesses would be valuable, I think we may need to go further and require Member States to provide for small businesses the same kind of mechanism to prevent the continued use of unfair terms as is required by article 7 of the Directive on Unfair Terms in Consumer Contracts. Our

---

[58] Law Commission and Scottish Law Commission Joint Report, *Unfair Terms in Contracts* (Law Com No 292, Scot Law Com No 199, 2005), Part 5. There would be a variety of exemptions where the small business does not seem to need protection, for example in markets that are already regulated or where the transactions are so large that even a small business will take advice.

[59] Written Statement by the Parliamentary Under-Secretary of State, Department of Trade and Industry, House of Lords, 25 July 2006, *Lords Hansard* Col WS165.

[60] Art 4:110.

[61] See PECL art. 4:118.

experience in the UK is that improving consumer rights under private law has had far less impact than the work of our Office of Fair Trading in encouraging (and if necessary requiring) businesses to remove unfair terms from their general conditions. The Law Commissions would have recommended a similar scheme for unfair terms in small business contracts had they been able to identify a body willing and able to take on the task.[62] A preventive mechanism needs to be considered at the European level. But of course this can only be done by way of a directive or regulation, not via an optional instrument. An optional instrument can only affect the private rights of the parties.

So I conclude that while an optional instrument would be valuable for small businesses and SMEs, it would need to be supplemented by EU legislation parallel to that for consumers.

4. A lingua franca of contract law within Europe

Even if the Commission does not pursue the idea of a CFR as a legislator's guide, were an optional instrument to be adopted, I believe that its terms and concepts would become accepted as the presumptive meaning of legal terms and concepts in European contract law. I think that gradually the same would happen for the terms of new EU legislation: it would add to interpret EU legislation in a way that did not refer to what would have become the European norm. But this does not mean that, after all, we don't need a CFR. The process I have just described would be a slow one and in the meanwhile there would very much less certainty than if the Commission were to press ahead with a CFR providing a full legislator's guide to general principles of contract law. I very much hope that with the support of stakeholders, colleagues and European Parliamentarians we can carry the CFR forward.

---

[62] See *Unfair Terms in Contracts* (above, n 55), paras 5.92–5.95.

Die Terminologie des italienischen Zivilgesetzbuches auf dem Gebiet der allgemeinen Vertragsbedingungen: Probleme der Übersetzung

Salvatore Patti (Rom)

I. Die „allgemeinen Bedingungen" im Codice civile

Das italienische Zivilgesetzbuch von 1942 war bekanntlich das erste Zivilgesetzbuch, das allgemeine Vertragsbedingungen und Verträge regelte, die mittels einseitig gestellter Formulare geschlossen werden.[1] Das Phänomen war in der Tat zu Beginn des letzten Jahrhunderts, insbesondere im Bereich der Banken und Versicherungen, in Erscheinung getreten, so dass die anderen großen europäischen Gesetzbücher nicht die Möglichkeit hatten, es zu berücksichtigen.[2]

An dieser Stelle soll davon abgesehen werden, die Probleme der Koordination oder gar Vereinbarkeit der neuen Bestimmungen mit der liberalen Ausrichtung des Gesetzbuches darzustellen, welches grundsätzlich dem bereits dem Gesetzbuch des Jahres 1865 in Italien eingeführten Modell des *Code civil* treu geblieben war. Zunächst ist vielmehr hervorzuheben, dass die neuen Artikel, die das Sachgebiet regeln, in das Gesetzbuch neue Begriffe eingeführt haben oder – und dies ist für die Übersetzung ein noch viel interessanterer Aspekt – Begriffe benutzt haben, denen eine andere Bedeutung zukam als diejenige, welche vorher im Gesetzbuch verwendet wurde.

Es handelt sich um die folgenden drei Artikel:
Art. 1341 – Allgemeine Vertragsbedingungen
Art. 1342 – Mittels Vordrucken und Formularen geschlossene Verträge
Art. 1370 – Auslegung gegen den Urheber der Klausel

---

[1] M. NUZZO, *Condizioni generali di contratto*, in N. IRTI (Hrsg.), *Dizionario di diritto privato*, I, *Diritto civile*, Mailand, 1980, 157 ff.; C.M. BIANCA, *Condizioni generali di contratto*, 1, *Diritto civile*, in *Enc. giur. Treccani*, VII, Rom ,1988, 1 ff; S. PATTI, *Le condizioni generali di contratto*, Padua, 1996, 1 ff.

[2] L. RAISER, *Das Recht der allgemeinen Geschäftsbedingungen*, Bad Homburg, 1935.

Art. 1341 enthält keine Definitionen und legt einzig die Voraussetzungen der Wirksamkeit von allgemeinen Vertragsbedingungen fest. Der Verzicht auf eine Definition stimmt mit der vom Gesetzgeber bevorzugten Technik überein, nach welcher die einzige Aufgabe der Gesetzgebung darin besteht, die Regelungen der Rechtsinstitute vorzuschreiben und die Aufgabe der Lehre darin, auf der Grundlage dieser Regelungen die entsprechenden Definitionen auszuarbeiten. Ausnahmen hiervon finden sich insbesondere im vierten Buch, welches Definitionen der einzelnen Vertragstypen enthält. Dies war jedoch für eine präzise gesetzliche Abgrenzung der einzelnen „Typen" erforderlich.

Die Definition der allgemeinen Vertragsbedingungen wurde also von der Lehre und der Rechtsprechung in gemeinsamer Übereinstimmung darüber entwickelt, dass mit diesem Ausdruck das Phänomen der einseitigen Vorgabe eines einheitlichen vertraglichen Inhalts benannt wird, der dazu bestimmt ist, zur Regelung einer Reihe von unbestimmten Rechtsbeziehungen zur Anwendung zu kommen.

Nützliche Hinweise für das Verständnis der gesetzlichen Regelung können der *Relazione al Codice civile*, den Motiven des Justizministeriums entnommen werden, in denen man insbesondere liest, dass die Verpflichtung von „Treu und Glauben (im objektiven Sinn)" das hier behandelte Sachgebiet der so genannten „Adhäsionsverträge" bestimmt.[3] Daraus ergibt sich also, dass es sich um Treu und Glauben im objektiven Sinn (und nicht im subjektiven Sinn wie zum Beispiel in Art. 1147 beim „gutgläubigen Besitz") handelt, ein Aspekt, der – wie man sehen wird – im Jahr 1996 bei der Umsetzung der Richtlinie über missbräuchliche Klauseln in Verbraucherverträgen in die italienische Rechtsordnung zum Diskussionsobjekt wurde. Ferner wird mit dem Begriff „Adhäsionsvertrag" ein Ausdruck verwendet, der im Gesetzestext zuvor nicht vorhanden war, wohl aber in der juristischen Literatur. In Bezug auf den Inhalt der einzelnen Artikel wird präzisiert, dass „besondere Formvorschriften dann für den Abschluss von Verträgen mittels Vordrucken und Formularen vorgesehen sind, welche von nur einer Partei gestellt werden oder für den Abschluss von Verträgen mit einem Verweis auf allgemeine Bedingungen".[4]

Aus der *Relazione al Codice civile* geht außerdem – wenn auch nur implizit – eine Erklärung für die systematische Stellung der neuen Artikel (kurz nach den ebenfalls neuen Vorschriften über die Verhandlungen und die vorvertraglichen Haftung) hervor. Man liest, dass „das Bedürfnis, die Einheitlichkeit des Inhalts aller Rechtsbeziehungen gleicher Natur zu gewährleisten um eine genauere Bestimmung des damit verbundenen Risikos zu erreichen, die sich bei der Verhandlung mit Kunden ergebenden Schwierigkeiten sowie das Bedürfnis, die Organisation und die Führung

---

[3] *Codice civile. Relazione del Ministro Guardasigilli*, Rom, 1943, 391.
[4] *Codice civile. Relazione del Ministro Guardasigilli* (Fn. 3), 391.

der Unternehmen zu vereinfachen, Unternehmer dazu veranlassen, Vordrucke zu stellen, deren Text vom Kunden nicht in Frage gestellt werden kann, wenn dieser nicht auf das Geschäft verzichten will. Eine solche Methode kann nicht nur deshalb als unrechtmäßig angesehen werden, weil sie Verhandlungen oder Diskussionen um einzelne Klauseln keinen Raum lässt, sondern dazu zwingt, bereits vorbestimmte Vereinbarungen zu akzeptieren. Die heutige wirtschaftliche Realität basiert auch auf einem schnellen Abschluss von Geschäften, was die Bedingung für eine Beschleunigung der Produktivität darstellt; diesem Bedürfnis ist die Notwendigkeit der freien Verhandlung, die oft unüberwindliche Hindernisse mit sich bringt, zu opfern".[5]

Man achte darauf, dass in diesem Zitat der Begriff „Bedingungen" (allgemeine Vertragsbedingungen), der in der Überschrift und dem Text des Artikels 1341 erscheint, nicht verwendet wird, sondern in Übereinstimmung mit der italienischen Tradition allein der Begriff „Klauseln".

Das Studium der *Relazione* ist schließlich interessant, weil aus ihr hervorgeht, dass die hier untersuchten Artikel Klauseln mit einer besonderen Härte für „nichtig" erklären, wenn hinsichtlich dieser nicht die besondere Aufmerksamkeit der annehmenden Partei (z.B. durch eine spezifische Zustimmung) vorliegt, während das Gesetz festlegt, dass „in jedem Fall solche Bedingungen keine Wirkung haben, hinsichtlich derer keine spezifische schriftliche Genehmigung vorliegt ..." und ein Teil der Lehre sowie der Rechtsprechung – auch auf der Grundlage dieses Wortlauts – davon ausgeht, dass es sich nicht um Nichtigkeit, sondern um Unwirksamkeit handelt.

Sowohl im Text des Artikels 1341, als auch in der *Relazione* tauchen also sowohl der Begriff „allgemeine Vertragsbedingungen" als auch der Begriff „Klausel" auf. Den ersten Begriff kannte die italienischen Rechtstradition zuvor nicht. Es kann davon ausgegangen werden, dass auch auf diesem Gebiet der Einfluss der deutschen Rechtslehre entscheidend war. Das Buch von Ludwig Raiser „Das Recht der allgemeinen Geschäftsbedingungen" aus dem Jahr 1935 war den italienischen Zivilrechtlern selbstverständlich bekannt, als sie sich der Abfassung des Zivilgesetzbuches des Jahres 1942 widmeten.

II. Unbekannte oder nicht erkennbare Klauseln, „lästige („vessatorie")" oder „belastende" („onerose") Klauseln

Das Schutzsystem, das durch die Artikel in das Gesetzbuch eingeführt wurde, ist ein Zweifaches. Der erste Absatz des Art. 1341 sieht vor, dass nur solche allgemeinen Vertragsbedingungen gegenüber der annehmen-

---

[5] *Codice civile. Relazione del Ministro Guardasigilli*, (Fn. 3), 391 f.

den Partei wirksam werden, welche diese kannte oder bei Anwendung der ordentlichen Sorgfalt kennen musste.

Ein Teil der Lehre ist der Ansicht, dass auch hier ein Fall von Nichtigkeit vorliegt,[6] aber es scheint nicht korrekt, sich vom Wortlaut der Vorschrift zu entfernen: Klauseln, die der annehmenden Partei auf der Grundlage der ordentlichen Sorgfalt nicht bekannt waren und nicht bekannt sein konnten, sind dieser gegenüber nicht wirksam, da sie nicht Bestandteil des Vertrags werden. Es liegt ein besonderer Fall des Zustandekommens eines Vertrags vor und das Gesetz wollte die Relevanz und die Wirkung einiger Klauseln vom Vorliegen wenigstens einer der genannten Voraussetzungen abhängig machen.

Ausgehend von dieser kurzen Darstellung zeichnen sich, soweit das Thema des Kongresses betroffen ist, für den Übersetzer große Schwierigkeiten ab: die Wahl zwischen dem Begriff Nichtigkeit und demjenigen der Unwirksamkeit stellt nicht nur eine sprachliche Wahl dar, sondern bedeutet vielmehr die Annahme einer der beiden oben dargestellten Interpretationen.

Noch interessantere Probleme stellen sich in Bezug auf den zweiten Absatz des Artikels 1341, der eine Reihe von Klauseln aufzählt, die „keine Wirkung entfalten, außer sie wurden spezifisch schriftlich genehmigt".

Diesbezüglich stellt die *Relazione* klar – und diese Präzisierung ist auch vom terminologischen Standpunkt aus relevant- , dass der zweite Absatz des Art. 1341 hinsichtlich der Klauseln, die spezifisch schriftlich genehmigt werden müssen, eine Aufzählung enthält, die sehr wohl einer erweiterten Auslegung zugänglich ist, jedoch nicht einer analogen Ausdehnung; der Annehmende muss diese „nicht nur dann spezifisch schriftlich genehmigen, wenn sie in Formularen enthalten sind, sondern auch, wenn sie Teil allgemeiner Verdingungsordnungen (capitolati generali) sind, auf die der Vertrag verweist".[7] Es wird der Begriff „allgemeine Verdingungsordnung" eingeführt und nicht derjenige der „allgemeinen Bedingungen" gebraucht, aber insbesondere wird nicht von „lästigen („vessatorie") Klauseln" gesprochen.

Wir sehen also, dass der Ausdruck der lästigen (vessatorie) Klauseln weder im Text der Artikel 1341 und 1342 vorhanden ist, noch in der *Relazione al codice civile* vorkommt. Von lästigen (vessatorie) oder belastenden (onerose) Klauseln sprechen dagegen die Lehre und die Rechtspre-

---

[6] S. hierzu, auch für einen Überblick über die verschiedenen Standpunkte, G. DE NOVA, *Nullità relativa, nullità parziale e clausole vessatorie non specificamente approvate per iscritto*, in Riv. dir. civ., 1976, II, 480 ff.; G.B. FERRI, *Nullità parziale e clausole vessatorie*, in Riv. dir. comm., 1977, I, 11 ff. In der Rechtsprechung s. Cass., 11.11.1974, Nr. 3508, in *Temi*, 1976, 413; Cass., 27.10.1987, Nr. 7925, in *Giur. it.*, 1988, I, 1, 1180.

[7] *Codice civile. Relazione del Ministro Guardasigilli*, (Fn. 3), 392.

chung in Bezug auf die im zweiten Absatz des Artikels 1341 aufgezählten Klauseln,[8] die nur dann wirksam sind, wenn sie spezifisch schriftlich von der annehmenden Partei genehmigt wurden. Die Frage wird – wie man nachfolgend sehen wird – nach der Umsetzung der Richtlinie über missbräuchliche (abusive) Klauseln vom 5. April 1993, Nr. 13, an Bedeutung gewinnen.

III. Verbraucherverträge: „missbräuchliche" („abusive") und „lästige" („vessatorie") Klauseln

Die Zeit vergeht, und auch die Gesetzbücher altern. Die moderne Ordnung des italienischen Zivilgesetzbuches erweist sich als nicht geeignet, einen angemessenen Schutz der schwachen Vertragspartei zu gewähren, insbesondere weil sie eine rein formale Kontrolle von lästigen (vessatorie) Klauseln auf der Grundlage der so genannten spezifischen Genehmigung durch besondere Unterschrift vorsieht, aber keine inhaltliche Kontrolle.

Die Lehre schlug der Rechtsprechung zunächst den Rückgriff auf das im Artikel 1375 für die Durchführung von Verträgen vorhandene Prinzip von Treu und Glauben vor. Nachdem sie von der gegenteiligen Einstellung der Rechtsprechung Kenntnis genommen hat, empfahl sie schließlich dem Gesetzgeber eine Reform insbesondere nach dem Vorbild des deutschen AGB Gesetzes von 1976.[9]

Auch dieser Vorschlag blieb ungehört, so dass erst die europäische Richtlinie von 1996 kommen musste, bevor man zu einer gesetzlichen Veränderung schritt.[10]

Im Zeitpunkt der Umsetzung der Richtlinie stellte sich insbesondere die Frage, ob die neuen Vorschriften in das Gesetzbuches oder aber in ein Sondergesetz aufgenommen werden sollten, da diese zweifelsohne Elemente enthielten, die gegenüber den Charakteristika des Gesetzbuches einen Bruch darstellten. Dennoch wurde der ersten Lösung der Vorzug gegeben, so dass sich darüber hinaus die Frage stellte, in welchen Teil des Gesetzbuches die neuen Bestimmungen eingefügt werden sollten.

---

[8] S. CESARO, *Condizioni generali di contratto ed elencazione delle clausole vessatorie*, in Riv. trim. dir. proc. civ., 1991, 55 ff.; Cass., 19.12.1969, Nr. 4011, in Mon. trib., 1970, 764.

[9] C.M. BIANCA, *Condizioni generali di contratto (tutela dell'aderente)*, in Digesto IV, Disc. priv., Sez. civ., III, Turin, 1988, 397 ff.; G. DE NOVA, *Le condizioni generali di contratto*, in P. RESCIGNO (Hrsg.), Trattato di diritto privato, 10, II, Turin, 1988, 101 ff.

[10] Vgl. S. PATTI, *La direttiva comunitaria sulle clausole abusive*, in Contratto e impresa, 1993, 71 ff.

Letztendlich wurde die These, die sogar eine Einordnung in das dem Schuldrecht gewidmete vierte Buch vermeiden wollte und eine Einordnung in den Teil des fünften Buches, der den Unternehmen gewidmet ist, bevorzugte, verworfen. Man entschied sich für eine Einordnung sofort nach den Vorschriften über den allgemeinen Teil des Vertrages (Art. 1469-bis ff) statt unmittelbar nach den Artikeln über die allgemeinen Vertragsbedingungen, wie von vielen vorgeschlagen worden war, um wenigstens eine gewisse Kontinuität zu bieten. Jedoch empfahl es sich bereits bei dem gesetzesfremden und nicht leicht mit den traditionellen Prinzipien des Gesetzbuchs zu vereinbarenden Begriff »Verbraucher«, einen Bruch im Inneren der Regelung über den Vertrag im Allgemeinen zu vermeiden und, wie gesagt, eine weniger verwirrende Art Anhang am Ende des Allgemeinen Teils und vor den Vorschriften über die einzelnen Vertragstypen zu schaffen.[11]

Allerdings tritt hier ein terminologisches Problem auf: das italienische Zivilgesetzbuch regelt bekanntlich nicht den Rechtsmissbrauch als allgemeines Prinzip, insbesondere wegen der Besorgnis, dem Richter einen zu großen Ermessensspielraum zu gewähren,[12] und die besonders nachteiligen Klauseln des zweiten Absatzes des Artikels 1341 wurden grundsätzlich weder durch die Lehre noch durch die Rechtsprechung als missbräuchlich (abusive) bezeichnet. Schließlich war dieses Adjektiv, das in vielen europäischen Ländern benutzt wird und aus diesem Grund auch von der Richtlinie gebraucht wird, in Italien nicht nur der Sprache des Gesetzgebers sondern auch derjenigen der Lehre und der Rechtsprechung fremd.

Das Gesetz verwendet daher bevorzugt den Ausdruck der lästigen (vessatorie) Klauseln und diese Wahl wurde sogar mit der Absicht gerechtfertigt, eine terminologische Einheitlichkeit mit den Artikeln 1341 und 1342 zu garantieren, die jedoch, wie oben gesagt, die Klauseln nicht qualifizieren und sich (im zweiten Absatz des Artikels 1341) darauf beschränken, jene Klauseln aufzuzählen, für die die so genannte spezifische Genehmigung erforderlich ist. Im Ergebnis wurde daher eine einheitliche Terminologie auf der Ebene der italienischen Lehre und der Rechtsprechung erreicht, aber ein Bruch mit der europäischen Terminologie und sogar der Terminologie des Gesetzbuches herbeigeführt.[13]

Allerdings wird der Begriff der missbräuchlichen (abusive) Klauseln – statt lästige (vessatorie) Klauseln – in einem der letzten Artikel gebraucht

---

[11] G. ALPA-S. PATTI, Introduzione, in G. ALPA-S. PATTI (Hrsg.), Clausole vessatorie nei contratti del consumatore, in Il Codice civile. Commentario, Mailand, 2003, 1 ff.

[12] Vgl. S. PATTI, Abuso del diritto, in Digesto IV, Discipline privatistiche, Sezione civile, I, Torino, 1987, 1 ff.

[13] ALPA-PATTI, Clausole vessatorie nei contratti del consumatore, (Fn. 11), 19 ff.

und daher stellt man auch innerhalb der Umsetzungsvorschriften keine einheitliche Terminologie fest.

Die neuen Vorschriften wurden schließlich aus dem Gesetzbuch ausgeschlossen und in das so genannte Verbrauchergesetzbuch aus dem Jahr 2005 aufgenommen (Art. 33–38). Hierbei handelt es sich um eine Sammlung von Gesetzen zum Schutz des Verbrauchers, in dem – unter anderem – die Umsetzungsvorschriften der Richtlinie über den Verbrauchsgüterkauf Aufnahme gefunden haben, die ebenfalls zunächst im Zivilgesetzbuch enthalten waren (Art. 1519-bis ff.) ,[14] bevor sie in das neue „Gesetzbuch" ausgelagert wurden.

IV. Das Prinzip von Treu und Glauben

Im Rahmen des hier behandelten Themas stellt das Prinzip von Treu und Glauben, auf das bereits bei der zitierten Richtlinie über missbräuchliche Klauseln in Verbraucherverträgen hingewiesen wurde, ein inzwischen sehr bekanntes Beispiel einer mangelnden Harmonisierung, die auf eine im Vergleich zu den anderen Sprachen abweichende Übersetzung der Richtlinie in das Italienische zurückzuführen ist, dar. Tatsächlich ist eine Klausel nach der Richtlinienversion in italienischer Sprache als missbräuchlich (abusive) einzustufen, wenn sie nicht Gegenstand einer individuellen Verhandlung war und zum Schaden des Verbrauchers „trotz Gutgläubigkeit" („malgrado il requisito della buona fede") ein bedeutendes Ungleichgewicht der vertraglichen Rechte und Pflichten der Parteien verursacht (Art. 3). Die italienische Richtlinienversion scheint also – auf der Grundlage ihres Wortlauts – auf Treu und Glauben im subjektiven Sinn Bezug zu nehmen. Dennoch haben bereits die ersten Kommentatoren hervorgehoben, dass es sich hierbei um einen offensichtlichen Übersetzungsfehler handelt, wobei sie feststellten, dass im Lichte der übrigen Versionen vielmehr anzunehmen sei, dass der europäische Gesetzgeber unter Berücksichtigung der in Europa über mehrere Jahrzehnte gewachsenen Erfahrung die Absicht hatte, das Sachgebiet durch eine Regelung von Treu und Glauben im objektiven Sinn zu normieren.[15]

---

[14] Vgl. S. PATTI (Hrsg.), *Commentario sulla vendita dei beni di consumo*, Mailand, 2004.

[15] R. SACCO, *Riflessioni di un giurista sulla lingua (la lingua del diritto uniforme, e il diritto al servizio di una lingua uniforme)*, in Riv. dir. civ., 1996, I, 58 ff.; S. PATTI, *Significato del principio di buona fede e clausole vessatorie: uno sguardo all'Europa*, in L. GAROFALO (Hrsg.), *Il ruolo della buona fede oggettiva nell'esperienza giuridica storica e contemporanea*, III, Padua, 2003, 59 ff.
Im deutschen Text der Richtlinie steht „entgegen dem Gebot von Treu und Glauben", im englischen Text „*contrary to the requirement of good faith*". Weni-

Was also wahrscheinlich lediglich als ein Versehen einzustufen ist, wurde bei der Umsetzung der Richtlinie dennoch nicht korrigiert, da der Wortlaut des ersten Absatzes des Artikels 1469-bis des Zivilgesetzbuches die Formel der italienischen Version der Richtlinie geändert und verkürzt hat und dadurch die Bezugnahme auf die Gutgläubigkeit im subjektiven Sinn eher noch verstärkte.

Da der Ausdruck „trotz Gutgläubigkeit" verwendet wurde, stellt man bei einer Beschränkung auf die wörtliche Auslegung fest, dass es sich um einen Hinweis auf Gutgläubigkeit im subjektiven Sinn handelt, ein Tatbestand fehlender Kenntnis, also Unkenntnis des missbräuchlichen Charakters der Klauseln des Verwenders.

Trotz des Ergebnisses, zu dem man bei einer wörtlichen Auslegung gelangt, hat sich die herrschende Lehre dennoch entschieden dafür ausgesprochen, dass es sich um ein im objektiven Sinn zu verstehendes Kriterium von Treu und Glauben handelt.[16] Diesbezüglich hebt die überzeugendste Argumentation hervor, dass vor dem Hintergrund des Ziels der Richtlinie, die Gesetzgebung der Mitgliedsstaaten auf dem Gebiet der Verbraucherverträge zu vereinheitlichen, die Bezugnahme auf ein Prinzip – das der Gutgläubigkeit (buona fede in senso soggettivo) – vermieden werden sollte, das trotz der teilweisen terminologischen Übereinstimmung nichts mit dem Prinzip von Treu und Glauben (buona fede in senso oggettivo) gemein hat. Ohne Zweifel handelt es sich bei letzterem um dasjenige Prinzip, das die Entwicklung der Kontrollsysteme von missbräuchlichen Klauseln in vielen Ländern der europäischen Union begleitet hat und das im Licht der Richtlinie in den meisten europäischen Rechtsordnungen das Wertungskriterium darstellt.

Schließlich erlaubt es die italienische Version, die auf der Grundlage der wörtlichen Formulierung dazu führt, von einer Gutgläubigkeit im subjektiven Sinn auszugehen, nicht, die angestrebte Harmonisierung zu verwirklichen. Es besteht darüber hinaus die Gefahr, dass das Prinzip von Treu und Glauben in Italien seine wichtigste Funktion als Sicherungsinstrument des Kontrollsystems, nämlich die Verhinderung der Umgehung der Kataloge von missbräuchlichen Klauseln, nicht mehr erfüllen kann.

Da andere Versionen der Richtlinie über die Verbraucherverträge ebenfalls – auch in diesem Punkt – nicht ganz eindeutig scheinen, ist das gegebene Beispiel ein guter Ausgangspunkt für die Beleuchtung des Pro-

---

ger zweideutig ist der französische Text: *„en dépit de l'exigence de bonne foi",* denn „*en dépit de*" kann abstrakt „trotz" oder „entgegen" bedeuten, während der Verweis auf die „*exigence*" davon ausgehen lässt, dass es sich um den guten Glauben im objektiven Sinne handelt.

16 S., auch für bibliographische Hinweise, UDA, *La buona fede nelle clausole abusive,* in ALPA-PATTI, *Clausole vessatorie nei contratti del consumatore,* (Fn. 11), 97 ff.

blems unter einem allgemeinen Gesichtspunkt. Konkret ist zu fragen, – da keine Richtlinienversion als „zwingend" angesehen werden kann – wie Richtlinien auszulegen sind, die in den verschiedenen Sprachen einen voneinander abweichenden Wortlaut besitzen.

Bekanntlich hat der Europäische Gerichtshof in zahlreichen Fällen die Notwendigkeit einer „richtlinienkonformen" Auslegung, unabhängig von den nationalen Rechtsordnungen, bekräftigt. Aber auch eine Auslegung, die sich getreu an dieser Regel orientiert, kann nicht zu dem gewünschten Ergebnis führen, wenn die Juristen in den einzelnen Ländern mit unterschiedlichen Texten arbeiten, die das Ergebnis voneinander abweichenden Übersetzungen sind.

Das Problem verschärft sich, da man, wie die Erfahrung zeigt, in jeder Rechtsordnung oft dazu neigt, diejenige Version einer Richtlinie, eines internationalen Vertrags oder einer internationalen Konvention in der eigenen Sprache für richtig zu halten. Nur im Fall von offensichtlichen Fehlern, wenn sich also die Ausführung in einer Sprache deutlich von allen anderen abhebt, wird ein Übersetzungsfehler relativ leicht akzeptiert und man kann folglich zu einer korrekten Auslegung gelangen. In den anderen Fällen hat der Europäische Gerichtshof ausgehend von dem Prinzip, nach dem alle Versionen gleichermaßen zwingend sind, bekräftigt, dass zunächst ein Vergleich der unterschiedlichen Versionen zu erfolgen hat, um den richtigen Sinn herauszufinden. Bleiben auch nach diesem Vergleich Zweifel bestehen, hat eine Analyse der Geschichte, der Systematik und des Ziels der Regelungen zu erfolgen. Von der wörtlichen Auslegung – die am meisten von einem möglichen Übersetzungsfehler abhängt – gelangt man also zu anderen Auslegungsregeln, zunächst zu dem teleologischen Kriterium.

Kritisch wurde bemerkt, dass die teleologische Auslegung auf diese Weise einen zu hohen Stellenwert einnehme, der den Auslegungsregeln für Gesetze in den Mitgliedsstaaten fremd sei und es darüber hinaus schwierig sei, das Ziel, das der europäische Gesetzgeber der Richtlinie habe zukommen lassen wollen, herauszufinden, wenn allen Versionen der gleiche Rang zugebilligt werde.[17] Daher wird vorgeschlagen, einer „Originalversion" vorherrschende Wirkung zukommen zu lassen und die Übrigen als reine Übersetzungen zu bewerten, um auf diese Weise die mit den verschiedenen Sprachen verbundenen Auslegungsschwierigkeiten zu lösen, da in jedem Fall auf einen einheitlichen Text Bezug genommen werde. Auf der anderen Seite kann nur eine „Parallelformulierung" in den verschiedenen Sprachen mit einer dauernden Kontrolle der Bedeutungsidentität dazu führen, dass man zu einer kohärenten und einheitlichen

---

[17] MARTINY, *Babylon in Brüssel? Das Recht und die europäische Sprachenvielfalt*, in ZEuP, 1998, 227, 239.

Auslegungsbasis gelangt. Aber in Wirklichkeit rühren viele der Versionen von einer Übersetzung aus dem Englischen, andere aus dem Französischen her.

V. Schlussbetrachtungen

Die italienische Erfahrung auf dem Gebiet der allgemeinen Vertragsbedingungen bestätigt schließlich die Schwierigkeiten, neue Begrifflichkeiten in einen Gesetzestext wie das Zivilgesetzbuch einzuführen, das auf der Sprache einer vergangenen geschichtlichen Epoche basiert und insbesondere an eine bestimmte Ideologie gebunden ist.

Das Problem wird, wie wir gesehen haben, besonders schwerwiegend, wenn die europäischen Richtlinien in die verschiedenen Sprachen der Mitgliedsstaaten übersetzt werden müssen. Die Auslegung der Umsetzungsgesetze der Richtlinien muss gesetzlichen Regeln folgen: Ein Jurist eines Mitgliedsstaats, der angehalten ist, seine Auslegungsregeln zu beachten, und der mit einem übersetzten Text arbeitet, kann abgesehen von den unvermeidbaren Übersetzungsfehlern eine Verschiebung zwischen der ursprünglichen Bedeutung des Textes und derjenigen, die er dem Text aufgrund der „Vermittlung" durch die Übersetzung gibt, bewirken.

Traditionell versucht man, die oben genannte Schwierigkeit zu überwinden, indem man die Übersetzung eines juristischen Textes einem Juristen anvertraut, der im Stande ist, die hermeneutische Dimension der Übertragung in eine andere Sprache als der des Gesetzestextes zu bewältigen. Tatsächlich kann es auch bei einer Übersetzung, die vollkommen dem Ausgangstext entspricht, der Fall sein, dass das exakte Verständnis der Bedeutung der Vorschriften nicht möglich ist. Der auslegende Übersetzer muss daher auch die Auslegungsregeln der Rechtsordnung kennen, aus der der zu übersetzende Text stammt, um die tatsächliche Bedeutung zu erfassen, die die Vorschriften in ihrer ursprünglichen Fassung besitzen.

In einer Staatenunion, die im Vergleich zu anderen historischen Erfahrungen eine bedeutende – oder besser, übermäßige – Anzahl von verwendeten Sprachen aufweist und die sich einer Verschärfung des Problems der Übersetzungen in Folge der geplanten Aufnahme weiterer Staaten gegenüber sieht, hängt die angestrebte Harmonisierung des Rechts auch von der kulturellen Vermittlung der auslegenden Übersetzer ab, die in der Lage sind, den „Erwartungshorizont" (ein Begriff von J. Esser) der Normempfänger wahrzunehmen. Aber insbesondere die Übersetzung von Richtlinien, die jeweils einzelne Sachgebiete zum Gegenstand haben und sich im Allgemeinen darauf beschränken, Wahlmöglichkeiten offen zu lassen, um die bestmögliche Einordnung der europäischen Regelungen in die nationalen Rechtsordnungen der Mitgliedsstaaten zu ermöglichen, lässt eine der Grenzen des europäischen Normensystems erkennen, welches einzelne Sachgebiete von zentraler Bedeutung für die Mitglieder „in Leopardenflecken" regelt und die Ausarbeitung von Prinzipien und allgemeinen Regeln verhindert, die möglicherweise als Basis für die Erstellung eines europäisches Gesetzbuch dienen könnten. Nur eine solche gemeinsame Basis könnte zumindest zum Teil zur Lösung der Übersetzungs- und Auslegungsprobleme beitragen, die gegenwärtig, häufig mit dürftigen Ergebnissen, hunderte von Übersetzern und Juristen beschäftigen.

Das Konzept der „Reasonableness" als Mittel zur Harmonisierung des Europäischen Vertragsrechts: Probleme und Perspektiven aus der Sicht des italienischen Rechtssystems

Stefano Troiano (Verona)

I. Einleitung

„Le phénomène nouveau ... est l'apparition dans divers domaines du droit privé, d'un nombre croissant de textes se référant expressément au raisonnable". Mit diesen Worten berichtete ein französischer Wissenschafter[1] Mitte der '80er Jahre vom Auftreten des Kriteriums des „raisonnable" („reasonable", „Vernünftigen") im französischen Privatrecht. Auf diese Weise wurde der Grundstein für eine der ersten Debatten zum Thema „Vernünftigkeit" im europäischen Privatrecht gelegt. Mehr als zwanzig Jahre später haben diese Worte nicht nur im Hinblick auf die französische Rechtsordnung, sondern im Hinblick auf alle kontinentaleuropäischen Rechtsordnungen, angefangen bei der italienischen und der deutschen, noch immer nicht an Aktualität verloren, denn seither hat sich das Kriterium der „Vernünftigkeit" im Privatrecht progressiv weiter verbreitet. Diese Entwicklung hat sogar eine Beschleunigung erfahren und erstreckt sich heutzutage mit stets wachsender Energie auf das gesamte europäische Vertragsrecht.

Im Rahmen der nachfolgenden Überlegungen soll auf der Grundlage dieser Vorbemerkungen analysiert werden, welche Rolle das Kriterium der „reasonableness" im europäischen Vertragsrecht derzeit spielt bzw. in Zukunft spielen kann. In diesem Zusammenhang wird dieser Begriff nicht als reines Bedürfnis der Rechtsauslegung oder -anwendung verstanden, sondern als spezifisches, unbestimmtes, normatives Kriterium des modernen europäischen Rechts, auf das der Gesetzgeber in einzelnen Gesetzesbestimmungen konkret verweist.

Da die vorliegende Untersuchung auf einen überschaubaren Bereich beschränkt werden muss, werden diese Aspekte im Folgenden hauptsäch-

---

[1] G. *Khairallah*, Le raisonnable en droit privé français. Développements récents, Revue trimestrielle droit civil 1984, 439 ff., 443.

lich vor dem Hintergrund des italienischen Rechtssystems analysiert.[2] Angesichts seiner Geschichte als kodifizierte Rechtsordnung romanistischer Abstammung hat das italienische Rechtssystem das Kriterium des „reasonable" bis vor kurzem zumindest auf gesetzgeberischer Ebene ignoriert und im Laufe der Zeit den Einsatz anderer Begriffe oder Generalklauseln (vor allem Treu und Glauben, Sorgfalt, Billigkeit) bevorzugt. Es stellen sich also folgende Fragen: Kann eine „neue" Generalklausel ohne nationale Wurzeln im engeren Sinne tatsächlich zur Harmonisierung des europäischen Rechts und zur Schaffung eines wirklich grenzüberschreitenden Begriffs beitragen? Oder ist sie dazu verurteilt, nach der Übernahme in die nationalen Kontexte eine wesentliche Wandlung im lokalen Sinne zu erfahren und auf diese Weise ihre vereinheitlichende Funktion weitgehend zu verlieren? Das Beispiel des italienischen Rechts, das für eine das gesamte europäische Vertragsrecht betreffende Entwicklung paradigmatisch ist, soll demnach einen Ausgangspunkt für eine Debatte über die Potenzialitäten und die Grenzen einer Harmonisierung des europäischen Vertragsrechts durch den Rückgriff auf Generalklauseln oder unbestimmte juristische Begriffe bieten.

II. Prämisse terminologischen und historischen Charakters

Die Entscheidung, zumindest eingangs und im Titel den englischen Ausdruck „reasonableness" an Stelle der deutschen bzw. italienischen Übersetzung dieses Begriffs, d.h. „Vernünftigkeit" bzw. „ragionevolezza, zu verwenden, hat zumindest drei Gründe.

Erstens ist im Ausdruck „reasonableness" im Unterschied zum entsprechenden deutschen Wort der lateinische Ursprung des Vokabels erkennbar, der auch in der juristischen Terminologie wertvolle Aufschlüsse über seine Bedeutung bietet. Zweitens hat die Verwendung des Ausdrucks trotz seiner lateinischen Wurzeln im angelsächsischen Recht mit Sicherheit eine weitaus solidere Tradition als in den kontinentaleuropäischen Rechtsordnungen unmittelbar romanistischer Abstammung. Man kann sogar behaupten – ohne eine Widerlegung dieser Aussage befürchten zu müssen –, dass das Konzept des „Vernünftigen" als gesetzliches Kriterium des Vertragsrechts (wie wir sehen werden, vor nicht allzu langer Zeit) gerade eben durch den Einfluss der Modelle des *Common Law* in den kodifizierten europäischen Rechtsordnungen Einzug gehalten hat: Die Wahl des englischen Ausdrucks soll also den (unmittelbaren) Ursprung des Konzepts unterstreichen. Drittens sind „Vernünftigkeit" und „ragionevo-

---

[2] Näher dazu S. *Troiano*, La „ragionevolezza" nel diritto dei contratti, Padova 2005. S. auch A. *Ricci*, La ragionevolezza nel diritto privato: prime riflessioni, Contr. impresa 2005, 619 ff.

lezza" zwar korrekte Übersetzungen des Ausdrucks „reasonableness", besitzen aber in der normativen Terminologie nicht immer die mit dem englischen Wort verbundene Vielfalt an Bedeutungen.[3] Es ist kein Zufall, dass der deutsche und der italienische Gesetzgeber bei der Übersetzung des reasonable-Kriteriums in den nationalen Gesetzestexten häufig die Verwendung von ihren Rechtsordnungen vertrauten Begriffen oder Klauseln bzw. andere Formeln bevorzugen, in denen die Bezugnahme auf das Konzept des Vernünftigen völlig wegfällt. Ein deutliches Beispiel hierfür ist die deutsche Übersetzung des Wiener Übereinkommens über den internationalen Warenkauf (bekanntlich stellt diese Übersetzung allerdings keinen offiziellen Text dar). Die insgesamt 47 Bezugnahmen auf das Konzept des „reasonable" in der englischen Version wurden in nur neun Fällen mit „vernünftig" oder einem davon abgeleiteten Wort übersetzt.[4] In allen anderen Fällen wurde der Verwendung von Ausdrücken wie: „angemessener Frist",[5] „unzumutbare Unannehmlichkeiten" (z.B. im Art. 34), „unverhältnismäßige Kosten" (auch im Art. 34), „ausreichend Gelegenheit" (z.B. im Art. 38), „ungebührlich hinauszögert" (Art. 88, Abs. 1), etc. der Vorzug gegeben und der Begriff auf diese Weise in eine Vielzahl unterschiedlicher Vokabeln zersplittert. Leider geht dadurch – auch zum Nachteil der zur Anwendung des Übereinkommens berufenen Fachleute – das Bewusstsein verloren, dass die verschiedenen Ausdrücke einen gemeinsamen Ursprung haben.[6]

---

[3] Nach J. *Schmidt*, Zur „reasonable person" in einem zukünftigen europäischen Privatrecht, in: Festschrift für Bernhard Großfeld, Heidelberg 1999, 1027 f., ist die Einführung des Wortes *„vernünftig"* in die deutsche Rechtsterminologie ein „fachsprachlicher Neologismus".

[4] Art. 8, Abs. 2 und 3, Art. 25: „vernünftige Person"; Art. 16, Abs. 2, lit. b, Art. 35, Abs. 2, lit. b, Art. 60, lit. a, Art. 79, Abs. 1: „vernünftigerweise"; Art. 44: „vernünftige Entschuldigung"; Art. 72, Abs. 2°: „vernünftig".

[5] Der Ausdruck „reasonable time" wird in 18 Artikeln verwendet.

[6] Der Umstand, dass der deutsche Gesetzgeber nur wenig mit der Vokabel *vernünftig* vertraut ist, bedeutet jedoch nicht, dass das Kriterium des „Vernünftigen" der deutschen Rechtserfahrung insgesamt fremd ist. Die wenigen Autoren, die sich mit diesem Thema auseinandergesetzt haben, sind zu der Schlussfolgerung gelangt, dass der Inhalt und die Funktionen, die der *reasonableness* im Common law zueigen sind, zumindest was die konkreten Anwendungen betrifft, auch im deutschen Recht eindeutig vorhanden sind (ausführlich dazu W. E. *Joachim*, The „Reasonable Man" in United States and German Commercial Law, 15 Comparative Law Yearbook of International Business 1992, pp. 341 et seq).

1. Die Herkunft des Wortes „reasonable"
   („ragionevole", vernünftig)

Nach dieser Prämisse terminologischen Charakters können wir uns nun besser auf die bisher nur angedeutete Herkunft des Wortes „reasonable" konzentrieren.

„Reasonable" und „reasonableness", „ragionevole" und „rationell" verraten ihre gemeinsame Abstammung von dem lateinischen Wort *ratio*, dessen ursprünglicher semantischer Kern eng mit dem konkreten Konzept von „Rechnung, Berechnung" verbunden ist.[7] Dieses Wort hat im Laufe der Zeit zahlreiche abstraktere Bedeutungen übernommen: Bereits im klassischen Latein wurde *ratio* als Synonym für „Grundlage, Grund, Motiv" verwendet, aber auch für den Ausdruck der menschlichen Fähigkeit zum Verständnis dieser Grundlage, d.h. als „Gedanke, Vernunft, Beurteilung". Der unterschiedliche Einsatz der Adjektive *rationalis* und *rationabilis* im Spätlatein[8] und dann der Wörter „razionale" (rationell) und „ragionevole" (vernünftig) in den neulateinischen Umgangssprachen ab dem Mittelalter bezeugt eine Sinnerweiterung, die die der Vokabel *ratio* seit jeher innewohnende abstrakt-konkrete Mehrdeutigkeit verstärkt. Das Konzept des „Rationellen" weckt die Vorstellung der Übereinstimmung mit einer „abstrakten Logik". Der Ausdruck „vernünftig" erinnert dagegen an ein „Gleichgewicht von Sachen oder Verhaltensweisen, das auf einen konkreten und menschlichen Maßstab bezogen ist" und sich am „allgemeinen Menschenverstand" inspiriert.[9] Auch die „Vernünftigkeit" als juristisches Beurteilungskriterium zeichnet sich grundsätzlich durch diese Merkmale aus: Sie tritt ebenfalls als eine Eigenschaft der pragmatischen Vernunft auf, die in die Realität eindringt und sich ihr anpasst, und im übertragenen Sinne den Stellenwert eines Synonyms für „Gerechtigkeit und Angemessenheit im Hinblick auf die konkreten Umstände" einnimmt.

---

[7] Dieser Sinn wurde im lateinischen *redde rationem* beibehalten, d.h. im konkreten Sinn „Rechnung legen" und im figürlichen Sinn „Rechenschaft ablegen".

[8] Eine erste Unterscheidung zwischen den Adjektiven *rationalis*, bezogen auf denjenigen, der die Vernunft einsetzt bzw. einsetzen kann („homo est animal rationale mortale"), und *rationabilis*, verstanden als Eigenschaft von Aussagen und Handlungen („quod ratione factum esse aut dictum": *Sankt Augustin, De Ordine* II, 11, 31) ist dem Heiligen Augustin zu verdanken.

[9] Zu dieser Unterscheidung siehe etwa *Khairallah* (Fn. 1) 457.

2. Die traditionelle Rolle der *reasonableness* im *Common Law*

Oft wird behauptet, dass das Kriterium der Vernünftigkeit „intensiv und in jeder Beziehung bis in sämtliche Ecken des Systems"[10] des *Common Law* „dringt", so dass namhafte Autoren unterstellen konnten,[11] dass das gesamte *Common Law* im Wesentlichen *right reason* ist.[12] In zahlreichen Fällen stützen die englischen Gerichtshöfe ihre Urteilssprüche sowohl im Bereich des öffentlichen Rechts, als auch im Bereich des Strafrechts und des Privatrechts auf das Kriterium der *reasonableness*.[13] In diesem zuletzt genannten Bereich nimmt das Kriterium der Vernünftigkeit in der Figur des *reasonable man* (oder der *reasonable person*) seine wichtigste Gestalt an. Die *reasonable person* – bei der es sich nach Aussage einiger um eine fiktive oder mythische Person handelt,[14] die Ausdruck einer „anthropo-

---

[10] G. *Criscuoli*, Buona fede e ragionevolezza, Riv. dir. civ. 1984, I, 725. Dazu auch N. *MacCormick*, On reasonableness, in: Les notions à contenu variable en droit, C. Perelman-R. Vander Elst (Hsg.), Bruxelles, 1984, 131 ff. e G. P. *Fletcher*, Comparative Law as a Subversive Discipline, American Journal of Comparative Law 1998, 683 ff.

[11] H. A. *Schwarz-Liebermann von Wahlendorf*, Le juge « législateur », L'approche anglaise, Revue internationale de droit comparé, 1999, 1110.

[12] Vgl. *Schwarz-Liebermann von Wahlendorf*, Les notions de *right reason* et de *reasonable man* en droit anglais, Arch. philo. dr., 1978, t. 23, 45: « Le droit anglais, dans sa conception originelle et profonde, est tout entier construit sur la notion de raison, sur la *reasonableness*, sur l'exigence d'être raisonnable. L'invocation de la raison expérimentale, d'une raison qui est le fruit de l'expérience, de l'observation, qui compare les phénomènes et qui en tire des conclusions, est véritablement le *life blood*, la vie du droit anglais, de sa structuration, de sa construction ». Vgl. dazu auch J. R. *Lucas*, The Philosophy of The Reasonable Man, 13 The Philosophical Quarterly 1963, 97.

[13] Vgl. *MacCormick* (Fn. 10) 132.

[14] Zu den verschiedenen Defininitionen der *reasonable person* in *Common law* („the anthropomorphic conception of justice", „the man of the Clapham omnibus", etc.) s. *Criscuoli* (Fn. 10) 726 f. S. etwa A. P. *Herbert*, Uncommon Law, London, 1935, p. 2 ss.: „The Common Law of England has been laboriuosly built about a mythical figure – the figure of 'The Reasonable Man'. ... He is an ideal, a standard, the embodiment of all those qualities which we demand of the good citizen ... This noble creature stands in singular contrast to his kinsman the Economic Man, whose every action is prompted by the single spur of selfish advantage and directed to the single end of monetary gain. The Reasonable Man is always thinking of others; prudence is his guide, and 'Safety First' ... is his rule of life". Dazu auch *MacCormick* (Fn. 10) 152: „The reasonable man, that convenient legal fiction, is of course no paragon of virtue. He is neither saint, hero not genius. He represents the Aristotelian virtue of pru-

morphen" Auffassung der Justiz ist – ist in der Regelung des *Tort of negligence* und auch in vielen Sektoren des Vertrags- und Schuldrechts erwähnt[15] und stellt das ideale Modell für auf sozialer Ebene akzeptable Verhaltensweisen dar, die sich am allgemeinen Menschenverstand und am Gleichgewicht inspirieren. Auf noch allgemeinere Weise wurde ausdrücklich behauptet,[16] dass das englische Vertragsrecht insgesamt als Instrument für die Realisierung der vernünftigen Erwartungen (*reasonable expectations*) der Parteien[17] aufgebaut ist, wobei mit vernünftigen Erwartungen nicht subjektive Wünsche, sondern objektiv begründete und sozialen Modellen der Normalität entsprechende Erwartungen gemeint sind.[18]

Historisch gesehen sind die Ursprünge des erfolgreichen Weges des Kriteriums der *reasonableness* im englischen Recht in der Entstehung des *Common Law* selbst zu sehen,[19] das, wie von vielen Seiten unterstrichen wird, seine Wurzeln im Naturrecht, verstanden als *Law of reason*, hat.[20] Hiermit ist jedoch nicht die abstrakte „vernünftige Vernunft" der formellen Logik, sondern eine pragmatische und auf die Erfahrung gestützte Vernunft gemeint. Dies entspringt der das angelsächsische Recht inspirie-

---

dence (*prudentia*, φρόνησις) in its ideal-typical form as a golden mean between over cautiousness and rashness ... is represented best in philosophy as the 'ideal impartial spectator' of Adam Smith, who derived the idea in part from David Hume".

[15] Beispiele zu dieser Fallgruppe in *MacCormick* (Fn. 10) 132; *Criscuoli* (Fn. 10) 726 ff.; J. *Steyn*, Contract Law: Fulfilling the Reasonable Expectations of Honest Men, Law Quarterly Review 1997, 440.

[16] So J. *Steyn* (Fn. 15) 433 ff.

[17] Zu diesem Thema s. statt aller B. J. *Reiter*-J. *Swan*, Contracts and the Protection of Reasonable Expectations, in: B. J. *Reiter*-J. *Swan* (Hsg.), Studies in Contract Law, Toronto 1980, vol. 1, 7. Vgl. auch M. *Hoch*, Is Fair Dealing a Workable Concept for European Contract Law?, Global Jurist Topics 2005, 1.

[18] *Steyn* (Fn. 15) 434.

[19] Nach G. *Weiszberg*, Le « Raisonnable » en Droit du Commerce International, Th. Paris II, 2003, Pace Database, Nr. 33, in: www.cisg.law.pace.edu (die Zitate beziehen sich auf die progressive Nummer der Paragraphen) geht die Entstehung dieses Standards auf das mittelalterliche Recht (XII. Jhdt.) zurück. L. A. *DiMatteo*, Contract Theory – The Evolution of Contractual Intent, East Lansing (Michigan) 1998, 22, vertritt die Auffassung, dass die Idee der *Reasonableness* seit der Epoche von Coke und Blackstone zur Tradition des *Common law* gehört. So auch G. K. *Gardner*, An Inquiry Into the Principles of the Law of Contracts, 46 Harvard Law Review, 1932, 3.

[20] So H. *Jaeger*, Introduction aux rapports de la pensée juridique et de l'histoire des idées en Angleterre, depuis la Réforme jusqu'au XVIIIe siècle, Arch. philo. dr. 1970, 13.

renden Vorstellung, dass einzig und allein die Erfahrung die Grundsätze für die rechtliche Betrachtung bieten kann.[21] An den Bedarf nach Vernünftigkeit, im hier dargestellten Sinne, knüpft die spätere Entwicklung des *Common Law* an, im Rahmen derer die von den *Courts of Equity* seit dem Ende des XIV. Jahrhunderts in ihren Entscheidungen angewandten Rechtsregeln gerade eben deshalb in das Rechtssystem der Präzedenzfälle aufgenommen wurden, um Abhilfe für zu unflexible und demnach unvernünftige Situationen zu schaffen.[22]

Der Einfluss des Vernünftigen auf das englische Recht ist jedoch nicht nur auf das Richterrecht beschränkt. Immer öfter wird die *reasonableness* nämlich in verschiedenen Formen in Gesetzen, *Statutes* oder in anderen Rechtsvorschriften autoritärer Herkunft erwähnt. Ein wichtiges Beispiel hierfür ist der *Reasonableness-Test* nach dem *Unfair Contract Terms Act* 1977.[23]

---

[21] *Schwarz-Liebermann von Wahlendorf* (Fn. 12) 44 f. Mit der Rolle der Erfahrung bei der Bildung der angelsächsischen Rechtsbetrachtung befasst sich auch eingehend *Khairallah* (Fn. 10) 460.

[22] *Weiszberg* (Fn. 19) Nr. 34. Die Vernünftigkeit der Lösung des konkreten Falls liegt insbesondere der Technik des *distinguishing* zugrunde (bzw. der Methode, bei der die Besonderheiten eines Falls herausgearbeitet werden, mit denen die Abweichung vom Präzedenzfall begründet werden kann), die von den Gerichtshöfen zur Abschwächung der manchmal unflexiblen Regel des *stare decisis* eingesetzt wird. Die Rechtsregel, die sich aufgrund der Autorität des Präzedenzfalls aufdrängt, drückt in der Tat nur die authentische *ratio decidendi* der gerichtlichen Entscheidung aus (und nicht dagegen die *obiter dicta*, denen nur reine Überzeugungskraft zuerkannt werden kann), aber von den Präzedenzfällen bzw. von der in ihnen ausgedrückten *ratio decidendi* kann der Richter abweichen, wenn die *distinction* ihrerseits *reasonable* ist (zur Unterscheidung zwischen *ratio decidendi* und *obiter dictum* siehe nur K. P. *Papadiamantis*, Le fondement et le Concept du Raisonnable en Droit; étude comparative entre les systèmes du Droit Continental et de la Common Law, Th. Paris X, 1990, 421 f.).

[23] Obwohl es sich um einen nur auf einige Verträge und auf eine ziemlich limitierte Typologie von Vertragsklauseln (die *exemption clauses*) begrenzten *Test* handelt, wird diese Anwendung des Kriteriums der „Vernünftigkeit" von der englischen Doktrin und Rechtsprechung für die Entwicklung des modernen *Law of contract* als überaus wichtig angesehen, insbesondere mit Bezug auf die Tendenz zu einem intensiveren Schutz der schwachen Vertragspartner. Siehe dazu die interessanten Bemerkungen von Lord Denning in *George Mitchell (Chesterhall), Ltd. v. Finney Lock Seeds Ltd.* [1983] 1 All. E.R., 113–117. Zum Unfair Contract Terms Act vgl. etwa A. *Brownsword*, The Unfair Contract Terms Act: A Decade of Discretion, 104 Law Quarterly Review 1988, 94 ff; H.

III. Die wachsende Bedeutung der *reasonableness* im italienischen bzw. europäischen Vertragsrecht

1. Allgemeiner Überblick

Das Thema der „ragionevolezza" (Vernünftigkeit) wurde in der italienischen Rechtstradition der letzten Jahrzehnte insbesondere auf dem Sektor des öffentlichen Rechts (z.B. Verwaltungsrecht, Strafrecht, Völkerrecht, etc.) eingehend untersucht, und zwar vor allem im Bereich des Verfassungsrechts, wo das Attribut „ragionevole" (vernünftig) bei der Prüfung der Verfassungsmäßigkeit einer Rechtsnorm zu einem grundlegenden Kriterium für ihre materielle Beurteilung geworden ist.[24] Vor nicht allzu langer Zeit ist das Interesse für diesen Begriff auch auf das Privatrecht übergegangen. Ausschlaggebend war in diesem Zusammenhang die ständig steigende Anzahl der Stellen, an denen die zivilrechtliche Gesetzgebung auf dieses Kriterium als Attribut für die Handlungen oder Verhaltensweisen Privater verweist. Diesbezüglich wird von vielen Seiten behauptet, dass die Vernünftigkeit bereits auf semantischer Ebene ein zweideutiger, flüchtiger, mehrsinniger Ausdruck sei: Oft folgt dieser Behauptung auch auf juristischer Ebene eine Abwertung des Begriffs mit der Begründung, dass er dem zu seiner Konkretisierung berufenen Ausleger vor allem angesichts der besonderen Bedeutung der konkreten Umstände bei der Beurteilung überaus großen Spielraum lässt.[25] Aber gerade die Unmöglichkeit, die „Vernünftigkeit" zu definieren und in feste und vorgegebene Grenzen zu zwingen, machen dieses Kriterium auch im Bereich des Privatrechts zu einem äußerst elastischen und flexiblen Instrument,[26] mit dem die Entscheidungsregel an die veränderlichen Umstände der konkreten Fälle angepasst und den Veränderungen der Gesellschaft Rechnung getragen werden kann.[27]

Beale, Unfair Contracts in Britain and Europe, in 42 Current Legal Problems 1989, 197 ff.

[24] Dazu J. *Luther*, Ragionevolezza (delle leggi), in: Digesto disc. pubbl., XII, Torino 1997, 342 ff.; L. *Paladin*, Ragionevolezza (principio di), in: Enc. dir. Aggiornamento, I, Milano 1997, 899 ff.

[25] *Criscuoli* (Fn. 10) 751) bezweifelt, dass es sich bei der Vernünftigkeit um ein „offensichtliches" Kriterium handelt, das „dem System der Rechtsordnung auf natürliche Weise innewohnt", und deshalb keine präzise Bedeutung hat.

[26] So *Weiszberg* (Fn. 19) n° 201.

[27] Wie Perelman, der Autor einiger grundlegender philosophischer Abhandlungen zum juristischen Kriterium des „Vernünftigen", unterstreicht, ist „déraisonnable" ... „ce qui est inadmissible dans une communauté à un moment donné" (C. *Perelman*, Le raisonnable et le déraisonnable en droit. Au-delà du positivisme juridique, Paris, 1984, 15).

Der Standard des „Vernünftigen" übernimmt sogar dank seiner extremen Anpassungsfähigkeit immer mehr die Rolle einer Schnittstelle bzw. eines Kompromisses zwischen verschiedenen Erfahrungen und wird dadurch zu einem wahren Instruments für die Harmonisierung des europäischen Vertragsrechts. Dieser Eindruck wird dadurch bestätigt, dass viele der Bezugnahmen auf das Kriterium der Vernünftigkeit, die heute in den nationalen (vor allem in den kontinentaleuropäischen) Rechtsordnungen vorhanden sind, entweder direkt dem Gemeinschaftsrecht oder einheitsrechtlichen internationalen Übereinkommen entspringen, d.h. das Ergebnis von Maßnahmen zur normativen Harmonisierung oder Vereinheitlichung auf grenzüberschreitender Ebene sind.[28] Im Rahmen dieses Prozesses werden also von außen Kriterien übernommen, die der jeweils betroffenen nationalen Rechtstradition fremd sind. Ist dies der Ursprung (zumindest eines Großteils) der normativen Bezugnahmen auf das Konzept des „Vernünftigen" im Vertragsrecht, sollte untersucht werden, wie sich dieses Kriterium nach seiner Übernahme in ein europäisches Rechtssystem des *Civil law*, in dem es traditionellerweise unbekannt ist, in das bestehende System des Vertragsrechts integriert und mit den anderen konsolidierten Konzepten interagiert, die dem Rechtsanwender in diesem Bereich zur Verfügung stehen.

2. Die Vernünftigkeit („ragionevolezza") im ursprünglichen Aufbau des italienischen Codice civile

Im ursprünglichen Aufbau des Codice civile sind der Ausdruck „ragionevolezza" (Vernünftigkeit) und die davon abgeleiteten Begriffe praktisch überhaupt nicht vorhanden. Die Bezugnahmen reduzieren sich letztendlich auf nur drei Bestimmungen über die zur Beantragung der Verschollenheitserklärung berechtigten Personen (Art. 49 Codice civile), die Befugnisse des Mandatars (Art. 1711, Abs. 2 Codice civile) und die Haftung des Pächters (Art. 1637 Codice civile). In diesen Bestimmungen wird insbesondere das Adverb „ragionevolmente" (vernünftigerweise) verwendet, das als Kriterium zur Qualifikation einer Auffassung oder Überzeugung eingesetzt wird und die objektive Relevanz dieser – an sich subjektiven und unergründlichen – Überzeugung eingrenzen soll.[29] Zwei weitere –

---

[28] Näher hierzu *Weiszberg* (Fn. 19).

[29] Art. 49 c.c. „jeder, der vernünftigerweise glaubt, hinsichtlich des Vermögens des Verschollenen Rechte zu haben, die von dessen Tod abhängig sind"; Art. 1711, Abs. 2, c.c., spricht von „Umständen, die dem Auftraggeber unbekannt sind", aufgrund welcher „vernünftigerweise anzunehmen ist, dass der Auftraggeber dazu seine Zustimmung erteilt hätte"; Art. 1637 c.c. nimmt Bezug

nur implizite – Bezugnahmen finden sich darüber hinaus in Art. 1365 Codice civile zum Thema Auslegung (wo eine „der Vernunft entsprechende" Auslegung erwähnt wird)[30] und in Art. 1435 Codice civile (wo von Gewalt die Rede ist, mit der eine „persona sensata", d.h. eine vernünftige Person, beeindruckt werden kann).[31] Es überrascht also keineswegs, dass vor nur zwanzig Jahren der Autor einer der ersten bahnbrechenden Studien, die in Italien dem Zusammenhang zwischen Treu und Glauben und Vernünftigkeit gewidmet wurden,[32] gerade eben aufgrund der spärlichen Verweise des Codice civile auf das Konzept des „Vernünftigen" behauptet hat, dass die entsprechenden Bestimmungen kein „Indiz für eine allgemeine Regel sind, die sich auf das Vertragsrecht insgesamt und umso weniger auf die umfassendere und allgemeinere Materie der Vermögensverhältnisse erstreckt".[33]

3. Die Vernünftigkeit in der heutigen italienischen Gesetzgebung und im europäischen Vertragsrecht

Auch wenn diese Überlegungen damals fundiert sein mochten, scheinen sie jedoch nicht mehr der Realität des heutigen italienischen Vertragsrechts zu entsprechen, denn in den letzten zwanzig Jahren hat der Gesetzgeber auf diesem Sektor immer öfter auf die „Vernünftigkeit" abgestellt. Ein Großteil dieser Entwicklung ist einerseits auf die Unterzeichnung von Übereinkommen in Sachen Einheitsrecht durch Italien und andererseits auf die durch die Eingriffe des Gemeinschaftsgesetzgebers im Interesse der Harmonisierung des Privatrechts ausgelöste Wandlung zurückzuführen. Die exponentielle Steigerung der Bezugnahmen auf die „Vernünftigkeit"

---

    auf „Zufälle, die die Parteien unter Einbeziehung des Orts und aller anderen Umstände vernünftigerweise hätten für wahrscheinlich halten können".

30 Nach dieser Vorschrift wird, falls in einem Vertrag zwecks Erklärung einer Vereinbarung ein Fall erwähnt ist, nicht davon ausgegangen, dass die nicht erwähnten Fälle, auf diese Vereinbarung „vernünftigerweise" erstreckt werden kann, ausgeschlossen sind. Für die Erklärung der Regel unter dem Gesichtspunkt der Vernünftigkeit s. Cass. 20.1.1983, n. 539; Cass., 3.10.1984, n. 4892; C. *Scognamiglio*, L'interpretazione, in: E. *Gabrielli* (Hsg.), I contratti in generale, II (in: Tratt. dei contratti Rescigno, Torino 2000, 924 ff.); *Bigliazzi Geri*, L'interpretazione del contratto, in: Il Codice civile. Commentario diretto da P. Schlesinger, Art. 1362–1371, Milano 1991, 190 f.

31 Der Text der Vorschrift ist Art. 1112 des französischen *Code civil* nachgebildet, wo von der „*personne raisonnable*" die Rede ist. Zu Art. 1112 *code civil* s. *Khairallah* (Fn. 19) 448.

32 *Criscuoli* (Fn. 10) 709 ff.

33 *Criscuoli* (Fn. 10) 751.

betrifft in erster Line den Codice civile, wo sich die Verweise in wenigen Jahren wortwörtlich multipliziert haben: z.B. in der Regelung des Agenturvertrags (vor allem nach der Umsetzung der Richtlinie 86/653/EEG über die selbständigen Handelsvertreter),[34] der Haftung des Gastwirts (infolge der Ratifizierung des europäischen Übereinkommens über die Haftung von Gastwirten vom 17.12.1962),[35] und im Gesellschafsrecht. In diesem Fall ist diese Erscheinung sowohl eine Folge der direkten Umsetzung zahlreicher Gemeinschaftsrichtlinien zum Gesellschaftsrecht, die ab den 70er Jahren bis heute erlassen wurden, als auch der umfassenden Reform des italienischen Gesellschaftsrechts, die in den Jahren 2003 und 2004 (s. d.lg. 17.1.2003, n. 6, d.lg. 30.12.2003, n. 394 und d.lg. 6.2.2004, n. 37) stattgefunden hat und mit der die italienische Rechtsordnung das Gesellschaftsrecht zu modernisieren und den bereits in den wichtigsten europäischen Ländern geltenden Regelungen anzugleichen beabsichtigte (s. insbesondere die Vorschriften in Sachen Gesellschaftsbilanzen[36] und Gesellschaftsfusion[37]).

---

[34] S. z.B. den Gebrauch des Adjektivs „ragionevole" (vernünftig), bezogen auf eine Frist oder einen Zeitraum, in Art. 1748, Abs. 3, c.c. und in Art. 1749, Abs. 1, c.c. Beide Artikel wurden in ihrer derzeitigen Formulierung im Rahmen der Umsetzung der Richtlinie 86/653/EEG über die selbständigen Handelsvertreter aufgenommen (d.lg. 10.9.1991, n. 303 und d.lg. 15.2.1999, n. 65).

[35] S. Art. 1783, Abs. 2, Nr. 3, c.c. (diese Bestimmung wurde anlässlich der Ratifizierung des europäischen Übereinkommens über die Haftung von Gastwirten vom 17.12.1962 abgeändert: s. Art. 3, Gesetz Nr. 316 vom 10.6.1978).

[36] Das Kriterium der Vernünftigkeit ist z.B. in der Regelung der Bewertungsrichtlinien für die Bilanzierung bzw. in Art. 2426, Abs. 1, c.c. erwähnt (in der durch die Gesetzesverordnung Nr. 127 vom 9.4.1991 abgeänderten Form. Mit dieser Gesetzesverordnung wurden die Richtlinien 78/660/EEG und 83/349/EEG über Jahresabschlüsse und konsolidierte Jahresabschlüsse von Kapitalgesellschaften umgesetzt), wo die Ausdrücke (Nr. 1) „dem Erzeugnis vernünftigerweise zurechenbarer Anteil" und (Nr. 11) „vernünftige Sicherheit" vorkommen. Im Hinblick auf die Bestimmungen, die im Rahmen der Reform des Gesellschaftsrechts eingeführt wurden, s. Art. 2427 bis c.c., in dem das Konzept der „vernünftigen Annäherung an den Marktwert" erwähnt ist.

[37] S. z.B. Art. 2501 bis, c.c. (der ebenfalls anlässlich der Reform des Gesellschaftsrechts eingeführt wurde) und insbesondere seine Abs. 2 und 4, wonach im Verschmelzungsplan einerseits „die Geldmittel, die für die Befriedigung der Verbindlichkeiten der sich aus der Verschmelzung ergebenden Gesellschaft vorgesehen sind" anzugeben sind und die „Vernünftigkeit" dieser Angaben andererseits von einem Sachverständigenbericht bestätigt werden muss. S. darüber hinaus Art. 2467, Abs. 2, c.c. zum Thema Rückzahlung von Finanzierungen („vernünftige Einlage").

Die Erscheinung betrifft aber ebenso die Sondergesetzgebung und die sog. sektorale Kodifizierung. Man denke vor allem an die Normen des neuen „Verbrauchergesetzbuches" (in Kraft getreten infolge der Gesetzesverordnung Nr. 206 vom 6. September 2005), das in einem koordinierten Text einen Großteil der Umsetzungsbestimmungen der Gemeinschaftsrichtlinien in Sachen Verbraucherschutz umfasst, die bis zum Vorjahr auf ungeordnete Weise zwischen Codice civile und Sondergesetzen aufgeteilt waren. Insbesondere sind in das Verbrauchergesetzbuch u.a. die – ursprünglich ebenfalls im Codice civile (in den Art. 1469 *bis* ff. und 1519 *bis* ss. Codice civile) enthaltenen – Bestimmungen über missbräuchliche Klauseln in Verbraucherverträgen und Garantien beim Verkauf von Verbrauchsgütern eingeflossen, in denen die Verweise auf das Kriterium der „Vernünftigkeit" (die im übrigen in der Regel bereits im Text der Richtlinien vorhanden waren, die durch diese Normen umgesetzt wurden bzw. in den Richtlinien 93/13/EEG und 99/44/EG) überaus zahlreich sind: Das Attribut der Vernünftigkeit wird hier z.B. auf Kündigungsfristen,[38] auf die Erwartung des Verbrauchers[39] und auf die Kosten für die Geltendmachung der als Garantie zustehenden Abhilfen bezogen[40] (auf diese Bestimmungen wird auch nachfolgend eingegangen. Die Anzahl der Bezugnahmen auf die „Vernünftigkeit" wäre sogar noch weitaus höher gewesen, wenn sich der mit der Umsetzung betraute italienische Gesetzgeber genauer an den Text dieser Richtlinien gehalten hätte. Das Wort „vernünftig" und

---

[38] S. Art. 33, Abs. 2, lit. h, Verbrauchergesetzbuch (Umsetzung der Richtilinie 93/13/CEE über mißbräuchliche Klauseln in Verbraucherverträgen): „si presumono vessatorie fino a prova contraria le clausole che hanno per oggetto o per effetto di: ... h) consentire al professionista di recedere da contratti a tempo indeterminato senza un ragionevole preavviso, tranne nel caso di giusta causa".

[39] Vgl. Art. 129, Abs. 2, lit. c, Verbrauchergesetzbuch, wonach unter den Bedingungen, unter denen die Übereinstimmung des Verbrauchsguts mit dem Vertrag vermutet wird, der Umstand genannt ist, dass die Sachen „eine Qualität und Leistungen aufweisen, die bei Gütern der gleichen Art üblich sind und die der Verbraucher vernünftigerweise erwarten kann, wenn die Beschaffenheit des Gutes und gegebenenfalls die insbesondere in der Werbung oder bei der Etikettierung gemachten öffentlichen Äußerungen des Verkäufers, des Herstellers oder dessen Vertreters über die konkreten Eigenschaften des Gutes in Betracht gezogen werden".

[40] Eine Abhilfe wird insbesondere dann im Vergleich zu einer anderen als „übermäßige Belastung" angesehen, wenn sie „dem Verkäufer gegenüber der anderen Abhilfe unvernünftige Kosten auferlegt, wobei zu berücksichtigen sind: a) der Wert, den die Sache hätte, falls keine Vertragswidrigkeit vorliegen würde; b) das Ausmaß der Vertragswidrigkeit; c) die Möglichkeit, dass ohne erhebliche Unannehmlichkeiten für den Verbraucher auf die alternative Abhilfe zurückgegriffen werden kann" (Art. 130, Abs. 4, c. consumo).

die von ihm abgeleiteten Begriffe wurden im Text der nationalen Umsetzungsbestimmungen nämlich nicht immer übernommen: Während z.B. die „Vernünftigkeit" in der Richtlinie 99/44/EG an sechs verschiedenen Stellen erwähnt wird,[41] reduzieren sich die Erwähnungen in den neuen Art. 128 ff. des Verbrauchergesetzbuches auf die beiden oben genannten, denn in den übrigen Fällen wurde das Kriterium der „Vernünftigkeit" durch die Verwendung von auf andere Parameter abstellende Formeln übersetzt,[42] z.B. auf die Sorgfalt.[43]

Neben dem Verbrauchergesetzbuch nehmen auch zahlreiche Sondergesetze auf die „Vernünftigkeit" Bezug, wie z.B. die Gesetze über die Finanzsicherheiten (in Umsetzung der Richtlinie 2002/47/EG eingeführt).[44] Besonders häufig, ja sogar systematisch, wird der Einsatz des Konzepts des „Vernünftigen" dann in den Übereinkommen über internationale Handelsverträge (und natürlich bei der entsprechenden nationalen Ratifizierung), angefangen von dem bekanntesten dieser Übereinkommen, d.h. dem Wiener Übereinkommen von 1980 über den internationalen Warenkauf (das in Italien 1985 ratifiziert wurde), in dem die Verweise auf die Vernünftigkeit dermaßen zahlreich sind (wer sie zählen möchte, käme auf immerhin 47 Erwähnungen: s. dazu oben II.) und eine derart umfassende Bandbreite an Funktionen übernehmen, dass viele Kommentatoren

---

[41] Siehe Art. 2, Abs. 2, lit. d; Art. 2, Abs. 3; Art. 2, Abs. 4, 1. Spiegelstrich; Art. 3, Abs. 3, Par. 1 und 3; Art. 3, Abs. 5.

[42] S. dazu S. *Ferreri*, La lingua del legislatore. Modelli comunitari e attuazione negli Stati membri, Riv. dir. civ. 2004, II, 560, 571.

[43] S. insbesondere die beiden Beispiele für die Übersetzung des Kriteriums der „Vernünftigkeit" in „ordinaria diligenza" (gewöhnliche Sorgfalt) in Art. 129, Abs. 3 und in Abs. 4, 1. Spiegelstrich, des Verbrauchergesetzbuches, worauf nachstehend eingegangen wird (s. unten IV.1.b). Weitere zwei Beispiele für die „Nationalisierung" des Kriteriums der Vernünftigkeit sind in der Umsetzung von Art. 3, Abs. 4, Par. 4, und Abs. 5 zu finden. Beide betreffen die Frist, innerhalb der der Verkäufer die Nachbesserungen oder Ersatzlieferungen vornehmen muss: Während die beiden Bestimmungen der Richtlinie auf eine „reasonable time" Bezug nehmen, hat es der italienische Gesetzgeber vorgezogen, das uns vertrautere Konzept der „termine congruo" (angemessenen Frist) zu verwenden (s. Art. 130, Abs. 5 und 7, lit. b des Verbrauchergesetzbuches). Eine analoge Entscheidung hat der deutsche Gesetzgeber bei der Umsetzung getroffen und dadurch im Vergleich zum italienischen Gesetzgeber ganz ähnliche Absichten preisgegeben (s. dazu unten, IV., 1., b).

[44] S. Art. 8, Abs. 1, d.lg. 21.5.2004, n. 170 (Umsetzung von Art. 4, Abs. 6, Richtlinie 2002/47/CE über Finanzsicherheiten): „die Ausübungsbedingungen der finanziellen Tätigkeiten und ihre Beurteilungskriterien sowie die gesicherten finanziellen Verbindlichkeiten müssen in wirtschaftlicher Hinsicht vernünftig sein".

von einer wahrhaften „Allgegenwärtigkeit" des Konzepts des „Vernünftigen" in dem Übereinkommen gesprochen[45] und dieses Konzept als (impliziten) allgemeinen Grundsatz des Übereinkommens angesehen haben.[46]

Die Vernünftigkeit kommt also nicht mehr in nur sporadischen und nebensächlichen Verweisen vor, sondern ist zu einem geläufigen Modell geworden. Der beharrliche Einsatz des Standards der Vernünftigkeit im Einheitsrecht und im Gemeinschaftsrecht verdeutlicht wie gesagt, dass die Tendenz dahin geht, diesem Begriff immer häufiger die Funktion eines Instruments für eine Annäherung der einzelnen Gesetzgebungen beizumessen. Eine bedeutende Bestätigung dafür bieten die derzeit laufenden Initiativen im Interesse der Harmonisierung des internationalen (und insbesondere des europäischen) Vertragsrechts, von den *Unidroit-Grundregeln der internationalen Handelsverträge* in der Neufassung von 2004,[47] in denen die „Vernünftigkeit" in ziemlich vielen und praktisch sämtliche Phasen der die Vertragsabwicklung betreffenden Bestimmungen erwähnt wird,[48] über die *Principles of European Contract Law*, die von der Kommission unter dem Vorsitz von Ole Lando ausgearbeitet wurden und in denen die „Vernünftigkeit" (allein in den ersten beiden Büchern) 65 Mal erwähnt[49] und darüber hinaus Gegenstand einer Definitionsnorm (Art. 1:302)[50] ist, bis hin zum Vorentwurf des *Code européen des contrats* der Akademie der europäischen Privatrechtler unter der Leitung von Giuseppe Gandolfi,[51] in dem der Ausdruck „vernünftig" ebenfalls (wenn auch weniger) häufig vorhanden ist und in der Form eines Attributs oder Adverbs auf subjektive Vertrauens-, Erwartungs-, Überzeugungszustände usw. oder auf die Gründe eines Verhaltens, häufiger aber auf Fristen oder Zeit-

---

[45] F. *Diesse*, La bonne foi, la coopération et le raisonnable dans la Convention des Nations Unies relative à la vente internationale de marchandises (CVIM), Journal du droit international 2002, 1, 82.

[46] S. *Fortier*, Le contrat du commerce international à l'aune du raisonnable, Journal de droit international 1996, 315, insb 316.

[47] S. J. *Bonell*, UNIDROIT Principles 2004 – The New Edition of the Principles of International Commercial Contracts adopted by the International Institute for the Unification of Private Law, 9 Uniform Law Review 2004, 6 ff.

[48] Vgl. etwa Art. 2.1.4(2)(b)); Art. 4.1(2); Art. 4.8(2)(d)); Art. 5.1.2(d).

[49] Zu einer aufmerksamen Klassifikation verschiedener Verweise zur „reasonableness" im CISG s. J. Schmidt (Fn. 3) 1017 ff.

[50] „Under these Principles reasonableness is to be judged by what persons acting in good faith and in the same situation as the parties would consider to be reasonable. In particular, in assessing what is reasonable the nature and purpose of the contract, the circumstances of the case, and the usages and practices of the trades or professions involved should be taken into account".

[51] V. *Accademia dei giusprivatisti europei*, Code européen des contrats, Avant-projet, (coord. G. Gandolfi), Livre premier, Milano 2004.

angaben bezogen wird.⁵² Dasselbe gilt für die von den noch laufenden Arbeiten der von Christian von Bar koordinierten *Study Group on a European Contract Code* (aber hier würde die Debatte angesichts ihrer Ausmaße den hiesigen Rahmen sprengen). Darüber hinaus wird es interessant sein, nach dem Abschluss der entsprechenden Arbeiten festzustellen, welche Rolle das Kriterium der Vernünftigkeit im zukünftigen *Common Frame of Reference* und insbesondere in den *Common Principles of European Contract Law (CoPECL)*, die derzeit vom *Joint Network on European Law* in Zusammenarbeit u.a. mit der *Study Group von Bar* und der *Acquis-Group* erstellt werden, spielen wird.

IV. Die Klassifikation der verschiedenen Verwendungen des Konzepts des „Vernünftigen" nach ihrer Funktion

Angesichts der Reichhaltigkeit und der Bedeutung der Erwähnungen ist es nicht allein zum Zwecke der Rekonstruktion erforderlich, eine erste Klassifizierung dieser verstreuten Bezugnahmen in einheitliche Gruppen vorzunehmen. Dabei wird unter Beibehaltung des hier gewählten Untersuchungsansatzes das italienische Rechtssystem als Modell eingesetzt. Am besten geeignet ist wahrscheinlich das Kriterium, das die dem Konzept des „Vernünftigen" in den verschiedenen Bestimmungen übertragene Funktion berücksichtigt. Vor diesem Hintergrund können die diversen Verwendungen dieses Konzepts in mindestens *drei* verschiedene Kategorien eingeteilt werden: A) als Modell, das den Grad und die Art der Bemühungen definiert, die von einer Person bei der Umsetzung eines bestimmten Ziels geschuldet sind oder verlangt werden können (insbesondere bei der Erfüllung einer Pflicht oder einer Obliegenheit); B) als Formel für die Zuweisung der Haftung für die Nichterfüllung einer Pflicht oder des Vertretenmüssens der Nichtbeachtung einer Obliegenheit; C) als Kriterium, das auf die Gewährleistung oder Wahrung des Vertragsgleichgewichts abzielt und deshalb dem Bedarf nach Kontrolle und Ausgleich der entgegengesetzten Interessen Rechnung trägt.

1. „Reasonableness" als Verhaltensmodell

Die funktionale Deklination der „Vernünftigkeit" als Verhaltensmodell findet ihren maximalen Niederschlag im Standard der „vernünftigen Per-

---

⁵² Vgl. etwa Artt. 6, Abs. 3; 12, Abs. 2; 17, Abs. 1; 61; art. 83, Abs. 1; Art. 94; Art. 92, lit. a; 92, lit. c; 93, lit. a; 93, lit. d; Artt. 15, Abs. 3, lit. b; 15, Abs. 4; 48, Abs. 1; 31, Abs. 3; 65, Abs. 1; 84, Abs. 1; 91, Abs. 1; 92, Abs. 1, lit. b; 96, Abs. 1, 114, Abs. 1.

son", der in der Norm manchmal ausdrücklich erwähnt oder nur angedeutet ist (im zuletzt genannten Fall aber dann im Rahmen der richterlichen Auslegung verdeutlicht wird). In diesen Fällen übernimmt die Bezugnahme auf das Vernünftige die Funktion, das *quantum* und das *quomodo* der Bemühungen anzugeben, die von der Partei gefordert sind oder verlangt werden können, um das Interesse Dritter zu verwirklichen oder um eine für den Schutz des eigenen Interesses erforderliche Voraussetzung zu schaffen. Mit anderen Worten dient die „Vernünftigkeit" als Verhaltensmodell der Bemessung und Beurteilung der geforderten Bemühungen. Angesichts dessen agiert die Vernünftigkeit in dieser konkreten Funktion also auf einer gemeinsamen Ebene mit anderen bekannten und unbestimmten Konzepten des Vertragsrechts: Insbesondere der Sorgfalt auf der einen Seite und Treu und Glauben im objektiven Sinn bzw. Korrektheit auf der anderen Seite.

a. Beispiele: Art. 8 Abs. 2 CISG („reasonable person")

Dies ist z.B. die Funktion, die dem Standard der „vernünftigen Person" im Bereich der Vertragsauslegungsregeln, angefangen von Art. 8, Abs. 2 CISG, anvertraut ist. Bekanntlich wird allgemein davon ausgegangen, dass sich der in dieser Norm enthaltene Verweis auf die *reasonable person* auf den objektiven und abstrakten Horizont des Erklärungsempfängers bezieht: Von einigen Seiten wird behauptet, dass hier genauer gesagt auf das objektive Modell[53] des *bonus paterfamilias*[54] abzustellen ist, d.h. auf die gewöhnliche Sorgfalt – eine Vorstellung, die dem kontinentaleuropäischen Juristen viel vertrauter ist –. Gleichzeitig wird jedoch darauf hingewiesen,[55] dass es sich um ein von den einzelnen nationalen Erfahrungen unabhängiges Modell handelt,[56] das darüber hinaus auf die Eigenschaften der auf dem Sektor des internationalen Handels gewerbsmäßig tätigen

---

[53] D.h. es ist auf den objektiven und abstrakten Horizont des Erklärungsempfängers abzustellen: dazu s. nur *F. Ferrari*, Art. 8 CISG, in Münchener Kommentar zum Handelsgesetzbuch, München 2004, Rn. 378; *Magnus*, Wiener UN-Kaufrecht (CISG), in Staudingers Kommentar zum Bürgerlichen Gesetzbuch mit Einführungsgesetz und Nebengesetzen, Berlin Neubearb. 2004, Art. 8, Rn. 17; *Brunner*, UN-Kaufrecht – CISG, Bern 2004, Art. 8, Rn. 6.
[54] Vgl. etwa *G. Eörsi*, General Provisions, in: *N. M. Galston-H. Smit* (Hsg.), International Sales , New York, 1984, 2 ff.
[55] *Diesse* (Fn. 45) 80.
[56] *Didier*, La Common Law en français: étude juridique et linguistique de la Common Law en français au Canada, Revue internationale de droit comparé 1991, 7, insb. 38.

Personen abzustimmen ist.[57] Die Regelung in Art. 8, die allerdings nicht isoliert geblieben ist, da sie sowohl von den Unidroit-Grundsätzen als auch von den *Principles of European Contract Law* übernommen wurde,[58] unterstreicht also in erster Linie den funktionalen Parallelismus zwischen den Konzepten der „vernünftigen Person" und dem Modell des sorgfältigen Vertragspartners. Will man jedoch die Grundlage der Auslegungsregel erforschen, nehmen die Kommentatoren auch häufig auf den Grundsatz von Treu und Glauben Bezug. Einer der deutschsprachigen Kommentare zu dem Übereinkommen vertritt die Auffassung, dass mit der Auslegung der Erklärungen der Parteien vielmehr ein „vernünftiges, mit Treu und Glauben vereinbares Resultat" erzielt werden sollte.[59] Demzufolge tritt bereits im Bereich der Auslegung das Problem auf, den Knotenpunkt (und dadurch eine präzise Rollenteilung) zwischen „Vernünftigkeit" auf der einen Seite und Sorgfalt und Treu und Glauben auf der anderen Seite zu ermitteln.

---

[57] S. F. *Ferrari*, Vendita internazionale di beni mobili. Art. 1-13. Ambito di applicazione. Disposizioni generali, in: Commentario del codice civile Scialoja e Branca, Bologna-Roma, 1994, Art. 8, 177, der vom „bonus paterfamilias des internationalen Handels" spricht.

[58] S. Art. 4.1 UNIDROIT Principles (2004): „(1) A contract shall be interpreted according to the common intention of the parties. (2) If such intention cannot be established, the contract shall be interpreted according to the meaning that reasonable persons of the same kind as the parties would give to it in the same circumstances". Auch in diesem Zusammenhang ist der Parallelismus zwischen „Vernünftigkeit" und dem Standard der Sorgfalt zwar nur angedeutet, aber trotzdem eindeutig. Dies wird durch die ständige Assoziierung zwischen „Vernünftigkeit" und Sorgfalt bestätigt, die sich wie ein unsichtbarer Faden durch den gesamten Text der Principles zieht (s. etwa Art. 5.1.4 (2), wonach „to the extent that an obligation of a party involves a duty of best efforts in the performance of an activity, that party is bound to make such efforts as would be made by a reasonable person of the same kind in the same circumstances"). Eine ähnliche Regelung ist auch im Art. 5:101 dei *Principles of European Contract Law* vorgesehen.

[59] *Brunner* (Fn. 53) Art. 8, Rn. 14. Ähnlich *Fioravanti*, Art. 8, in: C. M. *Bianca* (Hsg.), Convenzione di Vienna sui contratti di vendita internazionale di beni mobili, Commentario, Padova 1992, 35: „Die Auslegungsregeln nach Art. 8 stellen beide den Ausdruck und die Anwendung des fundamentalen Grundsatzes der *buona fede* dar, an denen sich die einheitliche Gesetzgebung insgesamt inspiriert".

b. „ragionevole affidamento" (vernünftiges Vertrauen) oder „aspettativa" (Erwartung), „ragionevole conoscenza" (vernünftige Kenntnis) bzw. „ignoranza" (Unkenntnis): Art. 129 Abs. 3 Verbrauchergesetzbuch (Art. 2 Abs. 3 Richtlinie 99/44/EG)

Der funktionale Parallelismus zwischen den Parametern der Vernünftigkeit und der Sorgfalt wird auch in jenen Bestimmungen deutlich, in denen die Vernünftigkeit mit Bezug auf subjektive Situationen einer Partei erwähnt wird, wie z.b. in den Ausdrücken „ragionevole affidamento" (vernünftiges Vertrauen) oder „aspettativa" (Erwartung), „ragionevole conoscenza" (vernünftige Kenntnis) bzw. „ignoranza" (Unkenntnis) usw. Unter diesen zahlreichen Beispielen, die in den Richtlinien und in den nationalen Bestimmungen gemeinschaftlicher Abstammung sowie in den Übereinkommen des einheitlichen Handelsrechts vorhanden sind, denke man insbesondere an die Regelung der Garantien beim Verbrauchsgüterkauf. Nach dem bereits erwähnten Art. 129 des Verbrauchergesetzbuches[60] (welcher diesbezüglich der Formulierung von Art. 2, Abs. 2, lit. d, Richtlinie 99/44/EG entspricht[61]), umfassen die Bedingungen, unter denen die Vertragsmäßigkeit der Verbrauchsgüter vermutet wird, die Tatsache, dass die Güter „eine Qualität und Leistungen aufweisen, die bei Gütern der gleichen Art üblich sind und die *der Verbraucher vernünftigerweise erwarten kann*, wenn die Beschaffenheit des Gutes und gegebenenfalls die insbesondere in der Werbung oder bei der Etikettierung gemachten öffentlichen Äußerungen des Verkäufers, des Herstellers oder dessen Vertreters über die konkreten Eigenschaften des Gutes in Betracht gezogen

---

[60] Ausführlicher dazu S. *Troiano*, Vendita di beni di consumo: la responsabilità da „dichiarazioni pubbliche", Responsabilità civile 2005, 1 ff.

[61] „Es wird vermutet, daß Verbrauchsgüter vertragsgemäß sind, wenn sie... d) eine Qualität und Leistungen aufweisen, die bei Gütern der gleichen Art üblich sind und die der Verbraucher vernünftigerweise erwarten kann, wenn die Beschaffenheit des Gutes und gegebenenfalls die insbesondere in der Werbung oder bei der Etikettierung gemachten öffentlichen Äußerungen des Verkäufers, des Herstellers oder dessen Vertreters über die konkreten Eigenschaften des Gutes in Betracht gezogen werden". Vgl. auch die englische Fassung: „Consumer goods are presumed to be in conformity with the contract if they ... – show the quality and performance which are normal in goods of the same type and which the consumer can reasonably expect, given the nature of the goods and taking into account any public statements on the specific characteristics of the goods made about them by the seller, the producer or his representative, particularly in advertising or on labelling").

werden".⁶² Dem Anschein nach handelt es sich erneut um ein mit dem Modell der Sorgfalt verbundenes Kriterium, das dahingehend zu verstehen ist, dass Qualitäten und Leistungen berücksichtigt werden, auf die ein Verbraucher unter Einsatz der Sorgfalt eines ordentlichen Familienvaters unter den konkreten Umstände vertrauen könnte.⁶³ Auch in diesem Fall wird die Norm aber zumindest in der italienischen Literatur von einigen als Ausdruck des objektiven Grundsatzes von Treu und Glauben angesehen.⁶⁴

Analoge Überlegungen gelten im Hinblick auf Abs. 3 des Art. 129 des Verbrauchergesetzbuches, wonach keine Vertragswidrigkeit vorliegt, wenn der Verbraucher zum Zeitpunkt des Vertragsabschlusses Kenntnis von der Vertragswidrigkeit hatte oder „unter Einsatz der gewöhnlichen Sorgfalt nicht in Unkenntnis darüber sein konnte".⁶⁵ Diesbezüglich ist hervorzuheben, dass die der Norm zugrunde liegende gewöhnliche Sorgfalt die Übersetzung der gemeinschaftsrechtlichen Formulierung „vernünftigerweise nicht in Unkenntnis" über die Vertragswidrigkeit „sein konnte" nach Art. 2, Abs. 3 der Richtlinie 99/44/EG⁶⁶ darstellt. Es ist

---

⁶² In der italienischen Fassung: „Si presume che i beni di consumo siano conformi al contratto se ... c) presentano la qualità e le prestazioni abituali di un bene dello stesso tipo, che il consumatore può ragionevolmente aspettarsi, tenuto conto della natura del bene e, se del caso, delle dichiarazioni pubbliche sulle caratteristiche specifiche dei beni fatte al riguardo dal venditore, dal produttore o dal suo agente o rappresentante, in particolare nella pubblicità o sull'etichettatura".

⁶³ Von der Erwartung des „durchschnittlich sorgfältigen Verbrauchers" sowie von einem „nicht schuldhaften Vertrauen, das in diesem durch die öffentlichen Erklärungen des Verkäufers oder des Herstellers geweckt wurde" spricht auch F. Bocchini, La vendita di cose mobili, in: Commentario del codice civile Schlesinger, Busnelli, Milano 2004, Artt. 1510–1536, 401, der diese Aussagen jedoch sofort danach auf die Ebene des objektiven guten Glaubens stellt. Im Hinblick auf die „Sorgfalt der Durchschnittsperson" s. auch E. Corso, La vendita dei beni di consumo, in Commentario del codice civile Scialoja e Branca, Galgano, Art. 1519 bis–1519 nonies, Bologna-Roma 2005, 77.

⁶⁴ S. Bocchini (Fn. 63) 401.

⁶⁵ Eingehend zu dieser Vorschrift S. Troiano, Art. 129, comma 3°, Codice del consumo, in: C. M. Bianca (Hsg.), La vendita dei beni di consumo, Padova 2006, 82 ff.

⁶⁶ Art. 2, Abs. 3 Richtlinie 99/44/EG: „Es liegt keine Vertragswidrigkeit im Sinne dieses Artikels vor, wenn der Verbraucher zum Zeitpunkt des Vertragsschlusses Kenntnis von der Vertragswidrigkeit hatte oder vernünftigerweise nicht in Unkenntnis darüber sein konnte oder wenn die Vertragswidrigkeit auf den vom Verbraucher gelieferten Stoff zurückzuführen ist" (Italienische Fassung: „non vi è difetto di conformità ... se, al momento della conclusione del contratto, il

aber kein Zufall, dass sich der italienische Gesetzgeber für die Bezugnahme auf die Sorgfalt entschlossen hat, denn diese Entscheidung knüpft an die Regeln an, die in Sachen Mängelgewährleistung bereits in den wichtigsten kontinentaleuropäischen Rechtssystemen vorhanden sind. Nur um die bedeutendsten Beispiele zu nennen, denke man an Art. 1642 des französischen *Code civil*,[67] an § 460 Abs. 2 des BGB alter Fassung[68] (d.h. der vor der zum 1.1.2002 erfolgten Modernisierung des Schuldrechts gültigen Fassung), an Art. 1491 des italienischen Codice civile[69] sowie an die Bestimmung nach Art. 35 CISG,[70] das für die Richtlinie 99/44 als primäres Modell fungiert hat und sich seinerseits an diesen Traditionen orientierte. Wenn man all diese Bestimmungen aufmerksam liest und dabei die Bedeutung berücksichtigt, mit der sie von Praxis und Doktrin üblicherweise ausgelegt und angewandt werden, stellt man abgesehen von den unterschiedlichen Ausdrücken für die Beurteilung der Erkennbarkeit der Vertragswidrigkeit erhebliche Gemeinsamkeiten fest, denn all diese Bestimmungen stellen ausdrücklich oder implizit auf das Parameter der *Sorgfalt* verweisende Regeln auf. Dies gilt in erster Linie für Art. 35, Abs. 3, CISG, der allgemein dahingehend verstanden wird, dass die Haftung des Verkäufers nur dann ausgeschlossen ist, wenn der Käufer die Vertragswidrigkeit zum Zeitpunkt des Vertragsabschlusses unter Einsatz

---

consumatore era a conoscenza del difetto o non poteva ragionevolmente ignorarlo, o se il difetto di conformità trova la sua origine in materiali forniti dal consumatore"; Englische Fassung: „There shall be deemed not to be a lack of conformity for the purposes of this Article if, at the time the contract was concluded, the consumer was aware, or could not reasonably be unaware of, the lack of conformity, or if the lack of conformity has its origin in materials supplied by the consumer").

[67] „Le vendeur n'est pas tenu des vices apparents et dont l'acheteur a pu se convaincre lui-même".

[68] „Ist dem Käufer ein Mangel der im § 459 Abs. 1 bezeichneten Art infolge grober Fahrlässigkeit unbekannt geblieben, so haftet der Verkäufer, sofern er nicht die Abwesenheit des Fehlers zugesichert hat, nur, wenn er den Fehler arglistig verschwiegen hat".

[69] „Non è dovuta la garanzia se al momento del contratto il compratore conosceva i vizi della cosa; parimenti non è dovuta, se i vizi erano facilmente riconoscibili, salvo, in questo caso, che il venditore abbia dichiarato che la cosa era esente da vizi".

[70] „Il venditore non è responsabile ... per un difetto di conformità dei beni che al momento della conclusione del contratto il compratore conosceva o non avrebbe potuto ignorare" („the seller is not liable ... for any lack of conformity of the goods if at the time of the conclusion of the contract the buyer knew or could not have been unaware of the lack of conformity").

eines minimalen Maßes an Sorgfalt erkennen konnte.[71] Auf die *Fahrlässigkeit* (insbesondere auf die *grobe* Fahrlässigkeit) nahm wie gesagt § 460 Abs. 2 des BGB a.f. ausdrücklich Bezug, aber dieselbe Formulierung wurde auch vom neuen § 442 Abs. 1, Satz 2 BGB übernommen, mit dem die Richtlinie 99/44/EG umgesetzt wurde und in dem ebenfalls von der Unkenntnis infolge *grober Fahrlässigkeit* des Käufers die Rede ist.[72] Der Parameter der Sorgfalt wird schließlich von der italienischen Lehre und Rechtsprechung für die Erklärung des Konzepts des „leicht erkennbaren" Mangels nach Art. 1491 Codice civile eingesetzt.[73] Ein solcher Mangel liegt dann vor, wenn der Mangel zum Zeitpunkt des Vertragsabschlusses unter Einsatz der *minimalen* Sorgfalt vom Käufer erkannt werden konnte.[74] Analoge Überlegungen gelten auch für die Auslegung des Konzepts der „vices apparents" durch die französische Rechtsprechung.[75]

c. „Vernünftige Maßnahmen", „vernünftiger Zeitraum" etc.

Die Funktion der Darstellung eines Verhaltensmodells, auf das die von der anderen Partei verlangten Bemühungen bezogen werden, ist darüber hinaus in all jenen und vor allem in internationalen Übereinkommen oftmals enthaltenen Bestimmungen zu finden, nach denen die Partei „vernünftige Maßnahmen"[76] ergreifen muss, um ein bestimmtes Ergebnis

---

[71] Mit anderen Worten haftet der Verkäufer nur dann nicht, wenn der Käufer bei der Prüfung des Zustandes der Ware grob fahrlässig gehandelt hat: *Magnus* (Fn. 53) Art. 35, Rn. 48; *Brunner* (Fn. 53) Art. 35, Rn. 20.

[72] „Ist dem Käufer ein Mangel infolge grober Fahrlässigkeit unbekannt geblieben, kann der Käufer Rechte wegen dieses Mangels nur geltend machen, wenn der Verkäufer den Mangel arglistig verschwiegen oder eine Garantie für die Beschaffenheit der Sache übernommen hat".

[73] Hierzu A. *Zaccaria*, Art. 1491 c.c., in: *G. Cian-A. Trabucchi*, Commentario breve del codice civile, Padova 2004, 7. Aufl., Rn. I, 1–3, 1464.

[74] Vgl. etwa *D. Rubino*, La compravendita, in: *Trattato di diritto civile e commerciale Cicu e Messineo*, Milano 1971, 2° ed., 783; *C. M. Bianca*, La vendita e la permuta, I, Torino 1993, 2° ed., 913 f. In der Rechtsprechung s. Cass., 18.12.1999, n. 14277, *Mass. Giust. civ.*, 1999, 2575; Cass., 2.4.1997, n. 2862; Cass., 23.5.1972, n. 1602.

[75] Vgl. z. B. *Cour de cassation*, 24.1.1984, *Bull. civ.*, 1984, IV, n° 34: „vices apparents sont ceux qu'une personne de diligence moyenne aurait découvert en procédant à des vérifications élémentaires".

[76] S. Art. 77 CISG: „Die Partei, die sich auf eine Vertragsverletzung beruft, hat alle den Umständen nach angemessenen Maßnahmen zur Verringerung des aus der Vertragsverletzung folgenden Verlusts, einschließlich des entgangenen Ge-

zu erreichen, oder innerhalb eines im Hinblick auf die Umstände „vernünftigen Zeitraums" handeln muss. Da diese Fälle an der ziemlich labilen Abgrenzung zwischen dem Bemühen unter Einsatz der Sorgfalt und dem Bemühen nach Treu und Glauben angeordnet sind, ist es im Zuge der Rekonstruktion allerdings überaus schwierig, die Grundlage des Verhaltensparameters zu erfassen.

Was z.B. die Fristen angeht, in deren Bereich die „Vernünftigkeit" am häufigsten verwendet wird (eine Aufzählung sämtlicher Erwähnungen wäre nicht nur nutzlos, sondern auch langweilig),[77] darf man sich nicht durch den Umstand täuschen lassen, dass in diesem Zusammenhang nur in wenigen Fällen direkt auf den Standard der „vernünftigen Person" oder des sorgfältigen Vertragspartners abgestellt wird.[78] In den meisten dieser Fälle kann diese Bezugnahme nämlich als *implizit* angesehen werden:[79] Wird z.B. von der Partei verlangt, die Mängel zur Vermeidung der Verwirkung des Rechts auf Geltendmachung der Abhilfen gegen die Vertragswidrigkeit innerhalb einer vernünftigen Frist anzuzeigen, ist es selbstverständlich, dass die Zeit gemeint ist, innerhalb der eine vernünftige Person unter denselben Umständen agieren müsste oder könnte. Der Ausdruck „vernünftige Frist" erscheint demnach als eine Ellipse, die ebenfalls auf ein Verhaltens*modell* verweist. Auch hier schwanken die in der Doktrin vertretenen Auffassungen ständig zwischen dem Konzept der Sorgfalt und den Parametern des objektiven Treu und Glaubens, was in einigen Fällen zu Unsicherheiten bei der Einordnung des geregelten Sachverhalts führt.[80]

---

winns, zu treffen (...)". S. auch die ähnlichen Regelungen in Artt. 85 und 86, Abs. 1, CISG.

[77] S. z.B. Art. 18, Abs. 2; Art. 33; Art. 47, Abs. 1; Art. 63, Art. 38; Art. 39; Art. 43; Art. 46, Abs. 2, Art. 73, Abs. 2. CISG.

[78] So z.B. Art. 5, Abs. 2 des Übereinkommens von Hamburg von 1978 über die Beförderung von Gütern auf See, wonach der Übergabetermin jener ist, „which it would be reasonable to require of a diligent carrier, having regard to the circumstances of the case".

[79] S. *Weiszberg* (Fn. 19) Nr. 249 : „le standard du vendeur ou de l'acheteur raisonnable est généralement sous-jacent compte tenu de l'examen des actions des parties".

[80] S. z.B. die „reasonable time", innerhalb der der Käufer die Vertragswidrigkeiten gegenüber dem Verkäufer anzeigen muss, um sein Recht auf Inanspruchnahme der Garantie i.S.v. Art. 39, Abs. 1 CISG nicht zu verlieren. Auch diese Regel wird von vielen Kommentatoren als Spezifizierung einer Pflicht zur Sorgfalt oder zu Treu und Glauben zu Lasten des Käufers erklärt (s. dazu *Fortier* (Fn. 46) 356). Eingehend zu dieser Vorschrift und ihrer Auslgeung in den einzelnen Staaten siehe nur *A. Veneziano*, Non Conformity of Goods in International Sales, A Survey of Current Case Law on CISG, Revue de droit des affaires in-

2. „Reasonableness" als Kriterium für die Haftungszuweisung

Eng mit den Ausführungen des vorstehenden Abschnitts verbunden ist die Verwendung des „Vernünftigen" als Kriterium für die Haftungszuweisung. In Wirklichkeit handelt es sich um zwei Seiten ein und derselben Medaille, da aus der Ermittlung des Grades und der Eigenschaft der geschuldeten Bemühungen auch die Anerkennung der Haftung zu Lasten desjenigen folgt, der das geforderte Ausmaß an Bemühungen nicht eingesetzt hat. Auch in diesem Fall ist die „Vernünftigkeit" durch die Nähe zu ähnlichen Begriffen belastet, wie dem Konzept der Fahrlässigkeit und der Arglist, im objektiven Sinne als Nichtbeachtung der Regeln der Korrektheit verstanden.

Diese Funktion ist in der Kernbestimmung der Regelung über die Zuweisung der Nichterfüllung des CISG (diese Bestimmung wurde auch in die Unidroit-Grundsätze[81] und in die Lando-Grundsätze übernommen[82]), bzw. in Art. 79, Abs. 1 besonders ausgeprägt. Der zweite Teil der Bestimmung, vor allem dort, wo auf eine Nichterfüllung Bezug genommen wird, die von der Partei „vernünftigerweise" nicht erwartet, vorausgesehen oder vermieden werden musste bzw. deren Folgen die Partei nicht überwinden musste, wird allgemein dahingehend verstanden, dass hier der Parameter der Sorgfalt des ordentlichen Familienvaters[83] bzw. der angloamerikanische, aber auf funktionaler Ebene gleichwertige Standard der *reasonable*

---

ternationales 1997, 51 und C. *Baasch Andersen*, Reasonable Time in Article 39(1) of the CISG – Is Article 39(1) Truly a Uniform Provision?, in: Pace Database, September 1998 (http://www.cisg.law.pace.edu/cisg/biblio/andersen.html).

[81] S. Art. 7.1.7, Abs. 1., Unidroit-Grundsätze 2004: „Non-performance by a party is excused if that party proves that the non-performance was due to an impediment beyond its control and that it could not reasonably be expected to have taken the impediment into account at the time of the conclusion of the contract or to have avoided or overcome it or its consequences".

[82] S. Art. 8:108 (1) Lando-Grundsätze (1998): „A party's non-performance is excused if it proves that it is due to an impediment beyond its control and that it could not reasonably have been expected to take the impediment into account at the time of the conclusion of the contract, or to have avoided or overcome the impediment or its consequences".

[83] S. *D. Tallon*, Art. 79, in: C. M. Bianca-M. J. *Bonell*, Commentary on the International Sales Law, Milano 1987, 580 f. und *Weiszberg* (Fn. 19) Nr. 448. S. auch *Magnus* ((Fn. 53) Art. 79, Rn. 8), nach dem sich Art. 79, Abs. 1 auf ein objektives Kriterium stützt, und nicht auf die Schuld im subjektiven Sinne, sondern auf das Verhalten, das eine vernünftige Person in derselben Situation an den Tag gelegt hätte (d.h. ebenso wie das Kriterium nach Art. 8, Abs. 2).

person[84] gemeint ist. Die Tendenz, die „Vernünftigkeit" als Kriterium für die Haftungszuweisung zu verwenden und sie in dieser Funktion der Sorgfalt gleichzustellen, wird schließlich auch durch den bereits erwähnten Art. 129, Abs. 4, lit. a des Verbrauchergesetzbuches bestätigt. Nach diesem Artikel sind die öffentlichen Äußerungen des Herstellers über die Eigenschaften des Gutes dann bedeutungslos, wenn der Verkäufer nachweisen kann, dass «er von der Äußerung keine Kenntnis hatte und auch unter Einsatz der gewöhnlichen Sorgfalt keine Kenntnis davon hätte erlangen können»:[85] Auch hier ist zu bedenken, dass in der Bestimmung auf die Sorgfalt (diligenza)[86] abgestellt wird, während in Art. 2, Abs. 4, 1. Spiegelstrich der Richtlinie 99/44/EG von einer Beurteilung nach dem Kriterium der „Vernünftigkeit"[87] die Rede ist.

3. „Reasonableness" als Kriterium für den Ausgleich der gegensätzlichen Interessen

In der legislativen Terminologie wird schließlich davon ausgegangen, dass sich die „Vernünftigkeit" auf das Maß oder den Inhalt der im Vertrag festgelegten Leistungen und auf deren in quantitativer oder qualitativer Hinsicht beurteiltes Gleichgewicht bezieht. Unter diesem Gesichtspunkt

---

[84] S. G. *Ponzanelli*, Art. 79, in: C. M. *Bianca* (Hsg.) (Fn. 59) 313.

[85] „Il venditore non è vincolato dalle dichiarazioni pubbliche di cui al comma 2, lettera c), quando, in via anche alternativa, dimostra che ... non era a conoscenza della dichiarazione e non poteva conoscerla con l'ordinaria diligenza".

[86] In diesem Fall handelt es sich deshalb um eine Haftung des Verkäufers aufgrund des Mangels der geschuldeten Sorgfalt bzw. aufgrund einer Schuld: E. *Schwarzenberg*, Art. 1519-ter, in: *L. Garofalo-V. Mannino-E. Moscati-P.M. Vecchi*, Commentario alla disciplina della vendita dei beni di consumo, Padova 2003, 236, Fn. 15. Zur Problematik s. auch C. *Caricato*, Art. 1519-ter, 4° comma, in: *S. Patti* (Hsg.), Commentario sulla vendita dei beni di consumo, Milano 2005, 161, die jedoch zu der unterschiedlichen Schlussfolgerung gelangt, dass diese Haftung zumindest im Hinblick auf das Wesen der Erscheinung von der Schuld unabhängig ist.

[87] „Der Verkäufer ist durch die in Absatz 2 Buchstabe d) genannten öffentlichen Äußerungen nicht gebunden, wenn er ... nachweist, daß er die betreffende Äußerung nicht kannte und vernünftigerweise nicht davon Kenntnis haben konnte". Italienische Fassung: „Il venditore non è vincolato dalle dichiarazioni pubbliche di cui al paragrafo 2, lettera d), quando ... dimostra che non era a conoscenza e non poteva ragionevolmente essere a conoscenza della dichiarazione". Englische Fassung: „The seller shall not be bound by public statements, as referred to in paragraph 2(d) if he ... shows that he was not, and could not reasonably have been, aware of the statement in question".

wird in zahlreichen Bestimmungen z.B. von „vernünftigem Preis", „unvernünftigen Ausgaben" oder „Kosten", „unvernünftigen Zwischenfällen", „vernünftigen Eigenschaften", usw. gesprochen. Dieser Einsatz des Ausdrucks kann nicht mehr – wie die vorstehend dargestellten – mit der Vorstellung in Einklang gebracht werden, dass hier die Bemessung der geschuldeten oder fälligen Bemühungen – bezüglich ihrer Modalitäten und Intensität – im Verhältnis zur Erreichung eines bestimmten Ergebnisses gemeint ist. Die „Vernünftigkeit" drückt in diesen Fällen vielmehr den Bedarf nach einer Sicherung des ursprünglichen Gleichgewichts zwischen den vertraglich geplanten Kosten und Belastungen aus bzw. dient der Wahrung oder Herstellung eines Gleichgewichts, das der Vertrag aus externen Gründen nicht erreicht hat. Hier wird also eine Verwendung des Kriteriums der „Vernünftigkeit" deutlich, die an jene Bedürfnisse nach wirtschaftlichem und normativem Gleichgewicht sowie nach vertraglicher Gerechtigkeit zu erinnern scheint, die in der italienischen Tradition normalerweise unter die Verwendung des Kriteriums der Billigkeit und zumindest teilweise auch des Grundsatzes von Treu und Glauben fallen.

Das CISG befreit z.B. die Partei von den *unreasonable expense* (Art. 85 und 86, Abs. 1) oder von den unvernünftigen Ausgaben für die Erhaltung oder die Veräußerung der Ware (Art. 86, Abs. 3).

Darüber hinaus ist die „Vernünftigkeit" z.B. in der Definition des Konzepts der „übermäßigen Belastung" der Abhilfen gemäß Art. 130, Abs. 3 und 4 des Verbrauchergesetzbuches erwähnt, der sich ausdrücklich (in Übereinstimmung mit Art. 3, Abs. 3, Para. 1, der hierdurch umgesetzten Richtlinie 99/44/EG) auf die „unvernünftige" Natur der vom Verkäufer zu tragenden Ausgaben stützt.[88]

V. Das Problem der Konkurrenz der „Vernünftigkeit" mit Sorgfalt, Treu und Glauben und Billigkeit

Nach dieser extrem synthetischen Darstellung der wichtigsten Funktionen, die der „Vernünftigkeit" in ihren konkreten normativen Verwendungen anvertraut zu sein scheinen, wird deutlich, dass die Einführung dieses Kriteriums – vor allem in den kontinentaleuropäischen Rechtsordnungen – in erster Linie ein Problem der Konkurrenz mit anderen Kon-

---

[88] Zu dieser Vorschrift s. G. *Amadio*, Art. 1519-quater, 1°, 2°, 3°, 4°, 5° e 6° comma, in: *Patti* (Hsg.) (Fn. 86) 214; A. *Zaccaria-G. De Cristofaro*, La vendita dei beni di consumo, Padova 2002, 76; G. *De Cristofaro*, La nuova disciplina codicistica dei contratti per la fornitura di beni mobili conclusi da consumatori con professionisti (Seconda parte), *Studium iuris*, 2002, 1324, Fn. 37; L. *Garofalo-A. Rodeghiero*, Art. 1519-quater, 7°, 8° e 10° comma, in: *Garofalo-Mannino-Moscati-Vecchi* (Fn. 86) 404.

zepten des Vertragsrechts aufwirft, da es sich hier um jene – vorstehend erwähnten – Funktionen handelt, die in diesen Rechtsordnungen – und darunter insbesondere in der italienischen – dem Treu und Glauben, der Sorgfalt und der Billigkeit vorbehalten sind.

Die grundlegende Frage, die genauer behandelt werden sollte, kann also folgendermaßen formuliert werden. Kann die „Vernünftigkeit" wirklich an die Stelle der klassischen und für die kontinentaleuropäischen Rechtsordnungen typischen Gliederung zwischen Treu und Glauben, Sorgfalt und Billigkeit treten? Besteht nicht die Gefahr, dass die Aufnahme dieser Instrumente in die allumfassende und elastische Formel der „Vernünftigkeit" durch den Wegfall einer komplexen Spezifizierung von Rollen – Klauseln und anderer Konzepte –, die das kontinentaleuropäische Recht im Laufe der Jahrhunderte mühevoll entwickelt hat, zu einer Einschränkung des begrifflichen Instrumentariums des Vertragsrechts führen könnte? Oder sollen wir diesem Prozess dagegen mit einer positiven Einstellung gegenübertreten, in der Überzeugung, dass die Qualitäten der „Vernünftigkeit", d.h. Flexibilität, Greifbarkeit und Pragmatismus, zur Abschwächung einiger Übermaße an Abstraktion und Starrheit beitragen können, die auf die exzellenten dogmatischen Konstruktionen zurückzuführen sind, die rund um die traditionellen Generalklauseln des Vertragsrechts in den kontinentaleuropäischen Rechtsordnungen ausgearbeitet wurden (vor allem Treu und Glauben)?

Diese Aspekte sind getrennt zu behandeln, und in erster Linie ist zu prüfen, ob die „Vernünftigkeit" wirklich die Voraussetzungen erfüllt, um ohne gravierende Probleme Sorgfalt, Treu und Glauben bzw. Billigkeit zu ersetzen.

I. Probleme und Grenzen der Assimilation Vernünftigkeit/Sorgfalt – Inhaltliche Differenzierung trotz funktioneller Gemeinsamkeit

Der Parallelismus Vernünftigkeit/Sorgfalt findet auf funktionaler Ebene ohne weiteres eine Rechtfertigung, da beide zum Ausdruck eines Verhaltensmodells geeignet sind und als Parameter für die Beurteilung der Haftung desjenigen, der von diesem Verhaltensmodell abweicht, eingesetzt werden können. Geht man jedoch von der funktionalen auf die inhaltliche Ebene über, wird die Distanz zwischen den beiden Parametern größer. Ein wichtiger Unterschied betrifft meiner Ansicht nach das Ausmaß der verlangten Bemühungen. Kommen wir erneut auf die Umsetzung von Art. 2, Abs. 3 der Richtlinie 99/44/EG in Italien zurück, wonach die Garantie des Verkäufers eines Verbrauchsguts für Vertragswidrigkeiten ausgeschlossen ist, wenn der Verbraucher „vernünftigerweise nicht in Unkenntnis darüber sein konnte". Die nationale Umsetzungsbestimmung

(Art. 129, Abs. 3 des Verbrauchergesetzbuches) betrifft dagegen wie gesagt Vertragswidrigkeiten, über die der Verbraucher „unter Einsatz der gewöhnlichen Sorgfalt nicht in Unkenntnis sein konnte": Die „Vernünftigkeit" wird also nicht nur mit „Sorgfalt" übersetzt, sondern es ist auch ein *präziser* Sorgfaltsgrad gefordert. Auch der deutsche Gesetzgeber hat unter Übernahme der Formulierung des früheren § 460 BGB a.F. die „nicht vernünftige Unkenntnis" der Richtlinie unter Bezugnahme auf einen genauen Sorgfaltsgrad übersetzt, hat aber – im Gegensatz zu seinem italienischen Kollegen – auf das Kriterium der *groben Fahrlässigkeit* des Käufers, d.h. des Mangels der minimalen Sorgfalt, abgestellt. Welcher der beiden Gesetzgeber ist dem Modell der Richtlinie am ehesten treu geblieben? Und hat es generell Sinn, bei der Übersetzung des Parameters der Vernünftigkeit einen *bestimmten Sorgfaltsgrad* anzugeben?

Auch dem CISG, das das wichtigste Modell der Richtlinie darstellt und das angesichts der zahlreichen Erwähnung der „Vernünftigkeit" einen Rahmen für eine bessere Festlegung des Inhalts dieses Parameters bieten könnte, sind scheinbar keine sicheren Angaben zu entnehmen. Der Grund hierfür besteht nicht so sehr in der nur impliziten Bezugnahme auf die Vernünftigkeit in der Bestimmung, in der die Art. 2, Abs. 3 der Richtlinie entsprechende Regelung enthalten ist, d.h. in Art. 35, letzter Abs. CISG.[89] Vielmehr ist dies darauf zurückzuführen, dass, wenn aus dem darin enthaltenen Parameter der Vernünftigkeit Schlüsse über den Grad des vom Käufer bei der Erkennung der Mängel der erworbenen Ware geforderten Bemühens gezogen werden sollen, viele Kommentatoren zu unterschiedlichen Ergebnissen gelangen als jene, die von der anderen Norm abgeleitet werden, in der der Standard der *reasonable person* (in diesem Fall ausdrücklich) im Übereinkommen aufscheint, und zwar in Art. 8, Abs. 2, über die Vertragsauslegung. Im ersten Fall wird wie gesagt auf die minimale Sorgfalt[90] des Käufers Bezug genommen, der das Recht auf Garantie nur dann verliert, wenn er bei der Prüfung der Ware grob fahrlässig[91] gehandelt hat. Im zweiten Fall tendiert man dagegen dazu, in der

---

[89] Wie bereits erwähnt wurde (s. oben bei § IV, 1, b), beschränkt sich Art. 35, Abs. 3, CISG auf den Ausschluss der Haftung des Verkäufers für Vertragswidrigkeiten, über die der Käufer „nicht in Unkenntnis sein konnte" (*„could not have been unaware of"*). Da jedoch von der herrschenden Meinung anerkannt wird, dass die Vernünftigkeit einen allgemeinen Grundsatz des Übereinkommens darstellt, kann davon ausgegangen werden, dass auch Art. 35 implizit auf diesen Parameter Bezug nimmt, wenn er entsprechend der allgemeinen Grundsätze ausgelegt wird, auf die sich die einheitsrechtliche Regelung stützt.

[90] S. dazu die oben (bei Fn. 73) erwähnten Autoren.

[91] Vgl. *Magnus* (Fn. 53) 365, und *J. O. Honnold*, Uniform Law for International Sales under the 1980 United Nations Convention, Deventer, 1991, 2. Aufl., 260. Zu dem Umstand, dass die Ware unter Berücksichtigung dessen, was auf

„vernünftigen Person" die abstrakte Personifizierung des *bonus pater familias* des internationalen Handels,[92] d.h. also der Person, die unter Einsatz der *normalen* oder *gewöhnlichen* Sorgfalt agiert, zu sehen.[93] Daraus folgt, dass die Erwähnungen des Vernünftigen in ein und demselben Text verschiedene Ausmaße an Bemühungen auszudrücken scheinen. Aus diesem Grund können aus diesem Modell keine einheitlichen und auf die Richtlinie 99/44/EG übertragbaren Schlüsse gezogen werden.

Diese Feststellung gibt in Wirklichkeit Aufschluss über die Bedeutung der Vernünftigkeit als Verhaltensstandard. Denn dadurch wird deutlich, dass die Vernünftigkeit als Begriff unbestimmten Inhalts eine operative Bedeutung übernimmt, die nicht *a priori* ermittelt werden kann, sondern jeweils vor dem Hintergrund des konkreten Einzelfalls präzisiert werden muss: Für die Beurteilung, ob das Verhalten dem vorgegebenen Modell entspricht, können zwar Richtlinien herangezogen werden, aber die eventuellen Ergebnisse dieser Beurteilung sind nicht voraussehbar, denn die Übereinstimmung mit dem Modell ist unter Berücksichtung der Umstände[94] und der Bedeutung zu prüfen, die diesen Umständen nach Maßgabe des normativen Kontexts, in denen das Parameter erwähnt ist, beizumessen ist. Die Vernünftigkeit als ein Verhalten vorzuschreiben bedeutet nicht, ein vorgegebenes Maß an Bemühungen festzulegen, sondern nur

---

dem Handelssektor des Käufers unter den gegebenen Umständen üblich ist, unter Einsatz der normalen Aufmerksamkeit geprüft werden muss, s. jedoch C. M. Bianca, Art. 35, in: *Ders.* (Hsg.) (Fn. 59) 150. Die von der Doktrin bevorzugte Auslegung stützt sich nicht nur auf den Wortlaut (sie folgt in der Tat der Bedeutung, die dem Ausdruck „could not have been unaware", wenn er „ought to have known" gegenübergestellt wird, normalerweise beigemessen wird [s. J. O. Honnold (Fn. 91) 260 und *Magnus* (Fn. 53) 666], sondern auch auf den Hinweis, dass die Mängel der Sache vom Verkäufer leichter festgestellt werden können. Diese *ratio* liegt auch vielen der nationalen Bestimmungen zugrunde (s. die bereits erwähnten § 460 BGB a.F., Art. 1642 *code civil*, art. 1491 c.c.), die ebenfalls weniger strenge Regeln für den Käufer vorsehen (s. oben bei Fn. 74).

[92] S. oben bei § IV, 1, a).

[93] Wie von namhaften Autoren unterstrichen wird (s. C. M. *Bianca*, Negligenza, in: Noviss. Dig. It., XI, Torino 1965, 190 ff.; M. *Giorgianni*, Buon padre di famiglia, in: Noviss. Dig. It., II, Torino 1958, 597), sind bei der Definition der „normalen" Sorgfalt *nicht alle* sozial relevanten Verhaltensweisen zu berücksichtigen, sondern nur jene, die auf sozialer Ebene als *sorgfältig* bzw. zweckmäßig erachtet werden: Daraus folgt, dass die durchschnittliche Sorgfalt einen *guten*, aber nich außergewöhnlichen Grad an Bemühungen ausdrückt.

[94] Dazu C. *Scognamiglio*, Clausole generali e linguaggio del legislatore: lo standard della ragionevolezza nel d.P.R. 24 maggio 1988 n. 224, Quadrimestre 1992, 65 ff., 70.

den *modus operandi*, den die Person bei der Wahl des an den Tag zu legenden Verhaltens beachten muss; es wird also ein „sorgfältiges" Verhalten gefordert, ohne aber einen bestimmten Sorgfaltsgrad vorzugeben. Mit dem Unterschied, dass sich die Vernünftigkeit, während die Sorgfalt nach unserer Tradition immer einer weiteren Spezifikation bedarf (minimal, gewöhnlich, des ordentlichen Familienvaters, etc.),[95] durch eine erhöhte Flexibilität auszeichnet, aufgrund der das Maß der geforderten Bemühungen je nach den im Einzelfall betroffenen Interessen und dem Grad des ihnen gesetzlich gewährleisteten Schutzes variieren kann: Mit anderen Worten je nach den gesetzlichen Rahmenbedingungen, in denen das Kriterium eingesetzt wird, und je nach der Grundlage der Regel, in der es erwähnt ist. In unserem Beispiel heißt das, dass zur Festlegung, auf welches Maß an Bemühungen sich die „vernünftige Unkenntnis" des Verbrauchers nach Art. 2 der Richtlinie bezieht, auf die *ratio* der Norm abzustellen ist: Angesichts der *ratio* des Verbraucherschutzes sollte in diesem Zusammenhang ausgeschlossen werden, dass vom Vertragspartner-Verbraucher zum Zeitpunkt des Vertragsabschluss bei der Prüfung der Ware ein Grad an Aufmerksamkeit verlangt werden kann, der sogar über den hinausgeht, der vom allgemeinen Käufer oder vom erwerbenden Händler im internationalen Warenkauf gefordert wird (d.h. mehr als die minimale Sorgfalt),[96] wie dies dagegen irrtümlicherweise vom italienischen Gesetzgeber verstanden wurde.[97]

Abgesehen vom konkreten Fall wird durch diese Ausführungen die Fragwürdigkeit einer mechanischen Identifikation zwischen Vernünftigkeit und Sorgfalt deutlich.

---

[95] S. S. *Rodotà*, Diligenza (dir. civ.), in: Enc. dir., XII, Milano 1964, 531: „der Ausdruck Sorgfalt wird nie ohne eine weitergehende Qualifikation verwendet".
[96] So mit Bezug zur Richtlinie 99/44/EG G. *De Cristofaro*, Difetto di conformità e diritti del consumatore, Padova 2000, 168; S. *Grundmann*, Art. 2, in: C. M. Bianca-S. Grundmann (Hsg.), EU Kaufrechts-Richtlinie – Kommentar, Köln 2002, 162.
[97] Der Fehler des italienischen Gesetzgebers könnte jedoch durch eine richtlinienkonforme Auslegung der internen Norm korrigiert werden (s. dazu S. *Troiano* (Fn. 65) 110 ff.). Ein Vertragsverletzungsverfahren gegenüber Italien wegen Verletzung der Pflicht zur konformen Umsetzung der Gemeinschaftsrichtlinien ist also ausgeschlossen. Zur Problematik s. auch V. *Larosa*, Art. 1519-ter, co. 3°, c.c., in: *Garofalo-Mannino-Moscati-Vecchi* (Fn. 86) 217.

2. Probleme und Grenzen der Assimilation Vernünftigkeit/Treu und Glauben

Gehen wir an dieser Stelle auf das Verhältnis zwischen der Vernünftigkeitsklausel und der Klausel über Treu und Glauben ein.

Die in Aussicht gestellte Abstandnahme von Treu und Glauben und die Übernahme dieses Grundsatzes in die allumfassende Klausel der „Vernünftigkeit" scheint eine Tendenz zu sein, die nach und nach im neuen Vertragsrecht und (im internationalen Handelsrecht) Fuß fasst und dem Bedürfnis nach dem Bau einer Brücke zwischen den kodifizierten Rechtsordnungen und dem *Common law* entspringt, wo der *Reasonableness* erheblicher Raum gewidmet ist, während – zumindest nach den gängigen Behauptungen – der Grundsatz von Treu und Glauben vernachlässigt wird.[98] Emblematisch für diese Tendenz ist die Entscheidung, die im holländischen Zivilgesetzbuch von 1992 getroffen wurde. Dieses Gesetzbuch sollte eine „starke" Diskussionsgrundlage für die auf die Harmonisierung des europäischen Privatrechts gerichteten Initiativen darstellen und darüber hinaus den Forderungen seitens der angelsächsischen Welt auf dem Kontinent entgegenkommen. Im holländischen Gesetzbuch wird die Vernünftigkeit der Billigkeit gleichgesetzt, und die beiden Konzepte werden in einem Zuge genannt (*redelijkheid en billijkheid*). Auf diese Weise soll der Grundsatz von Treu und Glauben (*goude trouw*, ein Begriff, der aus der gesetzgeberischen Terminologie gestrichen wurde)[99] als allgemeines Verhaltensgebot ersetzt werden, fast als wolle man hierdurch die Nutzlosigkeit einer rigorosen und mittelalterlichen *distinctio* zwischen Treu und Glauben, Billigkeit und Vernünftigkeit bestätigen.[100]

---

[98] Es wurde aber auch behauptet, dass der „kontinentale" Grundsatz von Treu und Glauben im Wesentlichen der Vorstellung einer Absicherung des vernünftigen Vertrauens (*reasonable reliances*) entspreche und daher im englischen System bereits unter allen Gesichtspunkten durch den objektiven *Standard* der *Reasonableness* realisiert sei: dazu Steyn (Fn. 15) 438 ff.

[99] S. z. B. Art. 6:52 BW. Dazu M. W. *Hesselink*, De redelijkheid en billijkheid en het europese Privaatrecht (Good Faith in European Private Law), Dordrecht, 1999, 27 ff.

[100] Auch der Text der Lando-Prinzipien enthält – ohne derart radikale Wege einzuschlagen – (wie gesagt in Art. 1:302) eine Definition der „Vernünftigkeit", die sich zum Teil mit Treu und Glauben deckt und die Absicht erkennen lässt, dass auf diese Weise ein Verbindungskonzept zwischen *Common law* und *Civil law* geschaffen werden soll, aber auch die problematische Erfassung ihrer besonderen funktionalen Spezifizität zu verstehen gibt. Zu dieser Vorschrift (deren Text oben in Fn. 50 zitiert ist) s. C. *Castronovo*, Un contratto per l'Europa, in: Principi di diritto europeo dei contratti, Parte I e II (it. Aufl. hsg. von C. Castronovo), Milano 2001, XXX.

Bereits in der Vergangenheit zeichnete sich in Italien jedoch vor dem Hintergrund des Interesses für die angelsächsische Welt der Bedarf nach einer Abstandnahme vom ethischen Grundsatz des Treu und Glaubens und seines Ersatzes durch die Vernünftigkeit ab, so dass alle gesetzlichen Verweise auf das erstgenannte Konzept als Bezugnahme auf die „Vernünftigkeit" hätten umgedeutet werden müssen.[101] Mit diesen Argumenten sollte die Zweckdienlichkeit eines Konzepts in Frage gestellt werden, das aufgrund seiner durch und durch ethischen Natur nicht mehr in der Lage sei, als Gebot in einer nicht mehr monolithischen Gesellschaft zu fungieren. Mangels einer dominanten moralischen Konzeption der sozialen Beziehungen könnte die Korrektheit, die den Launen und Ideologien der Richter ausgesetzt ist, für eine Vielzahl kollidierender Zwecke eingesetzt werden, die zwischen der individuellen Ethik, der Ethik des Marktes und einer solidaristischen Moral schwanken, welche in ihren extremen Erscheinungsformen in eine „Mystik des Kollektiven" übergehen würde. Aufgrund dieser Vorstellung sei die Vernünftigkeit – als nicht moralisches, sondern „amoralisches", neutrales und pragmatisches Kriterium definiert – „das einzig brauchbare und akzeptable Modell, mit dem – gerade eben dank seiner menschengerechten Dimension – das Gleichgewicht zwischen den entgegengesetzten Ansprüchen ermittelt werden kann".[102]

Der Versuch, die Beurteilung von Handlungen der Privatautonomie dem Personalismus der Richter zu entziehen und objektiven Parametern mit technischem Charakter zu unterwerfen, ist zwar mit Sicherheit lobenswert, aber der Vorschlag, den Treu und Glauben als ethischen Grundsatz aus dem Kontrollspektrum zu streichen, klingt keineswegs überzeugend. Durch die in Aussicht gestellte Lösung wird die Kontrolle über die in das Ermessen des Arbeitgebers fallenden Entscheidungen in eine rein prozedurale Kontrolle umgewandelt, die von der Beurteilung der getroffenen Entscheidungen losgelöst ist. Auf diese Weise entsteht letztendlich eine private Autorität, die sich den materiellen Kontrollen entzieht. Dieses Ergebnis scheint mit dem verfassungsrechtlichen Gleichbe-

---

[101] *Criscuoli* (Fn. 10) 732.
[102] Alle Zitate stammen aus *Criscuoli* (Fn. 10) 718 ff. Erst vor kurzem wurde die Eingliederung des Grundsatzes von Treu und Glauben in die Vernünftigkeit erneut mit völlig analogen Argumenten gefordert. In Italien wurde diesbezüglich der Standpunkt vertreten (*L. Castelvetri*, Correttezza e buona fede nella giurisprudenza del lavoro. Diffidenza e proposte dottrinali, Dir. lav e relaz. ind. 2001, 237 ff.), dass die Vernünftigkeit – ein technisches und neutrales Kriterium ohne ideologische Ausprägungen – an die Stelle von Treu und Glauben treten kann, um als Kontrollmaßstab für die Ausübung von diskretionären Weisungsrechten seitens des Arbeitgebers zu fungieren *L. Castelvetri*, Correttezza e buona fede nella giurisprudenza del lavoro. Diffidenza e proposte dottrinali, Dir. lav e relaz. ind., 2001, 237 ff..

rechtigungsgrundsatz zu kollidieren,[103] wonach auch in den Beziehungen zwischen Privaten die gegenseitige Parität einzuhalten ist. Sie geht darüber hinaus in eine völlig andere Richtung als die von der italienischen Rechtsordnung in den letzten Jahren eingeschlagene, um – auch faktische – privilegierte Stellungen abzuschaffen und die Entscheidungen Privater, die Ausdruck der missbräuchlichen Ausnutzung einer gesetzlich anerkannten bzw. faktisch entstandenen Dominanz sind, auch auf inhaltlicher Ebene einer Kontrolle zu unterwerfen.[104]

3. Probleme und Grenzen der Gleichsetzung von Billigkeit und Vernünftigkeit

Die Gleichsetzung von Billigkeit und Vernünftigkeit ist nicht nur in zahlreichen Studien über das eine oder andere Konzept und in der gesetzgeberischen Terminologie[105] vorhanden, sondern auch angesichts der Tatsa-

---

[103] Siehe nur C. M. *Bianca*, Le autorità private, Napoli 1977, auch in: *ders.*, Realtà sociale ed effettività della norma, Milano 2004, I, 1, 47 ff.

[104] In diesem Zusammenhang sind natürlich jene normativen Eingriffe größteils gemeinschaftsrechtlicher Abstammung gemeint, mit denen immer umfassendere Kontrollmechanismen gegen den Missbrauch von Vormachtstellungen beim Zustandekommen oder bei der Ausführung des Vertrages zum Schaden der schwächeren Vertragspartner eingeführt wurden.

[105] Man denke an die bereits erwähnte Formel des holländischen Zivilgesetzbuches, in der die beiden Kriterien in einem Zuge genannt sind: *redelijkheid en billijkheid*, und ihnen die Funktionen anvertraut sind, die in den Rechtsordnungen romanistischen Ursprungs traditionellerweise dem objektven guten Glauben vorbehalten sind. Eine analoge Assimiliation wude anlässlich des Kommentars zur Regelung der missbräuchlichen Klauseln in Verbraucherverträgen (s. Art. 3 Richtlinie 93/13/EG und Art. 33 Verbrauchergesetzbuch) in Aussicht gestellt, die nach Aussage namhafter italienischen Autoren „eine auf denselben Interessenausgleich wie die Billigkeit aufbauende Vernünftigkeits-Kontrolle der Verträge ausgelöst hätte" (s. *L. Mengoni*, Autonomia privata e costituzione, Banca borsa tit. cred. 1997, I, 16, und auch *ders.*, Problemi di integrazione della disciplina dei „contratti del consumatore" nel sistema del codice civile, in: Studi in onore di Pietro Rescigno, III, Diritto Privato, 2, Obbligazioni e contratti, Milano 1998, 543 f.). Andere haben allerdings im Hinblick auf diese Regelung von einer auf den objektiven guten Glauben gestützten Kontrolle der (normativen) „Billigkeit" des Vertrags gesprochen, wobei der objektive gute Glauben in diesem Zusammenhang „die Abwägung der entgegengesetzten Interessen dahingehend" erfordert, „dass die Rechte der einen und der anderen Partei angemessen berücksichtigt werden müssen" (C. M. *Bianca*, Le tecniche di controllo delle clausole vessatorie, in: C.M. *Bianca*-

che gerechtfertigt, dass der erste Begriff normalerweise als „Kriterium für die gerechte Abwägung der unterschiedlichen Interessen der Parteien im Hinblick auf den Zweck und die Natur des Geschäfts"[106] definiert wird und in dieser Definition eine weitreichende Übereinstimmung mit der Vernünftigkeit festzustellen ist, die sich ebenfalls auf eine „Abwägung von Interessen unter Berücksichtigung der konkreten Umstände" bezieht.

a. Abgrenzung des Problems: Die verschiedenen Erscheinungsformen der „Equità"

Das Problem der Unterscheidung zwischen den beiden Konzepten scheint sich in Italien nur bei einigen positiven Erscheinungsformen der Billigkeit und nur bei einigen normativen Verwendungen des Kriteriums der „Vernünftigkeit" zu stellen. In diesem Zusammenhang ist nämlich zu berücksichtigen, dass die Billigkeit in der italienischen Rechtsordnung in mindestens zwei unterschiedlichen Funktionen erwähnt ist.[107] In einigen Ausnahmefällen bezieht sich das Gesetz auf die Billigkeit als Kriterium, das der Richter anstelle des positiven Rechts zur Entscheidung des Rechtsstreits einsetzen kann (sog. „ersetzende" Billigkeit: equità sostitutiva).[108] In anderen Fällen wird die Billigkeit dagegen als Kriterium be-

---

G. Alpa (Hsg.), Le clausole abusive nei contratti stipulati con i consumatori, Padova 1996, 362).

[106] C. M. *Bianca*, Diritto civile, 3, Il contratto, Milano 2000, 2. Aufl., 518.

[107] Zu dieser Untescheidung s. z.B. V. *Varano*, Equità, 1) Teoria generale, in: Enc. giur. Treccani, XII, Roma 1989, 7 ff.; R. *Vecchione*, Equità (giudizio di), in: Noviss. Dig. It., VI, Torino 1960, 630 ff.; F. *Galgano*, Diritto ed equità nel giudizio arbitrale, Contratto e impr. 1991, 477 ff. Die Terminologie ist jedoch umstritten: s. dazu näher *Giusella Finocchiaro*, Il giudizio di equità nella giurisprudenza della Corte Costituzionale, Contratto e impr., 2005, 109 und G. *Alpa*, L'arte di giudicare, Roma-Bari 1996, 166 s.

[108] Die „ergänzende" Billigkeit wendet sich also nur an den Richter, dem es das Gesetz in bestimmten Materien und mit dem Einverständnis der Betroffenen ermöglicht, von der die Materie abstrakt regelnden Rechtsnorm abzuweichen und den Rechtsstreit unter Anwendung des allgemeinen Kriteriums der Abwägung der relevanten Interessen auf der Grundlage des sozialen Bewusstseins zu entscheiden (s. Art. 113, Abs. 2, 114, und 822 it. ZPO, hierzu vgl. E. *Grasso*, Equità (giudizio di), in: Dig. disc. priv., sez. civ., VII, Torino 1991, 443 ff.; *Giuseppe Finocchiaro*, L'equità del giudice di pace e degli arbitri, Padova 2001). Die ergänzende Billigkeit ist also kein unbestimmter Rechtsbegriff, sondern bietet die Möglichkeit, den Fall in Abweichung von – aber nicht im Widerspruch zu – den Normen zu entscheiden (hierzu s. F. *Gazzoni*, Equità e autonomia privata, Milano 1970, 153; M. *Franzoni*, Degli effetti del contratto, II,

zeichnet, das nicht an die Stelle des positiven Rechts tritt, sondern die Norm dahingehend ergänzt und präzisiert, dass die maßgeblichen Interessen nach dem sozialen Bewusstsein und unter Berücksichtigung der konkreten Umstände untereinander ausgeglichen werden (sog. „ergänzende" Billigkeit).[109] Auf diese Billigkeit bezieht sich z.B. Art. 1733 zur Ermittlung der geschuldeten Vergütung mangels einer entsprechenden Vereinbarung oder die Billigkeit gemäß Art. 1374 Codice civile, die, falls keine gesetzlichen Vorschriften und Handelsbräuche vorhanden sind, als Kriterium für die Vertragsergänzung eingesetzt wird. Offensichtlich ist, dass nur die sog. ergänzende Billigkeit eine problematische Überschneidung mit der Vernünftigkeit verursachen kann, denn in keiner der bekannten Anwendungen wird die Vernünftigkeit als Kriterium dargestellt, aufgrund dessen der Richter den Fall unabhängig von den entsprechenden Gesetzesbestimmungen entscheiden kann. Sie übernimmt vielmehr die Funktion einer Ergänzung des gesetzlichen Gebots, um die in der Norm (aufgrund einer präzisen Entscheidung) enthaltene Unbestimmtheit zu korrigieren.

Dies vorausgeschickt, erscheint die allumfassende Identifikation zwischen Vernünftigkeit und Billigkeit aber auch dann nicht gegeben, wenn sie nur auf die ergänzende Billigkeit beschränkt wird, denn es gibt wie gesagt Fälle, in denen die Vernünftigkeit zumindest auf funktionaler Ebene den Aktionsbereich der Sorgfalt und des Grundsatzes von Treu und Glauben abdeckt und ein Instrument für die Bemessung der Bemühungen darstellt, die zur Erreichung eines geschuldeten Ergebnisses (oder zur Erfüllung einer Obliegenheit) oder zur Wahrung der andernfalls ungeschützten Interessen Dritter gefordert sind. Mit anderen Worten ist der Vernünftigkeit ein Übermaß an Funktionen übertragen, angesichts dessen keine hundertprozentige Gleichstellung mit der Billigkeit möglich ist.

Integrazione del contratto. Suoi effetti reali e obbligatori, in: Commentario del codice civile diretto da Schlesinger, Artt. 1374–1381, Milano 1999, 112 ff.; s. dazu auch Corte Cost., 6.7.2004, n. 206, Nuove leggi civ. comm. 2004, 1224 ff.

[109] C. M. *Bianca* (Fn. 106) 518. Der Begriff der sog. „ergänzenden" Billigkeit umfasst nicht nur die Fälle, in denen die Billigkeit zu einer Vertragsergänzung führt (s. Artt. 1374 c.c., 1447, co. 2°, 1526, 1733, 2225 c.c.), sondern auch: 1) die sog. „auslegende" Billigkeit (Art. 1371 c.c.), ein Kriterium zur Ermittlung des Sinnes einer zweideutigen Vertragsklausel; 2) die sog. „korrigierende" Billigkeit (z.B. Art. 1384 c.c.), mit der ein alternatives Gleichgewicht zu dem von den Parteien festgelegten ermittelt wird oder die Klauseln zwecks Anpassung des Vertrags an neu eingetretene Umstände geändert werden; 3) und letztendlich die sog. „quantifizierende" Billigkeit (Art. 1226 c.c.), die dem Richter das Kriterium für die Berechnung des ersatzfähigen Schadens oder anderer wirtschaftlicher Größen vorgibt.

Nach dem Ausschluss der völligen Identifikation ist allerdings in den übrigen Fällen eine teilweise Überschneidung denkbar, d.h. wenn mit der Vernünftigkeit die Relevanz ursprünglicher Missverhältnisse oder eingetretener Veränderungen des vertraglichen Gleichgewichts begrenzt wird: Mit anderen Worten, wenn sie als Kriterium für die Gewährleistung des vertraglichen Gleichgewichts eingesetzt wird. Und im Hinblick auf diesen konkreten Aktionsbereich scheint das Kriterium der Vernünftigkeit zahlreiche und bedeutende Schnittstellen mit der Billigkeit aufzuweisen.

b. Vergleich mit der sog. „ergänzenden Billigkeit" („equità integrativa")

Auch die Vernünftigkeit drückt in dieser Anwendung ein generelles Bedürfnis nach einem Gleichgewicht zwischen Interessen aus, die unter Berücksichtigung der Umstände und des sozialen Bewusstseins abgewogen werden, und auch sie strebt nach dem gerechten Ausmaß und der konkreten Verhältnismäßigkeit. Im Hinblick auf die Vernünftigkeit wird – vielleicht konkreter als dies bei der zumindest auf traditionelle Weise verstandenen Billigkeit der Fall ist – auf ein Gleichgewicht abgestellt, das auf den allgemeinen Menschenverstand, d.h. der vernünftige Person bezogen ist. Auch in diesem Fall stehen wir – wie bereits bei der Billigkeit – vor einem unbestimmten Bedürfnis, das als solches keine Richtung vorgibt, wenn es nicht mit einer präzisen und sozial anerkannten Regel einhergeht. „Menschenverstand" und „Moderation" sind in der Tat alleine keine ausreichenden Orientierungshilfen für eine Beurteilung, denn sie geben keinen Aufschluss darüber, auf welche spezifischen Parameter die Beurteilung gestützt werden soll. Man muss sich also fragen, um „welche" Vernünftigkeit es geht: Eine an Kriterien des Marktes, der ausgleichenden Gerechtigkeit, der vertraglichen Solidarität oder an anderen Kriterien orientierte Vernünftigkeit? Insgesamt ist die Vernünftigkeit – ebenso wie die Billigkeit – ein neutrales Beurteilungsparameter, das mit einer menschlichen und pragmatischen Konzeption der Gerechtigkeit verbunden ist, aber aufgrund seiner Neutralität auf präzisere Ziele ausgerichtet werden muss, da die Vernünftigkeit eine unterschiedliche Verhaltensregel erfordert, innerhalb der sie ihre Wirkung entfalten kann. Darüber hinaus ist sie aus denselben Gründen ein unbestimmtes Beurteilungskonzept, mit der Aufgabe, den Inhalt einer Norm zu ergänzen, aber keine Generalklausel (bzw. autonome Quelle von Rechten und Pflichten): Sie setzt also eine primäre Norm voraus, die aufgrund objektiver und vom sozialen Bewusstsein ableitbarer Parameter ihren Entwicklungsrahmen und ihren Sinn vorgibt. Wie bei der Billigkeit ist die Beurteilung der Umstände also auch im Falle der Vernünftigkeit nicht allein der Sensibilität des Richters überlassen, sondern hängt von der Bedeutung der auf das Kriterium verweisenden Norm ab:[110] Die *ratio* der Norm (und die darin ausgedrückten Wertvorstellungen) leiten den Rechtsanwender also bei der Festlegung der maßgeblichen Umstände und bei der Ermittlung des idealen Ausgleichs zwischen den kollidierenden Interessen.[111]

VI. Vernünftigkeit als „Passepartout"?

1. Die Unmöglichkeit einer völligen Ersetzung von Sorgfalt, Treu und Glauben und Billigkeit mit dem Kriterium der Vernünftigkeit: Die Gefahr der „Verfälschung" dieser Kriterien und deren Verwandlung in untereinander austauschbare, bloße „Meinungsregeln"

Angesichts des bisher dargestellten, komplexen Rahmens muss man sich nun fragen, ob für die Vernünftigkeit in all ihren Erscheinungsformen eine einheitliche Definition vorgeschlagen werden kann.

Wenn die Vernünftigkeit mehrere Erscheinungsformen hat und jede dieser Erscheinungsformen die (je nach den verschiedenen Fällen mehr oder weniger fundierte) Gleichstellung mit dem einen oder anderen Grundkonzept des Vertragsrechts rechtfertigt, bedeutet dies im Gegenschluss, dass *keine* dieser Erscheinungsformen allein den entsprechenden

---

[110] S. dazu *N. Irti*, Crisi della legge e giudizio di equità, Dir. e società 1978, 373, nach dem der Richter bei der Entscheidung nach Billigkeit „nicht nur den inneren Stimmen Gehör schenkt oder wankelmütigen Launen bzw. persönlichen Neigungen folgt: Er muss seinen Blick stets aus sich hinaus lenken und das Recht in einem objektiven System an Verhältnissen erforschen".

[111] Der Umstand, dass das Urteil nach Billigkeit auf objektive Parameter (gestützt auf das Richterrecht, das effektive Recht oder die Praxis) zu beziehen ist, wird im übrigen von zahlreichen Autoren unterstrichen (vgl. *Varano* (Fn. 107) 11; *Franzoni* (Fn. 108) 140 f. e *N. Irti*, L'ordine giuridico del mercato, Bari-Roma 1998, 5 ff., 81 ff.) und auch von den Gerichtshöfen anerkannt (für die Bezugnahme auf die Marktparameter s. z.B. Cass., 9.10.1989, n. 4023). Deshalb scheint nunmehr die – seinerzeit in Italien ziemlich verbreitete – Vorstellung der Billigkeit als rein subjektives und vom Ermessen des Richters abhängiges Bewertungskriterium überholt zu sein. Die Billigkeit ist zwar ein mehrdeutiger Begriff, ihre Mehrdeutigkeit wird jedoch auf einer objektiven Beurteilungsebene deutlich: Sie verweist mit anderen Worten auf mehrere objektive Wertparameter, die allgemein das soziale Bewusstsein betreffen, untereinander aber keineswegs übereinstimmen, vielleicht sogar im Widerspruch zueinander stehen, so dass nur die Auslegung der *ratio* der entsprechenden Norm dem Richter einen Aufschluss über die Verwendung des einen oder anderen Bewertungsparameters geben kann.

Inhalt abdeckt. Mit anderen Worten ist die Vernünftigkeit nicht Treu und Glauben, Sorgfalt, Billigkeit, aber in einem gewissen Sinne in jedem dieser Konzepte „präsent": Diese Feststellung hilft bei der Untersuchung des Grundproblems, das die Kategorie der Vernünftigkeit in der italienischen Rechtsordnung (und wahrscheinlich auch in anderen europäischen Rechtsordnungen) aufwirft, und zwar, ob ihr Bestehen als neue konzeptuale Figur berechtigt ist.

Nicht umsetzbar erscheint daher der Vorschlag, die „Vernünftigkeit" als vereinheitlichende Kategorie einzusetzen und darin Treu und Glauben, Billigkeit und Sorgfalt aufzunehmen, wenn man keine nachteiligen Kompromisse im Hinblick auf die Stabilität des Systems und die Sicherheit des Rechts eingehen will. Obwohl Treu und Glauben, Billigkeit und Vernünftigkeit einer gemeinsamen Wurzel entspringen und all diese Konzepte nach dem Ideal des „Gerechten" streben,[112] haben sie doch im Laufe der Zeit eine eigene Autonomie entwickelt: Treu und Glauben und Billigkeit mit dem Ziel der Harmonisierung der europäischen Rechtsordnungen im neutralen Konzept der „Vernünftigkeit" zu vereinigen, würde also einen Rückschritt gegenüber der historischen Entwicklung bedeuten, die sich dagegen von der Undifferenziertheit in Richtung der Spezialisierung der Institute bewegt.[113] Die Gefahr, die die synkretistische holländische Formel der *redelijkheid en billijkheid* heraufbeschwört, besteht – wie von einem namhaften italienischen Juristen behauptet wurde – in der „Verfälschung" von Treu und Glauben, Billigkeit und Vernünftigkeit, die innerhalb eines einzigen Konzepts in untereinander austauschbare, bloße „Meinungsregeln" verwandelt werden.[114]

---

[112] So *F. D. Busnelli*, Note in tema di buona fede ed equità, Riv. dir. civ. 2001, I, 537 ff., mit Verweis auf den spätklassischen Juristen Claudius Tryphoninus: „die Rechtshistoriker lehren uns, dass die Billigkeit den guten Glauben leitet und ausrichtet: *bona fides, quae in contractibus exigitur, summam aequitatem desiderat*".

[113] *Busnelli* (Fn. 112) 554. S. auch G. *Vettori*, Buona fede e diritto europeo dei contratti, Europa dir. priv. 2002, 931.

[114] *Busnelli* (Fn. 112) 554 f., der auf die Gefahr hinweist, dass die Vernünftigkeit „zu einer Art *Passpartout*" wird, „das also zuerst in einem Sinn und dann im völlig entgegen gesetzten Sinn verwendet werden kann": D.h. zuerst als Ausdruck „einer liberalistischen Orientierung in einem von der wirtschaftlichen Analyse des Rechts beherrschten Bereich" und dann dagegen als Grundsatz, „der sowohl von den gesetzgeberischen Vorgaben als auch von den Erklärungen der Parteien losgelöst ist und sich darüber hinwegsetzt" und es dem Richter ermöglicht „über die Anwendung der geschriebenen Norm" hinauszugehen, um „eine Art Moralisierung der Regelung des Geschäftslebens durchzusetzen". Hier wird klar zu der namhaften Doktrin Stellung bezogen, die in Italien dazu neigt, dem guten Glauben und der Billigkeit den Stellenwert rei-

2. Der Bedarf nach einer erneuten Grenzziehung zwischen den verschiedenen kardinalen Konzepten des Vertragsrechts

Diese Befürchtungen erscheinen zum Großteil gerechtfertigt. Die Vernünftigkeit kann den Grundsatz von Treu und Glauben nicht ersetzen, da sie aufgrund ihrer extrem hohen Undifferenziertheit nicht die Rolle eines Richtungsweisers für die Adressaten der Norm und den Richter übernehmen kann, die auch nur ansatzweise mit der Rolle von Treu und Glauben als ethischer Verhaltensgrundsatz vergleichbar ist.

Dies bedeutet jedoch nicht, dass man daraus den von einigen aufgestellten Schluss ziehen muss, wonach in unserer Rechtsordnung (oder im europäischen Vertragsrecht) kein Platz für den Begriff der Vernünftigkeit ist, dass sie mit anderen Worten „nicht die Stellung einer normativen Regel einnimmt, sondern in unserem System ein empirischer Begriff ist und bleibt, der in das Ermessen des Richters fällt".[115] Durch die steigenden Bezugnahmen auf das „Vernünftige" steht der Ausleger nämlich vor einem Hindernis, das realistischerweise nicht dadurch überwunden werden kann, indem der Vernünftigkeit im entstehenden harmonisierten europäischen Recht jede Anerkennung verwehrt wird. Der einzig mögliche Weg ist also die Untersuchung, ob die Vernünftigkeit eine ausreichend begrenzte und überschaubare technische Bedeutung übernehmen kann, um neben den bereits verwendeten Konzepten zu bestehen (ohne sich mit ihnen zu überschneiden); d.h., ob neue Grenzen ausgearbeitet werden können, innerhalb derer nicht nur die Unterscheidung zwischen „Treu und Glauben", „Billigkeit",[116] „Sorgfalt" erhalten bleibt, sondern nun auch zwischen diesen drei Klauseln und der neuen Klausel „Vernünftigkeit" unterschieden wird.

a. Die Neutralität der Vernünftigkeit vs. die ethische und verfassungsrechtliche Bedeutung von Treu und Glauben

In diesem Zusammenhang scheint außer Zweifel zu stehen, dass in erster Linie die ethische Bedeutung von Treu und Glauben und ihre Grundlage im verfassungsrechtlichen Grundsatz der sozialen Solidarität[117] (die auf

---

ner „Meinungsregeln" beizumessen: R. Sacco, in: R. Sacco-G. De Nova, Il contratto, II, Torino 1993, 414, 417.

[115] So Busnelli (Fn. 112) 555.

[116] S. L. Mengoni, Spunti per una teoria delle clausole generali, Riv. crit. dir. priv. 1986, 19: „Zu vermeiden ist, dass sich unter dem Deckmantel des guten Glaubens ein die gesetzliche Regelung abänderndes Billigkeitsurteil verbirgt".

[117] Busnelli (Fn. 112) 555. Zur engen Verbindung zwischen Treu und Glauben und dem Grundsatz der sozialen Solidarität gemäß Art. 2 Cost. s. S. Rodotà, Le

normativer Ebene einen primären moralischen Wert ausdrückt) wieder herzustellen ist, von der sie die spezifische Anwendung auf den Vertrag darstellt,[118] da sie als „vertragliche Solidarität" den Stellenwert eines Grundsatzes für die Überwindung einer egoistischen Vision des Vertrags und eines Bestrebens nach der Berücksichtigung der Interessen Dritter[119] auch über die Vereinbarungen hinaus[120] darstellt. Obwohl sich dieser Begriff gegen eine Funktionalisierung des Vertrages zu sozialen Zwecken wehren muss, erscheint es nämlich nicht möglich, sich eine reduzierte Version von Treu und Glauben, eine Art *editio minor* vorzustellen, die unter dem Deckmantel der „Neutralität" der Vernünftigkeit ebenfalls eine ideologische Orientierung verbirgt, insoweit sie nur eine technische und empirische Kontrolle der Handlungen Privater ermöglicht, die vom Verweis auf die Grundwerte der Rechtsordnung losgelöst ist und dadurch für eine spiegelbildähnliche, aber genau in die entgegengesetzte Richtung gehende Funktionalisierung des Vertrages nach den vorherrschenden Logiken des Markt verwendet werden kann.[121]

fonti di integrazione del contratto, Milano 1969, (ristampa integrata 2004), 150 ff.; vgl. auch A. A. *Dolmetta*, Exceptio doli generalis, in: Enc. giur. Treccani, XIII, Roma 1997, 9. In der italienischen Rechtsprechung vgl. etwa Cass. 18.7.1989, n. 3362; Cass. 13.1.1993, n. 343, Giur. it. 1993, I, 1, c. 2129; Cass. 19 giugno 1997, n. 5481; Cass. 24 marzo 1999, n. 2788, Giur. it. 1999, 1802.

[118] Dazu G. M. *Uda*, L'esecuzione del contratto secondo buona fede, Torino 2004, 56 ff.: „mit Bezug auf den Vertrag greift der verfassungsrechtlich verankterte allgemeine Solidaritätsgrundsatz mit Hilfe des guten Glaubens nach Art. 1375 c.c., der es in seiner Eigenschaft als *Generalklausel* ermöglicht, den Grundsatz selbst in geschuldeten Handlungen zu konkretisieren".

[119] S. C. M. *Bianca*, La nozione di buona fede quale regola di comportamento contrattuale, Riv. dir. civ. 1983, I, 209. *Uda* (Fn. 118) 83 ff. weist darauf hin, dass die in dieser Form konkretisierte Solaridarität nicht von der besonderen Funktion des Vertrags absehen kann: Die Befriedigung des *sozialen* Bedürfnisses nach Solidarität verwandelt sich also in die Befriedigung des *privaten* Interesses der Parteien.

[120] S. *Busnelli* (Fn. 112) 558 f., der auf eine Rückkehr zur authentischen Bedeutung des guten Glaubens hofft, „die infolge der 'Durchsetzung von durch die Anwendungspraxis ausgearbeiteten ... solidaristischen Werten' in der Lage ist, 'eine internationale Vereinheitlichung des Rechts ... als Zeichen eines steigenden Bedarfs nach Gerechtigkeit seitens unserer Gesellschaft zu bewirken'".

[121] Der Ausdruck „vertragliche Solidarität" ist also kein banaler Widerspruch in sich, sondern im Gegenteil eine bedeutungsreiche Formel, die einerseits ausdrückt, dass die Entwicklung dahin geht, dass die Konzeption der Vertragsfreiheit immer mehr den Werten einer modernen Gesellschaft entspricht, und andererseits die Rolle des Vertrags verstärkt, insoweit sie eventuellen anormalen oder abwegigen Verwendungen dieses Mittels eine Grenze setzt und dem-

b. Die Unterscheidung zwischen Sorgfalt und Treu und Glauben

Angesichts des bereits erwähnten Parallelismus zwischen Vernünftigkeit (in einigen ihrer Erscheinungsformen) und Sorgfalt könnte die Übernahme von Treu und Glauben in das vereinigende Konzept der Vernünftigkeit auch die traditionell anerkannte Unterscheidung zwischen Sorgfalt und Treu und Glauben gefährden. Diese – alles andere als nutzlose – Unterscheidung zieht eine genaue Grenze zwischen Konzepten mit unterschiedlichen Inhalten und Funktionen,[122] denn die Sorgfalt gibt den Grad der Bemühungen an, der gefordert ist, um ein in Beziehungen oder in einem konkreten Schuldverhältnis geschütztes Interesse abzusichern (dies setzt also voraus, dass der Schutz des Interesses bereits im Vertrag oder durch eine andere Quelle geregelt ist),[123] und der Grundsatz von Treu und Glauben dagegen eine autonome Verhaltensregel ausdrückt, durch den einerseits der Bereich der schutzwürdigen Interessen auf einige weitere sonst ungeschützte Interessen ausgedehnt wird[124] und andererseits auch angegeben wird, welcher Grad an Bemühungen (bzw. welches Ausmaß an

---

zufolge die Gefahr mindert, dass der Vertrag von der einen Partei zur Ausnutzung der anderen Partei verwendet wird.

[122] Zu dieser Unterscheidung s. C. M. *Bianca*, Diritto civile, 4, L'obbligazione, Milano 1990, 89; *Rodotà* (Fn. 117) 152 ff.; U. *Breccia*, Diligenza e buona fede nell'attuazione del rapporto obbligatorio, Milano 1968; L. *Mengoni*, Obbligazioni di „risultato" e obbligazioni di „mezzi", Riv. dir. comm. 1954, I, 368 ff.

[123] Die Sorgfalt ist also keine autonome Pflicht, sondern ein Kriterium für die Festlegung des Inhalts der bereits in anderen Normen vorgesehenen Pflichten. Wie *Rodotà* (Fn. 117) 153 ff. schreibt, ist die Sorgfalt ein Kontrollinstrument für die Aktivität des Schuldners, die nur das *wie* der Leistung betrifft und deshalb „nicht als Quelle – eigenständiger oder akzessorischer – Pflichten angesehen werden kann". Die Sorgfalt ist vielmehr nur (ebenda 160) ein „Kriterium für die Haftung gegenüber einer *bereits* in ihrer Gesamtheit bestimmten Leistung, d.h. sie setzt einen unter allen Aspekten festgelegten Inhalt voraus", so dass „die Unterscheidung zwischen Sorgfalt und Treu und Glauben nicht offensichtlicher sein könnte: Denn die erste betrifft nur das Ausmaß der Bemühungen des Schuldners, die Übereinstimmung seines Verhaltens mit dem geschuldeten; die zweite dagegen die Entstehung des geschuldeten Inhalts".

[124] Diese Funktion fehlt bei der Sorgfalt, die sich darauf beschränkt, den Inhalt der Leistung vor dem Hintergrund des Gläubigerinteresses zu bestimmen. Ein Merkmal von Treu und Glauben ist dagegen die Funktion der Wahrung weiterer Interessen, die nicht direkt vertraglich geschützt sind. Treu und Glauben dient zwar der vollen Realisierung der Interessen der Parteien, schützt aber nicht (direkt) das Interesse der Gegenseite an der Leistung: In diesem Zusammenhang ist die Partei nicht nach Treu und Glauben sondern gemäß Sorgfalt verpflichtet (so *Bianca* (Fn. 106) 505 f.).

Augenmerk, Aufmerksamkeit, Vorsicht, Fachkenntnis, usw.) zur Wahrung dieser Interessen eingesetzt werden muss: Da es sich um die Erweiterung des Bereichs der Pflichten der Partei (bzw. eine Minderung der Rechte, die ihr der Vertrag abstrakt zuerkennt) handelt, entspricht der Grad meiner Meinung nach einer abgeschwächten Pflicht, die nicht so weit geht, dass von der Person eine erhebliche Aufopferung des eigenen Interesses verlangt werden kann.[125] Ist diese Unterscheidung korrekt, dann birgt der allumfassende Einsatz der Vernünftigkeit erneut die Gefahr, dass Differenzierungen wegfallen, deren Existenz dagegen angesichts der Unterschiedlichkeit der entsprechenden Interessen begründet ist.

c. Die Rollentrennung zwischen Billigkeit und Treu und Glauben

Aufgrund der Überschneidung und Konkurrenz zwischen „Vernünftigkeit" und Treu und Glauben einerseits und zwischen „Vernünftigkeit" und Sorgfalt andererseits könnte der Wegfall der Billigkeit durch Aufnahme in die „Vernünftigkeit" auch die Rollentrennung zwischen Billigkeit und Treu und Glauben[126] in Frage stellen, die dagegen eindeutig in der Gesetzgebung zahlreicher europäischer Rechtsordnungen vorhanden ist (s. für Italien die Art. 1374 und 1375 Codice civile). Die Billigkeit, ein rein ergänzendes Kriterium,[127] das nur zur Integration der von den Parteien nicht festgelegten Aspekte der vertraglichen Regelung[128] Anwendung findet, entfaltet auch dort, wo es gesetzlich erwähnt ist, seine Wirkung (nur) als Kriterium zur Begrenzung der Rechte und Pflichten der Parteien: Mit anderen Worten schafft es keine neuen juristischen Posi-

---

[125] Zur Grenze der erheblichen Aufopferung des eigenen Interesses s. *Bianca* (Fn. 106) 506; V. *Roppo*, Il contratto, in: Trattato di diritto civile Iudica e Zatti, Milano 2001, 497; *Uda* (Fn. 118) 104 ff. Obwohl dieser Standpunkt in Italien von einigen Autoren (vgl. z.B. A. *D'Angelo*, La buona fede, in: Trattato di diritto privato Bessone, XIII, Il contratto in generale, 4, Torino 2004, 81) kritisiert wird, findet er in der höchstrichterlichen italienischen Rechtsprechung umfangreiche Anerkennung (vgl. Cass. 23.5.2002, n. 7543, Foro it. 2003, I, c. 557; Cass. 27.9.2001, n. 12093, Foro it. 2001, I, c. 3541; Cass. 20 aprile 2004, n. 3775, Foro it. 1995, I, c. 1296).

[126] Zu dieser Unterscheidung s. *Gazzoni* (Fn. 108) 284 ff.; *Rodotà* (Fn. 117) 205 ff.; *Bianca* (Fn. 106) 520 ff.

[127] Vgl. G. *Schiavone*, Approfittamento e lesione *infra dimidium*, Napoli 2004, 58 ff.

[128] Mangels eines gesetzlichen oder durch einen übergeordneten Grundsatz bestimmten Verbots steht es den Parteien also frei, das am besten für ihre Interessen geeignete Gleichgewicht zwischen den Leistungen zu wählen (*Schiavone* (Fn. 127) 44).

tionen, sondern trägt dazu bei, vor allem auf quantitativer Ebene (aber s. dazu unten bei VII.2) den Inhalt der vom Vertrag geschützten juristischen Positionen zu definieren. Der Grundsatz von Treu und Glauben, der ebenfalls einen Ausgleich der entgegengesetzten Interessen bewirkt, stellt dagegen ein Kriterium der Gerechtigkeit dar, das sich an einem höheren Wert orientiert (wie gesagt der vertraglichen Solidarität)[129] und in der Lage ist, als Generalklausel zu wirken, bzw. den Bereich der Rechte und Pflichten zu erweitern (und über die bereits vertraglich geschützten Interessen hinauszugehen) und die Ausübung von Rechten und die Erfüllung von Pflichten, die dem Vertrag entspringen, zu begrenzen.[130]

VII. Schlussfolgerungen – Die mögliche Doppelrolle des Kriteriums des „Vernünftigen" im Vertragsrecht

Die Tatsache, dass ein Ersatz von Sorgfalt, Treu und Glauben und Billigkeit durch das Kriterium des „Vernünftigen" ausgeschlossen wird, bedeutet jedoch nicht, dass dieses Kriterium keine Rolle im italienischen bzw. europäischen Vertragsrecht spielen kann. Es kann meiner Meinung nach sogar eine doppelte Rolle übernehmen.

1. Das „Vernünftige" als Gleichgewichtskomponente innerhalb des Grundsatzes von Treu und Glauben und der Sorgfalt

Einerseits kann davon ausgegangen werden, dass die Vernünftigkeit, anstatt die bereits erwähnten Kernbegriffe des Vertragsrechts zu ersetzen, mit einer genauer begrenzten Bedeutung eine „Gleichgewichtskomponen-

---

[129] Für all diese Bemerkungen s. *Bianca* (Fn. 106) 520.
[130] Nach *Mengoni* (Fn. 122) 283 f., kann Treu und Glauben „angesichts dessen, dass das Gläubigerinteresse umfassender als vertraglich vorgegeben geschützt wird", eine Erweiterung der „Position der schuldnerischen Pflicht" auslösen oder „die Position des Schuldners durch den Ausschluss sämtlicher Verhaltensweisen, hinsichtlich derer der Anspruch des Gläubigers im Widerspruch zu den Grundsätzen der sozialen Solidarität stehen würde, einschränken". In Italien ist jedoch noch immer umstritten, ob Treu und Glauben eine Vertragsergänzung auslöst oder in Form einer nachträglichen Beurteilung des Verhaltens der Parteien greift: Zu dieser Debatte, die jedoch in der jüngeren Doktrin weniger umfassend ist, s. z. B. *Bianca* (Fn. 119) 205 ff.; *Rodotà* (Fn. 117) 137 ff.; *D'Angelo* (Fn. 125) 37 ff.; *U. Natoli*, L'attuazione del rapporto obbligatorio e la valutazione del comportamento delle parti secondo le regole della correttezza, Banca borsa tit. cred. 1961, I, 169 ff., *L. Bigliazzi Geri*, Buona fede nel diritto civile, in: Dig. disc. priv., sez. civ., II, Torino 1988, 172 ff.

te" darstellen kann, die „innerhalb" des Grundsatzes von Treu und Glauben und der Sorgfalt wirkt und eine Zusatzfunktion übernimmt. Auch Treu und Glauben und Sorgfalt ist die Komponente des gerechten Ausmaßes und der Abwägung der Interessen unter Berücksichtigung des Einzelfalls nicht fremd. Insbesondere wird die vom Schuldner geforderte Sorgfalt nach einem Kriterium der Verhältnismäßigkeit und Angemessenheit auf das Interesse des Gläubigers bezogen und in der Regel durch die Normalität begrenzt, die an den konkreten Umständen, in denen die Leistung erbracht werden muss, bemessen wird. Unter Normalität wird allerdings kein mittelmäßiges Bemühen verstanden, sondern ein für die Erreichung des Ziels (die Befriedigung des Interesses des Gläubigers) angemessenes Bemühen, auch wenn der Schuldner dadurch sein eigenes Interesse aufopfern muss. Nach dem Grundsatz von Treu und Glauben muss sich die Partei zwar um die Wahrung des Nutzens der anderen Vertragspartei bemühen und ihr den Vorrang gegenüber der vollen Realisierung des eigenen Interesses einräumen, da es sich aber um den Ausgleich zwischen einem geschützten Interesse und dem ansonsten vertraglich „nicht geschützten Nutzen" (Dritter) handelt, legt er das Gleichgewicht wie gesagt an der Grenze der erheblichen Aufopferung des eigenen Interesses fest.

In beiden Fällen beinhaltet der Parameter der Sorgfalt bzw. das Gebot der Korrektheit den Bedarf nach einem vernünftigen Schnittpunkt zwischen den kollidierenden Interessen: Und dieses Bedürfnis wird vom Gesetzgeber heute immer öfter durch den Verweis in präzisen Bestimmungen auf das Kriterium des „Vernünftigen" ausgedrückt.[131] All diese Fälle sind auf ein einziges Schema zurückzuführen, denn in jedem davon ermittelt die Vernünftigkeit je nach dem normativen Kontext einen unterschiedlichen Ausgleich zwischen den kollidierenden Interessen. Das Verständnis des Gleichgewichts ist wiederum durch die *ratio* der Regel vorgegeben, in der die Vernünftigkeit als Bedürfnis nach vertraglichem Gleichgewicht Anwendung findet.[132]

---

[131] Hierbei handelt es sich um die Fälle, in denen das Gesetz fordert, dass die Partei innerhalb einer „vernünftigen Zeit" tätig wird oder „vernünftige Maßnahmen" ergreift oder eine Tatsache „vernünftigerweise voraussehen konnte" bzw. „vernünftigerweise in Kenntnis darüber sein musste".

[132] Nicht vorstellbar ist also eine von der normativen *ratio* losgelöste „Vernünftigkeit", denn die Vernünftigkeit ist in all ihren Erscheinungsfromen ein Kriterium des Gleichgewichts, das – da es alleine nicht zum Ausdruck des für den Ausgleich einzusetzenden Werts geeignet ist – eine andere allgemeine Verhaltensregel benötigt, innerhalb der es wirken kann: Eine dieser Normen ist z.B. diejenige, nach der ein an der Korrektheit orientiertes Verhalten an den Tag zu legen ist oder nach der die Erfüllung unter Einsatz der Sorgfalt des ordentlichen Familienvaters zu erbringen ist. In diese Richtung scheint auch die von

2. Das „Vernünftige" als Kriterium, das sich faktisch mit der Billigkeit überschneidet – Vorschlag für eine Unterscheidung: „Vernünftigkeit" als Kontrollinstrument für das „normative" Gleichgewicht des Vertrags

Problematischer ist dagegen die Abgrenzung der Rollen zwischen Vernünftigkeit und Billigkeit, denn in einigen spezifischen Verwendungen (bzw. wenn sie als Instrument für das vertragliche Gleichgewicht eingesetzt wird) ist die erste kaum von der zweiten zu unterscheiden.

Diese mangelnde Unterscheidbarkeit ist also zur Kenntnis zu nehmen, und es sind die erforderlichen Schlüsse daraus zu ziehen. Die wichtigste Schlussfolgerung betrifft den Umstand, dass die Vernünftigkeit in dieser Bedeutung denselben Grenzen zu unterwerfen ist, denen die Billigkeit in der nationalen Rechtsordnung als rein ergänzende Quelle unterliegt, wie im Hinblick auf das italienische Recht aus Art. 1374 Codice civile und den Bestimmungen, die mit Bezug auf einzelne Sachverhalte auf die vertragliche Unbilligkeit eingehen, ersichtlich wird.[133]

Art. 1:302 der Lando-Grundsätze gebotene Definition zu gehen, über die *Castronovo* (Fn. 100) XLIII f., schreibt: Während „die Vernünftigkeit ein direkter Ausdruck der praktischen Vernunft ist, besteht der gute Glauben in einer ihr auferlegten Verhaltensregel". Und: „Die Überordnung des guten Glaubens gegenüber der Vernünftigkeit wird ... im Hinblick auf die Definition deutlich, wo der gute Glauben der Vernünftigkeit Inhhalt verleiht: ... der gute Glauben ist maßgeblich für die Festlegung, was vernünftig ist"; daraus folgt, dass „während der gute Glauben eine ergänzende Funktion hat und Pflichten auslöst, die Vernünftigkeit die Ausführungsmodalität betrifft, mit der diese Pflichten am besten erfüllt werden".

[133] Dem Vernünftigkeitskriterium des materiellen Vertragsgleichgewichts kann also nur die Funktion einer zusätzlichen Ergänzung zuerkannt werden, wie dies bereits bei der Billigkeit nach Art. 1374 c.c. der Fall ist. Darüber hinaus ist davon auszugehen, dass diese – ebenso wie die Billigkeit – den Vertrag nicht dahingehend korrigieren kann, dass dem von den Parteien festgelegten Gleichgewicht das vom Richter ermittelte Gleichgewicht übergeordnet oder die Ungültigkeit des Vertrags oder einzelner Klauseln verkündet wird. Dies kann nur dann der Fall sein, wenn das materielle Gleichgewicht des Vertrags durch einen anderen, übergeordneten Grundsatz kontrolliert werden kann. Einer dieser Grundsätze ist z.B. der von Treu und Glauben beim Zustandekommen der Vereinbarung, wonach keine unvernünftigen Vereinbarungen oder Klauseln aufgenommen werden dürfen (bzw. Vereinbarungen oder Klauseln, die für die Gegenseite eine übermäßige Belastung darstellen: s. die gemeinschaftsrechtliche Regelung in Sachen missbräuchliche Klauseln), da diese Ausdruck eines Missbrauchs der Vertragsgestaltungsgewalt sind, der von einem Vertragspartner zum Schaden des anderen begangen wird.

Gleichzeitig erscheint es jedoch möglich, über die bloße Feststellung der Übereinstimmung zwischen Billigkeit und Vernünftigkeit (die wie gesagt nur im Hinblick auf diese Funktion vorliegt) hinauszugehen, um – wenn auch nur auf rechtspolitischer Ebene – einen Vorschlag zu unterbreiten, damit das Kriterium der „Vernünftigkeit" im positiven Recht unterschiedlich und gezielter eingesetzt werden kann. In diesem Zusammenhang kann nämlich hervorgehoben werden, dass die Vernünftigkeit, auch wenn sie als Kriterium für das inhaltliche Gleichgewicht wirkt, zwar mit der Billigkeit übereinstimmt, aber in gewisser Weise über diese hinausgeht, da sie aufgrund ihrer Undifferenzierbarkeit sämtliche Forderungen nach Gleichgewicht und gerechtem Ausmaß zwischen entgegengesetzten Interessen umfassen kann, und zwar auch über den Bereich der Festlegung des „wirtschaftlichen" Inhalts der Leistungen hinaus. Sie greift nämlich nicht nur bei der Ermittlung der Vergütung für eine entgeltliche Tätigkeit (vernünftige Vergütung) oder des Höchstbetrags, ab dem der Verkäufer nicht zur Übernahme der Kosten der Nachbesserung oder Ersatzlieferung verpflichtet werden kann (unvernünftige Kosten), d.h. in Fällen, in denen sie sich mit dem traditionellen Konzept der im wirtschaftlich/quantitativen Sinne verstandenen „Billigkeit"[134] deckt, sondern dient auch als Kontrollinstrument für das „normative" Gleichgewichts des Vertrags.[135]

Um eine Begriffsduplikation zu vermeiden, die für die Kohärenz des Systems kaum von Vorteil wäre, wäre es – wenn auch nur *de iure condendo* – vorstellbar, dem technischen Begriff der „Billigkeit", wie die Tradition des Konzepts vorgibt und ein Großteil der Verwendungen der Billigkeit in einzelnen Bestimmungen des Codice bestätigt, die Aufgabe zu übertragen,

---

[134] Nach *Bigliazzi Geri* (Fn. 130) 186, hat die Billigkeit nach Art. 1374 c.c. „nicht ein qualitatives, sondern quantitatives Urteil zur Folge, da es auf das wirtschaftliche Gleichgewicht der gegenseitigen Leistungen abzielt". So auch *Gazzoni* (Fn. 108) 110 ff.

[135] Die Vernünftigkeit erstreckt sich also sowohl auf das sog. wirtschaftliche Gleichgewicht bzw. das Verhältnis des Werts zwischen den jeweiligen Vorteilen und Opfern, zu denen sich die Parteien verpflichten, als auch auf das sog. normative Gleichgewicht des Vertrags bzw. auf „die vertragliche Ordnung, in der Rechte, Pflichten, Obliegenheiten, Haftungen und Gefahren zugewiesen werden" (so *D'Angelo* (Fn. 125) 165). Das ist z.B. der Fall bei der Regelung der missbräuchlichen Klauseln, wo allerdings nicht *ex professo* von „Vernünftigkeit" (sondern von „significativo squilibrio di diritti ed obblighi", d.h. „unangemessener Benachteiligung": Art. 3 Richtlinie 93/13/EG und Art. 33 cod. consumo) die Rede ist, die materielle Kontrolle der Missbräuchlichkeit der Klauseln aber von mehreren Seiten eben als eine Kontrolle der Vernünftigkeit verstanden wird.

das sog. wirtschaftliche Gleichgewicht zu beurteilen, und die „Vernünftgkeit" dagegen als Kriterium für die Beurteilung des sog. normativen Gleichgewichts des Geschäfts[136] einzusetzen.

---

[136] Ein analoges Unterscheidungskriterium wurde kürzlich vorgeschlagen von P. *Perlingieri*, Equilibrio normativo e principio di proporzionalità nei contratti, in: L. *Ferroni* (Hsg.), Equilibrio delle posizioni contrattuali ed autonomia privata, Napoli 2002, 49 ff., und F. *Casucci*, Il sistema giuridico „proporzionale" nel diritto privato comunitario, Napoli 2001, 25, die die „Verhältnismäßigkeit" (aber dasselbe könnte meiner Ansicht nach auch für die „Billigkeit" gelten) als Kriterium für den gerechten Ausgleich zwischen gleichartigen und quantitativen Vergleichselementen nennen; die „Vernünftigkeit" würde dagegen einen Ausgleich zwischen verschiedenartigen und nicht vergleichbaren Elementen erfordern, die nicht quantifizierbare Interessen (z.B. keine Vermögensinteressen) betreffen und einer qualitativen Beurteilung bedürfen.

Traces of Paulian Action in Community Law

Antoni Vaquer[1] *(Lleida)*

I. The existing Acquis

There is neither specific regulation of Paulian Action in the Acquis nor any provision which expressly mentions this remedy for creditors against gratuitous dispositions made by their debtors. Nevertheless, the European Court of Justice has referred to

> "national rules which, in the member States, provide that certain acts of a debtor to the detriment of the interests of creditors and, in particular those which are of a fraudulent nature vis-à-vis creditors, either cannot be pleaded against the creditors or may be set aside under procedures specifically prescribed for that purpose".[2]

Some years later, the same European Court of Justice has dealt with the Paulian action as regulated in French law *(action paulienne)* and has used similar words to describe it:

> "The action paulienne, however, is based on the creditor's personal claim against the debtor and seeks to protect whatever security he may have over the debtor's estate. If successful, its effect is to render the transaction whereby the debtor has effected a disposition in fraud of the creditor's rights ineffective as against the creditor alone".[3]

> "As has been stated in paragraph 17 above, an action such as the action paulienne under French law seeks to protect whatever security the creditor may have by requesting the court having jurisdiction to render

---

[1] Professor of civil law, University of Lleida. This contribution is part of the research group AGAUR 2005SGR00199 funded by the regional Government of Catalonia.

[2] Judgment of 1 March 1983, Case 250/78, *Deka Getreideptodukte GMBH & Co v European Economic Community*, [1983] ECR 421, para 15.

[3] Judgment of 10 January 1990, Case C-115/88, *Mario P. A. Reichert and others v Dresdner Bank* (Reichert I), [1990] ECR I-27, para 12.

the transaction whereby the debtor has effected a disposition in fraud of the creditor's rights ineffective as against the creditor".[4]

These last two decisions refer to preliminary rulings in relation to the exercise before the French courts of the French rule of the Paulian action in a lawsuit filed by a German plaintiff against some German defendants. Therefore, the description of the Paulian action given in the judgment could only relate to French law. However, in the *Deka* case, the European Court of Justice emphatically considered that

"those national rules constitute the expression of a general principle common to the laws of the member States".

The expression of the judgment is a little confusing, since it is not easy to ascertain whether the "general principle common to the laws of the member States" is the sole fact of the existence of a remedy called Paulian action or whether it also embraces its legal regime, which is at least outlined. This paper aims to scrutinize the accuracy of the ECJ's statement, i.e. whether the Paulian action is a remedy common to the European legal systems and, yet further, whether a common core of law is identifiable. However, another relevant legal instrument must be taken into account. The European Regulation 1346/2000 on insolvency proceedings[5] establishes that the law of the State of the opening of proceedings shall determine "the rules relating to the voidness, voidability or unenforceability of legal acts detrimental to all the creditors" (art. 4(2)(m)). Moreover, it is repeatedly stated that different provisions of the same Regulation "shall not preclude actions for voidness, voidability or unenforceability as referred to in art. 4(2)(m)" (art. 5(4), 6(2), 7(3)). The purpose of this provision is that claims based on general private law remain unaffected, so that the *lex fori concursus* governs the question of avoidance of transactions.[6] Since it is assumed that most of the legal systems provide remedies to challenge transfers of property made by debtors before their insolvency is judicially declared, the wording seems to catch all variations encompassing the effects of the Paulian action, which is the traditional remedy available to defrauded creditors. This paper will especially focus on whether these three legal concepts – voidness, voidability, unenforceability – are applicable to the Paulian action, and whether such statement is compatible with the aforementioned characteriza-

---

[4] Judgment of 26 March 1992, Case C-261-90, *Mario Reichert and others v Dresdner Bank* (Reichert II), [1992] ECR I-2149, para 28.
[5] OJEC L160 of 30 June 2000.
[6] Miguel Virgós Soriano, Francisco J. Garcimartín Alférez, *Comentario al Reglamento europeo de insolvencia*, Madrid: Thomson-Civitas, 2003, p. 135.

tion made by the European Court of Justice. Issues of conflict of laws deriving from the aforementioned judgments, however, are beyond the scope of this essay.[7]

II. Paulian action within and outside bankruptcy proceedings

The mention of "the rules relating to the voidness, voidability or unenforceability of legal acts detrimental to all the creditors" in the European Insolvency Regulation implies a distinction between the genuine Paulian action and the actions intended to restore the debtor's assets within the insolvency proceedings. I refer to the genuine Paulian action in order to identify the modalities of this action originating in Roman law and regulated in most European Civil Codes, aimed at protecting the creditor against detrimental acts of the non-merchant debtor. The same Paulian action has evolved into specific remedies inside the insolvency proceedings. The aim here is the reconstruction of the merchant's estate patrimony in favour the pool of creditors; hence, the requirements and the effects of these actions are sensibly distinct. It is a collective proceeding for the purpose of reorganisation or liquidation of the assets and affairs of a merchant. This implies that the centre of interest is the bankrupt's estate, not single creditors.

Provided that the aim of challenging the acts and transactions carried out by the merchant debtor is to recover as many assets as possible in order that the chances of satisfaction of the creditors increase, the main effect of the claim is the reintegration of the merchant's estate. This is expressed by means of different terms in European domestic laws. In France, the Act No 2005-845, of 26 July 2005, has modified the law, which speaks, on the one hand, of "voidness of certain acts" (*"nullité de certains acts"*) in article L. 632-1 et seq. Commercial Code. This voidness is deemed to be a "nullité de droit". Therefore, the transaction or the act carried out by the insolvent undertaking is absolutely void.[8] On the other hand, art. L632-2 Code de Commerce lays down that certain payments "may be annulled", provided that those who have dealt with the debtor were aware of the company no longer being able to meet its liabilities.

---

[7] See Joaquim-J. Forner Delaygua, "The Actio Pauliana under the ECJ – a critical look on Reichert II", in Reiner Schulze, Gianmaria Ajani (ed.), *Gemeinsame Prinzipen des Europäischen Privatrechts / Common Principles of European Private Law*, Baden-Baden: Nomos, 2003, p. 291; Paul J. Omar, *European Insolvency Law*, Aldershot: Ashgate, 2004; Jona Israël, *European Cross-Border Insolvency Regulation*, Antwerpen-Oxford: Intersentia, 2006.

[8] See Frédéric Bicheron, *La dation en paiement*, Paris: Editions Panthéon-Assas, 2006, p. 477.

French authors refer now to a "nullité facultative",[9] a term that can be equated to optional voidability. According to art. L. 632-4 Commercial Code, the effect of a claim for voidness is to "reconstitute the debtor's assets".[10]

In Germany the term used by the Insolvency Act (*Insolvenzordnung*) is "Anfechtung", meaning "avoidance". The possibility of avoiding a transaction is called "Anfechtbarkeit", which can be translated as "voidability". The act is not absolutely void, but can be challenged in order to exclude its legal consequences. Although the character of such "Anfechtung" (§ 129 et seq. InsO) has been disputed, currently most authors consider that, according to the "schuldrechtlichen Theorie" (*personal obligation theory*), the insolvency administrator[11] can claim reintegration of the disposed assets *in natura*; if reintegration *in natura* is not possible, restoration is by reference to the value of the disposed assets.[12]

So far I have identified "voidness" and "voidability", two of the terms mentioned in the European Insolvency regulation. For "unenforceability" it appears that one has to turn to Italian and Spanish law. Both countries have re-enacted their insolvency regulations. In Spain, the Insolvency

---

[9] Guillaume Wicker, "La période suspecte après la loi de sauvegarde des entreprises", *Revue des procédures collectives*, nº 12, March 2006, 12; François Vinckel, "Le nouveau régime de la période suspecte dans la loi nº 2005-845 du 26 juillet 2005 et le décret nº 2005-1677 du 28 décembre 2005: une réforme en trompe l'œil", *La Semaine Juridique. Édition Enterprise et Affaires*, nº 3, 19 January 2006, 118; André Jacquemont, *Droit des enterprises en difficulté*, 4th ed., Paris: Litec, 2006, pp. 270 et seq., n. 516. The author is much indebted to Prof. Judith Rochfeld for valuable assistance with French doctrine.

[10] This is the main difference with the legal regime of the *action paulienne*. Already the legal reform carried out in 1985 replaced the consequences of the successful claim. Instead of declaring the act non-opposable to the creditors, the new legislation established the nullity of such acts. See Alain Bénabent, *Droit civil. Les obligations*, 10th ed., Paris: Montchrestien, 2005, n. 861; Jacquemont, *Droit des enterprises en difficulté*, pp. 261–262, 274, n. 493–494, 525.

[11] This is a direct translation of the German *"Insolvenzverwalter"*. The English equivalent is "trustee in bankruptcy". However, the term "trustee" is not appropriate here as it is related to the trust concept, which in turn in related to the division between legal and beneficial ownership of property in common law, which is not recognised in the civil law systems of Europe.

[12] Jörg Dauernheim, § 129, in Klaus Wimmer (ed.), *Frankfurter Kommentar zur Insolvenzordnung*, 4th ed., München: Luchterhand, 2006, pp. 918 et seq, paras. 3–9; Gerhart Krefr, § 129, in Dieter Eickmann *et al*, *Insolvenzordnung*, 4th ed., Heidelberg: C.F. Müller Verlag, 2006, pp. 752 et seq., paras. 64–76. See also Reinhard Bork, *Einführung in das Insolvenzrecht*, 4th ed., Tübingen: Mohr Siebeck, 2005, pp. 120–122, paras. 223–226.

Act was passed in 2003, whilst in Italy the legal reform occurred in two phases, first the *Decreto-legge* of 14 March 2005 and later the *Decreto legislativo* of 9 January 2006. Nevertheless, it has to be stressed that "unenforceability" is maybe not the best term. Enforceable implies that an act or a transaction becomes binding and refers to a party to an at least intended legal relationship.[13] The Spanish translation employs "inoponibilidad", the French translation "inopposabilité", and the Italian one "inopponibilità", which could be translated into English as "non-opposability", a word that would better highlight the fact that it refers to someone who has not been a party to the contract or legal relationship. As the ECJ rightly pointed it out, the main effect is that such acts "cannot be pleaded against the creditors".[14]

In Spain, the character of the claim against third parties in possession of a bankrupt's assets is disputed. Most of the authors link this claim in one way or another related to the Paulian action. They can speak of a special Paulian action[15] or even of a rescission based on lesion.[16] Therefore, the legal regime should be the same, at least in its main features, to that of the Paulian action. In fact, the Preamble of the Insolvency Act qualifies the remedy as "restoration claims aimed at rescinding the detrimental acts". Nevertheless, it has been said, not without reason, that if the effects of the claim within the insolvency proceedings were the same as those of the Paulian action, the outcome would be unsatisfactory, since the aim is the reconstruction of the bankrupt's estate.[17] On the contrary, the Paulian action does not amount to reintegration of the assets, as we will see later on.

---

[13] See paradigmatically in this sense James Gordley (ed.), *Enforceability of promises in European contract law*, Cambridge: Cambridge University Press, 2001.

[14] *Ante* footnote 2 and corresponding text.

[15] Guillermo Alcover Garau, "Aproximación al régimen jurídico de la reintegración concursal", in Rafael García Villaverde, Alberto Alonso Ureba, Juana Pulgar Ezquerra (ed.), *Derecho concursal*, Madrid: Dilex, 2003, p. 333; Elena Sivetti, art. 71, in Faustino Cordón Moreno (ed.), *Comentarios a la Ley Concursal*, Cizur Menor: Aranzadi, 2004, pp. 550–553. Ángel M. López y López, "La acción revocatoria concursal: perfiles generales", in *Estudios sobre la Ley Concursal. Libro homenaje a Manuel Olivencia*, t. IV, Madrid: Marcial Pons, 2005, pp. 4159 et seq., also considers that the remedy implies a rescission of the act acquainted with the Paulian action enshrined in the Civil Code, but nevertheless in his opinion the revocatory effect is total.

[16] Guillermo Ripoll Olazábal, art. 71, in Miguel Ángel Fernández-Ballesteros (ed.), *Proceso concursal práctico*, Madrid: Iurgium, 2004, p. 379.

[17] Fernando Crespo Allué, art. 73, in Juan Sánchez Calero, Vicente Guilarte Gutiérrez (ed.), *Comentarios a la legislación concursal*, t. II, Valadolid: Lex Nova, 2004, pp. 1416 et seq.

By contrast, Italian scholars seem to agree on the legal consequences of the *revocatoria fallimentare*. The consequences of Paulian Action and *revocatoria fallimentare* are deemed to be the same, and this approach finds legal support in art. 64 *Legge Fallimentare*.[18] According to that provision, certain acts have no effect against the creditors (*"sono privi di effetto rispetto ai creditori"*).

A similar situation is that of Dutch law. The *actio pauliana* is regulated both in the Civil Code (art. 3:45 to 3:48 BW) as well as in the *Faillissementswet* (art. 42 et seq.). As a peculiarity, it does not require a lawsuit, since an extrajudicial declaration suffices, although usually the matter will be brought to court where the parties disagree on the validity of the *actio pauliana*. The legal consequences are basically the same, and only some of the requirements are different.[19] Therefore, it is time to turn to the form of Paulian action in (some of) the European legal systems.

III. Paulian action and the protection of creditors

The Paulian action is a well-known remedy protecting creditors against gratuitous acts carried out by the debtor to their detriment. Its origins go back to Roman law.[20] This action has experienced an interesting evolu-

---

[18] Maria Rosaria Grossi, *La riforma della Legge Fallimentare*, Milan: Giuffrè, 2005, p. 6, 7.

[19] A.S. Hartkamp, in Jeroen Chorus, Piet-Hein Gerver, Ewoud Hondius, Alis Koekkoek (ed.), *Introduction to Dutch law*, 3rd ed., The Hague: Kluwer Law International, 1999, p. 146; Peter J.M. Declercq, *Netherlands Insolvency Law*, The Hague: TMC Asser Press, 2002, pp. 135 et seq.

[20] Current opinion suggests that the phrase *actio pauliana* conceals a Justinian fusion of two classic remedies for the protection of creditors: *in integrum restitutio ob fraudem*, and *interdictum fraudatorium*. Paulian action, forged in Justinian's compilation, presupposed two assumptions: (i) *eventus damni* or detriment to the creditor – arising from the debtor's diminution of assets as a result of an act of gratuitous alienation by the debtor –, and (ii) *consilium fraudis* or intention by the debtor to defraud the creditors' rights by diminishing the debtors' saleable assets, generally thought to occur in conjunction with the acquirer's knowledge of such intention or *scienta fraudis*. See further Theodor Kipp, "Impugnación de los actos «in fraudem creditorum», en Derecho romano y en el moderno Derecho alemán, con referencia al Derecho español", (1924) *Revista de Derecho Privado* 1; Antonio Butera, *De l'azione pauliana o revocatoria*, Torino: UTET, 1934, pp. 25-27; Hans Ankum, "«Interdictum fraudatorium» et «restitutio in integrum ob fraudem»", in: *Synteleia Vincenzo Arangio-Ruiz*, v. II, Napoli: Jovene, 1964, pp. 145-146; Biondo Biondi, *Istituzioni di diritto romano*, Milano: Giuffrè, 1972; Giovanbattista Impallomeni, "Azione revocatoria (dirit-

tion from the necessity of proving the debtor's intention of defrauding the creditors to a more objective approach in which the core requirement is the detriment to the creditor's position. At the same time, legislative acts have tried to find a balance between protecting the creditors' interests and the certainty of economic transactions.

I. France

The *Code civil* dedicates its art. 1167 to the Paulian action, which establishes that creditors "peuvent aussi, en leur nom personnel, attaquer les actes faits par leur débiteur en fraude de leurs droits". Such sparse regulation in the *Code civil* soon caused a doctrinal debate about the effects of the success of the Paulian action. On one hand, some authors defended the purely revocatory nature of the action. Others, to a greater or lesser extent, considered that there was no revocatory effect in as much as the contract between the debtor and a third party was and continued to be valid. Therefore, the only effect was that the creditor could pursue the alienated goods despite these being part of the third party's assets.[21] The storm of debate amongst commentators has since clamed and there is now

---

to romano)", *Novissimo Digesto Italiano*, II, pp. 148–149; Xavier d'Ors, *El interdicto fraudatorio en el derecho romano clásico*, Roma: CSIC, 1974; Max Kaser, *Das römische Privatrecht*, zweiter Abschnitt, München: Beck, 1975, pp. 94–95; Vincenzo Arangio-Ruiz, *Istituzioni di diritto romano*, Napoli: Jovene, 1976, pp. 145–146; Mario Talamanca, "Azione revocatoria (dir. rom.)", in: *Enciclopedia del diritto*, I, pp. 883 et seq.; Antonio Guarino, *Diritto privato romano*, 10th ed., Napoli: Jovene, 1994, pp. 1028–1029.

[21] A comparison can de drawn between, on the one hand, Duranton, and, on the other hand, Demolombe or Aubry & Rau. Alexandre Duranton, *Cours de droit civil français*, vol.VI, 4th ed., Bruxelles: Société Belge de Librairie, 1841, no. 574, considered that "par l'annullation ou révocation des actes, les biens rentrent dans le domaine du débiteur, comme s'ils n'en étaient jamais sortis (...) Les biens ainsi rentrés dans son patrimoine sont donc le gage commun de tous les créanciers". By contrast, Charles Demolombe, *Traité des contrats ou des obligations conventionnelles*, 2nd ed., Paris: Hachette, 1871, 245 et seq., no. 247: "cette révocation est relative, et (...) elle n'a lieu que dans l'intérêt du créancier demandeur, afin seulement d'empêcher que cet acte lui soit opposable". Similarly, Charles Aubry, Charles Rau, *Cours de droit civil français*, v. IV, 5th ed., Paris: Marchat et Billart, 1902, § 313, p. 234, thought that "[l]'admission de l'action paulienne contre un acte d'aliénation, tout en opérant revocation de cet acte, ne fait pas reentrer dans le patrimoine du débiteur les biens par lui aliénés: elle a seulement pour effet de rendre possible l'exercise du droit de gage établi par l'art. 2092".

consensus that the paulian action is one of *inopposabilité*. The aim of the action is believed to be no other than redressing any losses caused to the creditor as a consequence of the debtor's act of alienation. Therefore, "[i]l suffit que l'acte frauduleux soit privé d'effets à l'égard du ou des créanciers lésés, et dans la mesure du préjudice subi", that is, "l'*inopposabilité* de l'acte à ceux auxquels il porte préjudice".[22] Thus, the detrimental act continues to be valid amongst the parties, and the remnant after restoring any losses to the creditor, remains property of the acquirer.

2. Italy

The Italian Civil code of 1942 establishes explicitly in art. 2901 on the *azione revocatoria*, that "creditors, albeit their credit being subject to terms or conditions, can request that any gifts made by their debtors to the creditors' detriment, be declared void in relation to the said creditors". Scholars consider that this article states the *relative ineffectiveness* of the debtor's detrimental act. That is, the transferred property is not reinstated to the debtor's assets, but remains within the acquirer's assets subject to execution by the creditor. Creditors are thus immunised against the effects of their debtors' acts, since these are not to their detriment, despite the act remaining valid and effective for each party.[23]

---

[22] François Terré, Philippe Simler, Yves Lequette, *Droit civil. Les obligations*, 6th ed., Paris: Dalloz, 1996, pp. 1059–1060; Jacques Ghestin, *Traité de droit civil. Les obligations*, Paris: LGDJ, 1992, pp. 721 et seq.; Bénabent, *Droit civil. Les obligations*, p. 854 et seq.; Rémy Cabrillac, *Droit des obligations*, 2nd ed., Paris: Dalloz, 1996, p. 494; Philippe Malaurie, Laurent Aynès, Philippe Stofel-Munck, *Les obligations*, 2nd ed., Paris: Défrenois, 2006, p. 1148; Luc Grynbaum, *Droit civil. Les obligations*, Paris: Hachette, 2005, p. 117, no. 287; Jean-Pascal Chazal, "La acción pauliana en derecho francés", in: Forner Delaygua (ed.), *La protección del crédito en Europa*, pp. 73 et seq. (Spanish), pp. 177 et seq. (French); Muriel Fabre-Magnan, *Les obligations*, Paris: Presses Universitaires de France, 2004, pp. 464–465, no. 177, who explicitly sets out that "l'acte frauduleux n'ést rétroactivement révoqué et ne réintègre donc le patrimoine du débiteur que dans la mesure de ce qui est nécessaire pour désintéresser le créancier demandeur".

[23] Emilio Betti, *Teoría general de las obligaciones*, v. II, Madrid: Revista de Derecho Privado, 1970, especially p. 407–408; Alberto Trabucchi, *Istituzione di diritto civile*, 41th ed., Padova: CEDAM, 2004, pp. 597–598; Pietro Rescigno, *Manuale del diritto privato*, Milano: Ipsoa Kluwer, 2000, pp. 532–533; Paolo Zatti, Vittorio Colussi, *Lineamenti di diritto privato*, 6th ed., Padova: CEDAM, 1997, p. 357; Juan Antonio Fernández Campos, *Algunas consideraciones sobre la acción revocatoria en el derecho italiano*, (1997) Anuario de Derecho Civil 631; Paolo Gallo,

3. Spain

In Spain, the Paulian action appears in art. 1111 and 1291.3 of the *Código civil*. Traditionally, it was considered to produce a revocatory effect since art. 1295 and 1298, for example, refer to "devolution" of property. Currently, however, authors – clearly influenced by developments in France and Italy – almost unanimously defend the success of the Paulian action as translating into relative ineffectiveness or non-opposability of the detrimental act in relation to the creditor. Thus, the transaction is valid and effective between the parties, but creditors can claim the alienated assets as if they still belonged to the debtor to the extent necessary to satisfy their claims. If anything remains after satisfaction of the creditor, it belongs to the acquirer due to the validity of the detrimental transaction.[24]

4. The Netherlands

Creditors and the insolvency administrator may resort to the *actio pauliana*, outside a bankruptcy or within it, respectively. The legal consequences are deemed to be the same. The *actio pauliana* has retroactive effect. The detrimental act is considered never to have been performed, but annulment only benefits the party who invoked the *actio pauliana* and only to the extent necessary to cancel out the creditors' detriment.[25] Such

---

Istituzioni di diritto privato, Torino: Giappichelli, 1999, pp. 931–932; Pietro Trimarchi, *Istituzioni di diritto privato*, 16th ed., Milan: Giuffrè, 2005, pp. 533–534.

[24] Isabel Espín Alba, in Sjef van Erp, Antoni Vaquer (ed.), *Introduction to Spanish patrimonial law*, Granada: Comares, 2006, pp. 48 et seq; Luis Díez-Picazo, Antonio Gullón. *Sistema de derecho civil*, v. II, 9th ed., Madrid: Tecnos, 2005, pp. 214 et seq.; Ángel Cristóbal Montes, *La vía pauliana*, Madrid: Tecnos, 1997, especially pp. 183 et seq.; Juan Antonio Fernández Campos, *El fraude de acreedores: la acción pauliana*, Bolonia: Real Colegio de España, 1998; José Manuel Lete del Río, Javier Lete Achirica, *Derecho de obligaciones*, v. I, Cizur Menor: Thomson Aranzadi, 2005, pp. 276 et seq.; Franscisco Jordano Fraga, *La acción revocatoria o pauliana*, Granada: Comares, 2001; Francisco Rivero Hernández, in José Luis Lacruz Berdejo *et al.*, *Elementos de Derecho civil, II, Derecho de obligaciones*, v. 1, 3rd ed., Madrid: Dykinson, 2003, pp. 247–249; Francisco Javier Orduña Moreno, Silvia Tamayo Haya, *La protección patrimonial del crédito*, t. I, Cizur Menor: Thomson-Civitas, 2006, pp. 262 et seq.

[25] Declercq, *Netherlands Insolvency Law*, pp. 142–143; Sebastian Kortmann, Dennis Faber, Richard Nowak, Michael Veder, "National report for The Netherlands", in W.W. McBryde, A. Flessner, S.C.J.J. Kortmann (eds.), *Principles of*

legal consequences are derived from art. 3:45(4) BW, which expressly establishes same for the general *actio pauliana*, and from art. 42(1) *Faillissementswet* which states "for the benefit of the bankrupt estate". This may be called "relative nullity",[26] but in fact it is the same solution as in France, Italy or Spain, so that it can also be qualified as a remedy based on non-opposability of the detrimental act to the creditors.

IV. Germany

Germanic legal systems, as early as the Prussian *Allgemeines Landrecht*, did not incorporate the Paulian action into their civil codes.[27] Instead, this was regulated by insolvency laws. In particular, the law *betreffend die Anfechtung von Rechtshandlungen eines Schuldners außerhalb des Konkursverfahrens* (AnfG 21 July 1879) deserves special mention, since it embodies the actio pauliana. The AnfG uses the term *Anfechtung* but does not clarify the effects of the said impugnation of the act of alienation. Despite agreeing on its restitutory effect – given the parallel with the legal consequences of nullity, according to § 142 BGB – German authors defended different positions; from relative nullity *(relative Nichtigkeit)* to proprietary relative ineffectiveness *(relative dingliche unwirksamkeit)*.[28] From there the doctrine developed towards the idea that what is really important is that the goods disposed of must continue to guarantee fulfilment of the debtors' obligations, and are subject to the creditor's claim, despite the use in § 7 AnfG of the term *Rückgewähr*.[29] The AnfG of 1879 has been replaced by AnfG 1999. The current manifestation of the Paulian action in German law,[30] § 11 AnfG 1999, reaffirms the line of development mentioned above, since reference is made not to norms on *Anfechtung*, but to those

---

European insolvency law, Deventer: Kluwer Legal Publishers, 2003, pp. 511–512.

[26] Hartkamp, in Chorus *et al* (eds.), *Introduction to Dutch law*, p. 142; Declercq, *Netherlands Insolvency Law*, p. 142, who nevertheless later states (p. 143) that "the parties against whom the *actio pauliana* has effect have the obligation to return such assets to the trustee in bankruptcy"; this implies restoration of the assets, an effect closer to nullity than to non-opposability, a more efficient effect in bankruptcy, as has been said in the text.

[27] The exception was the Saxony Civil Code (§§ 1509 et seq.).

[28] See a summary of opinions in Rolf Möhlenbrock, *Die Gläubigeranfechtung im deutschen und spanischen Recht*, Frankfurt: Peter Lang, 1996, pp. 50–52.

[29] Möhlenbrock, *Die Gläubigeranfechtung*, pp. 52–55.

[30] Axel Flessner, "National report for Germany", in W.W. McBryde, A. Flessner, S.C.J.J. Kortmann (eds.), *Principles of European insolvency law*, pp. 349–350.

on unjust enrichment.[31] The obligational nature of the *Anfechtungsanspruch* is thus confirmed: the object of the creditor's action is to achieve satisfaction of the credit allowing, if necessary, the claim of goods that are no longer within the debtor's estate. This is however without claiming proprietary restitution – as opposed to what happens in impugnation within bankruptcy, where according to § 143 IO there is restitution of transferred property.[32] It is sufficient merely to allow the creditor to claim those goods that belonged to the debtor. The main goal is to satisfy the creditor, and in order to do so it is not necessary to reinstate the transferred goods to the debtor's estate, provided that the plaintiff is entitled to satisfy her credit by return of the alienated goods regardless their current ownership.[33]

V. A quick look at English law

As for English law, s. 423 of the Insolvency Act 1986 contemplates a similar case as that leading to in Paulian action:[34] transactions defrauding creditors. These are defined as "transactions entered into at an undervalue", such as donations and transactions without consideration or "for a consideration the value of which, in money or money's worth, is significantly less than the value, in money or money's worth, of the consideration provided by himself". Irrespective of the existence of a formal insolvency, the debtor has entered into a transaction with the purpose of

---

[31] § 11 AnfG 1999: "Was durch die anfechtbare Rechtshandlung aus dem Vermögen des Schuldners veräußert, weggegeben oder aufgegeben ist, muß dem Gläubiger zur Verfügung gestellt werden, soweit es zu dessen Befriedigung erforderlich ist. Die Vorschriften über die Rechtsfolgen einer ungerechtfertigten Bereicherung, bei der dem Empfänger der Mangel des rechtlichen Grundes bekannt ist, gelten entsprechend".

[32] As it has been said before, the aim is to restore the bankrupt's estate as if the detrimental act had not been taken place. See Kreft, § 143, in Eickmann *et al*, *Insolvenzordnung*, pp. 871 et seq.; Dauernheim, § 143, in Wimmer (ed.), *Frankfurter Kommentar zur IO*, pp. 1018 et seq.

[33] Mark Zeuner, *Die Anfechtung in der Insolvenz*, München: Beck, 1999, pp. 242 et seq.; Harald Hess, Michaela Weis, *Anfechtungsrecht*, 2nd ed., Heidelberg: Müller, 1999, pp. 252 et seq.

[34] According to Robert Stevens, "National report for England", in W.W. McBryde, A. Flessner, S.C.J.J. Kortmann, *Principles of European insolvency law*, p. 223, although English law does not know the *actio pauliana* by that name, there are a number of methods of clawing back assets which are functionally similar, being transactions defrauding creditors, the closest remedy to the civilian Paulian action.

putting assets beyond the reach of potential claimants or of otherwise prejudicing the creditors' interests. The concept of transactions at an undervalue can also be found in s. 339, which establishes a procedure for the retrospective avoidance of such transactions entered into by a person who is subsequently declared bankrupt. The distinction between these two sections is the requisite motive laid down in s. 423.[35] However, there are not many more similarities with the Paulian action. If one of the aforementioned acts is deemed executed with the intention of placing the goods out of reach of creditors or defrauding these in any way, the legal authority has the discretion to decide on a measure in accordance with provisions made by s. 425 in order to make good any detriment caused to the creditor (orders requiring any property transferred to be vested in any person, requiring persons to pay money in respect of benefits received from debtor, etc.). Irrespective of whether the court orders restitution of transferred property or directs that the proceeds of sale of said proerty be transferrred to the bankrupt's estate, the aim is to vest such money or property in the trustee in bankruptcy. This aim and, partially, the legal consequences of the remedy correspond with what could be considered typical effects of the Paulian action within bankruptcy on the Continent.[36] The remedies available purport to restore the position to what it would have been if the transaction had not been entered into and to protect those adversely affected by such transaction. But precisely the broadness of the judicial discretion prevents a total incompatibility with the continental approach based on the Paulian action.

VI. Catalonia

It is also convenient to devote some words to the civil law of Catalonia.[37] Catalonia's civil law does not contain any regulation of Paulian action. Instead, an objective system for the protection of creditors is established,

---

[35] Ian F. Fletcher, *The Law of Insolvency*, 3rd ed., London: Sweet and Maxwell, 2002, 8-083.

[36] Fiona Tolmie, *Corporate and personal insolvency law*, 2nd ed., London-Sydney-Portland: Cavendish, 2003, pp. 347 et seq.; Ian S. Grier, Richard E. Floyd, *Personal Insolvency: a Practical Guide*, 2nd ed., London: Sweet & Maxwell, 1993, pp. 137–139; Carmen Jerez Delgado, *Los actos objetivamente fraudulentos (la acción de rescisión por fraude de acreedores)*, Madrid: Civitas, 1999, pp. 94–98; Robert Stevens, Lionel Smith, "La acción pauliana en derecho inglés", in Forner Delaygua (ed.), *La protección del crédito en Europa*, pp. 95 et seq. (Spanish), pp. 195 et seq. (English); Fletcher, *The Law of Insolvency*, 8-068, 8-086.

[37] On the place of Catalan law within Spain see my introduction in van Erp, Vaquer (eds.), *Introduction to Spanish patrimonial law*, pp. 1 et seq.

which edges around the issue of fraud to concentrate exclusively on the creditor's detriment as a result of the gratuitous alienation. Art. 531-14 Civil Code of Catalonia sets out as the only effect of gifts made by debtors that of "no detriment" to creditors, which means that protection is founded on the non-opposability of the act of detriment to creditors.[38] The High Court of Catalonia has probably overemphasized the distinction between the Catalan indigenous remedy and the Paulian action. According to the decisions handed down on 6 December 2000 and 28 February 2005, non-opposability and Paulian action follow different paths, since the latter aims at challenging (ie rescinding) the gratuitous transactions carried out by the debtor, whilst the former only declares that such transactions are not detrimental to the creditor. The court concludes that because of their incompatibility the two remedies cannot be assimilated. However, the Court seems to ignore the modern approach of Spanish doctrine and case law referred to above *sub* 3.3. Moreover, the Catalan remedy protecting creditors from the detrimental acts carried out by their debtors is only an example of the historical developments of the Roman Paulian action in the search for a more efficient protection of creditors.

VII. Shifting from scienta fraudis to eventus damni

Any European standard handbook on the law of obligations still points out that there are two main prerequisites of a successful Paulian action, the existence of fraud by the debtor and of detriment to the creditor. However, since the Middle Ages, with the development of commercial activities, there has been an increasing need to find more flexible and agile methods of protecting creditors' interests than the Paulian action. Thus, across the whole of Europe, and beginning with local laws, a clear tendency emerged to objectivize the protection of creditors and gradually abandon fraud as a decisive element for the right to protection, and to

---

[38] José J. Pintó Ruiz, "La inoponibilidad y la constitución «Per tolre fraus»", in: *Estudios jurídicos en homenaje al profesor Luis Díez-Picazo*, t. II, Madrid: Civitas, 2003, pp. 2799 et seq.; Anna Casanovas Mussons, art. 19, and Ferran Badosa Coll, art. 58, in Anna Casanovas, Joan Egea, María del Carmen Gete-Alonso, Antoni Mirambell (eds.), *Comentari a la modificació de la Compilació en matèria de relacions patrimonials entre cònjuges*, Barcelona: Generalitat de Catalunya, 1995, pp. 165, 356; Maximino I. Linares Gil, "Inoponibilidad de las donaciones en el derecho civil catalán (Una propuesta de interpretación del artículo 340.3 de la Compilación de Catalunya)", (1998) *Revista Jurídica de Catalunya* 41; Antoni Vaquer Aloy, "Inoponibilidad y acción pauliana (La protección de los acreedores del donante en el art. 340.3 de la Compilación del Derecho Civil de Catalunya)", (1999) *Anuario de Derecho Civil* 1491.

focus more on the notion of detriment to the debtor's estate arising from acts of alienation carried out by debtors.[39]

The methods employed to strengthen the position of creditors were varied.[40] In Germany, for example, several local laws (Magdeburg, Bamberg, Lübeck) dealing with the disappearance of the debtor declared void any alienation of property to third parties, allowing the creditors to pursue the goods held by those third parties.[41] In Italy, presumptions of fraud proliferated within local statutes in order to facilitate recourse to the Paulian action.[42] In England, despite the fact that the Paulian action was never received, a statute from Edward III [50 Edward III, c. 6 (1376)] imposed a series of provisions aimed at avoiding fraud arising from gifts to friends and family, which eventually only applied to merchants [Law of 13 Elizabeth, c. 7 (1571)] and finally led to the regulation of bankruptcy.[43] In Catalonia, the Constitution *Per tolre fraus*, passed in 1503, simply established that unilateral gifts of a major part of the debtor's assets or in excess of five hundred florins, if these were not registered, did not produce any effect to the detriment of creditors.[44]

---

[39] See, in general, Kipp, "Impugnación" 10–11; Federico de Castro, "La acción pauliana y la responsabilidad patrimonial. Estudio de los arts. 1.911 y 1.111 del Código civil", (1932) *Revista de Derecho Privado* 203; Salvatore Pugliatti, *La trascrizione*, v. I, Milan: Giuffrè, 1957, pp. 154–157; Biondo Biondi, *Le donazioni*, Turin: UTET, 1961, pp. 433–434; Ángel Rojo, "Introducción al sistema de reintegración de la masa de la quiebra", (1979) *Revista de Derecho Mercantil* 40–44; Möhlenbrock, *Die Gläubigeranfechtung im deutschen und spanischen Recht*, pp. 18–22.

[40] See further my contribution "From *Revocation* to *Non-Opposability*: Modern Developments of the Paulian Action", in Hector MacQueen, Antoni Vaquer, Santiago Espiau (eds.), *Regional private laws and codification in Europe*, Cambridge: CUP, 2003, pp. 199 et seq.

[41] Alfred Schultze, "Über Gläubigeranfechtung und Verfügungsbeschränkung des Schuldners nach deutschem Stadtrecht des Mittelalters", (1920) 41 *ZSS (germanistische Abteilung)* 210 et seq.; Möhlenbrock, *Die Gläubigeranfechtung im deutschen und spanischen Recht*, pp. 32–33.

[42] Vincenzo Piano Mortari, *L'azione revocatoria nella giurisprudenza medievale*, Milan: Giuffrè, 1962.

[43] Louis Edward Levinthal, "The early history of English bankruptcy", (1919) 67 *University of Pennsylvania Law Review* 1; Sir William Holdsworth, *A History of English Law*, v. IV, London: Methuen & Co, reprint 1966, p. 480–481, v. VIII, pp. 229 et seq.; Fletcher, *The law of insolvency*, 1-014, 1-015.

[44] Ramon Maria Roca Sastre, "L'acció pauliana i la Constitució «Per tolre fraus»", (1935) *Revista Jurídica de Catalunya* 128–130; Vaquer, "Inoponibilidad y acción pauliana" 1492–1501.

More recently, case law and doctrine in Europe have softened the requirements for a successful Paulian action.[45] For example, in France the courts are satisfied with the mere awareness of the detriment that the debtor is causing to the creditor, so that the requirement of *scientia fraudis* is fulfilled with ease. Provided that the debtor knows her patrimonial situation, she must be aware of the negative consequences that the gratuitous act has for the creditor.[46] Likewise, the Spanish *Tribunal Supremo* states that "nowadays the Paulian action tends to be more objective despite a very subjective requirement like that of «consilium fraudis». (...) The subjective character of «consilium fraudis» has been softened by case law and scholars in order to make the Paulian action operative in practice. (...) It is enough to adduce evidence that the detrimental result was known or should have been known by the debtor".[47] Also in Italy fraud occurs when the debtor is aware of the detriment that the gratuitous act may cause.[48] In the Netherlands the burden of proof for knowledge of prejudice has been alleviated, whilst the courts have found detriment where the act of the debtor has not resulted in a decrease in the size of her assets, and where although a reasonable purchase price has been paid the proceeds would not have been available to the joint creditors as a means of recourse.[49]

Yet another development is worthy of attention. I have already mentioned that in the last twenty years most of the national insolvency acts have been thoroughly amended, including England (the Insolvency Act 1986 has been partially amended by the Insolvency Act 2000 and the Enterprise Act 2002), France, Germany, Italy, Scotland,[50] and Spain; the Dutch *Faillissementwet* has been most recently amended in 2005. Even the

---

[45] The same idea is expressed by William W. McBryde and Axel Flessner, "Principles of European insolvency law and general commentary", in W.W. McBryde, A. Flessner, S.C.J.J. Kortmann, *Principles of European insolvency law*, p. 54.

[46] See Bénabent, *Droit civil. Les obligations*, p. 591, citing recent French case law. See also Malaurie/Aynès/Stofel-Munck, *Les obligations*, n. 1145–1146.

[47] Tribunal Supremo 19 July 2005, westlaw-aranzadi RJ 2005/5342; 31 October 2002, RJ 2002/9735. See also Orduña Moreno, Tamayo Haya, *La protección patrimonial del crédito*, t. I, p. 224–225; Díez-Picazo, Gullón, *Sistema*, II, p. 215. Additionally, proof of fraud is unnecessary where the law establishes that certain acts are objectively detrimental to creditors; see Jerez Delgado, *Los actos objetivamente fraudulentos*.

[48] Trabucchi, *Istituzioni di diritto civile*, p. 712.

[49] Declercq, *Netherlands Insolvency Law*, pp. 139–140.

[50] William W. McBryde, *Bankruptcy*, Edinburgh: W. Green/Sweet & Maxwell, 2nd ed. 1995; Donna W. McKenzie Skene, *Insolvency Law in Scotland*, Edinburgh: T. & T. Clark, 1999.

European Union has devoted its efforts to insolvency by means of the Regulation 1346/2000. Legal reforms have aimed at a better protection of creditors. New lists of acts deemed to cause detriment have been drawn up. In France, operations dealing with stock options have been recently added to the list of *nullités de droit* (art. 632-1(8) Code de Commerce), whilst two more series of acts have supplemented the *nullités facultatives* (art. L632-2 Code de Commerce). The goal of this amendment is the more efficient restoration of the debtor's estate in order to safeguard either the situation of the company capable of continuing its activities or its liquidation.[51] The subjective fault of the debtor is irrelevant.[52] The goal of the legal reforms in Germany was the search for a more efficient regulation of *Anfechtung*.[53] §§ 130 to 137 InsO set down different acts that can be challenged which have in common the creditors' detriment.[54] In Spain the purpose has been modernisation and increased efficiency of the restoration claim as well. In fact, a series of different claims are established in favour of the creditors which try to cover as many detrimental acts as possible. Some acts are irrebuttably presumed as fraudulent (art. 71.2 *Ley Concursal*: gratuitous acts), other acts are only rebuttably presumed to cause detriment (art. 71.3 *Ley Concursal*: transactions with especially close persons to the debtor and the constitution of proprietary guarantees); detriment has to be specifically proved in relation to other acts (art. 71.4 *Ley Concursal*).[55] A noticeable evidence of the legislator's and courts' intention of making available to creditors as many remedies as possible is that the exercise of the Paulian action within the insolvency proceedings is not explicitly excluded at least in France[56] and Spain.[57]

---

[51] Jean-Pierre Arrighi, "Les nouveaux cas de nullités de la période suspecte", (2005) *Gazette du Palais* 2990. Vinckel, "Le nouveau régime de la période suspecte", 1118, stresses that the aim of the periodical reforms in this legal area is to improve the economic efficiency of the remedies.

[52] Jacquemont, *Droit des enterprises en difficulté*, p. 262.

[53] Kreft, in Eickmann et al, *Insolvenzordnung*, §129, para. 2. See also Christoph G. Paulus, "The new German Insolvency Code", (1998) *Texas International law Journal* 141.

[54] According to Kreft, in Eickmann et al, *Insolvenzordnung*, §129, para. 36, "Unabdingbare Vorausetzung jeder Anfechtung ist die objektive Benachteiligung der Insolvenz Gläubigern durch die Rechtshandlung". Similarly, Dauernheim, § 129, in Wimmer (ed.), *Frankfurter Kommentar zur IO*, p. 927, para. 36.

[55] See Alcover Garau, "Aproximación al régimen jurídico", pp. 325 et seq.; Ripoll Olazábal, art. 71, pp. 377 et seq.; María Linacero de la Fuente, *Las acciones de reintegración en la Ley concursal*, Madrid: Reus, 2005.

[56] Marc Sénéchal, "Qui peut ejercer l'action paulienne au tours d'une procedure collective?", (2002) *Droit 21* ER 017; Jacquemont, *Droit des enterprises en difficulté*, pp. 275–276.

By contrast, the Italian academic community has expressed strong criticism of the recent amendment of the *revocatoria fallimentare*. The "suspicious period" has been drastically reduced, so that only the transactions carried out within the last year or six months before the declaration of bankruptcy are legally presumed to be fraudulent.[58] Nevertheless, this seems to be the sole exception in a European landscape where national legislators try to strengthen the creditors' position.

Taking into account these developments, it would seem, therefore, more opportune to dispense with the notion of fraud and to focus exclusively on the prejudice caused to the creditor by the act of gratuitous alienation, as do many national laws partially and Catalan law completely. Prejudice is no more than a reduction of the debtor's assets below the level of her debts; that is, insolvency, or the inability of the debtor's estate to satisfy single or multiple creditors. Detriment must be measured in relation to the debtor's solvency at the time when the debt arose. Therefore, each creditor has her own solvency level. So, each act of gratuitous alienation is inherently detrimental, since it causes the loss of an element of the assets without any consideration to replace it. Detriment should suffice and fraud could be dispensed with as an independent requirement. Along these lines, it has to be remembered that the European Court of Justice in the aforementioned *Deka* case put the emphasis on detriment and referred to "acts of fraudulent nature" as a particular species of "acts to the detriment of creditors".[59] Similarly, the *Principles of European Insolvency Law* focus on detriment when considering the reversal of transactions.[60]

---

[57] Crespo Allué, art. 71, pp. 1400–1401; Ripoll Olazábal, art. 71, p. 382.

[58] Giorgio Schiano di Pepe, "La nuova revocatoria fallimentare", (2005) *Diritto Fallimentare e delle Società Commerciali* 798; Stefania Pacchi, "La reforma del derecho concursal italiano", 187 (2006) *Derecho de los Negocios* 7, 17–18. However, Grossi, *La reforma*, p. 63, considers that the reduction contributes to certainty and stability of legal relationships.

[59] *Ante* footnote 2 and corresponding text.

[60] According to § 8.1, "A juridical act unfairly detrimental to the creditors performed by the debtor within a certain period of time before the opening of the proceeding, is subject to reversal". Among acts subject to reversal, § 8.2 sets down transactions "with the intent of defrauding creditors". The *Principles of European Insolvency Law* are available at http://www.iiiglobal.org/country/european_union/PEILABIjournal_appended.pdf. See further on the *Principles* Axel Flessner, "Grundsätze des europäischen Insolvenzrechts", (2004) *Zeitschrift für europäisches Privatrecht* 887.

VIII. Concluding remarks

The European Court of Justice's assertion that most national legal systems contain some form of Paulian action is true.[61] It is also true that "those national rules constitute the expression of a general principle common to the laws of the member States". Moreover, two common principles can be identified. On the one hand, the fact of detriment is the core concept that allows resort to the Paulian action. On the other hand, the legal consequences of a successful exercise of the Paulian action either within or outside the insolvency proceedings, although textured by their respective legal traditions, amount to not totally dissimilar solutions. The consequences of a general Paulian action are neither voidness nor voidability, but non-opposability,[62] a legal term that is to be preferred to unenforceability. Non-opposability constitutes a compromise solution or balance between the owner's right of free disposition of her property and the protection of third parties who suffer detriment as a consequence of the act of disposition. This balance is founded on the basis of indemnity, both in relation to the validity and of the effectiveness of the act – the act remains valid and typically effective – in respect of third parties alien to the detrimental transaction. Creditors do not suffer any loss or prejudice in their legal position, since they can claim the alienated assets despite them belonging to a person other than the debtor. Non-opposability represents, in short, a mechanism of protection of third parties, in particular of the donor's creditors. This is a mechanism which is judicially less traumatic, since the detrimental act remains, from the point of view of validity and effectiveness, intact.

---

[61] As William W. McBryde and Axel Flessner, "Principles of European insolvency law and general commentary", p. 53, put it, "Legal systems commonly provide for a challenge of acts by the debtor prior to the opening of an insolvency proceeding". Other European civil codes with a regulation of Paulian action include, for example, Malta (art. 1144), Lithuania (art. 57), Portugal (arts. 610 et seq.), and Romania (art. 975).

[62] The distinction between Paulian action and non-opposability is to be found in the Civil Code of Québec. § 3 (of chapter 6, performance of obligations, sect. 3, protection of the right to performance of obligations, arts. 1631 et seq.) is entitled in French *"De l'action en inopposabilité"*, and in English *"Paulian action"*. Art. 1631 states that "the creditor who suffers prejudice through a juridical act made by his debtor in fraud of his rights (...) may obtain a declaration that the act may not be set up against him". See for further details Jean-Louis Baudouin, Pierre-Gabriel Jobin, *Les obligations*, 5th ed., Cowansville: Yvon Blais, 1998, p. 553; Vincent Karim, *Commentaires sur les obligations*, v. 2, Cowansville: Yvon Blais, 1997, pp. 367 et seq.

Nevertheless, specific developments of the Paulian action within insolvency proceedings need to be taken into account. Protection of creditors is still reinforced. Claims have a specific goal, that of reconstruction of the debtor's estate, so that all creditors can benefit from it. Hence, the annulment of the acts carried out by the debtor to the detriment of creditors is probably the most efficient solution. In fact, all the remedies in the national legal systems pursue the same aim based on the detrimental character of the debtor's acts: allowing the creditors to attack the disposed assets.

The European Insolvency Regulation makes explicit these approaches. It refers to three terms, voidness, voidability, and unenforceability, which embrace the legal consequences of a successful Paulian action in European national laws, either as contained in the Civil Codes or as developed in the insolvency legislation. Voidness and voidability are suitable for German, French and maybe Spanish law; unenforceability for Italian, French, Dutch and Spanish law; both could be compatible with English law. Although a deeper harmonisation is evidently possible, the foundations of a European regulation of the Paulian action are already recognisable.